MW00977757

"Information through Innovation"

Acumen Series

Acumen: Target Edition

DOS 6.2 Essentials	*Rod B. Southworth*
Windows 3.1 Essentials	*Michele Reader*
Word 6.0 for Windows	*Linda Ericksen*
Excel 5.0 for Windows	*LoriLee Sadler*
Access 2.0 for Windows	*Michelle Poolet and Michael Reilly*

boyd & fraser publishing company

I(T)P   An International Thomson Publishing Company

Danvers • Albany • Bonn • Boston • Cincinnati • Detroit • London • Madrid • Melbourne
Mexico City • New York • Paris • San Francisco • Singapore • Tokyo • Toronto • Washington

Publishing Process Director: Carol Crowell
Acumen Series Editor: Linda Ericksen
Development Editors: Cheryl Dukarich; Harriet Serenkin
Production Editor: Jean Bermingham
Composition: Gex, Inc.
Interior Design: Gex, Inc.
Cover Design: Richard Pepper/Flying Pepper Design
Manufacturing Coordinator: Carol Chase
Marketing Director: William Lisowski

 ©1995 by boyd & fraser publishing company
A division of International Thomson Publishing Inc.

 The ITP logo is a trademark under license.

Printed in the United States of America

 This book is printed on recycled, acid-free paper that meets
Environmental Protection Agency standards.

For more information, contact boyd & fraser publishing company:

boyd & fraser publishing company
One Corporate Place • Ferncroft Village
Danvers, Massachusetts 01923, USA

International Thomson Publishing Europe
Berkshire House 168-173
High Holborn
London, WCIV 7AA, England

Thomas Nelson Australia
102 Dodds Street
South Melbourne 3205
Victoria, Australia

Nelson Canada
1120 Birchmount Road
Scarborough, Ontario
Canada M1K 5G4

International Thomson Editores
Campose Eliseos 385, Piso 7
Col. Polanco
11560 Mexico D.F. Mexico

International Thomson Publishing GmbH
Konigswinterer Strasse 418
53227 Bonn, Germany

International Thomson Publishing Asia
221 Henderson Road
#05-10 Henderson Building
Singapore 0315

International Thomson Publishing Japan
Hirakawacho Kyowa Building, 3F
2-2-1 Hirakawacho
Chiyoda-ku, Tokyo 102, Japan

All rights reserved. No part of this work may be reproduced or used in any form or by any means—graphic, electronic, or mechanical, including photocopying, recording, taping, or information storage and retrieval systems—without written permission from the publisher.

Names of all products mentioned herein are used for identification purposes only and may be trademarks and/or registered trademarks of their respective owners. boyd & fraser publishing company disclaims any affiliation, association, or connection with, or sponsorship or endorsement by such owners.

1 2 3 4 5 6 7 8 9 10 MT 9 8 7 6 5

ISBN 0-7895-0199-6

Brief Contents

DOS 6.2 Essentials Contents

Windows 3.1 Essentials Contents

Word 6.0 for Windows Contents

Excel 5.0 for Windows Contents

Access 2.0 for Windows Contents

Preface

Welcome to the boyd & fraser family of *ACUMEN* authors, educators, and students who are participating in this vanguard of computer education. The *ACUMEN* series is both a well-integrated solution to the demands of the classroom and the foundation for the essential computer skills that today's students require for economic survival in the modern business world.

Computer literacy is essential in education and a growing number of professions. In the course of their careers, most individuals will have to learn more than a single application and, eventually, new versions of those applications. They will need to know how to integrate the applications to produce complex documents. They will need to work with other individuals to produce unified team projects.

The primary goals of the *ACUMEN* series are to instill confidence, build the skills and insight necessary to master the software application, develop a basic understanding of the concepts behind each task, and comprehend how different applications are often used interactively to complete a variety of tasks.

To meet these goals, *ACUMEN* introduces the concept of *active learning* that links all of the books in strategic and important ways. While other computer books isolate students in the world of a single application, *ACUMEN* students enter the real world of interactive computer technology.

Each text can be taught as a stand-alone course or combined in a unified syllabus. For example, the letters and plans written in the word processing application can be performed alone or combined with the financial projections and charts from the spreadsheet application. This information can then be applied to the product database from the database application to produce a complete business plan. In addition, optional group projects teach students how to work together in teams to produce the unified projects.

The *ACUMEN* structure, objectives, content, exercises, projects, and design are the product of extensive research, interviews, and field studies on what computer educators need to effectively teach both individual applications courses and fully integrated, comprehensive courses that cover a variety of applications.

The ACUMEN Solution: from Concept to Comprehension

▲ Quick Preview. Each *ACUMEN* begins with a short, pre-written program that demonstrates the application to the students and introduces a confidence-building real-world example.

Progressive Chapters. The chapters of each book are grouped into three distinct parts, with each chapter in a part progressively building on the preceding chapter.

 Fundamentals. Part I introduces the application and the basic skills required for competency. All of the chapters in this part cover the essential tasks necessary for using the program.

 Critical Thinking. Part II combines problem solving and critical thinking while adding skills required to produce useful work.

 Advanced Features. Part III combines advanced skills designed to improve productivity and proficiency.

 Conceptual Introductions. Each chapter begins with a list of objectives, a list of key terms and definitions, and a short, conceptual overview that clearly tell the student what will be covered in that chapter.

 Objectives Covered. The chapter objectives are each covered individually and are introduced with a brief why-this-is-important or explanatory paragraph. Each objective includes at least one hands-on exercise.

 Key Terms. New terms are printed in italic when first introduced. The term also is printed in bold in the margin of the text so that the student can make the connection between the definition in the *Key Terms* box and the use of the term in context.

 Self Evaluation. Each chapter ends with self-evaluation review questions, four Quick Projects, and two In-Depth projects. Projects are written so that two are specific to the chapter, two are continuing projects specific to the part, and two are *stretch* projects that require critical thinking.

 Part Projects. Each of the three parts ends with two comprehensive applications projects that combine the knowledge and skills learned in that part. One is an individual project and one is a team project.

 Linked Case Studies. Each applications title includes Case Studies that, while specific to the particular application covered in that book, are also part of an overall series project. The Case Studies can be used to link different applications and create actual business projects, with source materials drawn from the various applications.

 Boxed Sidebars and Special Features. To maintain student interest and show the effectiveness of the application in practical situations, each chapter contains at least one boxed sidebar and one special features box. Boxed sidebars provide human interest and real-world examples, while special features boxes emphasize an advanced or particularly interesting skill.

 Appendix on Windows. A special appendix introducing Windows to novice users is included at the back of each *ACUMEN* text. This Introduction to Windows gives the user an overview of basic Windows features and includes a hands-on tutorial.

Instructor's Materials

A comprehensive *Instructor's Manual* containing topic overviews, key terms, and solutions to all exercises and problems is available for each book. An *Instructor's Resource Disk* containing exercise and problem files, as well as all solutions files, is also available. The *Instructor's Resource Disk* contains data files that can be distributed to the user via disk or over a computer network. It also contains the integrated Case Studies and accompanying solutions, and a complete text-based copy of the *Instructor's Manual*.

Software Upgrades

ACUMEN adopters are eligible to participate in boyd & fraser's software upgrade program. Contact your sales representative for specific details.

Acknowledgments

The following reviewers helped shape this text by providing valuable comments:

Jackie Artmayer	Oklahoma City Community College
Ben Barnes	Mountain View College
Elizabeth Bates	Lynn University
Mitch Decker	Colorado Technical College
Paula Ecklund	Faqua School of Business
Joan Lumpkin	Wright University
Marie McCooey	Bryant Business School
Gail MonteCarlo	Gloucester Community College
Joyce Nielsen	
George Novotny	Ferris State University
Susan Therrien	
Kay Turpin	San Joquain Delta College

Special thanks go to Linda Ericksen, Series Editor, for her work on the entire list of *ACUMEN* series titles.

ACUMEN Series Titles

boyd & fraser is proud of the diversity, variety, and quantity of the computer education resources we offer designed to meet your instructional needs. New titles will be added for major software applications as the programs are released in new versions. Our current offerings include:

DOS:

DOS 6.22   ISBN 0-87709-971-5

WordPerfect 6.0 for DOS   ISBN 0-87709-956-1

Windows:

Windows 3.1   ISBN 0-87709-965-0

Windows 95   ISBN 0-7895-0349-2

Ami Pro 3.1 for Windows   ISBN 0-87709-962-6

Word 6.0 for Windows   ISBN 0-87709-959-6

WordPerfect 6.1 for Windows   ISBN 0-87709-953-7

Excel 5.0 for Windows   ISBN 0-87709-980-4

Lotus 1-2-3, Release 5 for Windows   ISBN 0-87709-974-X

Access 2.0 for Windows   ISBN 0-87709-983-9

Paradox 5.0 for Windows   ISBN 0-87709-968-5

QuattroPro 6.0 for Windows   ISBN 0-87709-977-4

Combined Applications:

Acumen: Target Edition:
DOS 6.2 Essentials, Windows 3.1 Essentials,
Word 6.0 for Windows, Excel 5.0 for Windows,
Access 2.0 for Windows   ISBN 0-7895-0199-6

Chapter 1

Overview of DOS

All computer systems require an operating system to direct the activities of the hardware. The primary objective of Chapter 1 is to introduce you to the Disk Operating System (DOS) used by most PCs. Additionally Chapter 1 teaches you the basic functions related to file management and command processing. This overview provides the necessary foundation to help you understand and use the DOS commands explained in this text. Specifically you will learn the major parts of DOS, understand how files are saved on disks, know the difference between internal and external DOS commands, and begin using DOS by booting the system.

INTRODUCTION TO DOS

An operating system is an integral part of all computer systems. It allows users like you to conveniently use the computer as a tool. For example, suppose you wanted to use your computer to create a term paper with a new word processing program. You would have to know how to load and execute the correct program. In addition, each application has to know how to save and retrieve disk files on your disk. This is all accomplished by the computer's disk operating system, called **DOS**.

DOS is the translator between the hardware and software. It coordinates and controls all the activities of the computer (see Figure 1-1). DOS contains a group of commands and programs that allow users to interact directly with the computer. For example, it provides an easy way to copy data from one disk to another, allowing you to conveniently make backup copies of important data.

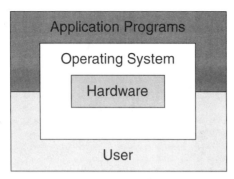

Figure 1-1 **The Role of an Operating System**

This chapter introduces you to a specific type of disk operating system called **MS-DOS** (also, **PC-DOS**). MS-DOS is Microsoft's version and PC-DOS is the same version written by IBM. The two operating systems are very similar and can be used on all IBM and IBM-compatible PCs. Because of the similarities between both operating systems, this text refers to either system simply as DOS.

BASIC DOS FUNCTIONS

DOS has three major functions. First, it controls the input and output operations of your computer. Second, it interprets and executes commands that you enter from your keyboard or other input devices. Third, it lets you permanently save files on disks and organize them effectively.

Control Input/Output Operations

All application programs share the same input and output problems. They all have to accept data from the keyboard, display data on the monitor, store data temporarily in main memory, store data permanently on disk, and retrieve data from disks. A great number of instructions are required to coordinate and control all these activities on a PC. Without an operating system, each application, such as a word processing or payroll program, would have to duplicate these instructions.

Interpret and Execute Commands

The command processor part of DOS interprets and executes the commands you enter. Without an operating system, you would have no effective way to communicate with the hardware and direct its activities.

Manage Files

Computer users are heavily involved with the file management role of DOS. For example, sometimes you need to list, save, rename, copy, or delete files on a disk. DOS provides a series of commands to allow both the user and the application programs to manage the multitude of disk files that are created over a period of time.

SAVING FILES WITH DOS

A **file** is a group of related records, where each **record** consists of an organized group of characters. Records are saved as part of a file. Records consist of either program instructions or data. Thus files are categorized as either program files or data files.

Because the files you create and work with in main memory are temporary, all operating systems must be able to save files on disk. Files become permanent only when you save them on disk. When you turn off the computer or otherwise lose power to main memory, everything in main memory is destroyed. DOS does not save files automatically. You can duplicate files by using the COPY command (see Chapter 4).

Although the process appears to be fairly simple, DOS goes through several important steps to save files. The following overview explains the process of saving files.

1. Before a disk can be used to store data, it must be specifically formatted by the operating system. The FORMAT command is used to properly define the areas on the disk for recording data. When you issue a SAVE command from an application program or directly from DOS, the operating system reads the directory portion of the disk to determine a suitable location to save the file.

2. If the file being saved is a new file, DOS tries to locate enough empty space to hold the file. If the file was previously saved on that disk, DOS replaces the contents of the old file on the disk with the contents of the file currently in main memory. Because DOS uses whatever areas it can find to save the data, the locations may not be adjoining. Files written in noncontiguous locations are called **fragmented files**. The additional disk head movement caused by fragmentation may slow down the reading and writing of these files considerably.

3. When a file has been saved, DOS updates a special area on the disk with system information. DOS uses this information to create a directory listing of files on a disk and to retrieve files when needed. This reserved area on disk is covered further in the explanation of the FORMAT command in Chapter 2.

MAJOR DOS PARTS

Before a DOS command can be executed, it must be loaded into the main memory of the CPU. Main memory is also called **Random Access Memory (RAM)**. Because DOS is too large to reside in RAM at one time, DOS commands are subdivided into two parts: the RAM-resident portion (that always resides in RAM) and a set of utility programs that remain on disk until they are needed. The RAM-resident portion is initially loaded into RAM when the computer is first turned on. Let's take a closer look at the major parts of DOS.

RAM-Resident Portion of DOS

The RAM-resident portion of DOS is made up of four specific files: the COMMAND.COM file and three DOS system files. The **COMMAND.COM** file contains many commonly used DOS commands. These commands let you list the filenames stored on a disk and let you copy, view, and delete files. DOS uses the two system files to translate general operating system commands into the specific input/output instructions that your computer hardware requires. When you list the files contained on your DOS disk, the three system files do not appear on the directory of files. Therefore, they are called **hidden files.**

Utility Programs

Whereas most of the common DOS commands are grouped into a single file (COMMAND.COM), the remaining DOS commands are stored in individual disk files, referred to as DOS **utility programs.** These programs (commands) are only loaded into RAM when they are needed. For example, the program used to format your disks (FORMAT.COM) is loaded into RAM only when it is being executed.

BOOTING DOS

Before you can use an operating system, you must load it from a secondary storage device such as a disk to the computer's main memory. Because not all parts of the operating system can be loaded at once, a process known as **booting the system** is used to load the controlling portion of the operating system. With hard disk systems, DOS looks for the DOS system files on the hard disk rather than on a floppy disk drive.

There are two general methods of booting any operating system. One method is called a **cold boot** because the computer is turned off prior to booting the operating system. The second method is termed a **warm boot** because the computer is already warmed up and was previously in use, but it needs to be rebooted. In both cases, DOS goes through the same process.

Cold Boot

Experience has shown that people learn best by doing. So go ahead and follow these steps to do a cold boot of DOS from a floppy disk. If you have a hard disk system, skip the first step and substitute all references to drive A with drive C.

1. Place the disk containing DOS in disk drive A with the latch securely closed. Drive A is usually either the top drive or the leftmost drive in PCs with two drives.
2. Turn on the power to both the monitor and the CPU.

3. The PC begins executing a small startup program permanently stored in the CPU that instructs it to do some diagnostic testing. The tests include checking the computer's RAM and keyboard interface to make sure they are functional. If it finds any problems, the program displays an appropriate error message on your screen.

4. If the computer passes the diagnostic checks, the startup program loads the DOS hidden files contained on the DOS disk in drive A. It also loads the file called COMMAND.COM into RAM from drive A. The COMMAND.COM file contains many of the DOS commands you will use. It is also responsible for interpreting and executing your commands. If you are working with a hard disk system, these system files are retrieved from the hard disk (drive C).

5. With floppy disk systems and some hard disk systems, DOS asks you to enter the correct date and time, so that it can keep track of the time with its own clock. Once you have entered the date and time, DOS displays the version number of the operating system and prompts you to enter a command. The default prompt for a floppy disk system is A:\>, where the A represents the default disk drive, the one containing the DOS disk. Figure 1-2 shows you how the screen might look if you entered a date of December 25, 1994, and a time of 2:35 pm. A:\> is the system prompt, which requests the next command. The underline character following A:\> represents the cursor on the screen. For illustrative purposes, the data you entered is shown in boldface.

```
Starting MS-DOS...
Current date is Sat 07-24-1994
Enter new date (mm-dd-yy): 12-25-94
Current time is 10:03:21.72a
Enter new time: 2.35p
Microsoft(R) MS-DOS(R) Version 6.20
            (C)Copyright Microsoft Corp 1981-1993.

A:\>
```

Figure 1-2   **Screen Display After Booting DOS**

The system date is entered using month, day, and year in the form of mm-dd-yy or mm/dd/yy. You can use a slash (/), a hyphen (-), or a period (.) to separate the date entries.

The system time is entered using hours, minutes, and seconds in the form of hh:mm:ss. The use of seconds (ss) is optional. You can enter time using the 24-hour system (military time) or the 12-hour system. To use the 12-hour system, key in the appropriate letter (a or p) after the time. Use the colon (:) or a period (.) to separate time entries. Thus you may enter 13.45, 13:45, 1.45p, or 1:45p to indicate 1:45 in the afternoon.

When you are finished entering a command or data, like the date or time, you need to press the Enter key to let the system know you are finished keying.

As long as DOS continues running, it keeps track of the time, automatically changing both the time and the date. Many systems today have a small battery and additional software to keep track of the date and time when the computer is turned off. When the system is booted, the system date and time can be set automatically from this battery-operated clock-calendar.

Warm Boot

The major difference between the two ways of booting the system is in how the boot process is initiated. In a cold boot, the computer is simply turned on to initiate the booting process. With a warm boot, the power is already on. It is advisable to use a warm boot whenever you can to minimize the possibility of damaging the electronic chips when the power is turned on. A warm boot is activated by pressing three keys simultaneously: the Control (Ctrl) key, the Alternate (Alt) key, and the Delete (Del) key. This combination of keystrokes is shown as Ctrl-Alt-Del.

To do a warm boot, press the Ctrl and Alt keys with your left hand, lightly tap the Del key with your right hand, and release all three keys. Most newer PCs have a Reset button that can be pressed to do a warm boot.

TYPES OF DOS COMMANDS

Because the full set of DOS commands is too extensive to be completely loaded into RAM, some commands are initially loaded into RAM and others remain externally stored on the DOS disk until they are needed. Thus DOS commands are classified as being either internal or external commands.

Internal Commands

The **internal commands** are contained in the COMMAND.COM file. Internal commands are available to DOS when the system is booted and a copy of the COMMAND.COM file is loaded into RAM. Because it is much faster to access commands from RAM, the designers of DOS chose many commonly used commands to be internal.

Essential internal commands include DIR, TYPE, and DEL. The DIR command is used to get a directory listing of files stored on a disk. The TYPE command is used to display the contents of non-executable files (e.g., MEMO.TXT) on the screen. The DEL command allows you to delete unwanted files from a disk. These internal commands are covered in Chapter 2.

External Commands

Because RAM must be used efficiently, **external commands** reside on the DOS disk as utility programs. They are only loaded into RAM when they are needed. The FORMAT command (see Chapter 2) is an example of an external command.

SUMMARY OF NEW TERMS

DOS is the disk operating system for IBM and IBM-compatible PCs. It consists of a set of system **files** stored on a disk, representing all of the commands needed to make the computer operate and run application programs. Four of the DOS files (COMMAND.COM and three hidden files) are copied into memory when the system is turned on, or booted. These are called **RAM-resident files** because they remain in memory until the power is turned off. The COMMAND.COM file contains commonly used DOS **internal commands**. The **hidden files** (files that do not show on a directory listing) provide DOS with the input and output instructions needed to direct the hardware. Less common DOS **external commands** reside on the DOS disk as utility programs. They are copied into memory as they are needed. Before you can issue any commands to a computer, the controlling portion of the operating system must be loaded to memory. This process, known as **booting** the system, loads the RAM-resident DOS files (COMMAND.COM and the two hidden files), requests the system date and time, and displays the system prompt. You can begin issuing commands at the **system prompt (A:\>)**. The term **warm boot** is used to describe the boot process when the computer is already turned on. Otherwise, the process is called a **cold boot**.

Review Questions

1. Why is an operating system necessary?
2. What does DOS mean?
3. Why are there two different types of DOS (MS-DOS and IBM DOS)?
4. What are the primary functions of DOS?
5. What does RAM-resident mean?
6. What is the function of the system information area of a disk?
7. What is an application program?
8. What are hidden files?
9. What is the purpose of hidden files?
10. What is the purpose of the COMMAND.COM file?

11. What does booting the system mean?

12. What happens to data in RAM when the power is turned off?

13. Why are some DOS commands referred to as being internal and others are called external?

14. What type of commands are contained in the COMMAND.COM file?

15. What process must be performed before files can be saved on a disk?

16. When you initiate a system boot, what happens after the diagnostic testing is completed?

17. What is the difference between a warm boot and a cold boot?

18. How do you activate a warm boot?

19. How would you enter a system date of February 14, 1995?

20. How would you enter a time of 2:35 pm?

Floppy Disk Lab Exercises

These exercises were developed for computers with two floppy disk drives. Drive A contains your DOS disk, and drive B is used for your data disk.

This first exercise has you do a warm boot; it assumes that the system is already turned on from work done previously in the chapter. If it is not already on, do a cold boot of your system before proceeding.

- With the DOS disk in drive A, use Ctrl-Alt-Del to boot DOS.
- Enter the current date in mm-dd-yy format (e.g., 4-15-94).
- Enter the correct time in hh:mm format (e.g., 11:07).
- Remember to press the Enter key (or Return) to cause the computer to act on your data.

This completes the Chapter 1 lab exercise. Remember to remove your floppy disks before you leave the computer. There are a variety of ways to leave your computer when you are finished, so ask your instructor how to exit your system.

Hard Disk Lab Exercises

These exercises were developed for computers with one hard disk and one floppy disk drive. Drive C contains your DOS disk, and drive A is used for your data disk.

This first exercise has you do a warm boot; it assumes that the system is already turned on from work done previously in the chapter. If it is not already on, do a cold boot of your system before proceeding.

- Use Ctrl-Alt-Del to boot DOS.
- Enter the current date in mm-dd-yy format (e.g., 4-15-94).
- Enter the correct time in hh:mm format (e.g., 11:07).
- Remember to press the Enter key (or Return) to cause the computer to act on your data.

This completes the Chapter 1 lab exercise. Remember to remove your floppy disk before you leave the computer. There are a variety of ways to leave your computer when you are finished, so ask your instructor how to exit your system.

Chapter 2

Beginning DOS Commands

Chapter 2 gets you started using DOS. You will learn how to format a disk, change the system date and time, get a directory listing of disk files, display the contents of disk files, and erase files from a disk.

FORMATTING DISKS WITH DOS

To save files on disk, the disk must be properly prepared to accept the data to be saved. New blank disks are "generic" and can be used with different operating systems. Therefore, each disk must be customized according to the requirements of DOS. This process is called **formatting** a disk. It includes the following:

1. Formatting creates addressable areas where data can be stored. Because each disk drive and operating system has its own addressing scheme, this activity is mandatory prior to saving files. Each of the 80 tracks on one side of most 3 ½-inch high-density floppy disks is divided into 18 sectors, for a total of 1440 sectors per side. A corresponding track and sector on both sides of a disk is called a **cluster**. It is the smallest addressable location on a disk. Typical cluster sizes are 512 and 1024 bytes, although cluster size varies with the type and density of the disk. Table 2-1 shows some of the different types of floppy disks.

2. Formatting checks every recording spot on the disk for damage, noting any clusters that are not acceptable for storing data.

3. Formatting creates a directory area and a **File Allocation Table (FAT)** on the disk. DOS uses these areas to keep track of saved files. Unacceptable disk clusters and the locations of each stored file are recorded in the disk's FAT.

Table 2-1   Floppy Disk Organization (Based on Disk Capacity)

	360KB	720KB	1.2MB	1.44MB	2.88MB
Disk size	5 ¼"	3 ½"	5 ¼"	3 ½"	3 ½"
Density type	low	low	high	high	extended
Sectors/track	9	9	15	18	36
Tracks/side	40	80	80	80	80
Bytes/cluster (allocation unit)	1024	1024	512	512	1024
Number of disks required to copy 10MB of data	29	15	9	8	4

HELP Command

Syntax: HELP [command name]

If you can't remember which DOS command to use, the **HELP command** may provide the information you need to jog your memory. When you enter HELP at the system prompt, the information available to you is equivalent to an abbreviated DOS manual.

The initial HELP screen, shown in Figure 2-1, displays the names of over one hundred DOS commands. Use the PgDn key to scroll through the commands. Place the cursor on the desired command name and press the Enter key to see information on the command's syntax and use. The essential HELP screen commands are:

- Use the Up arrow, Down arrow, PgUp, PgDn, and Tab keys to move the cursor to a command.
- Use the F1 key to get more information on using HELP. Press Esc at any time to exit from the current screen to a previous one. Press Esc multiple times to return to the initial HELP screen.
- At any time, press Alt, F, and X (one after the other) to exit HELP and return directly to the system prompt.

If you have booted DOS, enter HELP at the system prompt to see how it works. *Note:* DOS uses another command (QBASIC) that must be available for HELP to execute. When the initial HELP screen displays, do the following steps to find out information relating to the FORMAT command:

1. Press the Tab key once to move to the second column of commands.
2. Press the Down arrow key 11 times to select <Format> and then press the Enter key. Remember to use the Esc key if you make a mistake. Figure 2-2 shows the initial HELP screen for the FORMAT command.
3. Use the PgDn key to scroll through the displayed information about FORMAT. Then use the PgUp key 6 or 7 times to return to the top of FORMAT.

```
File  Search                                                          Help
─────────────── MS-DOS Help: Command Reference ───────────────────────────
Use the scroll bars to see more commands. Or, press the PAGE DOWN key. For
more information about using MS-DOS Help, choose How to Use MS-DOS Help
from the Help menu, or press F1. To exit MS-DOS Help, press ALT, F, X.

<What's New in MS-DOS 6.2?>

<ANSI.SYS>                 <Erase>                   <Nlsfunc>
<Append>                   <Exit>                    <Numlock>
<Attrib>                   <Expand>                  <Path>
<Batch commands>           <Fasthelp>                <Pause>
<Break>                    <Fastopen>                <Power>
<Buffers>                  <Fc>                      <POWER.EXE>
<Call>                     <Fcbs>                    <Print>
<Cd>                       <Fdisk>                   <Prompt>
<Chcp>                     <Files>                   <Qbasic>
<Chdir>                    <Find>                    <RAMDRIVE.SYS>
<Chkdsk>                   <For>                     <Rd>
<CHKSTATE.SYS>             <Format>                  <Rem>
<Choice>                   <Goto>                    <Ren>
<Cls>                      <Graphics>                <Rename>
<Command>                  <Help>                    <Replace>
<Alt+C=Contents> <Alt+N=Next> <Alt+B=Back>           |     N 00006:002
```

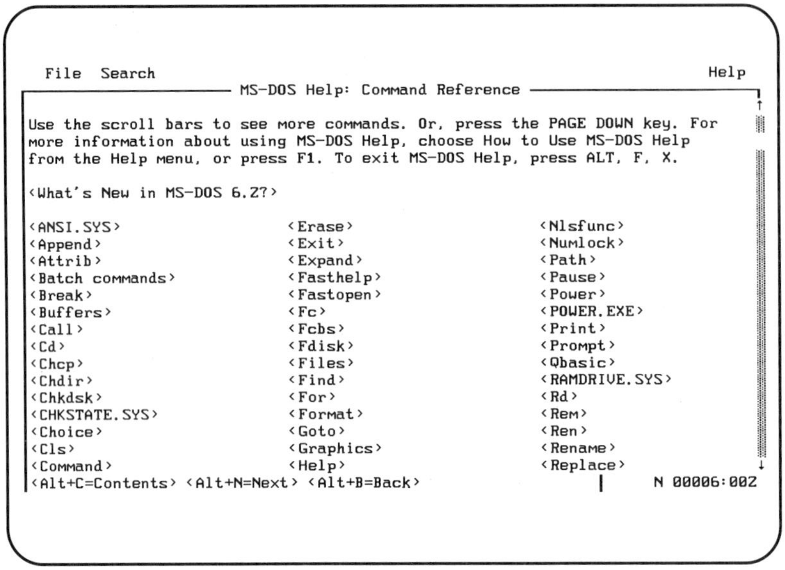

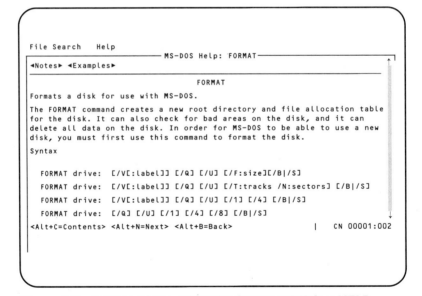

Figure 2-1 First HELP Screen

```
File Search   Help
──────────────────────── MS-DOS Help: FORMAT ─────────────────────────
◄Notes► ◄Examples►
───────────────────────────────────────────────────────────────────────
                              FORMAT
Formats a disk for use with MS-DOS.
The FORMAT command creates a new root directory and file allocation table
for the disk. It can also check for bad areas on the disk, and it can
delete all data on the disk. In order for MS-DOS to be able to use a new
disk, you must first use this command to format the disk.
Syntax

   FORMAT drive:  [/V[:label]] [/Q] [/U] [/F:size][/B|/S]
   FORMAT drive:  [/V[:label]] [/Q] [/U] [/T:tracks /N:sectors] [/B|/S]
   FORMAT drive:  [/V[:label]] [/Q] [/U] [/1] [/4] [/B|/S]
   FORMAT drive:  [/Q] [/U] [/1] [/4] [/8] [/B|/S]
<Alt+C=Contents> <Alt+N=Next> <Alt+B=Back>              |    CN 00001:002
```

Figure 2-2 Syntax of the FORMAT Command Using HELP

4. Make sure the cursor is on <Notes> and press the Enter key to access more detailed information about FORMAT. Use the PgDn key as required. Use the PgUp key to return to the top of FORMAT notes.
5. When the cursor is on <Examples>, press the Enter key to see some examples of using the FORMAT command. Press Esc 3 or 4 times to return to the initial FORMAT screen.
6. Press Alt, F, X to exit HELP and return to the system prompt.

View the syntax of the command you want to use by entering the command name along with the HELP command. For example, suppose you wanted help with the FORMAT command. Figure 2-2 shows you what displays when you enter the **HELP FORMAT command.** A space is used as a delimiter to separate parts of the command. Experiment using the HELP command, first with just HELP and then with specific commands that interest you. DOS commands can be entered in either upper- or lowercase characters. The commands HELP, help, and Help yield the same result.

The syntax of DOS commands used in this text will be much easier to follow than that provided by the online HELP feature. In an effort to simplify the process of understanding and using DOS, only the most common command parameters and options will be shown in this text. Bracketed items ([]) are optional. You can use the HELP command to obtain additional information if you need it.

FORMAT Command

Syntax: [d:][path]FORMAT d: [/F:size] [/S]

The **FORMAT command** prepares a disk to record data. All disks must be formatted before DOS can use them. Formatting a disk destroys all previously recorded data. During the format process for a 360KB disk, two write heads prepare 40 tracks (0–39) on each side for recording data. On other types of floppy disks, 80 tracks (0–79) are prepared. FORMAT examines each disk for defective sectors, making a note of any bad sectors on the FAT. The FORMAT command prompts you to enter a volume label to give your disk a name. In addition to establishing a disk directory and FAT, DOS randomly generates a disk serial number. This unique identifier changes only when the disk is reformatted.

To make a disk bootable, use the **/S option**. It formats the disk and copies to it three hidden system files and COMMAND.COM. The slash (/) identifies a command option to DOS. The term "switch" is also used to represent a command option. If you enter the FORMAT command without specifying a disk, DOS does not automatically format the default disk. This feature keeps you from reformatting your DOS disk accidentally.

The **/F option** specifies the size of the floppy disk to format. For example, you would use this option to format a 720KB disk in a 1.44MB floppy disk drive (i.e., /F:720). Due to the technical limitations of a low-density drive, you cannot format a 1.44MB disk in a 720KB disk drive. Figure 2-3 shows format using the /F option.

```
C:\DOS>format b:/s/f:720
Insert new diskette for drive B:
and press ENTER when ready...

Checking existing disk format.
Saving UNFORMAT information.
Verifying 720K
Format complete.
System transferred

Volume label (11 characters, ENTER for none)? dos62

      730,112 bytes total disk space
      199,680 bytes used by system
      530,432 bytes available on disk

        1,024 bytes in each allocation unit.
          518 allocation units available on disk.

Volume Serial Number is 141B-13E4

Format another (Y/N)?n

C:\DOS>
```

Figure 2-3 Screen Display of FORMAT with /F Option

FORMAT produces a status report on the screen with the following statistics for the formatted disk: total disk space, sectors marked as defective (if any), space allocated to the system files (when /S is used), the amount of space left for other files, and information about the allocation units.

Examples of Usage:

A:\> FORMAT b:/s
Formats the disk in drive B so that it contains the system files, making it bootable.

A:\> format b: /f:720
Formats the disk in drive B as a 720KB disk.

A:\> format/s
Rejected — disk parameter missing.

B:\> A:FORMAT B:
Formats the disk in drive B.

DEFAULT DISK DRIVE CONCEPT

In many instances, DOS needs to know what disk drive applies to the commands you enter. It uses a **default drive approach**. If you enter a command without a drive specification, DOS substitutes the default drive in its place. You specify the default drive. You can save a significant number of keystrokes by understanding this concept. *You need to specify a disk drive only if it is other than the default drive.*

DOS uses a disk drive coding scheme consisting of a letter and a colon. A: and B: are floppy drives, whereas C: and D: represent hard disk drives. DOS establishes the initial default drive as the disk drive that was used to boot the system: drive A for floppy disk systems and drive C for hard disk systems. You can easily change the default to another drive. When you boot DOS and see the A:\> prompt, the A:\ refers to the default disk drive and its root directory. The > symbol in the DOS system prompt lets you know that DOS is ready to receive a command.

To change the default drive, enter a new disk drive letter followed by a colon. For example, the command B: entered at the A:\> prompt, changes the default disk. Once entered, the default drive becomes drive B (the second floppy drive) and the system prompt is displayed as B:\>.

FILE NAMING CONVENTIONS

DOS uses all parts of the filename to tell it where to search for a specified file. The **full filename** consists of four parts: the disk drive containing the file, the path, the filename, and the filename extension. Brackets are used to identify the parts of the full filename that are optional. Only the filename itself is required. The full filename is as follows:

```
[d:][path]filename[.ext]
```

The first part of the full filename, **[d:]**, specifies the disk drive. To specify a drive, enter the drive letter followed by a colon. If you omit the drive designator, DOS substitutes the default disk drive.

The next part, **[path]**, represents the subdirectory containing the file and is covered in Chapter 5.

DOS requires a **filename** that is 1–8 characters long. Filenames can be made up of numeric digits, alphabetic letters, and certain special characters. Avoid using any of the special characters, except the hyphen (-), which can be used to make filenames more readable. Do not use spaces or punctuation marks.

The final part of the full filename is an optional **extension [.ext]**. It is 1–3 characters long and uses the same set of characters valid for filenames. If an extension is used, it must be preceded by a period (e.g., A:JONES89.DOC). The extension indicates the type of file. Filename extensions to aid in keeping track of files. For example, you can use .DOC, .WP, or .TXT for word processing files and .WK1 or .WKS for worksheet files.

When creating filenames, use meaningful titles. You can code a great deal of information into your filenames. For example, a set of memos on a new bottling plant could be named BOTTLE1.DOC, BOTTLE2.DOC, etc. If the memo dates were critical, they could be named BOTmmdd.DOC, where mmdd represents the month and day a memo was created. When disk directories are displayed in filename sequence, the memos would appear listed together chronologically. As the number of files grows, the benefits of care and foresight in creating filenames becomes more significant.

When you assign extensions, abide by the standard, commonly used extensions. Many of these are listed in Table 2-2.

Table 2-2 **Standard Filename Extensions**

EXECUTABLE FILES (executed by entering filename only with no extension):

.BAT	Batch file (file containing executable commands)
.COM	Machine language program file (limited to 64KB)
.EXE	Machine language program file (larger than COM files)

TEXT FILES (not executable, but can be displayed on screen):

.BAK	Backup text file
.BAS	BASIC program file (needs compiling first)
.DAT	Data file
.DBF	dBASE file
.DOC	Documentation file
.HLP	Help file (contains help instructions)
.INI	Initialization file (such as DOSSHELL.INI)
.PRN	Printer file (can be modified prior to printing)
.SYS	System ASCII file (such as CONFIG.SYS)
.TXT	Text file

OTHER FILES (not executable and not in a form that can be displayed):

.DEF	Program definition (setup) file
.FON	Font file
.GIF	GIF graphics image file
.OVL	Overlay file (used by large programs)
.PIF	Program information file (memory allocation in Windows)
.SYS	System binary file (such as ANSI.SYS)
.TIF	TIFF graphics image file
.WK1	Lotus 1-2-3 worksheet file
.WPG	WordPerfect graphics file

DISK DIRECTORY LISTING

When you get a **directory listing** on your screen, DOS displays more than just the filenames. The file size in bytes (where 1 byte stores 1 character) and a **date stamp** are displayed for each file. The date stamp is the date and time that each file was last changed on the disk. As the number of files becomes large, the correct date stamp becomes extremely useful. This is why it is important to enter the date and time correctly whenever DOS is booted.

DIR (Directory) Command

Syntax: DIR [d:][filename[.ext]] [/Ax] [/Oy] [/P] [/W]

The **DIR command** displays a directory, or listing, of the files on a specified disk. It includes the volume identification, the name of each file, the size in bytes of each file, the date and time each file was last modified, and the amount of free space left on the disk. If you do not designate a disk drive, DOS uses the default drive. If you specify a filename, the directory is limited to only that name. Because the filename can contain wildcard characters, the directory can be limited to a specific group of files. Wildcards are explained in the next section.

Use the **/A option** to selectively list files based on file attributes. For example, because hidden files are not normally included on DIR listings, the command DIR /AH can be used to list hidden files. The following attribute values may be substituted for x in the preceding syntax of the DIR command:

H|-H
Lists files that are (hidden | not hidden).

R|-R
Lists files that are (read-only | not read-only).

You can use the **/O option** to list directory files sequentially in a variety of ways. The eight sequences (or orders) that may be substituted for y in the preceding syntax are as follows:

D|-D
Orders by date (oldest to newest | newest to oldest).

E|-E
Orders alphabetically by extension (ascending | descending).

N|-N
Orders alphabetically by name (ascending | descending).

S|-S
Orders by size (smallest to largest | largest to smallest).

Use the **/P option** to cause the computer to pause during the display of the directory when the screen is full. It continues displaying again after you press any key to signal that you are ready to continue. Figure 2-4 shows what the screen might look like using the pause option with a directory in ascending sequence by filename. The first two <DIR> entries on the listing are system files that DOS uses to keep track of subdirectory information on the disk.

Use the **/W option** to display the directory in a "wide" format. With this format, filenames only display five columns across. Figure 2-5 shows a directory with the /W option.

```
Volume in drive C is PENWORTH
 Volume Serial Number is 1AF4-8878
 Directory of C:\DOS

.                <DIR>      01-01-80  10:57p
..               <DIR>      01-01-80  10:57p
DBLSPACE BIN     51214 03-10-93   6:00a
FORMAT   COM     22717 03-10-93   6:00a
NLSFUNC  EXE      7036 03-10-93   6:00a
ANSI     SYS      9065 03-10-93   6:00a
ATTRIB   EXE     11165 03-10-93   6:00a
CHKDSK   EXE     12907 03-10-93   6:00a
EDIT     COM       413 03-10-93   6:00a
EXPAND   EXE     16129 03-10-93   6:00a
MORE     COM      2546 03-10-93   6:00a
MSD      EXE    158470 03-10-93   6:00a
QBASIC   EXE    194309 03-10-93   6:00a
RESTORE  EXE     38294 03-10-93   6:00a
SYS      COM      9379 03-10-93   6:00a
UNFORMAT COM     12738 03-10-93   6:00a
NETWORKS TXT     23444 03-10-93   6:00a
README   TXT     61857 03-10-93   6:00a
OS2      TXT      6358 03-10-93   6:00a
Press any key to continue . . .
```

Figure 2-4   Screen Display of Sorted DIR with Pause (/P) Option

```
[.]              [..]             DBLSPACE.BIN     FORMAT.COM       NLSFUNC.EXE
ANSI.SYS         ATTRIB.EXE       CHKDSK.EXE       EDIT.COM         EXPAND.EXE
MORE.COM         MSD.EXE          QBASIC.EXE       RESTORE.EXE      SYS.COM
UNFORMAT.COM     NETWORKS.TXT     README.TXT       OS2.TXT          DEBUG.EXE
FDISK.EXE        DOSSHELL.VID     DOSSHELL.GRB     CHOICE.COM       MODE.COM
DEFRAG.EXE       GORILLA.BAS      DEFRAG.HLP       DOSSWAP.EXE      EGA.CPI
EGA.SYS          HIMEM.SYS        MEM.EXE          XCOPY.EXE        DOSSHELL.INI
DELTREE.EXE      MOVE.EXE         NIBBLES.BAS      RAMDRIVE.SYS     SMARTDRV.EXE
QBASIC.INI       DOSHELP.HLP      DOSSHELL.COM     DOSSHELL.EXE     FASTHELP.EXE
EDIT.HLP         HELP.HLP         FASTOPEN.EXE     HELP.COM         PRINT.EXE
QBASIC.HLP       SHARE.EXE        SETVER.EXE       APPEND.EXE       DELOLDOS.EXE
DISKCOMP.COM     DISKCOPY.COM     DRIVER.SYS       FC.EXE           FIND.EXE
GRAPHICS.COM     GRAPHICS.PRO     LABEL.EXE        SMARTMON.EXE     SMARTMON.HLP
SORT.EXE         LOADFIX.COM      REPLACE.EXE      SUBST.EXE        TREE.COM
DOSKEY.COM       VFINTD.386       MSBACKUP.EXE     MSBACKUP.OVL     MSBACKFB.OVL
MSBACKFR.OVL     CHKSTATE.SYS     UNDELETE.EXE     MSBACKDB.OVL     MSBACKDR.OVL
MSBACKUP.HLP     DBLSPACE.EXE     MSBCONFG.OVL     MSBCONFG.HLP     MEMMAKER.HLP
MEMMAKER.INF     INTERLNK.EXE     INTERSVR.EXE     MSCDEX.EXE       DBLSPACE.HLP
DBLSPACE.INF     DBLSPACE.SYS     DBLWIN.HLP       DOSSHELL.HLP     EMM386.EXE
MEMMAKER.EXE     SIZER.EXE        MONOUMB.386      MSTOOLS.DLL      MSAV.EXE
MSAV.HLP         MSAVHELP.OVL     MSAVIRUS.LST     VSAFE.COM        COMMAND.COM
       105 file(s)     4232182 bytes
                       4620288 bytes free

C:\DOS>
```

Figure 2-5   Screen Display of Sorted DIR with Wide (/W) Option

Examples of Usage:

`A:\> Dir`
Displays a directory of all files on the default disk drive.

`A:\> DIR B: /AR`
Displays a directory to include all read-only files on drive B.

`A:\> Dir b:/p`
Displays the drive B directory, pausing whenever the screen fills up.
Note: The slash serves as a command delimiter.

`A:\> dir /w`
Displays filenames on the default drive in wide format.

`A:\>` Displays filenames on drive B, sequenced by filename, in wide format, pausing after each screen.

`A:\> dir a:dog*.*`
Displays directory of drive A, of only those files with filenames that begin with DOG.

`A:\> dir *.doc/o-d`
Displays all .DOC files on drive A in new-to-old sequence by date.

WILDCARD CHARACTERS

Wildcard characters, like jokers in a card game, can be used to represent any characters in DOS commands. The most common DOS wildcard character is the asterisk (*), representing a group of characters.

The best way to understand wildcard characters is by example. To display a directory of all files on drive A that begin with LTR and that have a .DOC extension, enter the following command: DIR A:LTR*.DOC. In this example, the asterisk substitutes for any group of characters, so that LTRSMITH.DOC, LTR4.DOC, and LTRBILL3.DOC would all display the directory. Wildcard characters can also be used with optional filename extensions.

Examples of Usage:

`DIR A:TEXT.*`
Lists all files on drive A with a filename of TEXT, regardless of extension.

`DIR B:P*.TR* /W`
Lists in wide format any filename on drive B starting with P and having an extension starting with TR.

Try the following examples using your DOS disk by entering the commands at the system prompt. Remember that these commands may be entered using either upper- or lowercase characters.

```
DIR
```
Lists all files on the default disk.

```
DIR *.EXE
```
Lists just those with an extension of .EXE.

```
DIR S*.*
```
Lists all files that begin with an S.

MORE BEGINNING DOS COMMANDS

DATE Command

```
Syntax: DATE [mm-dd-yy]  or  DATE [mm/dd/yy]
```

The **DATE command** lets you change the system date. If you specify a new date, the system date changes immediately. If you omit this optional parameter, the system displays the current date and prompts you to enter a new date. Press the Enter key if you do not want to change the date. If you enter an invalid date, you are prompted to enter a correct date.

Examples of Usage:

```
A:\> DATE 3/4/94
```
Changes the system date to March 4, 1994.

```
A:\> date 03-04-94
```
Also changes the system date to March 4, 1994.

```
A:\> Date
```
Displays the current date and prompts you to change it.

TIME Command

```
Syntax: TIME [hh:mm[:ss]]
```

The **TIME command** changes the system time. It is important to keep the correct date and time on the system because it is recorded in the directory information for each file you save. If you omit the optional parameters, the current system time displays and you are prompted to change it. To leave the time unchanged, press the Enter key. If you enter an invalid time, the system prompts you to enter a correct time.

Examples of Usage:

```
A:\> TIME 8:30
```
Changes the system time to 8:30 am.

```
A:\> time 14:15
```
Changes the time to 2:15 pm.

```
A:\> TIME 2.15P
```
Also changes the time to 2:15 pm.

```
A:\> TIME
```
Displays the current time and prompts you to enter a new time.

DEL (Delete) Command

```
Syntax: DEL [d:]filename[.ext]
```

The **DEL command** deletes the specified disk file. If the drive designator is not specified, DOS assumes the default drive. You can use wildcard characters in the filename and extension, but do so with caution because multiple files can quickly be deleted with a single command. If you use *.* to specify the files, all the files on the designated disk will be deleted. When you attempt to delete all the files on a disk, the DEL command gives you some measure of protection against eliminating files by mistake. It pauses to ask you if you are sure. You are not allowed to delete read-only files or DOS hidden files.

The term "delete" may be misleading because files are not physically deleted from a disk file. DEL causes the file's entry on the disk directory to be flagged as deleted and the appropriate clusters in the FAT are shown as no longer being allocated.

Examples of Usage:

```
A:\> DEL B:MEMO.TXT
```
Deletes the MEMO.TXT file from drive B.

```
A:\> DEL memo.*
```
Deletes all files named MEMO from drive A regardless of extension.

```
B:\> del *.txt
```
Deletes all files on drive B with a .TXT extension.

TYPE Command

```
Syntax: TYPE [d:]filename[.ext]
```

The **TYPE command** displays the contents of a "listable" file on the standard output device, normally the monitor. It does not alter files. This command should be used for text files only, not command files with an .EXE or .COM extension. Wildcard characters are not allowed in the TYPE command.

Examples of Usage:

```
A:\> TYPE B:READ.ME
```
Displays on the screen the contents of READ.ME, stored on drive B.

```
A:\> type read.me
```
Displays on the screen the contents of READ.ME, stored on drive A.

```
A:\> TYPE AUTOEXEC.BAT >PRN
```
Types the contents of AUTOEXEC.BAT, redirecting the output from the screen to the printer; this is a handy technique for getting a printout of a text file.

SUMMARY OF NEW TERMS

The **HELP command** provides information about the syntax of DOS commands. Before data can be stored on a disk, the disk must be formatted to record files. DOS uses the **FORMAT command** to establish **clusters** where data can be stored. FORMAT sets up a directory and **File Allocation Table** on the disk to help DOS keep track of files.

DOS tries to make it easier to enter commands by automatically converting all characters to uppercase and by using the **default disk concept**. It assumes that the files referred to in the commands are on the default disk unless you tell it otherwise. The **full filename**, used to identify files stored on disk, is made up of at least three parts: an optional disk drive designator, a 1–8 character filename, and an optional 1–3 character extension preceded by a period. The extension is very useful in classifying the type of file on directory listings.

The **DIR command** is used to display a listing of files on a disk. By using **wildcard characters** with the DIR command, you can limit the listing to a specific group of files. The **DATE command** and **TIME command** are used to change the system date and time. The **DEL command** lets you delete files from a disk. The **TYPE command** lets you view the contents of text files.

Review Questions

1. What is a disk cluster?
2. What does the command DIR B:/P do when executed?

3. What is the purpose of the FORMAT command?

4. What is a filename extension and how does DOS identify it?

5. What are some common extensions for listable files?

6. What are some common extensions for executable files?

7. Why might you want to use the /F option with FORMAT?

8. What is the benefit of using wildcard characters in the DIR command?

9. Which command removes the filename from the disk directory but does not actually erase the file from the disk?

10. Which option displays a directory listing on the screen with multiple filenames on a line?

11. What command would you enter to get a directory listing of all files on drive B with an extension of .DOC sequenced by descending file size?

12. What command do you enter to change the system time to 4:00 pm?

13. What type of file is considered "listable" with TYPE?

14. What command would you enter to display all the hidden files on drive A?

15. How can you change the system date once the system is booted?

16. What special areas are created on a disk when it is formatted?

17. What is the structure of the full filename?

18. What part of the full filename is always required?

19. Explain the default disk drive concept.

20. At the B:\> system prompt, what command is entered to change the system prompt back to A:\>?

Floppy Disk Lab Exercises

1. Format a data disk to contain the DOS system files:

   - Enter FORMAT B:/S/F:n, where n = the type (capacity) of the disk being formatted (refer to Table 2-1).
   - When prompted, insert a blank disk in drive B and press Enter.
   - Enter your name when prompted to enter a volume label.
   - Enter N when prompted to format another disk.

Figure 2-6 shows you what the screen should look like when you finish formatting your blank disk.

```
C:\DOS>format b:/s/f:720
Insert new diskette for drive B:
and press ENTER when ready...

Checking existing disk format.
Saving UNFORMAT information.
Verifying 720K
Format complete.
System transferred

Volume label (11 characters, ENTER for none)? dos62

        730,112 bytes total disk space
        199,680 bytes used by system
        530,432 bytes available on disk

        1,024 bytes in each allocation unit.
          518 allocation units available on disk.

Volume Serial Number is 141B-13E4

Format another (Y/N)?n

C:\DOS>
```

Figure 2-6 Screen Display of the FORMAT Command

2. The COPY CON command, covered in Chapter 4, can be used to quickly create a text file from the keyboard:

- Enter COPY CON B:READ.ME (or copy con b:read.me).

- Then enter the following text, pressing the Enter key at the end of each line. If you have already pressed the Enter key at the end of a line, you cannot correct any errors in that line. You must press the Ctrl-C key to cancel the COPY command and start all over.

```
When entering DOS commands, the commands and parameters
<Enter> must be separated by delimiters.  Delimiters are
normally <Enter> either spaces or commas.  They can be
used interchangeably <Enter> in any command (e.g., COPY
A:OLDFILE,B:).  <F6><Enter>
```

- After typing the last line, press the F6 function key (to tell DOS you are done with the copy operation) and press Enter. F6 generates a Ctrl-Z character (^Z) that identifies the end of a text file to DOS. This text is now stored on the disk in drive B with the filename of READ.ME.

Figure 2-7 shows the result of the COPY CON command.

3. Display a disk file on the monitor:

- Enter DIR B: (to verify that your file was stored). This listing should include READ.ME plus the COMMAND.COM file placed there during formatting with the system option.

- Enter TYPE B:READ.ME to display the contents of your text file on the monitor.

```
A:\>COPY CON B:READ.ME
When entering DOS commands, the commands and parameters
must be separated by delimiters.  Delimiters are normally
either spaces or commas.  They can used interchangeably
within any command (i.e., COPY A:OLDFILE,B:).^Z
        1 file(s) copied

A:\>
```

Figure 2-7 Screen Display of COPY CON

4. Delete a file from a disk. Before you experiment with the DEL command, use the COPY command (Chapter 4) to make a copy of an existing file:

- Enter COPY B:READ.ME B:READ.BAK (to make a copy).
- Enter DIR B: (to verify that the file was copied).
- Enter DEL B:READ.BAK (to delete READ.BAK).
- Enter DIR B: (to verify that the file was deleted).

Your screen should look similar to that shown in Figure 2-8.

```
Volume in drive B is SOUTHWORTH
Volume Serial Number is 0D39-14E9
Directory of B:\

COMMAND   COM        54,619 09-30-93    6:20a
READ      ME            221 01-29-94    1:34p
READ      BAK           221 01-29-94    1:34p
        3 file(s)        55,061 bytes
                        528,384 bytes free

A:\>DEL B:READ.BAK

A:\>DIR B:

 Volume in drive B is SOUTHWORTH
 Volume Serial Number is 0D39-14E9
 Directory of B:\

COMMAND   COM        54,619 09-30-93    6:20a
READ      ME            221 01-29-94    1:34p
        2 file(s)        54,840 bytes
                        529,408 bytes free

A:\>
```

Figure 2-8 Screen Display of DEL and DIR

5. Change the default disk drive:

- Enter B: (to switch default to drive B).
- Enter DIR (to get a directory of the default disk, drive B).

- Enter DIR A:/W/ON (to get a wide listing of filenames on drive A in name sequence).
- Enter A: (to change the default drive back to drive A).

Don't be concerned if several lines have scrolled off the top of your screen. Your screen should look similar to Figure 2-9.

```
B:\>DIR

Volume in drive B is SOUTHWORTH
Volume Serial Number is 0D39-14E9
Directory of B:\

COMMAND   COM         54,619 09-30-93    6:20a
READ      ME             221 01-29-94    1:34p
        2 file(s)        54,840 bytes
                        529,408 bytes free

B:\>DIR A:/W/ON

 Volume in drive A is DOS62
 Volume Serial Number is 0C38-12E9
 Directory of A:\

CHKDSK.EXE      COMMAND.COM     DISKCOPY.COM    FORMAT.COM      MOVE.EXE
UNDELETE.EXE    UNDELETE.INI
        7 file(s)       148,081 bytes
                         66,560 bytes free

B:\>
```

Figure 2-9   Screen Display of DIR

6. Enter DATE and follow the prompts to change the current system date to December 25, 1994. Use the TIME command to change the system time to 1:45 pm. Most users enter hh:mm only (e.g., 13:45) and ignore the seconds.

7. Bonus exercise:

- Use the DATE command to enter the current date. Then use the TIME command to make sure that the system time is correct.
- Use the COPY CON command to create a new file called B:EX2.TXT. It should contain the following five lines of text, entered one line at a time, pressing the Enter key at the end of each line shown. After typing the last line of text, press the F6 key and then the Enter key.

```
The Lotus 1-2-3 software package, as the name implies,
has <Enter> three logical and integrated parts: spread-
sheets, graphics, <Enter> and data management.
Integration means that you do not <Enter> have to leave
the spreadsheet portion, for instance, to get <Enter> to
the graphing or data management portions. <F6><Enter>
```

- Use the TYPE command to display this newly created file.

- Using DOS wildcard characters, delete all files on drive B with a filename of EX2 and any extension. Before you press the Enter key, be sure your command is keyed correctly or you may delete more files than you intend. One file should be deleted. Display a directory listing to check the status of files on drive B. It should look similar to Figure 2-8.

This completes the Chapter 2 lab exercises. Don't forget to remove your floppy disks before you leave the computer.

Hard Disk Lab Exercises

1. After booting DOS, change to the subdirectory containing your DOS commands. See your instructor for specific instructions. Format a data disk that will contain the DOS system files as follows:

   - Enter FORMAT A:/S/F:n, where n = the type (capacity) of the disk being formatted (refer to Table 2-1).
   - When prompted, insert a blank disk in drive A and press Enter.
   - Enter your name when prompted to enter a volume label.
   - Enter N when prompted to format another disk.

Figure 2-6 shows you what the screen should look like when you finish formatting your blank disk.

2. The COPY CON command, covered in Chapter 4, can be used to quickly create a text file from the keyboard:

   - Enter COPY CON A:READ.ME (or copy con a:read.me).
   - Then enter the following text, pressing the Enter key at the end of each line. If you have already pressed the Enter key at the end of a line, you cannot correct any errors in that line. You must press the Ctrl-C key to cancel the COPY command and start all over.

```
When entering DOS commands, the commands and parameters
<Enter> must be separated by delimiters.  Delimiters are
normally <Enter> either spaces or commas.  They can be
used interchangeably <Enter> in any command (e.g., COPY
A:OLDFILE,B:). <F6><Enter>
```

   - After typing the last line, press the F6 function key (to tell DOS you are done with the copy operation) and press Enter. F6 generates a Ctrl-Z character (^Z) that identifies the end of a text file to DOS. This text is now stored on the disk in drive A with the filename of READ.ME.

Figure 2-7 shows the result of the COPY CON command.

3. Display a disk file on the monitor:

 - Enter `DIR A:` (to verify that your file was stored). This listing should include READ.ME plus the COMMAND.COM file placed there during formatting with the system option.
 - Enter `TYPE A:READ.ME` (to display the contents of your text file on the monitor).

4. Delete a file from a disk. Before you experiment with the DEL command, use the COPY command (Chapter 4) to make a copy of an existing file:

 - Enter `COPY A:READ.ME A:READ.BAK` (to make a copy).
 - Enter `DIR A:` (to verify that the file was copied).
 - Enter `DEL A:READ.BAK` (to delete READ.BAK).
 - Enter `DIR A:` (to verify that the file was deleted).

Your screen should look similar to that shown in Figure 2-8.

5. Change the default disk drive:

 - Enter `A:` (to switch default to drive A).
 - Enter `DIR` (to get a directory of the default disk, drive A).
 - Enter `DIR C:/W` (to get a wide listing of drive C).
 - Enter `C:` (to change the default drive back to drive C).

Don't be concerned if several lines have scrolled off the top of your screen. Your screen should look similar to Figure 2-9.

6. Enter `DATE` and follow the prompts to change the current system date to December 25, 1994. Use the TIME command to change the system time to 1:45 pm. Most users enter hh:mm only (e.g., 13:45) and ignore seconds.

7. Bonus exercise:

 - Use the DATE command to enter the current date. Then use the TIME command to make sure that the system time is correct.
 - Use the COPY CON command to create a new file called A:EX2.TXT. It should contain the following five lines of text, entered one line at a time, pressing the Enter key at the end of each line shown. After typing the last line of text, press the F6 key and then the Enter key.

```
The Lotus 1-2-3 software package, as the name implies,
has <Enter> three logical and integrated parts: spread-
sheets, graphics, <Enter> and data management.
Integration means that you do not <Enter> have to leave
the spreadsheet portion, for instance, to get <Enter> to
the graphing or data management portions. <F6><Enter>
```

- Use the TYPE command to display this newly created file.
- Using DOS wildcard characters, delete all files on drive A with a filename of EX2 and any extension. Before you press the Enter key, be sure your command is keyed correctly, or you may delete more files than you intend. One file should be deleted. Display a directory listing to check the status of files on drive A. It should look similar to Figure 2-8.

This completes the Chapter 2 lab exercises. Don't forget to remove your floppy disk before you leave the computer.

Chapter 3

Additional DOS Commands

Chapter 3 has three major objectives. The first objective is to review the most common error messages so you will know what to do if an error occurs. Another major objective is to show how DISKCOPY and COPY can be used to make backup copies of important files. The last objective of Chapter 3 is to show you how to use four more essential DOS commands: CHKDSK, RENAME, UNDELETE, and VER.

COMMON DOS ERROR MESSAGES

Commands you enter may be rejected by DOS, resulting in the error message **"Bad Command or Filename."** This message can occur when the command was not spelled correctly, or DOS cannot find the command. If this error message appears, simply retype the command correctly.

If you attempt to read a disk and no disk is in the designated drive or the drive latch is open, you get the following two-line error message, where X is the disk drive with the error:

```
Disk error reading Drive X

Abort, Retry, Fail?
```

If you get this message, correct the problem and enter R to retry. You can also enter A to abort the command, or F to let the disk operation fail without aborting the command. It is not advisable, however, to Fail (F) error messages, nor should you change disks before responding with R.

The space between the read/write heads and the surface of the disks is incredibly small. Therefore, any movement of the disk drive when the disk is operating can be very destructive. When you attempt to access damaged data or read an unformatted disk, you see the following message displayed:

```
General Failure reading Drive X

Abort, Retry, Fail?
```

THE IMPORTANCE OF BACKUP

All disks may be subject to damage from time to time. Files on floppy disks can become unreadable due to fingerprints, dirt, and improperly adjusted read/write heads. Hard disk drives can be severely damaged if they are moved without the read/write heads parked correctly. Static electricity can disrupt the data that is magnetically recorded on all disks. Therefore, you should periodically back up important files, especially if they are difficult to re-create. You can easily back up individual files using the COPY command. The DISKCOPY command is generally used to back up an entire disk.

DISKCOPY Command (External)

```
Syntax: [d:]DISKCOPY d:[d:] [/V]
```

DISKCOPY is an external command that resides on the DOS disk. It is used to copy the entire contents of one floppy disk to another floppy disk. It copies the directory portion of the disk, the File Allocation Table, and all files. The **/V option** directs DOS to verify that the disk was copied correctly. Because DISKCOPY makes an exact duplicate of the source disk, it does not require that the target disk be formatted. It cannot be used to duplicate a hard disk.

Two potential problems can occur when using DISKCOPY. By attempting to make an duplicate copy of the source disk, it is possible for data from good clusters to be copied into corresponding clusters on the target disk that are damaged. DOS cannot retrieve data written in bad clusters. Therefore, you should always include the /V option when using DISKCOPY.

The second limitation of DISKCOPY is that fragmented files on the source disk are written in the same fragmented clusters on the target disk. The COPY command, covered next, eliminates both of the problems inherent with DISKCOPY.

Examples of Usage:

```
A:> DISKCOPY A: B: /V
```
Makes an exact copy of the disk in drive A onto a disk in drive B.

```
A:> diskcopy a:
```
Makes a copy of the first disk inserted into drive A onto a second disk inserted into drive A when prompted.

COPY Command (Internal)

Syntax: `COPY [d:]filename[.ext] [d:][filename[.ext]]`, where the first filename is the source file and the second filename (optional) is the target file (the new file being created).

The **COPY command** lets you make copies of disk files to a previously formatted disk. It facilitates making backup or working copies of files without destroying existing files. However, the copy operation replaces any files on the target disk with the same name as the target file with the contents of the source.

If you omit either disk device designator, [d:], DOS substitutes the default device. If you omit the optional target filename, the system uses the same filename as the source file.

You can copy a group of files with a single command by using wildcard characters in filenames with the COPY command. For example, to copy all files on drive A with an extension of .DOC to drive B, enter:
`COPY A:*.DOC B:`

If you specify the source file as CON (CONsole keyboard), the target file contains characters you enter from the keyboard. Type characters as you would from a typewriter, pressing the Enter key at the end of each line. Lines are limited to 127 characters each. DOS uses Ctrl-Z to mark the end of a text file. To stop recording characters and to insert the Ctrl-Z character, press the F6 function key followed by the Enter key. For example,
`COPY CON A:KBFILE.TXT` (followed by lines of text and F6)

Examples of Usage:

`A:\> COPY *.* B:`
Copies all files on the default disk, drive A, to the disk in drive B, without renaming files.

`A:\> copy B:*.DOC`
Copies all files on drive B with an extension of .DOC to the default disk.

`A:\> Copy filea.doc b:filea.bak`
Copies FILEA.DOC on drive A to drive B, renaming it FILEA.BAK.

`A:\> copy con b:read.me`
Creates a file on drive B named READ.ME consisting of lines of data entered from the console.

`A:\> COPY A:*.DOC B:*.BAK`
Copies all files on drive A with a .DOC extension to drive B, renaming them with an extension of .BAK.

```
A:\> COPY FILEA.DOC PRN
```
Copies a text file to the printer.

MORE ESSENTIAL DOS COMMANDS

CHKDSK (Check Disk) Command (External)

Syntax: [d:][path]CHKDSK [d:][filename[.ext]] [/F] [/V]

The **CHKDSK command** produces a disk status report for a specified disk and lists the memory status of the system. The **/F option** fixes problems in the File Allocation Table. The **/V option** displays the full filenames of all files on a specified drive. After checking the disk, CHKDSK displays any error messages, followed by a status report. Figure 3-1 is an example of a CHKDSK report for a 720KB floppy disk.

The hidden files in the status report represent the DOS system files that are hidden from normal directory lists. The bottom portion of the report lists the memory status of a computer with 640KB of RAM. The difference between the 655,360 bytes of total memory shown in Figure 3-1 and the 560,656 bytes free is about 95KB, the amount of RAM space allocated to the resident portion of DOS and the space required to load and execute CHKDSK.

```
C:\DOS>chkdsk b:

Volume SOUTHWORTH  created 01-17-1994 12:42p
Volume Serial Number is 141B-13E4

     730,112 bytes total disk space
     144,384 bytes in 3 hidden files
      59,392 bytes in 5 user files
     526,336 bytes available on disk

       1,024 bytes in each allocation unit
         713 total allocation units on disk
         514 available allocation units on disk

     655,360 total bytes memory
     560,656 bytes free

Instead of using CHKDSK, try using SCANDISK.  SCANDISK can reliably detect
and fix a much wider range of disk problems.  For more information,
type HELP SCANDISK from the command prompt.

C:\DOS>
```

Figure 3-1   **Sample CHKDSK Report**

A file is written to contiguous clusters (allocation units) if the first unallocated space is big enough to hold it. Otherwise, DOS uses whatever clusters it finds to store a file, skipping over allocated clusters. Consequently files become fragmented.

If you specify a filename or group of files, CHKDSK displays the number of noncontiguous areas occupied by the file(s). Wildcard characters may be used in the filename. For example, you can use *.* to determine the extent of file fragmentation on a given directory of a disk. You can use the DEFRAG command (Chapter 5) to unfragment files. This process is recommended to improve access speed.

Lost allocation clusters are parts of files shown as allocated in the File Allocation Table (FAT), even though they are absent in the directory. This discrepancy occurs because of some malfunction during the file saving process. It can happen if electrical power is lost or if the computer is reset during a disk write operation.

You can use the /F option to combine lost clusters on a disk into a file named FILEnnnn.CHK, where nnnn is a unique number. This is a good command to use periodically. When the FAT is corrupted, it cannot accurately track files on disk. Whenever CHKDSK /F finds any lost clusters, you will see an error message similar to this:

```
6 lost clusters found in 2 chains.

Convert lost chains to files (Y/N)?
```

In this example, CHKDSK determined that lost data came from two different files (or two parts of the same file). If you respond "Y," a .CHK file is created for each chain. If a .CHK file created by CHKDSK is listable, you can use TYPE to view the lost data. After identifying the lost data, you should delete all .CHK files to make room for other files on the disk. If you respond "N," DOS removes the lost clusters, but it doesn't save the contents.

When you use CHKDSK *without the /F option* and errors are detected, you must run it again with the /F option to fix those errors. If CHKDSK reports problems, fix them before continuing to use the disk. The problems only get worse if you wait. You should use CHKDSK whenever the following conditions exist:

- Unexpected data appears within a file or on a directory listing.
- A program fails to run as it should.
- You suspect disk damage after major problems, such as a power failure or a system lockup.

Beginning with Version 6.2 of DOS, an improved disk repair command was added to replace the limited "fix" capabilities of CHKDSK. This command, called SCANDISK, should be used to fix any errors reported by CHKDSK.

Examples of Usage:

```
A:\> CHKDSK
```
Displays a status report for the default drive.

```
A:\> chkdsk /f
```
Displays a status report for drive A and fixes any errors found in the FAT.

```
A:\> b:chkdsk a:*.*
```
Loads CHKDSK from drive B, displays a status report for drive A, and lists any fragmented files found on drive A.

```
A:\> chkdsk B:read.me
```
Displays a status report for drive B and displays the number of noncontiguous areas contained in READ.ME.

```
C:\WORD\FILES> CHKDSK *.*
```
Displays a status report identifying any fragmented files found in the C:\WORD\FILES subdirectory.

RENAME (REN) Command (Internal)

```
Syntax: RENAME [d:]filename[.ext] filename[.ext]
```

The **RENAME command** changes the name of the file specified in the first parameter to the filename given in the second parameter. A drive designator is not allowed in the second parameter and is rejected if entered. RENAME gives you an easy way to make disguised copies of important files. For example, a spreadsheet file called BUDGET.WK1 could be renamed WORK.EXE. A shortened and commonly used version of RENAME is **REN**.

Examples of Usage:

```
A:\> RENAME b:ltr1.doc ltr1.bak
```
Renames ltr1.doc on drive B to ltr1.bak.

```
A:\> ren Ltr1.doc ltr1.bak
```
Renames ltr1.doc on drive A to ltr1.bak.

```
A:\> REN *.TXT *.DOC
```
Renames all files with a .TXT extension to have a .DOC extension.

```
A:\> ren ltr1.doc *.bak
```
Renames ltr1.doc on drive A to ltr1.bak, using wildcard characters to save keystrokes.

UNDELETE Command (External)

Syntax: `[d:][path]UNDELETE [[d:]filename[.ext]] [/LIST]`

The **UNDELETE command** restores files deleted with the DEL command. You can selectively undelete files by specifying the filename(s). Wildcard characters are permitted. If no filenames are supplied, UNDELETE lets you restore all deleted files, prompting you for confirmation on each file. The /LIST option lists deleted files, but it does not undelete any files.

UNDELETE only restores deleted files if the space freed up in the FAT has not yet been used by other files. *Whenever you accidentally delete a file, use the UNDELETE command immediately, before the data gets overwritten.* Figure 3-2 shows you a screen display of an UNDELETE operation.

```
UNDELETE - A delete protection facility
Copyright (C) 1987-1993 Central Point Software, Inc.
All rights reserved.

Directory: A:\
File Specifications: *.*

    Delete Sentry control file not found.

    Deletion-tracking file not found.

    MS-DOS directory contains     1 deleted files.
    Of those,    1 files may be recovered.
Using the MS-DOS directory method.

     ?ESTFILE TXT       140  7-24-93 11:01a  ...A  Undelete (Y/N)?Y
     Please type the first character for ?ESTFILE.TXT: T

File successfully undeleted.

A:\>
```

Figure 3-2   Screen Display of an UNDELETE Process

Examples of Usage:

`A:\> undelete b:/list`
Lists any deleted files on drive B.

`A:\> UNDELETE B:*.DOC`
Lets you restore any deleted .DOC files on drive B.

Using the DOS Shell to Undelete Files

The Undelete option is included in the Disk Utilities submenu in the Main program menu area. It can be used to identify the deleted files in the currently selected directory (the one highlighted in the Directory Tree). The default command parameter in the text box is the /LIST option. Generally you should execute the command with this option before attempting to undelete a file.

To undelete a file in the current directory, enter the appropriate parameter into the text box, such as *.* or *.BAK. If the undelete process was successful, you should tell DOS to reread the disk's directory to include the undelete file(s) on the File List. This is done by choosing the Refresh option on the Tree pull-down menu.

There could be a deleted file on your current DOS directory. Use the Undelete option (with /LIST as the parameter) to find out which files on the DOS directory have a deleted status. After identifying the deleted file(s), use the Undelete option to undelete one of them. Then refresh the screen to cause the undelete file(s) to be included in the File List.

VER (Version) Command (Internal)

Syntax: VER

The **VER command** displays the DOS version number being used on the screen (e.g., MS-DOS Version 6.20). If you boot your system with one version of DOS and then attempt to execute external DOS commands from a disk with a different version, you may get an "Incorrect DOS Version" error message. The VER command is used to identify the DOS version used to boot your system.

SUMMARY OF NEW TERMS

It is not uncommon to have error messages flash on the screen when you are using DOS. The most common message is **"Bad Command or Filename."** This simply means that DOS cannot recognize the command entered, or it cannot find the command. It is also possible for files on disks to become damaged (not readable). Therefore, it is recommended that backup copies (duplicates) be made of important files from time to time. The **DISKCOPY command** makes copies of all files on one disk to another disk. To avoid problems associated with DISKCOPY, you can use the COPY command. The **COPY command** copies selected files from one disk to another, or makes a copy on the same disk, using a different filename. If you experience problems with a disk, you can use the **CHKDSK command** to determine the extent of file fragmentation and to report on the overall status of file space. The **RENAME command** gives files a new name, without copying the file. The **UNDELETE command** recovers a previously deleted file if the original space it occupied on disk has not yet been used to store another file. The **VER command** quickly identifies the version of DOS in use.

Review Questions

1. What is the function of brackets in this text for describing command formats?
2. What is the function of the slash in this text for describing command formats?
3. What is a delimiter and why is it required?
4. What does the message "Bad Command or Filename" mean?
5. Why should you use the /V option with DISKCOPY?
6. Why is it important to back up files occasionally?
7. What does the COPY CON command let you do?
8. What happens when you enter the following command?
   ```
   COPY TEST.TXT B:
   ```
9. What is the benefit of using wildcard characters in the COPY command?
10. What happens when you enter the following command?
    ```
    COPY *.TXT B:*.BAK
    ```
11. What happens if you include a disk drive designator on both parameters of the RENAME command?
12. What command is used to fix lost allocation clusters?
13. What DOS command lists all deleted files on drive B?
14. Under what circumstances would you be able to successfully undelete a previously deleted file?
15. What are fragmented disk files?
16. How can you determine the amount of file fragmentation on a disk?
17. How can you improve access speeds of disks that contain fragmented files?
18. What is the primary difference between using the COPY command and the DISKCOPY command?
19. Which DOS command lists all files on a disk and displays the full filenames?
20. Under what circumstance can you get the message "Incorrect DOS Version?"

Floppy Disk Lab Exercises

1. Boot DOS (drive A) and insert your data disk in drive B. Then enter DIR B: to refresh your memory of the files on drive B. Two files that were previously created in the Chapter 2 lab exercises, COMMAND.COM and READ.ME, should display.

2. Enter COPY B:READ.ME B:READ.BAK to create a copy of READ.ME
   with a different extension. What would happen if you entered the
   command without the last parameter (B:READ.BAK)? DOS would have
   substituted the default disk and used the source filename, creating the
   backup copy on drive A with the same name.

3. Enter DIR B: to get a current directory listing of your data disk. Enter
   REN B:READ.BAK TEST.TXT to change the filename of READ.BAK
   on your data disk. Enter DIR B: to verify the name change. Your
   screen should look similar to Figure 3-3.

```
Volume in drive B is SOUTHWORTH
   Volume Serial Number is 0D39-14E9
   Directory of B:\

COMMAND  COM        54,619 09-30-93    6:20a
READ     ME            221 01-29-94    1:34p
READ     BAK           221 01-29-94    1:34p
        3 file(s)          55,061 bytes
                          528,384 bytes free

A:\>REN B:READ.BAK TEST.TXT

A:\>DIR B:

  Volume in drive B is SOUTHWORTH
  Volume Serial Number is 0D39-14E9
  Directory of B:\

COMMAND  COM        54,619 09-30-93    6:20a
READ     ME            221 01-29-94    1:34p
TEST     TXT           221 01-29-94    1:34p
        3 file(s)          55,061 bytes
                          528,384 bytes free

A:\>
```

Figure 3-3 **Screen Display of DIR**

4. Enter VER to see what DOS version you are using.

5. Enter CHKDSK to get a status report of the default drive (A:). Now enter
   CHKDSK B:*.* to get a status report of your data disk, directing the
   system to check for any fragmented files. Your display screen should
   look similar to Figure 3-1, with the added message "All specified
   file(s) are contiguous."

6. Use CHKDSK with the /V option to get a listing of all the files on your
   DOS disk. Then use it to view the files on your data disk.

7. Use the COPY command to create two new files as follows:
   COPY B:READ.ME B:TEST.1
   COPY B:READ.ME B:TEST.2

Using wildcard characters, delete all the files on drive B that have a filename of TEST. Enter UNDELETE B:/LIST to see what files are deleted on
your data disk. Your screen should look similar to Figure 3-4. Then enter
UNDELETE B:TEST.* to restore them. Follow the instructions to undelete

files and restore the first character of each filename (T). Get a directory listing of drive B to verify that the files were restored.

```
A:\>UNDELETE B:/LIST

UNDELETE - A delete protection facility
Copyright (C) 1987-1993 Central Point Software, Inc.
All rights reserved.

Directory: B:\
File Specifications: *.*

     Delete Sentry control file not found.

     Deletion-tracking file not found.

     MS-DOS directory contains     3 deleted files.
     Of those,     3 files may be recovered.

Using the MS-DOS directory method.
          ?EST     TXT     218   7-24-93 10:48a   ...A
          ?EST     1       218   7-24-93 10:48a   ...A
          ?EST     2       218   7-24-93 10:48a   ...A

A:\>
```

Figure 3-4   Screen Display of UNDELETE

8. Bonus exercise:

   ▪ Using the RENAME command, change all files on drive B with a filename of TEST (and any extension) to NEWNAME. Use wildcard characters whenever possible. Use the DIR command to confirm the results.

   ▪ Copy all files on drive B with a filename of NEWNAME to a filename of TEST on drive B, without changing the filename extension. Display all the files on drive B to confirm that the operation was successful.

   ▪ Delete all files on drive B with a filename of NEWNAME and use the DIR command to verify the results. The directory listing should look similar to Figure 3-4.

This completes the Chapter 3 lab exercises. When you are done, be sure to remove your disks.

Hard Disk Lab Exercises

1. Boot DOS (drive C) and insert your data disk in drive A. Then enter DIR A: to refresh your memory of the files on drive A. Two files that were previously created in the Chapter 2 lab exercises, COMMAND.COM and READ.ME, should display.

2. Enter COPY A:READ.ME A:READ.BAK to create a copy of READ.ME with a different extension. What would happen if you entered the command without the last parameter (A:READ.BAK)? DOS would have substituted the default disk and used the source filename, creating the backup copy on drive A with the same name.

3. Enter DIR A: to get a current directory listing of your data disk. Enter REN A:READ.BAK TEST.TXT to change the filename of READ.BAK on your data disk. Enter DIR A: to verify the name change. Your screen should look similar to Figure 3-3.

4. Enter VER to see what DOS version you are using.

5. Enter CHKDSK to get a status report of the default drive (C:). Now enter CHKDSK A:*.* to get a status report of your data disk, directing the system to check for any fragmented files. Your display screen should look similar to Figure 3-1, with the added message "All specified file(s) are contiguous."

6. Use CHKDSK with the /V option to get a listing of all the files on your DOS disk. Then use it to view the files on your data disk.

7. Use the COPY command to create two new files as follows:

   COPY A:READ.ME A:TEST.1
   COPY A:READ.ME A:TEST.2

   Using wildcard characters, delete all the files on drive A that have a filename of TEST. Enter UNDELETE A:/LIST to see what files are deleted on your data disk. Your screen should look similar to Figure 3-4. Then enter UNDELETE A:TEST.* to restore them. Follow the instructions to undelete files and restore the first character of each filename (T). Get a directory listing of drive A to verify that the files were restored.

8. Bonus exercise:

   ■ Using the RENAME command, change all files on drive A with a filename of TEST (and any extension) to NEWNAME. Use wildcard characters whenever possible. Use the DIR command to confirm the results.

   ■ Copy all files on drive A with a filename of NEWNAME to a filename of TEST on drive A, without changing the filename extension. Display all the files on drive A to confirm that the operation was successful.

   ■ Delete all files on drive A with a filename of NEWNAME, and use the DIR command to verify the results. The directory listing should look similar to Figure 3-4.

This completes the Chapter 3 lab exercises. When you are done, be sure to remove your disk.

Chapter 4

Hard Disk Commands

The first objective of Chapter 4 is to show you how to work with hard disks and subdirectories. This includes eight essential hard disk commands: MD, CD, RD, MOVE, PATH, PROMPT, DEFRAG, and MSAV. The second objective is to present a variety of useful techniques for managing hard disk systems.

HARD DISK CONSIDERATIONS

When you first use a hard disk system, you should notice two significant improvements over processing with floppy disks. First, the speed at which data can be transferred with hard disks is 10–20 times faster than it is with floppy disks. The second improvement is the amount of data that can be stored on hard disks. A 40MB hard disk can hold the equivalent of one hundred floppy disks.

The use of hard disks creates two considerations that are not as relevant when using floppy disks. The first consideration is the need for a good power supply that does not permit loss of electrical power. A temporary power loss can cause the disk's read/write heads to "crash" on the surface of the disk, causing permanent damage.

A second consideration is the need to periodically back up the data stored on your hard disk to floppy disks. Hard disk users tend to overlook this process. Get into the habit of backing up your hard disks regularly. You will be glad you did the day you turn on your computer and hear a noise like a spoon in a blender.

DIRECTORIES AND SUBDIRECTORIES

Because large amounts of data can be stored on a hard disk, it is extremely helpful to divide the total space into uniquely named areas. Each area can be reserved to store a group of files, allowing you to organize and classify files by area. DOS uses a **root directory** and optional **subdirectories** (directories within a directory) to keep track of the name and location of all files on disk. The term "directory" is often used in place of "subdirectory." You can establish directories for floppy disks, but the use of directories is more practical for hard disks.

One way to visualize directories is to compare a 40MB hard disk to a set of 100 low-density floppy disks. Conceptually each directory could represent a single floppy disk, without the physical limitations of 360KB, however. Like floppy disks, each directory could be devoted to a given application, like word processing, spreadsheets, accounting, and so on. Just as you change floppy disks, you can change to another directory. Additionally, just as commands like DEL, DIR, and COPY all relate to a given floppy disk, such commands also apply to a given directory.

You can organize and control hundreds of files on hard disk by adopting a tree-structured file directory system. Every disk has a root directory. The root directory branches into directories. The directories, in turn, can branch into further directories in a hierarchy much like that of a family tree. Each directory is assigned a unique name using the same rules we use with filenames. Floppy disks files are often organized manually by recording selected groups of files on a disk and identifying each disk with a label. Directories provide a big advantage in that they let you organize files on a hard disk "electronically." Within each directory, you can add files and create new directories. Figure 4-1 shows a graphic example of a tree-structured directory.

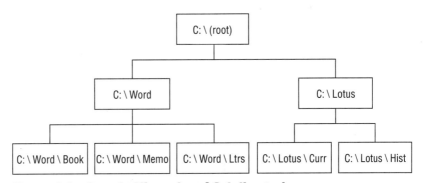

Figure 4-1   Sample Hierarchy of Subdirectories

In Figure 4-1, the root directory is divided into two directories: one for word processing and one for spreadsheets. The word processing directory, WORD, is further subdivided into three directories: one for a manuscript, one for memos, and one for letters. You can navigate through this structure by starting at the root and traveling down any of the desired branches to get to the desired directory.

DOS uses the **backslash** (\) to identify a directory name. Thus the file BOSS.DOC stored on the MEMO directory is identified with the full name C:\WORD\MEMO\BOSS.DOC. The full filename identifies a path of directories that DOS must take to find the file in the hierarchy. If the path is not included in the filename, the system looks for the file on the current directory. The backslash at the beginning of the path directs DOS to begin the path with the root directory. If the \ is not included, the path begins with the current directory. If the file you need is not on the current directory, you must provide DOS with the path to find it. This path must be part of the full filename, just as the disk designator is supplied when a file is not on the default drive.

Set up directories so that program files are separate from data files. This way, users can easily back up the directories containing data files without having to back up the unchanged program files. Directories containing program files only need to be backed up once, unless new programs have been added.

DOS has several commands that allow you to create and use directories. Any reference to the **current directory** refers to the directory in which you are currently working. You can change to another directory at any time. Entries on a directory include filenames and directory names. Directories are identified on a directory listing with the symbol <DIR>. The following recommendations should help you correctly set up the directory structure on a hard disk:

- Do not clutter up your root directory with lots of programs or data files. Generally just a few files need to be in the root directory: hidden files, COMMAND.COM, and any other files required to boot your system.
- Do not assign extensions to your directory names.
- Do not create directories more than 2 or 3 levels below the root directory.
- Give your directories short but meaningful names such as \DOS, \UTIL, \WORD, \DB, \SS, and so on.
- Do not give a file the same name as its directory name.

DOS COMMANDS RELATED TO DIRECTORIES

MD (Make Directory) Command (Internal)

Syntax: MD [d:]path

The **MD command** creates a new directory on the disk. You may create as many directories as you want, but too many can cause confusion. Each directory can contain both filenames and directory names that occur on other directories, but names must be unique within a directory.

Examples of Usage:

`C:\> MD \word`
Creates a directory named WORD one level down from the root directory.

`C:\> md \word\MEMO`
Creates a directory named MEMO one level down from the directory named WORD.

`C:\> Md games`
Creates a directory named GAMES one level down from the current directory.

CD (Change Directory) Command (Internal)

`Syntax: CD [d:][path]`

The **CD command** changes from the current directory to another one. The path is used to identify the new directory. For example, if you want to change to the root directory, you enter CD\. A leading backslash (\) in the path directs DOS to start the path at the root directory. Usually you want to start the path name at the root directory to make sure DOS is able to find it. You can enter the CD command with no parameters to display the current directory.

In directory listings, you see dot and double-dot directory entries:

`.   <DIR> 8-15-94 9:45a`

`..  <DIR> 8-15-94 9:45a`

The dot entry represents the current directory, and the double-dot entry represents the parent directory, one level up from the current directory. The double-dot entry can facilitate changing to the parent directory. For example, the command CD .. entered from the LOTUS\CURR directory changes to the LOTUS directory.

You can save keystrokes by recognizing that the symbols \ and .. are considered delimiters in DOS commands, just like a space and the slash (/). Thus the command CD\ is interpreted the same as CD \. Likewise, the command CD.. is the same as CD ...

Examples of Usage:

`C:\> CD \`
Changes to the root directory.

`C:\> Cd`
Displays the current directory.

```
C:\> cd\word\memo
```
Changes to the directory named MEMO on the WORD directory, starting from the root directory.

```
C:\> CD WORD\MEMO
```
Changes to the directory identified as MEMO on the WORD directory, starting from the current directory.

RD (Remove Directory) Command (Internal)

```
Syntax: RD [d:]path
```

The **RD command** removes a directory from disk. Before you can remove a directory, all files within that directory must be deleted and any subdirectories must be removed. Before attempting to remove the current directory, you must first change to another directory. You cannot remove the root directory.

Examples of Usage:

```
C:\> rd \word\memo
```
Removes the directory named MEMO from the WORD directory.

```
C:\> RD\WORD
```
Removes the directory named WORD from the root directory.

```
C:\> rd memo
```
Removes the directory named MEMO from the current directory.

MOVE Command (External)

```
Syntax: MOVE [d:][path]filename[.ext] [d:][path]
        filename[.ext], where the first parameter is the file(s) being
        moved (copied and deleted), and the second parameter is the
        new name and/or location.
```

The MOVE command lets you move one or more files from one location to another, renaming them if required. It is equivalent to using the COPY command, followed by the DEL command. In addition, this command lets you rename a directory.

Examples of Usage:

```
C:\> MOVE A:TEST.TXT B:TEST.BAK
```
Removes TEST.TXT from drive A, copying it to drive B and renaming it TEST.BAK.

```
C:\> move a:test.txt b:
```
Removes TEST.TXT from drive A, copying it to drive B without changing its name.

```
C:\> MOVE \UTILITY \UTIL
```
Renames the UTILITY directory on drive C to UTIL.

PATH Command (Internal)

```
Syntax: PATH [d:][path][;path][;path]
```

The command you want to execute may not always be on the current directory. The **PATH command** tells DOS the directories (and the order) to search to find a command that is not on the current directory. The commands it can search for include the DOS external commands and application programs, such as WP, LOTUS, or dBASE. The following considerations apply to the PATH command:

- PATH locates files that can be executed only, such as files that have an extension of .COM or .EXE.
- Typing PATH with no parameters displays the current path.
- Entering PATH with just a semicolon tells the system you do not want any search path.
- Issuing a PATH command does not change the current directory.
- If you boot DOS without executing a PATH command, and you have your DOS commands in a directory called MSDOS (or DOS), DOS will automatically create a search path for \MSDOS (or \DOS).

Examples of Usage:

```
C:\> Path \DOS6
```
Directs the system to look on the directory named DOS6, if it cannot find the desired command on the current directory.

```
C:\> PATH\word\ltrs
```
Directs the system to look on LTRS within WORD to find the external command it is looking for, if it is not on the current directory.

```
C:\> path
```
Displays the current search path setting.

```
C:\> Path ;
```
Deletes any previous search path setting.

```
C:\> PATH \;\UTIL;\DOS
```
Directs DOS to search three directories in the order given: root directory, \UTIL, and \DOS.

PROMPT Command (Internal)

```
Syntax: PROMPT [text],
```
where text is a variable-length string of characters. Text may

contain special strings in the form of $c, where c represents one
of the following options:

d	system date
g	the > character
n	current drive
p	current drive and directory
t	system time

The **PROMPT command** lets you change the system prompt from the
default (A:\>) to whatever you want to make it. If you enter PROMPT with
no text, the system reverts to show the current drive (ng). If you do not
set the prompt when the system is booted, DOS defaults to show the current drive and directory (pg). Figure 4-2 shows the effect on the screen
of executing the following four examples of PROMPT.

Examples of Usage:

`A:\> PROMPT Command?`
Changes the system prompt from A:\> to Command?.

`A:\> prompt DATE = $D`
Changes the system prompt to display DATE = followed by the system date.

`A:\> prompt Hi Fred $n$g`
Displays Hi Fred followed by A>.

`A> PROMPT`
Returns to the current drive prompt (ng).

```
A:\>PROMPT Command?

Command?prompt DATE = $D

DATE = Sat 07-24-1993prompt Hi Fred $n$g

Hi Fred A>PROMPT

A>
```

Figure 4-2   **Screen Display of PROMPT**

USING THE SHELL WITH DIRECTORIES

Using the DOS Shell to Change Directories

To change to a different directory, just select the new directory in the
Directory Tree. When you start the shell, only the first-level directories are
displayed. A plus sign (+) next to a directory name indicates that the directory contains one or more subdirectories. If a subdirectory you want to

change to is not included in the tree listing, you can expand the directory listings as follows:

KEYBOARD: Select the directory you want to expand and press the plus (+) key.

MOUSE: Click on the plus sign (+) next to the name of the appropriate directory.

To view *all directory levels* on the current disk, choose the **Expand All option** from the **Tree pull-down menu**. When a directory is expanded, a minus sign (–) displays next to the directory name. To collapse a directory, you can use the same process for expanding with one exception: Use a minus sign in place of a plus sign.

Using the DOS Shell to Create Directories

To simplify the process of creating a subdirectory, it is best if you select the parent directory as the current directory first. Then choose the **Create Directory option** from the **File pull-down menu**. After entering the subdirectory name in the text box, press the Enter key (or click on the OK command button) to create the new directory.

Using the DOS Shell to Remove Directories

The DOS shell has a feature that is not available from the command line. To remove an empty directory, select the directory (using the keyboard or mouse) and press the Del key. If the selected directory is empty, DOS asks you to confirm that you wish to delete it. Press Y (or select Yes) to remove the directory.

HARD DISK MANAGEMENT

One of the most difficult areas of DOS to master is the effective control and management of all the files that accumulate on hard disks. Several techniques can be employed to better manage the way you work with hard disk systems. Table 4-1 provides a good overview of these techniques.

Table 4-1 Hard Disk Management Techniques

- Develop good file naming conventions to help you better organize files.
- Use standard filename extensions to aid in classifying file types.
- Make backup copies of important data files regularly.
- Organize hard disk files into logical tree subdirectories.
- Place data files in a separate subdirectory from program files. This will shorten the time required to back up only your data files. Program files do not need to be backed up on a regular basis.
- Use AUTOEXEC.BAT and CONFIG.SYS files to customize your boot process.
- Limit your root directory files to only those used for booting, such as the COMMAND.COM, CONFIG.SYS, and AUTOEXEC.BAT files.

- Use the PATH command in an AUTOEXEC.BAT file to tell DOS where to look to find program files that are not in the current directory.
- Use the DIR command regularly to verify which files are in the current directory.
- Use DIR*. to display directory names in the current directory. Directory names do not have extensions.
- Use CD.. to change to the parent directory in the tree, one up from the current directory.
- Use SCANDISK periodically to fix any lost allocation clusters on the disk.
- Use DEFRAG periodically to eliminate file fragmentation your hard disk.
- Use MSAV periodically to locate and remove any computer virus from your system.
- Delete any unnecessary backup (.BAK) and temporary (.TMP) files from your hard disk.
- If you have only one floppy drive, create a temporary directory on your hard disk to serve as a transfer area for copying files from one floppy disk to another.
- Use a backup power supply to ensure a good supply of power to your computer. This will minimize any physical damage to your hard disk and/or loss of data.

The DEFRAG and MSAV Commands

Table 4-1 refers to two very useful DOS 6.2 utility programs, DEFRAG and MSAV. DEFRAG is used to optimize disk performance. It locates and eliminates file fragmentation on both floppy and hard disks. One option (/F) defragments files and ensures that the specified disk contains no empty spaces between files. Another option (/U) defragments files, but leaves empty spaces (if any) between files. Consequently, running DEFRAG with the /U option (the default) is faster. For best results, we recommend that you always use DEFRAG with the /F option.

In recent years, computer viruses have caused havoc among computer users. When a computer is infected, all files on its hard disk may be damaged. In most cases, computers are infected by using a floppy disk that contains a virus. Fortunately, the DOS 6.2 command MSAV scans your computer for known viruses. You can specify which drive(s) to scan. MSAV also scans RAM looking for infected memory.

To help it work efficiently, MSAV automatically creates a file called CHKLIST.MS. This file keeps track of file information, comparing it with new information to see if any files were changed (infected). Similar to DOSSHELL.INI, MSAV also creates a file (MSAV.INI) to keep track of how it operates.

As mentioned in Table 4-1, DOS uses two special files—CONFIG.SYS and AUTOEXEC.BAT—to modify the way it runs. When DOS is booted, the system looks for these files in the root directory of the disk used to boot DOS.

The CONFIG.SYS File

Immediately after the COMMAND.COM file and the hidden system files are loaded into RAM, DOS looks for the **CONFIG.SYS file.** The entries in this file let you specify how your system should operate and be configured. Typically CONFIG.SYS lets you control the way memory is used and install device driver programs for controlling other devices. It is a text file of system commands that can be quickly created with the COPY CON command. Here are the two CONFIG.SYS file entries most often used:

```
BUFFERS = nn

FILES = nn
```

In the BUFFERS entry, nn is the number of input/output buffers needed to improve disk performance. A high number of buffers tells DOS to read a larger than usual chunk of data from your disk. The next time your program needs data, DOS checks to see if it is already in the RAM buffer. If it is, access is almost immediate. A setting of 20–25 buffers suits most circumstances.

In the FILES entry, nn is the number of files that can be used at any one time by your programs. Because database applications often require 20 files open at the same time, the recommended number of open files is 25–30.

The AUTOEXEC.BAT File

The last step in the boot process is to execute an optional **AUTOEXEC.BAT file**. This file can simplify the boot process by executing a set of commands automatically. Figure 4-3 shows the contents of a typical AUTOEXEC.BAT file. It prompts the user to enter the correct system date and time, defines the search path for DOS, and then executes a spreadsheet program file named PAYROLL.EXE.

```
DATE
TIME
PATH C:\DOS;C:\UTIL;C:\WORD
PAYROLL
```

Figure 4-3 **Sample AUTOEXEC.BAT File**

SUMMARY OF NEW TERMS

Hard disk systems are significantly different from floppy disk systems. Not only are they much faster than floppy disks, but they can store much more data than a single floppy disk. Floppy disks are normally used to store backup copies of important hard disk files. Because so many files can be stored on a single hard disk, it is divided into **subdirectories.** The term directory is often used to refer to a subdirectory. The **backslash** (\) identifies a directory name. DOS commands let you make a directory (**MD**), change to a directory (**CD**), and remove a directory (**RD**). The **MOVE command** moves one or more files to a given location. It can also be used to rename directories. Just as DOS needs to know which floppy disk to search to find a file, it needs to know the directory (path) to locate a hard disk file. If the path is not included in a command, DOS uses a default path. The **PATH command** defines the default path. The **PROMPT command** defines how the DOS system prompt is displayed. **DEFRAG** is a DOS utility that removes file fragmentation from a disk. Another utility, **MSAV**, is used to detect and remove computer viruses from your system. A special file (**CONFIG.SYS**) improves the way files are processed in RAM. When DOS is booted, entries in the CONFIG.SYS file configure (modify) the system. The last step in the boot process involves another optional special file, the AUTOEXEC.BAT file. DOS automatically executes commands in an **AUTOEXEC.BAT file**.

Review Questions

1. How are files arranged or organized on hard disks?
2. What is the default system prompt?
3. What is meant by a "hierarchy of subdirectories"?
4. What advantages do hard disks have over floppy disks?
5. How are subdirectories designated in DOS?
6. What is a DOS path?
7. Why might you want to have relatively short directory names?
8. Which command allows you to switch from the current directory to another directory?
9. How do you switch to the root directory?
10. How can identical filenames (e.g., FORMAT.COM) exist multiple times on the same hard disk?
11. If the current directory is C:\WORD\MEMO (see Figure 4-1), what command is entered to create a directory named DOS as a part of the root directory?
12. What happens when the command MOVE A:xyz B:ABC.XYZ is entered, and the search path is correct?
13. What DOS command is used to detect a computer virus on your computer?
14. If multiple directories are included in a search path, which one is searched first?
15. How are multiple directories specified in the PATH command?
16. What command is used to view the current search path?
17. What DOS command eliminates any existing file fragmentation and how does it work?
18. What is the DOS command to a customized system prompt displaying the system date, system time, and the correct directory followed by the ">"?

19. Why is it beneficial to have program files in separate directories from data files?

20. What is the double-dot (..) entry on a directory listing?

Floppy Disk Lab Exercises

To keep from interfering with an existing hard disk structure, directories are created and used on a floppy disk.

1. Make a hierarchy of directories on drive B according to Figure 4-1 of this text as follows:
   ```
   A:\> MD B:\WORD
   A:\> MD B:\WORD\BOOK
   A:\> MD B:\WORD\MEMO
   A:\> MD B:\WORD\LTRS
   A:\> MD B:\LOTUS
   A:\> MD B:\LOTUS\CURR
   A:\> MD B:\LOTUS\HIST
   ```

2. Copy one of the files currently residing on the root directory of drive B to each of the seven directories created in Exercise 1, for example, COPY B:READ.ME B:\WORD.

3. Check out your new directory structure by entering:
   ```
   A:\> DIR B:
   ```
   Lists files and directories in the root directory.
   ```
   A:\> DIR B:\WORD
   ```
   Lists all files and directories in \WORD; the screen should look similar to Figure 4-4.

```
   Directory of B:\
COMMAND   COM          54,619 09-30-93    6:20a
READ      ME              221 01-29-94    1:34p
WORD           <DIR>          01-29-94    1:49p
LOTUS          <DIR>          01-29-94    1:50p
        4 file(s)         54,840 bytes
                         515,072 bytes free

A:\>DIR B:\WORD
Volume in drive B is SOUTHWORTH
Volume Serial Number is 0D39-14E9
Directory of B:\WORD
   .           <DIR>          01-29-94    1:49p
   ..          <DIR>          01-29-94    1:49p
BOOK           <DIR>          01-29-94    1:50p
MEMO           <DIR>          01-29-94    1:50p
LTRS           <DIR>          01-29-94    1:50p
READ      ME              221 01-29-94    1:34p
        6 file(s)            221 bytes
                         515,072 bytes free

   A:\>
```

Figure 4-4 **Screen Display of Directories in \WORD**

4. Make the current directory MEMO:
`A:\> B:`
Changes the default drive to B to minimize keystrokes.
`B:\> CD\WORD\MEMO`
Makes MEMO the current directory.
`B:\> DIR`
Tests the change to the desired directory only.
`B:\> CD\`
Changes back to the root directory.
`B:\> DIR`
Lists all files and directories in the root directory.

5. Delete the directory named HIST:
`B:\> DEL \LOTUS\HIST\*.*`
Deletes all files from HIST first.
`B:\> RD \LOTUS\HIST`
Removes HIST directory.

6. Set up a path to your DOS external commands:
`B:\> PATH A:`
Sets the path to include drive A.
`B:\> CHKDSK`
Tests the path, noting that DOS finds CHKDSK on drive A after first searching drive B.

7. Change the system prompt to display a message with the system date. Enter the following command:
`PROMPT It is $d$g What is your command?`
Execute a few commands (such as DIR, VOL, and VER) to experience the new system prompt.

8. Change the system prompt to display the current directory. Then change to several directories to see the effect:
`B:\> PROMPT $P$G`
`B:\> CD\WORD`
`B:\> CD\LOTUS\CURR`
`B:\> CD\`

9. Move B:\Lotus\READ.ME to the WORD directory on drive B, renaming it READ.TXT:
`B:\> MOVE \LOTUS\READ.ME \WORD\READ.TXT`
Using the CD and DIR commands, verify that the move was successful.

10. Bonus exercise:

   - Copy at least two files from the root directory of drive B to the WORD directory created in Exercise 1.
   - Create a directory (TEMP) from the root directory of drive B.
   - Change to TEMP, copy all files from B:\WORD to TEMP, and use the DIR command to verify the copy process. Use wildcard characters whenever possible to save keystrokes and minimize errors.

■ Remove the TEMP directory. Did you remember to delete the files in TEMP first?

This ends the Chapter 4 lab exercises. Remove your disks when you are done, and remember that "practice is the best teacher."

Hard Disk Lab Exercises

To keep from interfering with an existing hard disk structure, directories are created and used on a floppy disk.

1. Make a hierarchy of directories on drive A according to Figure 4-1 of this text as follows:
   ```
   C:\DOS> MD A:\WORD
   C:\DOS> MD A:\WORD\BOOK
   C:\DOS> MD A:\WORD\MEMO
   C:\DOS> MD A:\WORD\LTRS
   C:\DOS> MD A:\LOTUS
   C:\DOS> MD A:\LOTUS\CURR
   C:\DOS> MD A:\LOTUS\HIST
   ```

2. Copy one of the files currently residing on the root directory of drive A to each of the seven directories created in Exercise 1, for example, `COPY A:READ.ME A:\WORD`.

3. Check out your new directory structure by entering:
   ```
   C:\DOS> DIR A:
   ```
   Lists files and directories in root directory.
   ```
   C:\DOS> DIR A:\WORD
   ```
   Lists all files and directories in \WORD; the screen should look similar to Figure 4-4.

4. Make the current directory MEMO:
   ```
   C:\DOS> A:
   ```
   Changes the default drive to A to minimize keystrokes.
   ```
   A:\> CD\WORD\MEMO
   ```
   Makes MEMO the current directory.
   ```
   A:\> DIR
   ```
   Tests change to the desired directory only.
   ```
   A:\> CD\
   ```
   Changes back to the root directory.
   ```
   A:\> DIR
   ```
   Lists all files and directories on the root directory.

5. Delete the directory named HIST:
   ```
   A:\> DEL \LOTUS\HIST\*.*
   ```
   Deletes all files from HIST first.
   ```
   A:\> RD \LOTUS\HIST
   ```
   Removes HIST directory.

6. Set up a path to your DOS external commands:
   `A:\> PATH C:\`
   Sets the path to the root directory on drive C.
   `A:\> CHKDSK`
   Tests the path, noting that DOS does not find CHKDSK on drive C after first searching drive A. To make it work, reenter CHKDSK after setting the path correctly (i.e., C:\DOS).

7. Change the system prompt to display a message with the system date. Enter the following command:
   `PROMPT It is $d$g What is your command?`
   Execute a few commands (such as DIR, VOL, and VER) to experience the new system prompt.

8. Change the system prompt to display the current directory. Then change to several directories to see the effect:
   `A:\> PROMPT $P$G`
   `A:\> CD\WORD`
   `A:\> CD\LOTUS\CURR`
   `A:\> CD\`

9. Move A:\LOTUS\READ.ME to the word directory on drive A, renaming it READ.TXT:
   `A:\> MOVE \LOTUS\READ.ME \WORD\READ.TXT`
   Using the CD and DIR commands, verify that the move was successful.

10. Bonus exercise:

    - Copy at least two files from the root directory of drive A to the WORD directory created above.

    - Create a directory (TEMP) from the root directory of drive A.

    - Change to TEMP, copy all files from A:\WORD to TEMP, and use the DIR command to verify the copy process. Use wildcard characters whenever possible to save keystrokes and minimize errors.

    - Remove the TEMP directory. Did you remember to delete the files in TEMP first?

This ends the Chapter 4 lab exercises. Remove your disks when you are done, and remember that "practice is the best teacher."

DOS 6.2 Essentials Index

Chapter 1

Getting Started with Windows

Windows is an *operating system* that works with DOS (the Disk Operating System) to make it easier to use your computer. DOS controls your computer's hardware, such as disk drives and printers, and helps it work with the various application programs you use. In the past, users had to learn DOS commands to be able to use their computer efficiently. This could be difficult, because DOS commands had to be memorized. DOS uses a *command-line interface*, meaning you have to type the commands you want to enter. The commands are entered at a *prompt*, such as C:\>. Windows eliminates this memorization by using a *graphical user interface (GUI)*, pronounced "gooey." A graphical interface uses pictures, or *icons*, to represent various applications and files, and a pull-down menu system that allows you to select various commands.

In addition to the GUI, there are other Windows features that make Windows easier to use. Windows applications, such as word processing or spreadsheet programs, all use similar commands to perform basic functions. For example, printing and saving files is very similar in all Windows applications, which makes it easier to learn to use new applications. Also, with Windows you can open more than one file at the same time. You can open multiple files within an application, and also have more than one application window open on your screen. The applications all work together, so that you can copy text from your word processing document and paste it into a spreadsheet document, making it very easy to transfer information between applications.

Windows gets its name from the appearance of the open applications on your screen. They appear in *windows*, which are rectangular boxes that enclose the documents. These windows all have common features, such as a menu bar and various buttons that you will learn to use later in this topic.

Although Windows makes your computer easier to use, it works with DOS, so it still follows some DOS procedures. You will need a basic understanding of DOS, including the rules for naming files, and how *directories* help organize a disk. This book will give you a basic understanding of these concepts.

Starting Windows

Many computers are set up so that Windows starts when you turn on the computer. If you see a DOS prompt, such as C:\> or F:\>, type win and press (↵ ENTER). If you have problems starting Windows, see your instructor for specific steps for your computer.

When Windows starts, the Program Manager window appears on your screen. This window is shown in Figure 1.1.

Program Manager is the starting point for all Windows applications. Instead of entering special commands to start programs, select applications from the Program Manager.

Program Manager icon

If you do not see the Program Manager window on your screen, but see the Program Manager icon, move the mouse pointer to the icon and click the left mouse button twice. This opens the Program Manager into a window. Check with your instructor if you have problems displaying the Program Manager.

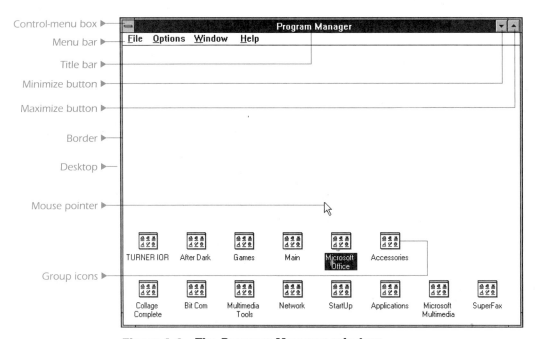

Figure 1.1   The Program Manager window

Using the Mouse

Windows was designed to be used with a *mouse*, which, after some practice, makes it easier to open applications and select options from a menu. You can also use the keyboard to select various commands, but using the mouse is often the fastest method.

To use the mouse, slide it across your desk. The mouse pointer moves in the same direction. After you have positioned the mouse pointer, there are three actions you can perform:

Click	Press the left mouse button and release it quickly.
Double-click	Press and release the left mouse button quickly twice.
Drag	Hold down the left mouse button and slide the mouse across your desk. This moves the selected icon or window. When the icon or window is repositioned, release the mouse button to drop it in the new location.

You will see the terms *click*, *double-click*, and *drag* used throughout this book. Unless the instructions specifically say to click the right mouse button, click the left button.

If you prefer to use the mouse with your left hand, see your instructor for instructions to switch the functions of the left and right mouse buttons.

Starting Applications

Start Windows applications from the Program Manager window. All of the applications are located within *group icons* that appear in this window. To open a group icon, double-click on this icon. A window appears, showing *program-item icons* that represent applications you can open. Figure 1.2 shows examples of program-item icons in the Accessories group window. Double-click on the program-item icon you want to open. The application window appears on your screen.

Program-item icon ▶

Figure 1.2   The Accessories group window

Minimizing, Maximizing, Restoring, and Closing Windows

An application icon

When you open an application or a file, the application is loaded into your computer's *memory,* or *RAM,* which is a temporary work area in your computer. Opening multiple windows can clutter your desktop. To reduce the clutter without closing a window, *minimize* the window. Minimizing changes the window to an *application icon* that appears at the bottom of your desktop. The application is still loaded into your computer's memory, but the window is no longer taking up space on your desktop. Minimizing a window can save several steps, since you don't have to open the group icon, then the program-item icon, then the document.

To see more of a specific window, you can *maximize* it, so it fills the screen. Figure 1.3 shows a maximized window.

The Maximize button is now a Restore button. Click this button to restore the window to its previous size.

To close an application window, double-click on its Control-menu box (the minus sign on the left of the window's title bar), or choose File, Exit from the menu bar.

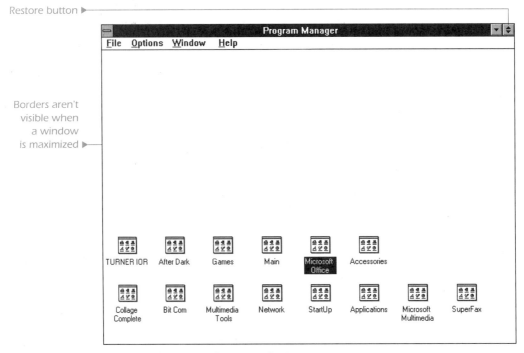

Figure 1.3 **A maximized window**

Resizing Windows

The two-headed arrow indicates you are positioned on a window border

In addition to using the Minimize and Maximize buttons to change the size of your windows, you can customize the window size by using the window borders. When you position the mouse pointer on a border, the pointer changes to a two-headed arrow.

Hold down the left mouse button, and drag the border to the left or the right to change the window size. When you have changed the window to the size you want, release the mouse button. You can change the size of two borders at the same time by positioning the mouse pointer on a window corner (the pointer becomes a diagonal two-headed arrow), then dragging the corner to a new position.

To move a window instead of resizing it, position the mouse pointer on the window's title bar. Drag the window to a different location on your desktop.

Using the Menu Bar

A menu bar appears across the top of most application windows. Use menu commands to perform functions such as opening and saving files, changing fonts, and printing. To open a menu, click the menu option, or press ⎇ALT⎊ and type the underlined letter (often referred to as the *mnemonic letter* or *hotkey*). See Figure 1.4 for an example of the File menu.

Dimmed option ►

Ellipsis ►

Figure 1.4   The File menu

Click a menu command to select it, or type the underlined letter. Some menu options are followed by an ellipsis (.   .   .). Choosing one of these commands displays a dialog box, which means Windows needs more information to complete the command. If a menu command is dimmed (light gray), it is not available at that time.

Key names next to a menu command, such as ⎇SHIFT⎊+⎇F5⎊, are *shortcut keys*. Press these keys to perform the command without opening the menu.

If you accidentally open the wrong pull-down menu, just click the correct menu option, or use the left and right arrow keys to move to the menu option you want. To close a menu without choosing a command, click outside the pull-down menu, or press ⟨ALT⟩ twice.

Using Scroll Bars

Scroll bars appear in a window when there is more information in the window than currently appears. A *vertical scroll bar* appears along the right edge of the window when more information can be displayed above or below the current information. If more information is to the right or left of the current display, a *horizontal scroll bar* appears along the bottom edge of the window. In Figure 1.5, vertical and horizontal scroll bars appear because there are group icons to the right and above what currently appears in the File Manager window.

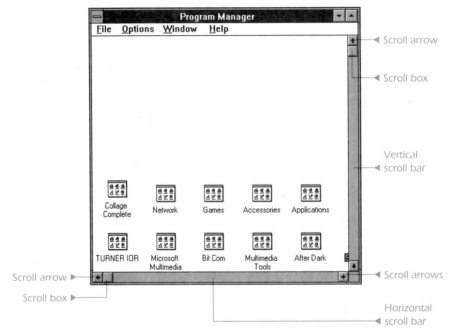

Figure 1.5 **Scroll bars appear in the File Manager window**

Scroll arrows appear along each side of the scroll bar. Click a scroll arrow to move in the direction the arrow is pointing. The *scroll box* indicates your relative location in the window. If the scroll box is at the top of the scroll bar, you are seeing the top of that window. If the scroll box is at the bottom, next to the down arrow, you have reached the bottom of the window. You can also drag the scroll box to move to a different position in the window.

Exiting Windows

After you have finished working with Windows, close any open application windows. Exit Windows by double-clicking on the Control-menu box
in the Program Manager window, or by choosing File, Exit Windows from
the menu bar. Choose OK when you are asked to confirm the Exit command.

Summary of New Terms

Windows is an operating system that works with DOS to control how your
computer's hardware and software work together. Instead of a command-line
interface, Windows uses a Graphical User Interface (GUI), using pictures
(icons), to represent applications and files. The GUI makes Windows easier
to learn. Open Windows applications from the Program Manager window.

Windows is designed to be used with a mouse. To open an application, use
the mouse to double-click on a group icon. The group window opens, displaying program-item icons, which represent applications. Double-click on
the program-item icon you want to use to open this application. Use the
mouse to make selections from a menu bar. The left mouse button is used
to click or double-click an icon or command. You can also drag windows
and icons to different locations on your desktop. You can minimize an
open window, changing it to an application icon that appears at the bottom of your desktop. If you maximize a window, it expands to fill your
screen. The Restore button returns the window to the size it was before it
was maximized. You can also customize the window size by dragging the
window borders.

The menu bar is used to make it easy to select commands for applications.
You can use the mouse or the keyboard to make selections from the menu
bar. Scroll bars appear in a window when there is more information in the
window than what is currently displayed. Click the scroll arrows to move
in that direction in the window. The scroll box indicates your relative
position in the window.

Review Questions

1. What is the purpose of an operating system?
2. Why is DOS sometimes difficult to use?
3. What type of interface does Windows use?
4. Why does this interface make the Windows operating system easier to use?
5. What are two other features that make Windows easier to use than DOS?
6. Why do you still need a basic understanding of DOS to use Windows?

7. What command do you type to start Windows from the DOS prompt?
8. What window appears on your screen when you start the Windows program?
9. What does it mean to double-click a mouse button?
10. How do you open an application from the Program Manager window?
11. How do you drag an icon?
12. When you open a file, where is the data stored?
13. What is the purpose of minimizing a file?
14. What happens when you maximize a window?
15. Why does a scroll bar appear in a window?
16. What is the first key you press to select a menu command with the keyboard?
17. What does it indicate if a menu option is followed by an ellipsis (. . .)?
18. Why are some menu commands dimmed?
19. What are the key names, such as (SHIFT)+(F5), listed next to some menu commands called, and what is their purpose?
20. How do you exit Windows?

Lab Exercises

Complete the following exercise to practice the procedures explained in this topic.

1. Start the Windows application, if necessary.
2. If the Program Manager window is maximized (you will see the Restore button in the top right corner of the window), click the Restore button to return it to its previous size.
3. With the Program Manager window on your screen, use the mouse to point to each of the following window components:
   Control-menu box
   Minimize button
   Maximize button
   Border
4. Minimize the Program Manager window.
5. Open the window by double-clicking the minimized icon.
6. Open the Accessories group, then the Write application.
7. Close the Write window, then the Accessories group window.
8. Change the Program Manager window size by dragging the window borders.

9. Drag the lower-right Program Manager window corner to make the window smaller, so that scroll bars appear in the window.

10. Use the scroll arrows to move up and down and left to right in the Program Manager window.

11. Drag the scroll box to move through the window.

12. Drag the window corner again to make the Program Manager window larger.

13. Move the Program Manager window to different locations on your desktop by dragging the window's title bar.

14. Click on each of the following menu options:

    File

    Window

    Help

15. Choose File, Exit Windows from the Program Manager menu bar to exit Windows.

16. When a dialog box appears, confirming you want to exit Windows, click OK.

17. Start Windows again by typing win at the DOS prompt and pressing ⏎ ENTER .

18. If you do not plan to continue working in Windows, exit Windows now.

Chapter 2

Using Dialog Boxes

When you select a menu command that is followed by an ellipsis (. . .), a *dialog box* appears on your screen. A dialog box is a window in which you enter additional information so that Windows can process the command. For example, when saving a file for the first time, a dialog box appears for you to enter the file name and location (directory and disk drive). When you print a file, you can specify various print options in a dialog box, including the number of copies to print and the margins of the printed document.

In this topic, you will learn how to use the basic components of dialog boxes. All dialog boxes are composed of one or more of these components. After you have a basic understanding of how each of these works, you will find it easy to enter information into the dialog boxes you see when using Windows and Windows applications. You will also learn how to save and open files, and how to use the Windows Help system.

Using Command Buttons

Two command buttons appear in almost every dialog box: OK and Cancel. *Command buttons* are rectangular buttons that are labeled with the function they perform. To select a command button, click the button you want. If you choose the OK command button, the information you entered into the dialog box is processed. For example, if you choose OK after typing a name for a file you are saving, the file is then saved with the name you entered. If you click Cancel, the dialog box is closed without processing the information.

You will often see the Help command button in a dialog box. To see Help information about the dialog box you are using, click this button. More about the Help system is explained later in this topic.

Setup...

Clicking this command button displays another dialog box

Many other command buttons may appear in a dialog box. If you see a command button with an ellipsis, for example Options . . ., and choose this button, another dialog box appears.

Using Option Buttons

Option buttons, also called radio buttons, appear in a dialog box when you have a choice of only one of a group of options. Figure 2.1 shows option buttons in the Write application Print dialog box. You can choose only one option in the Print Range group. To choose an option button, click on the option you want or hold down ALT and then type the underlined letter next to the option. The selected option appears with a black circle inside the option button.

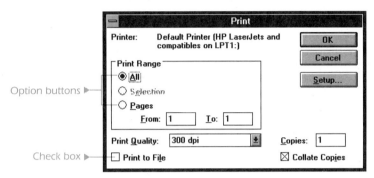

Option buttons ►

Check box ►

Figure 2.1   **Option buttons and check boxes are used in this dialog box**

Using Check Boxes

Check boxes also appear in the dialog box shown in Figure 2.1. Check boxes appear when you can select any number of a group of options. You can select all of the options, none of the options, or any combination. To select a check box, click on the box, or hold down ALT and type the underlined letter next to the box. An X appears in a selected check box. To remove the X, click the check box again.

Using Text Boxes

Text boxes appear in a dialog box when you need to enter information such as a file name. An example of a dialog box is shown in Figure 2.2.

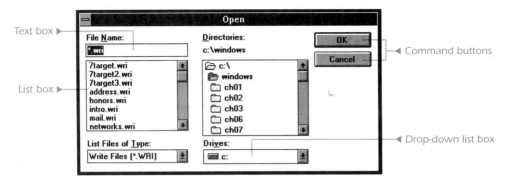

Figure 2.2   **The Open dialog box**

To type information into a text box, first select the text box by clicking in the box or by holding down the ⌐ALT⌐ key, then typing the underlined letter next to the box. When the text box is selected, a blinking *insertion point* appears within the box. This insertion point indicates where text you type will be entered. You can press the ⌐← BACKSPACE⌐ key to delete text to the left of the insertion point, or the ⌐DELETE⌐ key to remove text to the right of the insertion point. If you want to select all the text currently in a text box, double-click in the box, or hold down the left mouse button and drag across the text. When you type new text, it will replace all of the text you have highlighted.

To enter information into a text box, you can simply type what you want to enter. Often there is a list box below a text box where you can choose various options. List boxes are described in the following section.

Using List Boxes

List boxes are used when you have a choice of various options that you can select. For example, when you are opening a file, a list of all the files in the selected directory appears in the list box. You can choose an item from the list box by clicking on the item you want. The selected item appears in a text box above the list box.

A *scroll bar* often appears along the right side of a list box. If the arrows on the scroll bar are black, not gray, this indicates that there are more options in the list that do not currently appear. Click the up arrow to move up in the list. If you click the down arrow, you will move down through the list of options. The scroll box indicates your relative position in the list. For an example of a list box with a scroll bar, see Figure 2.3.

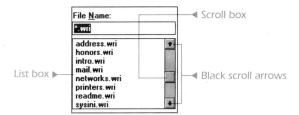

List box ►

Figure 2.3 **The scroll box indicates you are seeing the middle of the list**

Using Drop-down List Boxes

Drop-down list boxes are similar to list boxes, except that all of the options do not appear in the dialog box. Click the underlined arrow to the right of the drop-down list box to display additional choices. If all of the choices do not appear in the list, you will see black scroll arrows. When you have located the option you want, click this option. The drop-down list closes, and the option is entered into the box.

Saving and Opening Files

When working on a document, it is stored in short-term memory, or RAM. If you do not save the document to a floppy or hard disk, it will be lost if you exit the application or turn off your computer.

When you save a document, it is also referred to as a *file*. You must give this file a name so that you can access it later. When naming a document, follow DOS naming rules. A file name is one to eight characters long, and cannot include a space. Many applications automatically add a three-character *extension* onto the file name, separated from the file name by a period. You also cannot use the special characters " . / \ [ ] : * < > + = ; , ?. The easiest way to make sure the file name is allowable is to use only letters or numbers and no spaces.

To save a file, choose File, Save from the menu bar. The Save As dialog box, shown in Figure 2.4, appears in your screen.

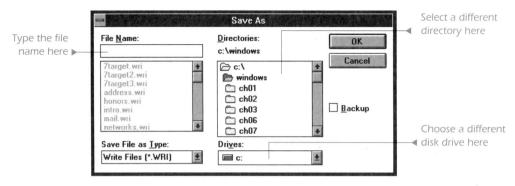

Type the file name here ▶

Select a different directory here ◀

Choose a different disk drive here ◀

Figure 2.4 **The Save As dialog box lets you enter a file name and location**

Type the file name in the File Name text box. If you want to save the file to a different directory, double-click the directory in the Directories list box. Click the Drives drop-down list box to save the file to a different disk drive.

After you have saved a file to a disk, choosing the File, Save command automatically saves the file with the same name and in the same location. A dialog box does not appear. If you want to change the file name or location, choose File, Save As. The Save As dialog box appears for you to make your changes.

Using the Help System

Windows and Windows applications offer access to Help in a variety of ways. You can get Help by clicking the Help button in some dialog boxes. You can also choose a Help option from the menu bar in most applications. After you choose Help, a pull-down menu appears on your screen.

The Help pull-down menu

To see a general list of your Help choices, choose the Contents command. A dialog box appears, listing general Help topic categories. You can also display the Contents window by pressing [F1] in most applications. Click one of the categories in the Contents window to display additional information. When you see underlined text in a different color, you can click this text to display additional information. This underlined text is called a *jump*. When the mouse pointer is positioned on a jump, it appears as a pointing finger (see Figure 2.5).

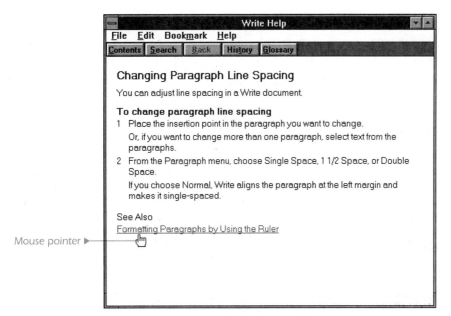

Mouse pointer ▶

Figure 2.5   A Write Help window

You can also click terms with a dotted underline. A box appears, giving you a definition of this term. To close this box, click outside of the box.

To search for help on a specific item, choose Search for Help on . . . from the Help pull-down menu. The Search dialog box, shown in Figure 2.6, appears.

Type the topic for which you want Help in the first text box, then click the Show Topics button. A list of related Help windows appears in the bottom list box. Click the topic you want to display, then click the Go To button. A Help window with information on the topic you selected appears. To close this window, double-click on the Control-menu box.

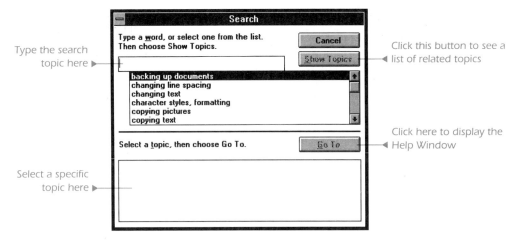

Type the search
topic here ▶

Click this button to see a
list of related topics ◀

Click here to display the
Help Window ◀

Select a specific
topic here ▶

Figure 2.6 **The Search dialog box**

Summary of New Terms

Dialog boxes appear on your screen when you need to enter more information for Windows to process a command. There are different components common to dialog boxes. Command buttons are labeled with their function, and appear in almost all dialog boxes. You will see option buttons if you must choose only one option in a group. Check boxes appear when you can choose different combinations of options. A text box is used to enter text, such as a file name. After selecting text, the insertion point appears in a text box. The insertion point indicates where text you type will be inserted. A list box appears if you can choose from a list of options. A black scroll bar appears next to a list box if all of the choices do not display. Click scroll arrows to move through the list box. The scroll box indicates your relative location in the list. When you click a drop-down list box, a list of your choices "drops down" in the dialog box.

When naming Windows application files, you must follow DOS naming conventions. The file names can be from one to eight characters long. The File, Save command is used to save files to a disk. Windows offers an extensive Help system that you can access through some dialog boxes, or by choosing Help from a menu bar. You can use the Contents command to locate the Help information you want, or use the Search for Help on command to find specific information. Jumps are underlined text in a Help window. When you click a jump, additional Help information appears.

Review Questions

1. Why do dialog boxes appear on your screen?
2. How do you select a text box?
3. What appears in a text box when it is selected?
4. How can you select all of the text in a text box?
5. If a scroll bar next to a list box is gray, what does this mean?
6. Why would the scroll box appear in the middle of the scroll bar?
7. How do you display the information in a drop-down list box?
8. What happens if you choose the OK command button?
9. If you click a command button that displays an ellipsis, what happens?
10. How many option buttons can you choose?
11. How do you know which option button is selected?
12. How do you remove the X from a check box?
13. Why do you need to save a file?
14. How long is the extension that applications automatically add to a file name?
15. Can you use an equal sign (=) in a file name?
16. How do you select a different disk drive when saving a file?
17. If you want to save a file with a different name, what command do you choose from the menu bar?
18. What are two ways you can display the Help Contents window?
19. What happens when you click underlined text in a Help window?
20. If you want to search for information on a specific topic, what command do you choose from the Help pull-down menu?

Lab Exercises

Complete the following exercise to practice the procedures explained in this topic.

1. Start Windows, if necessary.
2. Open the Accessories group icon, then the Write application.
3. Type your name and address in the Write document.
4. Insert the formatted floppy disk provided by your instructor into your floppy drive.
5. Choose File, Save.
   - The Save As dialog box appears.

6. Type address in the File Name text box.

7. Click the Drives drop-down list box.

   ■ A list of the disk drives available on your computer appears.

8. Click the letter for your floppy drive.

   ■ The drive letter appears in the drop-down list box.

9. Click OK to save the file.

10. Choose File, Print from the Write document menu bar.

    ■ The Print dialog box appears on your screen.

11. Click the Setup . . . command button.

    ■ The Setup dialog box appears.

12. Change the Orientation to Landscape by clicking this option button.

13. Click the Options . . . command button.

    ■ The Options dialog box appears on your screen.

14. Click the Help command button to display a Help window for this dialog box.

15. Close the Help window.

16. Click OK in the Options dialog box and the Setup dialog box to go back to the Print dialog box.

17. Check the Print to File check box.

18. Click OK to print the document to a file. Printing a document to a file saves a copy of the document with commands that can be used to print the file from DOS.

    ■ The Print to File dialog box appears.

19. Type addprt in the text box, then click OK.

20. The document is printed to a file that is saved on your floppy disk.

21. Choose Help, Contents from the Write menu bar.

22. Select Change Page Layout from the Contents window.

    ■ The Change Page Layout Help window appears.

23. Click the Back button near the top of the window to return to the Contents window.

24. Select each of the following topics from the Contents window:

    Change Tabs by Using the Ruler

    Copy, Cut, and Paste Text

    Add Headers, Footers, and Page Numbers

25. From the Add Headers, Footers, and Page Numbers Help window, click the underlined header term.

    ■ A box appears, giving the definition of header.

26. Click outside this box to close it.

27. Close the Help window.

28. From the Write menu bar, choose Help, Search for Help on.
    - ■ The Search dialog box appears.
29. Type printing in the text box.
30. When printing documents is highlighted in the list box, click Show Topics.
31. Because only one topic appears in the bottom list box, Printing Documents is automatically highlighted. Click Go To to see the Help information on this topic.
    - ■ The Help window appears on your screen.
32. Close the Help window.
33. Close the Write document window, then the Accessories group window.
34. If you do not plan to continue working in Windows, exit Windows now.

Chapter 3

Working with Multiple Windows

One of the major advantages of working with Windows is that you can open more than one window at a time. If you are typing a letter in a word processing application, you can open your spreadsheet application to look at data you are referring to in the letter. Many applications also allow you to open multiple windows within that application so you can easily switch back and forth between different letters or spreadsheets, for example.

Although working with multiple windows can be a real time-saver, it can also get to be very confusing! If you have six windows open on your desktop, it can be difficult to locate the one you want. In this chapter, you will learn various techniques for arranging, locating, and activating your open windows.

Arranging Group Windows

When you open a group icon, a *group window* appears on your desktop, displaying the program-item icons in that group. See Figure 3.1 for an example of a group window.

Often, you will have several group windows open on your desktop and need to locate a specific group window. Arrange the open group windows by *cascading* or *tiling* them. The Cascade and Tile options appear in the Program Manager window on the Window pull-down menu.

When you cascade the windows, the windows appear stacked diagonally, with the title bar for each window visible. Cascaded group windows are shown in Figure 3.2.

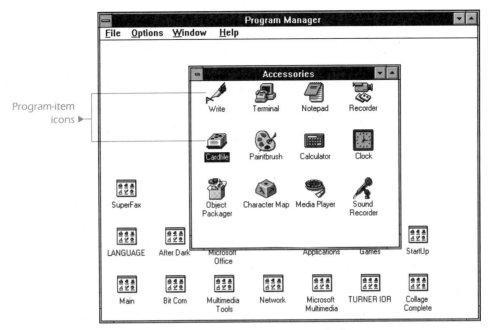

Program-item icons ▶

Figure 3.1   The Accessories group window

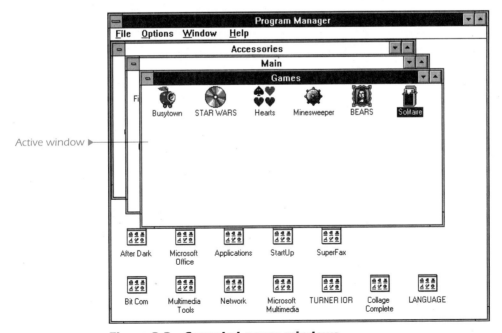

Active window ▶

Figure 3.2   Cascaded group windows

Activate the window you want by clicking any part of that window. The window you select moves to the front of the stack and the title bar is highlighted.

You can also arrange group windows by tiling them. Tiling arranges the windows side-by-side, in equal-size windows. See Figure 3.3 for an example of tiled group windows.

Active window ▶

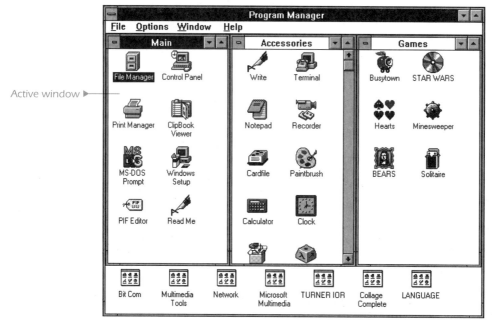

Figure 3.3 Tiled group windows

To activate a tiled window, just click any part of the window you want. The active window appears with a highlighted title bar.

The Arrange Icons option on the Window menu arranges the group icons in the Program Manager window into orderly rows. If you choose Cascade or Tile from the Window menu, the group icons are automatically arranged at the same time.

Opening Multiple Application Windows

Often you will want to open several different *application windows*, which are windows that contain software applications such as Microsoft Word for Windows or Microsoft Excel. Opening more than one application window allows you to work in a spreadsheet while your word processing application is open. The Window Cascade and Window Tile commands from the Program Manager do not arrange your application windows; these commands arrange only the open group windows. In the following sections you will learn different ways to manage your open application windows.

Switching to Different Applications

If you can see any part of an application window on your screen, you can activate it by simply clicking the window. The window is moved to the front of your desktop. If the application window is not visible, you can cycle through the open windows by holding down the ALT key, then pressing TAB . The name of an application window appears in the center of your screen. See the example in Figure 3.4.

Figure 3.4   Press Alt+Tab to display a box with an application name

Press TAB again while still holding down the ALT key and a different application window name appears. Keep pressing the TAB key until the application you want to activate appears in the box. When you release the ALT key, this application window moves to the front of your desktop.

Using the Task List

Windows Task List allows you to activate or close any open application window, and to cascade or tile these windows on your desktop. To display the Task List window, double-click any part of your *desktop background*, which is the area behind the open windows. If the desktop background is not visible, hold down the CTRL key and press ESC to open the Task List. The Task List is shown in Figure 3.5.

The list box displays the names of all of the open application windows. If all of the open windows do not appear in the list, scroll bars appear. To activate a different application window, highlight the window in the list box, then choose Switch To, or double-click the application you want to activate.

Close the selected application window by choosing the End Task button. If you choose the Cancel button, the Task List window is closed. You can also press ESC to close the Task List without making a selection.

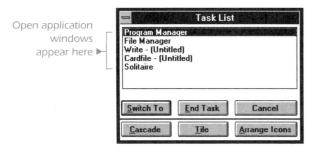

Open application
windows
appear here ▶

Figure 3.5   **The Task List allows you to arrange application windows**

To arrange the application windows, you can choose either Cascade or Tile. Cascaded application windows are shown in Figure 3.6.

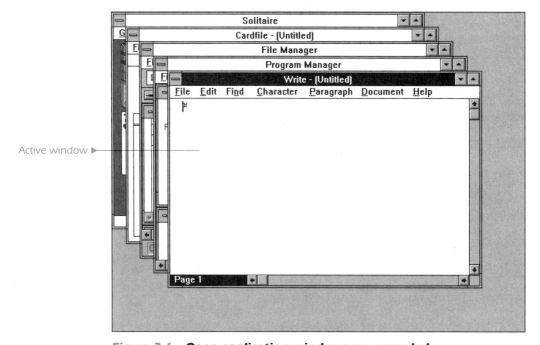

Active window ▶

Figure 3.6   **Open application windows are cascaded**

If you prefer to Tile the application windows, they appear as shown in Figure 3.7.

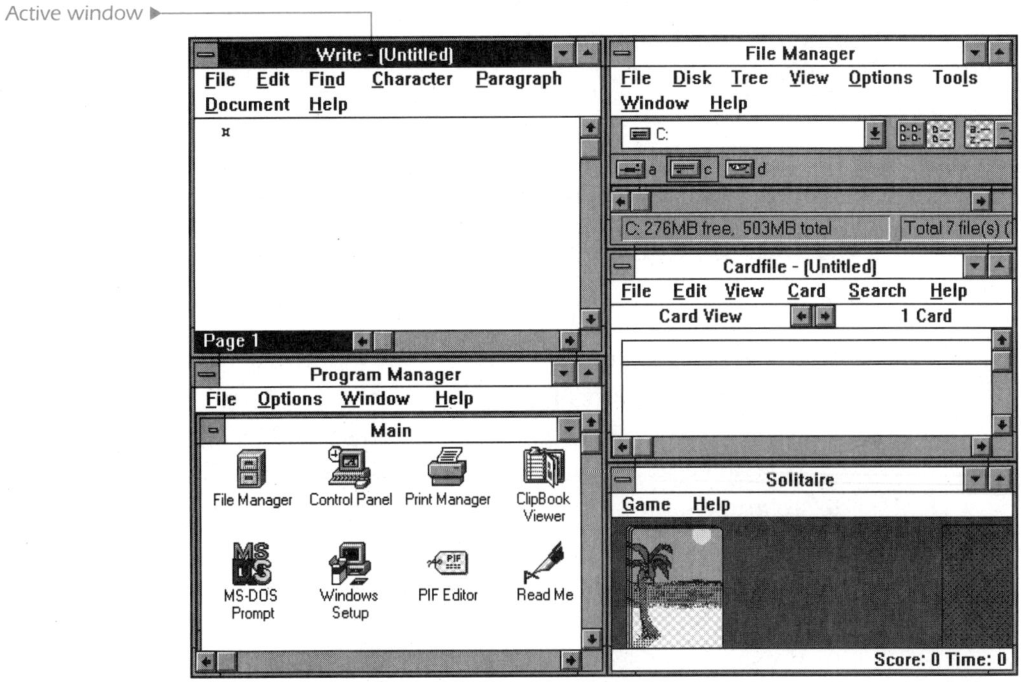

Active window ▶

Figure 3.7 Tiled application windows

Activate a cascaded or tiled application window by clicking any part of the window. The active window appears at the front of your desktop with a highlighted title bar.

If you choose the Arrange Icons option on the Task List, the *application icons* on your desktop are arranged. Application icons are the icons that appear at the bottom of your desktop when you minimize an application window. Choosing Cascade or Tile from the Task List automatically arranges these application windows.

Summary of New Terms

A group window is opened when you double-click a group icon in the Program Manager. The group window contains program-item icons, representing the applications available in this group. If you have multiple group windows open, you can make it easier to locate windows by tiling or cascading them from the Window menu in Program Manager. If your group icons have become disorganized, you can rearrange them by choosing Arrange Icons from the Window menu.

An application window is the window that contains an open application. Using the Window options from the Program Manager does not arrange application windows. Press ⌐ALT⌐ + ⌐TAB⌐ to cycle through the open application windows. You can also use the Task List to activate or close a different window, or to Cascade or Tile the application windows. The Arrange Icons option on the Task list arranges the application icons on your desktop. Application icons represent application windows you have minimized.

Review Questions

1. What is a group window?
2. If you can see part of a group window, how can you activate it?
3. What menu in Program Manager allows you to arrange group windows?
4. If you want to stack the group windows so that each window's title bar is visible, what command do you choose?
5. To arrange the group windows side-by-side, in equal-size windows, what command do you select?
6. What does the Arrange Icons command do?
7. What is an application window?
8. If you cannot see an open application window, what keys do you press to cycle through your open windows?
9. When you are cycling through open windows and the application window you want appears in a box on your desktop, how do you activate this window?
10. What is the Task List?
11. What are two ways to display the Task List on your screen?
12. If you do not see an open application listed in Task List's list box, how do you locate it?
13. What are two ways to activate an application window from Task List?
14. What two choices do you have for arranging open application windows?
15. What is an application icon?
16. How can you organize application icons into rows on your desktop?
17. If windows are cascaded, how do you know which window is active?
18. How do you know which tiled window is active?
19. Is the Accessories window a group window or an application window?
20. Is the Write window a group window or an application window?

Lab Exercises

Complete the following exercise to practice the procedures explained in this chapter.

1. Start Windows, if necessary.

2. From the Program Manager window, open the following group windows in the order given by double-clicking the group icons:

   Accessories

   Main

   Games

   ■ If you cannot see a group icon after opening a window, move the window by pointing to the title bar and dragging the window out of your way.

3. Choose Window, Cascade from the Program Manager menu bar.

   ■ The windows are cascaded. Your screen should look similar to Figure 3.2. The window that was active when you chose the Cascade command appears at the top of the stack.

4. Activate the Accessories group window.

5. Activate the Main group window. If necessary, Cascade the windows again so you can see the Main window to activate it.

6. Choose Window, Tile from the menu bar.

   ■ The group windows are tiled on your screen, as shown in Figure 3.3.

7. Activate each of the tiled windows.

8. Drag two of the remaining group icons to the right of the Program Manager window.

9. Choose Window, Arrange Icons to rearrange the group icons.

10. In the Accessories group window, open the Write application and the Cardfile application. You may need to drag open application windows to different locations to find the program-item icon.

11. In the Main group window, activate the File Manager.

12. In the Games group window, activate Solitaire.

13. Switch to the Write application window by pressing (ALT) + (TAB). Continue holding down (ALT) and pressing (TAB) until the Write application appears in the box on your screen, then release (TAB).

14. Switch to the File Manager application window by pressing (ALT) + (TAB).

15. Open the Task List by double-clicking your desktop background if it is visible, or by pressing (CTRL) + (ESC).

    ■ The Task List appears on your screen. It should look similar to Figure 3.5.

16. Activate the Write application by selecting the application from the list, then choosing Switch To. You can also double-click the application name in the list box.

   ■ The Write application window appears at the front of your desktop.

17. Open the Task List again, and choose the Cascade button to cascade the application windows.

18. Click any part of the Solitaire window to activate it.

19. Open the Task List, and choose Tile to tile the application windows.

20. Activate each of the tiled windows.

21. Click the Minimize button in the Solitaire and Cardfile windows.

   ■ Application icons appear at the bottom of your desktop.

22. Drag the application icons to different locations on your desktop.

23. Use the Arrange Icons button in the Task List to rearrange the application icons.

24. Close the Write application from the Task List by selecting Write, then choose the End Task button.

25. Open the Task List, then choose Cancel to close it without making a selection.

26. Close all of the open applications using the Task List. Do not close the Program Manager window.

27. Close all of the group windows by double-clicking on each Control-menu box.

28. Choose Window, Arrange icons to reorganize your group icons.

29. If you do not plan to continue working in Windows, exit Windows now.

Chapter 4

Using the File Manager

Windows uses the File Manager application to help you manage files and directories on your disks. You can perform file and disk maintenance operations including displaying the contents of a disk or directory, formatting floppy disks, creating new subdirectories, and copying, moving, and deleting files. Because the File Manager uses icons to represent your disks, subdirectories, and files, it is easy to see what is on a disk and to arrange the disk contents. In this topic, you will learn how to work with the File Manager.

Opening the File Manager

Open the File Manager from the Main program group. After you open File Manager, you will see a window similar to Figure 4.1. Your screen may look somewhat different, depending on the File Manager settings.

Disk drive icons ▶

Open directory ▶

Directory tree ▶

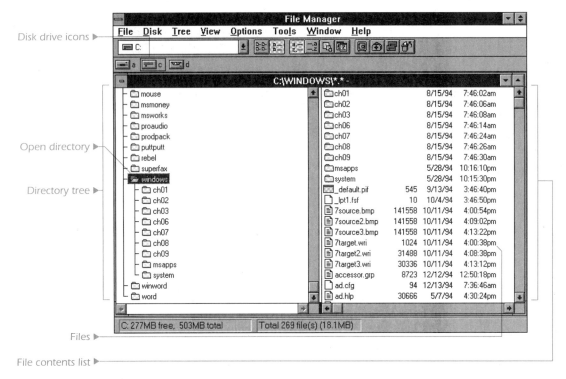

Files ▶

File contents list ▶

Figure 4.1 **The File Manager window**

Commands on the View menu let you customize the display of the File Manager window. Choose Tree and Directory to see both the *tree* (directory structure) and *directory* (file listing), as shown in Figure 4.1. To see information about each file on the right side of the window, including the file name, size (in bytes), and date and time last saved, choose All File Details. You can also determine the order in which files are sorted by choosing one of the Sort by commands.

The active area of the File Manager window is highlighted. Activate a different section of the File Manager window by clicking the area you want, or by using the TAB key.

The selected subdirectory is indicated by an open folder. The files along the right side of the window are the files in the selected subdirectory. Click a different subdirectory to display its contents.

If you insert a new floppy disk, the information on your screen may not be updated automatically. Press the F5 key to refresh the screen.

Turning on Confirmation Prompts

When first learning to use the File Manager, you may want to turn on the Confirmation Prompts. If these prompts are turned on, an additional dialog box appears to confirm your actions when you are formatting disks, copying or moving files, or deleting files or directories. To turn on the Confirmation Prompts, choose Options, Confirmation from the File Manager menu bar. The Confirmation dialog box appears (see Figure 4.2).

Check each of the boxes that describes the action for which you want to display a confirmation dialog box. The Mouse Action box displays confirmation when you drag files to different locations to move or copy the files. If you turn on the Disk Commands confirmation, a confirmation dialog box appears when you format a disk.

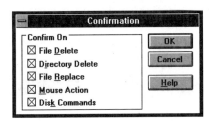

Figure 4.2   **The Confirmation dialog box**

Changing to a Different Drive

To see the contents of a different drive, click once on the drive icon. Before clicking a floppy drive icon, make sure you have inserted the floppy disk.

Opening and Closing a Directory Window

If you are copying or moving files, it is easier if you open a window for the directory you are copying *from* and a window for the directory you are copying *to*. To open additional windows within the File Manager, double-click the drive icon you want to display or choose Window, New Window from the menu. Arrange these windows using the commands on the Window pull-down menu. If you are using Windows for Workgroups, you have the option of tiling the windows horizontally or vertically. If you are using Windows 3.1, the Tile command tiles the windows horizontally. Figure 4.3 shows three horizontally tiled windows.

Close the additional windows by double-clicking on each window's Control-menu box. One window must always remain open in the File Manager, so you cannot close the last window.

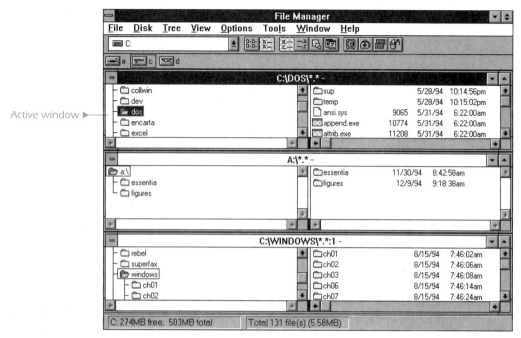

Active window ▶

Figure 4.3   **Three windows are open**

Formatting a Floppy Disk

Before you can use a floppy disk, it must be *formatted*. Formatting a disk erases any information currently on the disk and prepares it to store new files. You can buy disks that are preformatted for an IBM or compatible computer, or you can format floppy disks using the File Manager. To format a floppy disk, use the Disk, Format Disk command. A dialog box appears for you to enter additional information (see Figure 4.4).

Enter the drive where the disk is located, and the disk capacity. If you want to add a label to this disk, type a label up to 11 characters in the Label text box. To make a system disk, check the Make System Disk box. A system disk contains files that can be used to boot your computer. If the Quick Format box is selected, the disk is not searched for bad sectors before being formatted. Use this option if you are reformatting a disk that you are sure does not have bad sectors. You cannot choose this option if a floppy disk is being formatted for the first time.

After formatting a disk, File Manager automatically creates a *root directory* on this floppy disk. A root directory appears on all disks, and is the starting point for creating other directories. The root directory is represented by a backslash (\).

When the format is complete and the root directory is created, File Manager displays a message box telling you how many bytes should be available for the disk, and how many bytes are actually available. These numbers should match. If there is a big difference between the numbers, there are many bad areas on the disk. You should get a new floppy disk and not use the one with the bad areas. Click Yes in this message box if you want to format another floppy disk. If you are finished formatting, click No.

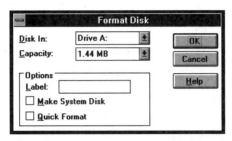

Figure 4.4   **The Format Disk dialog box**

Creating a Directory

Windows uses subdirectories to divide a hard disk to organize your files. Think of a subdirectory as a file folder used to hold related files and documents. Usually a software application has its own subdirectory. This subdirectory may be divided into additional subdirectories to group related files within that application. Create additional subdirectories from the File Manager by selecting the directory in which you want to create the new subdirectory. This directory is called the *parent* directory. Choose the File, Create Directory command. The Create Directory dialog box, shown in Figure 4.5, appears on your screen.

Type the name of the directory you want to create in the Name box. The name can be up to eight characters. Click OK to create the new subdirectory. The subdirectory appears as a folder under the parent directory. The terms directory and subdirectory are often used interchangeably.

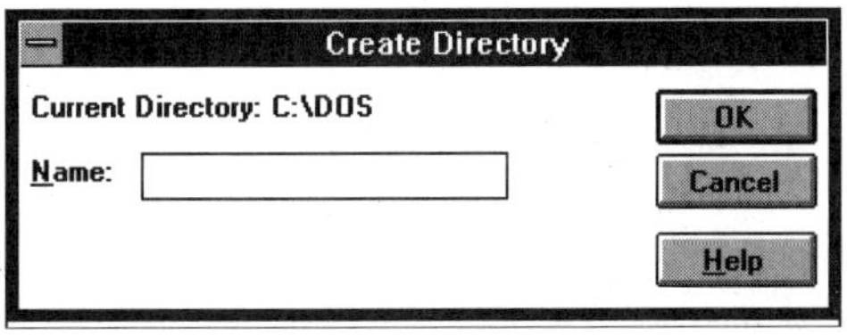

Figure 4.5   **The Create Directory dialog box**

Selecting Files and Directories

You can move, copy, delete, and rename files and directories from the File Manager window. The first step in performing any of these operations is to select the files or directory. To select a single file or directory, click the file or directory you want. The name is highlighted with a colored bar. If you want to select more than one adjacent file, click the first file you want. Move the mouse pointer to the last file, and hold down SHIFT while clicking the left mouse button once. All of the files between the first and last file are selected (see Figure 4.6).

To select nonadjacent files, select the first file, then select any additional files by holding down the CTRL key while clicking the left mouse button. All of the files you click are selected (see Figure 4.7). If you accidentally select the wrong file, while holding down the CTRL key, click the file again. The file is deselected.

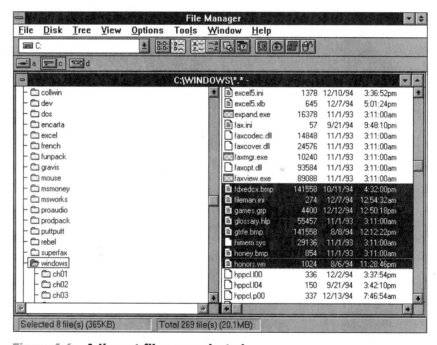

Figure 4.6 *Adjacent files are selected*

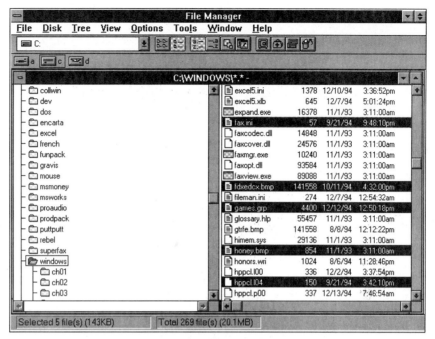

Figure 4.7 **Nonadjacent files are selected**

Copying Files

Copying files makes a duplicate of the files in a different location, such as in a different subdirectory or on a different disk. Often you will copy a file from your hard disk to a floppy disk. To copy files, first open windows showing the current location of the files and the location to which you want to copy. For example, to copy a file from drive C to drive A, open a window for each of these drives. Select the file(s) you want to copy, then position the mouse pointer on any of these files. Hold down the CTRL key, then press the left mouse button. Drag the files to the new location. When you are copying files, you will notice that a document with a plus sign in it appears next to the mouse pointer. Release the mouse button, then the CTRL key to drop the files in the new location.

You can also use the Copy command on the File menu to copy files to a different location.

Moving Files

Moving files follows the same procedures as copying files, except to hold down the SHIFT key while dragging the files to the new location. When you move files, the document that appears next to the mouse pointer does not contain a plus sign.

You can also move files by choosing the File, Move command.

Renaming Files and Directories

To change the name of a selected file or directory, you can use the File, Rename command. When you choose this command, the Rename dialog box, shown in Figure 4.8, appears on your screen.

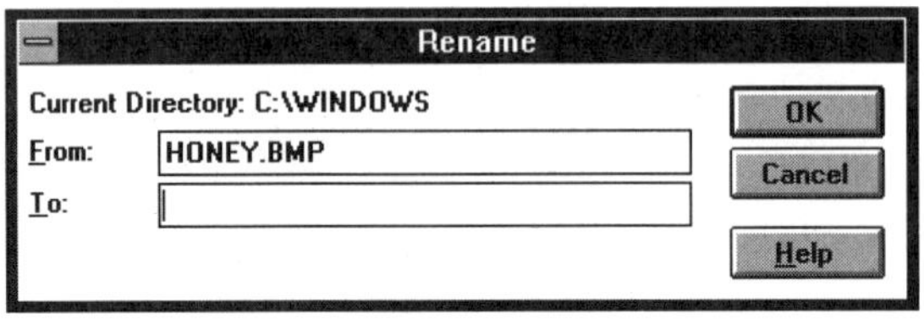

Figure 4.8 **The Rename dialog box**

The file or directory you have selected appears in the From text box. In the To text box, type the new name for the file. Click OK to rename this file.

To rename more than one file, you must use *wildcard* characters. Wildcards are characters that replace other characters in a file name. The asterisk (*) wildcard (often referred to as "star"), replaces any number of characters in a file name. The question mark (?) wildcard replaces zero or one characters. For example, the file name test*.doc refers to all files that start with the letters *test*, have any characters after that, and end with the .doc extension. The file test?.doc refers to those files that start with test, have zero or one characters after test, then end with the .doc extension. The file name *.* refers to all files: any file name, with any extension.

To change the extension on a group of files at the same time, rename these files using wildcards. For example, to change a group of files with the .doc extension to the .wri extension, select all of the files you want to change, then choose File, Rename. When the Rename dialog box appears, type *.wri in the To text box. This changes only the extension on the selected files, and leaves the original file name intact.

Deleting Files

Deleting files permanently removes the files from the disk. You should periodically deleted unneeded files to clean up your disk and to free disk space. After selecting the file(s) you want to delete, press the DELETE key on your keyboard, or choose File, Delete from the menu bar. The Delete dialog box, shown in Figure 4.9, appears on your screen.

The current directory appears at the top of the dialog box, and the name of the file or files you selected appears in the Delete text box. Check to see that you are deleting the correct file, then click OK.

If you have turned on the Confirmation prompts, a second dialog box appears, confirming that you want to delete the selected file. After verifying that you are deleting the correct file, click OK. The file is removed from your disk.

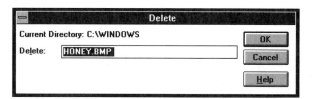

Figure 4.9   The Delete dialog box

To delete a subdirectory and all of the files in that directory, select the directory icon before choosing the Delete command. The Confirmation dialog box appears for each file in the directory unless you click the Yes to All button to delete all of the files in the directory without further confirmation.

Summary of New Terms

The File Manager application is used to manage files and directories on your disks. Turn on Confirmation Prompts in the File Manager to provide additional confirmation before executing commands such as moving, copying, or deleting files. After opening the File Manager, display a different disk drive by clicking the drive icon you want. To display additional windows, double-click the drive icon or choose Window, New Window from the menu bar.

A floppy disk must be formatted before you can use it. Formatting the disk erases any information currently on the disk and prepares it to store files. If you do not buy preformatted disks, use the Disk, Format Disk command to format your disks. A root directory is automatically created after the disk is formatted.

Subdirectories are divided sections of your disk that are used to store related files. Subdirectories are represented in the File Manager by folder icons. You can create additional subdirectories by selecting the parent directory (the directory under which you want to create the new subdirectory), and choosing the File, Create Directory command.

Before copying, moving, or renaming files, you must select the files. To select an individual file, click the file you want. To select adjacent files, click the first file, then press (SHIFT) while clicking the last file. Nonadjacent files are selecting by pressing the (CTRL) key while selecting each file.

To copy (duplicate) files, hold down the (CTRL) key and drag the file icons to the new location, such as a different directory or disk. Move files by holding down (SHIFT) while dragging the file icons. You can also use the Copy and Move commands on the File menu.

Change the name of selected files by using the Rename command on the File menu. To change more than one file name at a time, you must use wildcard characters. The asterisk (*) wildcard replaces any number of characters. The question mark (?) wildcard replaces zero or one characters.

Deleting a file permanently removes it from your disk. To delete files, select the files then press the (DELETE) key or choose File, Delete.

Review Questions

1. In which program group is the File Manager located?
2. Which command do you choose from the View menu to see both the directory structure and file listing?
3. Which key can you use to activate a different section of the File Manager window?
4. Why do you turn on Confirmation Prompts?
5. If you turn on the Disk Commands confirmation prompt, when does the confirmation dialog box appear?
6. How do you display a different disk drive?
7. How do you display a different disk drive in an additional window?
8. On which menu are the commands located to arrange your directory windows?
9. Why do you need to format a floppy disk?
10. Can you use the Quick Format option the first time you are formatting a floppy disk?
11. What does a folder icon represent in the File Manager?
12. How many characters can you use in a directory name?
13. How do you select a single file?
14. How do you select more than one adjacent file?

15. Which key do you hold down when selecting nonadjacent files?
16. While moving files to a new location, which key do you hold down when dragging the files?
17. Which command is used to change the name of a file?
18. How many characters does the asterisk wildcard replace?
19. What file name can you use to represent all files?
20. How can you delete an entire subdirectory and all of the files in the subdirectory?

Lab Exercises

Complete the following exercise to practice the procedures explained in this topic.

1. Start Windows, if necessary.
2. Open the Main Program group, then the File Manager application.
   - The File Manager window appears on your screen. If more than one window is open in the File Manager, close the additional windows.
3. Choose View, Tree and Directory to display both the directory structure and the directory listing.
4. Choose View, All File Details to display all of the information about the files, including the file size and date and time saved.
5. Choose View, Sort by Name to sort all of the files in alphabetical order.
   - Your screen should look similar to Figure 4.1. If it looks very different, check with your instructor.
6. Choose Options, Confirmation from the menu bar.
   - The Confirmation dialog box appears.
7. Make sure all of the boxes are checked, then click **OK**.
   - This turns on all of the confirmation prompts.
8. Insert a floppy disk into your floppy drive, then choose Disk, Format disk.
   - The Disk Format dialog box appears.
9. Make sure the correct drive letter and capacity appear in the dialog box, then click **OK**.
   - The Confirm Format confirmation box appears.
10. Click Yes to continue with the format.
11. When the format is complete, a box appears telling you the total disk space and the number of bytes available on this disk. Click No because you do not want to format another disk.

12. Click once on the floppy drive icon to see the contents of your floppy disk.

13. Double-click on the hard drive icon to see a second window, showing the contents of your hard disk.

14. Arrange the windows using the commands on the Window menu. If you are using Windows for Workgroups, try tiling the windows Vertically, then Horizontally. If you are using Windows 3.1, tiling arranges the windows horizontally.

15. Activate the floppy drive window by clicking the folder in the tree listing. The folder will be labeled **a:** or **b:**.

16. Choose File, Create Directory to create a directory off of the root directory.

    ▪ The Create Directory dialog box appears.

17. Type class in the Name text box, then click **OK**.

    ▪ The class directory is created and appears with a folder icon below the root directory.

18. Open the class directory by clicking this folder icon.

19. Activate the Windows subdirectory in your hard drive window.

20. Select the **arcade.bmp** file from the file listing in the hard drive window.

21. Use the scroll arrows to move down through the file listing.

22. Locate the calc.hlp file. Hold down (SHIFT), then click the **calc.hlp** file.

    ▪ The arcade.bmp file, calc.hlp, and all the files between the two files are selected.

23. Go back to the beginning of the file listing, and select the first file you see that ends with the **.bmp** extension.

24. Scroll through the file listing, and select any other **.bmp** files you see by holding down (CTRL) while clicking each file. Continue selecting files until you have selected five files.

25. Copy these files to the **class** directory on your floppy disk by holding down (CTRL) and dragging the files to the new location.

    ◆ A confirmation dialog box appears on your screen.

26. Check to be sure you are copying the files to the correct location, then click Yes.

27. Close your hard drive window.

28. Open a second window for your floppy drive.

29. Tile these windows horizontally, so you can see both of them on your screen.

30. Select the root directory in the bottom window.

31. Select three of the files in the class directory in the top window.

32. Move these files to the root directory on your floppy drive by holding down (SHIFT) and dragging them to the second directory window.

   ■ A confirmation dialog box appears, confirming that you want to move the files.

33. Check to make sure you are moving files from the class directory to the root directory on your floppy drive, then click Yes. If you are moving the files incorrectly, click No, then select and drag the files again.

34. Select two of the files on your floppy disk with a .bmp extension.

35. Choose File, Rename.

   ■ The Rename dialog box appears.

36. Type *.doc in the To text box, then click **OK**.

   ■ The extensions of the selected files are changed to .doc.

37. Select the class directory on your floppy drive.

38. Choose File, Delete to delete this directory and all of the files.

   ■ The Delete dialog box appears.

39. Click **OK** in the Delete dialog box.

   ■ The Confirm Directory Delete dialog box appears.

40. Click Yes to confirm the directory deletion.

   ■ The Confirm File Delete dialog box appears.

41. Click Yes to All to delete all of the files in the directory, without further confirmation.

42. Close the File Manager window by clicking the **Control-menu box** to the left of the File Manager title bar.

43. If you do not plan to continue working in Windows, exit Windows now.

Windows 3.1 Essentials Index

Quick Preview

Microsoft Word 6 for Windows

Microsoft Word for Windows 6.0 is a popular word processing program. Word 6 is easy for beginners to use and has many powerful features. Professional documents are even easier in Word 6 because of a feature called Wizards. This Quick Preview shows you how to use a Word 6 Wizard to create an award document.

Activity 1: Starting Word 6

1. Start Windows.
2. If the Microsoft Office program is not open, double-click the Microsoft Office icon.
3. Locate and double-click the Microsoft Word icon.
4. When Word is running, read the Tip of the Day and click OK to clear the box.

Activity 2: Starting a Word 6 Wizard

1. Choose the File menu by pointing the mouse toward it and clicking, or by pressing (ALT) + (F).
2. From the File menu, choose New by pressing (↵ ENTER). (See Figure QP-1.)

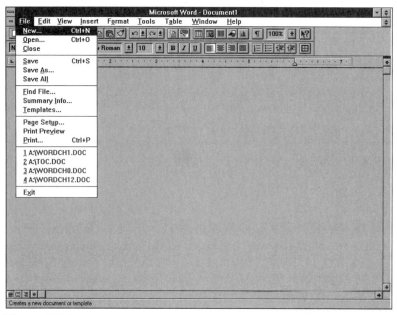

Figure QP-1 **The open File menu with the New option highlighted**

3. In the New dialog box, point and click the mouse on the Award Wizard in the Template list box. (See Figure QP-2.)

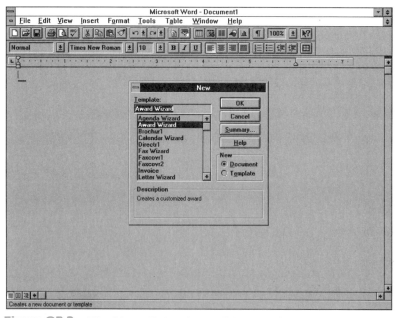

Figure QP-2 **The New dialog box with Award Wizard highlighted**

4. Click the OK button.

Activity 3: Using the Award Wizard

1. In the Award Wizard dialog box, select Decorative style by clicking the mouse on the radio button next to it. (See Figure QP-3.)

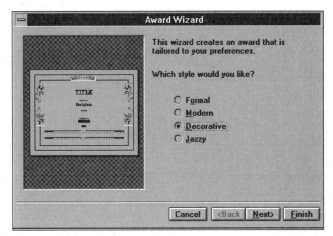

Figure QP-3   **Award Wizard dialog box with Decorative selected**

2. Click the Next button.

3. In the next Award Wizard dialog box, choose Landscape for the print direction.

4. Choose No in the preprinted border section. (See Figure QP-4.)

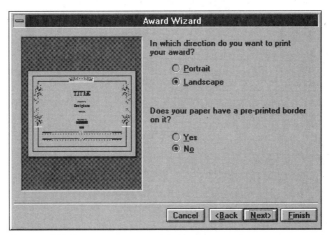

Figure QP-4   **Screen with Landscape direction and No selected**

5. Click the Next button.

6. Click the mouse in the Type name text box at the end of any existing name.

7. Press the Backspace key enough times to erase the existing name.

8. Type your name.

9. Click the mouse in the Award text box at the end of any existing award name.
10. Press the Backspace key enough times to erase the existing text.
11. Type Word Processing Award. (See Figure QP-5.)

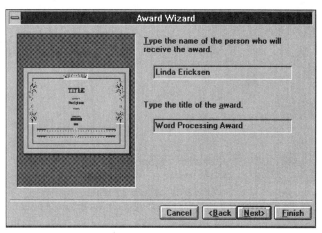

Figure QP-5   **Screen with Type name box and Award box filled in**

12. Click the Next button.
13. In the Type the names of the people who will sign the award box, type your instructor's name.
14. Leave the These are the people who will sign box blank. (See Figure QP-6.)

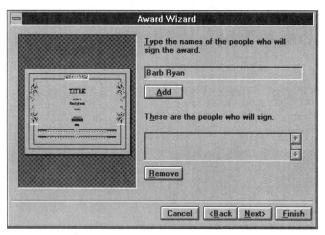

Figure QP-6   **Screen with the instructor's name filled in**

15. Click the Next button.
16. In the next Award Wizard dialog box, click the Presented by radio button.

17. In the text box, use the Backspace key to erase any existing text.

18. Type the name of your college or organization. (See Figure QP-7.)

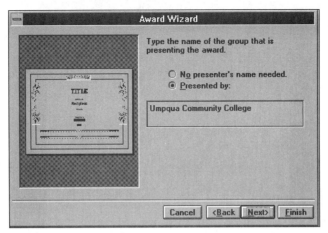

Figure QP-7 **Screen with Presented by selected and name filled in**

19. Click the Next button.

20. In the next Award Wizard dialog box, correct the date if it is incorrect by using the Backspace key and typing the correct date in the box.

21. In the Type additional text box, type the words For extraordinary work if they are not already in the box. (See Figure QP-8.)

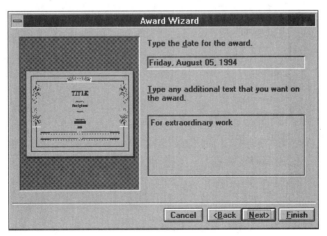

Figure QP-8 **Screen with date and additional text filled in**

22. Press the Next button.

23. In the checkered flag dialog box, click the No, just display the award button. (See Figure QP-9.)

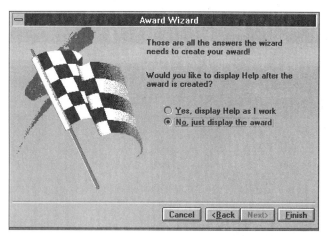

Figure QP-9   Screen with No option selected

24. Click the Finish button. (See Figure QP-10.)

Figure QP-10   Partial display of award

Activity 4: Viewing the Award

(Viewing the award requires a computer with 8MB of RAM.)

1. Choose the File menu.

2. From the File menu, choose Print Preview by typing the letter V. (See Figure QP-11.)

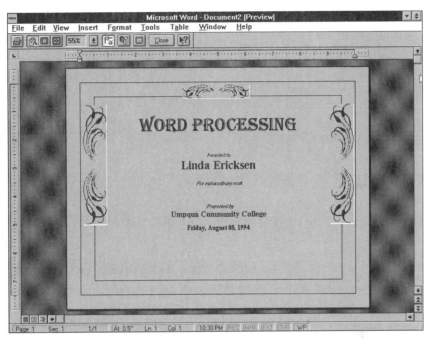

Figure QP-11 *Award displayed on Preview screen*

3. If you cannot see the entire award, click the Zoom Control button 43% ± and click the Whole Page option. (See Figure QP-12.)

Figure QP-12 *Screen with Zoom Control button selected and Whole Page option highlighted*

4. Choose the Close button.

Microsoft Word 6 for Windows Wizards

Microsoft Word 6 for Windows includes a feature called Wizards that can help you create documents. Wizards take you step by step through the process of creating common types of documents. You can create complicated documents with many enhancements even as you are just beginning to learn to use Word 6. From the File menu, choose New. In the Template box, select the wizard you want to use. Choose the OK button, and Word presents you with options to select or text to type in. When you are finished, you can edit, preview, print, or save the document like any other document. You can use Wizards to create invoices, memos, letters, FAX cover sheets, awards, and more.

As handy as Wizards are, however, they are not a substitute for learning to use Microsoft Word 6 for Windows. If you need to create a document for which Word did not create a Wizard, or if you want to edit the output of a document created using a Wizard, you need to know Word 6.

Activity 5: Printing the Award

(Printing the award requires a printer with sufficient memory.)

1. Choose the File menu.
2. From the File menu, choose Print by typing the letter P. (See Figure QP-13.)

Figure QP-13 **File menu with Print option highlighted**

3. In the Print dialog box, click OK. (See Figure QP-14.)

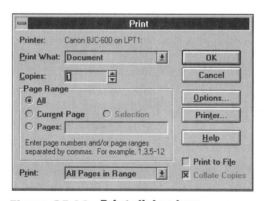

Figure QP-14 **Print dialog box**

Activity 6: Exiting Word 6

1. Choose the File menu.
2. From the File menu, choose Exit by typing the letter X. (See Figure QP-15.)

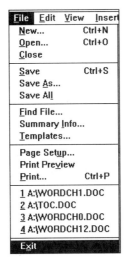

Figure QP-15 **File menu with Exit option highlighted**

3. In the Do you want to save changes to Document? dialog box, click No.

You have been exited from Microsoft Word 6 and returned to the Windows Program Manager.

Part 1

Fundamentals

Chapter 1

Introduction to Word 6 for Windows

Objectives

- Using the Mouse
- Starting Microsoft Word 6 for Windows
- Understanding the Elements of the Word 6 Screen
- Understanding the Top Part of the Screen
- Understanding the Document Window
- Understanding the Bottom Part of the Screen
- Using Help
- Exiting Microsoft Word 6 for Windows

Key Terms

TERM	DEFINITION
Word Processing Software	software that allows for creating, editing, printing, and saving text using a computer
Microsoft Windows	an operating environment, necessary to use Microsoft Word 6 for Windows
Program Manager	the Windows screen from which you start Word 6
Microsoft Office	program Group located in the Program Manager containing Microsoft Word 6
Icon	an image that represents an action and is usually a button
Toggle	a button that you click once to turn on and once again to turn off
Dialog Box	a box that displays options for you to select to provide a menu command with the additional information it needs
Clipboard	temporary storage area in Word that you can't see

word processing software

In this chapter, you learn about Microsoft Word 6 for Windows—*word processing software,* which is software that allows for creating, editing, printing, and saving text using a computer. You start the software, become familiar with all the screen elements including the menu system, and become comfortable with using the mouse or the keyboard to use the elements on the screen. You also become familiar with the online Help features available in Word 6. Finally, you exit the software. These are all the basics you need to begin writing your first document in Chapter 2 using Word 6 for Windows.

Objective 1: Using the Mouse

The mouse is a device that has become an easy-to-use alternative to the keyboard. It can be used to choose icons, to choose commands from menus, to move around a document, or to highlight text. In order to use the mouse to start the software, you need to know how it works.

Table 1-1 describes basic terms associated with correctly using the mouse.

Table 1-1   Mouse Commands

TERM	ACTION
Point	Move the mouse pointer over an item.
Click	Press and release the mouse button.
Double-click	Quickly press and release the mouse button twice.
Drag	Press and hold the mouse button as you move the mouse.

Unless otherwise indicated, always use the left mouse button.

When you use the mouse pointer in Word 6 for Windows, the pointer changes shape depending on what you are doing with it. When the mouse pointer is positioned over the document window or over text boxes in dialog boxes, it is an I-beam shape. When the mouse pointer is positioned over menus, rulers, or toolbars, the mouse pointer is a left-pointing arrow. (After you start the software, you will see the mouse change shapes as you go through Exercise 2.)

Objective 2: Starting Microsoft Word 6 for Windows

Microsoft Windows; icon

You can start Word 6 for Windows using a mouse or the keyboard. In either case, you go to the Microsoft Office program group in *Microsoft Windows* and use the Microsoft Word *icon* to start the program. (See Figure 1-1.)

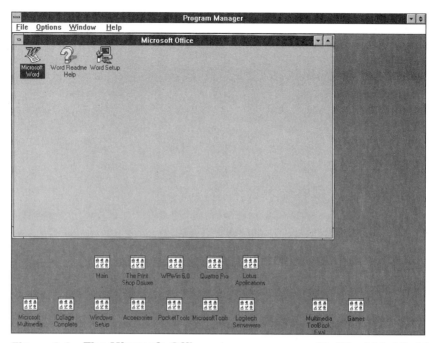

Figure 1-1   The Microsoft Office program group with Word highlighted

Program Manager; Microsoft Office
To start Word 6 using the mouse, double-click the mouse pointer on the Microsoft Office program in the Windows *Program Manager*. When the *Microsoft Office* program group opens, double-click the Microsoft Word icon.

To start Word 6 for Windows using the keyboard, hold down the Ctrl key and press the Tab key until the Microsoft Office title bar is highlighted. With Microsoft Office highlighted, press Alt-F, and then choose Open. The program group is opened. Use the arrow keys to highlight the Microsoft Word icon, and press Enter.

Each time you start Word 6, you will see a Tip of the Day. Microsoft includes these tips to make you a better user of the Word 6 for Windows software. You can look at other tips by selecting Next tip or, after reading the initial tip, you can choose the OK button or press Enter to close the box. (See Figure 1-2.) The Tip of the Day screen displays automatically each time Word is started unless the X is removed from the Show Tips at Startup box in the Tip of the Day dialog box.

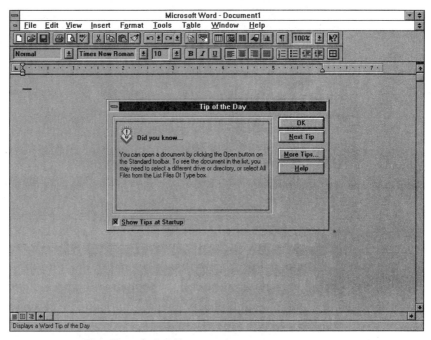

Figure 1-2 The Tip of the Day screen

Exercise 1: Starting Word

In this exercise, you start Word 6 for Windows.

1. If Microsoft Windows is not running, type Win at the DOS prompt.

2. With Windows Program Manager running, locate the Microsoft Office program group.

3. If you are using a mouse, double-click the Microsoft Word icon. If you are using the keyboard, highlight the icon by using (CTRL) + (TAB), press (ALT) + (F), choose Open, and use the arrow keys to highlight the Word icon and press (↵ ENTER).

4. When Word appears on the screen, read the Tip of the Day, and click OK to clear the box.

5. Keep Word on the screen for use in the next exercise.

Exercise 2: Using the mouse

In this exercise, you become familiar with the mouse.

1. Position the mouse pointer over the document window.
   The pointer becomes an I-beam.

2. Position the mouse pointer over the menus at the top of the screen.
   The pointer becomes a left-pointing arrow.

Objective 3: Understanding the Elements of the Word 6 Screen

When you start Word, a new, blank document appears on the screen. Along with the blank area where you will type your documents, the Word 6 screen has components that enable you to format, print, save, and enhance the documents you create. Understanding these screen elements is the way to learn how to use Word 6 for Windows. (See Figure 1-3.)

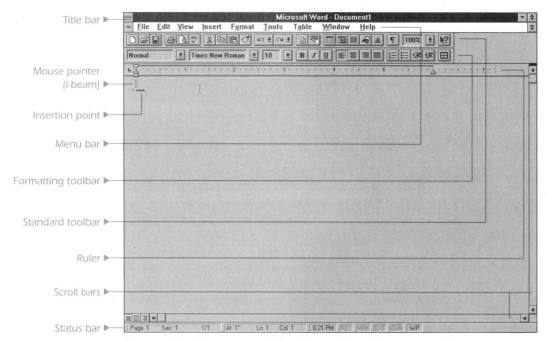

Figure 1-3 **The parts of the Word 6 for Windows screen**

The main Word 6 for Windows screen is divided into three parts. The first part contains the Title bar, Menu bar, toolbars, and ruler at the top of the screen. The second part, the document window, is the largest part of the screen and is where you type your documents. It contains the insertion point and has a scroll bar along the right side and another across the bottom. The third part, located at the bottom of the screen, contains the Status bar.

Objective 4: Understanding the Top Part of the Screen

The top part of the screen contains the Title bar, the Menu bar, the toolbars, and the ruler. These elements are all designed to help you use Word 6 for Windows efficiently.

Title bar

The Title bar is located at the top of the Word screen and contains the Application Control menu box; the name of the application—Microsoft Word; a name of a person, company, or school licensed to use the software (optional); the name of the active document; and the Minimize and Restore buttons. (See Figure 1-4.)

FEATURE

Shortcut menus

In Word, you can display shortcut menus which contain commands related to the item you are working with. Simply point to an item such as a paragraph and click the right mouse button. The shortcut menu displays in the document window. (See figure below.)

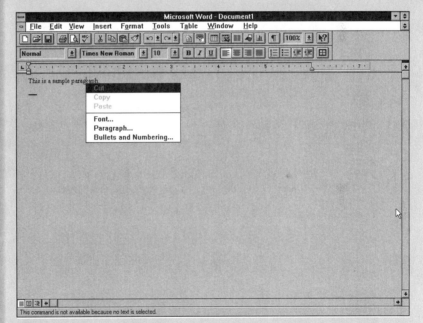

The shortcut menu displayed over the text in the document window

You can select a menu choice just as you would from any menu, or you can close the menu box without choosing a command by clicking anywhere outside the shortcut menu.

If you don't have a mouse, you can invoke the shortcut menu by pressing (SHIFT) + (F10). You can close the box by pressing (ESC).

Active document
name ▶

Application name ▶

Control menu ▶

Minimize button ▶

Restore/Maximize
button ▶

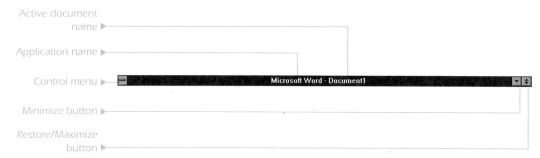

Figure 1-4   The parts of the Title bar

If you click the Control menu box, the menu shown in Figure 1-5 is displayed. The commands in the box are used to close Word, switch to other applications, and resize and move the Word window.

Figure 1-5   The Control menu box

If you click the Minimize button, Word is reduced to an icon. You must double-click the icon to return to Word. If you click the Restore button, the Word window is reduced on the screen. Simply click the button a second time to restore the full screen view.

Menu bar

The Menu bar is located below the Title bar, and contains the Document Control menu box, Word's command menus, and the Restore button, as shown in Figure 1-6.

Menu commands ▶

Document control
menu box ▶

Restore button ▶

Figure 1-6   The Menu bar

You use the Document Control menu box to size, move, split, and close document windows, and to move between windows. The Restore button on the Menu bar can be used to separate the active Word document from the

Menu bar so that you can drag the document on the screen. To restore the document to its original location, click the Document Maximize button.

You select commands from menus by using the mouse or the keyboard. To select a command with the mouse, click the left mouse button while pointing to the menu name. To select a command with the keyboard, press Alt + the underlined letter in the menu name. For example, press Alt + F to open the File menu and Alt + O for the Format menu.

Once the command is selected, a drop-down menu is displayed. Some commands carry out actions immediately, whereas other commands appear with an ellipsis, a check mark, a dot, or as dimmed text. Commands that are followed by an ellipsis (...) display a dialog box because more information is needed. Commands that are dimmed are not available at the current time. Commands that have a check mark or a dot indicate that they are turned on. (See Figure 1-7.)

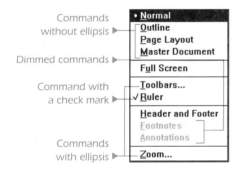

Figure 1-7 **View menu displaying the various types of commands**

You select commands from the drop-down menus by simply typing the underlined letter, pointing the mouse to the command, and clicking, or by using the arrow keys to highlight the command and pressing Enter. To deselect the menu you have selected, you can press the Esc key on the keyboard, or click the mouse while pointing outside the menu.

dialog boxes   Commands followed by ellipsis produce *dialog boxes* which provide options. Some dialog boxes are organized into categories, indicated with tabs, which look like file folders. To display a different category, click the tab. Lists of options are provided in dialog boxes. To select options, click one or more of the check boxes. To see a list of options, click an arrow and a drop-down list box results. You can select one option from the list. List boxes provide lists of options, and you can select one or click and drag to select more than one option in a list. When you are finished, click a command button, such as the OK, Cancel, or Help buttons, to carry out the action, cancel the action, or get help. (See Figure 1-8.)

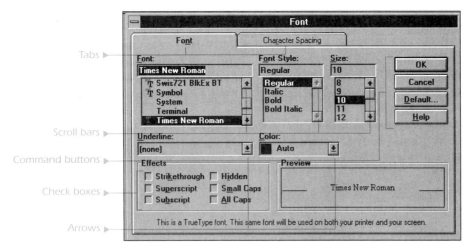

Tabs ►

Scroll bars ►

Command buttons ►

Check boxes ►

Arrows ►

Figure 1-8   **The Format Font dialog box**

To use dialog boxes using the keyboard instead of the mouse, press Ctrl + Tab to select Tabs, press the Tab to move to the various options, and then press Enter to carry out the action or press Esc to cancel.

Exercise 3: Selecting commands

In this exercise, you select and deselect menu choices.

1. With Word open, using either the mouse or the keyboard choose File Save As.
2. Choose the Cancel button.
3. If you have both a mouse and the keyboard available, redo the first two steps using the one you didn't use earlier.
4. Choose Format Paragraph.
5. In the Paragraph dialog box, choose the Cancel button.
6. Select the remaining menus, looking at the resulting drop-down menus. Cancel any menu choices.

Toolbars

Toolbars are quick ways to access commonly used commands using a mouse. Point to a button with the mouse and click the left button.

When you first start Word, the Standard and the Formatting toolbars are displayed just below the Menu bar. You can display or hide toolbars by selecting View Toolbars, or if at least one toolbar is visible, move the mouse pointer over a toolbar and click the right mouse button. Then select toolbars to display or deselect toolbars to hide. (See Figure 1-9.)

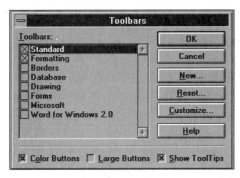

Figure 1-9   Toolbars dialog box with the Standard and Formatting toolbars selected

FEATURE

Checking text formatting with the Help button

If you click on the Help button 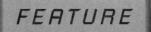 and then click on text in your document on screen, a pop-up bubble appears. The bubble contains information about the text's formatting. (See figure below.)

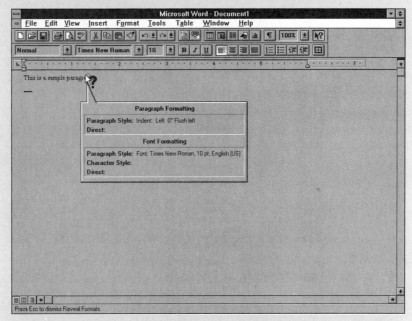

Paragraph and font formatting information provided in the pop-up bubble

Toolbars can be anchored, floating, or stacked. An anchored toolbar is locked to a specific location, whereas a floating toolbar is in a separate window that can be moved or sized. Stacked toolbars appear in the order you displayed them and can be dragged to a new location.

One handy feature of Word's toolbars is the ability to see a descriptive label of every tool. You simply move the mouse pointer over the button and wait for a few seconds; a Tooltip appears on the screen near the mouse pointer. At the same time, the Status bar, located at the bottom of the screen, provides an even more descriptive explanation of the button. For example, if you point to the Paint brush icon and wait a few seconds, a box appears by the pointer displaying "Format Painter." Along with that message, the Status bar displays the text, "Copies the formatting of the selection to a specified location." Until you are very familiar with the buttons, you should always wait for the Tooltip to appear so that you are sure you are selecting the correct button. (See Figure 1-10.)

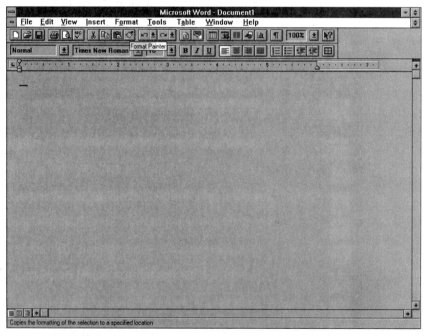

Figure 1-10   **Description of tool to which mouse is pointing with explanation in Status bar**

The buttons on the standard toolbar are shown in Table 1-2. Some tools, such as those on the Formatting toolbar, contain drop-down lists that work like the ones in dialog boxes, that is, click the arrow to see the list and then make a selection. (See Table 1-3.)

Table 1-2   The Standard Toolbar

BUTTON NAME	BUTTON	DESCRIPTION
New		Creates a new document based on the NORMAL template.
Open		Opens an existing document or template.
Save		Saves the active document or template.
Print		Prints the active document using the current defaults.
Print Preview		Displays full pages as they will be printed.
Spelling		Checks the spelling in the active document.
Cut		Cuts the selection and puts it on the *clipboard*.
Copy		Copies the selection and puts it on the clipboard.
Paste		Inserts the clipboard contents at the insertion point.
Format Painter		Copies the formatting of the selection to a specified location.
Undo		Reverses the last action—pressing ⊥ displays a history of the last actions.
Redo		Redoes the last action that was undone—pressing ⊥ displays a history of the last actions.
AutoFormat		Automatically formats a document.
Insert AutoText		Creates or inserts an AutoText entry, depending on the selection.
Insert Table		Inserts a table.
Insert Excel worksheet		If Excel is available, inserts a worksheet that can be used in Excel.
Columns		Changes the column format of the selected sections.
Drawing		Shows or hides the Drawing toolbar.
Insert Chart		Starts the Microsoft Chart Program, if it is available.
Show/Hide Paragraph		Shows or hides all nonprinting characters.
Zoom Control	100%	Scales the editing view—pressing ⊥ displays a list of view sizes.
Help		Lets you get help on a command or a screen region or examine text properties.

Table 1-3   **The Formatting Toolbar**

BUTTON NAME	BUTTON	DESCRIPTION
Style	Normal	Applies an existing style or records a style by example—pressing ⬇ displays options.
Font	Times New Roman	Changes the font of the selection—pressing ⬇ displays options.
Font Size	10	Changes the font size of the selection—pressing ⬇ displays options.
Bold	**B**	Makes the selection bold—is a *toggle*.
Italic	*I*	Makes the selection italic—is a toggle.
Underline	U	Formats the selection with a continuous underline—is a toggle.
Align Left		Aligns the paragraph at the left indent.
Center		Centers the paragraph between the indents.
Align Right		Aligns the paragraph at the right indent.
Justify		Aligns the paragraph at both the left and the right indent.
Numbering		Creates a numbered list based on the current defaults.
Bullets		Creates a bulleted list based on the current defaults.
Decrease Indent		Decreases the indent or promotes the selection one level.
Increase Indent		Increases indent or demotes the selection one level.
Borders		Shows or hides the Borders toolbar.

Exercise 4: Selecting and deselecting toolbars

In this exercise, you select and deselect toolbars.

1. Choose View Toolbars.
2. In the Toolbars dialog box, click on Borders and Database in the Toolbar section.
3. Choose OK.

   The screen adjusts to include all four toolbars.

4. Choose View Toolbars.
5. In the Toolbars dialog box, click on Borders and Database in the Toolbar section.
6. Choose OK.

The screen adjusts, removing two toolbars.

Ruler

The horizontal ruler is displayed immediately above the text editing area, allowing you to set tab stops, set indents for selected areas, change margins, and change column and table widths. To hide or redisplay the ruler, choose View Ruler.

Exercise 5: Hiding and displaying the ruler

In this exercise, you hide and redisplay the ruler.

1. Choose View.

   If the ruler is displayed on the screen, the Ruler command will have a check mark.

2. Choose Ruler.

   The ruler is removed from the screen display.

3. Choose View Ruler.

   A check mark is placed in front of the command, and the ruler is displayed again.

Objective 5: Understanding the Document Window

Until you start typing your document, the document window is blank. The insertion point is at the top left of the document because that is where the text you type will be inserted. As you type text, the insertion point moves with the text, showing you where the text you are typing will be inserted.

Scroll bars

Scroll bars appear at the right and bottom edges of the document window. The scroll boxes located in the scroll bars indicate your position in the document. That is, if the scroll box is at the top of the bar, you are at the top of the document; if the box is located away from the top, you see how far you are into the document. You can use the scroll bars to move around your document easily. Simply click the arrows. If you click the down arrow, you can view text below the insertion point. If you click the up arrow, you can view text located above the insertion point. You can click and drag the scroll box either up or down the document to move large distances in your document. Keep in mind that you are just *viewing* the text in other parts of your document; your insertion point doesn't move unless you actually move the insertion point to that location by clicking the mouse in a new location.

The horizontal scroll bar works the same way that the vertical scroll bar does, but it allows you to move horizontally in a document. The horizontal scroll bar also contains three buttons which change the document view from Normal to Page or Outline view. Normal view is the default and is the view you will use most of the time for creating and editing documents. Page Layout view displays the page as it will be printed and also allows editing. Outline view is useful if you organize your documents with a system of headers. When you switch to Outline view, all the headings and paragraphs are marked, thus allowing you to see the structure and make changes.

Microsoft Word Accessibility for People with Disabilities

The Microsoft Word documentation describes the Microsoft commitment to making software more accessible for people with disabilities. Microsoft provides products and services that support both people who are deaf or hard of hearing, and who are blind or have low vision.

Features built right into Microsoft Word 6 make it more accessible for people with disabilities. For example, you can zoom the screen to as much as 200%. Simply select the Down arrow on the Zoom Control button (`43%`) on the Standard toolbar) and select 200%. At 200% magnification, a 12-point type is almost 0.5 inch high on the screen. (See figure at top.)

You can also enlarge the buttons on the toolbar for easier viewing. Choose View Toolbars. In the Toolbars dialog box, select Large Buttons. The buttons increase in size. (See figure at bottom.)

Information and hints for customizing such aspects as keyboard layouts for people who can type with only one hand or for using a wand are available from Microsoft. (See Appendix D of the User's Guide for product information and phone numbers.)

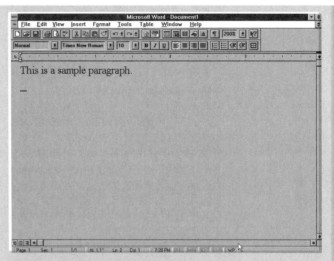

The screen zoomed to 200%

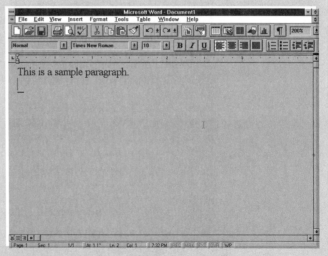

The buttons on the Toolbar enlarged

Objective 6: Understanding the Bottom Part of the Screen

The bottom of the screen, which is located below the horizontal scroll bar, contains the Status bar.

Status bar

The Status bar provides information about the current document or task. Here is an example of information in the Status bar:

DISPLAYED INFORMATION	MEANING
Page 4	Current page number
Sec 1	Current section of the document
4/4	Current page and the total number of pages
At 9.3"	Current location from the top of the page
Ln 54	Number of lines from the top of the page
Col 5	Number of characters from the left margin
1:10 PM	Current time

REC, MRK, EXT, OVR, and WPH are mode indicators. When they are dimmed, they are turned off; when they are bold, they are turned on. You can double-click to turn them on. For example, double-clicking OVR turns on Overtype mode. The mode indicators are as follows:

INDICATOR	MODE NAME
REC	Macro recorder
MRK	Revision marking
EXT	Extend selection
OVR	Overtype
WPH	WordPerfect Help

Exercise 6: Hiding and displaying the Status bar and scroll bars

In this exercise, you hide and redisplay the Status bar and the scroll bars.

1. Choose Tools Options.
2. In the Options dialog box, select the View tab, if necessary.
3. In the Window section of the dialog box, select Status Bar, Horizontal Scroll Bar, and Vertical Scroll Bar.

   The X is removed from the boxes.
4. Choose OK.

   The screen displays with the scroll bars and the Status bar removed.

5. Choose Tools Options.

6. In the Options dialog box, select the View tab, if necessary.

7. In the Window section of the dialog box, select Status Bar, Horizontal Scroll Bar, and Vertical Scroll Bar.

The X is placed in the boxes.

8. Choose OK.

The screen displays with the scroll bars and the Status bar displayed.

You can use the left half of the Status bar to display the Go To dialog box, which helps you move around a document quickly by moving the insertion point directly to a page, footnote, or other items. This is a very handy feature for long documents. Double-click any place on the left half of the Status bar and the Go To dialog box appears. (See Figure 1-11.)

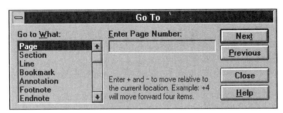

Figure 1-11 **Go To dialog box**

Objective 7: Using Help

Microsoft Word provides an extensive online Help feature, which can be accessed in various ways while working in Word. If you are currently in a dialog box and are uncertain as to what you should do, you can click the Help button. Every dialog box contains one. (See Figure 1-12.)

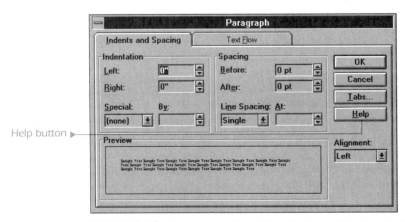

Figure 1-12 **An example of the Help button in a dialog box**

Exercise 7: Getting Help in a dialog box

In this exercise, you get help with a dialog box.

1. Choose File Save As.
2. In the Save As dialog box, click the Help button.
3. To quit Help, choose File Exit in the Help window.

You can choose Help from the Menu bar to view the Help menu. (See Figure 1-13.)

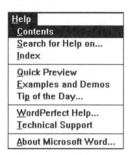

Figure 1-13   **The Microsoft Word Help menu**

You can get an overview of the Help feature by choosing Contents. You can get help on a specific topic by using the Search for Help on feature, or by choosing Index, and clicking on the first letter of the topic you want information about. Moving the mouse over a topic changes the pointer to a hand. Select a topic by clicking the hand pointer on the text.

Some words on the Help screen appear underlined with solid lines; click those words to get more information. Some words on the Help screen appear with dotted underlines; click those words to see a definition of the word.

Exercise 8: Using the Help menu

In this exercise, you use the Help menu.

1. Open the Help menu.
2. Choose Contents.
3. Choose the Help menu.
4. Choose How to Use Help. Read the information to become familiar with using the Help feature.
5. To quit Help, choose File Exit in the Help window, or double-click the close box (in the upper left corner of the Help window.)

You can get context-sensitive help by clicking the Help button on the Standard toolbar. The pointer appears with a question mark added to it. You can choose a command or item that you want help about. (See Figure 1-14.)

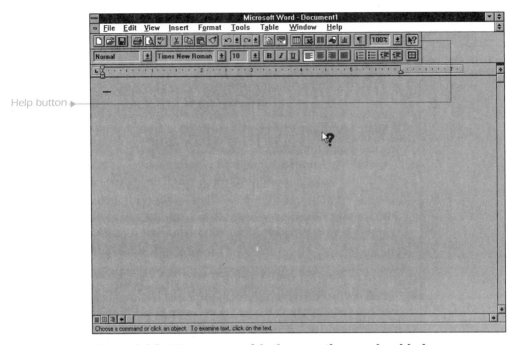

Help button ➤

Figure 1-14   The cursor with the question mark added

Exercise 9: Getting context-sensitive help

In this exercise, you use context-sensitive help.

1. Click the Help button 🖈❓ on the Standard toolbar.
2. Point to any button on the toolbar and click the mouse.

   Context-sensitive help is provided on the button you chose.

Objective 8: Exiting Microsoft Word 6 for Windows

When you are finished using Microsoft Word 6 for Windows, you should always exit from the software before you turn off the computer. To exit from the software, choose File Exit. If you didn't save the document you were working on or if you've made changes since the last time you saved, Word asks you if you want to save before exiting. You can save and exit, not save and exit anyway, or cancel the operation. (See Figure 1-15.)

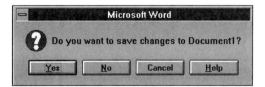

Figure 1-15 **Save before exiting prompt**

Exercise 10: Exiting Microsoft Word 6 for Windows

In this exercise, you exit Word 6 for Windows.

1. With Word 6 running, choose File Exit.

2. If you are asked about saving the document, click No.
   You are exited back to the Windows Program Manager.

Chapter Summary

In this chapter, you prepared yourself to start using Microsoft Word 6 for Windows. After starting the software, you became familiar with all the screen elements and the Help features. The chapter ended with learning how to correctly exit the software. You will use these features to create a document in Chapter 2.

Review Questions

True/False Questions

_____ 1. The Tip of the Day screen displays automatically each time Word is started unless the X is removed from the Show Tips at Startup box in the Tip of the Day dialog box.

_____ 2. You can only start Microsoft Word 6 for Windows by using a mouse.

_____ 3. If the mouse is pointed any place in the document window, it becomes an I-beam.

_____ 4. Page Layout view displays the page as it will be printed and also allows editing.

_____ 5. You can use the left half of the Status bar to display the Go To dialog box.

Multiple Choice Questions

_____ 6. The mouse pointer is a left-pointing arrow when positioned over
- A. menus.
- B. rulers.
- C. toolbars.
- D. All of the above.

_____ 7. To start Word 6 for Windows using the keyboard, hold down the Ctrl key and press Tab until the Microsoft Office title bar is highlighted. With Microsoft Office highlighted,
- A. you must click the mouse.
- B. press Alt-F, and then choose Open; the program group is opened. Use the arrow keys to highlight the Microsoft Word icon, and press Enter.
- C. press Ctrl-O to open.
- D. press the function key F1.

_____ 8. To select a command from menus, you can
- A. point and click to the menu choice.
- B. press a function key.
- C. press Alt + the underlined letter in the menu name.
- D. Both A and C.

_____ 9. If you want to deselect the menu you have selected, you can
- A. press Enter.
- B. press Esc.
- C. click the mouse while pointing outside the menu.
- D. Both B and C.

_____ 10. Commands that provide options are
- A. followed by ellipses.
- B. followed by check marks
- C. grayed.
- D. Both A and C.

Fill-in-the-Blank Questions

11. Software that allows for creating, editing, printing, and saving text using a computer is called _____ _____ software.

12. The Program Group located in the Program Manager containing Microsoft Word 6 is _____ _____.

13. The Windows screen from which you start Word 6 is called the _____ _____.

14. A(n) _____ is a button that you click once to turn on and once again to turn off.

15. A(n) _____ is an image that represents an action and is usually a button.

Acumen-Building Activities

Quick Projects

Project 1: Becoming Familiar with the Tip of the Day

1. Start Microsoft Word 6 for Windows.
2. From the Tip of the Day dialog box, choose More Tips.
3. Point the hand pointer to the first underlined green words <u>Navigating in Word</u> and click.
4. Read through the Navigating in Word tips.
5. When you are finished reading, choose File from the Word Help box.
6. Choose Exit from the drop-down menu.
7. From the Tip of the Day dialog box, choose OK to start Word.

Project 2: Becoming Familiar with the Toolbar

1. With Word 6 running, point the mouse pointer to the first icon on the Toolbar.
2. Hold it there until the Tooltip appears telling you the name of the button.
3. Notice that the Status bar has changed to provide you information on the button.
4. Repeat the process, looking at various buttons on both the Standard and Formatting toolbars.

Project 3: Using Go To from the Status Bar

1. With Word 6 running, double-click the mouse on the left half of the Status bar.
2. The Go To dialog box appears.
3. Drag the scroll box to the bottom of the Go to What section of the dialog box.
4. Notice all the objects that you can go to in your document.
5. Choose Close to exit the dialog box.

Project 4: Using the WP on the Status Bar

1. With Word 6 running, double-click the mouse on the gray WP on the Status bar. The Help for WordPerfect Users dialog box appears.
2. Point the mouse to Exit> in the Command Keys section.
3. Notice that the right part of the dialog box changes to provide information for WordPerfect users who press the function key F7 to exit the software on how to exit Microsoft Word 6.
4. Choose Close.

In-Depth Projects

Project 1: Using Word's Examples and Demos from the Help Menu.

1. With Word 6 running, choose Help.
2. Choose Examples and Demos.
3. Choose Proofing and Reviewing.
4. Choose Checking spelling.
5. Click the buttons: Find repeated words, Correct misspelled words, Add unique words, Check for spelling errors, and Ignore words.
6. Click on the Demo button.
7. Choose Start.
8. Keep selecting the Next> button to complete the demonstration.
9. Choose Close three times.
10. Choose File Exit from the Word Help box.

Project 2: Using the Help Index

1. With Word 6 running, choose Help.
2. Choose Index.
3. In the Word Help box, click the S.
4. Use the scroll arrows to move the pointer to the Spelling command (Tools menu).
5. Notice that the mouse pointer is the left-pointing arrow on that entry—that is just a heading. If you move the pointer over the options under the Spelling command, the pointer changes to a hand. You can use the hand pointer to select topics.
6. Point the hand pointer to description of and click.
7. From the Spelling command (Tools menu) box, click the hand on the green dotted-underlined words Standard toolbar. You see a definition of the Standard toolbar.
8. Click the mouse outside the box to close the Standard toolbar definition.

9. Use the downward-pointing arrow in the scroll bar to become familiar with the Spelling command's features.

10. When you are finished reading about the Spelling command, choose the Back button under the Word Help menu. You are returned to the main Index.

11. Continue to choose letters and then select features under each to read about.

12. When you are finished, choose File Exit from the Word Help box.

13. When you are finished working with Microsoft Word 6 for Windows, choose File Exit to exit properly. If you are asked if you want to save the document, choose No.

CASE STUDIES

Coffee-To-Go:

Preparing a Business Plan

In this case study, you will prepare a business plan for a start-up business called Coffee-To-Go. This small espresso stand will be located on a busy intersection in Eugene, Oregon. The location will provide drive-through access on the east side and walk-up access on the west side. The business will sell various types of coffee drinks and teas, as well as muffins and cookies.

You will be provided with the information to complete the business plan in the following chapters.

CASE STUDIES

Videos West:

Preparing a Business Plan

In this case study, you will prepare documents for a video business located in Fairbanks, Alaska. This business has operated a video rental store in downtown Fairbanks for two years. The owners of Videos West are planning to expand the business by including a retail line of special interest videos available to the entire state by mail order.

You will be provided with the information to complete the marketing of the new venture in the following chapters.

Chapter 2

Creating, Saving, and Printing a File

Objectives

- Creating a Document
- Moving Around the Document
- Inserting and Typing over Text
- Deleting Text
- Showing and Deleting Nonprinting Characters
- Saving a File
- Running the Spell Checker
- Printing a Document
- Opening a File

Key Terms

TERM	DEFINITION
Wordwrap	words that are automatically wrapped around to the next line when the current line is filled with text
Insert	text that is moved to the right making room for the new text that is typed
Overtype	text that is typed over the existing text
Nonprinting Characters	characters such as the space, tab, and paragraph marker
Directory	a location on a disk
Spell Checker	utility that compares the words in your document to the words listed in its dictionary file

In this chapter, you learn the basics necessary to produce a document using Microsoft Word 6 for Windows. First, you learn to create a document, editing your errors and checking your spelling. Next you learn to save the file to your disk for use later, and then you print the document. You also learn how to open the document so that you can use it the next time you return to Word 6.

Objective 1: Creating a Document

Every time you begin using Microsoft Word, a new document labeled Document1 is created. All you need to do to create a document is to start typing in Document1. The text is entered at the blinking insertion point, which is at the top of a new document. Word automatically *wordwraps* text to the next line when the text reaches the right margin, so you need only press Enter at the end of a paragraph. You can type your document and then make corrections or changes to it at any time.

wordwraps

Exercise 1: Creating a document

In this exercise, you create a document.

1. Start Microsoft Word as described in Chapter 1.
2. Type in the following document, pressing ⏎ ENTER only at the ends of paragraphs.

This is an invitation from your friends at Barbara's Yogurt to our most valuable customers. We desire your opinion on the latest and greatest flavor to be developed in our kitchens, so we are asking you to take part in our market survey. As a person who already greatly enjoys our yogurt, we think that your opinion is of great value.

Simply bring this letter to your local Barbara's Yogurt, and ask to be part of the survey. After you sample the new flavor, you will be given a survey form to fill out. Because we realize that your time is limited, you will be given a coupon for one free quart of any flavor yogurt for your trouble.

Objective 2: Moving Around a Document

You can use the scroll bars at the right and the bottom of the Word window to scroll to another part of the document; however, scrolling doesn't move the insertion point. So to insert, delete, or change text, you must move the insertion point to the desired location. The easiest way to move the insertion point is to position the I-beam pointer in the desired location and click the mouse. You can also use the keyboard to move the insertion point. Table 2-1 lists the keystrokes and their action.

Table 2-1   Moving the Insertion Point

KEYSTROKE	ACTION
← and →	One character left or right
↑ and ↓	One line up or down
CTRL + HOME	Top of document
CTRL + END	End of document
PAGE UP / PAGE DOWN	Up or down one screen
END	End of current line
HOME	Beginning of current line

Exercise 2: Moving around a document

In this exercise, you move the insertion point to a different location in the document.

1. Press CTRL + HOME to move to the top of the document.
2. Press ← ENTER.
3. Press ↑.
4. Type Barbara's Fine Yogurt and press ← ENTER three times.
5. Press CTRL + END to move to the end of the document.
6. Press ← ENTER three times.
7. Type Sincerely,
8. Press ← ENTER four times.
9. Type your name.
10. To practice using the mouse to move the insertion point, move the I-beam pointer to the "B" in "Barbara's" in the first paragraph and click the mouse.

Objective 3: Inserting and Typing Over Text

insert   When you want to add or *insert* text to your existing document, simply move the insertion point to where you want the text to appear and begin typing. To replace existing text rather than insert text, you can switch to

overtype   *overtype*. To change to overtype, either press the Insert key on the keyboard or double-click the OVR indicator on the Status bar. The OVR indicator is bold when it is turned on. To turn overtype off, either press the Insert key or double-click the OVR indicator a second time. (See Figure 2-1.)

Page 1   Sec 1   1/1   At 1"   Ln 1   Col 1   10:51 PM   REC   MRK   EXT   OVR   WP

Figure 2-1   The bold OVR indicator on the status line

Microsoft Corporation

Microsoft, the world's largest software company, was started in 1975 by Bill Gates and Paul Allen after Gates, 19 at the time, dropped out of Harvard. Besides producing Word 6 for Windows, Microsoft supplies the computer industry with systems and applications software for both IBM and compatible computers and the Apple Macintosh. Well-known, powerful software packages such as Windows, MS-DOS, Excel, Works, and Publisher plus many home products such as Money, Encarta, Bookshelf, and Beethoven have made Microsoft a billion-dollar corporation.

Located in Redmond, Washington, Microsoft has grown from about 30 employees in 1980 to over 8000 today. At least half of Microsoft's business is in international sales, and there are subsidiaries all over the world.

Unlike the heads of many such companies who have turned over the operation to others, Bill Gates still guides and shapes the future of Microsoft Corporation.

Exercise 3: Inserting and typing over text

In this exercise, you insert and type over existing text.

1. Using the document created in Exercise 1, move the insertion point to the "s" in "survey" in the second paragraph.

2. Type the word brief and press the spacebar.

3. Move the insertion point to the "Y" in "Yogurt" in the first paragraph and type Fine and press the spacebar. Repeat this step in the second paragraph. (See Figure 2-2.)

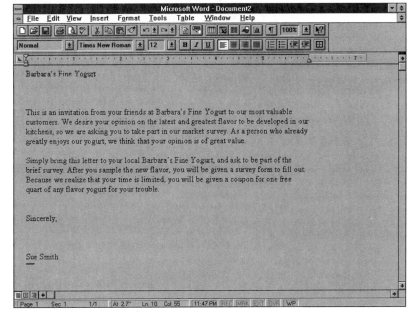

Figure 2-2 **The word "brief" inserted before "survey," and the word "Fine" before "Yogurt" in both paragraphs**

4. Move the insertion point to "l" in "limited" in the second paragraph.

5. Press the Insert key on the keyboard or double-click the OVR indicator on the Status bar.

6. Type the letters valuabl

7. Press the Insert key or double-click the OVR indicator.

8. Type the letter e to finish changing the word "limited" to "valuable."

9. Move the insertion point to the "t" in "trouble" in the second paragraph.

10. Press the Insert key or click the OVR indicator.

11. Type participation and press the period.

12. Press the Insert key or click the OVR indicator to turn off overtype. (See Figure 2-3.)

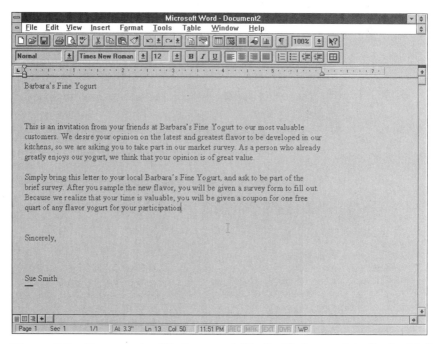

Figure 2-3   Document with the word "limited" changed to "valuable"

Objective 4: Deleting Text

You can correct simple typing mistakes by pressing the Backspace and Delete keys. The Backspace key erases characters to the left of the insertion point. The Delete key erases characters to the right of the insertion point.

Exercise 4: Deleting text

In this exercise, you erase text in a document.

1. Using the document just created, move the insertion point just after the "y" in "greatly" in the first paragraph.
2. Press the Backspace key eight times to remove the word and the extra space.
3. Place the insertion point on the "b" in "brief" in the second paragraph.
4. Press ⌈DELETE⌋ six times to remove the word and the extra space. (See Figure 2-4.)

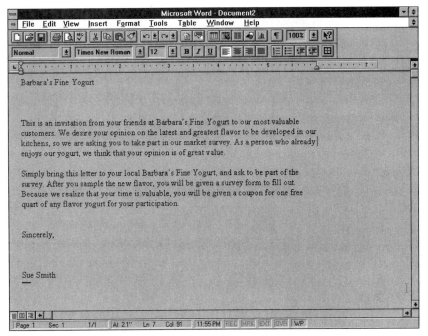

Figure 2-4 **Document with the words "greatly" and "brief" deleted**

Objective 5: Showing and Deleting Nonprinting Characters

nonprinting characters You can show all the *nonprinting characters* such as spaces, paragraph marks, and tab characters so that you can see whether you have typed in extra characters that need to be deleted. You click the Show/Hide button ¶ on the Standard toolbar to display the nonprinting characters. Click the button a second time to hide the nonprinting characters.

Exercise 5: Displaying and deleting nonprinting characters

In this exercise, you display and delete nonprinting characters.

1. Using the document just created, click the Show/Hide button ¶ on the Standard toolbar.
2. With the nonprinting characters showing, press `CTRL` + `END`.
3. Press `↵ ENTER` and then `TAB`. Then press the spacebar three times. Notice the character representing each of these keys.
4. Press the Backspace key to erase each of these characters.
5. Press the Show/Hide button ¶ to turn off the display.

FEATURE

AutoCorrect

Word 6 has the built-in capability to correct your most common typing errors as you type. For example, if you often type "teh" for "the," Word automatically changes it to the correct word as you type. You can see the built-in AutoCorrect entries by choosing Tools AutoCorrect. (See figure below.)

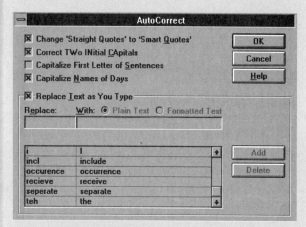

The AutoCorrect dialog box

Use the scroll bar on the list box to see the built-in entries that Word 6 corrects. You can also customize AutoCorrect by adding your regular typing errors in the Replace text box, with the correct version in the With text box and then clicking the Add button. The Formatted text button not only replaces the text, but also duplicates the formatting you include in the With text box. If you later change your mind about an entry, you can highlight it and press the Delete button to remove it.

If you often type long names that are difficult to type such as Umpqua Community College, you can store an abbreviation such as "uc," and it is automatically replaced for you when you type "uc." This can save you a lot of tedious typing.

To automatically correct as you type, place an X in the Replace Text as You Type check box. You can decide on other options to select such as Correct Two Initial Capitals or Capitalize Names of Days and place X's in the check boxes.

Objective 6: Saving a File

After creating a document, you will want to save it so that you have access to it at another time. When you save a document for the first time, you need to give it a meaningful name. Filenames can only be from one to a maximum of eight characters. You cannot include any of the following characters in filenames: spaces, periods, *, ?, :, [,], +, =, /, \, <, >. Word places the three-letter extension .DOC on your files immediately after the maximum of eight characters that you name your file. For example, if you want to name a report you created in October, you should think of a meaningful name that does not exceed eight characters and does not use any of the special characters in the preceding list. You could name it OCTRPT. Word would add the three-letter extension .DOC to the end, so the filename would be OCTRPT.DOC.

When you want to save your document, choose File Save As and type the name of the file in the dialog box. After the file has been given a name, you can continue to save as you work by choosing File Save or by clicking the Save button ![save] on the Standard toolbar.

You should save your file periodically while you are working so that if you experience a problem, you will have a current version of your file. Always save your file before you print, run special tools, or do a replace.

Exercise 6: Saving a document

In this exercise, you save a document.

1. Using the document you just created, choose File Save As.
2. In the Save As dialog box, type Barbara in the File Name section. (See Figure 2-5.)

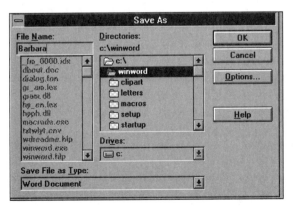

Figure 2-5 **The Save As dialog box with the filename typed in the File Name section**

3. Choose OK to complete the save.

The file you created in these exercises is now saved under the name BARBARA.DOC.

If you want to save a file to a disk drive other than the current one, you can choose a different drive in the Drives drop-down box. If you want to save a file to a *directory,* a location on a disk, other than the current one, you can choose a different directory in the Directories list box.

directory

Objective 7: Running the Spell Checker

One handy word processing feature is built-in spell checking capabilities. Microsoft Word 6 contains a *Spell Checker* which compares the words in your document to the words listed in its dictionary file. Words that are not on the list are highlighted as possible errors, and the Spelling dialog box appears, providing you with several options. (See Figure 2-6.)

Spell Checker

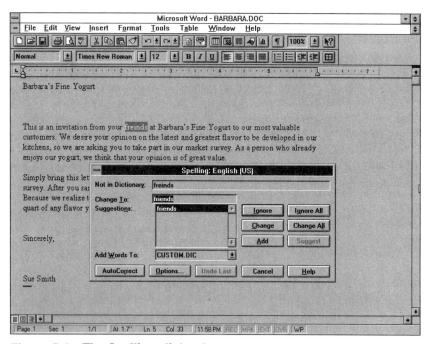

Figure 2-6   **The Spelling dialog box**

The misspelled word appears in the Not in Dictionary section of the dialog box. Word supplies alternatives in the Suggestions section, including one alternative that appears in the Change To section. You can click the Change button if the correct alternative is shown in the Change To section, or you can highlight any of the other alternatives you desire and then click the Change button. If you want to change every instance of the word in the document, you can choose Change All. If the word in the Not in Dictionary section is in fact correct, you can simply click the Ignore or Ignore All to skip it this once or to skip it entirely in this document, respectively.

The Add button allows you add words to the dictionary, so that words such as proper nouns or very technical terms will not continue to be highlighted. If you happened to select the wrong alternative and need to undo the correction, you can click the Undo Last button. If none of the displayed alternatives seems appropriate, you can use the Suggest button to ask Word to provide additional words if they are available.

If Word finds two identical words next to each other such as "... the the...," the second one is highlighted and the Change button becomes a Delete button. You can also click the Ignore button if you do want both words to appear in your document.

Word also highlights words that have mixed capitalization and numbers mixed with letters. You can correct or ignore these words as you would any highlighted word. If you want to change some of the spelling options, choose the Options button. Word provides options to ignore words with numbers mixed in, ignore words in uppercase, to turn off the suggest feature, and to add supplemental dictionaries.

You can choose the Cancel button to stop Word from checking spelling at any time. If you allow Word to complete the spelling check, you see the message: "The spelling check is complete" in the dialog box.

If the Spell Checker caught any errors, you should save your file again to update the saved version. You should always run the Spell Checker, but remember that you still need to read the document because a word is only highlighted if it is incorrectly spelled not if it is incorrectly used. For example, if you want to tell a person to "fill in the form" and you type "full in the from," no spell checker will catch these errors.

Exercise 7: Using the Spell Checker

In this exercise, you run the Spell Checker.

1. Using the document you just created, insert the following typing errors:
   a. Move to "friends" in the first sentence and change it to "freinds."
   b. Move to "your" in the second sentence and type your again so that it appears twice and then press the spacebar.
   c. Change "coupon" in the last sentence to "cupon."
2. Choose Tools Spelling or the Spelling button ⬚.
3. You should correct the three errors that you created along with any other errors that you might have in your document.
4. When the spelling check is complete, choose File Save or click the Save button ⬚.

Objective 8: Printing a Document

You can print your document at any time while you are working on it. You also can see what your document will look like when it is printed by choosing to preview before you print. Previewing the document allows you to make changes before you actually print on paper.

Exercise 8: Previewing and printing a document

In this exercise, you preview and then print a document.

1. Using the file just created, choose File Print Preview. You see what your document will look like when it is printed. (See Figure 2-7.)

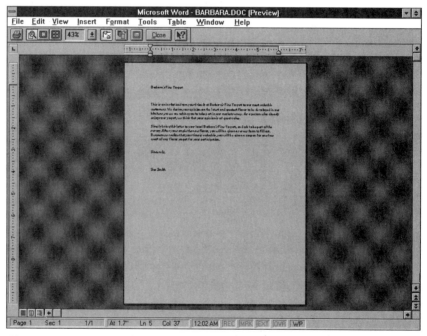

Figure 2-7 **The Preview screen**

2. Press ESC to leave the Preview screen.
3. To print the document, choose File Print.
4. Choose OK to send the document to the printer. (You will learn more about printing in Chapter 6.)
5. Close the file.

Objective 9: Opening a File

When you return to Microsoft Word, you might want to continue working on the same document. To do so, you would need to open the correct file. Word keeps track of the last files you have been working on and lists them at the bottom of the File menu. (See Figure 2-8.)

```
New...          Ctrl+N
Open...         Ctrl+O
Close

Save            Ctrl+S
Save As...
Save All

Find File...
Summary Info...
Templates...

Page Setup...
Print Preview
Print...         Ctrl+P

1 BARBARA.DOC
2 A:\WORDCH1.DOC
3 A:\TOC.DOC
4 A:\WORDCH0.DOC

Exit
```

Figure 2-8   **The File menu with the BARBARA.DOC file listed**

If the document you want to use is listed at the bottom of the File menu, you can type the number preceding it, or highlight it and click the mouse or press Enter. If the document you want to work with is not listed on the File menu, you must choose the Open command, and then select the file from the list in the File Name section of the dialog box by highlighting it and choosing OK. (See Figure 2-9.)

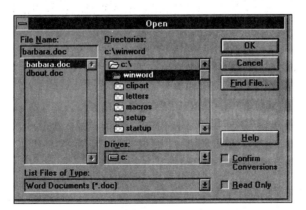

Figure 2-9   **The File Name section of the Open dialog box**

Exercise 9: Opening a file

In this exercise, you open a file.

1. Choose File.

2. From the File drop-down menu, type the number of the file you want to use from the bottom of the menu.

   The file appears on the screen.

3. Choose File Close to close the file.

4. Choose File.
5. Choose Open.
6. Select the BARBARA.DOC file from the File Name section of the dialog box.
7. Choose OK.

If the file you want to use is on a disk in a drive other than the current one, you can select a drive from the Drives drop-down box in the Open dialog box. If the file you want to use is in a different directory, you can change directories by selecting a different one from the Directory list box of the Open dialog box.

Chapter Summary

In this chapter, you learned all the basics necessary to create documents using a word processor. You created and edited a document, saved the document, checked the spelling, and printed the document. You also learned how to open a document that you saved so that you can return to it at another time. You will build on all these features in the second part of the book as you learn to enhance the documents that you create.

Review Questions

True/False Questions

_____ 1. When insert is turned on, text is moved to the right, making room for the new text that is typed.

_____ 2. A filename can have up to 18 characters.

_____ 3. Word keeps track of the last files you have been working on and lists them at the bottom of the File menu.

_____ 4. Wordwrap automatically places words on the next line when the current line is filled with text.

_____ 5. Previewing the document allows you to make changes before you actually print on paper.

Multiple Choice Questions

_____ 6. Which of the following names is a valid Word 6 filename?

A. My file.doc

B. My_file.doc

C. My*file.doc

D. All of the above.

_____ 7. Which of the following names is a valid Word 6 filename?

A. Memo2.doc

B. Memo 2.doc

C. Memo>>2.doc

D. None of the above.

_____ 8. To move to the top of your document, you can use

A. the Home key.

B. the Ctrl-Home combination.

C. the Insert key.

D. the Pg Up key.

_____ 9. To switch from Insert to Overtype or from Overtype to Insert, you can

A. click the OVR indicator on the Status bar.

B. press the Insert key.

C. press the Ctrl + Insert combination.

D. Either A or B.

_____ 10. To display the nonprinting characters, you would

A. choose Tools Autoformat.

B. choose Edit Paste.

C. choose the Show/Hide button on the Standard toolbar.

D. All of the above.

Fill-in-the-Blank Questions

11. When you turn on _____, text is typed over the existing text.

12. The _____ _____ utility compares the words in your document to the words listed in its dictionary file

13. Text will be entered at the blinking _____ _____, which is at the top of a new document.

14. Characters such as the space, tab, and paragraph marker are called _____ _____.

15. The _____ key erases characters to the left of the insertion point.

Acumen-Building Activities

Quick Projects

Project 1: Creating a Document

1. Create the following document:

Computer Files

A computer file is a collection of information stored as a unit and given a name. A document created using Microsoft Word 6 for Windows is saved as a file. In DOS, a filename consists of two parts: the filename, which can have up to a maximum of eight characters, and an extension, which can have a maximum of three characters. Microsoft Word places the three-letter extension DOC on files. The filename and the three-letter extension are separated with a period.

Files are saved on disks, either the hard disk or floppy disks. For easier management, disks are divided in sections called directories. You can compare a disk to a file cabinet and directories to the hanging folders which contain documents.

Therefore, a complete filename consists of the drive, the directory, the filename, and the three-letter extension. When you issue the File Save As command and type a file name such as DRIVE, Word will give it the three-letter extension .DOC and save it in the current directory and on the current drive. So its complete name might look something like this: C:\WINWORD\FILES\DRIVE.DOC.

2. Save the file as DRIVE.
3. Run the Spell Checker.
4. Proofread and correct any typing errors.
5. Save the file again.
6. Print the document and close it.

Project 2: Creating a Document

1. Create the following document:

   Ergonomics is the science of making your work
   environment healthy and comfortable. Avoiding back
   strain, eye strain, and wrist discomfort are important
   because Repetitive Stress Injuries are occurring at
   increasing numbers in today's offices.

   Start with a workstation that fits you; for example,
   make sure your feet touch the floor and don't dangle.
   Your chair should offer your spine plenty of support,
   so that after hours of working on the computer your
   back isn't frozen into a painful position.

   You might consider a glare filter for your monitor which
   can help avoid eyestrain, but at least be aware of the
   lighting in your work area. Lighting is an important
   factor in causing eye strain. The best guideline to
   follow for lighting or lamp positioning is to place your
   light source perpendicular to, or off to the side of,
   your monitor.

   You might also consider two add-ons for your wrists.
   The first is an ergonomic keyboard which is V-shaped
   and provides support for your wrists in a straight,
   natural position. The second is a palm rest for your
   mouse which provides support for repetitive use of
   the mouse.

   Don't forget to take breaks to rest your eyes,
   stretch your back, and relax your wrists.

2. Save the file as HEALTHY.
3. Run the Spell Checker.
4. Proofread and correct any typing errors.
5. Save the file again.
6. Print the document and close it.

Project 3: Creating a Document

1. Create the following document:

```
Microsoft's References

Microsoft Bookshelf for Windows is a CD-ROM reference
collection that includes the full text of the American
Heritage Dictionary (2nd College Edition), Bartletts'
Familiar Quotations, and the Concise Columbia Dictionary
of Quotations, the Concise Columbia Encyclopedia, and
Roget's II Electronic Thesaurus. It also includes recent
editions of the World Almanac and Book of Facts and the
Hammond Atlas.

This entire bookshelf is available for under $200,
and makes finding the correct information for school
papers fun and easy.

Bookshelf's interface makes jumping between books
in the collection easy and takes advantage of its
multimedia format. Bookshelf has audio clips such as
national anthems of countries and pronounces many of
the names of places for you. It also includes
animations in the encyclopedia.
```

2. Save the file as BOOK.
3. Run the Spell Checker.
4. Proofread and correct any typing errors.
5. Save the file again.
6. Print the document and close it.

Project 4: Creating a Document

1. Create the following document:

```
Not so many years ago, computers took up a whole
room and had to be specially cooled. The computer
revolution happened because computers became small
enough to fit on a desk and cheap enough that ordinary
people could afford them. These revolutionary computers
are known today as PCs for personal computer. The
personal computer refers to desktop computers which are
stationary and must have electricity in order to
function. Portable computers have been on the scene
for years, but they are now becoming powerful and
inexpensive so they are becoming very popular. Four
categories of portable computers are now available.
```

The first category includes the transportables which are the older version of a portable computer. They are still heavy and need electricity to function.

The second category is the laptop which should fit in your lap. This category has given way to the third category, notebooks. Notebook computers have the approximate dimensions of an 8.5 by 11 inch notebook and should be able to run on a battery for long periods of time. The average weight of a notebook computer is 6.5 pounds.

The fourth category of portable computers is the palmtop. These computers allow you to hold them in your hand, and they are capable of operating for long periods on battery power.

How small will computers continue to become—it's really anyone's guess.

2. Save the file as PALM.
3. Run the Spell Checker.
4. Proofread and correct any typing errors.
5. Save the file again.
6. Print the document and close it.

In-Depth Projects

Project 1: Creating a Document

1. Create a new document containing a list of all the information you would put in your résumé. That is, list all jobs that you have had, list all the education you have had, and list anything else that should be included. Don't worry about the format at this time, you will be learning how to format in the next section.
2. Save the file as RESUME.
3. Run the Spell Checker.
4. Proofread and correct any errors.
5. Save the document again.
6. Print out the document.

Project 2: Creating a Document

1. Create the following file:

Displaying a Document in Microsoft Word 6 for Windows

Word provides several ways to view a document: Normal
view, Outline view, Page Layout view, Print Preview, and
Master Document view. If you switch between the various
views, the insertion point remains in the same location
in your document, so that you don't lose your place.

Normal View

Normal view is for typing and editing. It is the
default view in Word 6. Normal view shows a simplified
version of a document and is the easiest place to
create, edit, and format a document. To switch to
Normal view, click the Normal View button on the
scroll bar, or choose Normal from the View menu.

Outline View

In Outline view, the document is collapsed to see only
the main headings. You must create your document with
headings in order to use this view successfully. To
switch to Outline view, click the Outline View button on
the scroll bar, or choose Outline from the View menu.

Page Layout View

Page Layout view is the WYSIWYG view, that is, What
You See Is What You Get. This view helps you see what
the final appearance of a document will be. Most people
don't work here because it may slow down editing and
scrolling. To switch to Page Layout view, click the
Page Layout View button on the horizontal scroll bar,
or choose Page Layout from the View menu.

Print Preview View

Print Preview view shows entire pages at a reduced
size. This view allows you to change the document
layout before you print. To switch to Print Preview,
click the Print Preview button on the Standard toolbar,
or choose Print Preview from the File menu.

Master Document View

Master Document view is used for creating a long document such as a book. You can bring together separate chapters into one master view. To switch to Master Document view, choose Master Document from the View menu.

2. Save the file as VIEW.
3. Run the Spell Checker.
4. Proofread and correct any errors.
5. Save the file again.
6. Print out the document.

CASE STUDIES

Coffee-To-Go:

Writing the Purpose Statement

In this chapter, you learned to enter text, save, and print a document. You can use those skills to start to create a business plan for Coffee-To-Go.

1. Type in the first part of the business plan as shown:

    Section One: The Business

    Purpose Statement

    Coffee-To-Go is seeking new start-up loans totaling $20,000 to purchase equipment and inventory; purchase and customize a portable building; lease the site; and help maintain sufficient cash reserves to provide adequate working capital to successfully operate a business.

    The $20,000 loan together with an additional $10,000 equity investment by the owner/operator will finance the start-up phase so that the business can become successful.

2. Move the cursor to the "b" in "business" at the end of the first paragraph. Type the word new and press the spacebar.
3. Move the cursor to the "s" in "successful" in the second paragraph. Change to Overtype mode and type the word profitable.
4. Move the cursor to the space after the word "new" in the first line. Press the Backspace key to erase the word and the space before it.
5. Move the cursor to the "h" in "help" in the first paragraph. Press DELETE five times to erase the word and the space following it.

6. Restore the deleted word "help."
7. Delete the word help again and don't restore it.
8. Save the file as Plan1.
9. Print the document.

CASE STUDIES

Videos West: **Writing a Marketing Letter**

In this chapter, you learned to enter text, save, and print a document. You can use these skills to create a marketing letter for Videos West.

1. Create the following letter:

```
Dear Friends,

Are you ready to enjoy your VCR more? Do you want to
learn new skills, improve your current skills, and
find more enjoyment right in your home?

Then our new interesting catalog of special interest
videos is the answer for you.

Some of the subjects offered on videocassette in our
catalog include: crafts and hobbies, business skills,
education, travel, medicine, gardening, exercise,
cooking, and so many more.

Our catalog contains over 3,000 titles for sale at
discounted prices. And if you act now, you will
receive a coupon for one free video of your choice.

To order the catalog, fill out the enclosed form and
mail it along with a $3 check or money order to:

                    Videos West
                    1121 Second St.
                    Fairbanks, AK 99701

Special interest videos can make a difference in the
way you work, play, and learn—you see it and hear it
at the same time. Expand your horizons today.

Sincerely,

Your name
```

2. Move to the "c" in "current" in the first sentence. Press the Backspace key five times to erase the word "your" and the extra space.

3. Move to the "i" in "interesting" in the second paragraph. Press DELETE twelve times to erase the word "interesting" and the extra space.

4. Move to the "m" in "medicine" in the third paragraph and type health and. Notice that the words are inserted before "medicine."

5. Move to the "e" in "exercise" in the third paragraph. Press INSERT, type fitness, and press DELETE once to erase the extra character.

6. Insert the current date at the top of the document.

7. Save the file as VCR.

8. Print the letter.

Acumen Fundamentals Milestone

Individual Project:

Creating a Long Document

1. Create the following document:

What Is Computer Memory?

Your computer contains two types of memory—RAM, random access memory, and ROM, read only memory.

ROM is a specialized memory which contains some of the instructions necessary to start the computer. Therefore, ROM is permanent and doesn't lose its contents when the computer's power is shut off. Although ROM performs important functions, its size and capability are not important to the user.

RAM, also known as main memory or primary storage, is temporary memory. That is, RAM is volatile, losing all its contents when the computer is turned off. RAM holds program instructions and data while you are working. For example, if you are working in Microsoft Word 6 for Windows, RAM must be able to hold enough of the operating system to function, enough of Windows to function, enough of Word 6 to do your word processing tasks, and enough of your document so that you can see it.

The size of your random access memory is very important. If you don't have enough, you can't even load a program. RAM is measured in bytes. A byte is the space necessary to store the equivalent of one character that you type. When a number describing RAM has a KB after it, the size is thousands of bytes. For example, 640 KB means 640,000 bytes of main memory. When a number describing RAM has a MB after it, the size is millions of bytes. For example, 4MB means 4 million bytes of main memory.

For a long time, people used computers with 640 KB of RAM. However, since the rise in popularity of Windows and the software that runs under Windows, such as Word 6, RAM has expanded in size to accommodate these powerful programs. Today, people purchase and use computers with 4 to 8 MB.

RAM memory resides in memory chips located inside your computer. A memory chip is an electronic circuit designed especially to hold data. These memory chips reside on the computer's motherboard, which is the large green circuit board that is located on the bottom of the computer. It is possible to add memory chips to a computer, but you should check your computer documentation before doing so.

2. Save the file as MEMORY.
3. Run the Spell Checker.
4. Proofread and correct any errors.
5. Print out the document.

Team Project:

Starting the Team Project

This project is intended for a team of people to work on. You start off in this section by coordinating and working on your own document. In the next two sections, you pull the individual parts together into one cohesive document.

Each team decides on the appropriate computer hardware purchase for a specific purpose. A list follows but is not exhaustive, so you might think of other examples.

Your job is to determine what computer should be purchased for an accounting office, a small desk-top publishing company, a secretarial workstation, or for a teacher.

First you will determine what software is necessary for these people to perform their jobs, then you will determine what computer system they should purchase. This system is to include the CPU with disk drives, mouse, monitor, printer, and other equipment as necessary for the particular job.

To get started, the team should decide on the appropriate software by talking to professionals in the field and by researching computer magazines. Then the members of the team should research an individual hardware component and write a description of the choice they have made. For example, one person researches monitors, another does printers, and each writes up the results using Word 6.

The individual recommendations at this point are individual files. The members of the team should each print their document. The entire team should read the files, and the team should comment on the content of all the research. When the research and writing of the individual sections is complete, they should all be printed and stapled together. This is the draft of the final report. You will continue to work on this report at the end of the next two sections of this book.

Part 2

Critical Thinking

Chapter 3

Working with Selected Text

Objectives
- Selecting Text
- Deleting and Restoring Selected Text
- Changing the Case of Selected Text
- Moving and Copying Selected Text
- Printing Selected Text
- Inserting the Date and Time

Key Terms

TERM	DEFINITION
Select	to highlight a body of text
Selection Bar	the area to the left of your document
Move Text	removing the text from its original location and placing it in a new location
Copy Text	leaving the text in its original location and making a copy of it in another location
Spike	a cut-and-paste tool in Word that enables you to remove several items from a document and then insert them as a group in a new location

When you create documents using a word processor, you can select groups of text with which to work. For example, if you want to delete an entire paragraph, it would take too long to hold down the Backspace or Delete key to do so. You can easily select the text and then delete it all at once. You may also decide to move or copy text from one part of the document to another. You simply select the text and then perform the move or copy. Sometimes a whole group of text may have the wrong capitalization. You can easily select it and use Word 6 for Windows to convert it to the appropriate capital letters. You might also want to print only one paragraph or one section of a long document. You can select it and issue the Print command.

Another handy feature in Word 6 is the ability to insert the current system date and time into documents. These fields update whenever the document is printed.

Objective 1: Selecting Text

select You can move, copy, delete, change, or print a block of text. You must first *select* the text or highlight the text, and then you can perform the desired action. You can select text using the mouse or the keyboard. To use the mouse to select text, you have several options:

ACTION	RESULT
Click and drag the mouse	Selects any amount of text.
Double-click on a word	Selects a word.
Hold Ctrl and click	Selects the current sentence.
Triple-click	Selects the entire paragraph.
Hold Alt and click and drag	Selects a vertical block of text.
Double-click EXT in the Status line	Turns on extend select; use arrow keys to select.

selection bar The area to the left of the text is called the *selection bar.* (See Figure 3-1.) You can use the mouse to select text by clicking in the selection bar as follows:

ACTION	RESULT
Click in the selection bar	Selects one line of text.
Drag in the selection bar	Selects lines of text.
Double-click in the selection bar	Selects the current paragraph.
Triple-click in the selection bar	Selects the entire document.

FEATURE

Nonbreaking or hard spaces
When you have two words such as a first name and a last name, and you do not want Word 6 to break a line between the two words, you can create a hard, or nonbreaking, space. You create a hard space by pressing Ctrl + Shift + spacebar instead of just pressing the spacebar between the words.

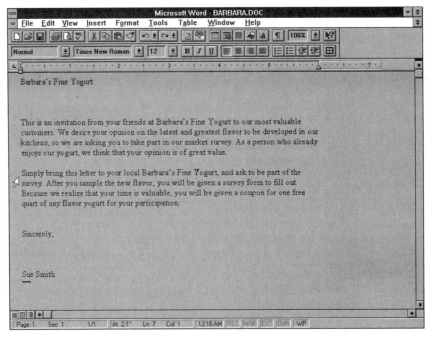

Figure 3-1   The pointer in the selection bar

You can also use the keyboard to select text; you have several options:

ACTION	RESULT
Shift + Left or Right arrow	Selects one character left or right.
Shift + Up or Down arrow	Selects one line up or down.
Shift + End	Selects to the end of the line.
Shift + Home	Selects to the beginning of the line.
Ctrl + Shift + Right arrow	Selects to the end of the word.
Ctrl + Shift + Left arrow	Selects to the beginning of the word.
Ctrl + Shift + Down arrow	Selects to the end of the paragraph.
Ctrl + Shift + Up arrow	Selects to the beginning of the paragraph.
Ctrl + Shift + PgUp or PgDn	Selects one screen up or down.
Ctrl + Shift + End	Selects to the end of the document.
Ctrl + Shift + Home	Selects to the beginning of the document.
F8 and then using arrow keys	Selects any amount of text.

You can cancel a text selection by clicking the mouse outside the selected text or by pressing any arrow key. If you have used the F8 key, press Esc and then an arrow key to deselect.

Using Emoticons

When people communicate using computers and the telephone lines, sometimes it is difficult to tell how a person means a statement. Without facial expressions or even voice inflections, emotions can easily be misread. Therefore, many people communicating on-line have started to include keyboard-produced pictorial representations of facial expressions called emoticons. These small pictures use common punctuation marks to create faces turned on their side.

Emoticons can represent smiley faces, tears, winks, or frowns. For example, you would type the characters

:-) to represent a smiley face.

:'(to represent tears.

;-) to represent a wink.

:-/ to represent a frown.

Exercise 1: Selecting and deselecting text

In this exercise, you select text and then deselect it.

1. Open the BARBARA.DOC file.

2. Using the mouse, click and drag over the first sentence of the first paragraph.

3. To deselect the text, click the mouse anywhere outside the first sentence.

4. Place the insertion point on the first word of the first sentence.

5. Press (F8).

6. Use ⊡ to highlight the sentence.

7. Deselect the text by pressing (ESC) and then an arrow key.

8. Practice using the previously listed keys to select and deselect text.

Objective 2: Deleting and Restoring Selected Text

Once text has been selected, it can be deleted by pressing the

Delete or Backspace keys, by choosing the Cut button 🔲 from the Standard toolbar, or by choosing Edit Clear.

If you select and delete text by mistake, you can restore it by selecting the

Undo button 🔲 on the Standard toolbar.

Exercise 2: Selecting and deleting text using the keyboard

In this exercise, you select, delete, and restore text using the keyboard.

1. Open the BARBARA.DOC file.

2. Move the insertion point to the "S" in "Simply" at the beginning of the second paragraph.

3. Press (F8) to activate EXT.

4. Press ⊡ six times. (See Figure 3-2.)

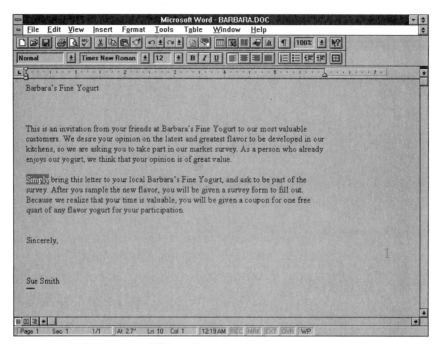

Figure 3-2 **The word "Simply" selected**

5. Press (DELETE).

   The word "Simply" is deleted.

6. Choose Edit Undo Clear.

   The word "Simply" is restored.

7. Press an arrow key to undo the selection.

8. Move the insertion point to the "i" in "invitation."

9. Press (CTRL) + (SHIFT) + (→).

   The entire word is selected.

10. Choose Edit Clear. The word "invitation" is deleted.

11. Choose Edit Undo Clear.

    The word is restored.

12. Press an arrow key to undo the selection.

Exercise 3: Selecting and erasing text using the mouse

In this exercise, you select, delete, and restore text using the mouse.

1. Move the I-beam to the word "letter" in the second paragraph.

2. Click and drag the mouse so that the word is selected.

3. Press the Backspace key.

   The word is deleted.

4. Click the Undo button on the Standard toolbar.

   The word is restored.

5. Click the mouse anywhere to undo the selection.

6. Move the mouse into the selection bar and click.

   The entire line next to where you clicked the mouse is selected.

7. Choose Edit Clear.

   The selected text is deleted.

8. Press the Undo button on the Standard toolbar.

   The selected text is undeleted.

9. Click the mouse anywhere to undo the selection.

10. Place the I-beam anywhere on the word "Because" in the second paragraph, and double-click the mouse.

    The entire word is highlighted.

11. Click the mouse anywhere else in the document to deselect the word.

Objective 3: Changing the Case of Selected Text

Once text is typed in and you realize that the case is not correct for the situation, you can easily change it. You select the text you want to change, and then choose Format Change Case. The Change Case dialog box gives you these five case options:

CASE	MEANING
Sentence case	Changes the initial letter in a sentence into a capital letter.
lowercase	Changes all the selected letters into lowercase.
UPPERCASE	Changes all the selected letters into uppercase.
Title Case	Changes the first letter of every selected word to a capital letter.
tOGGLE cASE	Changes the lowercase to uppercase and uppercase to lowercase for the selected case (in case you forgot to turn off Caps Lock).

Exercise 4: Changing the case of selected text

In this exercise, you change the case of selected text.

1. Using BARBARA.DOC, select the word "free" in the second paragraph.

2. Choose Format Change Case.

3. Select UPPERCASE from the Change Case dialog box. (See Figure 3-3.)

4. Choose OK, and press any arrow to deselect the word "FREE."

   The word "FREE" appears in uppercase.

5. Select the text "any flavor yogurt" in the second paragraph.
6. Choose Format Change Case.
7. Select Title Case from the Change Case dialog box.
8. Choose OK, and press any arrow to deselect the text.

   The text "Any Flavor Yogurt" appears with initial capital letters.

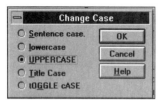

Figure 3-3 **The Change Case dialog box with UPPERCASE selected**

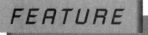

Inserting special symbols

In addition to the characters, numbers, and punctuation marks shown on the keyboard, Word 6 provides many symbols such as ™, ®, ©. You can insert these symbols into your document easily. Simply place the insertion point where you want the symbol to appear, and then choose Insert Symbol. The Symbol dialog box appears. (See figure below.) To enlarge a symbol for better viewing, click it.

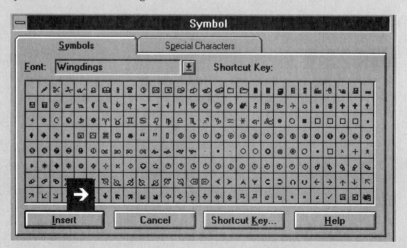

The symbol dialog box with an enlarged symbol

When you find the symbol you want, click the Insert button. If you don't see the one you are looking for, try selecting another font in the Font box. When you are finished, choose Close if you have inserted a symbol or Cancel if you decide not to insert a symbol.

Objective 4: Moving and Copying Selected Text

move text   You can move or copy text easily in Microsoft Word. To *move text* means to remove the text from its original location and place it in a new location.
copy text   To *copy text* means to leave the text in its original location and make a copy of it in another location.

Using drag-and-drop

If you want to move or copy text just a short distance in your document, the drag-and-drop method using the mouse is easiest. You simply select the text with the mouse, point the mouse to the selected text, and, holding down the left mouse button, drag the text. The mouse pointer changes to a dotted insertion point with a small dotted square under the left-pointing arrow. (See Figure 3-4.) Then release the mouse button, and the selection is moved to the new location.

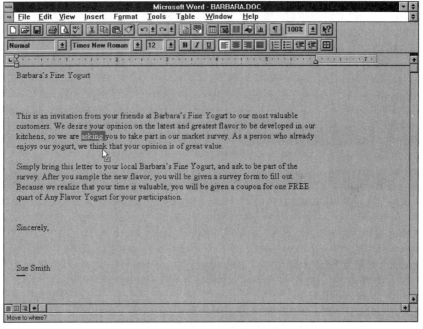

Figure 3-4   The mouse pointer with the dotted square and the dotted insertion point dragged to a new location to move selected text

To *copy text* using the drag-and-drop method, you select the text the same way you did to move it. However, hold down the Ctrl key as you point the mouse to the selected text and continue to hold the Ctrl key while you drag the selection to a new location.

Exercise 5: Using the drag-and-drop method to move and copy text

In this exercise, you use the mouse to drag and drop text.

1. Using BARBARA.DOC, select the first line of text.
2. Point to the selected line of text, and hold down the left mouse button.
3. Continuing to hold down the left mouse button, drag the dotted insertion point to the end of the first paragraph.
4. Release the mouse button.

   The text is placed after the first paragraph.
5. Click the Undo button.

   The text is restored to its original location.
6. Press any key to deselect the text.
7. Select the first line of text again.
8. Point to the selected text.
9. Hold down (CTRL) and hold down the left mouse button.
10. Continuing to hold down (CTRL) and the left mouse button, drag the dotted insertion point to the end of the first paragraph.
11. Release (CTRL) and the mouse button.

    The text is copied after the first paragraph.
12. Click the Undo button to delete the copy of the text.
13. Press any key to deselect the text.

Using Cut and Copy

If you want to move or copy text a long distance in a document, the Edit Copy or Edit Cut menu choices or the keyboard method are the easiest to use.

After you have selected text, choose Edit Cut to remove the selection from the document and place it on the Windows clipboard, or use Edit Copy to place the selected text on the clipboard without removing the original from the document. Then move the insertion point to the desired location for the text, and choose Edit Paste. The text that was placed on the clipboard is pasted into the document.

You can also use the Cut, Copy, and Paste buttons on the Standard toolbar. (See Figure 3-5.)

You use the toolbar buttons in the same way that you use the menu choices; that is, select the text first, and then click the Cut ✂ or Copy 📋 button. Move the insertion point to the desired location and click the Paste button 📋.

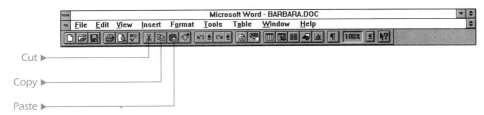

Figure 3-5   **The Standard toolbar**

Pasting text

Whether you choose Edit Paste or the Paste button ![Paste button], you can paste the contents of the clipboard in unlimited locations, an unlimited number of times. However, each time you select Cut or Copy from the menu or by using the buttons, the new selected text replaces the contents of the clipboard. If you accidentally replace the contents of the clipboard, you can click the Undo button on the Standard toolbar.

If you have placed large amounts of text, such as several paragraphs, on the clipboard and you try to quit Word, you will see a message asking if you want to save the contents of the clipboard. If you plan to use the contents again, you should save them.

Exercise 6: Using menu choices and the toolbar to move and copy text

In this exercise, you use menu choices and the toolbar to cut, copy, and paste text.

1. Using BARBARA.DOC, select the first line of text.
2. Choose Edit Cut.

   The line disappears from the document.
3. Move the insertion point to the end of first paragraph.
4. Choose Edit Paste.

   The text is inserted into the new location.
5. Choose Edit Undo Paste to remove the text.
6. Choose Edit Undo Cut and deselect the text.

   The text is returned to its original position.
7. Select the first line of text.
8. Choose Edit Copy.
9. Move the insertion point to the end of the first paragraph.
10. Choose Edit Paste.

    The text is copied to the new location.
11. Choose Edit Undo Paste.

    The copy of the text is removed from the document.

12. Select the first line of text.

13. Click the Cut button on the Standard toolbar.

14. Move the insertion point to the end of the first paragraph.

15. Click the Paste button on the Standard toolbar.

    The selected text is moved to the new location.

16. Choose Edit Undo Paste to remove the copied text.

17. Choose Edit Undo Cut.

    The text appears in its original location.

Using the keyboard to move and copy text

To use the keyboard method, you first select the desired text. Then you can press the F2 key to move text or press Shift + F2 to copy text. When you press F2, Word displays the Move to Where? message on the left end of the Status bar.

When you press Shift + F2, Word displays the Copy to Where? message. You simply move the insertion point to the desired location and press Enter to move or copy the selected text.

Exercise 7: Using the keyboard to move and copy text

In this exercise, you use the keyboard to move and copy text.

1. Using BARBARA.DOC, select the first line of text.

2. Press ⟨F2⟩.

3. Move the insertion point to the end of the first paragraph.

4. Press ⟨↵ ENTER⟩ to complete the move.

5. Choose Edit Undo Move.

6. Select the first line of text.

7. Press ⟨SHIFT⟩ + ⟨F2⟩.

8. Move the insertion point after the first paragraph.

9. Press ⟨↵ ENTER⟩ to complete the copy.

10. Choose Edit Undo Copy.

Using the Spike

Spike   The *Spike* is a cut-and-paste tool in Word that enables you to remove several items from a document and then insert them as a group in a new location. The Spike collects each item specified in the order they are selected. That is, the first item appears first, the second item second, and so on. When you insert the contents saved to the Spike, Word places each one in its own paragraph. You can view the contents of the Spike by choosing Edit Autotext and highlight Spike from the list box in the AutoText dialog box. When you insert the contents of the Spike, you can either clear the Spike or not clear the Spike.

Exercise 8: Using the Spike

In this exercise, you assemble text in the Spike and insert the text into a document.

1. Using BARBARA.DOC, select the first line of text.
2. Press (CTRL) + (F3) to remove the selected text to the Spike.
3. Move to the bottom of the document and select your name.
4. Press (CTRL) + (F3) to add the text to the text in the Spike.
5. Move the insertion point to the beginning of the document.
6. Choose Edit AutoText.
7. In the AutoText dialog box, highlight Spike if its not selected, and choose the Insert button.

   This inserts the text from the Spike and does not clear the Spike.
8. Choose File Close No.

   This closes the file without saving the changes that you have made to it.

If you make a mistake either putting text in the Spike or inserting text from the Spike, you can choose Edit Undo to undo insertions from or to the Spike.

Objective 5: Printing Selected Text

You can print selected text rather than an entire document. To do so, first select the desired text, and then choose File Print. In the Print dialog box, select Selection in the Page Range section and choose OK. (See Figure 3-6.) Only the selected range prints.

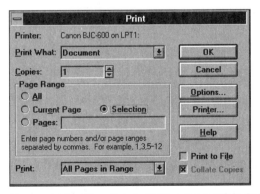

Figure 3-6   *The Print dialog box with Selection in the Page Range section selected*

Exercise 9: Printing selected text

In this exercise, you print only selected text.

1. Open the BARBARA.DOC file.
2. Select the second paragraph.
3. Choose File Print.
4. In the Page Range section of the Print dialog box, choose Selection.
5. Choose OK.

   Only the selected range is printed.
6. Close the document without saving.

Objective 6: Inserting the Date and Time

You can have Word 6 automatically insert the date and the time into a document. You choose Insert Date and Time. The Date and Time dialog box displays, showing you the formats in the Available Formats list box. (See Figure 3-7.)

Figure 3-7   **The Date and Time dialog box**

Word automatically updates the date or time when you print the document. If you do not want Word to update the date or time, clear the Insert As Field check box.

If you want to manually update the field, you can move the mouse pointer over the field and click the right mouse button. The shortcut menu displays, and you can choose the Update Field command.

Exercise 10: Inserting the date in a document

In this exercise, you insert the date into a document. (The current time is inserted in the same manner.)

1. Open the BARBARA.DOC file.
2. Move the cursor below the text "Barbara's Fine Yogurt."
3. Press Insert Date and Time.

4. In the Date and Time dialog box, select a date format.
5. Choose OK.

   The date is inserted into the letter.
6. Press Enter and type Dear Friends:
7. Save the document and close it.

Chapter Summary

In this chapter, you learned how to select text. After selecting text, you learned how to delete, move, copy, print, or edit the selection. You will see in Chapter 4 that selecting text has many more functions. You also learned to insert the date and time into documents.

Review Questions

True/False Questions

_____ 1. You must first select text before you can copy it.

_____ 2. You must always print the entire document when using Word 6 for Windows.

_____ 3. The Spike collects each item specified in the order they are selected.

_____ 4. Whether you choose Edit Paste or the Paste button, you can paste the contents of the clipboard in unlimited locations, an unlimited number of times.

_____ 5. You can cancel a text selection by clicking the mouse outside the selected text.

Multiple Choice Questions

_____ 6. You can select text using

A. the mouse.

B. the keyboard.

C. the Status bar.

D. All of the above.

_____ 7. The Sentence case menu choice changes
   A. the initial letter in a sentence into a capital letter.
   B. all the selected letters into lowercase.
   C. all the selected letters into uppercase.
   D. the first letter of every selected word to a capital letter.

_____ 8. To copy using the drag-and-drop method,
   A. select the text and hold down the Alt key as you point the mouse to the selected text and drag it to a new location.
   B. select the text and hold down the F8 key as you point to the selected text and drag it to a new location.
   C. select the text and hold down the Ctrl key as you point to the selected text and drag it to a new location.
   D. All of the above.

_____ 9. If you want to move or copy text a long distance in a document, you would use
   A. the Edit Copy or Edit Cut menu choices.
   B. the Cut or Copy buttons on the Standard toolbar.
   C. the drag-and-drop method.
   D. Both A and B.

_____ 10. To use the keyboard method to cut or copy text, you first select the desired text and then press
   A. F8 to move text or F9 to copy text.
   B. F1 to move text or F8 to copy text.
   C. F2 to move text or Shift + F2 to copy text.
   D. F8 to move text and Shift + F8 to copy text.

Fill-in-the-Blank Questions

11. The area to the left of the text is called the _____ _____.

12. A cut-and-paste tool in Word that enables you to remove several items from a document and then insert them as a group in a new location is the _____.

13. If you select and delete text by mistake, you can restore it by selecting the _____ button on the Standard toolbar.

14. To highlight a body of text in Microsoft Word 6 for Windows is called _____.

15. Each time you select Cut or Copy from the menu or by using the buttons, the new selected text _____ the contents of the clipboard.

Acumen-Building Activities

Quick Projects

Project 1: Deleting Text

1. Open the DRIVE.DOC file created in Quick Project 1 in Chapter 2.
2. Select the second paragraph.
3. Delete the second paragraph.
4. Print the document.
5. Close the file without saving it.

Project 2: Changing Case

1. Open the HEALTHY.DOC file created in Quick Project 2 in Chapter 2.
2. Select the words "Repetitive Stress Injuries" in the first paragraph.
3. Change the case to all caps.
4. Print the document.
5. Close the document without saving it.

Project 3: Moving Text

1. Open the BOOK.DOC file created in Quick Project 3 in Chapter 2.
2. Select the second paragraph.
3. Move the second paragraph after the third paragraph.
4. Print the document.
5. Save the file and close it.

Project 4: Copying Text

1. Open the PALM.DOC file created in Quick Project 4 in Chapter 2.
2. Select the first paragraph.
3. Copy the first paragraph to the end of the document.
4. Print the document.
5. Close the file without saving it.

In-Depth Projects

Project 1: Printing Selected Text

1. Open the VIEW.DOC file created in In-Depth Project 2 in Chapter 2.
2. Select the Print Preview section.
3. Move the Print Preview section to the end of the document.

4. Print the entire document.
5. Print only the Print Preview section.
6. Close the document without saving it.

Project 2: Using Copy and Move

1. Open the VIEW.DOC file created in In-Depth Project 2 in Chapter 2.
2. Select the Master Document section.
3. Move the Master Document section to the beginning of the document.
4. Select the Outline View section.
5. Move the Outline View section to the end of the document.
6. Print the document.
7. Close the file without saving it.

CASE STUDIES

Coffee-To-Go: **Writing the Description of the Business**

In this chapter, you learned many basic editing techniques. You will continue to create the business plan for Coffee-To-Go using those skills.

1. Open the Plan1 file.
2. Move the cursor to the end of the document.
3. Type in the next part of the business plan as shown:

Company Description

The Service

Coffee-To-Go will provide specialty coffee drinks along with various tea drinks. Besides the drinks, individually wrapped muffins and fresh-baked cookies will also be available.

Coffee-To-Go will be a permanent coffee and snack booth located on a busy intersection in downtown Eugene, Oregon. Coffee-To-Go will rely on both foot and automobile traffic that passes this location. Office and retail employees walk by this intersection on their way to work in the morning. Other patrons who are downtown for medical and legal appointments, for shopping, or for business in the various government buildings in the area also pass this intersection, providing potential for much walk-up business. Because one side of the booth will be accessible to automobiles, Coffee-To-Go will also attract commuters on their way to other locations. These factors will provide a year-round customer base from which to draw.

The Building

The building will be a portable building built to specifications at another site and installed permanently in the downtown location. The site will need to have water and electricity made available once the building is installed. The 15 x 20 foot building will have large sliding windows on the east and west sides to accommodate both the foot and automobile traffic. Large, colorful awnings will help with customer convenience during wet weather and will attract attention.

The interior of the building will be outfitted with espresso makers, burners, and other necessary equipment for the making of the drinks. Display shelves will contain the available food. The interior is designed for maximum efficiency for two people to work comfortably.

4. Select the first paragraph under Company Description and cut it out.
5. Paste the cut paragraph after the new first paragraph of this section.
6. Select the last two paragraphs and save them as Building.
7. Select and print the last two paragraphs.
8. Select the first paragraph.
9. Copy the selected paragraph to the end of the document.
10. Select the paragraph that was copied to the end of the document and delete it.
11. Save the file, using the name Plan1.
12. Print the entire document.

CASE STUDIES

Videos West: **Working with Text**

In this chapter you learned basic editing skills. You will apply those skills to the marketing letter.

1. Open the VCR file.
2. Select the first sentence in the first paragraph.
3. Cut the selected sentence.
4. Paste the sentence at the end of the first paragraph.
5. Select the mailing address at the end of the letter.
6. Copy the selected text to the top of the document. You will enhance it to create a letterhead in Chapter 4.
7. Select the first paragraph.
8. Delete the first paragraph.
9. Undelete the first paragraph.
10. Save the letter as VCR.
11. Print the letter.

Chapter 4

Enhancing a Document

Objectives
- Formatting Characters
- Formatting Paragraphs
- Dividing a Document into Sections
- Using Styles
- Changing Margins

Key Terms

TERM	DEFINITION
Format Characters	changing the appearance of text
Font	a set of characters of the same style
TrueType Fonts	fonts that appear on-screen as they will print
Paragraph	text that appears between two paragraph marks
Alignment	the way text lines up on the printed page
Line Spacing	the height of each line of text
Style	group of formats that you name and save

Once you have typed in your document and have edited it, you can enhance the way the text appears on the page. You can add attributes such as boldface and underlining to characters and even change the typeface and size of the font. You can increase the white space on the page by changing line spacing and margins, and you can change the format of paragraphs or sections of the document so that they align differently on the page. Once you have a set of enhancements that you want to use again, Word allows you to save them all together as a style.

Objective 1: Formatting Characters

format characters
To *format characters*, that is, to change the appearance of text you have already typed, you must select the text and then choose the formatting commands you desire. If you want Word to format text as you type it, you simply choose the formatting you desire and start typing. Word applies the formatting from the insertion point until you turn off or change the formatting. The formatting will appear on the screen. To change character formatting, choose Format Font. In the Font dialog box, select Font if it isn't already the active tab. (See Figure 4-1.)

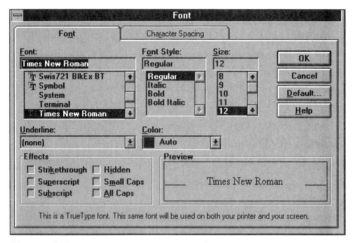

Figure 4-1 The Font dialog box

font
The Font list box in the dialog box provides you with a list of available fonts. A *font* is a set of characters of the same style. The fonts in the box appear with an icon of a printer, a double T symbol, or nothing in front of them. Fonts with the printer icon may not appear on the screen as they print; they are printer fonts. Fonts with the double T are *TrueType fonts*, and they appear on the screen as they will print. The fonts with nothing in front of them are simply screen fonts. The fonts that are available in the dialog box depend on your printer and are controlled by the Windows software. If you decide you want more fonts to choose from, you can install additional fonts using Windows.

TrueType fonts

The Font Style list box allows you to change text to be **bold**, *italic*, ***bold italic***, or regular. The Size list box provides font size alternatives. The Underline drop-down list box provides four ways to underline text:

OPTION	DESCRIPTION
Single	Places a single line under the selected text.
Words Only	Places a single line under each word of the selected text.
Double	Places a double line under the selected text.
Dotted	Places a dotted line under the selected text.

The Color drop-down list box provides color options for the selected text.

The Effects section provides these options:

OPTION	EFFECT
Strikethrough	Places a line through the middle of the text.
Superscript	Raises the text above the baseline.
Subscript	Lowers the text below the baseline.
Hidden	Hides the text both on the screen and when it is printed.
Small Caps	Changes all text to capitals that are the same size as the lowercase letters.
All Caps	Changes the text to uppercase.

Computer Bugs

Everyone has heard computer people refer to problems with their computers as bugs. There can be both software bugs or hardware bugs. The term *bug* actually came from an incident in the 1940s involving a real bug.

When an early computer called the Mark II stopped working, the staff at the Naval Surface Warfare Center in Dahlgren, Virginia, took the back off the machine to get a better look at the problem. What they discovered was a moth. They extricated the dead moth and attached it to the log book page along with a report of the incident. From that time on, computer problems have been referred to as bugs.

The Smithsonian Institution in Washington, D.C., is in possession of the famous bug and the computer log book from the 1940s.

The Preview box shows you how text will look. When you are pleased with the formatting you have chosen, you can click OK. If you click the Default button, Word asks you if you want to make the formatting the default, thus affecting all new documents that use this template.

Many of the formatting features are also buttons on the Formatting toolbar, so you can choose a font and font size from the drop-down box, or click the Bold, Italic, or Underline buttons as described in Chapter 1.

Exercise 1: Applying formats to existing text

In this exercise, you format existing text.

1. Open the BARBARA.DOC file.
2. Select the words "Barbara's Fine Yogurt" in the first paragraph.
3. Choose Format Font.
4. In the Font Style list box, choose Bold.
5. In the Size list box, choose 14.
6. In the Underline drop-down box, choose Single.
7. Choose OK to have the changes applied to the text.
   "Barbara's Fine Yogurt" appears boldfaced, underlined, and in 14 point.

8. Select the words "Barbara's Fine Yogurt" in the second paragraph.
9. On the Formatting toolbar, click the following buttons:

   ■ Bold button **B**

   ■ Underline button **U**

   ■ Size button **10** and choose 14.

10. Press any arrow to remove the highlighting. (See Figure 4-2.)
11. Save the document.

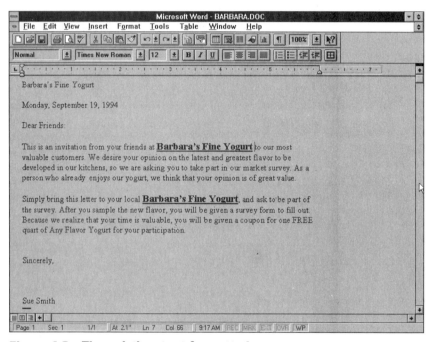

Figure 4-2 The existing text formatted

Exercise 2: Formatting text as it's typed

In this exercise, you format text as you type.

1. Using the BARBARA.DOC file, move the insertion point to the top of the document.
2. Delete Barbara's Fine Yogurt from the top of the document.
3. Move the insertion point back to the top of the document.
4. Choose Format Font.
5. Choose 14 from the Size list box.
6. Choose OK.
7. Click the Italic button *I* to turn on italic.

8. Type Barbara's Fine Yogurt and press (← ENTER).
9. Type 123 Bayview Ave. and press (← ENTER).
10. Type Ft. Lauderdale, Florida 33308 and press (← ENTER). (See Figure 4-3.)
11. Press (↓) several times.

    Notice that the previously typed text doesn't change to the new formatting.
12. Save the document.

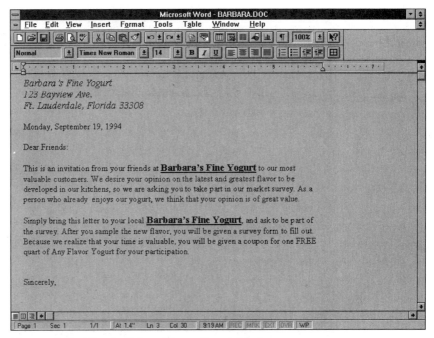

Figure 4-3   The inside address formatted

Changing and removing formatting

Changing or removing formatting that you have applied to text is easy. Simply select the text, turn off the undesired formatting, and choose the new format from the Format menu or click the button on the Formatting toolbar. For example, if you want to change formatting from bold to italic, select the bolded text and click the Bold button to turn off boldfacing and click the Italic button to turn on italic. If you simply want to turn off the bold feature, then select the text and click the Bold button.

Exercise 3: Changing formatting

In this exercise, you change the formatting of text.

1. Move the insertion point to the top of the document.
2. Select the first three lines.

3. Click the Italic button 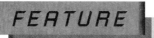 to turn off italic.

4. Click the Bold button **B** to turn on bold.

5. Choose Format Font.

6. Choose 16 from the Size list box.

7. Choose OK. (See Figure 4-4.)

8. Save the document.

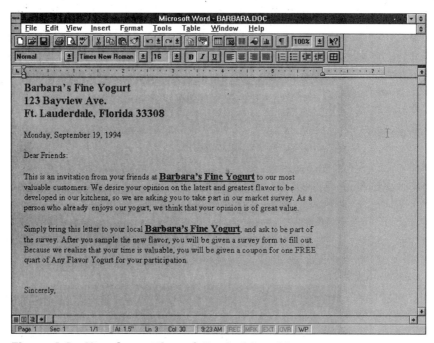

Figure 4-4   New formatting of the inside address

FEATURE

The AutoFormat feature

If you want Word 6 to provide formatting for your document, you can use the Autoformat feature. Simply type your document and then choose Format Autoformat. Word is able to recognize such elements as headings or lists and applies built-in styles to the elements. Word makes the changes to your document, but it also gives you the option to accept or reject the formatting changes.

Objective 2: Formatting Paragraphs

Formatting paragraphs in Word 6 is similar to formatting characters. However, Word applies the formatting to an entire paragraph. You position the insertion point any place in the paragraph you want to format, or you can select several paragraphs to format them at the same time.

paragraph A *paragraph* is defined in Word 6 as the text that appears between two paragraph marks. To display paragraph marks so that you can see where a paragraph begins and ends, you simply click the Show/Hide Paragraph button ¶ on the Standard toolbar. It doesn't matter where the insertion point is because Word shows the paragraph and space characters for the entire document. To turn off the Show/Hide Paragraph button, simply click the button a second time.

With the insertion point in the paragraph that you want to change or with several paragraphs selected, choose Format Paragraph. In the Paragraph dialog box, select Indents and Spacing if it isn't already selected. (See Figure 4-5.)

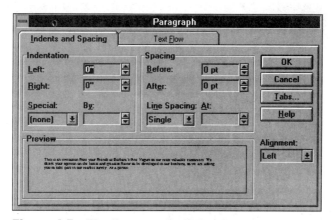

Figure 4-5 The Paragraph dialog box

Exercise 4: Showing paragraph symbols

In this exercise, you show the paragraph symbols so that you can tell how Word 6 defines paragraphs.

1. Use the BARBARA.DOC file.

2. Click the Show/Hide button ¶ on the Standard toolbar.

   The paragraph and space marks are visible in the document.

3. Click the button a second time to turn it off.

You will become familiar with two of the formatting options in this chapter: alignment and line spacing.

Alignment

alignment To change the *alignment* of text, that is, the way text lines up on the printed page, choose the Alignment drop-down list box. You are provided four ways to align text:

OPTION	DESCRIPTION
Left	Aligns the paragraph with the left margin only, producing a ragged right edge.
Centered	Aligns each line of the paragraph between the left and right margins.
Right	Aligns the paragraph with the right margin only, producing a ragged left edge.
Justified	Aligns each line of the paragraph with both the left and right margins.

(See Figure 4-6.)

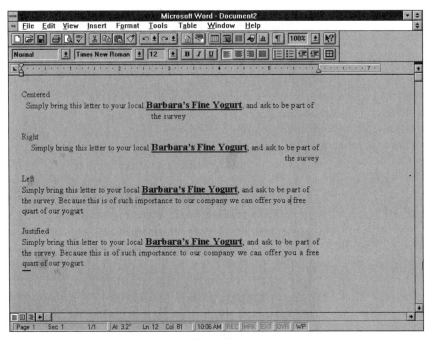

Figure 4-6 The results of the four alignment choices

The four alignment buttons on the Formatting toolbar can also be used to make the same changes to paragraphs as described in Chapter 1.

Exercise 5: Changing alignment

In this exercise, you change the alignment of text.

1. Using BARBARA.DOC, position the insertion point on the first line of the document.

2. Click the Show/Hide Paragraph button ¶.

3. Choose Format Paragraph.

4. Make sure Indents and Spacing is current, and choose Alignment.

5. Choose Centered and click OK.

   The first line of the document is centered.

6. Move the insertion point to the second line of the document.

7. Select that line and the line below it.

8. Choose the Center button ▦ on the Formatting toolbar.

   Both lines are centered. (See Figure 4-7.)

9. Click the Show/Hide Paragraph button ¶ to turn it off.

10. Save the document.

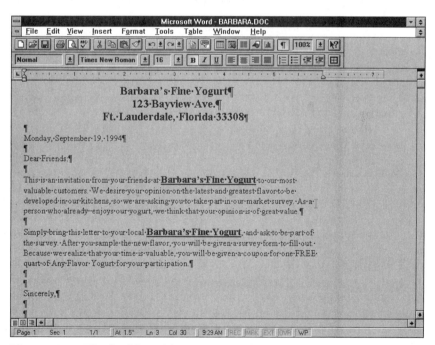

Figure 4-7   *The inside address centered*

Line spacing

Line spacing   *Line spacing* determines the height of each line of text. The Line Spacing drop-down list provides six options:

OPTION	DESCRIPTION
Single	Is the Word default and is based on the font size.
1.5 Lines	Increases spacing by one and one-half times, based on the font size.
Double	Increases spacing by two lines based on the font size.
At Least	Allows you to specify the minimum amount of space you want inserted between lines.
Exactly	Allows you to specify the exact amount of space you want inserted between lines.
Multiple	Allows you to type a number by which to multiply single line spacing, enabling such line spacing as triple spacing.

If you are going to change the spacing for more than one paragraph, you can use Edit Repeat Paragraph Formatting, but you must use it immediately.

Exercise 6: Changing line spacing

In this exercise, you change line spacing.

1. Using BARBARA.DOC, move the insertion point to the first paragraph.
2. Choose Format Paragraph.
3. In the Paragraph dialog box, choose Line Spacing.
4. Choose Double and OK.

   The first paragraph is double spaced.
5. Move the insertion point to the second paragraph.
6. Choose Edit Repeat Paragraph Formatting.

   The second paragraph is also double spaced.
7. Save and close the document.

Objective 3: Dividing a Document into Sections

When you start a document, it contains only one section, as indicated by the Sec 1 indicator on the Status bar. Sometimes you want to divide a document into sections to make formatting changes easier. For example, you might want a particular type of formatting in part of the document and another type of formatting in another part. Dividing the document into sections allows you to format a whole section at once.

You should create a new section when you want to change any of the following elements:

- Alignment
- Location of footnotes
- Contents and position of headers and footers
- Paper size
- Page orientation
- Margins
- Number of columns
- Format and position of page numbers

To divide the document, place the insertion point where you want the break to occur and choose Insert Break. The Break dialog box displays. (See Figure 4-8.)

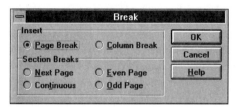

Figure 4-8   **The Break dialog box**

In the Section Breaks section of the Break dialog box, choose an option based on where you want the section break to begin.

OPTION	MEANING
Next Page	Word creates a page break at the point of the new section.
Continuous	Word creates the section break without a page break.
Even Page	Word begins the new section on the next even-numbered page.
Odd Page	Word begins the new section on the next odd-numbered page.

When you choose OK and return to your document, Word places an non-printing dotted line in the document to indicate the section break. Simply make the formatting changes you desire. You can delete a section break by selecting it and pressing the Backspace or Delete keys.

Exercise 7: Inserting and deleting sections in a document

In this exercise, you insert and delete section breaks into a document.

1. Open BARBARA.DOC.
2. Move the insertion point after the first paragraph of text.
3. Choose Insert Break.
4. In the Break dialog box, choose Next Page.

5. Choose OK.

   The document is divided into sections.

6. Select the section break.

7. Press (DELETE).

8. Close the document without saving it.

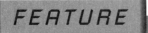

The AutoText feature

If you want Word 6 for Windows to automatically insert text, you would choose the AutoCorrect option. However, if you want to decide when to insert text, you should use the AutoText feature. AutoText is used for entries that you will insert less frequently than the AutoCorrect feature.

For example, if you always want "uc" replaced by the text "Umpqua Community College," you would use the AutoCorrect feature. However, you might not want "UCC" changed to "Umpqua Community College" every time you type it. So you could store the text "UCC" as AutoText, and you could choose to leave it UCC sometimes or to change it to Umpqua Community College sometimes.

You can access the AutoText dialog box by choosing Edit AutoText. (See figure below.) If you select text such as "UCC" and then choose Edit AutoText, you can give it the name UCC in the Name section of the dialog box. Later, when you want to use it, you can choose Edit AutoText, highlight the name of the AutoText, and choose Insert to place it in your document.

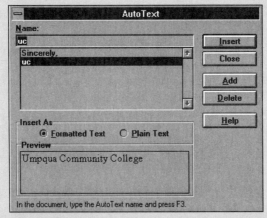

The AutoText dialog box

You can also use the Insert AutoText button ![button] on the Standard toolbar. Simply type the name of the saved AutoText such as UCC and press the Insert Autotext button. AutoText then replaces the name.

Objective 4: Using Styles

style   A *style* is a group of formats that you name and save. For example, if you want to format headings in a document a certain way, you could create a style for your headings and name it. Using the style on your headings ensures that all the headings in the document have identical formatting. If you change your mind about the heading's formatting, you simply edit the style, and all the text formatted with that style reformats automatically reflecting the changes.

You can access styles by choosing the Format Style command or by choosing the Style button ▏Normal   ▮▼▏ on the Formatting toolbar.

Word includes two types of styles: paragraph and character styles. Paragraph styles appear in boldface in the Styles list box, and they control all aspects of a paragraph's appearance, for example, font, size, spacing, alignment, and so on. Character styles are not boldfaced in the Styles list box, and they apply formats from the Format Font command such as font, size, and effects. (See Figure 4-9.)

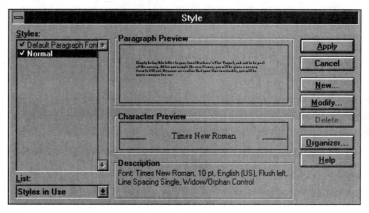

Figure 4-9   The Styles list box accessed with the Style button on the Formatting toolbar

When you begin typing a new document, Word applies the Normal style to each paragraph. The Normal style is defined as the 10-point Times New Roman font, single spacing, with left text alignment. Other built-in styles are provided such as various heading styles, and you can also create your own styles. Creating styles simply means telling Word to save certain formatting features so that you can use them as many times as you need.

Exercise 8: Creating a style

In this exercise, you create a style.

1. With a new blank document open, choose Format Style.
2. In the Style dialog box, choose New.

   The New Style dialog box appears as shown in Figure 4-10.

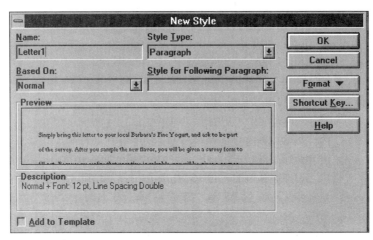

Figure 4-10   The New Style dialog box

3. In the New Style dialog box, type Letter1 in the Name text box.
4. Choose the Format button.
5. Choose Font.
6. In the Font dialog box, choose Bold in the Font Style section and 14 in the Size section and choose OK.
7. Choose the Format button.
8. Choose Paragraph.
9. In the Alignment drop-down box, choose Centered.
10. Choose OK twice.

    Notice that the style name Letter1 has been added to the Styles list. (See Figure 4-11.)

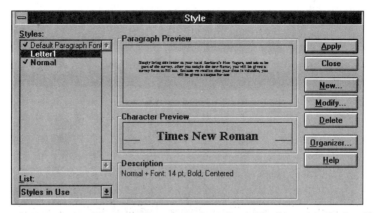

Figure 4-11   **The newly created style added to the Styles list**

11. Choose the Close button.

You use styles that you create the same way as you use preexisting styles. You simply select them.

Exercise 9: Using styles

In this exercise, you use a style.

1. With the same new blank document open, choose the Style button **Normal** ▼.

2. From the drop-down list, choose Letter1. (See Figure 4-12.)

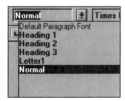

Figure 4-12   **The new style included in the drop-down list**

3. Type your name and notice that it is centered, bolded, and in 14-point type.

4. Close the document without saving.

Objective 5: Changing Margins

Word 6 assumes that you are working on an 8.5 × 11-inch sheet of paper with 1-inch margins on all sides. It is easy to change the margins in Word 6. You simply choose File Page Setup and change the appropriate margins in the Page Setup dialog box. (See Figure 4-13.)

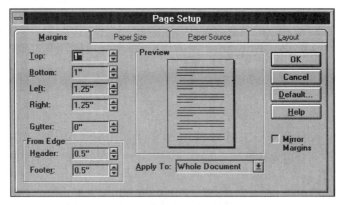

Figure 4-13 **The Page Setup dialog box**

The top, bottom, left, and right margins can all be increased or decreased by clicking the arrows. The Gutter option allows for extra space to be added to the inside margin for documents that will be bound. The Mirror Margins is for two-sided documents, so that a gutter will be added to the inside margin. The Apply To option lets you apply the margins to the whole document or from the insertion point forward. The Preview box shows what the changes you have made will look like. The Header and Footer options allow you to change the location of headers and footers in the margin.

Exercise 10: Changing margins

In this exercise, you change margins.

1. Open BARBARA.DOC.
2. Choose File Page Setup
3. In the Margins section of the Page Setup dialog box, click the upward facing arrows to increase margins and downward facing arrows to decrease the margins as follows:

MARGIN	SIZE
Top	3
Bottom	2
Left	.5
Right	1.5

4. Choose OK.

   The letter reformats to the new margins.
5. Close the document without saving.

Chapter Summary

In this chapter, you learned to enhance the text that you type by changing fonts, changing font size, or adding attributes such as boldface or underlines. You also learned to change line spacing, margins, and alignment of text. One very powerful feature of Microsoft Word 6 for Windows that was introduced is styles. You can save all the enhancements you make to text and use them again and again to ensure consistency.

Review Questions

True/False Questions

_____ 1. A paragraph is the text that appears between two page marks.

_____ 2. TrueType fonts appear on the screen as they will print out.

_____ 3. Justified alignment aligns each line of the paragraph with only the left margin.

_____ 4. A Style is a group of formats that you name and save.

_____ 5. Strikethrough text appears with a line through the middle of it.

Multiple Choice Questions

_____ 6. By choosing Format Font, you can change
   A. the font.
   B. the color.
   C. the underline option.
   D. All of the above.

_____ 7. By choosing Format Paragraph, you can change
   A. line spacing.
   B. the font.
   C. the underline option.
   D. All of the above.

_____ 8. You can display characters as
   A. hidden.
   B. superscript.
   C. strikethrough.
   D. All of the above.

_____ 9. To change margins in a document, you choose

    A. Format Paragraph.

    B. File Page Setup.

    C. Format Margins.

    D. All of the above.

_____ 10. The Line Spacing drop-down list provides the following options:

    A. Single, Double, Triple

    B. Single, Mixed, Triple, Quad

    C. Single, 1.5, Double, At least, Exactly, Multiple

    D. Single, 1.75, Double, Least, Mixed

Fill-in-the-Blank Questions

11. When you choose the _____ option, text appears lowered below the baseline.

12. When you choose the _____ option, text appears slanted.

13. When you _____ characters, you change the appearance of text.

14. _____ refers to the way text lines up on the printed page.

15. The _____/_____ button on the Standard toolbar shows the paragraph and space characters for the entire document.

Acumen-Building Activities

Quick Projects

Project 1: Formatting Existing Text

1. Open the DRIVE.DOC file created in Quick Project 1 in Chapter 2.
2. Center the title on the page.
3. Make the words "Microsoft Word 6 for Windows" italic.
4. Make the complete filename at the end of the document boldface.
5. Print the document.
6. Save and close the file.

Project 2: Formatting Existing Text

1. Open the HEALTHY.DOC file created in Quick Project 2 in Chapter 2.
2. Underline the word "Ergonomics" with a double underline.
3. Change the document so that it is double spaced.
4. Make the margins 2 inches at the left and right.
5. Right align the document.
6. Print the document.
7. Close the file without saving it.

Project 3: Formatting Existing Text

1. Open the file saved as BOOK.DOC in Quick Project 3 in Chapter 3.
2. Underline the words "Microsoft Bookshelf for Windows" with a single underline.
3. Place the following titles in italics:

   - American Heritage Dictionary (2nd College Edition)
   - Bartletts' Familiar Quotations
   - Concise Columbia Dictionary of Quotations
   - Concise Columbia Encyclopedia
   - Roget's II Electronic Thesaurus
   - World Almanac
   - Book of Facts
   - Hammond Atlas

4. Center the title.
5. Change the size of the font of the title to 24 points.
6. Justify the document.
7. Print out the document.
8. Save the file and close it.

Project 4: Formatting Existing Text

1. Open the PALM.DOC file created in Quick Project 4 in Chapter 2.
2. Change the spacing to triple.
3. Change the size of the font of the entire document to 18 points.
4. Make the alignment centered for the entire document.
5. Print the document.
6. Close the document without saving it.

In-Depth Projects

Project 1: Formatting Text Before You Type the Document

1. Open a new document.
2. Create letterhead for yourself. You should center your name, street address, city, state, and zip code.
3. Change the size of the font to at least 18 points.
4. Print the letterhead.
5. Save the file as Lhead.
6. Using the Lhead file, change the size of the font to 12 points for the body of the letter.
7. Write a business letter; for example, a letter of application, a letter about an order, or a letter about credit or insurance.
8. Print the letter.
9. Save the letter as Letter1.

Project 2: Formatting a Document

1. Open the VIEW.DOC file created in In-Depth Project 2 in Chapter 2.
2. Change the font of the title and make the size 18 points.
3. Center the title.
4. Bold the title.
5. Make all the headings the same font as the title, but make the size 14 points.
6. Underline all the headings with a single line.
7. Change the margins as follows:

Left	2 inches
Right	2 inches
Top	1.5 inches
Bottom	1.5 inches

8. Place the words "WYSIWYG What You See Is What You Get" in italics.
9. Double space the document.
10. Make the alignment justified.
11. Print the document.
12. Save the document and close it.

CASE STUDIES

Coffee-To-Go:

Writing a Market Analysis

In this chapter, you learned many techniques for formatting text. You will use those skills to continue to create the business plan for Coffee-To-Go.

1. Open the Plan1 file.
2. Move the cursor to the end of the document.
3. Type in the next part of the business plan as shown:

Market Analysis

Coffee-To-Go will be located in downtown Eugene, Oregon-- a city of about 120,000. All government buildings, numerous office buildings, and retail establishments are located in the area. The specific corner location was chosen because of the heavy foot traffic between available parking and the targeted businesses. This location has the added benefit of providing automobile access on the street side of the building, increasing customer potential.

Coffee drinking is currently on the rise in the United States, and coffee-related businesses are rated by National Business Review as the number two type of small business that is profitable to start.

Customers will be attracted by:

The convenient and attractive location with tasteful neon signs and colorful awnings.

A direct mailing to offices and retail establishments in the area.

Promotion in a local business bulletin produced weekly and distributed in the downtown area.

4. Format the words "National Business Review" to be in italics.
5. Continue to format as follows:

- Section One: The Business Plan should be centered, boldfaced, and the font enlarged to 16 points.
- Purpose Statement, Company Description, and Market Analysis should be underlined and the font enlarged to 14 points.
- Under the Company Description section, "The Service" and "The Building" should be underlined.

6. Justification should be set to produce a straight left edge and a ragged right edge.

7. Run the Spell Checker on the entire document.

8. Save the document as Plan1.

9. Print the document.

CASE STUDIES

Videos West: **Enhancing Text**

In this chapter, you learned to enhance a document by changing fonts, adding attributes, and changing alignments. You will apply those skills to enhance the marketing letter.

1. Open the VCR file.

2. Change the font of the mailing address at the top of the letter.

3. Center the mailing address at the top of the letter.

4. Underline the words "one free video" in the fourth paragraph.

5. Boldface the text "3,000 titles" in the fourth paragraph.

6. Justification should be set for a straight left edge and a ragged right edge.

7. Double space the letter.

8. Change the right and left margins to 1.5 inches.

9. Run the Spell Checker.

10. Save the letter as VCR.

11. Print the letter.

Chapter 5

Document Refinements

Key Terms

TERM	DEFINITION
Tab	a stop placed on the line
Indent	text that is pushed in or out from the left and right margins
Hanging Indent	lines after the first line that are indented by the amount you specify
Soft Page Break	a page break that Word automatically inserts when the current page becomes full
Hard Page Break	a page break inserted from the keyboard
Widow	the last line of a paragraph appearing at the top of a page
Orphan	the first line of a paragraph appearing at the bottom of a page
Header	text or graphics in the margin at the top of the page
Footer	text or graphics in the margin at the bottom of the page
Footnotes	notes at the bottom of the page used to provide more information about or explain text in a document
Endnotes	notes at the end of the document used to provide more information about or explain text in a document

Objective 1: Changing Tabs

tab A *tab* indents text a predefined measurement or number of spaces. Word 6 has tab stops set every 0.5 inch by default. You can use tabs by pressing the Tab key on the keyboard. If you have pressed the Show/Hide Paragraph button ¶ on the Formatting toolbar, you will see a small arrow on the screen for each time you press the Tab key.

You can change tab stops, but the change only affects the current paragraph. There are two ways to save time if you want to change tabs for several paragraphs. If the paragraphs are already typed in, select every paragraph before changing the tab stops. If the paragraphs aren't typed, set the tab stops for the first paragraph before you start typing. Then, when you press Enter to start a new paragraph, Word continues the formatting, which includes the tab stops, to the next paragraph.

Word includes four types of tabs: left aligned (the default), centered, right aligned, and decimal. A fifth option inserts a vertical line at the tab stop. They are each represented on the ruler by a unique character. Figure 5-1 shows the tab characters and the results of using each type of tab.

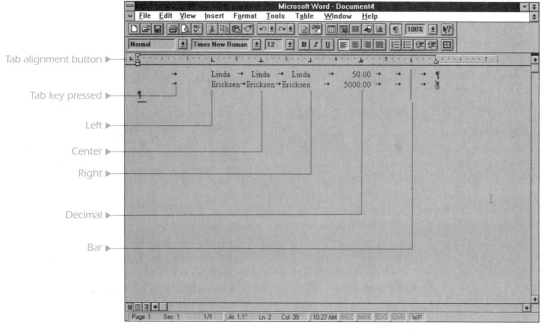

Figure 5-1   **The results of using the four types of tabs**

Setting and clearing tabs

Tabs can be set by using the ruler or by choosing Format Tabs and then making selections in the Tabs dialog box. Figure 5-2 shows the Tabs dialog box.

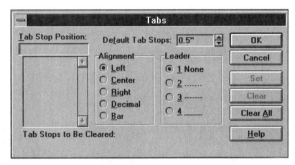

Figure 5-2   **The Tabs dialog box**

Using the Tabs dialog box

To change the default tabs, simply change the 0.5" in the Default Tab Stops box to another number such as 0.8". To create a new tab stop, type the new position into the Tab Stop Position text box. You can then click on the alignment option you want in the Alignment section. The Leader options insert dotted, dashed, or solid lines between tab stops. To set the tab, click the Set button. The tab position is inserted into the list box. Repeat this process for every new tab stop.

To remove all tab stops, click the Clear All button. To remove only certain tab stops, select one to be removed and click the Clear button. Repeat this process for all the tabs you want to clear.

Exercise 1: Setting tabs in the Tabs dialog box

In this exercise, you set and use tabs.

1. Open a new document, and click the Hide/Show Paragraph button ¶.
2. Press TAB and type your first name.
3. Press TAB, type your last name, and press ↵ ENTER.
   By default the tabs are set every 0.5 inch and are left aligned.
4. Choose Format Tabs.
5. In the Tabs dialog box, click the up arrow several times or type 2" in the Default Tab Stops box.
6. Press TAB and type your first name.
7. Press TAB, type your last name, and press ↵ ENTER. (See Figure 5-3.)

Telecommuting

Telecommuting is staying at home and using a computer, modem, phone lines, and fax to do your job. This trend is on the rise in the United States from about 3 million telecommuters in 1990 to over 7 million in 1993. The trend in telecommuting has shifted from clerical workers who could be closely monitored and their work easily measured to professionals who are self-motivated and work well independently.

Benefits for the employee include a better quality of life because less time is needed to commute to a job, allowing more time for other activities. Benefits for the organizations include savings on office space and equipment. Drawbacks for the individual include trying to find quiet space and manage time around family needs in a house, and lack of interaction with fellow employees.

8. Choose Format Tabs.

9. In the Tabs dialog box, type 5.9 in the Tab Stop Position text box and choose Set.

10. Type 7 in the Tab Stop Position text box, choose Set (if necessary), and then choose OK.

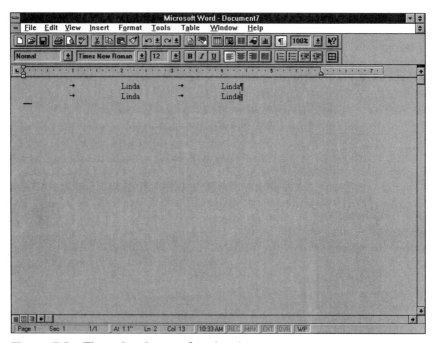

Figure 5-3 **The tabs change for the document**

Exercise 2: Removing tabs in the Tabs dialog box

In this exercise, you remove tabs.

1. Choose Format Tabs.

2. Select 5.9" in the Tab Stop Position text box.

3. Choose Clear.

4. Choose OK.

5. Close the document without saving it.

Using the ruler

Using the ruler can be a time saver for quick changes. You simply click the Tab Alignment button at the far left of the ruler. Keep clicking it until you see the type of tab you want to set. The tab stops and their buttons are as follows:

TAB SET STOPS	BUTTON
Left aligned	
Centered	
Right aligned	
Decimal	

Once you have selected the button for the appropriate tab, simply click on the ruler where you want the tab stop to occur.

To remove a tab stop from the ruler, drag the tab stop marker down below the ruler, and then release the mouse button. It will be deleted.

Exercise 3: Setting tabs using the ruler

In this exercise, you set tab stops using the ruler.

1. On a new document, click the Tab Alignment button enough times to select the Right Alignment button.
2. Point to the 2-inch marker on the ruler and click.

   A right-aligned tab appears at the 2-inch marker.
3. Click the Tab Alignment button enough times to select the Decimal Alignment button.
4. Point to the 5-inch marker on the ruler and click. (See Figure 5-4.)

Figure 5-4   The right and decimal markers on the ruler

5. Press TAB and type Amount.
6. Press TAB again and type 1.00 and press ↵ ENTER.
7. Press TAB twice, type 1,000,000.00, and press ↵ ENTER.

   Notice that the numbers line up on the decimal point because of the decimal tab.

Exercise 4: Removing tabs using the ruler

In this exercise, you remove tabs using the ruler.

1. Point to the decimal tab you set at the 5-inch marker on the ruler.
2. Drag it below the ruler.

   It disappears from the ruler.
3. Close the document without saving.

Objective 2: Indenting Text

indents

In the last chapter you learned to set margins. In this section you change a paragraph's *indents*, which can push text in or out from the left and right margins. The margins you set establish the overall width of the main text area as well as the space between the main text area and the edge of the paper. You use indenting to set off selected paragraphs from the rest of the document. Avoid pressing the Tab key or the spacebar numerous times to try to indent a body of text because the printed text will not be aligned properly. Word 6 supplies several easy-to-use options for indenting paragraphs.

FEATURE

Bookmarks

A bookmark is a Microsoft Word 6 feature that allows you to give a name to a location or item so that you can use the name at any time to locate the item.

First you select the item you want defined as a bookmark, then choose Edit Bookmark. The Bookmark dialog box displays. (See figure below.) Next type a name for the bookmark in the Bookmark Name text box and choose the Add button.

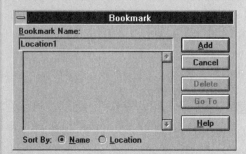

The Bookmark dialog box

To use the bookmark to move quickly to the text, choose Edit Bookmark, select the name of the bookmark, and then click the Go To button. When you are finished using bookmarks, simply click the Close button.

If you want to view all the bookmarks in a document, choose Tools Options. Select the View tab from the Options dialog box. In the Show section, place an X in the Bookmarks box. Word encloses each bookmark in square brackets. To remove the brackets, remove the X from the Bookmarks box.

Using the Paragraph dialog box

Position the insertion point where you want the indent to begin or select the paragraphs you want to indent. Choose Format Paragraph and the Paragraph dialog box appears. You can indent a paragraph from the left margin using the Left option. Select or type the distance you want to indent the paragraph from the left margin. To indent a paragraph from the right margin, select or type the distance in the Right option box. The Preview section shows the results of the indenting. (See Figure 5-5.)

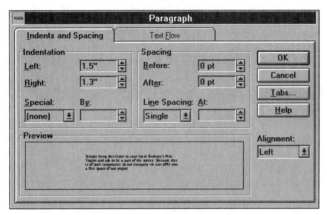

Figure 5-5 **New left and right indents with the results in the Preview section**

The Special option allows you to remove indenting, create a first line indent, or create a hanging indent.

To remove indenting, choose [none].

The First Line option indents the first line of a paragraph by the amount you specify in the By text box. (See Figure 5-6.)

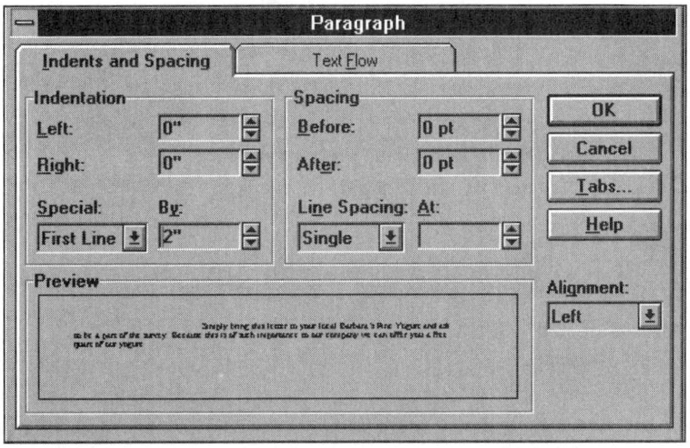

Figure 5-6 **The first line with a 2-inch indent**

Hanging Indent The *Hanging Indent* option indents the lines after the first line by the amount you specify in the By text box. (See Figure 5-7.)

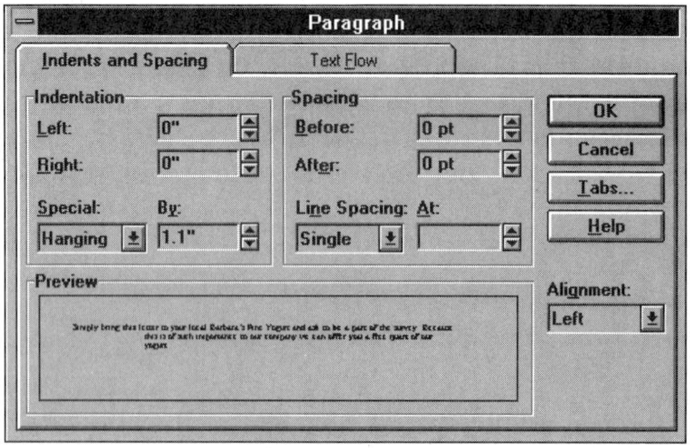

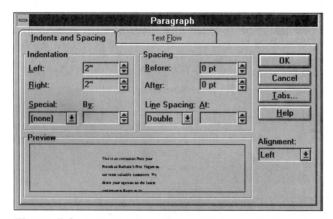

Figure 5-7 **A hanging indent**

Exercise 5: Creating indents using the paragraph dialog box

In this exercise, you create indents.

1. Open the BARBARA.DOC file and move the insertion point to the beginning of the first paragraph of the letter.

2. Choose Format Paragraph.

3. In the Paragraph dialog box, click the up arrow next to Left until the box reads 2".

   Notice that the Preview box shows the change.

4. Click the up arrow next to Right until the box reads 2".
   (See Figure 5-8.)

Figure 5-8 **The Preview box with indents from both margins**

5. Choose the Cancel button.

6. Choose Format Paragraph.

7. In the Paragraph dialog box, click the up arrow below the By box until it reads 2". (See Figure 5-9.)

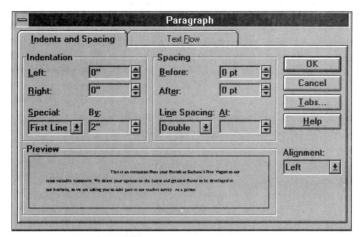

Figure 5-9   The Preview box with the first line indented 2 inches

8. Choose Special and then choose Hanging. (See Figure 5-10.)

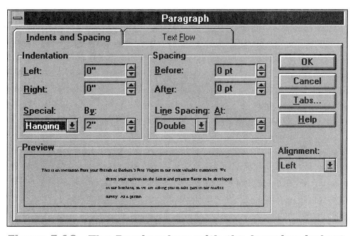

Figure 5-10   The Preview box with the hanging indent

9. Choose Cancel.

10. Close the document without saving it.

Objective 3: Inserting Page Breaks

soft page break

Word automatically inserts a page break when the current page becomes full. This is called a *soft page break* and appears as a dotted line across the screen. If you insert text above a soft page break, Word moves the soft page break to reflect the added text. If you delete text above a soft page break, Word moves the soft page break to reflect less text.

hard page break

Sometimes you want to create a page break in a location of your choosing. This is called a *hard page break*. To insert a page break, you simply position the insertion point where you want the break, choose Insert Break, and choose Page Break in the Break dialog box. This appears as a dotted line with the words "Page Break" on the line. (See Figure 5-11.)

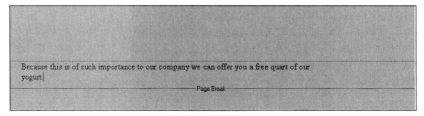

Because this is of such importance to our company we can offer you a free quart of our yogurt.

———————————————— Page Break ————————————————

Figure 5-11   A soft page break followed by a hard page break

If you decide that you don't want the hard page break, you can delete it by selecting it and pressing the Delete key. However, keep in mind that although you can't delete soft page breaks, because Word 6 inserts them when you have filled a page, you can control them as described in the next section.

Exercise 6: Inserting a page break

In this exercise, you insert a hard page break.

1. Open BARBARA.DOC and place the insertion point after the first paragraph.
2. Choose Insert Break.
3. In the Break dialog box, choose Page Break and OK.

   The document appears on two pages.
4. Leave the document on the screen for use in the next exercise.

Controlling soft page breaks

Sometimes the soft page breaks inserted by Word 6 might not be in a satisfactory location. Text you want to keep together is separated. You can control where Word 6 inserts page breaks by using the Format Paragraph command. Word provides four options on the Text Flow sheet of the Paragraph dialog box. (See Figure 5-12.)

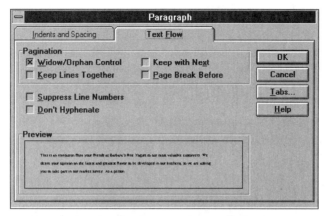

Figure 5-12   The Text Flow sheet of the Paragraph dialog box

The options in the Pagination section are as follows:

OPTION	DESCRIPTION
Widow/Orphan Control	A *widow* is the last line of a paragraph appearing at the top of a page, and an *orphan* is the first line of a paragraph appearing at the bottom of a page. This option prevents both from occurring.
Keep Lines Together	Keeps all lines in a paragraph together. If a whole paragraph does not fit on a page, Word moves the entire paragraph to the next page.
Keep with Next	Keeps two paragraphs together. This is useful to ensure that a heading isn't separated from a paragraph.
Page Break Before	Inserts a page break before text or a graphic to ensure that it is printed at the top of the next page.

widow
orphan

Exercise 7: Looking at the soft page break options

In this exercise, you look at the options for controlling soft page breaks.

1. Using the document on the screen, choose Format Paragraph.
2. Choose the Text Flow tab in the Paragraph dialog box.
3. Click the Help button.

   Word provides an explanation of the dialog box choices.
4. Close the Help window and close the Paragraph dialog box without making a choice.
5. Leave the document on the screen for use in the next exercise.

Objective 4: Including Page Numbers

Page numbers are an important part of longer documents. Word makes it easy to include page numbers and provides many options for formatting, positioning, and aligning page numbers in a document. To include page numbers, choose Insert Page Numbers. The Page Numbers dialog box provides options for number placement. (See Figure 5-13.)

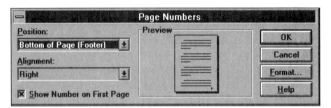

Figure 5-13 **The Page Numbers dialog box**

In the Position section, you can choose to locate the number at the top of the page, in a header, or at the bottom of the page. In the Alignment section, you are provided five options for aligning the numbers at the top or the bottom of the page. (See Figure 5-14.)

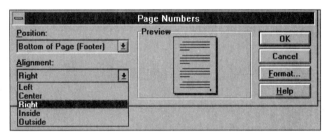

Figure 5-14 **The alignment options in the Page Numbers dialog box**

If you don't want a page number to occur on the first page of your document, deselect the Show Number on First Page.

Once you have decided on the location for the number on the page, you can decide what the numbers will look like by selecting the Format button. The Page Number Format dialog box appears, and you can choose a format from the Number Format section. (See Figure 5-15.)

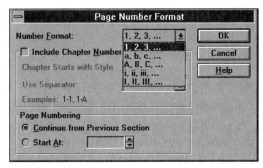

Figure 5-15   **The options in the Page Number Format dialog box**

Exercise 8: Including page numbers

In this exercise, you include page numbers in a document.

1. Move the insertion point to the top of the open BARBARA.DOC file.
2. Choose Insert Page Numbers.
3. In the Position section of the Page Numbers dialog box, choose Bottom of Page (Footer).
4. Choose all the Alignment options, one after the other, watching the Preview section to understand the choices.
5. Choose Left from the Alignment section.
6. Choose the Format button.
7. In the Number Format section of the Page Number Format dialog box, look at all the choices but choose 1,2,3 and click OK twice.
8. Choose File Print Preview.

    You will see the page numbers at the bottom left of the page.

9. Leave the document on the screen for use in the next exercise.

Objective 5: Including Headers and Footers

headers;
footers

You can include headers and footers in your documents. *Headers* are text or graphics in the margin at the top of the page, and *footers* are text or graphics in the margin at the bottom of the page. You can have as many headers or footers as you want in a document. Headers and footers can include text, page numbers, the date, and the time. When you choose View Header and Footer, your screen changes. Your document appears dimmed, and a header (or footer) area, defined by a nonprinting dashed box, is superimposed over your document along with the Header and Footer toolbar. (See Figure 5-16.)

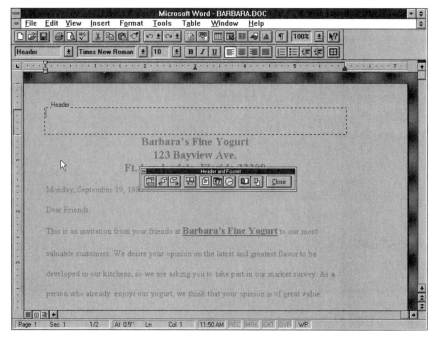

Figure 5-16 The Header box and the Header and Footer toolbar

The toolbar contains the following buttons:

OPTION	BUTTON	DESCRIPTION
Switch Between Header and Footer		Moves between Header and Footer box.
Show Previous		Shows header or footer created in a previous section.
Show Next		Shows header or footer created in a later section.
Same as Previous		Brings headers or footers created in a previous section into current section.
Page Numbers		Inserts page numbers.
Date		Inserts current date.
Time		Inserts current time.
Page Setup		Opens the Page Setup dialog box.
Show/Hide Document Text		Displays or hides the dimmed text.

Creating headers and footers

You can position text at the left or right margins, or in the center of the page. There are two preset tab stops in the Header and Footer box that will center and right align. Text typed at the left of the box aligns with the left margin. You can also set your own alignment by dragging the indent markers on the ruler.

You can format the text in a header or footer in the same way you would format any text. If you want to have different headers or footers on odd and even pages, or on the first page of a document, you click the Page Setup button. On the Layout tab, you can choose the Different Odd and Even option to have different headers or footers on all odd and even pages. You can choose the Different First Page option if you want a different header or footer on the first page of your document or if you do not want a header or footer on the first page—by leaving the header or footer area blank.

Exercise 9: Including a header in a document

In this exercise, you include a header in a document.

1. Move the insertion point to the top of the open BARBARA.DOC file.
2. Choose View Header and Footer.
3. Type Barbara's Fine Yogurt.
4. Press TAB.
5. Click the Date button .
6. Press TAB.
7. Click the Page Numbers button .
8. Choose Close.
9. Leave the document on the screen for use in the next exercise.

Editing and deleting headers and footers

If you decide to edit or delete a header or footer and you have more than one header or footer in the document, the insertion point must be in the section containing the header or footer you want to change. To edit a header or footer, choose View Header and Footer. When the box appears, you can edit the text you typed in just as you would in a document. To delete a header or footer, choose View Header and Footer, and when the box appears, select the entire header or footer and press the Delete key. To delete just an element of a header or footer such as the time, select only that element and press the Delete key.

Exercise 10: Editing a header

In this exercise, you edit a header.

1. Choose View Header and Footer.
2. When the Header box appears, select the date and press DELETE .
3. Choose the Time button 🕐. (See Figure 5-17.)
4. Choose Close.
5. Choose File Print OK.

   The file is printed.
6. Close the file without saving it.

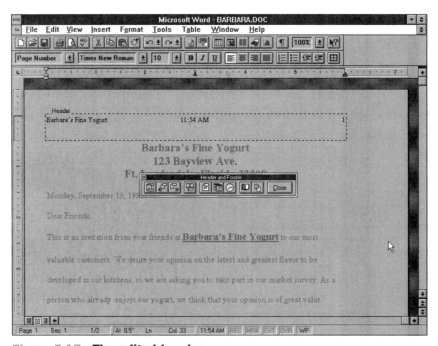

Figure 5-17   **The edited header**

Objective 6: Including Footnotes and Endnotes

footnotes

endnotes

Footnotes and endnotes are two types of notes used to provide more information about or explain text in a document. *Footnotes* usually appear at the bottom of the same page as the text they explain. A reference mark in the text alerts the reader to the footnote. *Endnotes* appear at the end of a section or at the end of the entire document. They are also accompanied in the text by a reference mark that alerts the reader to the endnote.

Creating and viewing footnotes and endnotes

Word automatically numbers and updates the notes. However, you can create your own custom reference marks, which cannot be updated. Notes can also be formatted as you would format any other text in a document.

When placing a footnote, the insertion point has to be to the right of the text that is being referenced. This is where Word will insert the reference mark. After locating the insertion point in the text, choose Insert Footnote. After selecting options in the Footnote and Endnote dialog box, you simply type the note in the note pane that opens, and Word places the reference in the text. (See Figure 5-18.)

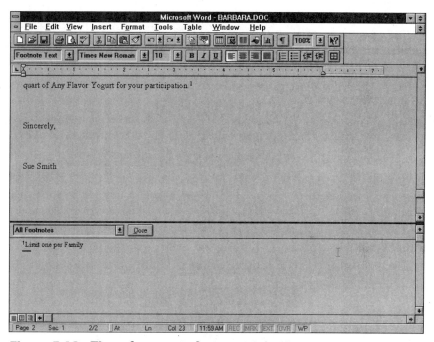

Figure 5-18 **The reference to footnote 1 in the text and the opened footnote pane**

Once you close the note pane, the footnote or endnote does not appear on the screen. You can view footnotes or endnotes in two ways: by double-clicking a note reference mark in the body of the document or by choosing View Footnotes.

Exercise 11: Creating and viewing a footnote

In this exercise, you create and view a footnote.

1. Open the BARBARA.DOC file and place the insertion point after the period following the word "participation" at the end of the end of the second paragraph.

2. Choose Insert Footnote.

3. Choose OK.

4. In the footnote pane, type Limit one per Family.

5. Choose Close.

   The screen shows the reference to the footnote but not the footnote.

6. To view the footnote, choose View Footnote.

7. Choose Close.

8. Save the document and leave it on the screen for the next exercise.

If you want footnotes or endnotes that are not automatically numbered, you can choose the Custom Mark option in the Footnote and Endnote dialog box. You must type in the character you want to use as a reference mark. You can type from one to ten characters in the text box. Another alternative to automatically numbered notes is to choose the Symbol button in the Footnote and Endnote dialog box. The Symbol dialog box appears, providing you with characters you can use as reference marks. (See Figure 5-19.)

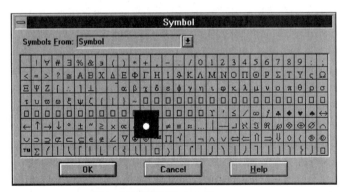

Figure 5-19   The Symbol dialog box

The Options button in the Footnote and Endnote dialog box allows you to change the numbering system that appears automatically. It also allows you to change the footnote's position on the page if you want the footnote to appear in a location other than at the bottom of the page.

Deleting, editing, and moving footnotes and endnotes

You may decide that you need to delete, edit, or move a footnote or endnote. If you want to delete a footnote or endnote, select the note reference and press the Delete key. If you want to move a note reference to a new location, drag the note reference to a new location. If it is an automatically numbered note, Word automatically renumbers any references as necessary, and all note text moves with the reference. You can also use Edit Cut or Copy and Paste from the menu or from the Standard toolbar to move or copy footnotes or endnotes.

To edit a footnote or endnote, view the note as described in the previous section and make any changes in the note window before choosing to close it. This changes the text of the note.

Exercise 12: Moving and deleting footnotes

In this exercise, you move and delete footnotes.

1. Using BARBARA.DOC, move the insertion point to the end of the first paragraph.
2. Choose Insert Footnote.
3. Choose OK.
4. In the footnote pane, type this is a footnote.
5. Choose Close.

    Notice that the original footnote renumbers to become number two. (See Figure 5-20.)

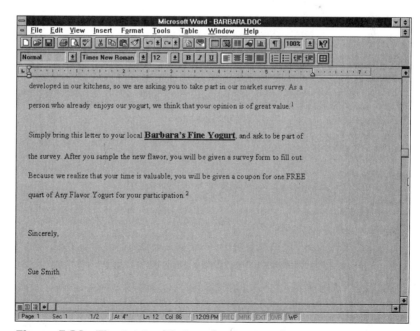

Figure 5-20   The text with two footnote references

6. Drag the second footnote to the end of the first sentence in the first paragraph.

   Notice that the references renumber again.

7. Select the first footnote reference and press (DELETE).

   The second footnote renumbers again.

8. Close the document without saving.

Chapter Summary

In this chapter you learned to make further refinements to your documents. Features such as headers, footers, footnotes, endnotes, and page numbers were added to your documents. Other enhancements to the text of your document include indenting text using tabs and indents, and inserting page breaks.

Review Questions

True/False Questions

_____ 1. A hanging indent indents the first line by the amount you specify.

_____ 2. Word 6 automatically inserts a soft page break when the current page becomes full.

_____ 3. A header is text or graphics placed in the margin at the top of the page.

_____ 4. An orphan is the first line of a paragraph appearing at the bottom of a page.

_____ 5. Footnotes provide more information about or explain text in a document.

Multiple Choice Questions

_____ 6. If you have pressed the Show/Hide Paragraph button on the Formatting toolbar and you press the Tab key, you will see

   A. a dot.

   B. a small arrow.

   C. a paragraph marker.

   D. a capital T.

_____ 7. In Word 6, you can align tabs
    A. at the left and right.
    B. at the center and on a decimal.
    C. justified.
    D. Both A and B.

_____ 8. If you insert text or delete text, Word adjusts the
    A. hard page break.
    B. soft page break.
    C. margins.
    D. All of the above.

_____ 9. You can automatically include which of these items in headers?
    A. The date
    B. Page numbers
    C. The time
    D. All of the above.

_____ 10. To view footnotes or endnotes, you would
    A. double-click a note reference mark in the body of the document.
    B. choose View Footnotes.
    C. just read them on the screen.
    D. Both A and B.

Fill-in-the-Blank Questions

11. _____ are stops placed on the line so that you can indent or align text.

12. A page break inserted from the keyboard is called a(n) _____ _____ _____.

13. A(n) _____ is the last line of a paragraph appearing at the top of a page.

14. Notes that appear at the end of a document and are used to provide more information about or explain text in a document are called _____.

15. To _____ is to push text in or out from the left and right margins.

Acumen-Building Activities

Quick Projects

Project 1: Refining a Document

1. Open the DRIVE.DOC file saved in Quick Project 1 in Chapter 4.
2. Insert hard page breaks after the first two paragraphs.
3. Add a header to the document that includes your name, the date, and the time.
4. Add page numbers to the bottom right of each page.
5. Print the document.
6. Close the file without saving it.

Project 2: Refining a Document

1. Open the HEALTHY.DOC file created in Quick Project 2 in Chapter 2.
2. Create a footnote after the word "ergonomics" that defines the term as the science of keeping the workplace healthy.
3. Create a second footnote after the term "Repetitive Stress Injuries" that defines the term as injuries resulting from excessive amount of repeated body motion.
4. Print the document.
5. Save the file and close it.

Project 3: Refining a Document

1. Open the BOOK.DOC file saved in Quick Project 3 in Chapter 4.
2. Indent the second paragraph 2 inches from the left margin.
3. Print out the document.
4. Indent the second paragraph 2 inches from both margins.
5. Print out the document.
6. Turn the second paragraph into a hanging indent, with all lines except the first indented 2 inches from the left margin.
7. Print out the document.
8. Indent the first line of the second paragraph 2 inches.
9. Print out the document.
10. Close the document without saving it.

Project 4: Refining a Document

1. Open a new file.
2. Create Tab stops at the following locations and with the following alignment:

1.2 inches	Left aligned
2.3 inches	Right aligned
3.3 inches	Centered
4.1 inches	Decimal

3. Press ⬚TAB after each item and type the following:

   Left

   Right

   Centered

   5.00

4. Press ↵ENTER.
5. Press ⬚TAB four times and type 5,000.00.
6. Print the document.
7. Close the file without saving it.

In-Depth Projects

Project 1: Refining a Document

1. Open the RESUME.DOC file created in In-Depth Project 1 in Chapter 2.
2. Use any enhancements you have learned so far to create a professional looking résumé. Don't forget to use a header, hanging indents, page numbers, fonts, centering, and any other feature you feel works for your résumé.
3. Print the document.
4. Save the file and close it.

Project 2: Refining a Document

1. Open the VIEW.DOC file saved in In-Depth Project 2 in Chapter 4.
2. Insert hard page breaks so that each heading starts a new page.
3. Insert page numbers in the bottom left of each page.
4. Include a header on every page that says "Microsoft Word 6 Views."
5. Print the document.
6. Save the file and close it.

CASE STUDIES

Coffee-To-Go:

Describing the Competition

In this chapter you learned to refine your documents. You will apply those skills to the business plan for Coffee-To-Go.

1. Open the Plan1 file.
2. Move the cursor to the end of the document.
3. Type in the next part of the business plan as shown:

The Competition

Currently, people in a five-block radius of the chosen location desiring a specialty cup of coffee have to enter a restaurant and drink the coffee there or wait by the checkout for a cup to go. The convenience of the chosen location will not only attract those customers who stop by a restaurant, but will attract those who currently would not go out of their way.

Because Coffee-To-Go will feature regular coffee drinks as well as specialty drinks such as espresso and lattes, people will be more inclined to stop on the way to work for a change from their same old coffee drink.

Because there are no bakeries in the downtown area, the addition of fresh baked goods such as muffins and cookies will also lure people from their current coffee stops at restaurants, which provide only commercial type cookies to go. The fresh baked goods will also attract customers who want a light lunch, don't have time to go to a restaurant, or in nice weather want to be outside during their break or lunch.

The particular services that Coffee-To-Go is attempting to provide are not really offered by anyone in the immediate area of downtown Eugene.

4. Move to the end of the Marketing Analysis section.
5. Make the last three paragraphs under Customers hanging indents.

6. Add a header to each page that says "Coffee-To-Go Business Plan."

7. Add page numbers to the document.

8. Create a footnote for *The National Business Review* in the Marketing Analysis section that says "March 1995, page 120."

9. Insert page breaks at the end of each of the following sections: Purpose Statement, Company Description, Market Analysis, and The Competition.

10. The words "The Competition" should match the font and formatting changes made to other headings in the document.

11. Save the document as Plan1.

12. Print the document.

CASE STUDIES

 **Videos West:**

Creating a Catalog

In this chapter, you learned to refine documents by creating hanging indents and adding headers. You will apply these and other skills you have learned to create a catalog for Videos West.

1. Open a new document.

2. Create the following document, using the hanging indent feature to create the indents:

Videos West Catalog

Sports and Outdoors:

Golf Like a Pro; Don't Let the Big Ones Get Away; Tips on Hunting; Hanggliding from the Peaks; Basketball Tips from Pros; Fly Fishing Techniques; Running Dogs with the Great Competitors; Skiing Your Best; Track and Field Tips; Baseball Tips; Tennis Pros Talk.

Fitness:

Tai Chi for Health; Jogging Tips; Backyard Trampolines for Fitness; Yoga for Your Health; Dance to Fitness; Celebrities Fitness Videos.

Health and Medicine:

Eating for Your Health; Addiction Awareness; Home
Remedies; Baby Proof Homes; Healthy Babies; Lifesaving
and Emergency Techniques; Quit Smoking on Your Own.

Finances:

Take Control of Your Financial Life; Start Your Own
Business; Evaluating Your Investments; Control Your Debt;
Buy Your Own Home.

Hobbies:

Knitting for Special Effects; Woodworking for Profit;
Christmas Crafts for Gifts; Turning Hobbies into a
Business; Leatherwork Techniques; Beaded Jewelry; Markets
for Handcrafted Items.

Languages:

Learn Spanish at Home; Speak French Like a Native;
Spanish in 30 Days; See and Hear Russian; Private Tutor
for Japanese; Hebrew at Home; Visit the Country and Learn
the Language From Your Home Series.

3. Create a header that says "Videos West Catalog."

4. Add a footer that says "Self-Improvement."

5. Save the file as VCR2.

6. Print the file.

Chapter 6

Printing

Key Terms

TERM	DEFINITION
Portrait Orientation	orients the paper vertically
Landscape Orientation	orients the paper horizontally

In this chapter, you learn about using the Page Setup dialog box to make changes to the page. You also learn more about printing your documents using Word 6 for Windows, including printing on different sized pages and on envelopes and labels.

Objective 1: Using the Page Setup Dialog Box

You used the Page Setup dialog box in Chapter 4 to change margin settings. You can also change the size, orientation, and source of the paper being printed on. To access the Page Setup dialog box, you choose File Page Setup. Choose the Paper Size tab to change the paper size and orientation. (See Figure 6-1.)

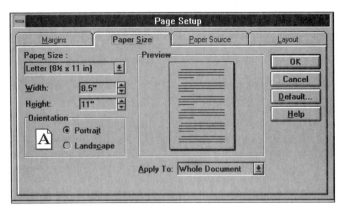

Figure 6-1   The Paper Size tab in the Page Setup dialog box

The Paper Size option provides preset, standard sizes based on the capabilities of your printer. You can also choose the Custom option, which allows you to print on a nonstandard size page.

Portrait;
Landscape   The Orientation option allows you to change from the default of *Portrait*, that is, vertical orientation, to *Landscape*, or horizontal orientation. This option is in effect for any size paper you choose.

The Apply To option allows you to have the size and orientation apply to the entire document or from the insertion point forward in the document.

Choose the Paper Source tab to change the paper source that your printer defaults to when printing. (See Figure 6-2.)

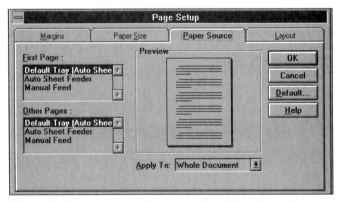

Figure 6-2   The Paper Source tab of the Page Setup dialog box

If your printer only has one tray of paper, use the Default Tray options. However, if you have more than one printer tray, you can set up your document to print the first page from one tray and all other pages from another tray. You might want to keep letterhead or envelopes in one tray for the first

What Is Shareware?

Shareware is a marketing strategy that allows you to try quality software before you pay for it. You pay a vendor a small fee for duplication and distribution costs, and you receive the program to try out. If you continue to use the program, you must send the author an additional payment, which entitles you to technical support, a printed manual, bonus programs, upgrades, or other benefits. The authors of shareware depend on your paying and registering the program so that they can continue to write and distribute programs.

Shareware catalogs are available from ads in most computer magazines. Ordering from a reputable shareware vendor guarantees that the programs you receive are virus free. Many fine utilities, graphics, games, and specialized business software are available.

page and print all others from a second tray with plain paper. To do this, simply designate the correct First Page and Other Pages options.

Exercise 1: Using the Page Setup dialog box

In this exercise, you change the paper size and orientation.

1. Open the BARBARA.DOC file, and place the cursor at the top.
2. Choose File Page Setup.
3. From the Page Setup dialog box, choose the Paper Size tab.
4. In the Paper Size drop-down box, choose Legal (8 1/2 × 14 in).
5. In the Orientation section, choose Landscape. (See Figure 6-3.) Notice that the Preview section reflects your changes.
6. Choose OK.
7. Use the scroll bar along the bottom of the document to see the text that is off the screen to the right.
8. To change the setting back to the original, choose File Page Setup.
9. On the Paper Size tab, choose Orientation Portrait.
10. Choose Letter (8 1/2 × 11 in) in the Paper Size drop-down box.
11. Choose OK. Document returns to the defaults.
12. Close the file without saving.

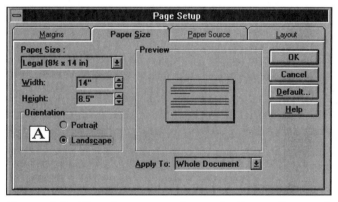

Figure 6-3 **The changes made to the Paper Size setting**

Objective 2: Selecting a Printer

Before you format a document, it is a good idea to select the printer that will print the document. The fonts available in Word 6 depend on the printer that will print the document. If you choose fonts and then choose a different printer, you may have formatting problems to correct in your document.

To select a printer, you choose File Print and then choose the Printer button. In the Print Setup dialog box, you can see the default printer. You can change the printer selection in the Printers list box. (See Figure 6-4.)

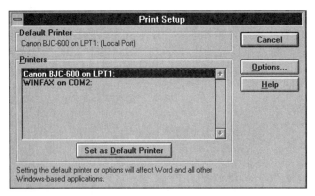

Figure 6-4 The Print Setup dialog box

By choosing the Options button, you can see the options available for your printer. (See Figure 6-5.)

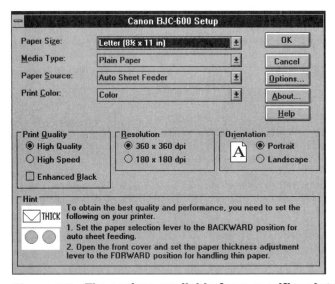

Figure 6-5 The options available for a specific printer

Exercise 2: Looking at the Print Setup dialog box

In this exercise, you look at the Print Setup dialog box.

1. Using a blank document, choose File Print.
2. Choose the Printer button in the Print dialog box.

3. In the Print Setup dialog box, choose the Options button.
   Notice the options available for your printer.
4. Choose the Cancel button three times.

FEATURE

Printing a bar code and FIM-A codes on an envelope
Envelopes that have machine-readable codes printed on them are
processed automatically by the U.S. Postal Service's automated mail-
handling equipment. Word 6 allows you to print two types of machine-
readable codes on envelopes. (This feature is available only if your printer
can print graphics.)

The first code is the POSTNET (POSTal Numeric Encoding Technique).
This is a bar code that represents the ZIP code and delivery point address.
The second available code is the FIM (Facing Identification Mark). The
FIM appears on preprinted courtesy envelopes provided to the recipient
and marks the front or face of the envelope during presorting.

To print either or both codes on envelopes, choose Tools Envelopes and
Labels. On the Envelopes tab, choose the Options button. Select the Delivery
Point Bar code and/or FIM-A Courtesy Reply Mail check boxes in the If
Mailed in the USA section. (See figure below.)

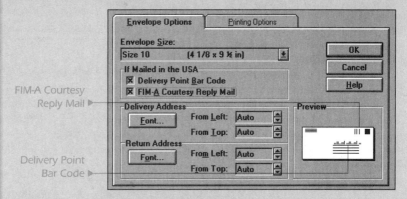

The Preview displaying both codes on the sample envelope

Objective 3: Using Print Preview

As you learned in Chapter 2, you can see what your document will look like before you print by choosing File Print Preview or choosing the Print Preview button ⎕ on the Standard toolbar.

The Preview screen includes a toolbar that enables you to make changes and print without having to return to another view. The options in the Print Preview toolbar are as follows:

OPTION	BUTTON	DESCRIPTION
Print		Prints the document using the defaults.
Magnifier		Magnifies an area.
One Page		Displays one page at a time.
Multiple Pages		Displays more than one page at a time.
Zoom Control	43%	Zooms in or out of the document.
View Ruler		Displays Ruler.
Shrink to Fit		Shrinks text to fit on fewer pages.
Full Screen		Displays document full screen.

Exercise 3: Using Print Preview

In this exercise, you use the Print Preview screen.

1. Open BARABARA.DOC, and move the insertion point after the first paragraph.
2. Choose Insert Break.
3. Choose Page Break from the Break dialog box, and choose OK.
4. Move to the top of the document, and choose File Print Preview. (See Figure 6-6.)
5. Choose the Multiple Pages button ⎕.
6. Click and drag the mouse over two pages in the grid that Word displays. Word displays the two pages when you release the button.

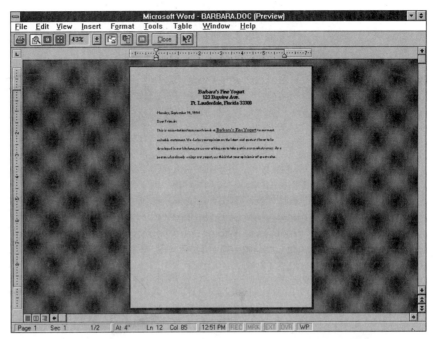

Figure 6-6   The document shown in the Print Preview screen

7. Click the One Page button 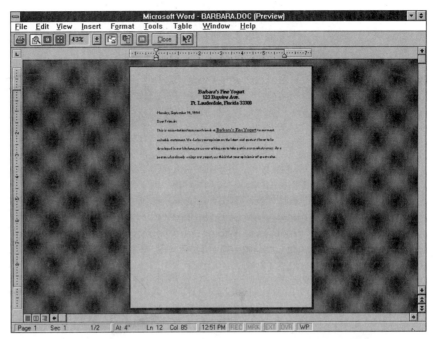.

8. Click on the Magnifier.

9. Move the magnifying glass pointer to a location on the page and click the mouse.

   The part of the page you clicked on becomes large.

10. Click the Zoom Control button.

11. Choose Whole Page.

12. Choose Close.

13. Close the file without saving.

Objective 4: Using the Print Command

If you are ready to print your document using the default settings, you can

click the Print button from either the Standard toolbar or from the Print Preview toolbar. If you need to change defaults, choose File Print, and the Print dialog box appears. (See Figure 6-7.)

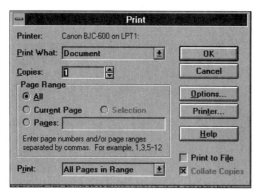

Figure 6-7 **The Print dialog box**

The Print What drop-down box provides options for printing. The Document option is the default and prints only the document. The other choices in the drop-down box, for example, styles that can be printed out with the document, are related to the document.

The Copies text box allows you to specify the number of copies of the document to print. You can use the arrows or type a number.

The Page Range section of the Print dialog box provides you with three choices: you can print the entire document by choosing All; you can print the page where the insertion point is located by choosing Current Page; or you can print a group of pages by choosing Pages and typing the page numbers in the text box.

The Print drop-down box provides options for printing only odd pages, even pages, or all pages, which is the default. The Print to File option prints the document to the disk rather than to a printer. The Collate Copies option collates multiple copies of the document as it prints out.

The Options button displays the Options dialog box. (See Figure 6-8.) The Printing Options section of the Options dialog box provides options for printing, for example, Reverse Print Order, which prints the document starting at the last page. The Include with Document section of the Options dialog box provides options that will print with the document, for example, Summary Info about the document, which includes such information as a word count of your document.

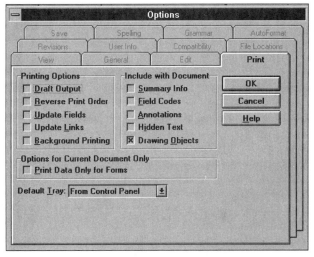

Figure 6-8 The Options dialog box

Exercise 4: Printing the document and summary information

In this exercise, you print the document and summary information.

1. Open the BARBARA.DOC file.
2. Choose File Print.
3. In the Print dialog box, choose Options.
4. Choose Summary Info in the Include with Document section.
5. Choose OK twice to print the document and the document summary.

Objective 5: Printing Envelopes

Word 6 has a built-in feature for creating and printing envelopes. If you are writing a letter, Word locates the mailing address and uses it as the envelope's Delivery address. If the letter contains several addresses, you should select the mailing address first before invoking any commands.

From the Tools menu choose Envelopes and Labels and select the Envelopes tab. (See Figure 6-9.) You can either accept the address in the Delivery Address box or edit it. You can choose Omit for no return address or accept or edit the address in the Return Address box.

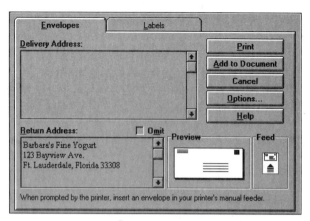

Figure 6-9 **The Envelopes tab of the Envelopes and Labels dialog box**

The Preview section shows the format of the envelope, and the Feed section demonstrates how the envelope should be fed into the printer.

You can click the Print button to print the envelope immediately. Alternatively, you can choose the Add to Document button to add the envelope to the beginning of the document. Then, when you print the file normally using File Print, both the document and the envelope will print.

If you choose the Options button on the Envelopes tab of the Envelopes and Labels dialog box, the Envelope Options dialog box displays. (See Figure 6-10.)

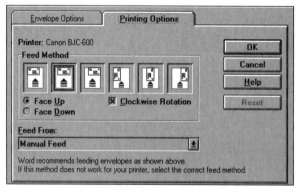

Figure 6-10 **The Envelope Options dialog box showing the Printing Options tab**

The Printing Options tab allows you to specify envelope feeding for your printer. The Envelope Options tab allows you to change the Envelope Size and formatting. (See Figure 6-11.)

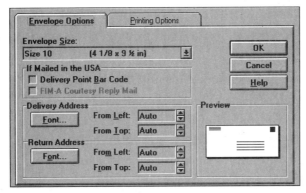

Figure 6-11   **The Envelope Options dialog box showing the Envelope Options tab**

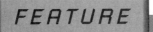

Routing a document online

If you are using Microsoft Word 6 on a network, you can make use of a handy feature to send documents to other people on the network. This feature is especially useful when you want others to review the document before it is finalized.

You use Microsoft Word along with Microsoft Mail or other compatible mail program to route the documents online. You have two options for routing. You can send a copy of the document to all the reviewers at the same time, or you can send a single copy that goes to each person in succession on a list that you provide. The latter routing feature allows each person to see the comments of all the previous reviewers.

When you are ready to send the document, you choose the Send command from the File menu. In the Routing Slip dialog box, you list the people who should receive the document and whether they all receive the document at the same time or one after the other. When they have made their comments or revisions, they use the same procedure to return it to you or send it on to the next person on the list.

Routing documents online saves having to print out multiple copies of documents in order to have other people review them, thus increasing productivity.

Exercise 5: Creating and printing envelopes

In this exercise, you create and print an envelope.

1. Open the BARBARA.DOC file.
2. Move the insertion point in the line before "Dear Friends."
3. Press ⏎ ENTER and then ↑.
4. Type your full name and press ⏎ ENTER.
5. Type your street address or post office box, and press ⏎ ENTER.
6. Type your city, state, and zip code, and press ⏎ ENTER.
7. Choose Tools Envelopes and Labels.
8. If your name and address do not appear correctly in the Delivery Address box, edit the box.
9. If Barbara's Fine Yogurt's address does not appear correctly in the Return Address box, edit the box.
10. Choose the Print button to print the envelope.
11. Close the file without saving.

Objective 6: *Printing Mailing Labels*

Word provides a built-in feature for printing mailing and other types of labels. You can choose from two mailing label options. The first prints an address on only one label. The second option prints the same address on every label of an entire sheet of labels.

To create and print labels, choose Tools Envelopes and Labels and choose the Labels tab. (See Figure 6-12.)

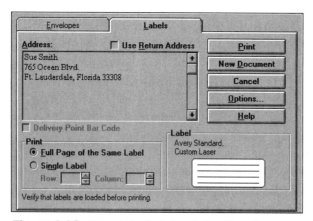

Figure 6-12 **The Labels tab of the Envelopes and Labels dialog box**

If the address in the Address section is not correct, you can edit it or type a different one. If you select Use Return Address, the return address appears.

From the Print section, you can choose to print Full Page of the Same Label or to print a Single Label.

The Options button displays the Label Options dialog box. (See Figure 6-13.)

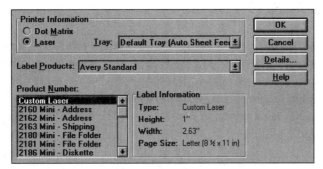

Figure 6-13   The Label Options dialog box

You can see additional information about the labels. For example, highlight Diskette in the Product Number list box. Then choose the Details button. A dialog box appears displaying information about the diskette labels. (See Figure 6-14.)

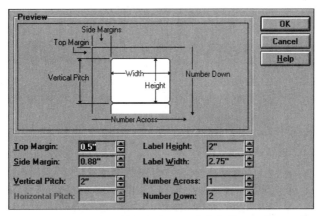

Figure 6-14   The dialog box with information about the diskette labels

Exercise 6: Creating and printing mailing labels

In this exercise, you create and print mailing labels.

1. On a blank screen, choose Tools Envelopes and Labels.
2. Choose the Labels tab.

3. In the Address box, type your name and complete address as they should appear on a label.

4. In the Print section, choose Single Label, and accept the default row and column.

5. Insert a sheet of labels into your printer if available.

6. Choose the Print button.

   One label prints out.

7. Close the file without saving.

Chapter Summary

In this chapter, you learned how to enhance your printouts. You can change the orientation of the paper, the size of the paper, and the location of the paper tray for letterhead paper. You learned how to increase your productivity by printing envelopes and labels.

Review Questions

True/False Questions

_____ 1. If you have more than one printer tray, you can set up your document to print the first page from one tray and all other pages from another tray.

_____ 2. Before you format a document, it is a good idea to select the printer that will print the document because the fonts available in Word 6 depend on the printer.

_____ 3. To print out a word count of your document, you would choose to print Summary Info.

_____ 4. The Print Preview screen makes use of the Standard toolbar to make changes to the document.

_____ 5. Printing Envelopes and Labels is located on the Tools menu.

Multiple Choice Questions

_____ 6. You can tell Word 6 to fit the document on one page by selecting which Print Preview button?

A. One page

B. Shrink to Fit

C. Full Screen

D. All of the above

_____ 7. If you are ready to print your document using the default settings, you can

A. click the Print button from the Standard toolbar.

B. click the Print button from the Print Preview toolbar.

C. choose File Print Preview.

D. Both A and B.

_____ 8. The options for printing mailing labels include

A. printing an address on one label.

B. printing one address on every label of an entire sheet of labels.

C. inserting a return address.

D. All of the above.

_____ 9. If you are writing a letter, Word locates the mailing address and uses it as the

A. envelope's Return address.

B. envelope's Delivery address.

C. filename.

D. Both B and C.

_____ 10. To view your document in Print Preview at 200%, you would choose which button?

A. Multiple Pages

B. Whole Page

C. Zoom Control

D. Magnifier

Fill-in-the-Blank Questions

1. _____ orientation is vertical page orientation.

2. _____ is horizontal page orientation.

3. Choose the _____ _____ tab of the Page Setup dialog box to change the paper source that your printer defaults to when printing.

4. The _____ _____ option in the Page Setup dialog box allows you to have the size and orientation apply to the entire document or from the insertion point forward in the document.

5. You can print the entire document, or you can print the page where the _____ _____ is located.

Acumen-Building Activities

Quick Projects

Project 1: Using Print Preview

1. Open the DRIVE.DOC file saved in Quick Project 1 in Chapter 4.
2. View the document on the Print Preview screen.
3. Magnify one section of the document.
4. Return to Whole Page view.
5. Print the document form the Print Preview screen.
6. Close the document without saving.

Project 2: Changing Orientation

1. Open the HEALTHY.DOC file saved in Quick Project 2 in Chapter 5.
2. Change the orientation from Portrait to Landscape, using the Page Setup dialog box.
3. Have the orientation change apply to the entire document.
4. Print the document.
5. Close the file without saving.

Project 3: Printing the Current Page Only

1. Open the BOOK.DOC file saved in Quick Project 3 in Chapter 4.
2. Insert a hard page break after the first two paragraphs.
3. Place the insertion point on the second page.
4. Print only the second page.
5. Close the file without saving.

Project 4: Printing Document Summary Information

1. Open the PALM.DOC file created in Quick Project 4 in Chapter 2.
2. Print the document and include the Summary Information with the printout.
3. Close the document without saving.

In-Depth Projects

Project 1: Creating and Printing an Envelope

1. Open the LETTER1.DOC file created in In-Depth Project 1 in Chapter 4.
2. Create an envelope to go with the letter.
3. Print the envelope.
4. Close the file without saving.

Project 2: Creating Mailing Labels

1. Open a new document.
2. Type in your full name, mailing address, city, state, and zip code.
3. Create a page of mailing labels using your name and address.
4. Print out the page of mailing labels.
5. Close the file without saving.

CASE STUDIES

Coffee-To-Go: **Printing Envelopes**

In this chapter, you learned to create envelopes. You will use those skills to create envelopes for the business plan for Coffee-To-Go.

1. Print envelopes to the following agencies and businesses that will receive the business plan or can provide assistance:

   U.S. Small Business Administration
   777 Oak St.
   Eugene, OR 97401

   Oregon Economic Development Commission
   P.O. Box 543
   Salem, OR 97502

   Service Corps of Retired Executives
   777 Oak St.
   Eugene, OR 97401

   Small Business Development Center
   Center College
   123 First St.
   Eugene, OR 97401

CASE STUDIES

 **Videos West** **Printing**

In this chapter, you learned to print documents using various formats. You will apply those formats to print the catalog file.

1. Open the VCR2 file.
2. Print the page in Landscape mode on regular size paper.
3. Print the page in Landscape mode on legal size paper.

Chapter 7

Using Writing Tools and Working with More Than One Document

Objectives

- Using the Go To Feature
- Using Find and Replace
- Using the Thesaurus
- Getting a Word Count
- Using the Grammar Checker
- Using Templates
- Combining Documents
- Adding Annotations

Key Terms

TERM	DEFINITION
Wildcards	characters that can stand for other characters just like wildcards in a card game and that are used to expand searching capabilities
Thesaurus	a list of synonyms that help your writing style
Template	a specially preformatted document
Annotations	notes in the body of the document that are viewed on the screen but are not printed with the document

In this chapter, you learn to use writing tools that help your writing style. You use the Thesaurus to find words to add variety to your writing and the Grammar Checker to help overcome grammar errors and improve your writing style. You learn to use such tools as Find and Replace, and the Go To commands. You are introduced to Word 6 templates and learn to how to create your own. You also learn about Word 6 features that can be useful when you are working in groups and need to combine documents and add annotations to documents.

Objective 1: Using the Go To Feature

The Go To feature helps you to move around your document easily and quickly. Instead of using the scroll bar to try to find a location, you can use the Go To feature to move to a specific location. You can access the Go To feature by choosing Edit Go To or by double-clicking the mouse on the left half of the Status bar. Both methods result in the display of the Go To dialog box. (See Figure 7-1.)

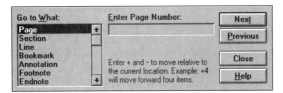

Figure 7-1 **The Go To dialog box**

In the Go to What list box, you can select the type of item to which you want to move. Then you must enter the name or the number of the specific item to go to. For example, if you selected Footnote as the item you wanted to go to, you would be prompted to enter the footnote number. If you chose Page, you would be prompted to enter the page number.

Then you click the Go To button to move to the desired location. You can also choose the Next or Previous buttons to move forward or backward to the next or previous item in the category. When you have reached the desired location, click the Close button.

Exercise 1: Using the Go To feature

In this exercise, you use the Go To feature.

1. Open the VIEW.DOC file saved in In-Depth Project 2 in Chapter 5, or any other multipage document you have saved.
2. Choose Edit Go To.
3. In the Go to What list box, select Page.
4. In the Enter Page Number box, type 3.
5. Click the Go To button.
6. Click the Previous button.
7. Click the Close button.
8. Close the file without saving.

Objective 2: Using Find and Replace

If you want to find specific text, formats, or special characters, you use the Find feature. If you want to find and replace text, formats, or special characters with other text or formats, you use the Replace feature.

What Is ASCII?

ASCII stands for the American Standard Code for Information Interchange. This system of codes for letters, numbers, and other symbols is the accepted standard computer code in the United States and the rest of the world.

When you type a character on your keyboard, the computer receives a series of electrical impulses. Each of these is translated into binary code, that is, a series of 0s and 1s representing the off and on electrical impulses. Every 0 and 1 is called a bit, and a group of 8 bits is called a byte. The computer translates every byte into a character. ASCII is the code used by the computer to translate bytes into the letters, numbers, and symbols. There are 127 standard ASCII numbers, which are understood by all computers and software. Extended ASCII adds another 128 numbers, which may mean different things to different computers.

The ASCII code allows text files to be transferred between computers or between different word processing programs. When you create a file on one computer in one word processing software, you save the file as a text or as an ASCII file. Then you can export it to another word processor. The second word processing program imports the file.

Word 6 for Windows provides an easy option for saving a file as an ASCII file. You simply choose File Save As, and the Save File as Type list box gives you several ways to save the file. To save a file as ASCII, select MS-DOS Text.

Find

You choose Edit Find to display the Find dialog box. (See Figure 7-2.)

In the Find What box, type the text you want to find. Then click the Find Next button to begin the search.

Figure 7-2 The Find dialog box

The matching text is highlighted in the document. The dialog box stays open on the screen even after the text you wanted to match is found. This gives you a chance to edit the document at the location of the first match and then move to the next match. When you are finished using the Find command, click the Close button to close the dialog box.

Word 6 searches the entire document. If you do not want to search through the entire document, you can specify search limits in the Search drop-down list box. (See Figure 7-3.) All, which is the default, searches the document, annotations, footnotes, endnotes, headers, and footers for matches. Up or Down searches the document only from the insertion point up to the beginning of the document or from the insertion point down to the end of the document.

Figure 7-3 The Search drop-down list box

The four options in the center of the dialog box, Match Case, Find Whole Words Only, Use Pattern Matching, and Sounds Like, provide flexibility in searches.

The Match Case option finds text with the same capitalization that you type into the Find What box. For example, if you select this option and type "Terry" in the Find What box, Word 6 will not find "terry."

The Find Whole Word Only option is only available when you type one word in the Find What box. It ensures that the entire word, not parts of words, is found. For example, if you select this option and type "the" in the Find What box, Word 6 will not match "them," "other," "their," or any other parts of words that match the text "the." If you search for "the" and do not select this item, Word will find parts of words.

wildcards   The Use Pattern Matching option allows you to use *wildcards* in the Find What box. Wildcards in Word 6 are like wildcards in a card game; that is, you use a character to represent other characters, allowing you to expand searching capabilities. The ? and * characters are wildcards or search operators that expand searching capabilities by providing flexibility. The ? (question mark) replaces any single character, and the * (asterisk) replaces any number of characters. (Other built-in operators are available in Word 6; for information on their use, consult the *User Manual* or the Help feature.) For example, if you want to find Objectives 1–9, you would select Use Pattern Matching, and type "Objective ?" in the Find What box. If you wanted to find all the words that started with "rec" and ended with "ve," you would type "rec*ve" in the Find What box.

The Sounds Like option matches words that sound the same as the word being searched for but are spelled differently. For example, if you select this item and type "Merry" in the Find What box, Word 6 will also find "Mary."

Word 6 provides the capability to search for text with specific formatting. For example, after you type the text to search for in the Find What box, you can click the Format button, and Word provides four options: Font, Paragraph, Language, and Style. (See Figure 7-4.)

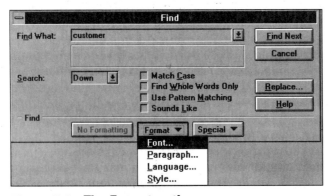

Figure 7-4   **The Format options**

If you choose the Font option, the Font dialog box displays, allowing you to format the text in the box. Any formatting selected will appear below the Find What box. The other three options work in the same way. For example, if you wanted to find a word that appears in italics in your document, you would type the word in the Find What box, and then click the Format button and choose Font. In the Font Style section of the Font dialog box, you would choose the italic feature. The word "italic" would then appear below the Find What box.

If you want to search only for formatting without any text, delete all text from the Find What box, leave the insertion point in the Find What box, choose the Format button, select the formatting you want to find, and proceed with the search. For example, if you wanted to find where the font was changed in your document, you would delete all text from the Find What box and click the Format button. You would choose Font. In the Font section of the Font dialog box, you would specify the name of the font to look for.

If you type text with formatting in the Find What box and you want to remove all formatting, choose the No Formatting button to search for the text with no formatting. For example, if you wanted to find a word in italics and later you want to find the same word without the italics format, you would remove the formatting by clicking the No Formatting button.

The Special button allows you to search for special characters. You simply click the Special button and select one of the special characters. (See Figure 7-5.)

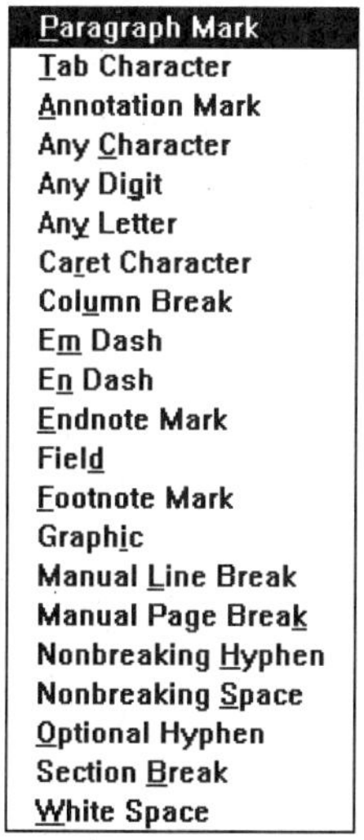

Paragraph Mark
Tab Character
Annotation Mark
Any Character
Any Digit
Any Letter
Caret Character
Column Break
Em Dash
En Dash
Endnote Mark
Field
Footnote Mark
Graphic
Manual Line Break
Manual Page Break
Nonbreaking Hyphen
Nonbreaking Space
Optional Hyphen
Section Break
White Space

Figure 7-5 **The Special characters option**

Exercise 2: Using Find to search for text

In this exercise, you find text.

1. Open the BARBARA.DOC file.
2. Choose Edit Find.
3. In the Find dialog box, type yogurt in the Find What box.
4. Choose the Find Next button.

   The first instance of the word "yogurt" is highlighted.

5. After viewing the first match, choose the Find Next button again.
6. Click the Cancel button.
7. Leave the document open to use in the next exercise.

Exercise 3: Using Find to search for text with formatting

In this exercise, you search for text that is formatted.

1. Using BARBARA.DOC, choose Edit Find.
2. In the Find dialog box, type fine.
3. Click the Format button.
4. Choose Font.
5. In the Font dialog box, select Single from the Underline drop-down box.
6. Click OK to close the Font dialog box.
7. Choose Find Next to start the search.

   The first instance of the word "fine" underlined is highlighted in the document.

8. Click the Cancel button.
9. Leave the document open to use in the next exercise.

Exercise 4: Using Find to search for formatting

In this exercise, you search for formatting only.

1. Using BARBARA.DOC, choose Edit Find.
2. Delete all text in the Find What box, and leave the insertion point in the box.
3. Click the Format button.
4. Choose Font.
5. In the Font dialog box, select Bold in the Font Style section.
6. Choose OK to close the Font dialog box.
7. Choose Find Next to start the search.

   The first instance of boldfacing is highlighted in the document.

8. Click the Cancel button.
9. Leave the document open to use in the next exercise.

Exercise 5: Using wildcards to search for text

In this exercise, you use a wildcard to expand searching capabilities.

1. Using BARBARA.DOC, choose Edit Find.
2. In the Find dialog box, type yog* in the Find What box.
3. Select Use Pattern Matching.
4. Choose the Find Next button.

    The first instance of a word matching the pattern is highlighted.

5. After viewing the first match, choose the Find Next button again.
6. Choose the Close button.
7. Leave the document open to use in the next exercise.

Replace

Sometimes you will want to search for a word or group of words so that you can replace them with other words. For example, if you spelled your customer's name Erickson and her name is Ericksen, you could search through a contract and quickly replace the wrong spelling with the correct one.

You can choose Edit Replace to search for text, formatting, or special characters, and then replace them. You specify text and formatting in the Replace dialog box in the same way that you do in the Find dialog box. (See Figure 7-6.)

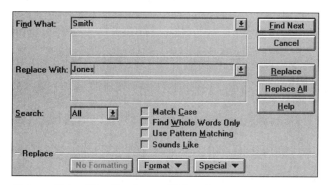

Figure 7-6   The Replace dialog box

WARNING   Before using the Replace feature, always save your document.

Fill in the Find What box in the Replace dialog box, following the same guidelines you used for the Find dialog box. Then fill in the Replace With box with the text, formatting, text with formatting, or special character that you want to appear in the document. Choose the Replace button to replace only the next occurrence of the item and obtain user confirmation, or choose the Replace All button to change all occurrences without user confirmation. It is safer but slower to use the Replace button because you have the opportunity to reject a replacement of a word. It is faster but more dangerous to use the Replace All button because all instances are replaced immediately.

Exercise 6: Using the Replace feature

In this exercise, you use the Replace feature.

1. Using BARBARA.DOC, choose Edit Replace.
2. In the Replace dialog box, type fine in the Find What box.
3. Type quality in the Replace With text box.
4. Click the Replace All button.
5. Click the Close button.

   All instances of "fine" have been changed to "quality."
6. Close the document without saving.

Objective 3: Using the Thesaurus

Thesaurus Word 6 provides a *Thesaurus*. You can use it to find synonyms for words or phrases to achieve variety in your writing style. Select the word or phrase you want to look up, or simply place the insertion point in a single word, and choose Tools Thesaurus. The Thesaurus dialog box displays on the screen. (See Figure 7-7.)

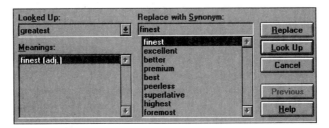

Figure 7-7 The Thesaurus dialog box

The word or phrase you selected appears in the Looked Up box, and the synonyms for the word appear in the Replace with Synonym list box. If the word has multiple meanings, which appear in the Meanings list box, you can select a different meaning to see a different list of synonyms.

You can highlight a word in the Meanings list box or in the Replace with Synonym box and click the Look Up button to display a list of synonyms for that word. When you have found the replacement you want, click the Replace button. If you decide not to replace the word, click the Cancel button.

Exercise 7: Using the Thesaurus

In this exercise, you use the Word 6 Thesaurus.

1. Open a new document and type big.
2. Select the word.
3. Choose Tools Thesaurus.
4. Highlight various meanings from the Meanings list box to see different lists of synonyms.
5. Highlight the word you want to use in the Replace with Synonym list box.
6. Click the Replace button.

    The word "big" is replaced on screen with the synonym that you chose.

Objective 4: Getting a Word Count

Word 6 provides an option for seeing statistics about your document, which include the number of pages, number of words, number of characters, number of paragraphs, and the number of lines in the active document. You choose Tools Word Count to automatically see the statistics. Select the check box at the bottom of the dialog box to Include Footnotes and Endnotes in the statistics. (See Figure 7-8.)

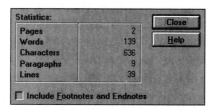

Figure 7-8   **The Word Count dialog box**

Exercise 8: Using Word Count

In this exercise, you use the Word Count option.

1. Open the VIEW.DOC file saved in In-Depth Project 2 in Chapter 5, or any long document you have saved.
2. Choose Tools Word Count.

    The Word Count dialog box displays the statistics.
3. Click the Close button.
4. Close the document without saving.

Objective 5: Using the Grammar Checker

Word 6 includes a tool for checking your grammar. Word identifies sentences that contain possible errors and suggests improvement. By default, the Grammar Checker checks both grammar and spelling from the insertion point forward in the document.

To use the Grammar Checker, move the insertion point to the beginning of the section you want checked and choose Tools Grammar. The Grammar Checker displays a dialog box, depending on the error detected. (See Figure 7-9.)

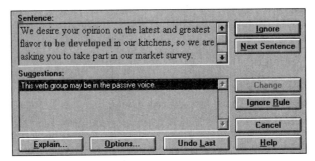

Figure 7-9 **The Grammar dialog box**

You can choose the Explain button to see a more detailed explanation of the error. (See Figure 7-10.)

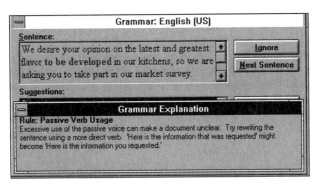

Figure 7-10 **Explanation of the highlighted error**

In the Grammar dialog box, you can choose the Change button to accept the suggested change; you can ignore the suggestion with the Ignore button; you can ignore the rule throughout the document with the Ignore Rule button; you can continue the grammar check with the Next Sentence button; you can reverse the last change with the Undo Last button.

When the grammar check is complete, Word 6 displays the Readability Statistics dialog box. (See Figure 7-11.) The Counts section provides the same statistics as the Tools Word Count menu option. The Averages section provides more statistics about the average word, sentence, and paragraph length. The Readability section shows the reading level or difficulty based on standard readability formulas. It also provides information on the use of passive sentences in your document.

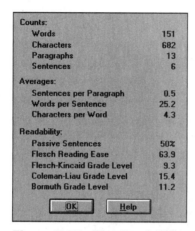

Figure 7-11 **The Readability Statistics dialog box**

To change options such as whether certain features such as the Spell Checker or readability level are in effect, you can choose the Options button from the Grammar dialog box, or you can choose Tools Options and then select the Grammar tab. (See Figure 7-12.)

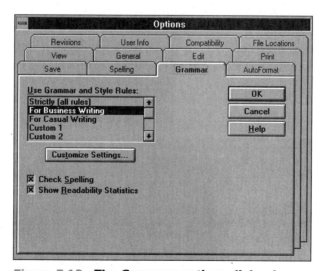

Figure 7-12 **The Grammar options dialog box**

In the Use Grammar and Style Rules list box, you are provided with rule groups from which you can select to tell Word the type of grammar and style rules to use in your document. The Strictly option observes all grammar and style rules. The For Business Writing option observes all grammar rules, but it does not observe all style rules. The For Casual Writing option observes most grammar rules, but it observes only basic style rules. The Custom 1 and 2 options allow you to customize what Word checks for in you writing. When you choose the Customize Settings button, the Customize Grammar Settings dialog box is displayed. (See Figure 7-13.)

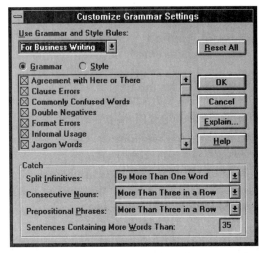

Figure 7-13 The Customize Grammar Settings dialog box

You can select rules from the Grammar and Style list boxes, or see explanations of the selections with the Explain button.

Exercise 9: Using the Grammar Checker

In this exercise, you use the Word 6 Grammar Checker.

1. Open the VIEW.DOC file saved in In-Depth Project 2 in Chapter 5, or any other multipage document you have saved.
2. Choose Tools Grammar.
3. Choose to change some style and grammar errors and to ignore others as you work through the document.
4. When you are finished, note the reading level in the Readability Statistics dialog box.
5. Choose OK to complete the check.
6. Close the document without saving.

Objective 6: Using Templates

template   A *template* is a preformatted document. It is necessary to have a template in effect in order to have a font, font size, margins, tabs and other features set up for you. By default, you base every new document in Word 6 on the template named Normal. Instead of using the Normal template, you can choose to use one more suited to a specific job. Word 6 provides many built-in templates, or you can create your own.

Word 6 Wizards are templates that prompt the user through the creation of a document, such as the award created in the Quick Preview chapter of this book. With templates that are not wizards, there is no prompting.

A template can store styles, macros, and customized settings for use with certain types of documents. Word 6 provides templates for common documents such as memos and business letters, and you can create others.

To use a template, choose File New. Then select a template from the Template list box in the New dialog box. (See Figure 7-14.) The selected template is described in the Description section. Click the OK button, and Word copies the information to the new document.

Figure 7-14   **The New dialog box**

When you choose the New button ⬚ from the Standard toolbar, Word automatically opens the new document based on the Normal template and does not display the New dialog box to enable you to change templates.

Exercise 10: Using a template

In this exercise, you use a Word 6 template.

1. Choose File New.
2. Choose Faxcovr1 in the Template list box.
3. Create the fax cover sheet.

4. Print the document.

5. Save the document as MYFAX and close the file.

6. Choose File New.

7. Select other templates from the Template list box to become familiar with the available templates.

You can create your own templates for your specific word processing needs. To create a template from scratch, choose File New. In the New dialog box, choose the Template button and then click OK. In the template document window, you can set up the formats and text as you want them. When you are finished creating the template, choose File Save As. You must give the template a name, and it is automatically saved with the three-letter extension DOT and placed in the template subdirectory.

Objective 7: Combining Documents

If you are working on a group project and each member has written part of the document, or if you need to compile your monthly reports into a year-end report, you can combine these different files into one document.

If you want to combine two or more documents into one document, you can do so by placing the insertion point at the location where you want the file to appear, and choosing Insert File. You simply select the file you want to add from the File Name list box in the File dialog box. (See Figure 7-15.) The document is inserted at the insertion point. You can move the insertion point to another location and repeat the process to insert another file.

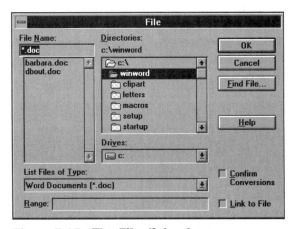

Figure 7-15   **The File dialog box**

Exercise 11: Inserting a file into another file

In this exercise, you combine two files.

1. Open the VIEW.DOC file saved in In-Depth Project 2 in Chapter 5, or any other multipage document you have saved.
2. Place the insertion point at the end of the document.
3. Choose Insert File.
4. Highlight the PALM.DOC file or any other file you have saved.
5. Click OK.

   The PALM.DOC file is added to the bottom of the VIEW.DOC file.

6. Close the file without saving.

FEATURE

Using the Revision feature

Word 6 allows you to see how a document has been revised. This is especially useful if several people are working on the same document. Text that is inserted into the original document can appear underlined, and text that is deleted from the original document can appear formatted for strikethrough.

You simply choose Tools Revisions. The MRK indicator in the Status bar becomes bold, and the Revisions dialog box appears. In the Revisions dialog box, you can choose to Mark Revisions While Editing, Show Revisions on Screen, or Show Revisions in Printed Document. (See figure below.)

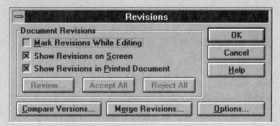

The Revisions dialog box

If you want to change the formatting of the revisions, you can choose the Options button in the Revisions dialog box.

Objective 8: Adding Annotations

annotations If several people are working on a document, they might want to include *annotations* or notes in the body of the document that are viewed on the screen but are not printed with the document. In Word 6, an annotation consists of two parts: first, the annotation mark, which is the initials of the author and the number of the annotation, and second, the note or the actual annotation.

You simply place the insertion point where you want to annotate the document and choose Insert Annotation. Word automatically inserts the annotation mark (initials and the number) at the insertion point and opens the Annotation window where you can type the desired note. You simply close the window when the note is complete. (See Figure 7-16.)

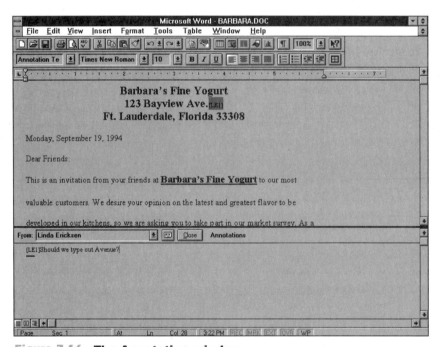

Figure 7-16 The Annotation window

To find annotations in a document, open the document. Choose Edit Go To. In the Go To What list box, select Annotation, and in the Enter Review's Name drop-down box, select the correct name. Then choose the Next or Previous button to move to the correct annotation. To see the contents of the annotation, choose View Annotations. When you are finished reading the note, choose the Close button.

Exercise 12: Adding annotations to a document

In this exercise, you add an annotation to a document.

1. Open the VIEW.DOC file saved in In-Depth Project 2 in Chapter 5, or any other multipage document you have saved.
2. Move the insertion point to the end of the first paragraph.
3. Choose Insert Annotation.
4. In the Annotation window, type This paragraph needs more work!
5. Click the Close button.
6. Keep the document open for the next exercise.

Exercise 13: Finding and viewing annotations

In this exercise, you find the annotation you inserted in Exercise 12 and read the contents.

1. Using the VIEW.DOC file, move the insertion point to the beginning.
2. Choose Edit Go To.
3. Choose Annotation in the Go To What list box.
4. In the Enter Review's Name drop-down box, select the correct name.
5. Click the Next button.
6. Click the Close button.
7. Choose View Annotations.

   The Annotation window opens, so that you can see the contents of the note.
8. Close the Annotation window.
9. Close the document without saving.

Chapter Summary

In this chapter, you learned to improve your writing style using Word 6. You learned to search for text or formats and replace them with other text or formats, and you learned about the Go To feature. You learned to use the Thesaurus, the Word Count feature, and the Grammar Checker. You also combined documents and placed annotations in a document.

Review Questions

True/False Questions

_____ 1. You can use the Go To feature to go directly to annotations.

_____ 2. Word 6 never searches for text or formats in footnotes when you use the Find or Replace commands.

_____ 3. The Find Whole Word Only option is not available when you type in more than one word in the Find What box.

_____ 4. Word 6 provides a Thesaurus, which lists synonyms for words or phrases.

_____ 5. Word 6 inserts a document at the insertion point.

Multiple Choice Questions

_____ 6. A Word 6 annotation consists of

A. the annotation mark.

B. a note.

C. a footnote.

D. Both A and B.

_____ 7. Word 6 automatically gives a template name the three-letter extension

A. DOC.

B. TEM.

C. DOT.

D. WP6.

_____ 8. The Grammar Checker can check for

A. all usage rules.

B. business usage rules.

C. casual usage rules.

D. All of the above.

_____ 9. If you want to search for the word "perceive," and you cannot remember how to spell the word, you could search for

A. per?

B. perc??ve

C. ?ve

D. All of the above.

_____ 10. If you select this option and type "out" in the Find What box, Word 6 will not match "shout" or "about."

    A. Find Whole Word Only

    B. Use Wildcard

    C. Sounds like

    D. All of the above

Fill-in-the-Blank Questions

11. _____ _____ are search operators that expand searching capabilities.

12. A(n) _____ is a list of synonyms that help your writing style.

13. A(n) _____ is a specially preformatted document.

14. _____ are notes in the body of the document that are viewed on the screen but are not printed with the document.

15. You can use Find and Replace to search for _____, _____, and _____.

Acumen-Building Activities

Quick Projects

Project 1: Using the Thesaurus

1. On a blank document type small.

2. Use the Thesaurus to find alternatives.

3. Choose an alternative.

4. Close the file without saving.

Project 2: Using Search and Replace for Text

1. Open the VIEW.DOC file saved in In-Depth Project 2 in Chapter 5.

2. Search for the word "view" and replace it with "window."

3. Print the document.

4. Close the file without saving.

Project 3: Using Search and Replace for Formatting

1. Open the VIEW.DOC file saved in In-Depth Project 2 in Chapter 5.

2. Search for the word "view" and replace it with "view" bolded and in italics.

3. Print the document.

4. Close the file without saving.

Project 4: Using a Template

1. Open a new document.
2. Open the Letter1 template.
3. Create a letter using the template.
4. Print the document.
5. Close the file without saving.

In-Depth Projects

Project 1: Creating a Template

1. Create a template for a document type you use often, for example, for your assignments for a class or a letter or memo type you use often.
2. Save the file as a template.
3. Use the template to create a document.
4. Print the document.
5. Close the file without saving.

Project 2: Combing Documents

1. Open the HEALTHY.DOC file created in Quick Project 2 in Chapter 2.
2. Move the insertion point after the first paragraph.
3. Insert the PALM.DOC file created in Quick Project 2 in Chapter 2.
4. Print the new document.
5. Close the file without saving.

CASE STUDIES

 Coffee-To-Go: **Writing the Loan Analysis**

In this chapter, you learned to search for text and replace it with new text. You will use that skill to change the name of the business from Coffee-To-Go to Coffee-On-The-Go. You will also create a second document.

1. Open the Plan 1 file as document one.
2. Create a new document as a second document.
3. In the new document create a decimal tab located five inches from the left edge of the paper.
4. Type in the Loan Analysis as shown:

Loan Analysis

The $20,000 will be used as follows:

Purchase of building	$8,000.00
Lease of property (1 year)	6,000.00
Customizing building	1,000.00
Electricity and Water to site	4,000.00
Awnings	1,000.00
Total:	$20,000.00

Personal Investment of $10,000 will be used as follows:

Equipment:

Coffee makers	$2,000.00
Supplies—cups, napkins, etc.	500.00
Cleaning supplies	25.00

Inventory:

Coffee, tea, etc.	1,000.00
Baked goods	275.00

Marketing:

Mailing	200.00
Local advertising	500.00
Working Capital	5,500.00
Total:	$10,000.00

5. Save the Loan Analysis as Loan.
6. Select the Loan Analysis section and copy it to the bottom of the business plan.
7. Create a page break above the Loan Analysis section in the business plan.
8. Change the font and attributes of the words Loan Analysis so that this heading matches the other headings in the business plan.
9. The business name can't be Coffee-To-Go and must be changed to Coffee-On-The-Go; the word processor can do this for you. Search for every instance of Coffee-To-Go in the entire business plan. Either include the header in the search or edit the header.
10. Save the file as Plan1.
11. Print out only the Loan Analysis section.

CASE STUDIES

Videos West: Using Multiple Documents

In this chapter, you worked with more than one document. You will use that concept here to pull information from one file to another.

1. Open the VCR file.
2. Open the VCR2 file as a second document.
3. Select the mailing address from the VCR file.
4. Copy the selected text to the top of the VCR2 file.
5. Save the VCR2 file.
6. Print out the VCR2 file.

Acumen Critical Thinking Milestone

Individual Project:

Enhancing the Document

1. Open the MEMORY.DOC file created in Individual Project 1 at the end of Part 1.
2. Search for the word "memory" and replace it with the word "storage."
3. Center, bold, and change the font size of the title.
4. Make the alignment justified.
5. Add a header that includes your name.
6. Add a hard page break after the third paragraph.
7. Add page numbers in the lower right corner of the page.
8. Add a footnote at the end of the last paragraph, which says If you are uncertain about adding memory, take the computer back to the dealer you bought it from.
9. Print the document.
10. Save the document as MEMORY1.DOC.

Team Project:

Combining and Annotating the Document

In Team Project 1 at the end of Part I, each individual researched part of the topic and typed their findings.

1. Combine all the documents into one document.
2. Provide each participant with a copy of the combined file.
3. Each participant should add two annotations to the document.
4. The group should meet to view the annotations and revise the document.
5. Extra credit: Use Tools Revisions, described in the Feature box in this chapter. Choose to Mark Revisions While Editing, and Print the document showing the revisions.

6. Once the group has created a complete document, place a title on the document that is centered and bold, and increase the font size.

7. In the document place a header that reflects the content.

8. Create footnotes for any referenced material.

9. Add page numbers.

10. Make the alignment left.

11. Run the Grammar Checker and improve the writing, and check the readability level.

12. Print the document.

13. Save the document as TEAMPRO.DOC.

Part 3

Advanced Features

Chapter 8

Graphics, Frames, and Drawing

Objectives

- **Creating Frames**
- **Adding Borders, Shading, and Captions to Frames**
- **Inserting Graphics**
- **Drawing Objects**
- **Using WordArt**
- **Creating a Dropped Cap**

Key Terms

TERM	DEFINITION
Frames	containers for text or graphics in Word 6
Linked Objects	objects that are stored in the source file (Word 6 stores only the location of the source file and displays a representation of the linked data.)
Embedded Objects	objects that are part of the Word 6 document
Dropped Cap	a large, initial, capital letter

In this chapter, you learn to use Word 6 tools to add graphics, frames, and other enhancements to your text. These visual features help make the message of the text clear to the reader by setting off important text or adding graphics that have visual impact.

Objective 1: Creating Frames

Frames are containers for text or graphics in Word 6. You can place any object except a footnote, endnote, or annotation in Word 6 in a frame. You can place the frame any place on the page. To display the frame's location on the page and see its actual size, you need to be in Page Layout view; simply choose View Page Layout.

You can create an empty frame and add text or graphics to it, or you can select an item and place it in a frame. To insert a frame into a document, choose Insert Frame. The pointer changes to a crosshair to enable you to draw the frame on the screen. You position the crosshair pointer where you want the top left corner of the frame, click the mouse, and drag diagonally, sizing the frame. When you release the mouse button, the frame is displayed on the screen with the insertion point in the frame and a border around the outside. (See Figure 8-1.) If you want to place text in the frame, you can simply start typing.

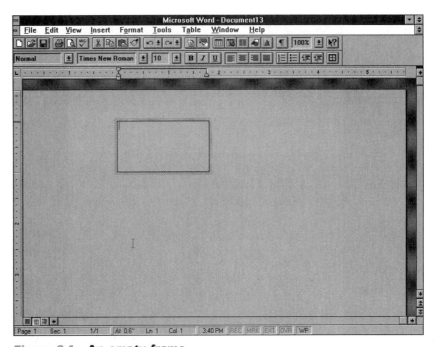

Figure 8-1   An empty frame

Exercise 1: Creating a frame and placing text in the frame

In this exercise, you create a frame and type text into the frame.

1. Open a new document.
2. Choose View Page Layout.
3. Choose Insert Frame.
4. Drag the crosshair to create a frame of about 2 inches by 2 inches.

5. Type the following text into the frame: This is a Microsoft Word 6 Frame
   The text appears in the frame.
6. Keep the document on the screen for the next exercise.

If you want to move or resize the frame, you must select the frame. To select the frame, first point to the border of the frame, noting that the pointer changes to a positioning pointer. Then click the mouse to select the frame. The selected frame has eight sizing handles around its edge. (See Figure 8-2.)

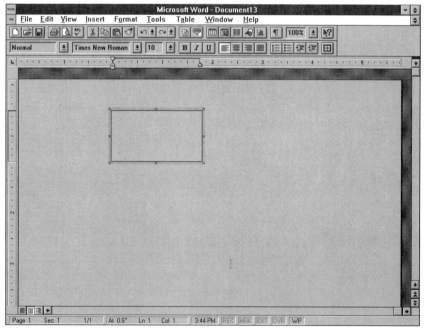

Figure 8-2   A selected frame with sizing handles

You can resize a selected frame with the mouse by pointing to a sizing handle and dragging the arrow that points in the desired direction. For example, if you point to the sizing handle on the top of the box, the handle changes to an upward-pointing arrow; if you drag the arrow upward, the height of the box changes. If you want to change the width and height of the frame simultaneously, point to a corner sizing handle, and then drag the diagonal arrow.

You can move the frame to a new location by pointing to the frame border and clicking and dragging the positioning pointer to the desired location.

You can resize and position the frame in an exact location using the Frame dialog box. To access the Frame dialog box, you can double-click the frame border or you can choose Format Frame. (See Figure 8-3.)

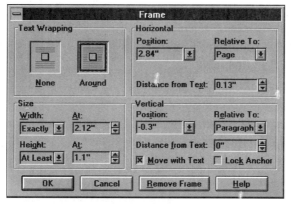

Figure 8-3 **The Frame dialog box**

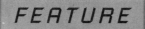

Printing special text and graphics on an envelope
To print special text and graphics on an envelope, choose Tools Envelopes
and Labels. On the Envelopes tab, change the Delivery or the Return
address as necessary, and then choose Add to Document. Switch to page
layout view and type any special text you want on the envelope. You can
insert a graphic by choosing Insert Picture or use the Drawing tools to create a graphic. You can position the text or graphic by placing it in a frame
and dragging it to the desired location.

After you have designed the envelope, you can save it and print it with
the document, or you can save it to use again later. To save it for later use,
select the text, choose Edit AutoText, name it EnvelopeExtra1, and choose
the Add button. You can save two AutoText entries for use on envelopes
as EnvelopeExtra1 and EnvelopeExtra2.

All envelopes created with the current template will automatically contain the graphics or text you saved as EnvelopeExtra1 or EnvelopeExtra2.
If you do not want to include either of the EnvelopeExtra formatting, use a
different template or delete the Autotext entries in the AutoText dialog box.

You can change the size of the box in the Size section of the dialog box by
specifying the Width and the Height. You can choose from Exactly or Auto
for the width, and from Exactly, Auto, or At Least for the height. Exactly
allows you to type an exact measurement in the At box; Auto adjusts for
the tallest or widest item in the frame; At Least allows you to specify a
minimum height.

You can specify an exact location for the frame on the page by using the Horizontal and Vertical sections of the Frame dialog box. If you choose Position in the Horizontal section, the drop-down box displays, and you can select from Left, Right, Center, Inside (on the inside edge of the margin), or Outside (on the outside edge of the page). If you choose Position in the Vertical section, the drop-down box displays, and you can select from Top, Bottom, or Center of the page. In the Relative To drop-down boxes, you can select whether to position the frame relative to the Margin, Page, Paragraph, or Column.

You can specify whether the frame should move with the paragraph that you inserted the frame into, or whether the frame should be locked to a location on the page by choosing either the Move with Text or the Lock Anchor option.

The Text Wrapping section of the Frame dialog box allows you to specify whether you want text to appear on the same lines as the frame. If you do, choose the Around option, or if you want text only above and below the frame, choose the None option. If you wrap text around the frame, you can specify the distance between the text and the frame in the appropriate Distance from Text boxes.

The Remove Frame button removes the frame but leaves the contents of the frame. If you want to delete both the frame and the contents, select the frame and press the Delete key.

Exercise 2: Resizing and moving the frame

1. Using the frame just created, click on the border to select the frame.
2. Place the mouse pointer over the side sizing handle and drag horizontally to change the width of the box.
3. Place the mouse pointer over the top sizing handle and drag vertically to change the width of the box.
4. Place the mouse pointer over the corner sizing arrow and drag diagonally to change both the width and height simultaneously.
5. Point the mouse pointer at the frame so that you see the positioning pointer and then click and drag the frame to a new location.
6. With the frame selected, choose Format Frame.
7. Change the Width and the Height by typing in a measurement.
8. Change the Horizontal and Vertical positions by typing in positions.
9. Select OK.

    The frame appears in the location and the size you specified.
10. Keep the document on your screen for use in the next exercise.

Objective 2: Adding Borders, Shading, and Captions to Frames

You can change the default border Word 6 uses to enclose a frame, add shading to a frame, and include a caption with a frame.

Borders

When you create a frame, Word 6 encloses it in a simple box border. You can change or remove the border by using the Borders toolbar. Simply click the Borders button [≡][↓] on the Formatting toolbar to display the Borders toolbar, which includes the options described in Table 8-1.

Table 8-1   The Borders Toolbar

OPTION	BUTTON	DESCRIPTION
Line Style	¾ pt ⎯⎯⎯⎯ [↓]	Lists available line styles.
Top Border	⬜	Applies the line to the top.
Bottom Border	⬜	Applies the line to the bottom.
Left Border	⬜	Applies the line to the left edge.
Right Border	⬜	Applies the line to the right edge.
Inside Border	⊞	Applies the border to the inside edge of the margin.
Outside Border	⊡	Applies the border to the outside edge of the margin.
No Border	⬚	Removes all borders.
Shading	⬜ Clear [↓]	Applies shading.

You can also choose Format Borders and Shading, activate the Borders tab, and make selections in the dialog box. (See Figure 8-4.)

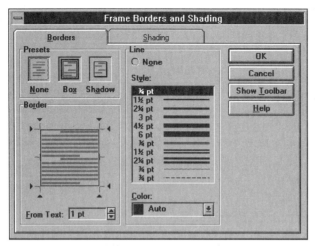

Figure 8-4 **The Borders tab of the Frame Borders and Shading dialog box**

To apply a border to a frame, first select the frame, then select a line style, and finally click the appropriate button to apply it.

Shading

You can also add shading to a frame. Note, however, that graphics (which you will learn to use in Objective 3) inserted into a frame cannot be shaded. If the frame contains both text and a graphic, only the text will be shaded.

You can click the Shading button ☐ **Clear** ⬇ on the Borders toolbar or you can choose Format Borders and Shading and click the Shading tab. (See Figure 8-5.)

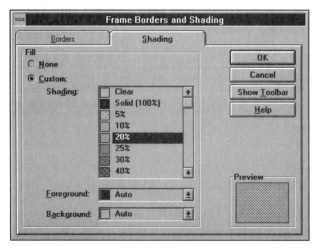

Figure 8-5 **The Shading tab of the Frame Borders and Shading dialog box**

Punched Cards: From Weaving to Computers

In the early 1800s, Joseph-Marie Jacquard invented a loom for weaving fabric that used punched cards. The cards were punched and hooked together to make patterns as the fabric was woven. The punched cards fed the right colors of thread through the holes.

In the mid 1800s, Charles Babbage invented a machine called the Analytical Engine. The machine was to follow instructions fed to it on punched cards. The machine was so complex for the technology of the time that it was never finished; however, Babbage and Lady Augusta Ada Byron, the Countess of Lovelace, recorded their efforts and thoughts on programmable machines.

In 1890 Herman Hollerith constructed an electro-mechanical machine to help tabulate the census of the United States. Hollerith's Tabulating Machine used punched cards. The cards allowed electricity to pass through the holes, turning on motors which moved the counters which tabulated the totals for the census.

Contemporary computers use the binary numbering system because it represents the electrical states on and off with the digits 0 and 1. It's only in the last 15 to 20 years that punched cards have been replaced by other means of inputting data and programs into computers, but the concept is actually the same.

Captions

You can add captions to frames to explain their contents. The caption becomes part of the frame and moves with the frame if you change its location. To add a caption, select the contents of the frame, and then choose Insert Caption. The Caption dialog box displays. (See Figure 8-6.)

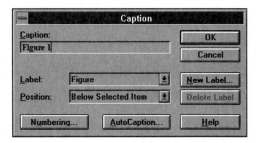

Figure 8-6   The Caption dialog box

In the Caption section, you can type the desired text after the label Figure 1. To change to a different label, either choose one from the Label drop-down box, or click the New Label button and type in a new one. You can change the numbering style of the captions by clicking the Numbering button.

You can place the caption either Below the Selected Item or Above the Selected Item in the Position drop-down box.

Objective 3: Inserting Graphics

You can easily insert graphics into your Word 6 documents. Graphics can be drawings you create in another application, drawings you purchase such as clip art, or images that are scanned. Word 6 can bring in most of the common graphic file formats such as PCX, BMP, WMF, TIF, or GIF.

You can insert a graphic into a frame, by itself into a document, or copy it from the clipboard. To insert a graphic into a frame, simply create a frame, select it, and then choose Insert Picture. To insert a graphic into a document but not in a frame, you place the insertion point where you want the graphic to appear and choose Insert Picture. The Insert Picture dialog box displays. (See Figure 8-7.)

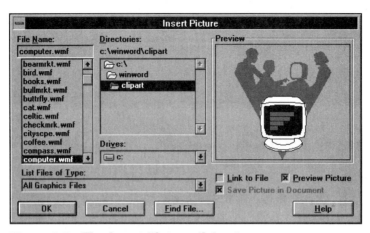

Figure 8-7 **The Insert Picture dialog box**

In the File Name section, you must type or select the name of the graphic file and then select the correct directory in the Directories section, along with the correct drive in the Drives section. If the Preview Picture check box is selected, Word displays the selected image. If you want to keep the size of the current file from getting too large, you can store a link to a graphic, rather than storing the entire image, by selecting Link to File.

If you have an image in another Windows application that you want to use in Word 6, simply open the other application and copy the graphic to the Windows clipboard. Then open Word 6, position the insertion point where you want the image to appear, and choose Edit Paste.

Exercise 3: Adding a graphic to a document

In this exercise, you add a graphic to a document.

1. Open a new document.
2. Choose Insert Picture.
3. In the Insert Picture dialog box, select a graphic image. Change the drive or directory as needed.
4. Choose OK.

   The graphic appears at the top of the document.
5. Keep the document open for use in the next exercise.

Once you have placed a graphic in a document, you can size, crop, and scale it using the mouse or the Picture dialog box. To modify a graphic, you must first select it. Eight sizing handles appear when it is selected.

To size a graphic using the mouse, click and drag a corner handle to keep the image in proportion, or click and drag one of the middle handles to stretch the image out of proportion.

To crop the image using the mouse, hold down the Shift key while you drag the handles either inward to crop or outward to add white space. The mouse pointer changes to a cropping tool when you press the Shift key.

To size, crop, or scale the image using the Picture dialog box, choose Format Picture. The Picture dialog box displays. (See Figure 8-8.)

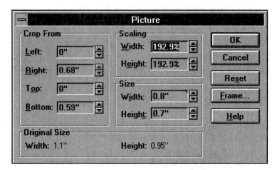

Figure 8-8　**The Picture dialog box**

You can crop the image by placing measurements in the Left, Right, Top, and Bottom text boxes. You can size the image by placing measurements in the Width and Height boxes, and you can scale by placing percentages in the Width and Height boxes. If you want to restore the graphic to its original settings, choose the Reset button.

If you want to move a graphic to a different location in the document, it must be in a frame. Then you can select the frame and drag it to the new location.

Exercise 4: Modifying a graphic

In this exercise, you size and crop the graphic image.

1. Using the image inserted into the document in the previous exercise, select the image by clicking on it with the mouse pointer.
2. Drag the corner handles outward to increase the size of the graphic proportionally.
3. Hold down the Shift key and drag a handle inwards to crop the graphic.
4. Close the file without saving.

Objective 4: Drawing Objects

You can draw new objects and edit drawn objects by clicking on the Drawing button on the Standard toolbar to display the Drawing toolbar, which displays at the bottom of the screen between the Status bar and the horizontal scroll bar.

To draw an object, click the drawing tool button and draw the object. For example, to draw an rectangle, click the rectangle drawing tool. This allows you to draw one rectangle. If you want to draw several of the same object, double-click the button and the drawing tool stays in effect until you click another tool. For example, if you want to draw several rectangles, double-click the rectangle tool and you can draw as many as you wish.

After you select the drawing tool by clicking or double-clicking it, place the pointer where you want the object to appear and click the mouse. Move the mouse on the screen and click it again to create the object. For example, if you want to draw a line, click the mouse on the screen at one end of the line, move the mouse the desired length of the line, and click the mouse a second time. The Drawing toolbar contains the buttons shown in Table 8-2.

Table 8-2 **The Drawing Toolbar**

OPTION	BUTTON	DESCRIPTION
Line		Draws lines.
Rectangle		Draws rectangles.
Ellipse		Draws an ellipse.
Arc		Draws an arc.
Freeform		Draws freeform objects.
Textbox		Places text behind or in front of the text layer.
Callout		Explain items in an illustration.
Format Callout		Formats the callout.
Fill Color		Fills an object with color.
Line Color		Changes the line color.
Line Style		Changes the line style.
Select Drawing Objects		Selects the object.

continued

Table 8-2 continued

OPTION	BUTTON	DESCRIPTION
Bring to Front		Brings the selected image to the front.
Send to Back		Sends the selected image to the back.
Bring in Front of Text		Brings the object in front of the text layer.
Send Behind Text		Sends the object behind the text layer.
Group		Groups objects.
Ungroup		Ungroups objects.
Flip Horizontal		Flips the image horizontally.
Flip Vertical		Flips the image vertically.
Rotate Right		Rotates 90 degrees to right.
Reshape		Reshapes a freeform image.
Snap to Grid		Aligns objects on a grid.
Align Drawing Objects		Aligns objects.
Create Picture		Opens the picture editing window.
Insert Frame		Creates a frame.

Exercise 5: Using the drawing tools

In this exercise, you create drawn objects.

1. Open a new document.
2. Choose View Page Layout.
3. Click the Drawing button on the Standard toolbar.
4. Click the Line button and draw a line.
5. Click several other drawing tools and draw the objects.
   The objects appear on the screen.
6. Close the document without saving it.

If you have not selected an object and choose Format Drawing Object, the Drawing Defaults dialog box displays. You can change the default settings for the line and fill styles for objects you will draw. (See Figure 8-9.)

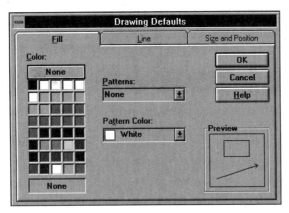

Figure 8-9 **The Drawing Defaults dialog box**

If you select an object and choose Format Drawing Object, the Drawing Object dialog box displays. You can change the selected object's size, location, fill pattern, and line color.

Object linking and embedding (OLE)

linking;
embedding

You can include objects created in other applications in Word 6 using *linking* and *embedding*. The main difference between the two is where the data is stored. Embedded objects become part of the Word 6 document. Linked objects are stored in the original file. Word 6 stores only the location of the original or source file and displays a representation of the linked data in the Word document.

To embed an object, position the insertion point where you want the object to appear and choose Insert Object. In the Object dialog box, choose the Create New tab, and select the type of object you want to create, or choose Create From File tab to embed an existing file.

To create a link from a Word 6 document to a file in another application, that application must support dynamic data exchange (DDE) or object linking and embedding (OLE). (Check the documentation for that application to determine if it does.) Open the application where the source file is located and save the file. Then select the information in the source file, and copy it to the clipboard. Activate Word 6 with the document that you want to link as the active document. Position the insertion point where you want the information and choose Edit Paste Special. In the Paste Special dialog box, click the Paste Link and select the correct format in the As list box.

To control how Word 6 updates links, choose Edit Links. In the Links dialog box, you can choose Automatic to have the link updated every time the source file changes, or you can choose Manual to have it updated only when you make it happen.

Objective 5: Using WordArt

WordArt is one of several supplementary applications included with Microsoft Word 6 for Windows. These applications use object linking and embedding (OLE) to create and add objects to a Word 6 document. After you insert an object, you can put it in a frame, size it, move it, and edit it. You can fit text into a variety of shapes and give text a variety of effects.

Choose Insert Object, and choose the Create New tab. In the Object Type section of the dialog box, choose Microsoft WordArt 2.0. (See Figure 8-10.)

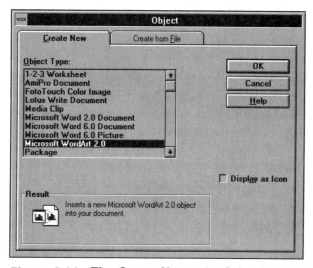

Figure 8-10 **The Create New tab of the Object dialog box**

Word 6 displays the WordArt toolbar, a text entry box, and menu bar. The options in the toolbar are shown in Table 8-3.

Table 8-3 **The WordArt Toolbar**

OPTION	BUTTON	DESCRIPTION
Line and Shape	— Plain Text	Displays containers to put text into.
Font	Times New Roman	Changes the font.
Font Size	10	Changes the font size.
Bold	B	Makes the selection bold.
Italic	I	Makes the selection italic.
Even Height	Ee	Makes the entire selection the same height.

continued

Table 8-3 continued

OPTION	BUTTON	DESCRIPTION
Flip		Flips the selection.
Stretch		Stretches the selection.
Alignment		Changes the alignment of the selection.
Character Spacing		Changes the spacing of the selection.
Special Effects		Provides special effects.
Shading		Adds shading to the selection.
Shadow		Adds a shadow to the selection.
Border		Add a border to the selection.

You simply type the text you want to format into the text entry box, and then select the text effects from the toolbar. When you are finished formatting the text, click the mouse in the Word document. The text is inserted into the document, and you are returned to Word 6. If you want to edit the formatted text, double-click on the text.

Exercise 6: Using WordArt

In this exercise, you use WordArt to format text.

1. Open a document.
2. Choose Insert Object.
3. In the Object dialog box, choose the Create New tab.
4. In the Object Type section, select Microsoft WordArt 2.0.
5. Choose OK.
6. In the text entry box, type your first and last name.
7. Click the Line and Shape button.
8. From the Line and Shape box, select various shapes: Arch Up, Arch Down, Slant up, Triangle, and others.
9. Choose other formatting buttons.

10. When you are finished formatting, click outside the box in your document.

    You are returned to Word 6.

11. Close the document without saving.

Objective 6: Creating a Dropped Cap

You can format the first character of a paragraph to be a large initial or dropped capital letter. You can choose to have a single letter or a word as a dropped cap. Word places the letter or the word in a frame, and the text that follows wraps beside the frame.

To make a letter into a dropped cap, position the insertion point in the paragraph where you want the dropped cap to appear and choose Format Drop Cap. The Drop Cap dialog box appears. (See Figure 8-11.)

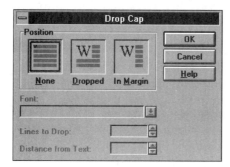

Figure 8-11   **The Drop Cap dialog box**

In the Position section, choose either Dropped or In Margin. In the Font box, select a font. For the best results, choose a TrueType font. In the Lines to Drop box, you can specify the height of the letter, and in the Distance from Text box, you can specify the amount of space you want between the dropped capital letter and the following text in the paragraph.

When you complete your selections in the dialog box, Word 6 asks if you want to switch to page layout to view the dropped cap.

If you select any part of the first word before choosing Format Drop Cap, Word 6 makes the entire first word large.

If you want to remove the drop cap effect, move the insertion point into the paragraph, and choose Format Drop Cap. In the Drop Cap dialog box, choose None.

Chapter Summary

In this chapter, you learned to add frames to documents that can hold text, graphics, or special characters and to add borders, shading, and captions to the frames. You learned to insert predrawn graphics and to draw your own. You also learned about two features to enhance text, WordArt and the Drop Cap command.

Review Questions

True/False Questions

_____ 1. You can create an empty frame and add text or graphics to it, or you can select an item and place it in a frame.

_____ 2. When you create a frame, Word 6 encloses it in a simple box border.

_____ 3. You can also add shading to a frame; however, text inserted into a frame cannot be shaded. If the frame contains both text and a graphic, only the graphic will be shaded.

_____ 4. Embedded objects become part of the Word 6 document.

_____ 5. Linked objects are stored in the source file, and Word 6 stores only the location of the source file but displays a representation of the linked data.

Multiple Choice Questions

_____ 6. You can

    A. insert a graphic into a frame.

    B. insert a graphic by itself into a document.

    C. copy a graphic from the clipboard.

    D. All of the above.

_____ 7. If you select any part of the first word before choosing Format Drop Cap, Word 6 will

    A. make the entire first word large.

    B. remove the drop cap effect.

    C. make the first letter large.

    D. make the selected text large.

_____ 8. To draw an object, using Word 6
      A. buy a drawing program.
      B. click the drawing tool button and draw the object.
      C. choose Insert Drawing.
      D. Both B and C.

_____ 9. Graphics can be
      A. drawings you create in another application.
      B. drawings you purchase, such as clip art.
      C. images that are scanned.
      D. All of the above.

_____ 10. You can edit a graphic image by
      A. sizing it.
      B. cropping it.
      C. scaling it.
      D. All of the above.

Fill-in-the-Blank Questions

11. _____ are containers for text or graphics in Word 6.
12. A(n) _____ _____ is a large initial letter.
13. You can add _____ to frames to explain their contents.
14. You can fit text into a variety of shapes and give text a variety of effects using _____.
15. If you want to move or resize the frame, you must _____ the frame.

Acumen-Building Activities

Quick Projects

Project 1: Adding Graphics to a Document

1. Open the DRIVE.DOC file created in Quick Project 1 in Chapter 2.
2. Place the insertion point in the second paragraph.
3. Insert a graphic that compliments the contents of this document.
4. Print the document.
5. Save the file as DRIVEGR.DOC.

Project 2: Editing Graphics

1. Open the DRIVEGR.DOC file created in Quick Project 1 in this chapter.
2. Place the graphic you inserted in a frame if it isn't already in one.
3. Change the frame border.
4. Add a caption to the frame.
5. Move the graphic to the third paragraph.
6. Print the document.
7. Close the file without saving.

Project 3: Creating a Dropped Cap

1. Open the BOOK.DOC file created in Quick Project 3 in Chapter 2.
2. Make the "M" in Microsoft, which is the first word in the first paragraph, a dropped cap.
3. Print the document.
4. Close the file without saving.
5. Reopen the document named BOOK.DOC.
6. Make the entire word "Microsoft," which is the first word in the first paragraph, a large initial word.
7. Print the document.
8. Close the file without saving.

Project 4: Using Draw

1. Open a new document.
2. Choose the Drawing button on the Standard toolbar.
3. Create a drawing of your choosing.
4. Print the document.
5. Save the file as DRAWING.DOC.

In-Depth Projects

Project 1: Creating a Letterhead

1. Open a new document.
2. Create a letterhead for yourself—either your business or your personal address.
3. Use any formatting necessary—font changes, centering, etc.
4. Print the letterhead.
5. Create an envelope.
6. Print the envelope.
7. Add a graphic image to the letterhead—either bring in an existing graphic or create one using the Drawing feature.

8. Print the letterhead.
9. Save the file as LHEAD2.DOC.

Project 2: Creating a Logo

1. Open a new document.
2. Create a logo for your company or school using the WordArt feature to format the text.
3. Print the logo.
4. Save it as LOGO.DOC.

CASE STUDIES

 **Coffee-On-The-Go:**   **Creating a Cover Page**

In this chapter, you learned to use graphics and lines. You will apply those skills to creating a cover page for the business plan for Coffee-On-The-Go.

1. Open the Plan1 file.
2. Move the cursor to the beginning of the document.
3. Create a page break and move up into the new first page.
4. Create a title page for the business plan and do the following:

   Create a border around the edge of the page.

   Center, boldface, and increase the font size of the text: Coffee-On-The-Go.

   Center and increase the font size of the text: Business Proposal.

   If you have a graphic of a steaming cup of coffee available, retrieve it onto the cover page and center it.

   Center the words: Submitted by: your name.

   Center the words: Date: the current date.

   Suppress the page number.
5. Save the entire file as Plan1.
6. Print only the title page.

CASE STUDIES

 **Videos West:** **Adding Lines and Graphics**

In this chapter, you inserted lines and graphics into a document. You will use the line feature to create a small form.

1. Open a new document.
2. Using lines and borders, create a form for the customer to fill out to receive a catalog.
3. The form should include the customer's name, address, city, state, zip code, and phone number.
4. The form should also include the company name, address, and phone number: Videos West, 1121 Second Ave, Fairbanks, Alaska 99701 800-344-1234.
5. Retrieve an appropriate graphic to create a logo on the form for the business.
6. Save the form as VCR3.
7. Print the form.

Chapter 9

Creating a Mail Merge

Key Terms

TERM	DEFINITION
Mail Merge	combining source data with a form letter to personalize documents
Form Letter	a document that contains text and other items that remain the same for each letter
Data Source	the information that changes in each letter
Merge Fields	fields that instruct Word where to print information from the data source into the form letter
Fields	categories of data in the data source
Header Row	first row of the data source file which lists the names of the fields
Record	a row of the data that produces a unique form letter
Query	a set of instructions describing the data records you want from the data source
Sort Keys	fields upon which you base a sort

mail merge;
form letter;
data source

In this chapter you learn how to personalize letters, envelopes, and mailing labels using the mail merge feature. To create a *mail merge,* you must create a form letter and a data source. The *form letter* is a document that contains text that remains the same for each letter. The *data source* is the information that changes in each letter. A merge in Word 6 has three steps: creating a form letter, creating a data source, and merging the two together. In this chapter, you learn to do all three steps.

Objective 1: Creating a Form Letter

merge fields

The first step of the merge process is to create a form letter or a main document. This document contains text that remains the same for each letter and will contain the *merge fields*, which tell Word where to print information from the data source into the form letter.

To start the merge process, you choose Tools Mail Merge. The Mail Merge Helper dialog box displays, showing you the three-step process. (See Figure 9-1.)

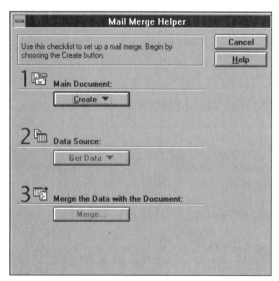

Figure 9-1   **The Mail Merge Helper dialog box**

Click the Create button. A drop-down list displays the four types of merge documents: Form Letters, Mailing Labels, Envelopes, and Catalog. After selecting the document type, you must choose to make the active window the main document or create a new main document. If you start from a new document, simply choose to make the active window the main document. Word then displays the type of merge and the name of the main document under the Create button in the Mail Merge Helper dialog box.

Exercise 1: Creating the main document

1. Open a new document.
2. Choose Tools Mail Merge.
3. In the Mail Merge Helper dialog box, click the Create button.
4. Choose Form Letters from the drop-down list box.
5. Click the Activate Window in the prompt box.

   The Mail Merge Helper dialog box displays the type of merge and the name of the file under the Create button.
6. Keep the Mail Merge Helper on the screen for use in the next exercise.

Objective 2: Specifying the Data Source

You actually type the form letter after you create the data source. Therefore, after creating the main document, you complete the second step of the process, which is to create the data source. The data source contains the information that will change in each letter. You can open an existing data source file, or you can create a new one.

fields

header row

record

When you create a data source file, Word 6 stores the information in a table. The columns in the table are the *fields* or categories of data. The first row of the table lists the names of the categories or fields and is called the *header row* in Word 6. The data to be merged is stored in rows under the header row. When you merge the form letter and the source data file, each row or *record* produces a unique form letter.

For example, if you want to create a customer mailing list, you would start by identifying all the information you should put in the source file about each person. All the categories of data such as name and address are the fields or columns in the table. You need to give each field a name, and that name appears in the header row. Each row under the header row is used to input the information about one customer, so each row becomes a record.

It is a good idea to put some thought into designing your data source file so that you can easily access your data. For example, inputting the name Mr. John Smith in a single Name field will make your letters appear awkward because you will not be able to use parts of his name. If you divide up the data into small fields, and place Mr. in a Title field, John in a FirstName field, and Smith in a LastName field, you can use the individual fields in any way you want.

To create a data source file, continue with the second step in the Mail Merge Helper dialog box by clicking the Get Data button. The drop-down box displays the choices: Create Data Source, Open Data Source, and Header Options. Choose Create Data Source, and Word displays the Create Data Source dialog box. (See Figure 9-2.)

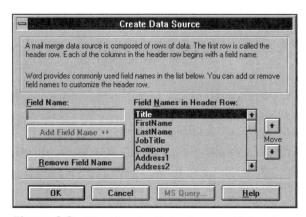

Figure 9-2   The Create Data Source dialog box

You use the Create Data Source dialog box to create the field names for the data source, and Word 6 provides a list of common field names in the Field Names in Header Row list box. As you look through the list and find fields that do not apply, highlight the field name in the Field Names in Header Row list box and click the Remove Field Name button. If you need to include fields that are not in the list, type the field name in the Field Name text box and click the Add Field Name button. When you type field names, you cannot include spaces.

If you want to change the order of the field names, highlight the field you want to move and click the up or down Move arrows.

When you are finished creating the list of field names, click OK. Word displays the Save Data Source dialog box.

After you type a name for the file in the File Name text box and click the OK button, Word displays a prompt box asking if you want to Edit Data Source or Edit Main Document. You can do either activity at this point, that is, create the letter or type the data into the data source.

Exercise 2: Creating a data source file

In this exercise, you create a data source file.

1. Continuing with the merge from Exercise 1, choose the Get Data button.
2. Choose Create Data Source.
3. In the Field Names in Header Row list box in the Create Data Source dialog box, highlight Address2.
4. Choose the Remove Field Name button.
5. Repeat steps 3 and 4 to remove the JobTitle, Company, Country, and WorkPhone fields.
6. In the Field Name text box, type Age.
7. Click the Add Field Name button.
8. Repeat steps 6 and 7 to add a field named Sex.
9. Highlight Age and use the Move up arrow to place it after the LastName field.
10. Choose OK.
11. In the Save Data Source dialog box, type Customer in the File Name text box.
12. Choose OK.
13. In the prompt box, choose the Edit Data Source button.
14. Keep the file on-screen for use in the next exercise.

Objective 3: Adding Records to the Data Source

Once you choose to Edit Data Source, Word 6 displays the Data Form dialog box. (See Figure 9-3.) You use the dialog box to enter the data into the data source. Make sure that you fill in each field correctly.

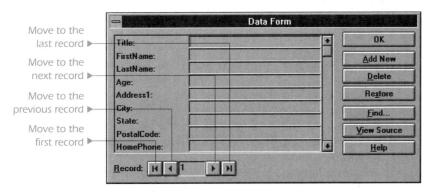

Figure 9-3 **The Data Form dialog box**

Language Dictionary

When checking spelling in a document, you can select the language that you want Word 6 to use. Simply choose Tools Language. The Language dialog box provides the language options. (See figure below.) If the language you desire is not available, you may need to load it with the Setup feature.

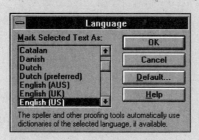

The Language dialog box

You can move from field to field by clicking the mouse in the text boxes, or by pressing the Enter or Tab keys to move forward and the Shift + Tab key combination to move backward. Use the scroll bar to see all the data fields. When you have entered all the data for the record, choose the Add New button to display a blank form for the next record.

To delete the current record, press the Delete button. To cancel changes made to the current record, click the Restore button. To find data in a field, choose the Find button.

You can move forward or backward through the records by using the Record arrow buttons, or by typing the record number in the box. You can move to the previous or next record, or you can move to the first or last record in the table.

If you click the View Source button, Word 6 displays the data table. (See Figure 9-4.)

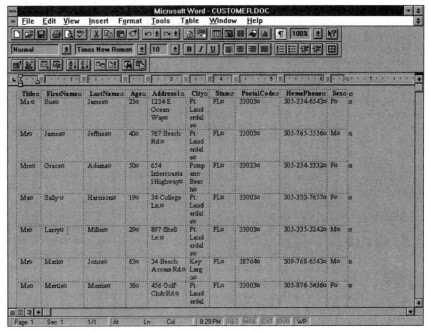

Figure 9-4   **The records displayed as a table**

Exercise 3: Adding records to the data form

In this exercise, you add records in the Data Form dialog box.

1. Type the following record, pressing ⌐ ENTER after each field:

   ```
   Title        Ms
   FirstName    Sue
   LastName     James
   Age          25
   Address1     1234 E. Ocean Way
   City         Ft. Lauderdale
   State        FL
   PostalCode   33003
   HomePhone    305-334-6543
   Sex          F
   ```

2. Click the Add New button.

3. Repeat steps 1 and 2 to input the following records:

```
Title        Mr                    Title        Mrs
FirstName    James                 FirstName    Grace
LastName     Jeffries              LastName     Adams
Age          40                    Age          50
Address1     767 Beach Rd.         Address1     654 Intercostal Highway
City         Ft. Lauderdale        City         Pompano Beach
State        FL                    State        FL
PostalCode   33003                 PostalCode   33023
HomePhone    305-765-5556          HomePhone    305-234-3332
Sex          M                     Sex          F

Title        Ms                    Title        Mr
FirstName    Sally                 FirstName    Larry
LastName     Harrison              LastName     Miller
Age          19                    Age          29
Address1     34 College Ln.        Address1     897 Shell Ln
City         Ft. Lauderdale        City         Ft. Lauderdale
State        FL                    State        FL
PostalCode   33003                 PostalCode   33003
HomePhone    305-333-7657          HomePhone    305-335-3242
Sex          F                     Sex          M

Title        Mr                    Title        Ms
FirstName    Mark                  FirstName    Mertle
LastName     Jones                 LastName     Morris
Age          63                    Age          56
Address1     34 Beach Access Rd.   Address1     456 Golf Club Rd.
City         Key Largo             City         Ft. Lauderdale
State        FL                    State        FL
PostalCode   38764                 PostalCode   33003
HomePhone    309-768-6543          HomePhone    305-876-5436
Sex          M                     Sex          F

Title        Mr
FirstName    Henry
LastName     Hamilton
Age          36
Address1     987 Bay View
City         Ft. Lauderdale
State        FL
PostalCode   33003
HomePhone    305-234-9876
Sex          M
```

4. Click the View Source button.

The table is displayed on the screen.

5. Keep the file active for use in the next exercise.

Using the Database toolbar

When you choose the View Source button, Word 6 displays the entire data source table and displays the Database toolbar. (See Figure 9-5.) You can use the Database toolbar to add, edit, and sort records. (See Table 9-1.)

Figure 9-5   **The Database toolbar**

Table 9-1   **The Database toolbar**

OPTION	BUTTON	DESCRIPTION
Data Form		Opens the Data Form dialog box.
Manage Fields		Opens the Manage Fields dialog box.
Add New Record		Adds a Record to the data source.
Delete Record		Deletes selected record from data source
Sort Ascending		Sorts on one field in ascending order.
Sort Descending		Sorts on one field in descending order.
Insert Database		Inserts records from another data source.
Update Fields		Updates and displays data.
Find Record		Displays the Find in Field dialog box.
Mail Merge Main Document		Makes the main document active.

Exercise 4: Using the Database toolbar to add records

In this exercise, you add more records to the data source using the Database toolbar.

1. Continuing with the data source created, click the Add New Record button .

2. Type the following record:

Title	Ms
FirstName	Tiffany
LastName	Williams
Age	17
Address1	Sunset Ave.
City	Ft. Lauderdale
State	FL
PostalCode	33003
HomePhone	305-334-5436
Sex	F

3. Click the Data Form button 🖼.

4. In the Data Form dialog box, choose OK.

5. Click the Mail Merge Main Document button 🖼.

   The main document is displayed.

6. Keep the file on the screen for use in the next exercise.

Objective 4: Writing the Form Letter

You can now create the form letter that you will later merge with the data source. The form letter or main document contains the text that will not change from letter to letter and the merge codes for the data that will change from letter to letter.

You simply type and edit the text and graphics that you want to appear in each letter. When you come to a place such as the inside address or the salutation that will change in each letter, you insert the merge codes, making sure to include proper spacing and punctuation. By default, Word 6 displays the merge codes within chevrons (<< >>). These are special characters that Word inserts and cannot be typed by the user. (See Figure 9-6.)

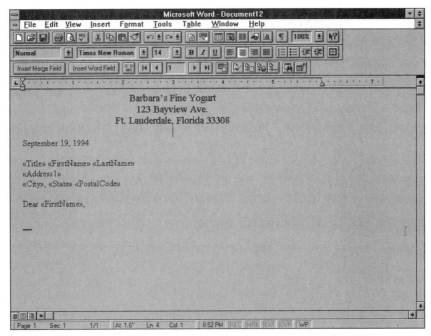

Figure 9-6 **The merge codes as placed in chevrons by Word 6**

Word 6 displays the Mail Merge toolbar in the main document window, which helps you create the form letter. (See Table 9-2.)

Table 9-2 **The Mail Merge toolbar**

OPTION	BUTTON	DESCRIPTION
Insert Mail Merge Field	Insert Merge Field	Displays a drop-down box of the fields in the data source.
Insert Word Field	Insert Word Field	Displays a drop-down box of Word fields.
View Merged Data	«»ABC	Displays merged data instead of field codes.
First Record	◀	Displays the first record instead of field codes.
Previous Record	◀	Displays the previous record instead of field codes.

continued

Table 9-2 continued

OPTION	BUTTON	DESCRIPTION
Go to Record	`1`	Displays a specific record.
Next Record	▶	Displays the next record instead of field codes.
Last Record	▶❙	Displays the last record instead of field codes.
Mail Merge Helper		Displays the Mail Merge Helper.
Check for Errors		Checks main document and data source for field name errors.
Merge to New Document		Merges to a document.
Merge to Printer		Opens the Print dialog box.
Mail Merge		Opens the Merge dialog box.
Find Record		Finds and previews a record.
Edit Data Source		Displays the Data From dialog box.

Exercise 5: Creating the form letter

In this exercise, you create a form letter.

1. In the main document window, type

   Barbara's Fine Yogurt

   123 Bayview Ave.

   Ft. Lauderdale, Florida 33308

2. Increase the font size to 14 and center the text to create a letterhead.
3. Press ⏎ ENTER twice.
4. Return to normal font size and alignment.
5. Choose Insert Date and Time, select a date option from the Available Formats section of the Date and Time dialog box, and click OK.
6. Press ⏎ ENTER twice.
7. Click the Insert Merge Field button `Insert Merge Field`.
8. Select Title from the drop-down box.
9. Press the spacebar.
10. Click the Insert Merge Field button `Insert Merge Field`.
11. Select FirstName from the drop-down box.

12. Press the spacebar.
13. Click the Insert Merge Field button Insert Merge Field .
14. Select LastName from the drop-down box and press ⏎ ENTER .
15. Click the Insert Merge Field button Insert Merge Field .
16. Select Address1 from the drop-down box and press ⏎ ENTER .
17. Click the Insert Merge Field button Insert Merge Field .
18. Select City from the drop-down box, type a comma, and press the spacebar.
19. Click the Insert Merge Field button Insert Merge Field .
20. Select State from the drop-down box and press the spacebar.
21. Click the Insert Merge Field button Insert Merge Field .
22. Select PostalCode from the drop-down box and press ⏎ ENTER twice.
23. Type Dear and press the spacebar.
24. Click the Insert Merge Field button Insert Merge Field .
25. Select FirstName from the drop-down box, type a comma, and press ⏎ ENTER twice.
26. Type the following text:

   This is an invitation from your friends at Barbara's Fine Yogurt to our most valuable customers.

27. Press the spacebar after the period.
28. Click the Insert Merge Field button Insert Merge Field .
29. Select FirstName from the drop-down box, type a comma, and press the spacebar.
30. Type the rest of the letter:

   We desire your opinion on the latest flavor to be developed in our kitchens, so we are asking you to take part in our market survey. As a person who already greatly enjoys our yogurt, we think that your opinion is of great value.

   Simply bring this letter to your local Barbara's Fine Yogurt, and ask to be part of the survey. After you sample the new flavor, you will be given a survey form to fill out. Because we realize that your time is valuable, you will be given a coupon for one free quart of any flavor yogurt.

31. Press ⏎ ENTER three times and type Sincerely,.
32. Press ⏎ ENTER four times and type your name. (See Figure 9-7.)

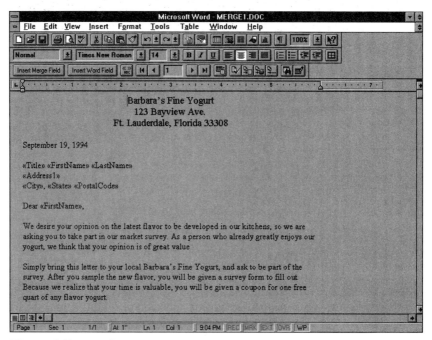

Figure 9-7 **The form letter with the merge codes**

33. Choose File Save As and give it the name Merge1.

34. Keep the document on the screen for use in the next exercise.

Objective 5: Merging the Documents

Once both documents are created, you can merge them together. You can merge single records or all records with the form letter, and you can merge to the printer or to another file.

Make the main document the active window, and click the View Merged Data button. Word displays the information from the first record in the data source in the form letter. You can choose to view other records in the form letter by clicking the First Record button, the Previous Record button, the Go to Record button, the Next Record button, and the Last Record button. You can print only the document previewed on the screen by choosing File Print.

To merge all the records with the form letter, you have two options. You can either merge the letters and data source to a separate file so that you can see every letter by clicking the Merge to New Document button [image], or you can merge the letters and the data source to the printer by clicking the Merge to Printer button [image].

Exercise 6: Merging all the letters to the printer

In this exercise, you merge all the records in the data source with the form letter and send the output to the printer.

1. With the main document active, click the Merge to Printer button [image].
2. In the Print box, choose OK.
3. Keep the document on the screen for use in the next exercise.

Objective 6: Editing the Data Source and the Form Letter

You will need to make changes to both the records in the data source and to the form letter from time to time. You edit the form letter just as you would any document you created using Word 6.

To change the contents of a field, simply move the insertion point to the field, use the Delete or Backspace keys, and type in the desired information. You edit the data source by using the Database toolbar. You can add fields, rename fields, add records, delete records, sort records, find records, and bring in data from another file.

Objective 7: Creating Envelopes

After you have created all the form letters, you will want to merge the names and addresses to envelopes or labels. You can create envelopes by creating another main document and choosing to create envelopes.

Start from a new document and choose Tools Mail Merge. From the Mail Merge Helper, choose the Create button, and from the drop-down list, choose Envelopes. (See Figure 9-8.) When Word presents you with the prompt box, choose the Active Window button.

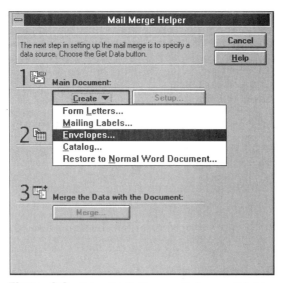

Figure 9-8   **The Mail Merge Helper with Envelopes highlighted**

In the Mail Merge Helper, you are ready to specify a data source. Because you want the envelopes to use the same data as the letters, you do not want to create a new data source file. Choose the Get Data button, and from the drop-down box, select Open Data Source. The Open Data Source dialog box displays, and you must select the data file.

Word displays another prompt box asking if you want to create the main document, in other words, the envelopes. Click the Set Up Main Document button. The Envelope Options dialog box displays. (See Figure 9.9.)

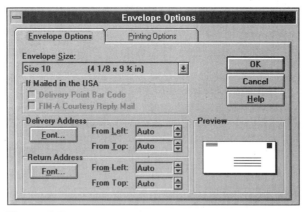

Figure 9-9   **The Envelope Options tab of the Envelope Options dialog box**

On the Envelope Options tab, you must select an envelope size from the Envelope Size drop-down list. You can change the fonts and positions of the Delivery and Return addresses, and you can preview the changes in the Preview section.

**What Is The
Information Highway?**

When people talk about a future society linked by tele-communications systems that circle the globe, providing text, sound, and video images at the speed of light, they usually call it the Information Highway. In reality, a highway called the Internet already exists.

The Internet began in 1969 as a single network called ARPANET. Developed by the Advanced Research Projects Agency of the U.S. Department of Defense, ARPANET was designed to allow researchers to share major hardware and software resources located at remote computer centers.

As other telecommunication networks developed throughout the 1970s and 1980s, it became advantageous to link them to the Internet. By 1990, ARPANET was replaced by the National Science Foundation Network, NFSNET.

Currently NSFNET operates as a high-speed backbone for the Internet, a superhighway accessed by slower, regional networks. The Internet consists of over 5000 connected networks extending to all seven continents. Between five and ten million people use the Internet directly, and over fifteen million users can exchange messages between the Internet and interconnecting networks.

The Internet provides various ways of sending messages from sending E-mail to being part of a discussion group. It provides a user remote login at a distant computer, and it provides file transfer from one machine to another.

On the Printing Options tab, you will have various options, based on the selected printer. Once you have finished making any selections in the Envelope Options dialog box, you are presented with the Envelope Address dialog box. (See Figure 9-10.)

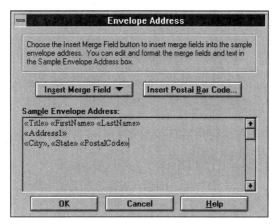

Figure 9-10 **The Envelope Address dialog box**

In the Envelope Address dialog box, you choose the appropriate merge fields to appear on the envelope by clicking the Insert Merge Field button and selecting the field from the drop-down box. Remember to include spaces and punctuation as you did in the form letter. If you want to insert the POSTNET bar code, click the Insert Postal Bar Code button.

After creating the address in the Envelope Address dialog box, click OK and you are returned to the Mail Merge Helper. Choose Edit under the Main Document, and Word displays the envelope. If a return address is displayed and you have preprinted envelopes, you can delete the return address.

Simply click the Merge to Printer button [icon] to print the envelopes.

Exercise 7: Merging envelopes

In this exercise, you merge the data source with envelopes.

1. Open a new document.
2. Choose Tools Mail Merge.
3. In the Mail Merge Helper, click the Create button.
4. From the drop-down list, choose Envelopes.
5. From the prompt box, click the Active Window button.
6. In the Mail Merge Helper, click the Get Data button.
7. From the drop-down list, choose Open Data Source.

8. From the Open Data Source dialog box, select the CUSTOMER.DOC file and click OK.

9. From the prompt box, click the Set Up Main Document.

10. On the Envelope Options tab of the Envelope Options dialog box, select the correct envelope size from the Envelope Size drop-down list.

11. Click the OK button to accept the defaults.

12. In the Envelope Address dialog box, click the Insert Merge Field button, select Title from the drop-down list, and press the spacebar.

13. Click the Insert Merge Field button, select the FirstName field, and press the spacebar.

14. Click the Insert Merge Field button, select the LastName field, and press ⏎ ENTER.

15. Click the Insert Merge Field button, select the Address1 field, and press ⏎ ENTER.

16. Click the Insert Merge Field button, select the City field, type a comma, and press the spacebar.

17. Click the Insert Merge Field button, select the State field, and press the spacebar.

18. Click the Insert Merge Field button and select the PostalCode field.

19. Click OK.

20. In the Mail Merge Helper dialog box, click the Edit button under the Main Document section and select Envelope.

21. From the Main Document choose the Merge to Printer button to print the envelopes.

22. Close the documents and save the envelope file as ENVELOPE.DOC.

Objective 8: Creating Mailing Labels

You can also create mailing labels rather than envelopes using the Mail Merge Helper, and the steps are similar.

Open a new document, and choose Tools Mail Merge. From the Mail Merge Helper, choose the Create button, and from the drop-down list, choose Mailing Labels.

When Word presents you with the prompt box, choose the Active Window button. In the Mail Merge Helper, you are ready to specify a data source. Because you want the labels to use the same data as the letters, you do not want to create a new data source file. Choose the Get Data button, and from the drop-down box, select Open Data Source. The Open Data Source dialog box displays, and you must select the data file.

Word displays another prompt box asking if you want to create the main document, in other words, the labels. Click the Set Up Main Document button. The Label Options dialog box displays. (See Figure 9-11.)

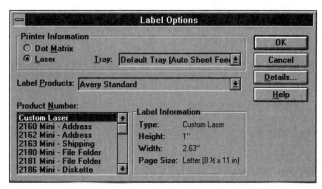

Figure 9-11   **The Label Options dialog box**

You must specify the type of printer in the Printer Information section, the brand of label in the Label Products section, and the type of label in the Product Number section.

Word opens the Create Labels dialog box, and you enter the fields on the label by choosing the Insert Merge Field button. After you have created the label and returned to the Mail Merge Helper dialog box, you can either choose Edit the main file and choose the Merge to Printer button on the toolbar, or you can choose the Merge button under Merge the Data with the Document on the Mail Merge Helper screen. (See Figure 9-12.)

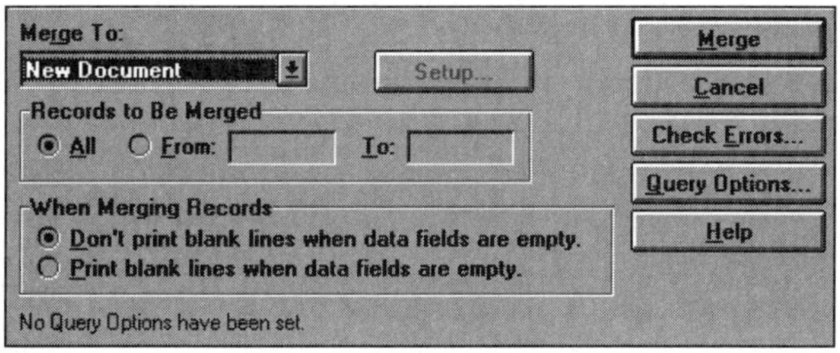

Figure 9-12   **The Merge dialog box**

Select the Merge To drop-down box to direct the labels to a New Document or the Printer, and then click the Merge button.

Using the Merge dialog box, you can merge only certain records using the From and To text boxes to designate record numbers. You can choose to Print blank lines when data fields are empty, or Don't print blank lines when data fields are empty. You can have Word check for field name errors by clicking the Check Errors button, and you can use the Query Options, which are described in Objective 9.

Objective 9: Querying the Data Source

By default, Word 6 merges all the records from the data source with the form letter, labels, or envelopes. At times you will want to specify a set of instructions for Word to follow to match records in the data source. These instructions are called a *query*.

For example, you might want to target sales to a certain age or gender, or you might want to send a letter to customers who owe more than a certain amount of money, or students who have a certain grade point. All these operations are possible in Word 6.

You can access the Query Options dialog box two ways: either choose the Query Options button in the Merge dialog box, or click the Query Options button in the Mail Merge Helper. Using either method displays the Query Options dialog box. (See Figure 9-13.)

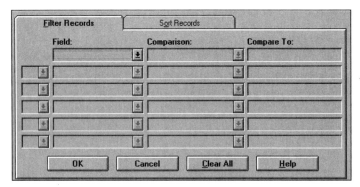

Figure 9-13 **The Filter Records tab of the Query Options dialog box**

On the Filter Records tab, you use the Field drop-down box to choose the field to set the field to query, such as State. In the Comparison drop-down box, you choose the operator, such as Equal To. In the Compare To text box, you type in the text or numbers that you want to compare with, such as Florida. In this example, only people who live in Florida would be part of the merge.

To start the query operation, click the OK button. To remove all previous queries, click the Clear All button. Note that there are several rows of drop-down boxes and text boxes. This allows you to create complex queries, using And and Or to combine them.

Exercise 8: Querying the data source for text

In this exercise, you query the data source for only the women.

1. Open the MERGE1.DOC file.
2. Choose Tools Mail Merge.

3. Choose the Query Options button in the Mail Merge Helper dialog box.
4. On the Filter Records tab, click the Field drop-down box.
5. Select Sex.
6. Click the Comparison drop-down box.
7. Select Equal To.
8. In the Compare To text box, type F.
9. Choose OK.
10. In the Mail Merge Helper, choose the Merge button.
11. In the Merge dialog box, choose to merge to the Printer or Merge to a New Document.

    Only records of female customers are merged.

Objective 10: Sorting Data Records

You can sort data records before you merge them with the form letter. This is a handy feature to use, for example, for bulk mailings that need to be grouped by zip code for the post office.

Sort keys   You can sort data on up to three sort keys. *Sort keys* are fields upon which you base the sort. For example, if you are going to sort a database by name, you would want to sort first by last name, then by first name within last name, and then by middle initial within first name and last name. All the Smiths would appear sorted by first name, and all the Sue Smiths would be further sorted on middle initial.

You can arrange records in alphabetic or numeric order, depending on the data in the field. You can sort in Ascending order, that is, numbers from smallest to largest and letters from A to Z. You can sort in Descending order, that is, numbers from largest to smallest and letters from Z to A.

Exercise 9: Sorting the data records

In this exercise, you sort the records in the data base.

1. With the main document active, choose Tools Mail Merge.
2. Choose the Query Options button.
3. Choose the Sort Records tab.
4. In the Sort By box, select LastName.
5. Choose Ascending.
6. In the Then by box, select FirstName.
7. Choose Ascending.
8. Choose OK.

   The data records are sorted by first name within last name.

Chapter Summary

In this chapter, you saw the power of the Mail Merge feature. You created a customer data source file and merged it with a letter similar to the letter created in Chapter 1. However, this letter was addressed to the specific person. You also created envelopes and labels for the letters. Finally, you were shown the query feature, allowing you to merge customers that met a certain condition.

Review Questions

True/False Questions

_____ 1. Combining source data with a form letter to personalize documents is known as a mail merge.

_____ 2. The first row of the data source file, which lists the names of the fields, is called the form letter.

_____ 3. The categories of data in the data source are called fields.

_____ 4. The Mail Merge Helper dialog box guides you through creating all types of merged documents.

_____ 5. Word 6 helps you find fields in the form letter that are not in the data source.

Multiple Choice Questions

_____ 6. You can merge data with

A. form letters.

B. mailing labels.

C. envelopes.

D. All of the above.

_____ 7. A form letter contains

A. a header row.

B. merge fields.

C. the data source.

D. All of the above.

_____ 8. A query consists of

    A. a field to query.

    B. an operator.

    C. text or numbers that you want to compare.

    D. All of the above.

_____ 9. The data source consists of

    A. envelope specifications.

    B. label specifications.

    C. fields.

    D. All of the above.

_____ 10. You can print merged letters to

    A. everyone in the data source.

    B. a single record.

    C. any group based on a query.

    D. All of the above.

Fill-in-the-Blank Questions

11. A document that contains text and other items that remain the same for each letter is called a(n) _____ _____.

12. The information that changes in each letter is stored in the _____ _____ file.

13. A(n) _____ is a row of data which produces a unique form letter.

14. _____ _____ instruct Word where to print information from the data source into the form letter.

15. A set of instructions describing the data records you want from the data source is called a(n) _____.

Acumen-Building Activities

Quick Projects

Project 1: Creating the Data Source

1. Create a data source that contains the following fields with the following records:

```
Title        Professor        Title        Chancellor
FirstName    John             FirstName    Mary
LastName     Jones            LastName     Hayes
Address1     123 First St.    Address1     876 Pine St.
City         Toledo           City         Toledo
State        Ohio             State        Ohio
PostalCode   45678            PostalCode   45678

Title        Dean             Title        Mr
FirstName    Jack             FirstName    Harry
LastName     Miller           LastName     Smith
Address1     547 Oak St.      Address1     789 Cleveland
City         Maumee           City         Toledo
State        Ohio             State        Ohio
PostalCode   45665            PostalCode   45678

Title        Ms               Title        Professor
FirstName    Sue              FirstName    Alice
LastName     Harper           LastName     Spencer
Address1     123 River St.    Address1     876 Lake St.
City         Toledo           City         Columbus
State        Ohio             State        Ohio
PostalCode   45678            PostalCode   45543
```

2. Name the file TEACHERS

Project 2: Creating a Form Letter

1. Create a letterhead for Toledo Community College.
2. Create a form letter that uses the fields from the TEACHERS data source for the inside address and salutation.
3. The body of the letter should consist of the following text:

```
As a member of the Toledo Community College Faculty
Association, you are invited to attend a pleasant and
informative breakfast on Sept. 1, 1995.

Former graduates of the college, local businesses, and
government agencies will all be represented on a panel
which will look at the issue of applied academics.

FirstName, we hope you will come support this effort.


Sincerely,
```

(Type your name)
4. Name the letter COLLEGE.

Project 3: Merging the Data Source and the Form Letter

1. Merge the data source, TEACHERS, and the form letter, COLLEGE.
2. Print one letter to each person.

Project 4: Creating Mailing Labels

1. Use the data source, TEACHERS.
2. Create one mailing label for each person in the data source.
3. Print the labels.

In-Depth Projects

Project 1: Using the Mail Merge in a Job Search

1. Create a data source of employers. You can include businesses, government agencies, or any other job source.
2. Create a form letter that consists of a letterhead for yourself and merge codes to create an inside address and the salutation.
3. Write a form letter that you would actually send to employers.
4. Merge the data source and the form letter and print the letters.
5. Create envelopes for the data source, printing the envelopes.

Project 2: Using the Query Option

1. Use the TEACHERS data source and the COLLEGE form letter created in the Quick Projects in this chapter.
2. Use the query feature to send the letter only to teachers who live in Toledo.
3. Print the letters.

CASE STUDIES

Coffee-On-The-Go: **Creating a Direct Mailing**

In this chapter, you learned to use the merge feature. You will use those skills to send a marketing letter to specific people.

1. Create the following database:

```
Joe Smith                    Dr. Mary Jones
Attorney-at-Law              Eugene Medical Plaza
123 Ninth St.                567 Second St.
Eugene, OR 97401             Eugene, OR 97401
```

```
Albert Barry               Sue Brown
U.S. Bank                  Center College
987 Pearl St.              123 First St.
Eugene, OR 97401           Eugene, OR 97403

Barb Swan                  Mary Barns
Attorney-At-Law            The Federal Building
456 Oak St.                876 Main St.
Eugene, OR 97401           Eugene, OR 97403

Norman White               George Williams
Investments Plus           Golds Travel Agency
651 Main St.               345 Oak St.
Eugene, OR 97401           Eugene, OR 97401

Dr. Will Peters            Henry Jones
Eugene Medical Plaza       The Federal Building
567 Second St.             876 Main St.
Eugene, OR 97401           Eugene, OR 97401
```

2. Save the database as Names.

3. Create a new document.

4. Create the following form letter:

   Create a letterhead for Coffee-On-The-Go which has an enlarged font. Include a graphic of a steaming cup of coffee if possible. The address is 700 Oak St., Eugene, OR 97401. Date the letter with the current date.

   Insert the correct codes to create an inside address to each person in the database.

   Individualize each letter by inserting the firstname code after the word Dear.

   Type the letter as follows:

   We are pleased to announce the opening of Coffee-On-The-Go. Our new concept in convenience for the downtown Eugene community will feature specialty coffee drinks such as espressos and lattes in convenient cups for busy people.

   We also feature muffins and cookies from the famous Ann's Bakery, baked fresh every morning.

   To become acquainted with our new business located on the corner of Oak and 7th St., simply bring in this letter for a free coffee drink of your choice.

   Sincerely,

   (Your name)

5. Save the file as Letter.
6. Merge the Names file and the Letter file.
7. Create mailing labels from the database.

CASE STUDIES

Videos West:

Creating a Personal Mailing

In this chapter, you learned to create a mail merge. You will apply those skills to create a marketing letter addressed to specific people.

1. Open a new document.
2. Create the following database:

```
Mary John                    Mark Allen
P.O. Box 234                 P.O. Box 788
Tanana, AK 99501             Nikolai, AK 99602

Albert Sams                  Robert Willams
P.O. 763                     P.O. Box 654
McGrath, AK 99670            Ruby, AK 99643

Mary Black                   Sue Smith
P.O. Box 890                 P.O. Box 345
Tanana, AK 99501             Arctic Circle, AK 99832

Joyce Roberts                Rob Anderson
P.O 321                      P.O. Box 675
Tanana, AK 99501             Arctic Circle, AK 99832

Bob Jones                    Ruby Smith
P.O. Box 456                 P.O. Box 123
Takotna, AK 90601            Tanana, AK 99501
```

2. Save the files as VCR4.
3. Open the VCR file.
4. Replace "Dear Friends" with an inside address and a salutation to the individual.
5. Save the letter as VCR5.
6. Sort the database by zip code.
7. Merge the letter and the database to create the mailing.
8. Print mailing labels for the database.
9. Select only those customers living in Tanana.
10. Print out a list of the Tanana customers.

Chapter 10

Working with Lists, Columns, Hyphenation, and Tables

Objectives
- Creating Bulleted and Numbered Lists
- Creating Multilevel Lists
- Creating Newspaper-Style Columns
- Using Hyphenation
- Creating Tables

Key Terms

TERM	DEFINITION
Newspaper-Style Columns	columns in which text flows from the bottom of one column to the top of the next column
Table	a grid of rows and columns which can contain text, numbers, or graphics
Cell	the intersection of a column and row

In this chapter, you learn to create bulleted and numbered lists, create newspaper-style columns, use hyphenation, and create, modify, and format tables. You also learn to add a formula to a table for performing calculations on numbers in a table.

Objective 1: Creating Bulleted and Numbered Lists

Many times you will create a document that has a list of items that could be set off with bullets or numbers to emphasize the information. With Word 6, you can create either bulleted or numbered lists easily.

You can apply either list feature to your text by pressing the Bullets button or the Numbering button on the Formatting toolbar; typing the list, which is then formatted with bullets or numbers; and finally pressing the same toolbar button a second time to turn off the list feature.

Alternatively, you can type the list, select it, and then press either the Bullets button ▦ or the Numbering button ▦. The text will appear as a numbered or bulleted list, as shown in Figures 10-1 and 10-2.

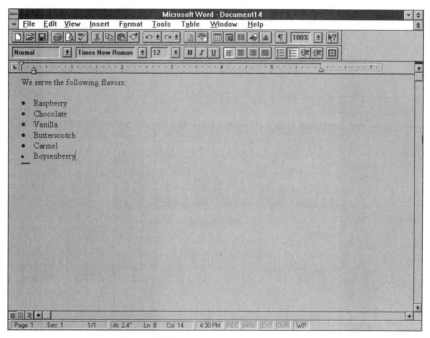

Figure 10-1   A bulleted list

What Is Virtual Reality?

Virtual reality (VR) is an experience not a technology. It is a computer-mediated experience made up of 3-dimensional objects that can be interacted with randomly in a place that exists only in cyberspace.

The most common virtual reality device today is the head-mounted display, which places images directly in front of your eyes and blocks out the real world. This head gear also records where you are looking so that the image can change to reflect your point of view. Other input devices, such as a specialized glove, record movement and allow you to manipulate objects.

One of the leaders of VR, Ivan Southerland developed the first head-mounted device in 1970. It displayed an image of a cube that changed perspective as the user moved. Since those beginnings, VR has come a long way. In December 1993, NASA attempted to repair the Hubble space telescope. The mission required six trips outside the space shuttle, each lasting more that six hours, during which astronauts removed, replaced, and repaired many of the flawed parts. The success of this mission was due partly to a VR simulation in which the astronauts had practiced the repairs before leaving Earth.

Virtual reality has moved into the arcade game market but is also slowly moving into business areas such as architecture. For example, an architect can build a model of a large building and have clients walk through the model, making changes specific to their purposes. The clients' specific needs are met, and the model is used many times for many purposes.

The future of virtual reality seems bright with aerospace and medical applications leading the way.

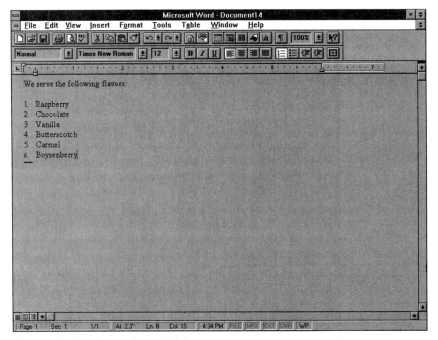

Figure 10-2   A numbered list

You can remove bullets and numbers from a list by selecting the list and then pressing the Bullets button or the Numbering button.

You can convert numbers to bullets or bullets to numbers by selecting the list you want to change and then clicking the button for the desired feature. For example, if you have a numbered list and want it to appear with bullets, select the numbered list and click the Bullets button on the Formatting toolbar.

Exercise 1: Creating a bulleted list

In this exercise, you create a list.

1. Open a new document.
2. Type in the following text:

   ```
   We serve the following flavors:
       Raspberry
       Chocolate
       Vanilla
       Butterscotch
       Caramel
       Boysenberry
   ```

3. Select the list, that is, from Raspberry through Boysenberry.

4. Click the Numbering button ⊞ on the Formatting toolbar.
   The list is numbered.

5. Select the list, that is, from Raspberry through Boysenberry.

6. Click the Bullets button ⊞ on the Formatting toolbar.
   The list appears with bullets.

7. Keep the document on the screen for use in the next exercise.

Modifying bullets or numbers

You can change the appearance of the bullets or the numbers in a list. You select the list you want to modify, and then choose Format Bullets and Numbering. You can change the numbering style on the Numbered tab and the bullets on the Bulleted tab. (See Figures 10-3 and 10-4.)

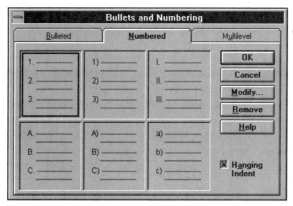

Figure 10-3 The Numbered tab of the Bullets and Numbering dialog box

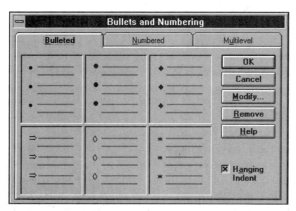

Figure 10-4 The Bulleted tab of the Bullets and Numbering dialog box

If you choose the Modify button on either tab, you can choose to create your own numbering or bullet style. (See Figure 10-5.)

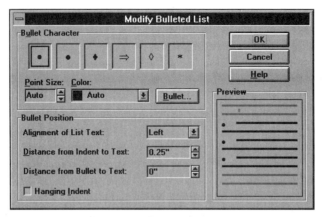

Figure 10-5 **The Modify Bulleted List dialog box**

If you choose the Bullet button in the Modify Bulleted List dialog box, you can select from all the special symbols available in the Symbol dialog box. (See Figure 10-6.)

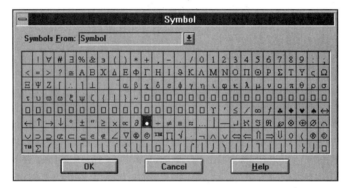

Figure 10-6 **The Symbol dialog box**

Exercise 2: Modifying bullets

In this exercise, you modify the bullets in the list you created.

1. Using the list created in Exercise 1, select the list.
2. Choose Format Bullets and Numbering.
3. On the Bulleted tab, choose a different bullet style and choose OK.
4. Close the document without saving.

Objective 2: Creating Multilevel Lists

You can create many types of complex lists such as outlined lists by choosing the Multilevel tab in the Bullets and Numbering dialog box. Word predefines six types of multilevel formats, and you can create your own by modifying any of the predefined types. (See Figure 10-7.)

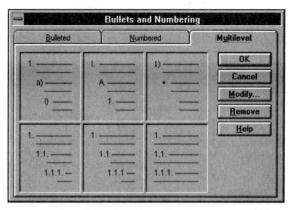

Figure 10-7 **The Multilevel tab on the Bullets and Numbering dialog box**

After selecting the appropriate style and turning it on, type the list. To create the indents, use the Increase Indent button on the Formatting toolbar. To promote items, that is, move them back toward the left margin, use the Decrease Indent button on the Formatting toolbar.

Exercise 3: Creating a multilevel list

In this exercise, you create a multilevel list.

1. Open a new document.
2. Choose Format Bullets and Numbering.
3. Choose the Multilevel tab.
4. Click the first example outline and click OK.
5. Type Chapter 10 and press (↵ ENTER).
6. Type Creating Bulleted and Numbered Lists and press (↵ ENTER).
7. Press the Increase Indent button on the Formatting toolbar.
8. Type Creating Bulleted and Numbered Lists and press (↵ ENTER).
9. Type Modify Bullets or Numbers and press (↵ ENTER).
10. Press the Decrease Indent button on the Formatting toolbar.
11. Type the following text, pressing (↵ ENTER) and the proper Decrease or Increase Indent button after each one:

    Creating Multilevel Lists
    Creating Newspaper-Style Columns
    Creating Columns of Varying Widths
        Using Hyphenation

12. Close the document without saving.

Objective 3: Creating Newspaper-Style Columns

newspaper-style columns

You can format text to appear in *newspaper-style columns*, that is, columns with text that flows from the bottom of one column to the top of the next column. You select the text you want to appear in columns of equal width, and click the Columns button on the Standard toolbar. The column box opens under the button, and you drag to select the number of columns you want. (See Figure 10-8.)

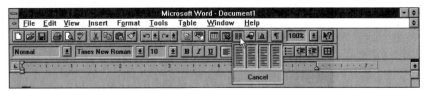

Figure 10-8 **The Columns button and the column box**

If you do not select any text and click the Columns button, Word 6 turns the entire document into columns of equal width.

You can view the columns on the screen in Page Layout view or on the Print Preview screen.

Exercise 4: Creating newspaper-style columns

In this exercise, you create newspaper-style columns.

1. Open the VIEW.DOC file.
2. Click the Columns button on the Standard toolbar.
3. Select three columns by dragging the mouse to select three columns in the box.
4. Choose View Page Layout.

   The document appears in three columns.
5. Close the file.

Creating columns of varying widths

To create columns of unequal width, choose Format Columns. The Columns dialog box appears. (See Figure 10-9.)

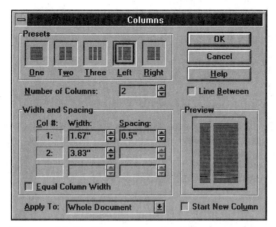

Figure 10-9 **The Columns dialog box**

You can then create two unequal columns by choosing the Left or Right presets. The Left preset makes the left column narrower than the right column, and the Right preset makes the right column narrower than the left column.

To create more than two columns of unequal width, select the number of columns you want in the Number of Columns box. Remove the selection from the Equal Column Width box, and in the Width and Spacing section, type or select the correct measurements in the Width and Spacing for each column.

The Apply To drop-down box allows you to apply the column feature to the Whole Document or from This Point Forward in the document.

The Line Between check box adds a vertical line between columns of text.

Exercise 5: Creating columns of unequal width with lines

In this exercise, you create columns of unequal width and add lines between the columns.

1. Open the VIEW.DOC file.
2. Choose Format Columns.
3. In the Columns dialog box, select 3 in the Number of Columns box.
4. Remove the selection from the Equal Column Width box.
5. In the Width and Spacing section, make Col #1: 2.5 inches, Col #2: 1.5 inches, and Col #3: 1 inch.
6. Select the Line Between box.
7. Choose OK.

8. If you aren't in Page Layout view, choose View Page Layout.

   The document appears in three unequal columns with lines between the columns.

9. Close the document without saving.

On-Line Forms

Word 6 provides features for creating forms that others can fill in on-line. First, you create the form using the table feature or any other formatting you want. Then you position the insertion point where the user will fill in data. You choose Insert Form Fields.

Word provides three types of form fields: text form field, check box form field, and a drop-down form field. There are six types of text form fields: text, numbers, date, the current date, current time, and calculation. You would choose one of these if you wanted the user to type in text, numbers, or a date, or if you want Word to provide the system date or time, or to perform a calculation. The check box field prompts the user to provide a yes or no response. The drop-down form field presents the user with a list of items from which to choose.

This feature can be used in any business situation in which a user fills in forms, such as retail sales or phone sales where on-line forms are used and could be streamlined by using any or all of the form fields to speed up data entry and reduce errors.

Objective 4: Using Hyphenation

Hyphenation splits words at the end of a line of text and inserts a hypen into the word. This feature allows you to fit more text on a line and is especially useful when you are placing text into columns so that you do not end up with columns that contain an excessive amount of white space at the end of the lines. Word 6 hyphenates your document beginning wherever the insertion point is positioned. To turn on hyphenation, choose Tools Hyphenation. The Hyphenation dialog box appears. (See Figure 10-10.)

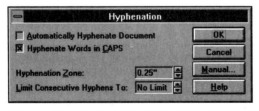

Figure 10-10 **The Hyphenation dialog box**

If you select the Automatically Hyphenate Document check box, Word 6 hyphenates as you type. If you select the Hyphenate Words in CAPS check box, which is the default, Word 6 hyphenates capitalized words.

By default, the Hyphenation Zone is set at 0.25". A word that falls in the zone and is too long to fit on the line is hyphenated. The larger you make your hyphenation zone, the less frequently Word 6 will have to hyphenate words in your document. The smaller you make your hyphenation zone, the more frequently Word 6 will have to hyphenate words in your document.

The Limit Consecutive Hyphens To option limits the number of consecutive lines of text that can contain hyphens.

To start automatic hyphenation, choose OK. To see every word that Word 6 proposes to hyphenate, click the Manual button. (See Figure 10-11.) The Manual Hyphenation box appears superimposed on your document.

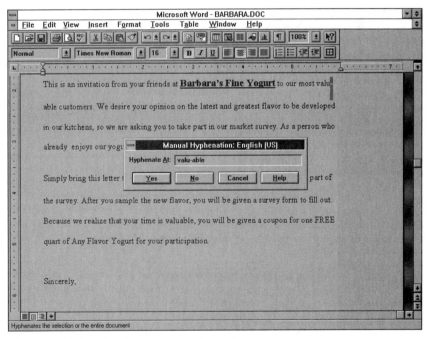

Figure 10-11   **The Manual Hyphenation box**

Word displays the word in the text box with the proposed hyphenation indicated. You select Yes to hyphenate the word as Word 6 has proposed. You select No to leave the word alone. You can move the hyphen with the arrows or mouse and then choose the Yes option. Cancel will cancel hyphenation.

You can also hyphenate a document after you have typed it. Move the insertion point to the beginning of the document and turn on hyphenation. The document will be hyphenated.

Objective 5: Creating Tables

table   You can use the *table* feature to place text, numbers, or graphics in a grid of columns and rows. Tables are used in a document to place data side by side for emphasis or to be more easily understood. The intersection of a column **cell**   and a row in a table is called a *cell*. You can size, format, shade, and even perform math in a table, making this a very useful and versatile feature.

Creating a table

You can create a table by positioning the insertion point where you want the table and pressing the Insert Table button ⊞ on the Standard toolbar. Word 6 displays a box which allows you to choose how large you want the table to be. You simply select the correct number by dragging the mouse to the correct size. (See Figure 10-12.)

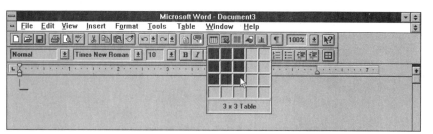

Figure 10-12 **The Insert Table box**

You can also use choose Table Insert Table to place a table in a document. The Insert table dialog box displays. (See Figure 10-13.)

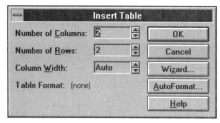

Figure 10-13 **The Insert Table dialog box**

You can specify the Number of Columns, Number of Rows, and the Column Width in the Insert Table dialog box. If you click on the Wizard button, the Table Wizard dialog box opens. (See Figure 10-14.)

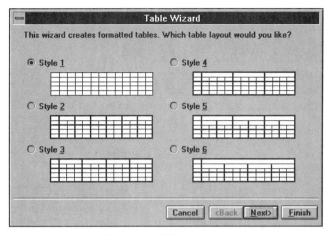

Figure 10-14   The Table Wizard box

The six styles in the Table Wizard box provide you with options of formatted tables.

If you choose the AutoFormat button in the Insert Table dialog box, you can choose from the predefined formats for the table shown in the Preview section of the Table AutoFormat dialog box. (See Figure 10-15.)

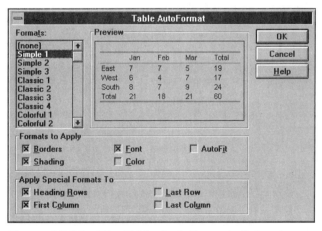

Figure 10-15   The Table AutoFormat dialog box

The table displays on the screen as a grid marked by dotted gridlines. If the gridlines are not displayed, choose Table Gridlines to display the lines on the screen. These lines do not print, but you can add borders that will. (You will learn to add borders later in this chapter.)

To display the end-of-cell marks and the end-of-row marks, click the Show/ Hide button ¶ on the Standard toolbar. (See Figure 10-16.)

Dotted gridlines ▶

End-of-cell marker ▶

End-of-row marker ▶

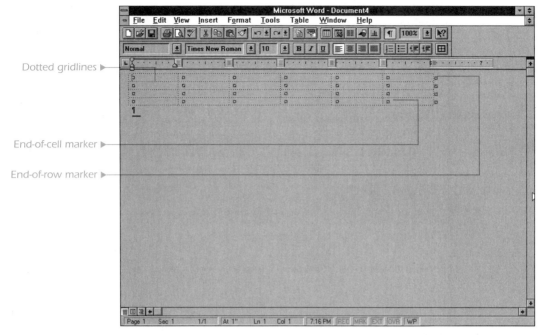

Figure 10-16 **Visible dotted gridlines, end-of-row marks, and end-of-cell marks**

Exercise 6: Creating a table

In this exercise, you create a table and display the gridlines and markers.

1. Open a new document.

2. Click the Insert Table button [img] on the Standard toolbar.

3. Drag the mouse to make the table 5 X 5.

4. If the gridlines are not displayed, choose Table Gridlines.

5. Click the Show/Hide button [img] on the Standard toolbar.

   The table is displayed with the gridlines and the end-of-cell and end-of-row markers.

6. Keep the document on the screen for use in the next exercise.

Moving around the table and adding data

To move around the table, click the mouse in the desired cell. You can also use the Tab key, the Shift + Tab key combination, or the arrow keys.

To place text, numbers, or graphics in the table, move the insertion point to the correct cell and enter the data as you normally would in any document. You also edit and format the data as you normally would.

Text wraps within the cell as you type, and the cell height increases to accommodate the data. If you press the Enter key, you start a new paragraph within the same cell. If you want to insert a tab within a cell, you must press the Ctrl + Tab key combination.

Exercise 7: Moving around the table and adding data

In this exercise, you move the insertion point to the desired cell and type in text.

1. Using the table created in the previous exercise, make sure the insertion point is in the top left corner cell.
2. Type Item and press (TAB).
3. Type Description and press (TAB).
4. Type Price and press (TAB).
5. Type Quantity and press (TAB).
6. Type Total and press (TAB).
7. Keep the document on the screen for use in the next exercise.

Modifying a table

You can modify tables in many ways. For example, you can add and delete rows and columns; you can delete the entire table; and you can split and merge cells together.

To select a cell, point to the left edge of the cell until the mouse pointer becomes a right-pointing arrow, and then click the mouse.

To work with rows or columns, you must select the row or column. To select a row or column, position the insertion point in the table in the row or column with which you want to work, and choose Table Select Row or Select Column.

If you selected a row, the Table menu changes to Insert Rows, and if you selected a column, the Table menu changes to Insert Columns. The new row is inserted above the selected row and the new column to the left of the selected column.

You can also use the mouse to select multiple rows or columns, and Word 6 will insert the same number of rows or columns. For example, if you select three columns and then choose Table Insert Column, Word will insert three columns to the left of the selected columns.

If you position the insertion point in the bottom right cell and press the Tab key, Word 6 will add a new row at the bottom of the table.

To delete a table, use the mouse to select the entire table, or place the insertion point in the table and choose Table Select Table. Then press the Delete key.

To delete a row or column from a table, select the rows or columns, and then choose Table Delete Columns or Delete Rows. If you select a group of cells, choose Table Delete Cells. Word displays the Delete Cells dialog box. (See Figure 10-17.)

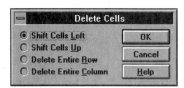

Figure 10-17   The Delete Cells dialog box

Choose Shift Cells Left to shift cells left after you delete the selected cells; choose Shift Cells Up to move cells up after you delete the selected cells; choose Delete Entire Row or Delete Entire Column to delete the entire row or column.

You can join adjacent cells together into one cell by selecting the cells that you want to merge and then choosing Table Merge Cells. This feature allows you to create heading rows for the table.

You can split cells with the Table Split Cells feature. Select the cells that you want to split, and when you choose the command, Word displays the Split Cells dialog box so that you can specify how many columns you want the cells split into.

Exercise 8: Modifying a table

In this exercise, you modify a table.

1. Using the table created in the previous exercises, move the insertion point to the top left corner.
2. Choose Table Insert Rows.

    A new row is added to the top of the table.
3. Choose Table Select Row.

    The new row is selected.
4. Choose Table Merge Cells.

    The top row is now one cell.
5. Type Barbara's Fine Yogurt.
6. Choose Format Paragraph.
7. In the Alignment section, choose Centered.

    The title is centered in the cell.
8. Keep the document on the screen for use in the next exercise.

Formatting tables

You can format tables by adding borders that will print and shading to cells by placing the insertion point in the table and choosing Table AutoFormat. (See Figure 10-15.) In the Formats list box, you can select a table design. In the Formats to Apply and the Apply Special Formats To sections, you select the check boxes for the features you want to apply.

You can add borders and shading to individual cells in the table by selecting the cells and then choosing either Format Borders and Shading or the Borders button ▦ on the Formatting toolbar.

If you are using the table feature in Word 6 for a large table that will print on more than one page, you can have Word repeat the heading on every page. Simply select the row or rows that you want repeated on every page and choose Table Headings.

Adding formulas to tables

You can add formulas to tables that perform calculations. For example, if you want to use the Word 6 table feature to create an invoice, you could have Word calculate the totals for you.

To perform calculations, you must know how Word sets up a table. Each row is numbered from the top of the table starting with the number one. Each column is given a letter designation starting from the left edge of the table and beginning with the letter A. Any cell in the table can be named by figuring its column letter and row number, for example, D6 or B3.

To write a formula you simply figure what cell locations you want in the formula and what operations should take place to produce the desired results. For example, to multiply quantity times price, you must determine the cell locations of the quantity and price and then include the correct operator. (The operators are + for addition, – for subtraction, * for multiplication, and / for division.) If quantity is in C3 and price is in C4, you would want to multiply C3 times C4. Since the asterisk indicates multiplication, the formula would be C3*C4. However, that is not complete because all formulas in Word 6 must start with an equal sign. Therefore, the correct formula would be =C3*C4.

Word also provides built-in functions that help when summing rows or columns. To perform calculations in a table, place the insertion point in the table and choose Table Formula. The Formula dialog box displays. (See Figure 10-18.)

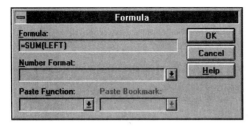

Figure 10-18 **The Formula dialog box**

Word proposes a formula in the Formula text box. If it is not the correct formula for your purposes, backspace over it, leaving only the equal sign. You can then either write a formula of your own, or you can choose a built-in function from the Paste Function drop-down list.

In the Number Format drop-down list, you can choose what the numbers should look like when calculated.

Exercise 9: Performing calculations in a table

In this exercise, you add formulas to the table.

1. Using the table created in the previous exercises, place the insertion point in cell A3.
2. Type A101 and press TAB.
3. Type Chocolate Chip and press TAB.
4. Type 5.50 and press TAB.
5. Type 3 and press TAB.
6. Choose Table Formula.
7. In the Formula dialog box, delete the formula from the Formula list box, leaving the equal sign.
8. Type C3*D3.
9. In the Number Format drop-down list, choose the $#,##0.00 format.
10. Choose OK.

    The formula computes the price times the quantity for the item and formats the result for currency format. (See Figure 10-19.)

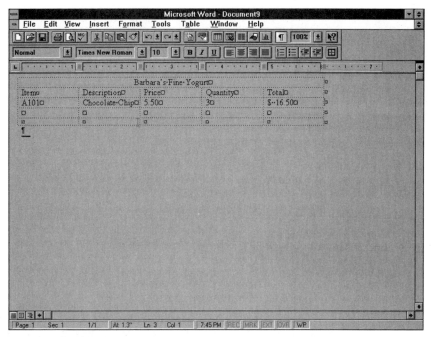

Figure 10-19 **The table displaying the results**

11. Move to cell A4, type Z177, and press (TAB).
12. Type Chocolate and press (TAB).
13. Type 4.75 and press (TAB).
14. Type 7 and press (TAB).
15. Choose Table Formula.
16. In the Formula dialog box, delete the formula from the Formula list box, leaving the equal sign.
17. Type C4*D4.
18. In the Number Format drop-down list, choose the $#,##0.00 format.
19. Choose OK.
20. Keep the table on the screen for use in the next exercise.

Exercise 10: Adding a function to a table

In this exercise, you use a built-in function to calculate numbers in a table.

1. Using the table created in the preceding exercise, move the insertion point to the bottom right corner cell.
2. Choose Table Formula.

   Because you are at the bottom of a column, Word suggests the formula =SUM(ABOVE). This is the correct formula. Word also proposes a format.

3. Select the same currency format shown in Step 9 of Exercise 9 and choose OK.

The table will now compute the total for more than one purchase.

4. Save the table as TABLE1.

5. Keep the table on the screen for use in the next exercise.

If you change some of the numbers that Word 6 is using to perform the calculation, you can select the cell with the formula and press the F9 key to recompute the results.

Exercise 11: Recalculating the table

In this exercise, you change a number and have Word recalculate the formula.

1. Using the TABLE1 table, move to cell D4.

2. Delete the number and type 5, and type the number 2.

3. Move to cell E4.

4. Select the cell.

5. Press (F9).

The formula recomputes.

6. Close the file without saving.

Chapter Summary

In this chapter, you learned to enhance text by creating lists that contain bullets or numbers. You learned to turn text into newspaper-style columns and use hyphenation to keep from having too much white space in the columns. You learned to create, modify, and format tables of data. You also learned how to calculate numbers in a table.

Review Questions

True/False Questions

_____ 1. You cannot convert a bulleted list into a numbered list once it is created.

_____ 2. You can create columns of equal width or unequal width in Word 6.

_____ 3. When you use the hyphenation feature, you fit less text on the line.

_____ 4. A table displays on the screen as a grid marked by dotted grid-lines which do not print.

_____ 5. A table formula must start with an equal sign.

Multiple Choice Questions

_____ 6. To create an outline in Word 6, you would choose
   A. Format Outline.
   B. the Outline button.
   C. Format Bullets and Numbering then the Multilevel tab.
   D. Both A and B.

_____ 7. To create the indents in a multilevel list, you would
   A. press the Increase Indent button.
   B. choose Edit Indent.
   C. press the Decrease Indent button.
   D. press the Zoom Control button.

_____ 8. If you want a table to print with lines, you choose
   A. Table Gridlines.
   B. Format Borders and Shading.
   C. the Borders button on the Formatting toolbar.
   D. Both B and C.

_____ 9. Once a table is created, you can modify it by
   A. adding rows and columns.
   B. deleting rows and columns.
   C. splitting and merging cells.
   D. All of the above.

_____ 10. If you want to subtract the discount in F6 from the total sale in F5, the formula would be
   A. F6-F5.
   B. F5-F6.
   C. =F5-F6.
   D. =F5/F6.

Fill-in-the-Blank Questions

11. Each row in a table is _____ from the top.

12. Each column in a table is given a(n) _____ designation starting from the left edge of the table.

13. Text flows from the bottom of one column to the top of the next column in _____-_____ columns.

14. A(n) _____ is a grid of rows and columns that can contain text, numbers, or graphics.

15. The intersection of a column and row in a table is called a(n)
_____.

Acumen-Building Activities

Quick Projects

Project 1: Creating a Bulleted List

1. Open the BOOK.DOC file.
2. Edit the first paragraph so that the seven books are listed in the form of a bulleted list.
3. Print the document.
4. Save the file as BULLET.DOC.

Project 2: Creating a Numbered List

1. Open the BOOK.DOC file.
2. Edit the first paragraph so that the seven books are listed in the form of a numbered list.
3. Print the document.
4. Close the file without saving.

Project 3: Modifying a Bulleted List

1. Open the BULLET.DOC file.
2. Change the style of bullets used in the list.
3. Print the document.
4. Close the file without saving.

Project 4: Creating a Multilevel List

1. Create the following multilevel list:

   A.Yogurt
      1.Basic ingredients
      2.Nutrition analysis
   B.History of its use
      1.Neolithic herdsmen let milk stand in clay pots
      2.Spread from Middle East to Far East, Russia, and
        into Europe and beyond
   C.Uses
      1.Symbol of courage
         a)Given to warriors to give courage or strength
         b)Given to pregnant women

2. Print the document.
3. Save as OUTLINE.DOC.

In-Depth Projects

Project 1: Using Columns

1. Open the VIEW.DOC file. Remove any page breaks from the document.
2. Change the document so that the entire document is in two equal columns.
3. Print the document.
4. Close the file without saving.
5. Open the VIEW.DOC file.
6. Change the document so that the entire document is in three columns of unequal width.
7. Place a line between the columns.
8. Turn on hyphenation.
9. Print the document.
10. Close the file without saving.

Project 2: Creating a Table

1. Create a table of the following information:

   Total Sales Per Month

January	February	March	Total
3,250	4,875	3,900	

2. Format the table so that the title row is shaded.
3. Add a border to the table.
4. Include a formula that will total the three month's sales in D3.
5. Format the numbers for currency.
6. Print the table.
7. Save as SALES.DOC.

CASE STUDIES

Coffee-On-The-Go: **Creating a Table**

In this chapter you learned to create tables. You will use those skills to create a menu for Coffee-On-The-Go.

To create a table featuring the coffee drinks and their prices, follow these steps:

1. Open a new document.
2. Create the following table:

```
                          Coffee-On-The-Go
                     We Roast Our Own Coffee Daily
     Coffee               Description                      12oz    16oz
     house coffee         regular or decaf                  .75
     espresso             two shots                          .75    1.00
     Cappuccino           espresso with hot foamed milk     1.50    1.75
     Latte                espresso with frothy steamed milk 1.50    1.75
     Latte Royale         latte with flavoring              1.75    2.00
     Latte Steamer        steamed milk with flavoring       1.25    1.50
     Mocha Supreme        espresso, chocolate, and cream    1.75    2.00
     Mexican Mocha        espresso with Mexican chocolate   1.75    2.00
     Tea                  hot or iced                        .75    1.00
```

3. Save the file as Coffee.

4. Print the file.

CASE STUDIES

Videos West: **Creating a Brochure**

In this chapter you learned to create lists and use columns. You will use those skills to create a brochure for Videos West.

1. Open a new document.

2. Using the columns feature, set up three columns in landscape mode.

3. Create a brochure that could be mailed by itself to customers. It should include the form (turned sideways) saved as the file VCR3; some of the video descriptions saved as the file VCR2; and the letterhead in the VCR file.

4. Enhance the document to create a pleasing brochure.

5. Save the file as VCR6.

6. Print the document.

Chapter 11

Using Advanced Features

Objectives
- Creating an Index
- Creating a Table of Contents
- Managing Files
- Opening a Document Created in Another Application
- Saving a Word 6 Document in Another File Format

Key Terms

TERM	DEFINITION
Index	a listing of page numbers for an item in a printed document
Cross-Referenced Index Entry	an index entry that refers to another index entry
Table of Contents	a list of the headings that appear in the document in the order in which they appear along with the page number

In this chapter, you enhance long documents by learning to create an index and a table of contents for a document. You learn to manage files you create using Microsoft Word 6. You also learn to bring in documents created in other applications and to save Word 6 files so that you can use them more easily in other applications.

Objective 1: Creating an Index

index   An *index* provides page numbers for items in a printed document so that a reader can find information more easily. An index is usually alphabetized and placed at the end of the document. For example, when you are uncertain about how to do something in Word 6, you flip to the back of this book and look up the command or concept in the alphabetized list which tells you which page it is located on in this book. In Word 6, you can create an

cross-referenced index entry index that has main entries, subentries, as well as cross-references. A *cross-referenced index entry* refers the reader to another index entry, for example, "See Software."

You create an index using Word 6 by selecting the text for the index, formatting the text, and then compiling the index. In an index, you can include text from footnotes and endnotes as well as text in the body of the document. If you make changes to the document after creating the index, Word updates the page numbers in the index.

Marking index entries

To mark text for an index, select the text you want indexed, and then choose Insert Index and Tables. Word opens the Index and Tables dialog box. (See Figure 11-1.)

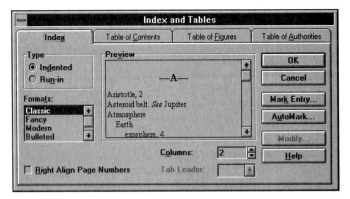

Figure 11-1   The Index tab of the Index and Tables dialog box

Choose the Mark Entry button, and the Mark Index Entry dialog box opens. (See Figure 11-2.)

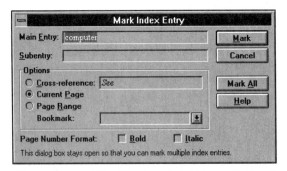

Figure 11-2   The Mark Index Entry dialog box

If you did not select the text, you can type it in the Main Entry text box, or you can edit selected text that appears in the text box.

What Is FAT?

FAT, or the File Allocation Table, is the index or system that DOS, the disk operating system, uses to keep track of your files. It records the files, unused disk space, and space depleted by damaged sectors. The FAT is created when you format a disk.

If the FAT is damaged, your hard drive can no longer locate any of the files saved on it, and they are essentially lost. As a safety measure, DOS places two copies of the FAT on a disk in case one is damaged.

You can create a subentry by typing the text in the Subentry text box. If you want to include more than one subentry, type them in the text box, separating one from the other with a colon.

In the Options section, the default Current Page should be selected. If you want to create a Cross-reference, type the cross-reference in the text box after the word "See."

You can choose to have the page numbers Bold, Italic, or both by selecting them in the Page Number Format section.

You can then choose the Mark button to mark just this instance of the text, or choose the Mark All button to mark all instances of the same text in the document. Word inserts an Index Entry field, or XE field, in the document formatted as hidden text, that is, it will not appear on the screen. You can see the hidden field by clicking the Show/Hide button ¶ on the Standard toolbar. You can get more information about the XE field by positioning the insertion point in the field and pressing the F1 key.

The Mark Index Entry dialog box stays open so that you can move through the document marking entries. Simply click on the dialog box to make it active, and close it when you have finished marking all entries.

Exercise 1: Marking text for an index

In this exercise, you mark text to appear in an index.

1. Open the VIEW.DOC file.
2. Move the insertion point to the beginning of the document, and select the text "normal view" in the first sentence.
3. Choose Insert Index and Tables.
4. On the Index tab of the Index and Tables dialog box, choose the Mark Entry button.

   The text "normal view" should appear in the Main Entry text box of the Mark Index Entry dialog box.
5. Choose the Mark All button.
6. With the Mark Index Entry open on the screen, select the text "outline view" in the first sentence.
7. Choose the Mark All button.
8. Repeat steps 6 and 7 for the following text:

   ```
   page layout view
   print preview
   master document view
   ```

insertion point
scroll bar
WYSIWYG
Standard toolbar
View menu

9. Close the Mark Index Entry dialog box.

10. Press the Show/Hide button 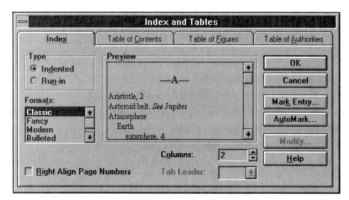 to see the XE entries.

11. Press the Show/Hide button to hide the entries.

12. Keep the document active for use in the next exercise.

Formatting and compiling the index

The index will appear wherever the insertion point is, so you must position the insertion point where you want the index to appear before you compile it. Choose Insert Index and Tables. With the Index tab selected, choose the formatting desired for the index. (See Figure 11-3.)

Figure 11-3   The Index tab of the Index and Tables dialog box

In the Type section, you can choose Indented to have subentries indented on separate lines under the main entry, or choose Run-in to have subentries listed one after the other on a single line.

In the Formats list box, choose a style for the index. You can see the results in the Preview section.

Choose Right Align Page Numbers to have the page numbers line up at the right edge of the page; choose the Tab Leader if you want to select dots to precede right-aligned page numbers.

The Columns box allows you to specify the number of columns for the index.

When you are finished formatting, choose OK. Word 6 inserts the index into the document at the insertion point.

Exercise 2: Formatting and compiling the index

In this exercise, you format and compile an index for the words you marked in Exercise 1.

1. Using the VIEW.DOC with the words marked in Exercise 1, move the cell pointer to the end of the document.
2. Choose Insert Break.
3. In the Break dialog box, make sure Page Break is selected and choose OK.
4. Type Index.
5. Choose Format Paragraph.
6. Choose Alignment Centered, and choose OK.
7. Press (↵ ENTER) twice.
8. Choose Insert Index and Tables.
9. On the Index tab, make sure that Indented is selected in the Type section.
10. In the Formats list box, choose Formal.
11. Choose OK.

   Word inserts the index.

12. Save the document and close it.

If the index appears as an INDEX field code instead of appearing on the screen, press the Shift + F9 keys to convert the codes to the index.

Objective 2: Creating a Table of Contents

table of contents

You can create a table of contents using Word 6 so that readers can easily find information in the body of the document. A *table of contents* lists the headings that appear in the document in the order in which they appear, accompanied by the page number. A table of contents usually appears at the beginning of the document.

If you create the table of contents after you create the index, you can include the index and the page number it appears on in the table of contents.

If you create your document using the built-in heading styles (Headings 1 through 9) to format the headings in your document, creating a table of contents is quite easy. However, you can create a table of contents even if you did not use the built-in styles for the headings.

Creating a table of contents with built-in heading styles

Position the insertion point where you want the table of contents to appear. Choose Insert Index and Tables. Choose the Table of Contents tab in the Index and Tables dialog box. (See Figure 11-4.)

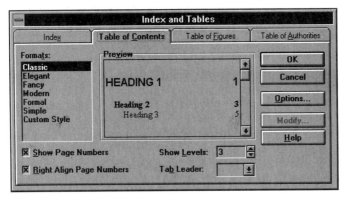

Figure 11-4   **The Table of Contents tab of the Index and Tables dialog box**

In the Formats list box, select the desired format. The Preview section displays examples of the format.

Choose Show Page Numbers to display page numbers in the table of contents. Choose Right Align Page Numbers to have the numbers appear at the right edge of the page. Choose a Tab Leader if one is desired for right-aligned numbers. Choose Show Levels to specify the number of heading levels you want to display in the table of contents.

Once you have finished formatting the table of contents, choose OK to compile the table of contents. It appears at the location of the insertion point. If you see the TOC field codes instead of the table of contents, press Shift + F9 to display the table.

Exercise 3: Creating a table of contents

In this exercise, you create a table of contents for a document created using the built-in heading styles.

1. Open the VIEW.DOC file.
2. Place the insertion point on the line with the title.
3. Choose the Style button `Normal ▼` and select the Heading 1 style.
4. Move the insertion point on the line with the heading Normal View.
5. Choose the Style button and select Heading 2.
6. Repeat Steps 4 and 5 for the following headings:

```
Outline View
Page Layout View
Print Preview
Master Document
Index
```

7. Move the insertion point to the top of the document.

8. Choose Insert Break.

9. In the Break dialog box, make sure Page Break is selected and choose OK.

10. Type Table of Contents.

11. Choose Format Paragraph.

12. Choose Alignment Centered.

13. Press ⏎ ENTER twice.

14. Choose Insert Index and Tables.

15. Choose the Table of Contents tab.

16. In the Formats section, choose Formal.

17. Choose the following if they aren't selected: Show Page Numbers and Right Align Page Numbers.

18. Select a dot leader in the Tab Leader box.

19. Choose OK.

    The table of contents is compiled and appears in the document.

20. Save the document and close it.

Creating a table of contents using styles other than the built-in styles

To create a table of contents for a document in which you used styles other than the built-in styles to format the headings, you must tell Word 6 what styles you applied to your document. For example, if you created a template that uses styles to format headings in the document, you must define which style applies to which level of entry in the table of contents.

Position the insertion point where you want the table of contents to appear. Choose Insert Index and Tables. Choose the Table of Contents tab in the Index and Tables dialog box. (See Figure 11-5.)

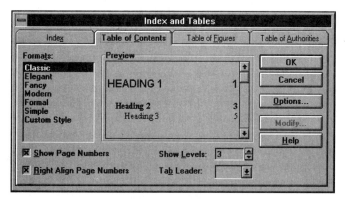

Figure 11-5   *The Table of Contents tab of the Index and Tables dialog box*

After choosing the format for the table of contents, choose the Options button. The Table of Contents Options dialog box displays. (See Figure 11-6.)

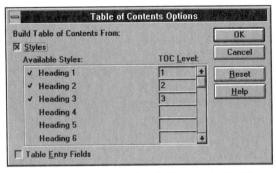

Figure 11-6 **The Table of Contents Options dialog box**

Simply find the styles you applied to your document and type the number in the box to the right of the style name to indicate the level in the table of contents. For example, if you have a style called Header and it should be level one, type the number 1 in the box to the right of the name.

Once you have all the styles numbered correctly, you should delete any level numbers from styles you do not want to have to appear in the table of contents. Click OK twice to compile the table of contents.

Updating a table of contents

If you make changes to the document such as changing headings, you will need to update the table of contents. Place the insertion point in the table of contents and choose Insert Index and Tables. You can make any changes to the formatting that you want, and when you press OK, Word 6 asks if you want to replace the selected table of contents. Select OK to replace the old table of contents with the new one. (See Figure 11-7.)

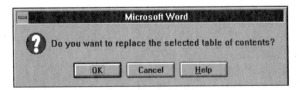

Figure 11-7 **Word 6 query**

As an alternative method of updating the table of contents, place the insertion point in the table of contents and click the right mouse button. From the shortcut menu, select the Update Field option. (See Figure 11-8.)

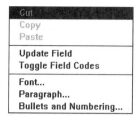

Figure 11-8   **The shortcut menu**

The Update Table of Contents dialog displays. (See Figure 11-9.)

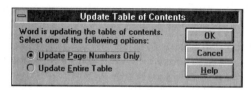

Figure 11-9   **The Update Table of Contents dialog box**

You can choose to Update Page Numbers Only or to Update Entire Table.

Objective 3: Managing Files

Word 6 provides options to help avoid information loss. You can choose to have Word save a backup copy of every file you create. You select this option by choosing Tools Options and the Save tab. Select Always Create Backup Copy. (See Figure 11-10.)

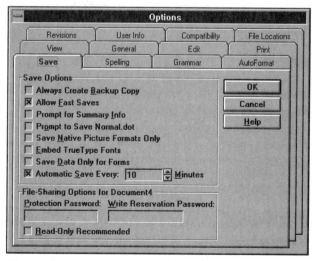

Figure 11-10   **The Save tab of the Options dialog box**

If you select the Always Create Backup Copy option, you still must save your document in the normal way. Word creates a second copy of the saved file, giving it the three-letter extension BAK. For example, if you have created a document named VIEW.DOC, Word creates a second copy of the file, naming it VIEW.BAK. Then if something happens to the VIEW.DOC file, you can open the next-to-last version named VIEW.BAK.

If you select the Automatic Save Every option, Word saves a temporary copy of the document you are working on as often as you specify. (See Figure 11-10.) For example, if you type a 10 in the text box, Word saves a temporary copy of the document every ten minutes. If you experience a power outage eight minutes after an autosave has taken place, you have only lost eight minutes of your work. If there is a power failure or other such problem, Word displays the documents that were open at the time of the problem the next time you return to Word 6 and adds the word "Recovered" to the document name.

The Allow Fast Saves option is a time-saving option. It can only be used if you have not selected the Always Create Backup Copy Option because instead of saving the entire document, it only saves the changes you have made. This option is also not available if you are working on a network.

If you select the Prompt for Summary Info option, Word displays the Summary Info dialog box when you save a document for the first time. (See Figure 11-11.)

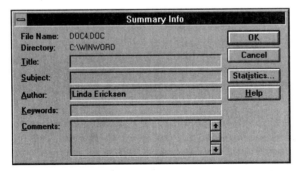

Figure 11-11   **The Summary Info dialog box**

You also see this same dialog box if you choose File Summary Info. In the Summary Info dialog box, you can include information about the document such as the Author, Keywords, and Subject which are saved with the file. You can also see statistics about the document such as the file size, the amount of editing time, and the author by pressing the Statistics button. (See Figure 11-12.)

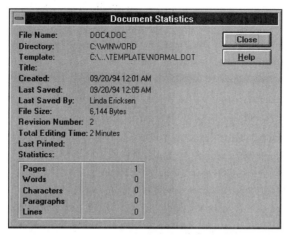

Figure 11-12 **The display of the statistics for the current document**

Protecting documents

The Save tab of the Options dialog box (see Figure 11-10) also contains options in the File-Sharing Options section for protecting documents from change. (This same dialog box is displayed if you choose File Save As and press the Options button.)

If you want to keep other users from opening a document, assign the document a password in the Protection Password text box of the Save tab. You simply type a password of up to 15 characters and click OK. Word then displays the Confirm Password dialog box. (See Figure 11-13.) You must type the same password in the Reenter Protection Password text box. Word displays the password as asterisks as you type so that your password is not visible on the screen.

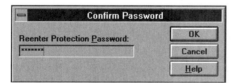

Figure 11-13 **The Confirm Password dialog box with the password displayed as asterisks**

If you want to allow other users to see the document but not allow them to save changes to the document, assign the document a password in the Write Reservation Password text box of the Save tab. You will again see the password as asterisks and be asked to reenter it. If a user does not know the correct password, the document is opened as a read-only document.

If you want to recommend that the document be a read-only document but do not want to require it, select the Read-Only Recommended option of the Save tab. When the user opens the file, Word recommends that it be a read-only file.

If you save a file with a password and then want to remove the password or change it, you must open the file, choose File Save As, and choose the Options button. Select the asterisks that represent the password and press Delete to remove the password or type the new password. You will be asked to reenter the new password in the Confirm Password dialog box.

You open a file saved with a password just as you would open any file. You are prompted for the password. (See Figure 11-14.)

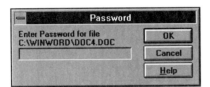

Figure 11-14   **The Password dialog box**

If you type the password incorrectly, Word displays a message telling you that the password is incorrect and that the file cannot be opened. (See Figure 11-15.)

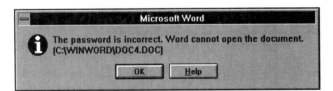

Figure 11-15   **Word 6 message**

Exercise 4: Saving a file with a password

In this exercise, you save a file with a password.

1. Open a new file.
2. Type your name and address.
3. Choose File Save As.
4. Choose the Options button.
5. In the Protection Password text box, type dog.
6. Choose OK.
7. In the Reenter Protection Password text box, type dog.
8. Choose OK.
9. In the File Name section of the Save As dialog box, type PASS and choose OK.
10. Choose File Close.

The file is given the name PASS.DOC and can only be opened by someone who knows the correct password.

Exercise 5: Opening a file saved with a password

In this exercise, you open the file saved with the password.

1. Choose File Open.
2. In the File Name list box of the Open dialog box, select PASS.DOC and choose OK.
3. In the Enter Password for File text box, type cat and choose OK.
   Word is unable to open the file. Click OK.
4. Choose File Open.
5. In the File Name list box of the Open dialog box, select PASS.DOC and choose OK.
6. In the Enter Password for File text box type dog and choose OK.
   Word opens the file.

You will want to use this feature only when you want to keep information confidential, and you will need to remember your own passwords because they are not listed anywhere in Word 6 for you.

FEATURE

Cross-references

Word 6 provides an option for creating cross-references to headings, which were formatted with built-in styles, to footnotes, endnotes, figures, or tables. Simply type in the text that introduces the cross-reference, such as "See also." Then choose Insert Cross-Reference. Word displays the Cross-reference dialog box. (See figure below.)

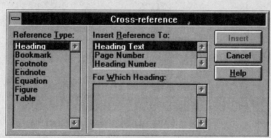

The Cross-reference dialog box

In the Reference Type list box, select the type of item you want to refer to. In the Insert Reference To box, select the type of information about the item that you want Word to insert in the document, such as Page Number. In the For Which box, select the specific item. Choose Insert to the cross-reference in the text.

Finding files

One of the most frustrating parts of working on computers is not being able to find files you have created. Word 6 provides the File Find File feature, which displays the Find File dialog box. (See Figure 11-16.) You can also display the Find File dialog box by choosing File Open and then pressing the Find File button.

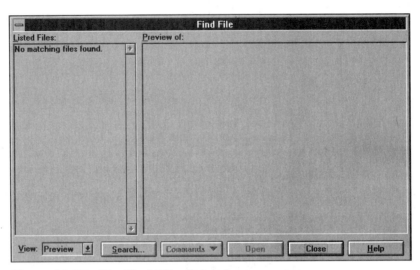

Figure 11-16 **The Find File dialog box**

The Find File feature searches for files that have been saved by searching for the filename, author, specific text in the document, or by the date the file was created or last modified. The first time you choose File Find File, the Search dialog box appears so that you can specify File Name and Location search criteria. (See Figure 11-17.)

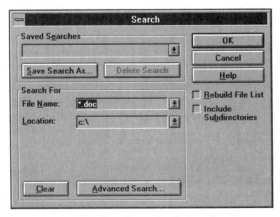

Figure 11-17 **The Search dialog box**

After you define the File Name and Location search criteria in the Search dialog box, Word uses the same information for its searches. Instead of displaying the Search dialog box every time you choose File Find File, Word displays the Find File dialog box immediately and uses the last information in the Search dialog box. However, if Word displays the Find File dialog box and you want to change the File Name or Location information, press the Search button and the Search dialog box will display.

In the Search For section of the Search dialog box, you can type a specific filename in the File Name text box, or you can select a type of file to search for by choosing one from the File Name drop-down box.

In the Location box of the Search dialog box, you must select a drive to search. If you know a specific subdirectory or you want to type a path to search, you can type that in also. However, the easiest method is to select the Include Subdirectories option, and Word will search all subdirectories on the designated drive.

When you press OK, Word displays the Find File dialog box with the matching files displayed in the Listed Files box, and Word displays a view of the highlighted document, which can be a Preview, a File Info view, or a Summary view. A Preview of the file allows you to move around in the document. A File Info view provides information about the listed files. A Summary view provides the document summary information.

To change views, choose the View drop-down box and select a view. If you locate the file you are searching for, select it and press the Open button. If the file you are looking for did not appear, you can press the Search button and redefine the File Name or Location, or choose the Advanced Search button in the Search dialog box, and the Advanced Search dialog box will display. (See Figure 11-18.)

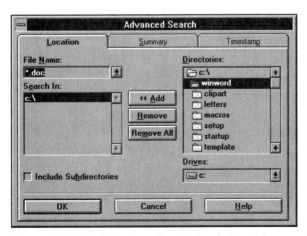

Figure 11-18 **The Location tab of the Advanced Search dialog box**

You can add directories and delete directories from the search with the Add and Remove buttons.

By choosing the Timestamp tab of the Advanced Search dialog box, you can search for the date a file was created or last saved. By choosing the Summary tab of the Advanced Search dialog box, you can search for files based on information in the document summary.

In any Summary Info field, you can use the wildcards and operators described in Table 11-1 to search for specific text:

Table 11-1 **Searching for Text**

WILDCARD OR OPERATOR	DESCRIPTION
? (question mark)	Matches any single character. Sm?th to match Smith or Smyth.
* (asterisk)	Matches any number of characters. Sm* matches Smith, Smyth, or Smithsonian.
" " (quotation)	Matches characters in quotation marks literally. "?" to match a question mark.
, (comma)	Logical OR. CA,WA matches CA or WA.
& (ampersand) or (space)	Logical AND. CA WA or CA & WA to match both.
~ (tilde)	Logical NOT. ~CA excludes CA from search.

Exercise 6: Searching for a file

In this exercise, you search for a file.

1. Choose File Find File.
2. If the Find File dialog box displays, press the Search button.
3. In the Search dialog box, choose the File Name drop-down box and choose Word Documents (*.doc).
4. In the Location box, select the correct drive for your configuration.
5. Select the Include Subdirectories option.
6. Choose OK.

   All files created as part of this book should be listed in the Listed Files section of the Find File dialog box.
7. If Preview is not selected in the View section, select it to view a document.
8. Choose Close when you are finished.

Document management features of Find File

You can perform document management tasks using the Find File feature. For example, you can delete, copy, sort, or print a file or a group of files. Choose File Find File. In the Find File dialog box, press the Commands button to display the options. (See Figure 11-19.)

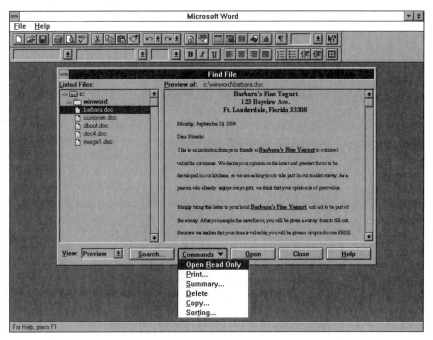

Figure 11-19   The Find File commands

Choose the Sorting option to sort the files in the Listed Files box. When you choose Sorting, the Options dialog box displays, allowing you to specify how Word should sort and display the files. (See Figure 11-20.)

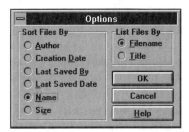

Figure 11-20   The Options dialog box for sorting

If you want to delete, copy, print, or open a file as read-only, you can specify that command. If you want to perform the action on a group of files, you can hold down the Ctrl key as you click each filename. To extend select a group of filenames, click the first filename, hold down the Shift key, and click the last filename.

Objective 4: Opening a Document Created in Another Application

If you want to open a document created in another application, you can simply open it, telling Word what kind of file it is by choosing the appropriate type in the List Files of Type section of the Open dialog box. (See Figure 11-21.)

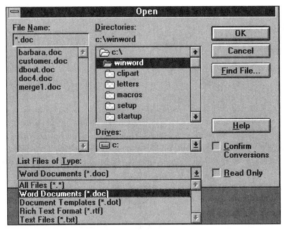

Figure 11-21   The List Files Type drop-down box of the Open dialog box

Word converts most types of documents automatically. If, however, Word 6 cannot convert the document, it displays the Convert File dialog box. (See Figure 11-22.)

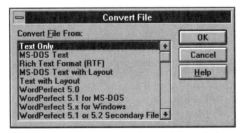

Figure 11-22   The Convert File dialog box

Select the appropriate file format listed in the Convert File dialog box, and then choose OK. Word 6 converts and opens the document. If the file did not convert correctly, close the file without saving it, and try again using a different format.

Objective 5: Saving a Word 6 Document in Another File Format

You can save documents that you create using Microsoft Word 6 for Windows in other file formats for use in earlier versions of Microsoft Word or for use in different applications.

Save the file using File Save As. In the Save As dialog box, choose the appropriate type from the Save File as Type drop-down box. (See Figure 11-23.)

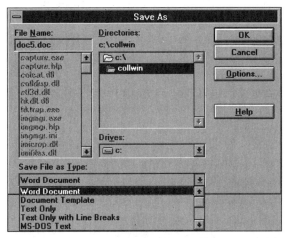

Figure 11-23   **The Save File as Type drop-down box**

Chapter Summary

In this chapter, you learned about many of Word's advanced features. You learned to enhance long documents with an index and a table of contents. You also learned to manage files by using such features as File Find to search for files. You learned to protect files with passwords. You opened documents created in other applications and saved files to be used in other applications.

Review Questions

True/False Questions

_____   1. A table of contents is usually alphabetized and placed at the end of the document.

_____   2. Word inserts an Index Entry field, or XE field, in the document formatted as hidden text.

_____ 3. If you create the table of contents after you create the index, you can include the index and the page number it appears on in the table of contents.

_____ 4. By choosing the Summary tab of the Advanced Search dialog box, you can search for files based on information in the document summary.

_____ 5. Word displays the password as asterisks as you type so that your password is not visible on the screen.

Multiple Choice Questions

_____ 6. In Word 6, you can create an index that has
   A. main entries.
   B. subentries.
   C. cross-references.
   D. All of the above.

_____ 7. If you select the Always Create Backup Copy option and save a file named LETTER.DOC, Word 6 will save another file named
   A. LETTER.BAC.
   B. LETTER.BAK.
   C. BACK.LETTER.
   D. LETTER.BACK.

_____ 8. By choosing the Timestamp tab of the Advanced Search dialog box, you can search for
   A. the date a file was created.
   B. the date the file was last modified.
   C. the system date.
   D. Both A and B.

_____ 9. A table of contents
   A. lists the headings that appear in the document.
   B. lists headings in the order in which they appear.
   C. lists headings accompanied by the page number.
   D. All of the above.

_____ 10. If you want to search for both black and block, you could use the wildcard search
   A. bl?ck.
   B. bl&ck.
   C. bl@ck.
   D. bl,ck.

Fill-in-the-Blank Questions

11. A(n) _____ provides page numbers for items in a printed document.

12. A(n) _____-_____ index entry refers to another index entry.

13. A(n) _____ _____ _____ lists the headings that appear in the document in the order in which they appear, accompanied by the page number.

14. If you want to allow other users to see the document but not allow them to save changes to the document, assign the document a _____.

15. The _____ _____ feature searches for files that have been saved by searching for the filename, author, specific text in the document, or by the date the file was created or last modified.

Acumen-Building Activities

Quick Projects

Project 1: Creating an Index

1. Open the PALM.DOC file.
2. Mark the following words for the index:

   ```
   computer
   desktop
   portable
   transportable
   laptop
   palmtops
   ```

3. Choose an index format.
4. Compile the index on a separate page at the end of the document.
5. Print the document.
6. Save the file as PALM1.DOC.

Project 2: Creating a Table of Contents

1. Open the PALM1.DOC file created in Quick Project 1.
2. Place headings in the document before each paragraph.
3. Format the headings, using built-in styles.
4. Choose a format for the table of contents.

5. Compile the table of contents at the beginning of the document on a separate page.
6. Print the document.
7. Save the file as PALM2.DOC.

Project 3: Saving a File with a Password

1. Open a new document.
2. Type one paragraph of your choosing.
3. Save the file as PASSWRD.DOC with the password SAFE.
4. Close the file.
5. Open the file using the password.
6. Close the file.

Project 4: Deleting a File

1. Using the File Find File feature, locate the PASSWRD.DOC file.
2. Using the password SAFE, preview the document.
3. Using the Delete command, delete the file.

In-Depth Projects

Project 1: Creating a Complete Document

1. Find a magazine article of interest to you.
2. Type it using Word 6.
3. Use any editing features necessary to make the copy of the article perfect, for example, spell check.
4. Format the article, changing fonts, sizes, centering the title, and so on.
5. Footnote the title, citing the source.
6. Double space the article so that it runs at least 2 to 3 pages.
7. Save the article with an appropriate name.

Project 2: Enhancing the Document

1. Open the article you created in In-Depth Project 1.
2. Mark recurring and important words for the index.
3. Create the index on a separate page at the end of the document.
4. Place the title "Index" at the top center of the page.
5. Create headings in the document if they were not part of the original.
6. Format the headings, using built-in styles.
7. Create a table of contents at the beginning of the document on a separate page.

8. Place the title "Table of Contents" at the top center of the page.
9. Print the document.
10. Save and close the file.

CASE STUDIES

Coffee-On-The-Go:

Creating a Table of Contents

In this chapter, you learned to use advanced features. You will apply those skills to create a table of contents for the business plan for Coffee-On-The-Go.

1. Open the Plan1 file.
2. Insert a page break after the title page to create a new page 2.
3. Type Table of Contents. Center and enlarge the font to 16.
4. Create a table of contents for the entire business plan, using the section headings and subheadings. Include the page numbers.
5. Print the table of contents.
6. Save the Plan1 document.

CASE STUDIES

Videos West:

Creating an Invoice

In this chapter you learned to use advanced features. You will apply what you have learned in this chapter and the preceding chapters to create an invoice for Videos West.

1. Open a new document.
2. Copy the letterhead from the VCR file.
3. Use the line or table feature to create a blank invoice. It should include the following categories: Item Number, Item Description, Price, Quantity, Total Price.
4. Use the math features to place formulas in the table to multiply Price times Quantity, to add up the ordered videos, to add postage to the total, to add tax to the total, and to create a Grand Total.
5. Save the file as VCR7.
6. Print the file.

Chapter 12

Creating Equations, Graphs, and Macros

Objectives
- **Creating Equations**
- **Creating Graphs**
- **Recording Macros**
- **Running Macros**
- **Editing and Deleting Macros**
- **Customizing Word 6**

Key Terms

TERM	DEFINITION
Slots	dotted boxes that allow you to add elements to an equation
Cell	each box in a Graph data sheet
Datapoint	each cell in a Graph data sheet that contains data
Dataseries	datapoints that are grouped together in a Graph data sheet
Macros	programs that automate Word 6
WordBasic	Microsoft Word macro language
Template Macros	macros that are available only for a particular template
Global Macros	macros that are available for every document

In this chapter, you learn to use two of the supplementary applications included with Word 6, the Equation Editor and Graph. You also learn to record, run, and edit macros. These macros can be assigned to toolbar buttons, to menus, or to shortcut keys. After creating buttons and menu options, you return Word 6 to its original settings.

Objective 1: Creating Equations

You use the Equation Editor to include special characters such as exponents, square root signs, integrals, or other mathematical symbols in your documents. The Microsoft Word Equation Editor not only inserts the symbols into your document, but it also formats the symbols appropriately, such as superscripting and reducing the font size of an exponent.

You choose Insert Object. On the Create New tab, select Microsoft Equation 2.0 from the Object Type list. Word displays the Equation Editor toolbar and menu bar. (See Figure 12-1.) The top row of the toolbar contains symbols that can be inserted into an equation. The bottom row of the toolbar contains the containers, or fences, that contain the data.

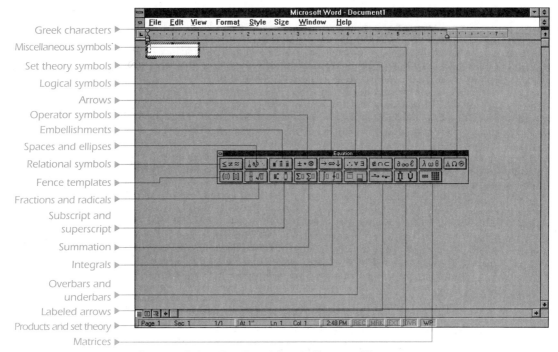

Figure 12-1 **The Equation Editor toolbar**

To create an equation, place the insertion point where you want the equation to appear, click the appropriate button, and then drag to select the item you want.

Slots *Slots* are the dotted boxes that appear allowing you to add elements to the equation. Slots expand as you type numbers, text, or symbols. Complex equations may consist of may different slots.

Equations are stored in Word 6 as embedded objects, which means that you can double-click an equation to edit it.

Exercise 1: Creating an equation

In this exercise, you create an equation.

1. On a new document, choose Insert Object.
2. On the Create New tab, select Microsoft Equation 2.0 from the Object Type list.
3. Create the following equation:

$$x^3 + \frac{a}{b}$$

4. Close the document without saving.

Word 6 provides extensive on-line help for the Equation Editor, including step-by-step instructions.

Objective 2: Creating Graphs

Word 6 also includes a supplementary application called Graph, which creates charts. This feature helps you make complex numeric data easier to understand by presenting it visually. With Graph, you can enhance all types of documents with bar, column, line, pie, and other types of charts. The charts are saved as embedded objects, which means that you can double-click a Graph chart and change the characteristics of the chart.

You invoke the Graph program by choosing Insert Object. The Object dialog box displays, and you choose the Create New tab. In the Object Type list box, choose Microsoft Graph and choose OK. Alternatively, you can click the Insert Chart button on the Standard toolbar to invoke the Graph program. Both methods open Graph over your Word document. The Graph application has two windows: the Chart window and the Datasheet window. The Chart window contains the chart of your data. (See Figure 12-2.) The Datasheet window contains the data to be charted. (See Figure 12-3.)

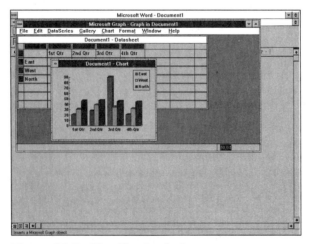

Figure 12-2 The Chart window

Writing a Computer Program

A program is a list of instructions for the computer to carry out to perform a certain task. A simple task might be written in a macro language, and a complex task such as writing a complete software application would be written in a programming language.

There are various programming languages which are used for different jobs. However, a computer really only understands one language, that is, machine language, or binary code. In fact, programs written in the early days of computing had to be written in binary code. Because programming with zeros and ones was so error prone, other languages were developed. Today programs are written in other languages but are translated into machine language for the computer to understand.

Assembly language is one step up from machine language. Instead of using the zeros and ones of binary code, a programmer could use codes that resembled English. Other languages that resemble English even more are called high-level languages. They include BASIC, COBOL, FORTRAN, PASCAL, C, and many others.

Newer languages that are powerful and user friendly such as Microsoft's Visual BASIC are becoming available. These languages feature tools within the program that help programmers create graphics and menus.

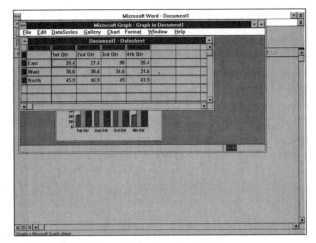

Figure 12-3 **The Datasheet window**

By default, Graph already has data in the Datasheet window, and the data is plotted as a graph in the Chart window. The data can be edited to change the chart.

To create charts, Word 6 offers two methods: you can turn a table into a chart, or you can create a chart by typing data directly into the datasheet.

Creating a chart from a Word 6 table

To create a chart from a table, select the table and then click the

Insert Chart button on the Standard toolbar ![chart icon], or choose Insert Object and select Microsoft Graph from the Object Type list on the Create New tab. The chart appears in the Graph window, and it can be modified there. When you exit from the Graph window, the chart is inserted in the document immediately following the table.

Exercise 2: Creating a chart from an existing table

In this exercise, you create a table and then have Word create a chart from the table information.

1. In a new document, create the following table:

	Qtr 1	Qtr 2	Qtr 3	Qtr 4
Smith	2000	2500	2800	1200
Jones	2400	1800	2600	1400
Brown	1900	2200	2300	1300
Hill	2300	3000	1800	1100

2. Select the table.

3. Click the Insert Chart button ▦ on the Standard toolbar.

4. Choose File Exit and Return, Yes Update Graph.

   The chart is inserted immediately below the table.

5. Save the file as CHART1.DOC and close it.

Creating a chart from data not in a table

To create a chart from data that is not in a Word 6 table, position the insertion point at the location in the document that you want the chart to appear, and choose Insert Object. On the Create New tab, select Microsoft Graph.

cell; datapoint; dataseries   When the datasheet appears, type information into it that you want Graph to chart. The datasheet is divided into 4000 rows and 256 columns, into which you can enter numbers and labels. Each box in the datasheet is called a *cell*, and each cell that contains data is called a *datapoint*. The datapoints are grouped together into *dataseries*. You can select a cell or a group of cells to change the numbers or labels in the cells.

By default, Graph enters series data in rows, so if you use the default set-up, type the data series names down the first column and the category names across the first row. Then, enter the data for each series across each row.

The category names typed into the first row of the datasheet appear along the x-axis of the chart, and the data series names typed in the first column appear in the legend. You should leave the top left cell of the datasheet blank because Graph does not plot that cell.

Exercise 3: Creating a chart from data not appearing in a table

In this exercise, you create a chart from data that does not appear in a Word 6 table.

1. Open a new document.

2. Choose Insert Object.

3. On the Create New tab, select Microsoft Graph.

4. On the datasheet tab, insert the following data:

	Qtr 1	Qtr 2	Qtr 3	Qtr 4
North	50000	48000	60000	55000
South	60000	50000	50000	46000
East	70000	68000	66000	60000
West	58000	63000	70000	66000

5. Choose File Exit and Return Yes Update Graph in Document.

   The chart displays in the document.

6. Save the document as CHART2.DOC.

You can also import data from another application by choosing File Import Data. Graph converts the data from the other application such as Lotus 1-2-3, based on the file's three-letter extension.

Changing chart types

Graph provides twelve types of charts—seven two-dimensional and five three-dimensional. Table 12-1 shows the chart types and their uses.

Table 12-1 **Chart Types**

CHART TYPE	USES	VARIATION
Column	Shows variation over a period of time.	Stacked and 100%
Bar	Shows figures at a specific time.	Stacked and 100%
Line	Shows trends over a period of time.	
Pie	Shows relationship of parts to the whole.	
Area	Shows how values change in proportion to the total over a period of time.	100%
XY (Scatter)	Shows relationship between values in different groups.	
Combination	Combines up to four axes to compare data.	
3-D Column	Shows a 3-D view of a column chart.	
3-D Bar	Shows a 3-D view of a bar chart.	
3-D Line	Shows a 3-D view of a line chart.	
3-D Pie	Shows a 3-D view of a pie chart.	
3-D Area	Shows a 3-D view of an area chart.	

By default, Graph plots charts as column charts. To change the chart type, choose the Gallery menu, and then choose a chart type. A Chart Gallery dialog box displays showing the range of formats for that chart type. (See Figure 12-4.)

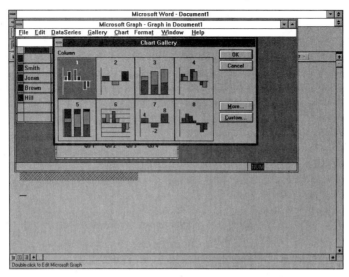

Figure 12-4   The Chart Gallery dialog box

Exercise 4: Changing chart types

In this exercise, you look at the chart types available in Graph.

1. Open the CHART1.DOC file.
2. Double-click the chart.
3. Click the Chart window to make it the active window.
4. Choose Gallery Line.
5. Select chart number 4.

   The chart appears as a line chart. Notice that the same data is charted. It simply appears in a different format.

6. Choose Gallery Pie.
7. Select chart number 5.

   The chart appears as a pie chart.

8. Choose Gallery 3D Line.
9. Choose chart number 1.

   The chart appears as a 3-D chart.

10. Choose File Exit and Return.
11. Keep the chart on the screen for use in the next exercise.

Adding titles to a chart

You can add a title to the chart so that the chart is more self-explanatory. Choose Chart Titles. The Chart Titles dialog box displays.

Select Chart and click OK. A title object appears on the chart screen. Simply type the title and press Esc or click the mouse outside the title to remove the handles.

FEATURE

Outline View

Outline view provides you with a different way of looking at your document. You see the same document but with the structure and organization made apparent. You switch to Outline view by choosing the Outline View button ▦ on the horizontal scroll bar, or by choosing View Outline. When you switch to Outline view, Word displays the Outline toolbar. (See figure below.)

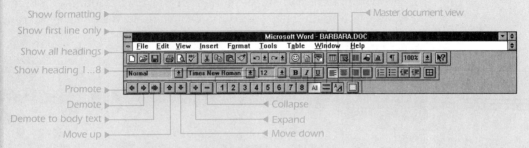

Show formatting ▶
Show first line only ▶
Show all headings ▶
Show heading 1...8 ▶
Promote ▶
Demote ▶
Demote to body text ▶
Move up ▶

◀ Master document view
◀ Collapse
◀ Expand
◀ Move down

The Outline toolbar

Word displays the document with symbols that reflect the level of the text. (See figure below.)

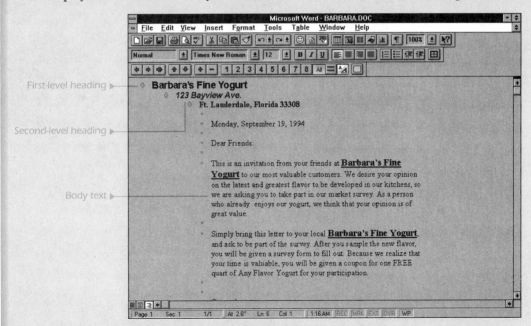

First-level heading ▶
Second-level heading ▶
Body text ▶

A document in Outline view

You can use the toolbar in Outline view to see a collapsed view of the document, to quickly scroll through the document, and to rearrange sections. The Outline view feature comes in handy for long documents.

Objective 3: Recording Macros

Macros are programs that automate Word 6. Macros increase productivity by saving time and avoiding errors. They consist of a sequence of steps that you perform repeatedly in Word 6. You record the steps as a group and assign the macro a name or assign the macro to a toolbar, a menu, or to shortcut keys. Macros range from a simple series of keystrokes to a complex program using the Word macro language, *WordBasic*.

WordBasic

To record a macro, you start the macro recorder by double-clicking the REC indicator on the Status bar, or choosing Tools Macro. The Macro dialog box displays. (See Figure 12-5.)

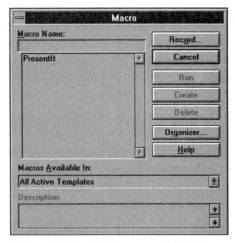

Figure 12-5 **The Macro dialog box**

In the Macro dialog box, choose the Record button. The Record Macro dialog box displays. (See Figure 12-6.)

Figure 12-6 **The Record Macro dialog box**

template macros; global macros   Word 6 has two types of macros: macros that are available only for a particular template, *template macros*, and macros that are available for every document, *global macros*. In the Make Macro Available To drop-down box in the Record Macro dialog box, you can choose to make a macro a template or a global macro. The default is to assign the template to the Normal template, thus making it a global macro.

In the Record Macro Name text box, type a name for the macro or use the name that Word suggests. Type a description of the macro in the Description box. When you choose OK to close the dialog box, you are returned to your document. Word displays two buttons on the screen over your document.

They are the Macro Stop ◼ and the Macro Pause ‖◉. Every action you perform is recorded as part of the macro until you stop recording the macro with the Macro Stop button or pause recording the macro with the Macro Pause button.

Exercise 5: Creating a macro

In this exercise, you create a simple macro and give it a name.

1. Open a new document.
2. Choose Tools Macro.
3. In the Macro dialog box, choose Record.
4. In the Record Macro dialog box, type the name Closing in the Record Macro Name section.
5. Make sure that All Documents is selected in the Make Macros Available To section.
6. In the Description text box, type letter closing.
7. Choose OK.
8. Type Sincerely, press ⏎ ENTER four times, type your full name, press ⏎ ENTER, and type a title for yourself.
9. Click the Stop button ◼ on the Macro toolbar.
10. Close the document without saving. (You will run the macro in Objective 4.)

You can assign the macro to a toolbar button, a menu, or to shortcut keys on the keyboard. You do so in the Assign Macro To section of the Record Macro dialog box by choosing Toolbars, Menus, or the Keyboard. Selecting any of these assign buttons opens the Customize dialog box. (See Figure 12-7.)

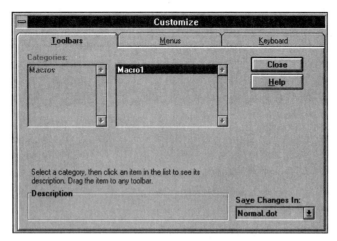

Figure 12-7 **The Toolbars tab of the Customize dialog box**

If you choose to assign the macro to a toolbar, Word displays the Toolbar tab of the Customize dialog box. On the Toolbar tab, you click and drag the macro name from the list box to a toolbar. When you release the mouse button, the Custom Button dialog box displays. (See Figure 12-8.) You can choose a button or choose to use the Text Button Name provided by Word 6 in the text box. Then you choose the Assign button.

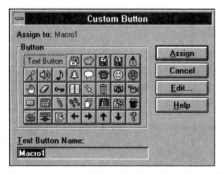

Figure 12-8 **The Custom Button dialog box**

If you choose to assign a macro to a menu, Word opens the Customize dialog box with the Menus tab active. (See Figure 12-9.)

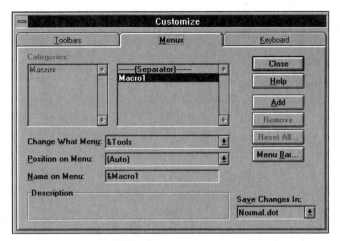

Figure 12-9   **The Menus tab of the Customize dialog box**

Choose a menu from the Change What Menu drop-down list; choose a position on the menu from the Position on Menu drop-down list. You can edit the Name on Menu if you need to. If you choose the Menu Bar button, you can create your own menu to contain macros. The Menu Bar dialog box displays. (See Figure 12-10,)

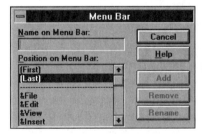

Figure 12-10   **The Menu Bar dialog box**

In the Name on Menu Bar text box, type a name for the menu, and in the Position on Menu Bar list box, select a position for the menu option. Choose the Add button to complete the process.

If you choose Keyboard in the Assign Macro To section of the Record Macro dialog box, Word displays the Keyboard tab of the Customize dialog box. (See Figure 12-11.)

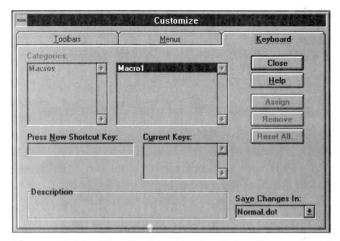

Figure 12-11   **The Keyboard tab of the Customize dialog box**

In the Press New Shortcut Key text box, press the keys that you want to assign to the macro. If the key combination is already assigned to another command, Word will indicate that the keys are not available by displaying the Currently Assigned To section, which tells what the keys are used for. The key combination appears in the Current Keys list box. Choose Close to Record.

When you return to your document after assigning the macro to a toolbar, a button, or the shortcut keys, or simply giving it a name, Word displays the Macro Stop button ▪ and the Macro Pause button ❙❙◉. You can press the Pause button to pause the recording. Click it a second time to resume recording.

When you are finished recording the macro and want to turn off record, you can click the Stop button or double-click the REC indicator on the Status bar, or you can choose Tools Macro and click the Stop Recording button.

Exercise 6: Recording a macro and saving it to shortcut keys

In this exercise, you record a macro and save it to shortcut keys.

1. Open a new document.
2. Choose Tools Macro.
3. In the Macro dialog box, choose Record.
4. In the Record Macro dialog box, you can leave the name Macro1 (or the number of the macro suggested) in the Record Macro Name section.
5. Make sure that All Documents is selected in the Make Macros Available To section.

6. In the Description text box, type supervisor's closing.

7. Choose Keyboard in the Assign Macro To section.

8. On the Keyboard tab of the Customize dialog box with the insertion point in the Press New Shortcut Key section, press (CTRL) + (ALT) + (X).

9. In the Currently Assigned To section, the message should read [unassigned]. If something is assigned to these keys, try a different key combination.

10. Choose the Assign button.

11. Choose Close.

12. Type Sincerely, press (↵ ENTER) four times, type your supervisor's name, press (↵ ENTER), and type your supervisor's title.

13. Click the Stop button ■ on the Macro toolbar.

14. Close the document without saving. (You will run the macro in Objective 4.)

Exercise 7: Recording a macro and saving it to a toolbar button

In this exercise, you record a macro and save it to a toolbar button.

1. Open a new document.

2. Choose Tools Macro.

3. In the Macro dialog box, choose Record.

4. In the Record Macro dialog box, leave the name Macro2 (or the number suggested) in the Record Macro Name text box.

5. Make sure that All Documents appears in the Make Macro Available To section.

6. In the Description text box, type inside address.

7. Choose Toolbar in the Assign Macro To section.

8. On the Toolbars tab of the Customize dialog box, click and drag Macro2 from the list box up to the center of the toolbar.

   A blank button appears on the Standard toolbar, and the Custom Button Toolbar dialog box appears.

9. In the Custom Button Toolbar dialog box, choose the Happy Face button.

10. Click the Assign button. (See Figure 12-12.)

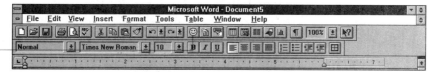

Happy Face button ▶

Figure 12-12   The Happy Face button on the Standard toolbar

11. Choose Close.

    You are returned to your document, and the macro is recording your keystrokes.

12. Type your street address; press (↵ ENTER); type your city, state, and zip code; and press (↵ ENTER) twice.

13. Double-click the REC indicator on the Status bar to stop recording.

14. Close the document without saving. (You will run the macro in Objective 4.)

Exercise 8: Creating a macro and assigning it to a menu

In this exercise, you create a macro and assign it to a menu.

1. Open a new document.

2. Choose Tools Macro.

3. In the Macro dialog box, choose Record.

4. In the Record Macro dialog box, leave the name Macro3 (or the number suggested) in the Record Macro Name text box.

5. Make sure that All Documents appears in the Make Macro Available To section.

6. In the Description text box, type Letterhead.

7. Choose Menu in the Assign Macro To section.

8. Choose the Menu Bar button.

9. In the Menu Bar dialog box, type &Macros in the Name on Menu Bar.

10. In the Position on Menu Bar list box, select {Last}.

11. Choose the Add button.

12. Choose Close.

13. On the Menu tab of the Customize dialog box, the Change What Menu box should read &Macros.

14. The Position on Menu Bar list box should read {Auto}.

15. In the Name on Menu box, type &Letterhead.

16. Choose the Close button.

    You are returned to your document, and the macro is recording your keystrokes.

17. From the Font button, choose BrushScript.

18. From the Font Size button, choose 16.

19. Click the Center button.

20. Type your name; press (↵ ENTER); type your street address; press (↵ ENTER); type your city, state, and zip code; and press (↵ ENTER).

21. Turn off the macro record feature by pressing the Stop button ■ on the Macro toolbar.

22. Close the document without saving.

Objective 4: Running Macros

Running a macro is very easy. You position the insertion point in the document at the location you want the macro results to appear, and then invoke the macro. If you assigned shortcut keys to the macro, simply type the shortcut keys and the macro will run. If you assigned the macro to a button on the toolbar, simply click the button. If you assigned the macro to a menu, choose the menu and select the desired macro just as you would any command in Word 6. If you simply gave the macro a name, choose Tools Macro, select the macro, and choose Run.

Exercise 9: Running macros

In this exercise, you run the macros you created.

1. Open a new document.

2. Press CTRL + ALT + X or the keystroke combination that you assigned to the macro.

3. Press ← ENTER twice.

4. Click the Happy Face button on the Standard toolbar.

5. Press ← ENTER twice.

6. Choose Macros Macro3.

7. Press ← ENTER twice.

8. Choose Tools Macro.

9. In the Macro dialog box, select the Closing macro.

10. Click the Run button.

Objective 5: Editing and Deleting Macros

You can edit macros by choosing Tools Macro. In the Macro dialog box, select the macro you want to edit and click the Edit button. Word opens the macro editing window and displays the macro commands. (See Figure 12-13.)

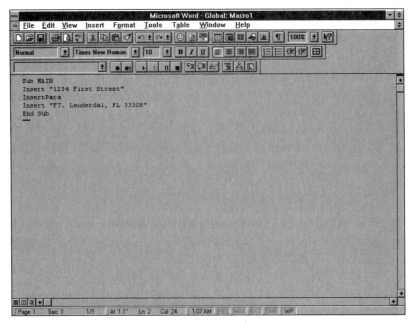

Figure 12-13 The macro editing window

You can edit the macro using the toolbar or the WordBasic macro language. You can delete a macro by choosing Tools Macro. In the Macro dialog box, select the macro that you want to delete and click the Delete button. Word 6 will ask you to confirm the deletion of the macro.

Exercise 10: Deleting macros

In this exercise, you delete the macros you have created.

1. Open a new document.
2. Choose Tools Macro.
3. In the Macro dialog box, select Closing.
4. Press DELETE .
5. Choose Yes to confirm deletion.
6. Repeat Steps 2 and 3 for Macro2 and Macro3.
7. Close the Macro dialog box.

The macros are deleted, but the menu addition and added buttons remain on the screen. You will learn how to remove these in Objective 6.

Objective 6: Customizing Word 6

You can customize Word 6 by adding and deleting items to menus and toolbars and by changing the items that display on the screen.

You can add a button to a toolbar by choosing Tools Customize. On the Toolbars tab of the Customize dialog box, select a category for the type of button, for example, File. You then select a button and drag it to the toolbar, positioning it where you want it. The button is added where you designated.

You can add a command to a menu by choosing Tools Customize. On the Menus tab of the Customize dialog box, select Categories for the type of menu, for example, Edit. In the Commands box, select the specific item you want to add, and select the menu to which the item should be added, its position, and the text you want on the menu. Choose the Add button and the command is added to the menu.

If you make changes to the menus and to the toolbars and want to restore Word 6 to its original setting, you can do so easily. To reset menus, choose Tools Customize. On the Menus tab, choose the Reset All button. To reset toolbars, choose View Toolbars. In the Toolbars list box in the Toolbars dialog box, select the toolbar you want to restore to its original settings and click the Restore button.

Exercise 11: Deleting the unwanted buttons and commands

In this exercise, you restore Word 6 to its original settings by deleting the button and menu you just created.

1. Choose Tools Customize.
2. On the Menus tab of the Customize dialog box, choose Reset All, and Yes to Reset menu assignments.
3. Click the Close button.

   The Macros menu disappears from the screen.
4. Choose View Toolbars.
5. In the Toolbars list box in the Toolbars dialog box, select the Standard toolbar.
6. Click the Reset button.
7. In the Reset toolbar dialog box, choose OK.
8. In the Toolbar dialog box, choose OK.

   The Happy Face button disappears from the screen.

Chapter Summary

In this chapter, you learned about two of the supplementary programs that come with Microsoft Word 6: Equation Editor and Graph. You created equations and created charts using these applications and embedded them in a Word 6 document. You also created macros by simply giving one a name and by attaching others to menus, toolbar buttons, and shortcut keys. You ran the macros, edited the macros, and deleted the macros. You also customized the screen display in this chapter.

Review Questions

True/False Questions

_____ 1. Slots are dotted boxes that allow you to add elements to an equation.

_____ 2. A line chart shows relationship of parts to the whole.

_____ 3. You can customize Word 6 by adding and deleting items to menus and toolbars.

_____ 4. A macro will run at the position of the insertion point an unlimited number of times.

_____ 5. Template macros are available by default for every document.

Multiple Choice Questions

_____ 6. The chart window in Graph contains

   A. the chart of your data.

   B. the data to be charted.

   C. the gallery of charts.

   D. Both A and B.

_____ 7. The Datasheet window contains

   A. the chart of your data.

   B. the data to be charted.

   C. the gallery of charts.

   D. Both A and B.

_____ 8. Equations and charts created with the Equation Editor and Graph

A. cannot be edited.

B. are stored in Word 6 as static object.

C. are stored in Word 6 as embedded objects.

D. Both A and B.

_____ 9. You can create a macro and assign it to

A. any general name.

B. a menu.

C. a toolbar or shortcut keys.

D. All of the above.

_____ 10. You can turn off the macro record feature by

A. clicking the Stop button on the Macro Record toolbar.

B. double-clicking the REC indicator on the Status bar.

C. choosing Tools Macro and click the Stop Recording button.

D. All of the above.

Fill-in-the-Blank Questions

11. Each box in a Graph datasheet is call a(n) _____.

12. Each cell in a Graph datasheet that contains data is called a(n) _____.

13. Datapoints are grouped together in a Graph datasheet into _____.

14. _____ are programs that automate Word 6.

15. _____ is the Microsoft Word macro language.

Acumen-Building Activities

Quick Projects

Project 1: Creating an Equation

1. Open a new document.

2. Create the following equation:

$$\sqrt{(a+b)} * c^2$$

3. Print the document.

4. Close the file without saving.

Project 2: Creating a Graph from a Table

1. Open a new document.
2. Create the following table:

	Game 1	Game 2	Game 3
Jim	185	215	225
Sue	213	175	240
Mary	165	200	215
John	200	150	185
Alice	175	230	200

3. Select the table.
4. Create a chart from the information in the table.
5. Print the document.
6. Save the document as BOWL.DOC

Project 3: Creating a Macro

1. Open a new document.
2. Create a macro that centers your school or business name on the page and changes the font and the font size.
3. Attach the macro to a button and add the button on the Standard toolbar.
4. Test the macro by running it.
5. Print the results.

Project 4: Deleting a Macro and Removing a Button

1. Use the Macro created in Quick Project 3.
2. Delete the macro.
3. Remove the button from the Standard toolbar.

In-Depth Projects

Project 1: Creating a Memo Macro

1. Open a new document.
2. Create a macro that is a memo template, enhancing the text and placing it on the page in an appropriate place.
3. Assign the memo macro to a new menu named Utility.
4. Print the memo.
5. Close the file without saving.
6. Test the macro by running it and print the results.

Project 2: Enhancing a Document with a Chart

1. Open the article document that you created in In-Depth Projects 1 and 2 of Chapter 11.
2. Add a table to the document.
3. Create a chart from the table.
4. Add a title to the chart.
5. Print the document.
6. Save the file.

CASE STUDIES

Coffee-On-The-Go:

Creating a Macro

In this chapter, you learned to create macros. You will use those skills to create a macro for Coffee-On-The-Go.

1. Write a macro that creates a letterhead for Coffee-On-The-Go. The letterhead should include font changes, formatting, a line, a graphic if available, and immediately below it the current date. The address is 700 Oak St., Eugene, OR 97401.
2. Save the macro as Head.
3. Test the macro and print it.

CASE STUDIES

Videos West:

Macros

In this chapter, you learned to create macros. You will apply those skills by creating a macro for Videos West.

1. Open a new document.
2. Create a macro to create the letterhead for Videos West. The letterhead should include the address 1121 Second Ave., Fairbanks, Alaska 99701.
3. Include a graphic in the letterhead if possible.
4. Enhance the letterhead by changing the font and the size.
5. Include a line that separates the letterhead from the rest of the document.
6. Save the macro as VCR.

Acumen Advanced Features Milestone

Individual Project: ### Polishing the Document

1. Open the document MEMORY1.DOC created in Project 1 at the end of Part 2.
2. Add a graphic to the document.
3. Add a table to the document.
4. Create a bulleted list in the document.
5. Create an index for the document.
6. Create a table of contents for the document.
7. Create a chart for the document.
8. Print the document.
9. Save the document as MEMORY2.DOC.

Team Project: ### Polishing the Document as a Team

1. Open the TEAMPRO.doc file created in Project 2 at the end of Part 2. Working as a group, add the following enhancements to the document:
2. Add a graphic to the document.
3. Add a table to the document.
4. Create a bulleted list in the document.
5. Create an index for the document.
6. Create a table of contents for the document.
7. Create a chart for the document.
8. Print the document.
9. Save the document as TEAMP2.DOC.

Index for Word 6.0 for Windows

Quick Preview

Excel 5.0 for Windows

Excel 5.0 is a spreadsheet program that can be used by people at all skill levels for recording and analyzing financial and scientific information. Excel is easy for beginners and has powerful features that help you organize data, perform calculations, and even display charts that illustrate the relationships in numerical data.

This Quick Preview shows you some of these features.

Activity 1:   Starting Excel and Opening a File

1. Start Windows.

   The Program Manager window appears.

2. Locate the Excel 5.0 program-item icon ▨ Microsoft Excel . It may be stored inside the Microsoft Office program group.

3. Double-click the Excel 5.0 program-item icon ▨ Microsoft Excel .

   Excel presents you with a new, blank worksheet, as shown below.

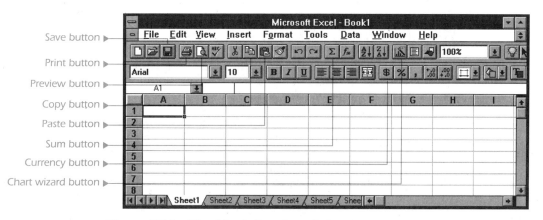

Save button ▶
Print button ▶
Preview button ▶
Copy button ▶
Paste button ▶
Sum button ▶
Currency button ▶
Chart wizard button ▶

Figure QP-1   The blank Excel worksheet

Activity 2: Entering Information into a Worksheet

The worksheet is divided into cells by gridlines. Each cell has an address. The cell in the upper left corner is in column A, row 1. Its cell address is A1.

1. Press ⊡ once.

   A black border appears around cell B1, indicating that the cell is selected. When you select a cell, you can enter or change information in that cell.

2. Press ⊡ once.

   The selected cell is now cell A1.

3. With cell A1 selected, type Sales and press ⎆ ENTER.

   The word *Sales* appears in cell A1, and cell A2 becomes the selected cell.

4. Press ⎆ ENTER again to make cell A3 the selected cell.

5. In cell A3, type Burns and press ⎆ ENTER.

6. In cell A4, type Carson and press ⎆ ENTER.

7. In cell A5, type Freelin and press ⎆ ENTER.

8. In cell A6, type Peters and press ⎆ ENTER.

9. Position the mouse pointer in cell B2, and click to select cell B2.

10. In cell B2, type January.

11. Make cell C2 the selected cell, and type February.

12. Make cell D2 the selected cell, and type March.

13. Make cell B3 the active cell, type 1521.93, and press ⎆ ENTER.

14. Finish entering the worksheet shown below.

Figure QP-2 **The basic Sales information**

15. Copy the values from February into March. To do this, select cell C3 and drag the mouse pointer down to cell C6 so that cells C3 through C6 are highlighted.

16. Click the Copy button 🖺 in the toolbar.

17. Make cell D3 the selected cell. and click the Paste button 📋 in the toolbar.

The data from cells C3 to C6 is copied into cells D3 through D6.

Activity 3: Adding Formulas

Now that you have entered data into the worksheet, you can use a formula to help fill in the worksheet. Assume that sales in April were up by 6% from sales in March. You will write a formula that will multiply the March sales figures by 1.06.

1. Make cell E2 the selected (active) cell, and type April.

2. Make cell E3 the active cell, type the formula =D3*1.06, and press ⏎ ENTER.

   This formula tells Excel that the contents of cell E3 are to be equal to the contents of cell D3, multiplied by 1.06. Excel places the new value in cell E3.

3. Make cell E3 the active cell again, and click the Copy button 📋 in the toolbar.

4. Make cell E4 the active cell and drag the mouse pointer down through cell E6 so that cells E4, E5, and E6 are selected.

5. Click the Paste button 📋 in the toolbar. Press ESC.

   The formula from cell E3 is copied into cells E4 through E6.

Activity 4: Performing Quick Addition

Assume that all sales staff are reviewed at the beginning of May by their supervisor. One of the top priorities of the review is to examine the sales record of each employee. To do this quickly, you can total the sales for each person using the Sum button Σ.

1. Make cell F2 the active cell and type the label Subtotal, and press ⏎ ENTER.

2. Make cell F3 the active cell, and click the Sum button Σ.

   Excel places the formula =SUM(B3:E3) in cell F3. This formula means that Excel will add the values in cells B3, C3, D3, and E3 and place the result of that addition into cell F3.

3. Press ⏎ ENTER to confirm this formula.

   Excel places a new value, based on the result of the formula, in cell F3.

4. Copy the formula in cell F3 to cells F4 through F6. Make cell F3 the active cell, and click the Copy button 📋.

5. Select cells F4 through F6, and click the Paste button 📋.
   The Subtotal category is filled in for each salesperson.

Activity 5: Formatting Labels

Entering data and formulas is only part of setting up a worksheet. The worksheet must have a professional appearance, obtained by modifying the format of the cells.

1. Make cell B3 active, and drag the mouse pointer down and to the right so that cells B3 through F6 are all selected.

2. Click the Currency style button 💲 in the toolbar.
   The data for all values appear as #####. This is because the cell widths cannot accommodate the data.

3. Adjust the cell width for column B by moving the mouse pointer to the right boundary gridline of column B (the line that forms the right boundary of the column).
   The mouse pointer changes to a cross-hair.

4. Double-click the mouse button.
   The column width adjusts to accommodate the values in column B.

5. Repeat Steps 3 and 4 above for columns C, D, E and F so that all the data is visible.

Activity 6: Using the ChartWizard

Although your data is enhanced by attractive formatting, there is no substitute for the impact made by a chart. A chart quickly makes a point while raw worksheet data must be visually analyzed.

1. Select cells A2 through F6.

2. Click the ChartWizard button 📊 in the toolbar.

3. In the worksheet, select the range A8 through F20.
   A dialog box appears with Step 1 of the ChartWizard.

4. You have already selected the range of data to be charted, so click Next to move to the next step in the ChartWizard.
   The ChartWizard presents several types of charts from which to choose, with the Column chart already selected.

5. Accept the Column chart style by clicking Next.
   Step 3 of the ChartWizard appears, asking you to select a format.

6. Accept the chart format already selected by clicking Next.

   Step 4 of the ChartWizard appears, providing you with the opportunity to change the way the ChartWizard is interpreting your data.

7. The ChartWizard's interpretation is accurate, so click Next.

   The final step of the ChartWizard appears, asking you to enter a title for the Chart.

8. Move the mouse pointer to the white space beneath Chart Title, click the mouse button, and type Sales by Associate.

9. Click Finish.

   The ChartWizard closes, and a new chart appears on your worksheet.

Activity 7: Printing the Worksheet

A worksheet can be printed with all its data and formatting, as well as any charts you have created. Before printing anything, however, it's a good idea to preview your work.

1. Click the Preview button 🔍 in the toolbar.

   A miniaturized, full-page preview of your worksheet and chart appears on the screen.

2. Click Close to close the Print Preview.

3. Click the Print button 🖨 in the toolbar.

   Excel displays a message box telling you that it is printing your worksheet.

4. Collect your worksheet and chart from the printer. If you're sharing a printer with others, make sure that you get only your work.

Activity 8: Saving the Worksheet

Saving your work is an important part of the worksheet process. In this example, you will save your work under the file name preview.xls. The .XLS is the standard file extension for Excel 5.0 worksheets.

1. Insert a formatted floppy disk into drive A of your computer.

2. Click the Save button 💾 in the toolbar.

   Excel will enter the default file name book1.xls in the File Name field.

3. Press (← BACKSPACE) to delete this name, and then type preview.xls.

4. Click the Drives list box arrow, and select drive A.

5. Click OK to complete the save process.

   Excel displays a summary information box.

6. Click OK to bypass this box and return to your worksheet.

Activity 9: Exiting Excel

After you have finished working with Excel and have saved your file, it is safe to exit the program. You should always quit an application such as Excel when you have finished working with it to free up the computer's resources for other tasks.

1. Open the File menu by clicking it.

2. Drag the mouse pointer down to choose Exit.

   The program closes, and you are returned to the Windows desktop.

Part 1

Fundamentals

Chapter 1

Introduction to Microsoft Excel

Objectives

- Identifying Elements of the Software
- Using the Mouse and Keyboard
- Starting the Software
- Exploring Elements of the Screen
- Obtaining On-Line Help
- Exiting Excel 5.0

Key Terms

TERM	DEFINITION
Worksheet	a grid or matrix of rows and columns on a page
Column	the vertical lines, designated by letters, that separate each category of information in a worksheet
Row	the horizontal lines, designated by numbers, that separate each category of information in a worksheet
Cell	the intersection of a row and a column and the storage place for data in the worksheet
Cell Address	the column-row coordinate defining the location of a cell (for example, A7 is the cell located in column A, row 7)
Formula	a mathematical equation for executing a calculation
Chart	a graphical representation of data in the worksheet
Database	an organized table or list of data

TERM	DEFINITION
Sorting	the process of physically reorganizing information based on one or more criteria
Range	a group of contiguous (connected) cells identified by the address of the upper left cell and the lower right cell (for example, A3:D7)
Dialog Box	a small window that contains optional settings for a specific command
Hotkey	the underlined letter in a menu or command name that indicates the letter on the keyboard that can be typed to activate the menu or command
Icon	a picture representing a program or process in Windows
Boot	the term generally used for turning on the computer
Workbook	a group of related worksheets and charts saved under one file name in Excel
Ready Mode	the state that Excel is in when it is waiting for you to do something
I-beam	the blinking bar denoting the location where text will appear when you begin to type, also called the insertion point
Macro	a series of keystrokes and commands stored in a file and executed with a single keystroke or menu command.

Using a powerful tool like Microsoft Excel 5.0 for Windows can make many financial, record-keeping, and presentation tasks easier. Before you jump right in to using Excel, however, you need to know a few things about the program's capabilities and about the way the program works with your computer. Taking the time up-front to understand what you can do with Excel will save you hours of hunting around for that magic keystroke later on.

Objective 1: Identifying Elements of the Software

Excel has several elements that provide users with capabilities ranging from simple data management to complex computations. The three primary features of Excel are its worksheet capabilities, its charting capabilities, and its database capabilities. Advanced features such as the capability of writing and storing worksheet procedures make Excel a powerful tool for a wide range of users.

Exploring worksheets

worksheet   A *worksheet* is a grid of rows and columns. You work with many traditional worksheets on a daily basis. Your checkbook register is a good example of a worksheet. A checkbook register has columns for check numbers, dates, descriptions, debits, credits, and the balance. Figure 1-1 shows a portion of a checkbook register.

Column ▶

Row ▶

Cell ▶

	A	B	C	D	E	F
1	Check #	Date	Description	Debit	Credit	Balance
2	5274	9/2/94	Hardware store	$ 57.63		$2,701.73
3	5275	9/2/94	Grocery store	$ 102.83		$2,598.90
4	5276	9/3/94	Veterinarian	$ 78.20		$2,520.70
5		9/5/94	Pay check		$ 2,751.43	$5,272.13

Figure 1-1   A checkbook register is a good example of a worksheet

column

row

cell

cell addresses

Columns run vertically through the worksheet and generally contain heading information. In your checkbook register, horizontal lines separate each transaction—whether it's a check that you've written or, on those rare occasions, money that you have deposited. *Rows* run horizontally across the page. The intersection of a row and a column is called a *cell*. Thus, the blank space for you to type a check number, a date, a description, an amount, or a balance is a cell. In Excel, columns are labeled with letters, and rows are labeled with numbers. *Cell addresses* are identified by their column-row coordinates. In Figure 1-1, check number 5275 is in cell A3.

Calculating with formulas

Cell addresses are critical because they enable spreadsheet programs like Excel to do what they do best—make calculations. Examine Figure 1-1. When you write a check, you compute the new balance in your checkbook by subtracting the check amount from the previous balance. If you make a mistake in a computation, all your balance figures will be wrong until you correct the mistake. In Excel, however, you compute the balance by telling the program to subtract the amount in cell D3 from the balance in cell F2.

formula

You give this instruction in a *formula*, the mathematical equation for completing this operation. By using the cell address in the formula rather than the actual data in the cell, you can make changes to the data in any cell and Excel will automatically update all results, such as the balance total in the example. The formula to subtract the check in row 3 from the balance in row 2 of the checkbook worksheet is F2 − D3.

Exercise 1: Identifying cell coordinates

In this exercise, you will use Figure 1-2 to identify the cell coordinates of the remaining data in the worksheet.

	A	B	C
1	X		Z
2		Q	
3	31		
4			Y
5	Data		
6			

Figure 1-2   Cells are identified by their column-row coordinates

1. In the space below or on a blank sheet of paper, write down the cell address of the cell that contains the letter *Z*.
2. Determine and write down the cell addresses for the following cells:
   a. the cell containing the word *Data*
   b. the cell containing the number *31*
   c. the cell containing the letter *Y*
   d. the cell containing the letter *Q*

Representing data in charts

chart
After data has been entered into a worksheet, it can quickly be transformed into a *chart,* a graphical representation of numeric data in the worksheet. Numeric data is often much easier to understand when it is presented as a chart or graph. (The old adage "A picture is worth a thousand words" holds true today.) In Excel, you can choose a group of cells to be made into a chart and then use commands to create the chart. Figure 1-3 shows a small sales worksheet and two different charts that were created using the data in the worksheet. Excel has many chart styles and options available, and, with some basic understanding of the different chart types and a little practice, you'll be able to create effective charts that help you make your point.

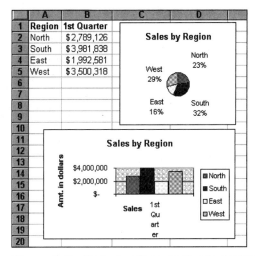

Figure 1-3 **Data is often easier to understand when it is displayed in a chart**

Organizing data in worksheets

database
Advanced worksheet packages such as Excel contain many database features to make data management easy and efficient. *Databases* are tables or lists which contain information organized by categories. In this respect, databases and worksheets are quite similar. Column headings such as

those mentioned in the preceding checkbook register example act as the standard categories, and information stored in rows and cells make up the database. The strength of a database package lies in its capability to organize information in a variety of ways and to produce professional-looking reports. Worksheets, on the other hand, are most useful for making calculations and determining the best answer based on analysis of the data.

sorting

range

Excel simplifies arranging or *sorting* rows of data in the worksheet by the contents of the columns. When you sort a worksheet, you must first select the *range* or group of connected cells to be included in the sort procedure. In almost all cases, you will want to select all the cells that contain data in the worksheet. After you have selected the range, you must determine on which column to sort and whether the data should be sorted in ascending (A...Z, 1...100) or descending (Z...A, 100...1) order. When you have set the sort options, Excel begins the sort process, rearranging your data as you specified.

Using the sales example shown in Figure 1-3, you could sort regions in ascending order, which would display the data in the alphabetical order East, North, South, and West. Alternatively, you could sort in ascending order on 1st Quarter Sales, which would display the data in the order East, North, West, and South.

Exercise 2: Examining sorted data

In this exercise, you will examine two small worksheets to determine what sort criteria were used to achieve the organizations shown.

1. Examine Figure 1-4, and answer the following questions.
   a. On which column is the worksheet sorted?
   b. Is the worksheet sorted in ascending or descending order?

	A	B	C	D
1	Student	Exam 1	Exam 2	Exam 3
2	Anderson	78	83	87
3	Bailey	72	80	86
4	Chaney	91	90	97
5	Henderson	98	99	99
6	Wilkerson	84	80	86

Figure 1-4   **The sorted Grades worksheet**

2. Examine Figure 1-5, and answer the following questions.
   a. On which column is the worksheet sorted?
   b. Is the worksheet sorted in ascending or descending order?

	A	B
1	House payment	830
2	Student loans	300
3	Credit cards	300
4	Food	300
5	Utilities	200
6	Miscellaneous	200
7	Automobile	125

Figure 1-5 **The sorted Budget worksheet**

Storing procedures in macros

macro

An advanced feature of Microsoft Excel is the capability of creating macros. *Macros* are holding places for several keystrokes and/or commands that can be invoked by one single keystroke or command. Macros help reduce the time you spend completing redundant tasks, or they can simplify complex tasks. If you have a formula or calculation that you use all the time, for example, you can create a macro to quickly activate the formula. Macros also help reduce the possibility of errors in complex worksheet tasks. You can use a macro to complete an operation with one keystroke rather than with several.

FEATURE

Linking and Embedding

Many current software applications have the capability of sharing data with one another. Two primary mechanisms are used to share data: linking and embedding. Linking data between documents causes the data in the remote document to be automatically updated any time data in the source document is changed. If a group of cells in an Excel worksheet were copied and linked into a Microsoft Word document and the Excel worksheet was changed, for example, the linked data in the Word document would also be changed. In this example Excel contains the source document and Word contains the remote document.

Embedding data from one application into another enables you to use the remote application to format and edit the data. Thus, if you copy and embed Excel worksheet data into a Word document, you can use Word to format or make changes to the way the worksheet data looks within the Word document (for example, center text on the page, wrap text around the worksheet fragment, and so on). These changes would not alter the Excel worksheet itself, only the data that had been embedded in the Word document. Linking and embedding are capabilities enabled by two software industry standards: the Object Linking and Embedding (OLE) standard and the Dynamic Document Exchange (DDE) standard. Applications must conform to at least one of these standards in order to use linking and embedding.

TIP   If you are familiar with DOS batch files, macros may be easy for you to grasp; they are basically the same thing.

Exercise 3: Writing a practice macro

Although you may think that macros are used only with computers, you might be surprised to find that you use macros every day in your language and actions. When someone asks you to sharpen a pencil, for example, you know that the request involves completing several steps, and you automatically complete each step in a certain sequence to accomplish the task. Thus, the command *sharpen a pencil* is really a macro for many small steps or subtasks. List each step required to sharpen a pencil. Test your "macro" by doing each step in the order you've given. Are any steps missing? Make sure that none of the steps are themselves macros with several subtasks. Edit your listing as necessary, and then check it against the one your instructor provides.

Objective 2: Using the Mouse and Keyboard

The mouse and keyboard provide you with powerful navigation and data input possibilities in Excel. You use the mouse primarily to make menu and button selections and to move from cell to cell within the worksheet. You use the keyboard primarily to enter data, although you can also use keyboard keys to issue commands and navigate around the worksheet. As you begin to work with the program, you will find a mouse-keyboard combination that works well for you.

When working with the mouse, you need three physical skills: click, double-click, and drag. Table 1.1 lists these three actions and their effects.

Table 1-1   Actions taken with the mouse

ACTION NAME	ACTION DESCRIPTION	RESULT
Click	Press and release the mouse button once	Makes a window or item active and executes some commands
Double-click	Press and release the mouse button twice in rapid succession (usually within one second)	Starts a program from a program-item icon or from a document icon
Drag	Press the mouse button down, move the mouse on the pad until the mouse pointer is in the desired location, and then release the mouse button	Moves objects around on the screen, makes selections from the menus, and selects ranges

If you have a mouse with two buttons, use the left button to make selections. If you have a three-button mouse, you will not use the middle button in Microsoft Excel. Figure 1-6 displays a *dialog box* with button commands and drop-down menus that enable you to customize a command. To invoke a button command, move the mouse pointer to the desired button and click once. To select an item from a drop-down menu, move the mouse pointer to the desired menu name, and drag the mouse pointer down the menu items. Highlight the command you want to select, and then release the mouse button.

dialog box

Click once to execute button commands ▶

Drag the mouse down the dropdown menu list until the desired item is highlighted. Release the mouse button ▶

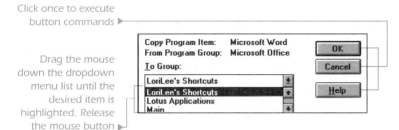

Figure 1-6 A dialog box with button commands and drop-down menus

Figure 1-7 shows a standard Windows menu. Every Windows menu and most commands contain one letter that is underlined. This underlined letter is often called a *hotkey* because it indicates the letter on the keyboard that can be used to activate the menu or command. Some commands are followed by an ellipsis (...) to indicate that a dialog box with additional options will appear when the command is selected.

hotkey

Underlined letters indicate hotkeys that will activate menus and commands from the keyboard ▶

Commands followed by an ellipsis (...) open a dialog box with additional settings ▶

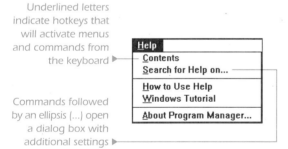

Figure 1-7 A standard Windows menu

To make a menu selection, move the mouse pointer to the desired menu name and drag down, displaying all available commands. Highlight the desired command, using the mouse to select it, and then release the mouse button.

To navigate from cell to cell in a worksheet, place the mouse pointer on the cell you want to make active and then click, or use the arrow keys on the keyboard to move to the desired cell. A border around the cell indicates that the cell is active (refer to Figure 1-1, cell A1).

To enter data into the worksheet, move to the desired cell by using either the mouse or the keyboard, and type the data you want to appear in that cell. Press ⏎ ENTER or click another cell to complete the entry.

Objective 3: Starting the Software

Now that you have an idea of the purposes and capabilities of Excel, it is time to actually start the program and get to work. Because many schools and businesses install specialized menu programs on their computers, you may need to ask your instructor or the lab consultant for specific instructions on starting Excel.

Starting Excel from the Program Manager

icon

Excel 5.0 is a Windows program; Windows must be running before you can start Excel. To start the Excel program, locate the Excel program-item *icon* (picture), shown in Figure 1-8, and double-click the icon. This icon is generally found under the Excel program group or the Microsoft Office program group.

Figure 1-8 **The Excel program-item icon**

Exercise 4: Starting Excel 5.0

In this exercise, you will start the Excel 5.0 program.

boot

1. Turn on (*boot*) your computer and start Windows, if necessary.

   The Program Manager window appears on the screen.

2. Locate the Excel program-item icon shown in Figure 1-8, and double-click the icon.

   The Excel program starts and displays the screen shown in Figure 1-9.

1. Title bar ►
2. Menu bar ►
3. Standard toolbar ►
4. Formatting toolbar ►
5. Cell address indicator ►
6. Formula bar ►
7. Worksheet area ►
8. Vertical scroll bar ►
9. Horizontal scroll bar ►
10. Sheet tabs ►
11. Status bar ►

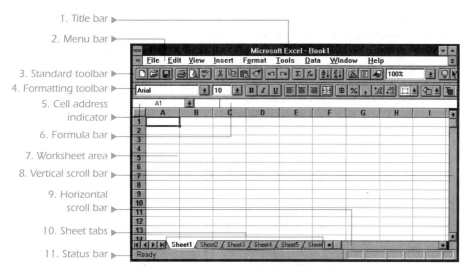

Figure 1-9   **The Excel program window**

Objective 4: Exploring Elements of the Screen

As you can see from Figure 1-9, the Excel screen has many elements. Starting at the top, Excel displays the program and document title in the title bar (1). If you have several windows open at one time, the title bar helps you determine which window is active. The menu bar or main menu (2) contains menu categories under which commands are located. Item three is the Standard toolbar. Excel contains thirteen toolbars that appear and disappear, depending on what you are doing at the time. You can see a definition of each button on the toolbar by resting the mouse pointer on top of the desired button. All toolbars provide quick access to frequently-used commands.

  Click the right mouse button on a toolbar to access additional toolbars.

The Formatting toolbar (4) is used to format text within the worksheet. Display of this toolbar is optional, so it may not appear on your Excel screen. The address of the active cell (5) is displayed in the left side of the Formula bar (6), and, when you begin to enter information into a cell, that **I-beam**   information will appear in the remainder of the formula bar as the *I-beam* moves to the right.

The worksheet area (7) takes up the majority of the screen. Recall from earlier discussions that the worksheet is where information is entered and organized. Notice that the columns are labeled with letters and the rows with numbers. You can see parts of the worksheet that lie outside the window boundary by using the horizontal and vertical scroll bars. You can drag the vertical scroll bar (8) down to see higher-numbered rows, or you can drag the horizontal scroll bar (9) to the right to see higher-lettered columns. You can click on the arrows in either scroll box to move in equal increments vertically or horizontally.

The final two lines on the screen are the Sheet tabs line (10) and the status bar (11). The Sheet tabs enable you to quickly move between related work **workbook** sheets saved in a *workbook*. The status bar tells you what Excel expects you to do next. Always look at this bar if you are uncertain of the next step to take. When Excel isn't waiting for you do to anything in particular, it **Ready mode** displays the word *Ready* (often called *Ready mode*) in the status bar to let you know that it is ready to accept the next command or action.

Exercise 5: Navigating the Worksheet and Menus

In this exercise, you will use the mouse and keyboard to move through and enter data into a worksheet and to practice making menu and dialog box selections.

1. With a new Excel worksheet on the screen, use the keyboard or mouse to move the mouse pointer to cell A3. Remember that if you are using the mouse, you must position the mouse pointer on the cell and then click to make the cell active.

2. Using either the mouse or the keyboard arrow keys, move to cell D7.

   Notice that the cell address indicator in the Formula bar changes each time you move into a new cell. If you have trouble visually locating where you are on the screen, check the cell address indicator in the Formula bar.

3. Using either the mouse or the keyboard arrow keys, move to cell C5.

4. Using the mouse, point to the File menu and click to display its contents.

   A list of commands appears beneath the menu name, with the first command highlighted.

5. Use ⬇ to highlight each command in the list.

6. Use the appropriate arrow key to select the Summary Info command, and press (↵ ENTER) to execute the command.

   A dialog box like the one shown in Figure 1-10 appears. Notice that the Author field is automatically filled in with the name under which the software is licensed. If you had completed a worksheet, you might want to include other summary information as well.

PC Popularity

If you wish that computers had never been invented or have wondered how they became so popular, the answer lies in the topic of this book—spreadsheets. When the first microcomputers hit the market in the late '70s, there wasn't much the average person could do with them. Very little software existed, and most of the people using computers were programmers. Then, in 1979, a product called VisiCalc was introduced by two business students from Harvard University who wanted to find a better way to do their accounting homework.

VisiCalc was the first worksheet program, and it changed forever the way businesses and individuals worked. With VisiCalc, you could enter numbers from an accounting ledger and create formulas to do complex calculations, such as income tax withholdings. If you made a mistake in one of the ledger entries, you could simply change the number in the cell and the formula would automatically recalculate to provide the correct figure. Accountants no longer had to recalculate entire ledgers to locate and correct errors—the spreadsheet did it for them.

Many computer historians and computer experts believe that personal computers would never have sold so many so fast if it weren't for that first worksheet program. So the next time you read about a wealthy software company or see a computer make calculations on the screen, remember that most of the fame and glory can be attributed to the spreadsheet.

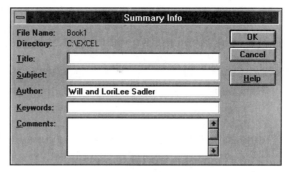

Figure 1-10 The Summary Info dialog box

7. TAB moves the I-beam from one field or button to the next. Press TAB six times to make the Cancel button active.

8. Press ↵ ENTER to execute the Cancel command so that the dialog box is closed with no changes.

9. Using the mouse, open the File menu again and choose the Summary Info command by dragging the highlight bar to that command and then releasing the mouse button.

10. Click Cancel to close the dialog box without making any changes.

11. Make cell A1 the active cell.

    A border appears around the cell.

12. Type your first name in the cell, and press ↵ ENTER.

    Excel makes cell A2 the active cell.

13. Using the arrow keys or mouse, make cell B1 the active cell, type your middle name, and press ↵ ENTER.

14. Make cell C1 the active cell, type your last name, and press ↵ ENTER.

15. Leave the worksheet on the screen for the next exercise.

NOTE   You should always leave the worksheet with which you have been working on the screen at the end of each exercise unless you are explicitly told otherwise. In many cases, you will work on the same worksheet for an entire chapter.

Objective 5: Obtaining On-Line Help

With each new version of Microsoft Excel, the on-line Help feature increases in both quality and quantity. You can access on-line Help from the Help menu in the menu bar or by pressing the F1 key. In Excel 5.0, you can get help from a Help contents listing, search for specific term or topic on which to get help, and look at the index of keywords and select help from that point. You can also work through Excel's on-line tutorial, called Quick Preview, to learn basic skills in several areas, and you can see examples and demonstrations of many worksheet operations by selecting the Examples and Demos option. This feature organizes Excel's capabilities starting with basic tasks and working through to advanced topics.

Exercise 6: Exploring Help

In this exercise, you will explore Excel's on-line Help system.

1. Select Help Contents from the main menu.

   A contents listing appears on the screen, with major content headings. Any word that is underlined (and a different color, if you're using a color monitor) is linked to more text.

2. From the contents listing, click on the text *Using Microsoft Excel.*

   A new listing appears.

3. Click on *Essential Skills.*

   The Essential Skills list appears.

4. Click on *Getting Information While You Work.*

   Topics on locating information while you work appear.

5. Click on *Overview of Using Help to Find the Information You Need.*

6. Read this information carefully. When you have finished, click the Contents button at the top of the window.

   You are returned to the main contents listing.

7. Click the Search button at the top of the Window.

   A dialog box similar to the one shown in Figure 1-11 appears.

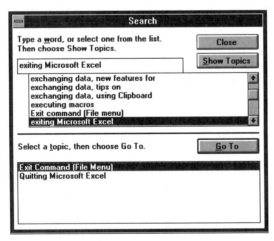

Figure 1-11 You can use the Search dialog box to select commands or tasks for which to find help

8. In the top field, scroll down to the topic *Exiting Microsoft Excel.*

 To move to a Help topic quickly, begin typing the topic name you are searching for.

9. Click the Show Topics button to see a list of available topics on exiting Excel. This list appears in the bottom field of the dialog box.

10. Select *Exit Command [File Menu]* and click the Go To button.

11. Read about the Exit command, and then close the dialog box by double-clicking in the Control-menu box in the top left corner of the Help window.

Objective 6: Exiting Excel 5.0

When you have finished working in any application, you must exit the application properly. As you know from the preceding exercise, you can exit Excel by selecting the menu commands File, Exit. You can also use the keyboard shortcut Alt+F4, or you can double-click in the Control-menu box at the top left corner of the Excel program window.

When you issue this command, Excel displays a message box like the one shown in Figure 1-12, asking if you want to save the changes in the file. If you answer Yes, Excel prompts you for a file name if you've never saved the file or saves the file to the file name that you have already given it. If you answer No, the program closes and any changes you made to the worksheet are lost. If you answer Cancel, Excel aborts the exit process and returns you to the worksheet. If you click on Help, Excel opens the Help screen on saving and exiting.

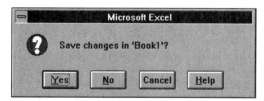

Figure 1-12 **Excel asks if you want to save changes before exiting**

> **⚡ WARNING** You should never turn your computer off without first exiting all open Windows applications and the Windows program itself. Some of the program's working files may become damaged if they are not properly closed before you shut down the system.

Exercise 7: Exiting Excel

In this exercise, you will exit the Excel program without saving the practice worksheet you created in this chapter.

1. From the File menu, choose Exit.

   A message box asking if you want to save your changes appears.

2. Click No because you do not want to save this practice file.

   The Excel window closes, and you return to the Program Manager window.

Chapter Summary

In this chapter, you learned how to start the Excel program and navigate through the worksheet and menu items. You examined the various on-line Help options and learned how to exit the program properly. You learned about the concept of cells and cell addressing and the distinction between rows and columns.

Review Questions

True/False Questions

_____ 1. A cell is the intersection of two columns.

_____ 2. Worksheets are most useful for making financial calculations.

_____ 3. Excel has aspects of database and presentation software.

_____ 4. The right button on the mouse is used to make menu selections.

_____ 5. You should always exit applications and Windows before turning off your computer.

Multiple Choice Questions

_____ 6. Which of the following are features available with Excel?
  A. worksheets
  B. charts
  C. sorting
  D. all of the above

_____ 7. Which of the following bars can be turned on or off in Excel?
  A. title bar
  B. status bar
  C. Formatting toolbar
  D. formula bar

_____ 8. In Excel, a range is
  A. a block of contiguous cells.
  B. a group of disconnected cells.
  C. a series of worksheets.
  D. both A and B

_____ 9. Command names followed by ellipses in menus indicate that
   A. another menu will appear.
   B. help is available on that command.
   C. that command is not available for execution.
   D. a dialog box will appear when the command is selected.

_____ 10. Excel Help provides which of the following?
   A. demos and explanations
   B. Quick Previews
   C. Index of Help
   D. all of the above

Fill-in-the-Blank Questions

11. Worksheet data is often more easily understood when transformed into a(n) _____.

12. The process that physically reorganizes data in a worksheet based on certain criteria is called _____.

13. The active cell in the worksheet is displayed in the _____ of the Formula bar.

14. When you have routine, complex worksheet operations to complete, it is best to create a _____ to ensure accuracy.

15. _____ is an element of Excel's on-line Help system that shows you what Excel can do without asking you to do anything.

Acumen-Building Activities

Quick Projects

1. Real-Life worksheets

1. Carry a notebook with you for the next four days.
2. Record all the examples of worksheets—traditional paper or computerized, that you encounter, starting with the checkbook example used in this chapter.

2. Checking out the worksheet market

1. From your school or local library's magazine (serial) collection, locate an article in a computer magazine that reviews and compares several spreadsheet programs.

2. Read the article and ratings carefully. Is Excel the spreadsheet product you would have chosen, based on the article?

3. Photocopy the article, and write a short explanation of why you would choose to use Excel or a different spreadsheet product, based on the information in the article.

3. Creating a worksheet from a chart

1. Locate a chart in your local newspaper or a favorite magazine. The chart can be a pie graph, line graph, or bar graph.

2. On paper, create a worksheet that could have been used to generate the chart. The worksheet should contain all the data shown in the chart.

4. Using Quick Previews

1. Use the Quick Preview feature of Excel Help to review Excel basics and information about on-line Help. In Excel, choose Help, Quick Preview.

2. Go through the preview for Getting Started and Getting Information While You Work.

3. Exit Help and the Excel program when you have finished.

In-Depth Projects

1. Tracking your transcript

For this project, you will create a paper worksheet that you will later transform into an Excel worksheet. The purpose of the worksheet is to keep track of all the courses you have taken in college, as well as the grades you received in those courses.

1. On paper, make column headings for semester, course number, course description, instructor, and final letter grade.

2. Enter information for one course in each row, using as many rows as necessary to record your college courses to the present time.

3. Save this paper for use in a later chapter.

2. Worksheets in your profession

1. Write a short paper (1-2 pages) explaining how worksheets are used or could be used in your profession. If you are studying to become a doctor, for example, explain how worksheets are used to track patient test results and histories.

2. Interview someone on the faculty in your department, and ask them how they use worksheets (and technology in general) in their teaching and professional work.

CASE STUDIES

Coffee-On-The-Go:

Introduction

Throughout this case study, you will prepare the financial section of a business plan for a start-up business called Coffee-On-The-Go. This small espresso stand will be located at a busy intersection in Eugene, Oregon. The one location will provide drive-through access on the east side and walk-up access on the west side. The business will sell various types of coffee drinks and teas, along with muffins and cookies.

You will be provided with the information to complete the financial section of the business plan in the chapters which follow.

CASE STUDIES

Videos West:

Introduction

Throughout this case study, you will prepare financial worksheets for Videos West. This video rental business located in Fairbanks, Alaska has been a successful business for two years. Recently, Videos West added a line of specialty videos for sale by mail order. The marketing effort has targeted the entire state for video sales, and the business is entering a growth period. The owners will use an electronic spreadsheet to keep a handle on the actual financial status of the business.

You will be provided with the information to complete the financial worksheets in the chapters which follow.

Chapter 2

Building a Worksheet

Objectives
- Entering Text in the Worksheet
- Navigating the Worksheet
- Entering Numbers in the Worksheet
- Entering Formulas in the Worksheet
- Entering Simple Functions in the Worksheet
- Editing Errors
- Saving the Worksheet
- Opening the Worksheet
- Printing the Worksheet

Key Terms

TERM	DEFINITION
Column Heading	text entered at the top of a column to explain its contents
Enter Box	the check mark box in the Formula bar that confirms a cell entry
Cancel Box	the X box in the Formula bar that cancels a cell entry
Left Justified	text or numbers that are aligned at the left edge of the cell
Right Justified	text or numbers that are aligned at the right edge of the cell
Default	settings which are in place when the software is shipped from the manufacturer to the customer
Function	a predefined formula that accepts input from the user and returns an answer
Argument	information entered by users into a function so that it can complete its operation
Syntax	the structure of a command or function

TERM	DEFINITION
Random Access Memory (RAM)	a temporary storage place in the computer that keeps data intact until a file has been saved. RAM is erased each time the computer is turned off.
Save	the process by which data stored in RAM is permanently written to a floppy drive or hard drive
Print Preview	a miniaturized view of the worksheet as it will appear when it is printed
function	The basis for all Excel operations is the data you enter in the worksheet. In this chapter, you will learn how to enter data in the worksheet, create simple formulas and *functions*, edit any errors that you might make, and save the worksheet to disk. You will also learn how to open an existing worksheet for further editing and how to print a worksheet.

Objective 1: Entering Text in the Worksheet

Entering data into the worksheet is fundamental to using Excel. You can't create a chart without data, and you can't reorganize data that doesn't exist. Before you begin to enter data, however, you need to think about the nature of the data and how it should be organized in the worksheet. After you have the data design worked out, you will begin to enter data into the worksheet and use the Excel tools to change the data so that it meets your needs exactly.

Designing the Worksheet

Most people decide to use a worksheet when they are faced with a particular question or problem. If you have trouble remembering when your bills are due, you might want to record their due dates in a worksheet. If you are watching a certain stock on the stock market, you could use Excel to track the stock's performance over a two-week trial period before investing. Whatever your goal, the first step in building a worksheet is to examine the kind of data that you will be managing and how you will use that data.

For some situations, the design phase will be as simple as determining the information that goes in columns and the information that goes in rows. For other, more complex problems, you will need to determine how the information is to be categorized and broken down into manageable elements and how the information will translate into a chart. In almost all cases, you may find that designing a worksheet on paper helps you determine the best organization strategy.

Exercise 1: Designing a price-comparison worksheet

Assume that a new wholesale buying club has opened in your area. You have heard from other sources that prices on some products are quite good while others are higher than daily and sale prices at standard discount and grocery stores. You decide to build a worksheet for comparing items you buy often so that you can determine what to buy at the wholesale club and what to buy at the regular retail store.

1. Determine what information you want to record.

   For this exercise, you need to track the product name, retail price, retail sale price, and wholesale club price.

2. Determine where information should be recorded (columns or rows).

   Because there are only four categories of information and potentially hundreds of items to be recorded, it is best to place the category headings in columns and the information for each item in rows.

3. On a piece of paper, construct the worksheet and make up a couple of rows of information to test the design.

4. Make any changes necessary to the design on paper, and save the paper for use later in this chapter.

Entering Text

After you have determined the basic design of the worksheet, you are ready to enter the column and row headings and data into the worksheet. It is best to first lay out the structure of the worksheet and then go back and enter the data.

As you learned in the last chapter, you enter data into a cell by making the cell active and then typing the information. The information you enter appears in the Formula bar as you type it. When you have finished entering the data for a particular cell, you can click in a new cell, press Enter or an arrow key, or click the *enter box,* as shown in Figure 2-1, to complete the text entry process. If you enter text in a cell and then decide you don't want the text to appear there, click the *cancel box* in the Formula bar to cancel the text entry for that cell.

enter box

cancel box

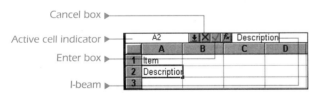

Figure 2-1   Click the enter box in the Formula bar to complete the text entry process

If you make a mistake when entering text, you can correct the text in the Formula bar. Use the mouse to select the error, and then type the corrected text.

Exercise 2: Entering the worksheet structure

column headings

In this exercise, you will enter the *column headings* for the price-comparison worksheet.

1. Boot your computer and start Excel, if necessary.
2. Make cell A1 the active cell, if it isn't already.
3. Type the word Item in the cell, and press (↵ ENTER).

    The word *Item* appears in cell A1, and cell A2 becomes the active cell.
4. In cell A2, type the word Description and click the enter box .
5. Continue inserting column headings and row data, as shown in Figure 2-2.

    Some letters may appear to be in the next column because the data is wider than the column itself. Don't worry about this for now.

	A	B	C	D	E
1	Item	Retail	Retail Sale	Wholesale	
2	Description	Price	Price	Price	
3					
4	Chicken				
5	Lettuce				
6	Coke				
7	Bread				
8	Gr. Chuck				
9	Milk				
10	Tissues				
11	Pens				
12	Light Bulbs				
13	Cereal				
14					

Figure 2-2 **The price-comparison worksheet**

Objective 2: Navigating the Worksheet

Excel offers several ways to move around a worksheet. The most obvious way is to place the mouse pointer on the cell you want to make active and click. You can also use the arrow keys on the keyboard to move up, down, left, and right within the worksheet. There are three special keys on the keyboard that you can also use in worksheet navigation. The Page Down key causes Excel to display rows that are currently not showing on the screen. The number of rows that are jumped depends on the size of your window and monitor. On a fifteen-inch monitor with a maximized Excel window, using Page Down moves your view down sixteen rows in the worksheet. The Page Up key causes Excel to display the next set of rows up from those that are currently showing on the screen. The Home key makes the cell in column A of the current row the active cell. Thus, if the active cell is D7 and you press the Home key, the active cell will become A7.

In addition to these keyboard and mouse navigation techniques, you can also use the Go To command located under the Edit menu to go to a specific cell. When you issue this command, Excel displays the Go To dialog box. The address of the active cell is automatically displayed in the dialog box. You can change this address to a new address by deleting the default cell address, typing the new cell address, and clicking OK to go directly to the specified cell.

 You can access the Go To dialog box quickly by pressing the F5 function key.

Exercise 3: Navigating the worksheet

In this exercise, you will practice moving around the worksheet that you created in Exercise 2 of this chapter.

1. Press ⌊PAGE DOWN⌋.

    Excel moves down several rows.

2. Press ⌊PAGE UP⌋.

    Excel moves back up in the worksheet.

3. Using the mouse, make cell D12 the active cell.

4. Press ⌊HOME⌋ to make cell A12 the active cell.

5. From the Edit menu, select Go To or press ⌊F5⌋.

    The dialog box shown in Figure 2-3 appears.

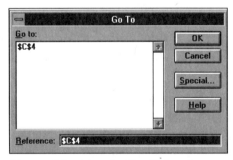

Figure 2-3   **The Go To dialog box**

6. Type the cell address A1 in the Reference field, and click OK.

    The active cell is now cell A1.

 You can press ⌊CTRL⌋ + ⌊HOME⌋ to quickly move to cell A1.

Objective 3: Entering Numbers in the Worksheet

Excel treats text (letters) and numbers quite differently. When letters are entered into a cell, Excel assumes that you do not want to make any calculations on those letters. However, when you enter numbers into a cell, Excel stores the numbers in such a way that calculations can easily be made on those numbers.

left justified
right justified

default

When you enter text into a cell, the text is begun at the left-most position within the cell (*left justified*). When you enter numbers, however, Excel aligns them at the right-most position in the cell (*right justified*) so that the decimals are aligned. You can change the alignment of both text and numbers, but these *default* settings (settings that are made when the program is shipped) indicate the most common use of each type of data.

Exercise 4: Entering numbers in the worksheet

In this exercise, you will enter the prices of ten items in the price-comparison worksheet.

1. With the price-comparison worksheet in the active window, make cell B4 the active cell.
2. Type the number 2.99 in cell B4.
3. Press ⊡ to make cell C4 active.
4. Type the number 2.49 in cell C4.
5. Using the mouse, make cell B5 the active cell.
6. Type the number 1.29 in cell B5.
7. Type the number .89 in cell C5.
8. Continue until you have entered all the data shown in Figure 2-4.

	A	B	C	D	E
1	Item	Retail	Retail Sale	Wholesale	
2	Description	Price	Price	Price	
3					
4	Chicken	2.99	2.49		
5	Lettuce	1.29	0.89		
6	Coke	6.29	5.99		
7	Bread	1.29	0.99		
8	Gr. Chuck	2.97	2.79		
9	Milk	3.62	2.99		
10	Tissues	1.29	0.99		
11	Pens	0.99	0.89		
12	Light Bulbs	3.49	3		
13	Cereal	3.49	3.25		
14					

Figure 2-4   Enter numbers into the price-comparison worksheet

Objective 4: Entering Formulas in the Worksheet

In Chapter 1, you learned that the real value of using a worksheet is its capability of making calculations based on formulas. Formulas are instructions that you give Excel to make a specific calculation. In school, you are taught to follow formulas to make a calculation. In Excel, you're the one who defines the formula, and Excel follows your instructions.

In Excel, most of the formulas you write will reference cell addresses rather than the actual data in the cells. To compute the difference between the retail price and the sale price of chicken in the price-comparison worksheet shown in Figure 2-2, for example, enter the formula =B4–C4. This formula tells Excel to subtract the value in cell C4 from the value in cell B4. Excel doesn't care what those values are, so you can change them at any time and the formula will still be accurate. If the regular retail price of chicken goes up, you can change that value and Excel will still compute the difference between the regular retail price and the retail sale price by using the simple formula =B4–C4.

Every formula in Excel begins with an equals sign (=). This sign tells Excel that the information you are entering into a cell is not regular data but rather a formula. Excel formulas use standard mathematical operators to make calculations. Table 2.1 displays a simple set of operators used frequently in formulas.

OPERATOR	OUTCOME
Plus sign (+)	adds the values in two or more cells together, for example, =B4+C4+D4
Minus sign (–)	subtracts the value in the second cell address from the first cell address, for example, =B4–C4
Multiplication sign (*)	multiplies the value in the first cell address by the value in the second cell address, for example, =B4*C4
Division sign (/)	divides the value in the first cell address by the value in the second cell address, for example, =B4/C4
Parentheses ()	groups operations so that they occur in the proper order, for example, =(B4-C3)/100

Exercise 5: Calculating the Wholesale Club price

In this exercise, you will complete the initial version of the price-comparison worksheet. Because the Wholesale Club sells items in bulk (large quantities or sizes), you must adjust the wholesale price so that you are comparing prices for the same quantities.

1. Make cell D4 the active cell.

2. The Wholesale Club sells chicken breasts in 5-pound bags for $9.99. Type the following formula in cell D4:

   =9.99/5

   The value 1.998 appears in cell D4. Notice that although the result of the formula appears in the cell, the formula appears in the Formula bar, as shown in Figure 2-5.

	A	B	C	D	E
1	Item	Retail	Retail Sale	Wholesale	
2	Description	Price	Price	Price	
3					
4	Chicken	2.99	2.49	1.998	
5	Lettuce	1.29	0.89		
6	Coke	6.29	5.99		
7	Bread	1.29	0.99		
8	Gr. Chuck	2.97	2.79		
9	Milk	3.62	2.99		
10	Tissues	1.29	0.99		
11	Pens	0.99	0.89		
12	Light Bulbs	3.49	3		
13	Cereal	3.49	3.25		

Figure 2-5 **The formula is displayed in the Formula bar, but the result appears in cell D4**

3. The Wholesale Club sells two heads of lettuce for $1.29. In cell D5, type the formula that will give the Wholesale Club's price for a single head of lettuce.

4. The Coke price listed in the retail and retail sale price columns is for cans of Coke by the case. The Wholesale Club sells a case of canned Coke for $6.19. Type 6.19 in cell D6.

5. The Wholesale Club sells two loaves of sandwich bread for $.99. In cell D7, type the formula that will compute the price of a single loaf of bread at the Wholesale Club.

6. The Wholesale Club sells ground chuck in ten-pound packages for $12.98. Type the formula in cell D8 that will compute the cost of a single pound of ground chuck.

7. Milk at the Wholesale Club is $5.18 for two gallons. In cell D9, type the formula that will compute the price of a single gallon of milk.

8. Facial tissues at the Wholesale Club are sold in packages of 12 boxes for $13.72. In cell D10, type the formula that will compute the price of one box of tissues.

9. Roller ball pens sell for $6.29 per box of 12 at the Wholesale Club. Enter the formula that will compute the price for one pen in cell D11.

10. Three-way light bulbs are sold in packs of eight at the Wholesale Club for $7.35. They're sold in packs of four at the retail stores. Compute the price of four light bulbs at the Wholesale Club in cell D12.

11. The Wholesale Club sells a 64-ounce box of Grape Nuts for $6.17. The regular and sale retail prices are for a 16-ounce box. Enter a formula in cell D13 that will compute the price of 16-ounces of cereal at the Wholesale Club.

Your worksheet should look identical to the one in Figure 2-6. If any of the numbers are different, go back and check your formulas to make sure that you have made the correct calculation.

	A	B	C	D	E
1	Item	Retail	Retail Sale	Wholesale	
2	Description	Price	Price	Price	
3					
4	Chicken	2.99	2.49	1.998	
5	Lettuce	1.29	0.89	0.645	
6	Coke	6.29	5.99	6.19	
7	Bread	1.29	0.99	0.495	
8	Gr. Chuck	2.97	2.79	1.298	
9	Milk	3.62	2.99	2.59	
10	Tissues	1.29	0.99	1.143333	
11	Pens	0.99	0.89	0.524167	
12	Light Bulbs	3.49	3	3.675	
13	Cereal	3.49	3.25	1.5425	

Figure 2-6   **The price-comparison worksheet with the wholesale prices in column D1**

Objective 5: Entering Simple Functions in the Worksheet

argument

In addition to formulas that you write yourself, Excel comes with hundreds of built-in *functions*. Functions are prewritten formulas that use information from you, perform an operation, and then return information to you. The information that you provide is called an *argument*. Some functions require only one argument while others require several. Examine this simple function: =AVERAGE (12, 15, 19, 27, 31). The equals sign tells Excel that you are entering an operation, not text or numbers. The word *AVERAGE* is the function name. It will return the average of each of the arguments (in this case, numbers) in the parentheses. When this function is entered into a worksheet cell, the average is computed and the result is displayed in the cell in which the function was written. The function itself is displayed in the Formula bar, as shown in Figure 2-7.

A1		=AVERAGE(12, 15, 19, 27, 31)			
	A	B	C	D	E	F
1	20.8					
2						

Figure 2-7   **The result of the function is shown in the worksheet while the function itself is displayed in the Formula bar**

Using the Function Wizard

The Function Wizard is a step-by-step aid for writing functions. Excel has two ways to access the Function Wizard. The fastest method is to click the Function Wizard button in the Standard toolbar. You can also access the Function Wizard by opening the Insert menu and choosing the Function command. Figure 2-8 shows the first step in the Function Wizard.

Instructions for current step in process ▶

Select a function category from this list ▶

Select a function from this list ▶

Function syntax ▶

Function explanation ▶

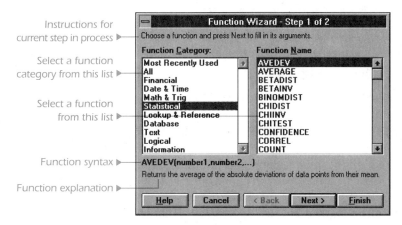

Figure 2-8   The Function Wizard assists you in selecting and writing functions

Nearly everything you need to know about writing a function is located in this dialog box—you just have to know where to look. The text at the top of the box tells you what you have to do for any given step. For this first step, you must select a function category from the Category list on the left side and then select a function to use from the Function Name list on the right side. The function name that is selected is explained below the two **syntax** lists. The function *syntax* or structure is given first, followed by a description of what the function does. When you have selected the function that you want, click Next to go to the next step in the process. In this example, click on AVERAGE in the Function Name list.

NOTE   Excel's on-line Help gives comprehensive information about each function available. If you are unsure of a function's purpose based on the short description given by the Function Wizard, click the Help button at any time to see more details.

Step 2 of the Function Wizard for the AVERAGE function opens a dialog box that enables you to enter the arguments for the function. Figure 2-9 shows this dialog box. The Value field displays the current result of the AVERAGE function, and this result changes each time you enter a new number or change an existing number. When you have finished entering the arguments for this function, click Finish. The value will appear in the cell in which you wrote the function, and the function will appear in the Formula bar (refer to Figure 2-7).

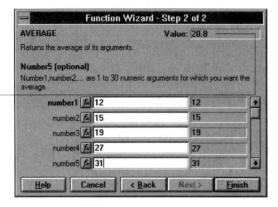

Value (result) changes
each time a new
argument is added
or changed ▶

Figure 2-9   **The second and final step in the function process**

Exercise 6: Writing a function with the Function Wizard

In this exercise, you will use the Function Wizard to write the AVERAGE function demonstrated in this chapter.

1. Make cell J4 the active cell.

2. Click Function Wizard 🔘 in the Standard toolbar, or from the Insert menu, choose the Function command.

    The Function Wizard Step 1 dialog box appears, as shown in Figure 2-8.

3. From the Function Category list, select Statistical.

4. From the Function Name list, select AVERAGE.

5. Click Next.

    The dialog box for the Function Wizard Step 2 appears, as shown in Figure 2-9.

6. In the number 1 field, type 12.

7. Press (TAB) to move to the number 2 field.

8. Type 15.

9. Complete the function dialog box, as shown in Figure 2-9.

    Make sure that your value is the same as the value shown in Figure 2-9. If it is not, double-check the numbers you have entered and make sure that you are using the AVERAGE function.

10. Click Finish to apply the function and close the dialog box.

    The function result appears in cell J4 while the function itself appears in the Formula bar.

Testing with functions

In addition to computing values with functions, you can also test data in a worksheet and tell Excel to complete one action if the test is true and a different action if the test is false. The most common test is the IF function. The IF function requires an argument that tests data. Using the price-comparison worksheet as an example, if you wanted to have Excel automatically print the words *retail* beside items in the worksheet with retail as the lowest price and *wholesale* beside items in the worksheet with wholesale as the lowest prices, you would say, "If the retail price is lower than the wholesale price, print *retail*; otherwise, print *wholesale*." This is almost exactly the syntax for the IF function except that you use cell addresses to define the items, and you use logical operators (<, less than; >, greater than; and =, equal to) rather than words for the test itself.

Exercise 7: Determining where to shop

In this exercise, you will use the IF function to automatically print *retail* or *wholesale,* depending on the best price for each item.

1. Make cell E4 the active cell.
2. Issue the command to insert a function.

   The Function Wizard dialog box appears.
3. From the Function Category list, select Logical.
4. From the Function Name list, select IF.

   The Step 2 dialog box appears, as shown in Figure 2-10.

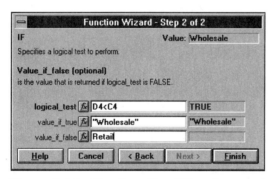

Figure 2-10   The Function Wizard prompts for the test, the result if true, and the result if false

5. In the Logical_Test field, type the test D4<C4.

   This tests to see whether the data in cell D4 is less than the data in cell C4.
6. Press TAB to move to the Value_If_True field.
7. Type Wholesale and press TAB.
8. In the Value_If_False field, type Retail.
9. Click Finish to apply the function and close the dialog box.

   The function returns the answer *Wholesale* in cell F4.

Objective 6: Editing Errors

It is easy to make errors when entering data into any system. People make errors in their checkbooks all the time. They skip checks and make mistakes with addition and subtraction. When this happens in the checkbook, making the correction is often as difficult as finding the error. Luckily, editing errors in a worksheet is quite simple, and, after the error is edited, no one will ever know something was amiss.

The most common errors are data entry errors in cells. When you find an error, you can correct it in one of two ways. You can overwrite the contents of the cell with the corrected data, or you can edit the erroneous characters directly in the cell or in the Formula bar. To overwrite the contents of a cell, make the cell active, type the new data, and press an arrow key or the Enter key. To edit a cell's contents in the Formula bar, anchor the I-beam to the right of the character or characters that are incorrect, highlight the characters to be changed, and type in the correct replacement characters. Click the enter box when you have finished making the correction.

Faith in Function

Spreadsheet programs became more popular in the mid-80s. Several interesting legal cases were tried regarding the validity and accuracy of these programs. Perhaps the most (in)famous case involved a fledgling software manufacturer who sold a spreadsheet program that was specially designed to help with payrolls of medium and large firms. An error in the tax-withholding function resulted in the underpayment of taxes for almost every employee in one medium-sized firm. Fined for underpayment by the IRS, the employees took the software company to court. The courts ruled that the software company was not liable for the error—that the employees were responsible for their own withholdings.

Exercise 8: Editing prices

In this exercise, you will change two prices and one of the row headings in the price-comparison worksheet.

1. With the price-comparison worksheet in the active window, make cell B8 the active cell.

2. Move the mouse pointer into the Formula bar and click so that the I-beam is anchored to the right of the *9* in *2.97*.

   Notice how the pointer changes from a cross to the I-beam when you move from the worksheet area into the Formula bar.

3. Press (← BACKSPACE) once to erase the *9*.

4. Type 8.

5. Click the enter box [✓].

   The retail price for ground chuck should be 2.87.

6. Make cell D7 the active cell.

7. Change the formula so that the wholesale price for two loaves

   of bread is 1.05 rather than .99, and then click the enter box [✓] when you have finished.

8. Change the row heading in cell A6 from Coke to the more generic term Cola.

Objective 7: Saving the Worksheet

**Random Access
Memory**

After you have entered data into a worksheet, you should save that worksheet to disk. For the preceding exercises, the work you have been doing has been stored in *Random Access Memory* (RAM), a temporary holding place for data and instructions in the computer. The contents of RAM are completely erased each time the computer is turned off or when there is an interruption in power. For this reason, you must instruct Excel to store the file in a more permanent location, usually a hard disk or a floppy disk, for safe keeping.

Save

Version 5.0 of Excel stores worksheets in workbooks, enabling you to store related groups of worksheets under the same file name. You will work with multiple worksheets in a later chapter. There are two commands in Excel (and in most Windows applications) to store files to disk; both are found under the File menu. Use the *Save As* command when you want to declare a new or different file name for a file on which you are working. Use *Save* to store a file without changing its name. It is generally best to use the Save As command when you save a file for the first time, when you want to save backup copies of files under a different file name, or when you want to save a file as a different file type for use with another application. After you have saved a file for the first time, you should save about every twenty minutes to protect your work from unexpected interruptions.

TIP You can also press (CTRL) + (S) or click the Save button in the standard toolbar to save a file.

When you are finished working with a file and have saved your work, you can close the file by issuing the Close command which is located under the File menu. The Close command removes the file's contents from RAM and frees your workspace for other documents.

FEATURE

Sample the Goods!

Although most people are able to write relatively simple formulas, the vast majority find it difficult to write formulas that include complex operations. The makers of Excel realized this early on and have shipped a group of sample worksheets that have difficult formulas (many of which include functions) already written. The sample worksheets are generally installed in a subdirectory of the Excel directory and contain worksheets that enable you to figure the amortization rate on a home mortgage and use other complex functions "out of the box." So before you bang your head trying to get a common but complex calculation to work, check the functions list and sample worksheets that come with Excel and save yourself some time.

Exercise 9: Saving the price-comparison worksheet

In this exercise, you will save the price-comparison worksheet that you have been constructing in this chapter. Be sure to have a formatted floppy disk ready before you begin this exercise.

1. Place a formatted floppy disk in drive A of your computer.
2. From the File menu, choose Save As.

   A dialog box like the one shown in Figure 2-11 appears.

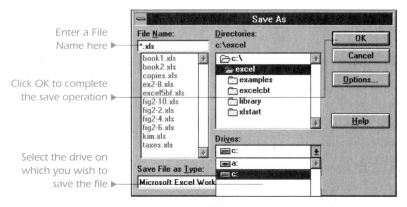

Figure 2-11   **The Save As dialog box**

3. Click on the asterisk in the File Name field to select it, and then type the file name pricomp. Leave the .XLS extension in place; it is the standard extension for Excel worksheets.
4. Click the drop-down arrow in the Drives field to display the available drives.
5. Click drive A, and make sure that the Directories field changes to indicate that drive A is the active drive.
6. Click OK to save the file.
7. From the File menu, choose Close.

   The price-comparison worksheet disappears from the screen.

Objective 8: Opening the Worksheet

As you have discovered, Excel displays a new, blank worksheet when you start the program. While this is fine if you want to create a new worksheet, it doesn't help when you need to use a worksheet that you created sometime earlier. To open an existing worksheet, click the Open button in the Standard toolbar, or access the File menu and choose the Open command. Regardless of which method you use, a dialog box almost identical to the Save As dialog box appears (see Figure 2-11). Select the drive, directory, and file name of the file to be opened, and then click OK. The file then appears in the Excel window.

Exercise 10: Opening the price-comparison worksheet

In this exercise, you will open the price-comparison worksheet. Be sure that the disk on which you saved the file in Exercise 9 is in drive A of your computer before beginning.

1. Click Open ![icon] on the Standard toolbar, or from the File menu, choose Open.

   A dialog box similar to the one shown in Figure 2-11 appears.

2. In the File Name field, type pricomp.xls.

3. Select drive A from the Drives drop-down menu.

4. Click OK to complete the open process.

   The pricomp.xls worksheet is displayed on the screen.

TIP A faster method of opening a file that has recently been closed is to select one of the recently opened file names listed at the bottom of the File menu, as shown in Figure 2-12.

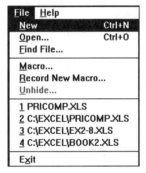

Figure 2-12 **To open a recently closed file, select the file name from the bottom portion of the File menu**

Objective 9: Printing the Worksheet

After you have carefully checked your worksheet for errors and have saved the worksheet, you can print the worksheet on a printer. Excel has many printing options—so many that all of Chapter 7 of this text is devoted to printing issues. In this chapter, however, you will learn the basic steps used in printing a worksheet.

Before you can print a worksheet, you must define the range of cells that are to be printed so that all cells in the worksheet (including the blank ones) do not get printed. To do this, make the top left cell in the worksheet the active cell, and then drag the mouse pointer down and right, to the bottom right cell that contains data. When you release the mouse button, the area of the worksheet that contains data should be highlighted.

Print Preview

After you have selected a range, you can see a preview of how the output will look by clicking the Print Preview command button or choosing File, Print Preview. Excel displays a print preview, in miniaturized form, of the actual printed output on the screen, as shown in Figure 2-13.

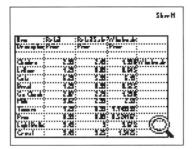

Figure 2-13   You can use the Print Preview option to ensure that the selected data will fit on the page

You can *zoom in* if necessary to actually read the data by moving the pointer, which has changed to a magnifying glass, over the worksheet area and clicking. Click a second time to *zoom out*. Click the Close button to close the preview window. To print the file, open the File menu and choose Print, or press Crtl + P. A dialog box like the one shown in Figure 2-14 appears.

Click here to print the selected range ▶

Click here to print all worksheets in workbook ▶

Change the number of copies to print ▶

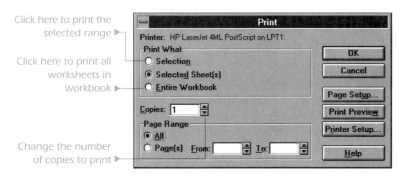

Figure 2-14   The Print dialog box

Make the appropriate selections in the Print dialog box, and click OK to send the data to the printer.

TIP   Click the Print button on the standard toolbar to quickly print the active worksheet.

Exercise 11: Printing the price-comparison worksheet

In this exercise, you will print two copies of the price-comparison worksheet—one for yourself and one to turn in to your instructor.

1. Select the range A1 through E13 (usually expressed A1:E13).

2. Click the Print Preview button 🔲 , or from the File menu, choose Print Preview.

    The Print Preview window opens, as shown in Figure 2-13.

3. Move the magnifying glass over the worksheet, and click once to enlarge the worksheet.

4. Click the mouse a second time to reduce the worksheet to preview size.

5. Click Close.

6. From the File menu, choose Print.

7. In the Print dialog box, click Selection in the Print What portion.

8. Click the up arrow by the Copies field to increase the number of copies printed to 2.

9. Click OK to send the job to the printer.

10. Collect your documents from the printer. If you share a printer with others, be careful to retrieve only your work.

11. Quit Excel at this time, or continue with the problems at the end of this chapter.

Chapter Summary

This chapter could have been alternately titled "All I ever needed to know I learned in Chapter 2" because the fundamentals of creating, saving, editing, and printing a worksheet were all covered in this chapter. In addition to these basics, you learned the fundamental principles of writing formulas and using functions. In subsequent chapters, you will build on the information from this chapter to round out your knowledge of worksheets and of Excel.

Review Questions

True/False Questions

_____ 1. The Home key moves the cell pointer to cell A1.

_____ 2. Excel makes no differentiation between text and numbers.

_____ 3. All formulas in Excel must begin with the = sign.

_____ 4. Formulas are predefined functions in Excel.

_____ 5. When you save a file, the file is permanently written to disk.

Multiple Choice Questions

_____ 6. Which one of the following keys jumps from the active cell to a cell approximately 15 rows higher in the worksheet?

    A. Home

    B. End

    C. Page Up

    D. Page Down

_____ 7. When letters are entered into a cell, they are automatically placed

    A. at the left margin of the cell.

    B. at the right margin of the cell.

    C. in the center of the cell.

    D. none of the above

_____ 8. The IF function is also known as a(n)

    A. logical function.

    B. test.

    C. argument.

    D. both A and B

_____ 9. To quickly open a recently closed file,

    A. choose File, Open.

    B. select the file name from the File menu.

    C. double-click the file name in the File Manager.

    D. none of the above

_____ 10. Before printing a file on a printer, it is a good idea to

    A. save the file.

    B. preview the file.

    C. A and B

    D. none of the above

Fill-in-the-Blank Questions

11. The _____ symbol is used to represent multiplication.

12. In a formula, the values you enter are called _____.

13. The text AVERAGE(number1, number2, number3...number 30) is called the _____.

14. When you have finished editing a cell's contents in the Formula bar, click the _____.

15. How would you express the range of cells from A1 through D16? _____.

Acumen-Building Activities

Quick Projects

1. Keeping track of your schedule

1. In Excel, create a worksheet with column headings for the days of the week (starting in column B) and row headings in column A for times of the day.

2. Enter your schedule for the week in the appropriate cells, noting class times, work times, and any other obligations you have.

3. Save the file as schedule.xls.

2. Tracking your monthly budget

1. In Excel, create a worksheet that will help you keep track of your monthly income and expenses.

2. Enter the following column headings:

   Column A: Date

   Column B: Description

   Column C: Expense

   Column D: Income

   Column F: Balance

3. Enter a starting balance in cell F2, and then enter at least four rows of data.

4. Write a formula to compute the balance in each row of column F.

5. Save the file as budget.xls.

3. Managing your CD collection

1. Create a worksheet that will help you keep track of your growing CD (or LP or cassette tape) collection.
2. You should have column headings for the title, group or artist, and date released.
3. Enter at least ten rows of data into the worksheet.
4. Save the worksheet as music.xls, and print the worksheet.

4. Saving money

Use Excel to create a worksheet that will show you the advantages of saving a small amount of money each month for five years, with interest disbursed annually.

1. Make the heading for column A Year, for column B Amount Deposited, for column C Interest Earned, and for column D Total.
2. In cells A2 through A6, type the numbers 1 through 5, representing each of the five years.
3. In cell B2, type a formula that will compute the total of twelve deposits of $25 each.
4. In cell C2, type a formula that will compute the interest at 3.25%.
5. In cell D2, type the combined total of the data in B2 and C2.
6. In cell B3, carry the total from the prior year (cell D2) and add to that total deposits of $25 each for twelve more months.
7. Compute the interest at 3.5% in cell C3, and compute the annual total in cell D3.
8. Continue in this manner until you have computed the five-year total, including interest.
9. Save the worksheet as savings.xls.

In-Depth Projects

1. Taking stock of the stock market

Create a worksheet that will track the performance of a single stock over the course of one week. Make sure that you save the worksheet each time you enter new data.

1. The column heading for column A should be Day, for column B, Price; and for column C, Gain/Loss.
2. In cell A3, type the label Monday.
3. Enter Tuesday through Friday in rows 4 through 7.
4. Save the worksheet as stock.xls.

5. Record the price of your selected stock at closing each day.

6. In cell C4, write a formula that will compute the gain or loss in value over the previous day's closing price.

7. Write this formula in cells C5, C6, and C7, to complete the worksheet.

8. In cell A8, type the name of the stock you tracked for the week.

9. Save the worksheet again.

2. Creating a transcript worksheet

1. For this problem, create in Excel the transcript worksheet you created on paper in Chapter 1.

2. Add a final column heading to your worksheet called Point Value.

3. In the Point Value column, use the IF function to determine the grade point for each letter grade you have received (in other words, if the letter grade is an A, the point value is 4.0; if the letter grade is a B, the point value is 3.0). If you don't know the grade point assignments your school uses, check in the bulletin or ask your instructor.

4. Save the file as trnscrpt.xls.

CASE STUDIES

Coffee-On-The-Go:

Creating a Balance Sheet

In this chapter, you learned the basics of entering numbers, text, and formulas. You can create a balance sheet for Coffee-On-The-Go with these skills.

1. Create the balance sheet as shown below. Use formulas to compute the totals.

Balance Sheet

Coffee-On-The-Go

December 31,1995

ASSETS

Current Assets

Cash	10,000
Accounts Receivable	500
Inventory	1,000
Total Current Assets	$11,500

Fixed Assets

Building	8,000
Equipment	1,000
Fixtures	500
Less Accumulated Depreciation	(1,000)
Total Fixed Assets	$8,500

Other Assets	0
TOTAL ASSETS	$20,000

LIABILITIES

Current Liabilities

Accounts Payable	8,000
Payroll	2,000
Taxes	400
Total Current Liabilities	$10,400

Long-Term Liabilities

Long-Term Note	7,000
Total Long-Term Liabilities	$7,000

TOTAL LIABILITIES	$17,400
NET WORTH	$2,600

2. Save the balance sheet as balance.xls.
3. Print the worksheet.

CASE STUDIES

Videos West: **Creating a Forecast for the First Quarter**

In this chapter, you learned the basics of entering numbers, text, and formulas. You can create a forecast worksheet for Videos West with these skill.

1. Open a new worksheet.
2. In cell C1, type Videos West.
3. In cell C2, type Quarterly Forecast.
4. In cell A5, type REVENUE.
5. In cell A6, type Rental.
6. In cell A7, type Mail Order.

7. In cell A8, type Net Sales.
8. In cell A10, type Cost of Goods.
9. In cell A12, type Gross Profit.
10. In cell A14, type OPERATING EXPENSES.
11. Starting in cell A15, type the following labels and press the down arrow after each one: Salaries and Wages, Employee Benefits, Payroll Taxes, Insurance, Advertising, Rent, Utilities, Office Supplies, Postage, TOTAL EXPENSES, NET INCOME/LOSS.
12. In cell B4, type JAN and press (→).
13. In cell C4, type FEB and press (→).
14. In cell D4, type MAR and press (→).
15. In cell E4, type Total and press (↵ ENTER).
16. Move to cell B6 and type 9000 and press (→). (This is January's Rental Revenue.)
17. Repeat this process for each month by typing the following entries and pressing the right arrow after each one: 10000, 11000.
18. Move to cell B7, and type 2000 and press (→). (This is January's Mail Order Revenue.)
19. Repeat this process for each month by typing the following entries and pressing the right arrow after each one: 4000, 6000.
20. Move to cell E6, and total the three month's Rental Revenue.
21. Move to cell E7, and total the three month's Mail Order Revenue.
22. Move to cell B8, and total the Net Sales for January. Repeat this process for February, March, and the Total for the Quarter.
23. Save the file as revenue.xls.
24. Print the worksheet.

Chapter 3

Modifying the Worksheet

Objectives
- Erasing Data
- Widening Columns
- Moving Data
- Copying Data
- Inserting Columns and Rows
- Deleting Columns and Rows
- Recalculating Formulas
- Checking Spelling
- Naming Groups of Cells

Key Terms

TERM	DEFINITION
Clear	permanently removes the contents of selected cells
Cut	erases the contents of selected cells and temporarily stores the erased data in the Clipboard
Clipboard	temporary storage place for data that has been cut or copied, but can hold only one item at a time
Paste	retrieves cut or copied data from the Clipboard and places it in a new location in a worksheet
Move	transfers data from one location to another
Pointer Mode	the status of the mouse cursor when it is pointing to the border of a cell or range of cells
Drag and Drop	the procedure in which the mouse is used to select a cell or range of cells and drag those cells to a new location

TERM	DEFINITION
Relative Cell Addressing	the standard (default) method used by Excel to reference cells within a worksheet, enabling Excel to automatically adjust copied formulas to their new location, relative to the active cell. Relative cell addresses are denoted by their column-row coordinate (for example, A7).
Absolute Cell Address	an alternative cell reference method used by Excel to hold a specific cell in a formula constant, regardless of where it is copied to. Absolute cell addresses are denoted by dollar signs in front of the column and row coordinate (for example, $A$7).
Fill Handle	the small box at the lower right corner of the active cell. When dragged, this handle copies the contents of the current cell to adjacent cells.
Iteration	a setting which tells Excel the number of times it should attempt to resolve an error before issuing an error message
Radio Button	similar to a check box in a dialog box and used when only one option from a list may be selected
Spell Checker	a utility provided by Excel to check the spelling of words within a worksheet
Named References	a feature in Excel which enables you to give a name to a cell, group of cells, or a formula for easier reference

Now that you have learned the fundamental processes involved in creating a worksheet (entering data, saving the file, editing the file, using formulas and functions, and printing the file), you are ready to begin using Excel features that will make your data more readable and that will make your management of the data faster.

The first six objectives in this chapter all deal with changes you can make in the worksheet area. Erasing a worksheet cell leaves the cell truly void of information, not just blank. Widening columns becomes necessary when you have longer, more descriptive column headings. Moving and copying data are useful mechanisms for filling in your worksheet. Inserting and deleting columns and rows are often necessary if you decide to rearrange the data on the worksheet, have left something out of the worksheet, or have put too much into the worksheet.

The remaining three objectives in this chapter, recalculating formulas, checking spelling, and naming cells, are all helpful utilities that you will use throughout this text and in your daily work.

Objective 1: Erasing Data

Excel has several methods you can use to erase data from a cell or group of cells in the worksheet. The first method is to delete the data from the active cell using the Backspace or Delete key. The second method, which is gener-

clear   ally preferable to the first, is to *clear* the data. When data is cleared from a cell or range of cells, it is completely removed from the computer's memory and no trace of data is left in the cell or group of cells. If you accidentally clear data that you should have kept, you can retrieve the data by using the Undo command found in the Edit menu or by clicking the Undo button in the Standard toolbar.

Deleting cell data

To use the Backspace or Delete key to erase the data from a single cell, make the cell you want to erase the active cell, and then delete the cell's contents. Click the enter box to confirm the change.

Exercise 1: Deleting data from cells

In this exercise, you will open the Pricomp worksheet and delete data from one cell.

1. Boot your computer, start Windows, start Excel, and open the pricomp.xls worksheet created in the last chapter.
2. Make cell G3 the active cell.
3. Type your last name in the cell, and press ⏎ ENTER .
4. Make cell G3 the active cell again.
5. In the Formula bar, use DELETE or ← BACKSPACE to erase your last name.
6. Click the enter box .

   Your name is removed from the cell.

7. Click Undo ↶ , or from the Edit menu, choose Undo.

Clearing cell data

A better approach to deleting cell data is to clear the data from the cell. The Clear command is found under the Edit menu. Figure 3-1 shows the Edit, Clear menu and submenu. Four options are under the Clear command: All, Formats, Contents, and Notes. Because you are dealing only with data at this point, the option you will use for this chapter is the Contents option.

TIP   To quickly clear the contents of a range, select the range and press DELETE .

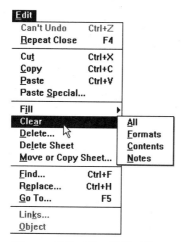

Figure 3-1 **The Edit Clear menu**

After you have issued the Clear command, the data in the selected cells disappears. If you realize that you need the data that you just cleared, you can unclear the data by using the Undo command. Again, this command retracts your last command or action, but you must use Undo immediately after completing the command you want to retract. If you issue several other commands and then realize you need to undo a command completed earlier, it is too late—Undo will not remember what you did several keystrokes ago.

Exercise 2: Clearing and undoing

In this exercise, you will clear a group of cells from the Pricomp worksheet and then retract the command to restore the cell data.

1. With the pricomp.xls worksheet in the active window on screen, select the range A1:D3.

    All cells between cell A1 and cell D3 should be highlighted.

2. From the Edit menu, choose Clear.

    The submenu shown in Figure 3-1 appears.

3. From the submenu, choose Contents.

    The contents of the cells in the selected range are cleared.

4. Click the Undo button ⟲, or from the Edit menu, choose Undo Clear.

    The contents of the cleared cells will be restored.

Objective 2: Widening Columns

It is often necessary to change the width of columns in a worksheet to accommodate the data. Even in the Pricomp worksheet, wider columns would make the data easier to read. Excel offers several ways to widen columns, but the easiest method is to use the Autofit Selection command. This command automatically adjusts the column width of the selected columns so that the data stored in them fits between the cell's boundaries (in other words, the column expands to accommodate the widest entry in that column). You also can adjust the width of one or more columns by dragging the column line right or left, at the top of the worksheet, as shown in Figure 3-2. Finally, you can adjust the column width of one or more columns by using the Column, Width commands from the Format menu.

Column width indicator ▶

Mouse pointer changes to a cross-hair ▶

	A	B	C	D	E
1	Item	Retail	Retail Sale	Wholesale	
2	Description	Price	Price	Price	
3					
4	Chicken	2.99	2.49	1.998	Wholesale
5	Lettuce	1.29	0.89	0.645	
6	Cola	6.29	5.99	6.19	
7	Bread	1.29	0.99	0.525	
8	Gr. Chuck	2.87	2.79	1.298	
9	Milk	3.62	2.99	2.59	
10	Tissues	1.29	0.99	1.143333	
11	Pens	0.99	0.89	0.524167	
12	Light Bulbs	3.49	3	3.675	
13	Cereal	3.49	3.25	1.5425	

Width: 11.00 — Bread

Figure 3-2 You can adjust column widths by dragging the column boundary line

TIP If you enter numeric data into a cell but Excel displays only a series of pound signs (########), the column is not wide enough to accommodate the value. To fix this, increase the column width and the value will be displayed.

Exercise 3: Changing column widths

In this exercise, you will practice using all three column-width adjustment methods in the Pricomp worksheet.

1. With the Pricomp worksheet in the active window, select the range A1:E13.

2. From the Format menu, choose the commands Column, Autofit Selection.

   The widths of each column will automatically adjust so that the contents of the columns fit within the cell boundaries. Notice that some columns decrease in width (column B, most notably) while others increase in width (column D, most notably).

3. Although all the data fits in column B, its significantly smaller width looks strange on the worksheet. Move the mouse pointer up into the letter portion of column B so that the pointer changes to a cross-hair (refer to Figure 3-2).

4. Drag the line that forms the right boundary of Column B to the right to increase the width in column B. Release the mouse button when the column is about as wide as column C.

   The column width for column B changes, and the worksheet looks more uniform.

5. Issue the necessary commands to make column A a specific width. Make cell A1 the active cell.

6. From the Format menu, choose Column, Width.

   A dialog box like the one shown in Figure 3-3 appears.

Column Width
Column Width: 9.57
OK
Cancel
Help

Figure 3-3   The Column Width dialog box

7. Select the number in the Column Width field and press ← BACKSPACE to delete the number.

8. Type a new column width setting of 11.

9. Click OK to apply the change and close the dialog box.

   Column A is now approximately eleven characters wide.

Objective 3: Moving Data

move

drag and drop

No matter how much preplanning you do for a worksheet, you will often discover that you need to *move* categories of data from one location to another within the worksheet. When you move data, the data is literally lifted from its original location and placed in a new location. Excel provides two easy methods for moving data. You can select a cell or group of cells and drag them to their new location (usually called *drag and drop*), or you can use the Cut and Paste commands from the Edit menu or Standard toolbar.

Dragging cells

Pointer mode

When a cell is active, you can move the contents of the cell by dragging the cell to a new location in the worksheet. Figure 3-4 shows an active cell with the mouse cursor in *Pointer mode*, which indicates that the cell is ready to be moved. Drag the cell to the new location, and release the mouse button.

Mouse cursor in
Pointer mode ►

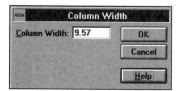

Figure 3-4   An active cell is ready to be moved

TIP   To select all the cells in a row, click on the row number of the row to be selected. To select all the cells in a column, click on the column letter of the column to be selected. To select an entire worksheet, click in the blank button to the left of column A and above row 1.

Exercise 4: Moving with drag and drop

In this exercise, you will drag and drop a portion of the Pricomp worksheet.

1. With the Pricomp worksheet in the active window, select all the cells in column A by clicking on the column letter at the top of the work-sheet area.

   The entire column is highlighted.

2. Position the mouse cursor at the top of cell A1 so that the cursor is in Pointer mode (refer to Figure 3-4).

3. Drag the column to column G.

   Your worksheet should look like Figure 3-5.

	A	B	C	D	E	F	G
							Item
1		Retail	Retail Sale	Wholesale			Item
2		Price	Price	Price			Description
3							
4		2.99	2.49	1.998	Wholesale		Chicken
5		1.29	0.89	0.645			Lettuce
6		6.29	5.99	6.19			Cola
7		1.29	0.99	0.525			Bread
8		2.87	2.79	1.298			Gr. Chuck
9		3.62	2.99	2.59			Milk
10		1.29	0.99	1.143333333			Tissues
11		0.99	0.89	0.524166667			Pens
12		3.49	3	3.675			Light Bulbs
13		3.49	3.25	1.5425			Cereal

Figure 3-5   The entire contents of column A are moved to column G

Using Cut and Paste

Although the drag-and-drop method of moving cells is fast and relatively simple, it works well only when you can see the portion of the worksheet from which you're moving files and the portion of the worksheet to which you're moving files at the same time. When you can't see both worksheet **cut** portions, you should cut and paste the cells. *Cut* and *paste* is the process **paste** of cutting data from a document and pasting the data into another portion of the same document or even a different document.

When data is cut, it is stored in a temporary holding place called the **Clipboard** *Clipboard*. The Clipboard can hold only one item at a time, so each time you cut something, the old item in the Clipboard is replaced by the new item. When you are ready to paste data, you issue the Paste command and the data is retrieved from the Clipboard and placed in the new location.

Exercise 5: Cutting and pasting cells

In this exercise, you will cut the data in column G and paste it back into column A of the Pricomp worksheet.

1. With the Pricomp worksheet in the active window, select the entire contents of column G by clicking on the *G* at the top of the worksheet area.

2. Click the Cut button ✂ on the Standard toolbar, or from the Edit menu, choose Cut.

   A dotted border appears around the cells that have been cut.

3. Make cell A1 the active cell.

4. Click the Paste button 📋 on the Standard toolbar, or from the Edit menu, choose Paste.

   The cut data is moved from column G and pasted back into column A.

Objective 4: Copying Data

The process of copying data is very similar to the process of moving data. However, the outcome is quite different. When you move data, you move a range of cells from one location to another so that only one version of those cells is in the worksheet. When you copy data, however, you make a duplicate set of the data and place it in a different location in the worksheet or in a different document altogether.

While copying data may seem pretty mundane, copying formulas is a whole different ball game. The process is the same, but the cell addresses in the formula adjust so that the formula is accurate in its new, copied location. Figure 3-6 shows a simple worksheet with exam scores for five people. In cell E2 is a formula that computes the average of the three exam scores. When this formula is copied to cell E3, the cell addresses in the formula will automatically change to compute the average of the range B3:D3. This change in the formula is caused by *relative cell addressing,* the method used by Excel to make the operations in the worksheet relative to the location of the active cell or cells. Thus, Excel updates the formula in the figure so that it is relative to the cells in row three of the worksheet.

relative cell addressing

E2	↨	=AVERAGE(B2:D2)		
A	**B**	**C**	**D**	**E**
1 Student	Exam 1	Exam 2	Exam 3	Average
2 Anderson	78	83	87	82.67
3 Bailey	72	80	86	
4 Chaney	91	90	97	
5 Henderson	98	99	99	
6 Wilkerson	84	80	86	

Figure 3-6 *The cell addresses in the formula will change when the formula is copied to a new cell*

Relative cell addressing is, in general, a time saving feature. It saves you time because it enables you to copy formulas without editing them for each new cell reference. There will be times, however, when you will not want a cell address to be relative—when you will want a cell address in a formula to remain constant regardless of the location to which the formula is copied. When this is the case, you must use an *absolute cell address*, an address you declare by placing dollar signs ($) in front of the column and row coordinates. In Figure 3-7, the commission rate in cell C3 should remain constant in all formulas which compute the commission rate. To make this cell address constant or absolute, you insert dollar signs before the column and row in the cell address. When the formula in cell C6 is copied, the cell address for each person will change, but the cell address for the commission rate will stay the same.

**absolute
cell address**

C6		=B6*$C$3	
A	**B**	**C**	**D**
1		Third Quarter Sales Figures	
2			
3 Commission rate:		0.05	
4			
5 Sales Rep	Total Sales	Commission	
6 Randy	$22,890.06	$ 1,144.50	
7 Jennifer	$27,682.12	$ 1,384.11	
8 JoAnne	$18,982.78	$ 949.14	
9 Jim	$13,512.31	$ 675.62	
10 Mike	$21,928.51	$ 1,096.43	
11 Melissa	$19,345.16	$ 967.26	

Figure 3-7 **The absolute cell address forces the commission rate cell to stay constant in the formula while all other cell addresses in the formula change when copied**

FEATURE

Absolutely!

If you're still uncertain about when to use absolute cell references and when to use relative cell references, think about the following analogy. You're driving in a strange town, looking for a friend's house. After circling the neighborhood for half an hour, you finally decide to stop and ask directions. You see a man mowing his lawn and signal him over to the car. You tell him you're looking for Augusta June's house. His first response is, "Oh, she lives two doors down." He has just given you a relative address. "Two doors down" is relative to your present location and won't help if you're five houses away or on the next block. The man continues by saying, "That's 1729 Arlington Road." This is the absolute address. 1729 Arlington Road is (hopefully) the only house in the town that has this address, and the address is valid regardless of where you are.

Copying cells with drag and drop

fill handle

You can copy cells using the drag-and-drop method discussed earlier in this chapter. If the copied cells are to be placed directly next to the original cells, you can use the *fill handle* (the small box at the lower right corner of the active cell) to fill the selected cells with copies of the original cell. If the copied cells will not be located next to the original cells, you must hold down the Control key while you drag the range of cells to their new location. When the copy of the range is situated in its new location, release the mouse button and then the Control key.

Exercise 6: Copying the IF formula

In this exercise, you will copy the IF formula that you created for the Pricomp worksheet in column E to the remaining cells in column E, using the drag-and-drop method.

1. With the Pricomp worksheet in the active window on screen, make cell E4 the active cell.

   In Figure 3-8, the fill handle is shown on the left, and the mouse cursor in Fill mode is shown on the right.

Mouse cursor
in Fill mode ▶

Fill handle ▶

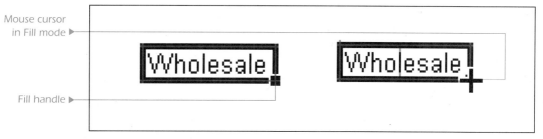

Figure 3-8   The fill handle and mouse cursor in Fill mode

2. Position the mouse cursor so that it changes to Fill mode, as shown in Figure 3-8.

3. Drag down, until the range E4:E13 is bordered by a gray rectangle.

4. Release the mouse button.

   Each cell in the range will contain the answer to the IF test. Look at cell E5. Notice that the formula changed so that it was relative to the data in row 5.

5. Carefully examine each of the remaining data cells in the column.

Copying cells to a different portion of the worksheet

When the destination for copied cells is not next to the source of the cells to be copied, you must use a different copying method than dragging and dropping. If you can see both the source cells and the destination cells on the screen, a fast way to copy cells is to select the cells to be copied, hold down the Control key, and drag the cells to their new location. The Control key forces Excel to make a copy of the selected data rather than to move the selected data.

A second alternative to drag and drop is to use the Copy and Paste commands in the Edit menu or on the toolbar. To do this, select the cells to be copied, issue the Copy command, move the mouse cursor to the destination point, and issue the Paste command.

TIP You can also use the CTRL + C and CTRL + V keys to copy and paste, respectively.

Exercise 7: Copying cells to a distant destination

In this exercise, you will practice copying cells using the drag-and-drop and copy-and-paste methods.

1. With the Pricomp worksheet in the active window, select the range A13:E13. Position the mouse pointer on any edge of the selected range, so the pointer becomes an arrow.

2. Hold down CTRL and drag the selected cells to A15. Release the mouse button, and then release CTRL.

   The selected cells are duplicated in row 15.

3. Select the range A15:E15.

4. Click the Copy command button , or from the Edit menu, choose Copy.

5. Make cell A17 the active cell.

6. Click the Paste button , or from the Edit menu, choose Paste.

   The data is copied into row 17.

7. Press ESC to deselect the cells in row 15.

8. Clear the data from rows 15 and 17, using whichever method described in Objective One of this chapter you prefer.

Objective 5: Inserting Columns and Rows

Occasionally, you will discover that you forgot a category or some data in a worksheet after you have entered a large portion of the worksheet. This happens all the time in a checkbook register—you skip a check number and must write it down at a later date. In Excel, you don't have to put a missed item at the end of the worksheet. You can insert a row or column where you need it so that your data is properly organized.

The commands to insert a row or column are located under the Insert menu. When you insert a column, Excel moves the current column and all subsequent columns to the right (in other words, column C becomes column D, column D becomes column E, and so on). Formulas are automatically changed. When you insert a row, Excel moves the current and all subsequent rows down (row 7 becomes row 8, row 8 becomes row 9, and so on). If you accidentally insert a column or row into the wrong location, remember to use the Undo command immediately.

Exercise 8: Inserting columns and rows

In this exercise, you will insert columns and rows into the Pricomp worksheet to make the data easier to read.

1. With the Pricomp worksheet in the active window, make cell B1 the active cell.
2. From the Insert menu, choose Column.
   The data in column B is shifted to column C, and the new column B is blank.
3. Make cell D1 the active cell, and insert a new column.
4. Make cell F1 the active cell, and insert a new column.
5. Make cell H1 the active cell, and insert a new column.
6. Set the width of the new (blank) columns to 2, using one of the methods described earlier in this chapter.
7. Make cell A5 the active cell.
8. From the Insert menu, choose Row.
9. Make cell A7 the active cell, and insert a new row.
10. Insert a row above rows 7, 9, 11, 13, 15, 17, 19, and 21, in that order.
    There should now be a blank row between each row of data in the worksheet.

Objective 6: Deleting Columns and Rows

Just as you occasionally leave data out of the worksheet, you occasionally put too much data into the worksheet. This generally happens when you set up a worksheet structure (column and row headings) and, after entering a few rows of data, realize that the structure doesn't fit the data.

To delete a column or row, click on the column letter or row number to be deleted to select the entire column or row, and then, from the Edit menu, choose Delete. The selected column or row is removed from the screen.

Exercise 9: Deleting blank rows and columns

In this exercise, you will delete the blank rows and columns you created in Exercise 8.

1. With the Pricomp worksheet in the active window, click on the letter *B* in the column letters to select the entire column.
2. From the Edit menu, choose Delete.

3. Repeat Steps 1 and 2 for columns C, D, and E, in that order. When you have finished, the worksheet should not have any blank columns.

4. Click the number 5 in the row numbers to select the entire row.

5. From the Edit menu, choose Delete.

   The blank row is deleted, and the remaining rows move up.

6. Repeat Steps 4 and 5 for rows 6, 7, 8, 9, 10, 11, 12, and 13. When you have finished, there should be no blank rows in the worksheet.

Objective 7: Recalculating Formulas

Excel automatically recalculates a formula every time data stored in the cells the formula uses is changed. You can change this and other calculation options in a special kind of dialog box called a *tab sheet*, shown in Figure 3-9. Tab sheets enable the writers of software to keep dialog boxes straightforward and relatively uncluttered by placing options for different settings on related sheets.

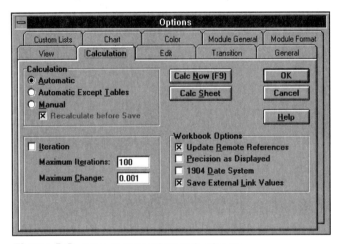

Figure 3-9 The Calculation tab sheet

iteration As you can see from the Calculation tab sheet, you can select when calculation occurs, how many times (*iterations*) Excel should attempt to resolve an error in a formula before it gives an error message, and workbook options such as updating remote references (references to other worksheets or linked objects).

Exercise 10: Changing calculation to Manual

In this exercise, you will change the calculation option to Manual so that the worksheet will only be recalculated when you give the command. You will then make a change in the Pricomp worksheet and issue the Recalculation command.

1. From the Tools menu, choose Options.

   The Options dialog box appears on the screen.

2. Click the Calculation tab to make it the active sheet.

   The Calculation tab sheet will move to the front, as shown in Figure 3-9.

radio button 3. In the Calculation portion of the sheet, click the *radio button* beside the Manual option.

4. Click OK to apply the settings and close the sheet.

5. In the Pricomp worksheet, change the formula in cell D7 to =2.10/2.

   Notice that the IF formula in cell E7 does not update, even though it should.

6. Press F9 to calculate the worksheet.

   Excel runs the IF test and changes the Wholesale result to Retail since the retail sale price is lower than the wholesale price.

7. Return to the Calculation tab sheet, and set the Calculation option to Automatic.

8. Click OK to close the tab sheet.

Objective 8: Checking Spelling

Spell Checker One of the more recent additions to spreadsheet programs is a *Spell Checker*. A Spell Checker checks the spelling of words in the worksheet and offers suggestions for corrections when it finds a word that is misspelled. Before Spell Checkers were integrated into spreadsheet programs, it was not uncommon to find spelling or typographical errors in important worksheets. This was due, in large part, to the fact that people were concentrating on the data (usually the numbers) in the spreadsheet and not looking for obvious errors like spelling errors.

Using the Spell Checker

In Excel, you can click the Spelling button in the toolbar or use the Tools menu to access the Spell Checker. The checker examines each word and, if no misspelled words are found, issues a message box saying that no errors were found. When the Spell Checker does find a word that it thinks is misspelled or that it cannot understand, it displays a dialog box similar to the one shown in Figure 3-10.

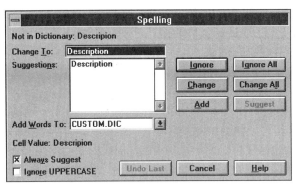

Figure 3-10 **The Spelling dialog box suggests alternatives for misspelled words**

 Press (F7) to begin a spell check of the current worksheet.

The Spelling dialog box has several options, which are discussed in Table 3.1.

Table 3-1 **The spelling options and their functions**

OPTION	DESCRIPTION
Ignore	Ignores a misspelled or special word one time
Ignore All	Ignores a misspelled or special word for remainder of the worksheet
Change	Changes the misspelled or special word to the selected word in the Change To or Suggestions field
Change All	Changes all occurrences of the misspelled word to the corrected word
Add	Adds the word not found in the dictionary to the specified dictionary so that it can be checked in the future
Suggest	Suggests a word when the Always Suggest option is turned off

When the Spell Checker locates a word not found in its dictionary, select one of the options in Table 3-1 to correct or ignore the word. The Spell Checker will then continue with its search, displaying words not found in its dictionary when necessary and ending with a completion message when it has searched the entire document.

Exercise 11: Checking the Pricomp worksheet

In this worksheet, you will edit several cells so that they contain spelling errors and then correct those errors using the Spell Checker.

1. With the Pricomp worksheet in the active window, make cell A2 the active cell.
2. Edit the word in cell A2 so that it reads Descripion.
3. Edit the word in cell D1 so that it reads Holesale.
4. In cell A15, type your last name. Click cell A1.
5. Click Spelling , or from the Tools menu, choose Spelling.

The Spell Checker will begin to run and will display the dialog box shown in Figure 3-10.

6. When the Spell Checker finds the typo *Descripion*, make sure that the Change To field is the correct spelling, and then click Change.

The word is corrected, and the Spell Checker moves on to the next word not found in the dictionary.

7. Continue with the Spell Checker, making the appropriate correction each time a word is not found. If the Spell Checker lists your last name as not found, click Add to add your last name to the dictionary.

8. When the Microsoft Excel dialog box appears, click OK to return to the worksheet.

Note that some common last names (for example, *Smith* and *Jones*) are already in the dictionary.

Objective 9: Naming Groups of Cells

named references

Another feature of spreadsheet programs is the capability of giving names to groups of cells or formulas. Remembering a range name like Sales is much easier than remembering the range D1:D7. *Named references* make formulas easier to read as well. The worksheet shown in Figure 3-11 is the same worksheet as the one shown in Figure 3-7 except that cell C3 has been named ComRate and the range of cells B6:B11 has been named Total_Sales. The formulas in cells C6 through C11 read: =ComRate*Total_Sales. A person who knows nothing about spreadsheets is much more likely to understand this formula than the formula with unnamed references.

Formula using named cell references ▶

Cell C3 is named ComRate ▶

The range B6:B11 is named Total_Sales ▶

	C6	▼	=ComRate*Total_Sales	
	A	**B**	**C**	**D**
1		Third Quarter Sales Figures		
2				
3	Commission rate:		0.05	
4				
5	Sales Rep	Total Sales	Commission	
6	Randy	$22,890.06	$ 1,144.50	
7	Jennifer	$27,682.12	$ 1,384.11	
8	JoAnne	$18,982.78	$ 949.14	
9	Jim	$13,512.31	$ 675.62	
10	Mike	$21,928.51	$ 1,096.43	
11	Melissa	$19,345.16	$ 967.26	

Figure 3-11   *The formula using named cell references is easier to read than the formula using unnamed cell references*

To name a cell, you must select the cell or range of cells to be named, and then define the name using the Name Define command under the Insert menu. A dialog box like the one shown in Figure 3.12 appears. After you have created a range name and are ready to use it in a formula, you can select the name from the name list box in the Formula bar, as shown in Figure 3-13.

Reduce, Reuse, Recycle!

Although naming cell references is a convenient way to remember ranges, it is really a way to reduce the amount of work you have to do, to reuse some of the work you've already done, and to recycle data into new and interesting figures. This chapter and most of this book will focus on working with a single worksheet in a workbook. However, Excel enables you to have multiple worksheets in one workbook. You could have your budget worksheet as sheet 1, your savings worksheet as sheet 2, and so forth—all stored in a workbook called Personal Finance. Each named cell reference you define can be used in any of the worksheets in a workbook. Thus, a cell named Total_Expenses in the budget worksheet could be used in the savings worksheet. So, while naming cells and ranges of cells makes it easy to remember them, it also enables you to use them efficiently in other worksheets.

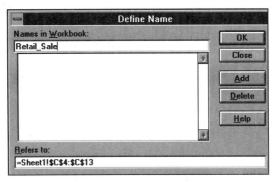

Figure 3-12 **The Define Name dialog box**

Figure 3-13 **The name list box provides quick access to all defined names for a workbook**

Exercise 12: Naming cells

In this exercise, you will use the Pricomp worksheet one last time (promise!) to name ranges of cells, and then you will use the named ranges in formulas.

1. With the Pricomp worksheet in the active window, select the range C4:C13.

2. From the Insert menu, choose Name, Define.

   A dialog box like the one shown in Figure 3-12 appears.

3. Type the name Retail_Sale in the field, as shown in Figure 3-12, and click OK to close the dialog box.

4. Select the range D4:D13.

5. From the Insert menu, choose Name, Define.

6. In the dialog box, define the name Wholesale and click OK to close the dialog box.

7. Make cell E4 the active cell.

8. In the Formula bar, place the I-beam to the right of the cell address D4 and press (← BACKSPACE) twice to delete the cell address.

9. Pull down the names list box in the Formula bar (refer to Figure 3-13 if necessary), and select the name Wholesale.

   The named reference Wholesale is pasted into the formula.

10. Place the I-beam to the right of the cell address C4 in the formula, and press (← BACKSPACE) twice to delete the cell address.

11. From the names list box, select the name Retail_Sale.

12. Click the enter box in the Formula bar to confirm the changes to the formula.

    The word *Wholesale* should appear in cell E4. If it doesn't, make sure that your ranges are named correctly and that the formula in E4 has been edited correctly.

13. Copy the edited formula in cell E4 to cells E5:E13, using the fill handle.

14. Save the file as price.xls.

Chapter Summary

In this chapter, you have learned important techniques for managing worksheets and data effectively and efficiently. You have learned how to plan the structure for a worksheet and how to move data around within that structure, using Cut, Copy, and Paste. You have also learned how to change the structure itself by inserting and deleting columns and rows. You know where the calculation options are in Excel and have become familiar with some of those settings, as well as the settings and options in the Spell Checker. Finally, you learned how to name groups of cells for ease of use in formulas.

Review Questions

True/False Questions

_____ 1. The Clear command temporarily deletes data from selected cells.

_____ 2. When data is copied, two versions of the same data exist.

_____ 3. The Clipboard can hold up to 16 items at one time.

_____ 4. When formulas are copied and then automatically adjust to their cell references, absolute cell addressing is in place.

_____ 5. When the Spell Checker notifies you that it can't find a word in its dictionary, you should always select Ignore.

Multiple Choice Questions

_____ 6. When you issue a command that you need to immediately retract, you should use which command?

A. Retract

B. Undo

C. Oops

D. Revert

_____ 7. When you insert a row into a worksheet, the row is inserted

A. above the active row.

B. below the active row.

C. in the active row.

D. at the top of the worksheet.

_____ 8. To quickly copy a cell or group of cells to an adjacent set of cells, use

A. Cut and Paste.

B. Copy and Paste.

C. Drag and Drop.

D. Ctrl+C, Ctrl+V.

_____ 9. When the formula =$D$3*F4 is copied from cell G4 to cell G5, it will change to

A. $E$4*G4.

B. $D$4*F5.

C. D4*G4.

D. $D$3*F5.

_____ 10. When the formula =D6+D7+D8 is copied from cell D10 to cell E10, it will

A. change to =E6+E7+E8.

B. not change.

C. change to =D9+D10+D11.

D. none of the above

Fill-in-the-Blank Questions

11. To store the contents of one or more cells in the Clipboard, use the _____ command.

12. To copy a cell or group of cells to an adjacent cell, use the _____ of the selected cell borders.

13. To select all the cells in a particular row, click the _____ .

14. To copy cells using the drag-and-drop method, you must hold down the ＿＿＿＿＿＿ key while dragging.

15. Before you can use a named reference, you must first ＿＿＿＿＿＿ the cell range and the name.

Acumen-Building Activities

Quick Projects

1. Editing your schedule

1. Open the schedule.xls worksheet created at the end of Chapter 2.
2. Adjust the column widths so that the columns are wide enough to accommodate the data in them.
3. Copy the range that has the days of the week to a new location in the worksheet (preferably underneath the current week's schedule).
4. Copy the times of day in column A to the new week's schedule.
5. Fill in the schedule for the second week.
6. Save the file as sched3.xls.

2. Editing the Budget worksheet

1. Open the budget.xls worksheet you created in Chapter 2.
2. Adjust the column widths so that they are wide enough to accommodate the data.
3. Name the range of cells in column A Date; in column B, Description; in column C, Expense; and in column D, Income.
4. Rewrite the formulas in column F so that they use the range names rather than the cell addresses.
5. Copy the balance formula to all cells in row F that have expenses.
6. Save the file as budget3.xls.

3. Checking the spelling of your CD collection

1. Open the file music.xls.
2. Adjust the width of any columns that are too narrow to accommodate the data.
3. Run the Spell Checker on the worksheet.
4. Add proper names to the dictionary, and correct any typographical errors you may have made.
5. Save the file as music3.xls.

4. Editing the Savings worksheet

1. Open the file savings.xls.
2. Adjust the width of any columns that are too narrow to accommodate the data.
3. Insert two blank rows at the top of the worksheet.
4. In cell A1, type the label Interest rate.
5. In cell B1, type the value: .035.
6. Edit the formula in column C for year 1 so that the interest rate (.0325) is deleted and in its place is an absolute cell address to reference the interest rate in cell B1.
7. Copy this formula to the cells in column C for rows 2 through 5.
8. Adjust the column width of column A, if necessary.
9. Save the file as savings3.xls.

In-Depth Projects

1. Editing the Stock worksheet

1. Open the file stock.xls.
2. Adjust the column widths so that the columns are wide enough to accommodate the data in them.
3. Insert a row at the top of the worksheet so that row 1 is blank.
4. Move the stock name in cell A9 to cell A1.
5. Copy the cells containing the row labels *Monday* through *Friday* to cell range A10:14.
6. Track the stock for a second week.
7. Copy the formulas to compute loss or gain from the first week's cells, making certain that the formula is accurate for the new cells.
8. Save the file as stock3.xls.

2. Editing your transcript

1. Open the file trnscrpt.xls.
2. Adjust the column widths so that they are wide enough to accommodate the data.
3. Name the range of cells containing letter grades Letter.
4. Edit the IF formula to compute the Point Value so that it uses the named reference rather than a cell address.
5. Copy this formula to the remaining rows in the Point Value column.
6. Save the file as trans3.xls.

CASE STUDIES

Coffee-On-The-Go: **Creating a Three-Year Projection**

In this chapter, you learned to modify a worksheet. You can now build a larger worksheet for Coffee-On-The-Go, using these skills to produce a three-year projection.

1. Create the three-year projection as shown. Use formulas to compute the totals.

Income Statement
Coffee-On-The-Go

	1995	1996	1997
INCOME			
Gross Sales	80,000	90,000	95,000
Cost of Goods	14,000	18,000	22,000
GROSS PROFIT	66,000	72,000	73,000
OPERATING EXPENSES			
Salaries	20,000	22,000	25,000
Benefits	1,200	1,300	1,500
Taxes	1,500	1,700	1,900
Advertising	5,000	5,000	5,000
Supplies	6,000	6,000	6,000
Insurance	4,000	4,500	5,000
Utilities	6,000	6,000	6,000
Licenses	2,000	2,000	2,000
Miscellaneous	2,000	2,000	2,000
Total Operating Expenses	47,700	50,500	54,400
Net Income (before Taxes)	18,300	21,500	18,600

2. Widen columns as necessary.
3. Use the Spell Checker.
4. Save the file as 3year.
5. Print the worksheet.

CASE STUDIES

Videos West: **Modifying the Forecast Worksheet**

In this chapter, you learned to modify a worksheet. You will apply those skills to the Revenue worksheet for Videos West.

1. Open the Revenue worksheet.
2. Move to column A, and widen the column to 20 characters.
3. Move to cell B10, and type 3000; in cell C10, type 4000; and in cell D10, type 5000.
4. Write a formula to figure Gross Profit for each month. Gross Profit is Net Sales minus Cost of Goods.
5. Starting in cell B15, type the following data, pressing ⬇ after each one: 3000, 200, 500, 300, 500, 1000, 200, 100, 400.
6. In cell B24, write a formula which totals January's Operating Expenses.
7. In cell B25, write a formula to figure the NET INCOME/LOSS. NET INCOME/LOSS is Gross Profit minus Total Expenses.
8. Insert a row above the NET INCOME/LOSS, at row 25.
9. Copy the data from cell B15 through cell B26 to columns C and D.
10. In cell E10, write a formula to total the Cost of Goods for the three months.
11. Copy the formula down column E to total all categories for the three months.
12. Delete any formulas in which the total blanks to 0.
13. Move to cell B7 and type 6000. Watch as the entire worksheet recomputes.
14. Save the file as revenue3.xls.
15. Print the worksheet.

Chapter 4

Formatting the Worksheet

Objectives

- Formatting Numbers
- Aligning Data in Columns
- Changing Fonts
- Changing Attributes
- Using Borders
- Using Patterns
- Protecting the Worksheet

Key Terms

TERM	DEFINITION
Center Justify	aligns data at the horizontal center of a cell
Justify	arranges data so that it takes up the entire horizontal space of a cell
Orientation	the direction in which text is printed or displayed on the screen
Wrap	Excel automatically creates a new line for data after the horizontal space of a cell has been filled with data in the first line
Font	the typeface used to display characters on the screen and in a printout
Pattern	a colored and/or shaded background that can be used to emphasize certain cells in a worksheet
Hatch Marks	lines that are part of a pattern
Password	a word or group of characters that act as a key to accessing data that has been protected

Up to now you have been working with worksheets using only the formatting that is done automatically, but Excel offers many tools to format both the worksheet itself and the data within the worksheet, and those tools are the focus of this chapter.

Numbers can be formatted in a wide variety of ways. In Excel, you can define the symbol that should precede or follow a number, the number of decimal places to be shown, and even the use of commas within large numbers. Although numbers are typically aligned along the right margin of the column, you can change this alignment for numbers and text as well. You **font** can also change the *font* and style of text and numbers within the cells to emphasize portions of your worksheet. You can define narrow or wide **patterns** lines to act as borders for your worksheet, and you can add *patterns* and colors to make the data easier to read and more meaningful.

In addition to changing the look of the worksheet, you can also change the accessibility of the worksheet. Excel enables you to protect your worksheet from accidentally deleting important formulas and from others using it inappropriately. You can assign a password to a worksheet or an entire workbook so that only those with the correct password can open the file. You can also lock cells so that they cannot be changed and hide formulas so that someone looking at your worksheet will not be able to see how you arrived at a specific figure.

Objective 1: Formatting Numbers

Because worksheets are used primarily to display numbers, Excel offers many different numeric formats from which to choose. Figure 4-1 shows the numeric formatting tools on the Formatting toolbar. In addition to those five options, you can use a set of cell-formatting tab sheets, accessed by choosing Format, Cells, to make many formatting decisions.

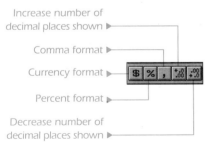

Increase number of decimal places shown ▶

Comma format ▶

Currency format ▶

Percent format ▶

Decrease number of decimal places shown ▶

Figure 4-1 **Five frequently-used numeric formats are available on the Formatting toolbar**

Using the numeric formatting buttons

The five numeric format buttons on the Formatting toolbar provide you with quick access to frequently used formats. To use any of these buttons, you must first select the cell or range of cells you want to format. Then click the appropriate button. You can format cells after data has been entered or before you enter data, whichever you prefer.

Exercise 1: Entering and formatting numbers

In this exercise, you will begin building a new worksheet to compare the cost of four-by-four sport utility vehicles.

1. Boot your computer, start Windows, and start Excel, if necessary.

2. With a new, blank workbook in the active window, enter the following worksheet shown in Figure 4-2.

	A	B	C	D	E	F
1						
2						
3						
4	Make	Model	Total Vehicle Cost	Interest Rate	Loan Period	Total Cost of Vehicle
5	Chevrolet	Blazer	21257			
6	Ford	Explorer	22837			
7	Isuzu	Trooper	20482			
8	Jeep	Cherokee	24912			
9	Land Rover	Land Rover	41908			
10	Mitsubishi	Monterro	24124			
11	Suzuki	Sidekick	16938			
12	Toyota	Land Cruiser	34861			

Figure 4-2   **The beginnings of the Truck worksheet**

3. Use the Autofit Selection command to automatically size the column widths.

TIP   The Autofit Selection shortcut is to double-click the vertical line separating column letters. Excel then automatically sizes the column widths.

4. Save the file as truck1.xls.

5. Select the range C5:C12.

6. Click the Currency button **$** in the Formatting toolbar.

   The values in column C are formatted with a dollar sign, commas, and a decimal point and two trailing decimals.

7. Select the range C5:C12 again, and click the Decrease decimal button **.00/.0** twice so that no decimal places are shown in this column.

8. Save the file again.

Formatting numbers using the Format Cell tab sheet

Although the numeric format buttons will meet most of your needs most
of the time, occasionally you may need to use other formatting options.
When this time comes, you can use the Format Cells dialog box, shown in
Figure 4-3. The numeric formatting options are grouped into categories on
the Number tab. When you click on a category, the available format codes
are displayed. To select a specific code, click on the code and then click OK.

Displays negative
values in parenthesis ►

Displays negative
values in red and
parenthesis ►

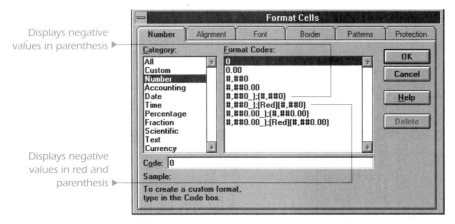

**Figure 4-3   The Number tab sheet offers many more formatting options
than are available on the Formatting toolbar**

Exercise 2: Formatting values using the Number tab sheet

In this exercise, you will continue to build the Truck1 worksheet and use
formatting options from the Number tab sheet.

1. With the Truck1 worksheet in the active window, enter the data shown
    in Figure 4-4, without any formatting, in columns D and E (for exam-
    ple, enter .049 in cell D5).

	A	B	C	D	E	F
F5			=(principle*rate*time)+principle			
1						
2						
3						
4	Make	Model	Total Vehicle Cost	Interest Rate	Loan Period	Total Cost of Vehicle
5	Chevrolet	Blazer	$ 21,257	4.90%	4	$ 25,423.37
6	Ford	Explorer	$ 22,837	5.50%	4	$ 27,861.14
7	Isuzu	Trooper	$ 20,482	6.00%	3	$ 24,168.76
8	Jeep	Cherokee	$ 24,912	3.80%	4	$ 28,698.62
9	Land Rover	Land Rover	$ 41,908	6.50%	4	$ 52,804.08
10	Mitsubishi	Monterro	$ 24,124	5.50%	4	$ 29,431.28
11	Suzuki	Sidekick	$ 16,938	6.50%	3	$ 20,240.91
12	Toyota	Land Cruiser	$ 34,861	6.00%	4	$ 43,227.64

Figure 4-4   The total cost of each vehicle, including interest

2. Name the cell range C5:C12 Principle.
3. Name the cell range D5:D12 Rate.

4. Name the cell range E5:E12 Time.

5. Select the cell range D5:D12.

6. From the Format menu, choose Cells.

   The Format Cells dialog box will appear.

7. Click the Number tab to bring that tab sheet to the front, if it is not already there.

8. From the Category listing, choose Percentage.

9. From the Format Codes listing, select 0.00% and click OK.

   The data in column D will be formatted as percentages with two decimal places.

10. In cell F5, enter a formula that will compute the total cost of the car over the loan period (interest plus initial cost of car).

    Hint: The formula is shown in the Formula bar of Figure 4-4.

11. Copy the formula in cell F5 to cells F6:F12, using whichever method you prefer.

12. Format the range F5:F12 as currency with two decimal places, using whichever method you prefer.

13. Save the file as truck2.xls.

Objective 2: Aligning Data in Columns

As you have discovered by this point, Excel has default settings for alignment in cells. Numeric data is aligned, by default, on the right while text data is aligned on the left. You can change the alignment of text and data by using the alignment buttons in the Formatting toolbar or by using the Alignment tab sheet.

Aligning text with the alignment buttons

center justify

There are four alignment buttons in the Formatting toolbar, as shown in Figure 4-5. You can use these buttons to align cell data at the left margin (left justify), in the center of the cell (*center justify*), at the right margin (right justify), and across a group of selected cells. As with numeric formatting, you can align the data in cells before you enter the data or after the data has already been entered. You should never attempt to manually place data in a certain location in the cell (in other words, to manually center a cell's contents using spaces, for example). The computer can do this task much more efficiently than you can, and, if you change the width of the column, Excel automatically realigns your data within the cell.

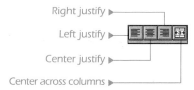

Right justify ▶
Left justify ▶
Center justify ▶
Center across columns ▶

Figure 4-5 The four alignment buttons on the Formatting toolbar

Exercise 3: Using the alignment buttons

In this exercise, you will use the alignment buttons in the Formatting toolbar to arrange the Truck worksheet.

1. With the truck2.xls worksheet in the active window, select the range A4:F4.
2. Click the Center justify button ▤ in the Formatting toolbar.

   The column headings are centered in the cell width. Notice that the column headings that take up the entire cell width do not change position since there is no room for them. Notice also that when one of the centered cells is the active cell, the Center justify button is on.

3. In cell A1, type the text Comparison of Popular 4x4 Sport-Utility Vehicles and press (← ENTER).
4. Select the range A1:F1, and click the Center across columns button ▦ in the Formatting toolbar.

   The worksheet title is centered across the selected cells.

5. Save the worksheet as truck3.xls.

Using the Alignment tab sheet

In addition to the four alignment buttons located on the Formatting toolbar, Excel offers other alignment options on the Alignment tab sheet. You can access the tab sheet by opening the Format menu and choosing Cells, and then clicking the Alignment tab. The Alignment tab sheet is shown in Figure 4-6. Table 4.1 describes the alignment options.

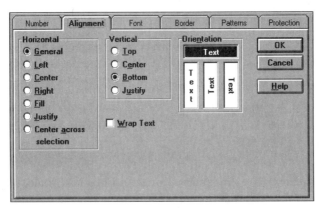

Figure 4-6 The Alignment tab sheet has many alignment options

Table 4-1 **The alignment options**

OPTION	PURPOSE
General	Aligns data according to Excel's general rules of alignment (default is left justify for text, right justify for values)
Left	Forces text to begin at the left margin of the cell
Center	Forces text to be evenly displayed between the left and right margins of the cell
Right	Forces text to end at the right margin of the cell
Fill	Fills the contents of the current cell with the same contents as the selected cell, creating a row of dashed lines or a separating line in a worksheet such as ———— or ======, for example
Justify	Justifies wrapped text so that all lines completely fill the column width
Center Across Selection	Centers the data in one cell across a group of selected cells

The Vertical alignment options tell Excel how to align text between the vertical edges of a cell. The default is for Excel to align text along the bottom edge of the cell. Table 4.2 describes each vertical alignment option.

Table 4-2 **The vertical alignment options**

OPTION	PURPOSE
Top	Aligns text in cells with the top of the cell
Center	Aligns text in the vertical center of the cell
Bottom	Aligns text with the bottom of the cell (the default setting)
Justify	Vertically centers wrapped text within the boundaries of a cell
wrap Wrap Text	Forces the cell height to expand as text exceeds the width of the cell so that one cell contains multiple lines of labels or values

orientation You can change the direction or *orientation* of text with the Orientation options. This option is especially handy when preparing a worksheet for a presentation since the directional text adds visual interest to the worksheet.

Exercise 4: Aligning text with the Alignment tab sheet

In this exercise, you will practice aligning text using options on the tab sheet.

1. With the truck2.xls worksheet in the active window, select cells A5:A12.
2. From the Format menu, choose Cells.
3. When the Format Cells dialog box appears, click the Alignment tab.

4. In the Orientation section of the tab sheet, select the last text option on the right in the second row (text has been turned 90-degrees clockwise from standard text).

5. Click OK.

   The make of each truck listed is turned on its side, creating taller rows.

6. Resize column A so that there is just enough room for the word *Make*.

7. Select cells C4:F4, and return to the Alignment tab sheet.

8. Click the Wrap Text option, and click OK.

9. Decrease the size of each of those columns so that there is enough room for the values in the columns.

   The text in the column headings will wrap, making the cells in row 4 taller and decreasing the amount of horizontal space the worksheet requires.

10. Save the file as truck4.xls.

Objective 3: Changing Fonts

Using different fonts is another method for emphasizing or de-emphasizing information in a worksheet. A *font* is the typeface used to present each character. There are artsy fonts and traditional fonts, fonts that are easy to read, and fonts that take some lessons in deciphering. The font you choose says a great deal about you and can make or break your presentation, based on its readability. Although there are a couple of ways to change the font of a cell or group of cells, the quickest way is to use the Font list box in the Formatting toolbar, as shown in Figure 4-7.

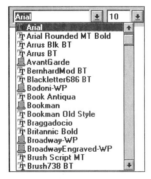

Figure 4-7   The Font list box in the Formatting toolbar

While fonts come in different shapes, they also come in different sizes. A larger font draws attention; a smaller font may make data go unnoticed. Font sizes can be changed from the Font Size list box in the Formatting toolbar. The larger the number in the list box, the bigger the character will be.

To change a font or a size, select the cell or cells you want to change, and then select the font and size you want from the list boxes.

Exercise 5: Changing fonts and sizes

In this exercise, you will change the font and size of several cells in the Truck worksheet.

1. With the truck4.xls worksheet in the active window, select cell A1.

   Although cell A1 looks blank, remember that the title of the worksheet was actually entered in this cell and then centered across the other cells.

2. From the Font list box in the Formatting toolbar, select a font of your choosing.

   The font changes after you make your selection.

3. Experiment with several different fonts until you find one that you think is easy to read and will make a good title.

4. From the Font Size list box in the Formatting toolbar, select size 12 so that the title is larger than the other text in the worksheet.

5. Save the file as truck5.xls.

Objective 4: Changing Attributes

Attributes are characteristics that can be applied to fonts to enhance their looks. Size is generally considered an attribute. Other common Excel options are **bold**, *italic*, and underline. These three attributes can be applied to any font in any cell by clicking the appropriate button in the Formatting toolbar, as shown in Figure 4-8.

Italic ▶
Bold ▶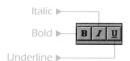
Underline ▶

Figure 4-8   You can select the bold, italic, and underline attributes from the Formatting toolbar

In addition to the Formatting toolbar attributes, the Font tab sheet enables you to make additional settings, as shown in Figure 4-9. The Font and Font Size list boxes in the Font tab sheet are the same as those on the Formatting toolbar. The Font Style list box has a greater number of options than the three buttons on the Formatting toolbar, and the number and types of styles available differ with each font. That is, each font family has its own set of associated styles and sizes. If a font looks good only in bold, italic, and underline, then those are the only three options available.

In addition to character font and style, you can also set the Underline (single, double, and so on), the Color, and Effects, such as ~~strikethrough~~, superscript, or subscript effects.

Using different-colored text is great if you have a color printer or are making a presentation by displaying worksheets from the computer onto a color monitor or with a color projection system. Colored text is also useful if you plan to have someone else examine your worksheet. Displaying certain cells in certain colors is sure to draw your audience's attention.

In the Font tab sheet, the selections you make will always show up as samples in the Preview portion of the tab sheet. Previewing makes it much easier to experiment with fonts and styles; you don't have to leave the dialog box to see how your text is going to look. When you have finished making selections in the tab sheet, click OK to apply the changes and close the sheet.

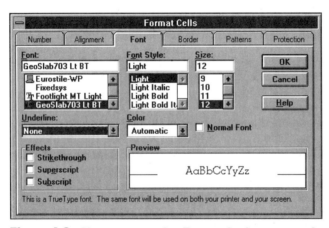

Figure 4-9   You can use the Font tab sheet to make many different choices affecting the Font

Exercise 6: Emphasizing data in the worksheet

In this exercise, you will continue to work with the Truck worksheet to emphasize data with font and style changes.

1. With the truck5.xls worksheet in the active window, select the range A4:F4.

2. Click the Bold button **B** in the Formatting toolbar to make the column headings boldfaced.

   The text of the column headings will increase in darkness and density.

3. Select the data in cells A5:B5.

4. From the Format menu, choose Cells, and click the Font tab to open the Font tab sheet shown in Figure 4-9.

5. Pull down the Color list box, and click on a color for the Chevrolet Blazer text.

6. Click OK to apply the change and close the tab sheet.

   The text in cells A5 and B5 are a different color.

7. Repeat Steps 3-6, selecting a different color for each truck make and model listed.

   Which colors stand out? Which ones fade into the background? If you were making a presentation to your boss about which truck you should get as the company vehicle, how you would change the colors so that the truck you want is easiest to spot?

8. Select the range A9:F9 and, using the Font tab sheet, make the row appear with strikethrough text since this truck is out of your budget.

9. Repeat Step 8 for the range A12:F12, since this truck is too expensive as well.

10. Save the file as truck6.xls.

Objective 5: Using Borders

Another way to emphasize portions of a worksheet is to add borders around a group of cells. A border can outline the entire cell or group of cells or appear on only one or two sides of the cell. It can be drawn using several different styles and, of course, you can select a different color for your border. You can use the Border button on the Formatting toolbar to display and select predefined border styles, or you can use the Border tab sheet (see Figure 4-10).

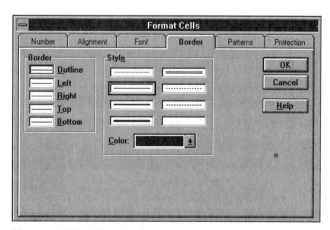

Figure 4-10 **The Border tab sheet**

You should be careful when using borders that you don't go overboard. It is very easy to make data confusing by having too many colors, styles, and additional elements such as borders. Use a light hand when it comes to worksheet formatting.

FEATURE

Know what you're paying for

Consumer laws in most states mandate that certain retailers such as car dealers and funeral home operators disclose all components of a purchase price. If you feel a merchant is hiding formulas from you, check with your state's Better Business Bureau about full disclosure laws in your area and the track record of the merchant with whom you are dealing.

Exercise 7: Adding a border to the Truck worksheet

In this exercise, you will add a border to the Truck worksheet that you have been developing.

1. With the truck6.xls worksheet in the active window, select the range A4:F4.
2. From the Format menu, choose Cells, and then click the Border tab.

   The Border tab sheet, as shown in Figure 4-10, appears.
3. Select an Outline border from the Border portion of the sheet.
4. Select the heaviest line weight (the one at the bottom left column) in the Style portion.
5. Select (or leave) the color black.
6. Click OK to apply the changes and close the sheet.

   A heavy black border appears around the column headings in row 4.
7. Now select the entire worksheet (cells A4:F12), and place a heavy black outline border around these cells.

   The entire worksheet is now bordered by a heavy black line.
8. Save the file as truck7.xls, and print the worksheet.

   Notice that the border makes the printed worksheet appear much cleaner than it would have without a border.

Objective 6: Using Patterns

The final element that can be added to an Excel worksheet to add visual interest is a *pattern* (sometimes called shading). Like colors and borders, patterns should be used sparingly. Patterns can be a background color for a **hatch marks**   cell, a background color with *hatch marks* (lines going in different directions) that form a pattern, or hatch marks themselves. Figure 4-11 shows the Patterns tab sheet. Note that a subset of available patterns can be selected using the Color button on the Formatting toolbar.

The password is...

In this era of networked computers and open information, a robust password is necessary for many applications. Your password is something that only you should know. Never give your password to a friend or relative, and don't store your password in an obvious place.

Good passwords consist of at least eight characters, with at least one of the characters being a number. Your password should not be found in any dictionary (English or foreign language), and should not be a slang word. Programs are available that enable computing administrators and computer hackers to check passwords for their "guessability," and curse words and proper names are at the top of almost every password checker program because people tend to use these most often. Your password is the key to your data and, in many cases, your communication system. If you feel that someone has guessed your password, change it immediately.

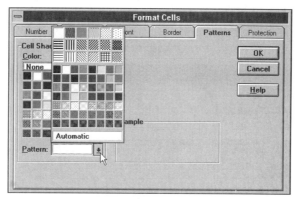

Figure 4-11   The Patterns tab sheet

Exercise 8: Adding a pattern

In this exercise, you will experiment with several patterns to emphasize your choice of trucks.

1. With the truck7.xls worksheet in the active window, select the row of the truck you would like to have as your company vehicle from the six trucks that are within your price range.

2. From the Format menu, choose Cells, and click the Patterns tab. The Patterns tab sheet, as shown in Figure 4-11, appears.

3. Click a color that you think will be appropriate as a background color.

4. From the Pattern list box, select a pattern that you think will be appealing. If you don't like any of the patterns, move the mouse pointer outside of the Pattern area and release it so that no selection is made.

5. Click OK to view your selection.

6. Experiment with several other backgrounds and patterns until you find one that you think looks best.

7. Save the file as truck8.xls.

Objective 7: Protecting the Worksheet

A final feature you can use to enhance your worksheet is to protect it. The Protection tab sheet, shown in Figure 4-12, enables you to lock the contents of a cell or cell range. Locking cells is a good way to prevent accidental deletion of important data or a formula. When a cell is locked, it cannot be altered in any way.

You also can use the Protection tab to hide a formula so that it doesn't appear in the Formula bar when a cell with the formula in it is made active. The capability of hiding formulas comes in handy in two specific situations: when you are teaching someone how to write formulas and don't want to give the answers away, and when you don't want someone to see how you actually arrived at a figure. Sales people will often hide formulas so that you can't see the markup, fees, or commission factored into the price of an item.

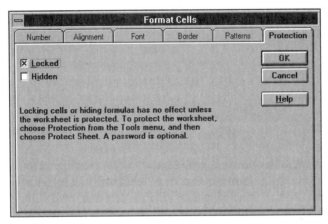

Figure 4-12   **The Protection tab sheet**

After you have selected cells to be locked or hidden, you must set the protection for the worksheet. You set this protection using the Protection, Protect Sheet commands from the Tools menu. When you make these selections, a dialog box like the one shown in Figure 4-13 appears. Excel enables you to set protection on the contents of the worksheet (data, formulas, charts, and macros), objects (graphics that have been pasted into the worksheet), and scenarios (problem-solving cases which haven't been discussed yet). Excel **password** also enables you to set a *password* for the worksheet. If you choose to use a password, you should write the password down and keep it in a safe place so that if you forget it, you can retrieve the password and your data won't be locked forever. In general, however, stealing data is like stealing a car. If someone really wants to steal, a password (or anti-theft device) is not going to stop them. If you have highly sensitive data in a worksheet, the best way to keep it safe is to store the worksheet on at least two floppy disks and keep those disks in two separate locations.

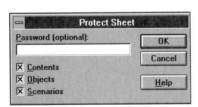

Figure 4-13   **The Protect Sheet dialog box**

Finally, if you need to make changes to cells that have been locked or hidden, you must first unprotect the worksheet using the Protection, Unprotect Sheet commands from the Tools menu.

Exercise 9: Protecting the Truck worksheet

In this exercise, you will set the protection for the Truck worksheet that you have been building, and then you will unprotect it.

1. With the truck8.xls worksheet in the active window, select the range F5:F12.

2. From the Tools menu, choose Protection, Protect Sheet.

   The Protect Sheet dialog box shown in Figure 4-13 appears.

3. In the Password field, type the word truck.

   The dialog box displays only asterisks as you type, preventing anyone who might be watching your screen from seeing your password.

4. Click OK.

   A dialog box like the one shown in Figure 4-14 appears. Read this dialog box very carefully.

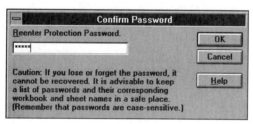

Figure 4-14   The Confirm Password dialog box

5. Retype the password truck, and click OK to apply the password.

6. Make cell F6 the active cell.

7. Open the Format menu.

   The Cells command is grayed out, meaning that it is not available.

8. Click the Bold button **B** in the Formatting toolbar.

   Excel issues an error message dialog box telling you that the cell is locked and the operation you chose cannot be done.

9. Click OK to close the error message box.

10. To unprotect the worksheet, choose Tools, Protection, Unprotect Sheet.

A dialog box like the one shown in Figure 4-15 appears, asking you to enter the password so that the sheet can be unprotected.

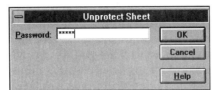

Figure 4-15 Enter the password in the Unprotect Sheet dialog box

11. Type the password truck, and click OK.

12. Complete Steps 6-8 again to verify that the protection has been removed, but click Undo to remove the boldface from cell F6.

13. Save the file as truck9.xls, and exit Excel at this time or continue with the problems at the end of this chapter.

Chapter Summary

In this chapter, you have learned the fundamentals of formatting worksheets and worksheet data in Excel. More importantly, you have learned where the formatting options are located and how to select and deselect them. You have learned to format various kinds of numeric values, to align data within cells and across cells, and to change the character attributes such as font, size, and color. You have also learned how to emphasize portions of a worksheet with borders and patterns. Finally, you have learned how to protect your worksheet by locking cells and hiding formulas.

Review Questions

True/False Questions

_____ 1. It is always a good idea to format numeric values with commas and dollar signs as you enter the data.

_____ 2. By default, text is left-justified when entered into an Excel worksheet.

_____ 3. All fonts have the same style attributes.

_____ 4. Patterns fill the background of selected cells.

_____ 5. Using a password is the best way to protect your data.

Multiple Choice Questions

_____ 6. Numeric data is automatically
  A. left-justified.
  B. center-justified.
  C. right-justified.
  D. justified across cells.

_____ 7. To change the direction text is displayed in a cell, you must change the
  A. orientation.
  B. rotation.
  C. navigation.
  D. page layout.

_____ 8. Fonts, borders, and patterns are changed in the Cell Format
  A. dialog box.
  B. menu.
  C. preferences file.
  D. button.

_____ 9. To prevent data in certain cells from being changed, you should
  A. hide the data.
  B. lock the data.
  C. change the Write attribute.
  D. password-protect the data.

_____ 10. It is best to use color in cells only when
  A. the worksheet will be displayed on a color monitor.
  B. the worksheet will be printed on a color printer.
  C. both A and B
  D. none of the above

Fill-in-the-Blank Questions

11. List the four types of justification that can be applied to a cell.

12. When Excel reaches the right boundary of a cell and automatically creates a new line for the remaining text, you can tell that the _____ feature is turned on.

13. To outline a cell or group of cells with a line or pattern, use the _____ tab sheet.

14. When a cell with a formula is the active cell but no formula appears in the Formula bar, _____ is turned on.

15. When you enter a password in Excel, the password is displayed as _____.

Acumen-Building Activities

Quick Projects

1. Formatting your schedule

1. Open the sched3.xls worksheet.
2. Make the days of the week for both weeks boldface, and adjust the column widths if necessary.
3. Select all cells containing data in the worksheet, and format the text so that it will wrap
4. Save the file as sched4.xls.

2. Formatting your budget

1. Open the budget3.xls worksheet.
2. Center the column headings.
3. Format all cells containing dollar amounts as currency with 2 decimal places displayed. Widen columns as necessary.
4. Format the text in column B (not the heading, just the data) in a small font size—8 or lower—so that you can get more information in the cell.
5. Save the file as budget4.xls.

3. Liven up your music

1. Open the music3.xls worksheet.
2. Center the data in all cells.
3. Create a double-line border around the entire worksheet.
4. Add a pattern to the group/artist column.
5. Save the file as music4.xls.

4. Protect your savings

1. Open the savings3.xls worksheet.
2. Hide the formulas in column D.
3. Lock the cells in column C.
4. Protect the worksheet with a password of your choosing.

5. Remember to record the password in a separate place.
6. Save the file as savings4.xls.

In-Depth Projects

1. Formatting the Stock worksheet

1. Open the stock3.xls worksheet and insert a blank row at row 2.
2. In cell A2, type the label # Shares.
3. In cell B2, type the value 300.
4. In cell D3 type the label Value.
5. In cell D5, compute the value of the stock by multiplying the number of shares by the day's closing price. Your formula should use only cell references—no actual values.
6. Place a green border around the day you should have sold the stock.
7. Place a dark gray border around the day you should have bought the stock.
8. Assign a light gray background to all cells in the worksheet with data.
9. Save the file as stock4.xls, and print the worksheet.

2. Formatting the Transcript worksheet

1. Open the trans3.xls worksheet.
2. Center the column headings, and boldface the data in column A.
3. Assign a pattern to each row in which the grade for the course listed is a B or above.
4. Change the color of the data in those rows so that it is complimentary to the pattern.
5. Change the color of the data in those rows in which the grade for the course listed is a D or below.

   Can you see a pattern of performance? Do you do better in science courses than arts and humanities courses? Are your grades lower in courses that gave a certain kind of exam (essay, for example)?
6. If you see a pattern, write a short one or two sentence description of the pattern in a blank column A cell that closely follows the transcript data.
7. Save the file as trans4.xls, and print the worksheet.

CASE STUDIES

Coffee-On-The-Go: **Creating an Annual Income Statement**

In this chapter, you learned to format and enhance the worksheet. You can now create a larger worksheet for Coffee-On-The-Go by creating a one-year projection.

1. Open a new workbook, and create the Income Projection for one year as shown. The worksheet will occupy columns A through O. Use formulas to compute totals.

Income Statement
Coffee-On-The-Go
Year: 1995

	Jan	Feb	Mar	Apr	May	Jun	Jul	Aug	Sept	Oct	Nov	Dec	TOTAL
INCOME													
Gross Sales	4,000	4,000	6,000	6,000	6,000	6,000	7,000	7,000	8,000	8,000	9,000	9,000	80,000
Cost of Goods	900	900	900	1,000	1,000	1,000	1,000	1,300	1,500	1,500	1,500	1,500	14,000
Gross Profit	3,100	3,100	5,100	5,000	5,000	5,000	6,000	5,700	6,500	6,500	7,500	7,500	66,000
OPERATING EXPENSES													
Salaries	1,200	1,200	1,200	1,200	1,300	1,300	2,000	2,000	2,000	2,200	2,200	2,200	20,000
Benefits	100	100	100	100	100	100	100	100	100	100	100	100	1,200
Taxes	100	100	100	100	100	100	100	110	140	150	200	200	1,500
Advertising	500	500	500	500	500	500	300	300	400	300	300	400	5,000
Supplies	500	500	500	500	500	500	500	500	500	500	500	500	6,000
Insurance	400	400	400	400	400	400	300	300	250	250	250	250	4,000
Utilities	500	500	500	500	500	500	500	500	500	500	500	500	6,000
Licenses	100	120	120	120	120	120	150	200	200	250	250	250	2,000
Miscellaneous	100	120	120	120	120	120	150	200	200	250	250	250	2,000
Total Operating Expenses	3,500	3,540	3,540	3,540	3,640	3,640	4,100	4,210	4,290	4,500	4,550	4,650	47,700

2. Format all values as currency with zero decimal places.
3. Save the file as income.xls.
4. Print out the worksheet, and close the file.

CASE STUDIES

Videos West: **Formatting the Spreadsheet**

In this chapter, you learned to format a worksheet. You will apply those skills to the Revenue spreadsheet for Videos West.

1. Open the Revenue3 worksheet.
2. Format the entire worksheet for the comma format with zero decimal places.
3. Format the NET INCOME/LOSS row for the currency format with zero decimal places.
4. Format column E for the currency format with zero decimal places.
5. Choose a different font in rows 1 and 2, and increase the size to 16 point.
6. Choose a different font in row 4, and increase the size to 14 point.
7. Underline the cells in rows 7 and 23.
8. Boldface the cells in row 26—the NET INCOME/LOSS.
9. Align the three month labels so that they are centered.
10. Place a border around the title of the worksheet in rows 1 and 2.
11. Save the file as revenue4.xls.
12. Print the worksheet.

Acumen Fundamentals Milestone

The Income Tax Worksheet

Now that you know a little bit about Excel, you have decided to record all
your income tax information in an Excel worksheet so that your tax data
will be well organized and easy to use when it is time to file your income
tax return. Create a worksheet that has headings for Income, Charitable Gifts,
Business Expenses, Medical Expenses, Child Care, and Other Deductions.
Within each heading, write a description of each item and its amount (for
example, under Charitable Gifts, you might have entries for Church and an
amount; Big Brothers/Big Sisters, followed by an amount; and so on). Use
formulas and functions to total the amounts in each category, and be sure to
format the data in the worksheet appropriately. Save the file as incometx.xls
and print the worksheet.

The Student Painters Worksheet

You and a small group of friends are interested in investigating the possibility
of operating a Student Painters franchise as a means of summer employment.
Each person in the group should prepare summary data on the amount of
money he or she needs to have to live on during the three months of the summer, as well as a goal to earn. The Student Painters literature suggests that you
should plan on painting 20 houses during the three months of summer break,
with an average cost of $1700 per house in your area for labor charges. Create
a worksheet that lists the amount of money each person in your group needs
to earn and the amount of money each person in your group would like to
earn. Total the amounts in these two columns with these column headings: #
of Houses Painted and Income. In the # of Houses Painted column, enter a
starting number of 20. In the Income column, write a formula to multiply
the number of houses painted by the average amount charged per house,
according to Student Painters. Compare the Income value with the amount
of money you need to earn as a group. Adjust the number of houses painted
number up or down until the Income value is close to the amount needed
by your group. Save the file as paint.xls. Print the worksheet.

Part 2

Critical Thinking

Chapter 5

Using Functions

Objectives

- Exploring Functions
- Using Statistical Functions
- Using Financial Functions
- Using Lookup and Reference Functions
- Using Date and Time Functions
- Using Logical Functions

Key Terms

TERM	DEFINITION
Function	a predefined formula that accepts inputs and returns a value or label
Argument	information necessary for functions to operate. Arguments can be cell ranges or actual data.
Relational Database	a group of related files in which data from separate files can be pulled together to form reports and perform search and lookup tasks
Lookup Value	the range or data that is searched for when using a lookup function to locate data
Table Array	the range of cells the lookup procedure scans
Row Index Number	the *n*th row in the table array in which a particular data item is located
Column Index Number	the *n*th column in the table array in which a particular data item is located

function   As you learned in Chapter 2, Excel provides you with over one hundred predefined formulas or *functions*. With the help of the Function Wizard, Excel's step-by-step function builder, you can use any of Excel's functions with ease.

Objective 1: Exploring Functions

Excel's built-in functions are separated into categories to make locating a specific function easier. Table 5-1 lists each function category and provides a brief description of the functions in that category.

Table 5-1   Functions and their descriptions

FUNCTION CATEGORY	DESCRIPTION
All	Lists all available functions
Financial	Performs analyses such as depreciation and loan payments
Date & Time	Performs analyses on date and time information and transforms date and time information into values which can be calculated
Math & Trig	Performs mathematical and trigonometric calculations
Statistical	Performs statistical tests on data
Lookup & Reference	Locates and utilizes data from multiple worksheets in calculations
Database	Performs calculations on a set of cells defined as a database
Text	Returns information about the text in a certain cell and transforms text for analyses
Logical	Performs tests on data and acts on the result of the test
Information	Returns information about a cell or group of cells, such as the format and field width

arguments

Functions can be entered into a worksheet in three ways. You can type the entire function into a cell, just as you would any other data. Of course, this method assumes that you know the syntax and *arguments* to be used in the function. You can use the Insert menu to insert a function. You can also click the Function Wizard button in the Standard toolbar. Choosing either one of the latter two commands opens the Function Wizard.

Typing a function

The fastest way to enter a function into a cell is to type the complete function into the desired cell of the worksheet, as you would any regular data. Because functions are really just prewritten formulas, you must begin a function the same way you begin a formula—with an equal sign (=). After the equal sign comes the function name itself, which is followed by the arguments for the function, enclosed in parentheses.

Exercise 1: Summing a group of values

In this exercise, you will enter a group of values into a new worksheet and then use the SUM function to find the total of those values.

1. Boot your computer and start Excel, if necessary.

2. With a new, blank worksheet in the active window, make cell B3 the active cell.

3. Type the value 1 into cell B3, the value 2 in cell B4, and the value 3 in cell B5.

4. Select the range B3:B5. Drag the fill handle down to cell B14, and release the mouse button.

   Excel automatically fills the blank cells with a continuation of the series of numbers 1, 2, 3 through the number 12.

5. In cell A16, type the label Total.

6. In cell B16, type the formula =SUM(B3:B14), and click the enter box ☑.

   The SUM function adds all the values in cells B3 to B14 and returns the total in cell B16.

7. Save the file as ex5-1.xls.

Using the SUM button

Because the SUM function is used so frequently, the makers of Excel decided to put a SUM function button on the Standard toolbar. To use the SUM button, make the cell in which you want the SUM formula to appear the active cell, and then click the SUM button. Excel attempts to guess the range you want summed (and it's usually right!), but sometimes you will need to define the range by selecting the group of cells to be summed. Regardless of how the range is entered, always double-check the range for accuracy. Click the enter box in the Formula bar to confirm the function.

Exercise 2: Using the SUM button

In this exercise, you will use the SUM button to sum the column of data created in Exercise 1.

1. With the worksheet you created in Exercise 1 of this chapter in the active window, move to cell A17.

2. Type the label Sum.

3. Make cell B17 the active cell, and click the SUM button Σ.

   Excel enters the function =SUM(B16). This is not a valid formula, and you must edit it to correct it.

4. Using the mouse, select the range B3:B14.

   The formula in cell B17 changes as you select the cells, indicating the range to be summed. The formula should be =SUM(B3:B14).

5. Click the enter box ☑ to confirm the formula.

   The value in cell B17 should be the same value in cell B16. If it isn't, check both formulas and edit the one with the mistake.

6. Save the file as ex5-2.xls.

Combining functions with other formula commands

Occasionally, you will want to combine a function with other formula components to come up with a result. To do this, use parentheses to show the priority of operations.

TIP The standard algebraic order of operations is first multiplication, then division, addition, and subtraction, in that order.

Exercise 3: Using SUM in a larger formula

In this exercise, you will combine the SUM function with other formula instructions to average the data in the worksheet.

1. Make cell A18 the active cell, and type the label Average. Adjust the column width if necessary.

2. In cell B18, type the formula =(SUM(B3:B14))/12, and click the enter box ☑.

   This formula tells Excel to calculate the sum of the numbers in the range first, then divide that sum by 12, and place the result in cell B18. The result should be 6.5.

3. Save the file as ex5-3.xls.

Using the Function Wizard

While typing a formula with a function is the quickest method for using formulas, it isn't always the most efficient. If you have to stop and think about the syntax for the formula for several minutes or "play around" with the formula to get it right, it is probably a better use of your time to use the Function Wizard.

Recall from Chapter 2 that the Function Wizard provides you with step-by-step instructions for building a formula that contains a function. You can access the Function Wizard by opening the Insert menu and choosing Function, or you can click the Function Wizard icon in the Standard toolbar.

FEATURE

Im"personal" statements

Because of the competition among credit card companies, many corporations are now adding phrases such as "We really appreciate the way you have paid on your account over the years." to customers' statements to make the customers feel appreciated. While the goal of these warm-fuzzy phrases is to make you think that the company appreciates you personally, you should realize that a fancy IF function is hard at work in the background to generate these kinds of statements. The function looks at your past payment history. If all your payments register as "on time," you get a warm fuzzy. If the company hasn't received your previous payment, the IF statement prints a notice telling you that the company wants your money. The days of true personal notes on your account statements are long gone.

When the Function Wizard dialog box opens, you must select the category and function name and then enter the necessary information, called arguments, for the function to run properly. When you have provided Excel with this information, the program places the correctly-formatted formula in the active cell and returns the result.

Exercise 4: Using the Function Wizard

In this exercise, you will use the Function Wizard to determine the minimum value in the list of values in the worksheet.

1. With the file ex5-3.xls still on the screen, type the label Minimum in cell A19 and the label Maximum in cell A20.

2. Make cell B19 the active cell, and click the Function Wizard f_x.

   The Function Wizard dialog box appears, as shown in Figure 5-1.

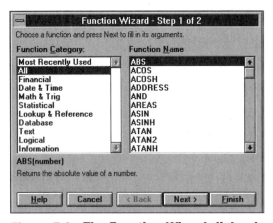

Figure 5-1   The Function Wizard dialog box

3. Select the Statistical category, and select the function name MIN.

4. Click the Next button to move to the next step.

5. In the Number 1 field, type the range B3:B14.

6. Click Finish to indicate that you have finished entering the arguments for the function.

   Excel executes the formula and places the result, 1, in cell B19.

7. Save the file as ex5-4.xls.

Using named cell references in a function

In addition to using regular cell addresses in a formula that is based on a function, you can also use named cell references. Using a named cell reference makes it very clear to both you and anyone else looking at the worksheet exactly what you have calculated.

Exercise 5: Editing formulas to include named references

In this exercise, you will name the numeric series in the worksheet and then edit the formulas to include the named range.

1. Select the range B3:B14, and define the range with the name Value_Series.
2. Edit the Formulas in column B using the new range name.
3. Save the file as ex5-5.xls.

Objective 2: Using Statistical Functions

Statistical functions are useful in a wide variety of situations. Table 5-2 describes statistical functions that are commonly used.

Table 5-2   Statistical functions and their descriptions

FUNCTION NAME	DESCRIPTION
AVERAGE	Returns the average (mean) of the values in a range
COUNT	Returns the number of values in a range
MAX	Returns the maximum value in a range
MEDIAN	Returns the value that is exactly in the middle of a range of values (in other words, half the values are higher than the returned value and half the values are lower than the returned value)
MIN	Returns the minimum value in a range
MODE	Returns the value that most frequently occurs in a range

Exercise 6: Managing a gradebook

In this exercise, you will create the worksheet shown in Figure 5-2 and then enter appropriate formulas to complete the worksheet, using statistical functions.

	A	B	C	D	E
1	Student	Exam 1	Exam 2	Exam 3	Average
2	Anderson	78	83	87	
3	Bailey	72	80	86	
4	Chaney	91	90	97	
5	Henderson	98	99	99	
6	Wilkerson	84	80	86	
7					
8	Mean				
9	Median				
10	Mode				

Figure 5-2   The Gradebook worksheet

1. Close the ex5-5.xls workbook, and open a new workbook on the screen.
2. Enter the worksheet shown in Figure 5-2, adjusting the columns as necessary.
3. Name the range B2:B6, Exam1; the range C2:C6, Exam2; and the range D2:D6, Exam3.

4. Name the range B2:D2, Anderson; the range B3:D3, Bailey; the range B4:D4, Chaney; the range B5:D5, Henderson; and the range B6:D6 Wilkerson.

5. In cell E2, use the Function Wizard and the AVERAGE function to write a formula that will compute the average for Anderson. Be sure to use the named reference in the formula.

6. Copy the Average formula for Anderson to Bailey, Chaney, Henderson, and Wilkerson in their respective rows in column E. Edit the copied formulas to include the appropriate range names.

7. In cell B8, write a formula using the AVERAGE function that will determine the average (mean) exam score for exam 1.

8. Write the same formula, using appropriate named references, in cells C8 through E8.

9. In cell B9, write a formula using the MEDIAN function that will determine the Exam 1 score that is precisely in the middle of the range of scores.

10. Repeat Step 9, changing named references, for cells C9 through E9.

11. In cell B10, write a formula using the MODE function that will determine the most frequent score for Exam 1.

   Excel returns the error #N/A since there are no duplicate scores in the range.

12. Repeat Step 11, changing named references, for cells C10:E10.

13. Save the file as ex5-6.xls.

14. Close the worksheet.

Objective 3: Using Financial Functions

Financial functions are used to analyze investments, securities, and annuities. They can also determine depreciation and calculate cash flows and loans. Table 5-3 describes commonly-used financial functions.

Table 5-3   Financial functions and their descriptions

FUNCTION	DESCRIPTION
DDB	Calculates the double-declining balance depreciation allowance of an asset
FV	Calculates the future value of a series of equal payments
IPMT	Calculates the cumulative interest on a periodic payment for an investment
IRR	Calculates the internal rate of return for a series of cash flows
NPER	Calculates the number of payment periods of an investment
NPV	Calculates the net present value for a series of cash flows
PMT	Calculates the payment amount needed to pay off a loan
PV	Calculates the present value of a series of equal payments
SLN	Calculates the straight-line depreciation allowance for one period

Text functions

A set of functions not discussed in this chapter but important nonetheless is the text category of functions. These functions perform operations on text in the worksheet and can provide real time savings when you are trying to make your data consistent. The LOWER and UPPER functions convert text in the specified cells to all lowercase or all uppercase. The PROPER function converts text to proper case, capitalizing the first letter of the text and making the remainder of text in lowercase. Finally, the SUBSTITUTE function enables you to search for text in the worksheet and substitute new replacement text. This function is especially useful if you have consistently entered text or a value incorrectly.

Using the Function Wizard to write financial functions

Financial functions are arranged to perform analyses in the following areas: annuities, bonds, capital-budgeting, depreciation, and single-sum compounding. Unlike statistical functions, in which you supply a range which is then calculated, financial functions may require several pieces of information. To calculate the amount of a loan payment, for example, three pieces of information are required: the principal amount, the interest rate, and the length of time in which the principal will be repaid. The Function Wizard prompts you for each piece of information needed to complete the formula.

Exercise 7: Paying off a credit card

Assume that you have just transferred the balance of an old, high-interest rate credit card to a new, lower-interest rate card. You have set a goal for yourself to have the entire balance paid off in three years.

1. Save and close any open worksheets on your screen.

2. Open a new worksheet.

3. Create the worksheet fragment shown in Figure 5-3.

Figure 5-3   **The credit balance worksheet fragment**

4. Make cell C4 the active cell, and click the Function Wizard button ![fx].

5. Select Financial from the category column and PMT from the function name column, and then click Next.

6. Complete Step 2 of the Function Wizard as shown in Figure 5-4. Note that since you will be making monthly payments, you must divide the interest rate by 12 to get the monthly interest rate rather than the annual interest rate.

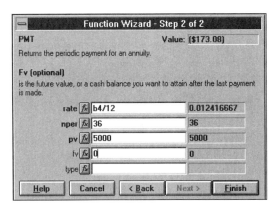

Figure 5-4 **The information to provide the Function Wizard**

7. Click Finish to complete the formula, and click the enter box in the Formula bar, if necessary.

Excel displays the value 173.08 in parentheses (and possibly the color red, depending on how your system is set up) indicating that this is a negative number or outgoing cash flow. This value shows that you must pay that amount each month to have a zero balance on your credit card at the end of thirty-six months.

8. Save the file as credit.xls, and close the worksheet.

Objective 4: Using Lookup and Reference Functions

Lookup functions are powerful tools that enable you to use data from one location in formulas in a different location. Lookup functions can be used to look for data within the same worksheet, within separate worksheets, and even separate workbooks. Lookup functions enable spreadsheet programs to have some of the same characteristics as *relational databases* because you can relate information from one file (worksheet) to another. Two commonly used Lookup functions are HLOOKUP and VLOOKUP.

relational databases

Locating values in rows with HLOOKUP

HLOOKUP stands for horizontal lookup. HLOOKUP uses the data in the top row of a range as a comparison value and then locates the specific data you request by searching down the column. The syntax for HLOOKUP is HLOOKUP(lookup_value, table_array, row_index_number). Let's examine each of these components.

lookup value
table array

row index number

The *lookup value* is the value to be compared against—the known value. The lookup value can be an actual value or a cell reference. The *table array* is the range which is to be searched. The table array typically is the range of the column in which data is to be found. Finally, the *row index number* is the row that contains the value to be returned. The number, however, is not necessarily the actual row number. If you defined the table array as

B2:B15 and you want to locate a total, which is stored in row 13, the row index number would actually be 12 because row 13 is the twelfth row in the array.

Exercise 8: Locating information with HLOOKUP

In this exercise, you will prepare a small payroll worksheet, shown in Figure 5-5, and then use the HLOOKUP function to locate data within the worksheet.

1. Save and close any open worksheets.

2. Open a new worksheet, and enter the data as shown in Figure 5-5, using a formula to arrive at the total take-home pay in column F.

	A	B	C	D	E	F
		After-Tax Salary	Medical Insurance	United Way	Other	Total Take Home
1	Employee					
2	Adams, M.	2416.66	13.72	24	50	2328.94
3	Dobson, C.	2511.32	67.33	25	150	2268.99
4	Jessema, R.	3641.98	67.33	32	150	3392.65
5	Robel, A.	3427.18	5.05	45	0	3377.13
6	Welty, W.	4105.38	98.63	40	150	3816.75

Figure 5-5   The Payroll worksheet

You create a formula to look up data within the worksheet.

3. Make cell A8 the active cell.

4. Click the Function Wizard button ![fx], select Lookup & Reference from the category column and HLOOKUP from the function name column, and then click Next to go to the next step.

Step 2 of the Function Wizard appears, as shown in Figure 5-6.

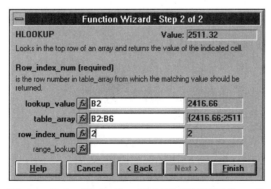

Figure 5-6   Data for the HLOOKUP function

5. Enter the arguments shown in Figure 5-6, and then click Finish to close the Function Wizard. Take the time to read the explanation of each argument on the screen as you enter it. Excel looks up the value you requested and places it in cell A8.

6. Save the file as payroll.xls.

Working with VLOOKUP

As you have just seen, HLOOKUP locates data by rows. VLOOKUP, on the other hand, locates data by columns. When you use the VLOOKUP command, you must tell Excel where to locate the data you want to find by defining the number of columns away from the reference column the data is located.

column index number

The syntax for the VLOOKUP function is quite similar to that of the HLOOKUP function except that the table array is generally the entire worksheet area rather than one column, and you use a *column index number* rather than a row index number to tell Excel where to find the data for which you are looking.

Exercise 9: Using VLOOKUP

In this exercise, you will work with the Payroll worksheet created in the preceding exercise and the VLOOKUP function to locate data in columns.

1. With the Payroll worksheet in the active window on the screen, move to cell B8.

    You will now write a formula using the VLOOKUP function that will locate the salary of a specific employee.

2. Click the Function Wizard button ![fx], select Lookup & Reference from the function category list and VLOOKUP from the function name list, and click Next to move to Step 2.

3. Complete Step 2 of the Function Wizard, as shown in Figure 5-7. Note that Excel provides the quotes in the lookup-value field. Be sure to read the explanation of each argument as you give it.

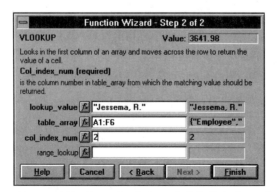

Figure 5-7 *Step 2 of the VLOOKUP function*

4. Click Finish to close the Function Wizard.

   Excel looks up the row that contains Jessema, R. in it, then moves to the specified column in the column number index (2, in this case), and locates the desired data.

5. Save the file as payroll2.xls.

Objective 5: Using Date and Time Functions

Date and time functions are used in conjunction with the internal calendar and clock on your computer. You can use date and time functions to return the current date and time or, more commonly, to transform a date or time expressed in text to a serial number which can be used in a calculation.

Obtaining the current date and time

You can use the NOW function to place the current date and time in a cell in a worksheet. This function comes in handy when you need to enter a date and time stamp as an entry in a worksheet. To use this function, make the cell in which you want the date and time to appear the active cell and then select the function from the Function Wizard. No arguments are necessary for this function.

Exercise 10: Using the NOW function

In this exercise, you will use the NOW function to place a date and time stamp beside payroll information in the Payroll2 worksheet.

1. With the Payroll2 worksheet in the active window, make cell G1 the active cell, and type the label Date/Time. Boldface the label, and adjust the column width if necessary.

2. Make cell G2 the active cell, and click the Function Wizard button .

3. From the category list, select Date & Time.

4. From the function name list, select NOW and click Next to continue.

5. Since the value of NOW is constantly changing, the Function Wizard displays the word *Volatile* in the value box of Step 2. Click Finish to complete the formula. The current date and time displays in cell G2.

6. Adjust the width of column G if necessary.

7. Save the file.

Calculating dates

In addition to getting system information, you can also use date and time functions to calculate the number of days between two dates. To do this, you must use the DAYS360 function and provide the Function Wizard with a start date and a stop date.

Exercise 11: Using the DAYS360 function

In this exercise, you will calculate the number of days between two dates in the Payroll worksheet.

1. Move to cell A10 in the Payroll2 worksheet.

2. Click the Function Wizard button f_x, and select the Date & Time category and the DAYS360 function.

   Step 2 of the DAYS360 function displays, as shown in Figure 5-8.

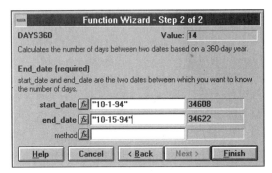

Figure 5-8 **Step 2 of the DAYS360 function**

3. Enter the dates as shown in Figure 5-8, making sure that you use quotation marks at the beginning and end of each date.

4. Click Finish to close the Function Wizard window.

   Excel displays the number of days between the two days given in cell A10.

5. Save the file as payroll3.xls.

6. Close the worksheet.

Objective 6: Using Logical Functions

In Chapter 2, you were briefly introduced to the most common logical function, the IF function. There are several other logical functions that are really useful. Table 5-4 describes commonly-used logical functions.

Table 5-4 **Logical functions and their descriptions**

FUNCTION NAME	DESCRIPTION
AND	Returns a value of true if both arguments joined by AND are true
IF	Performs a test on an argument and then returns different results if the argument is true or false
NOT	Reverses the logic of an argument
OR	Returns a value of true if one or more arguments is true

Using one logical function at a time

Each function listed in Table 5-4 can be used on its own to perform a test of some sort. When the test is passed, Excel prints the word *True* in the cell. When the test is failed, Excel prints the word *False* in the cell. If you want to test two or more arguments, for example, you use the AND or OR functions. The AND function requires that all arguments be true in order for the function to return True. If even one argument fails the test, the answer for the entire function will be False. OR, on the other hand, requires that only one of the list of arguments be true.

Exercise 12: Testing arguments

In this exercise, you will create a simple worksheet and use the AND and OR functions to test the data.

1. Save and close any open worksheets, and open a new workbook.

2. Create the worksheet shown in Figure 5-9. To minimize your work, be sure to use the fill handle to fill down each column after entering the first two values in each column.

	A	B	C	D	E
1					
2				AND	OR
3	1	2	3		
4	2	3	4		
5	3	4	5		
6	4	5	6		
7	5	6	7		
8	6	7	8		
9	7	8	9		
10	8	9	10		
11	9	10	11		
12	10	11	12		
13	11	12	13		
14	12	13	14		

Figure 5-9   A simple practice worksheet

3. Make cell D3 the active cell, and click the Function Wizard button f_{x}.

4. In the Function Wizard dialog box, select the Logical category and the AND function, and then click Next.

   The Function Wizard moves to Step 2.

5. In the Logical1 field, type b3>a3.

6. In the Logical2 field, type c3>b3.

7. Click Finish.

   Because both tests were true (the value in cell B3 is greater than cell A3 and the value in cell C3 is greater than Cell B3), the result *True* appears in the cell.

8. Make cell E3 the active cell, and click the Function Wizard button f_{x}.

9. In the Function Wizard, select the Logical category and the OR function, and then click Next.

   Step 2 of the Function Wizard appears on the screen.

10. In the Logical1 field, type b3>a3.

11. In the Logical2 field, type b3>c3.

12. Click Finish to close the Function Wizard.

    Excel displays *True* in cell E3 because at least one of the tests in the function was true (b3 is greater than a3).

13. Save the file as ex5-12.xls.

Combining logical functions

Each function listed in Table 5-4 can be used in conjunction with the IF function. If you want to test two sets of data, for example, you can write a formula like =IF((AND(B3>C3,B7>C7)),"deflation", "inflation"). This formula says that if the data in cell B3 is greater than the data in cell C3 and if the data in cell B7 is greater than the data in cell C7, print the word *deflation*. If either or both of the numbers in column C is greater than the numbers in column B, however, the test is failed and the word *inflation* should be printed. This capability of joining functions provides you with tremendous power in managing your data.

Exercise 13: Combining IF and AND

In this exercise, you will combine the IF and AND functions to generate results other than True and False.

1. Make cell F2 the active cell, and type the column heading IF/AND.

2. Make cell F3 the active cell, and type the following formula:
   =IF((AND(B3>A3,C3>B3)),"inflation", "deflation").

3. Click the enter box ☑ to confirm the formula.

   Excel displays the word *inflation* in cell F3.

4. Save the file as ex5-13.xls.

5. Quit Excel at this time, or continue with the problems at the end of this chapter.

Chapter Summary

In this chapter, you became more familiar with the functions that are available in Excel. You have learned that the Function Wizard is a valuable tool for writing and editing correct functions, and you have caught a glimpse of the power that functions provide you in the management of data.

Review Questions

True/False Questions

_____ 1. Functions are actually predefined macros.

_____ 2. The Function Wizard provides step-by-step instructions for creating formulas with functions.

_____ 3. All functions must begin with a plus sign (+).

_____ 4. Financial functions require a single argument.

_____ 5. Logical functions can be used alone or in conjunction with other logical functions.

Multiple Choice Questions

_____ 6. The Function Wizard button is located
   A. on the Formatting toolbar.
   B. in the File menu.
   C. on the Standard toolbar.
   D. in the status bar.

_____ 7. Which one of the following function categories tests data?
   A. Financial
   B. Date & Time
   C. Statistical
   D. Logical

_____ 8. To calculate the number of days between two dates, use the
   A. NDAYS financial function.
   B. DAYS360 date & time function.
   C. DateToSerial date & time function.
   D. subtraction operator with no function.

_____ 9. When combining functions with other calculations in a formula, what symbol must you use to show order of operation?
   A. parentheses
   B. commas
   C. exclamation points
   D. semi-colons

_____ 10. Which one of the following functions returns the value that most frequently occurs in a range?

A. MEAN

B. MEDIAN

C. MODE

D. FREQ

Fill-in-the-Blank Questions

11. To determine the minimum value in a range of cells, use the _____ function from the _____ category.

12. To determine the amount of multiple equal payments to pay off a loan, use the _____ function from the _____ category.

13. To print the current date and time, use the _____ function from the _____ category.

14. To find data in a column, use the _____ function from the _____ category.

15. To test the "trueness" of values in four different cells, use the _____ function from the _____ category.

Acumen-Building Activities

Quick Projects

1. Making a savings plan

For this problem, you will create a worksheet and use a function to determine the amount of money you must save each month to reach a savings goal of $7,500 in four years, of $7,500 in three years, of $7,500 in two years, and of $7,500 in one year.

1. Start Excel, and open a new workbook.

2. Create the worksheet shown in Figure 5-10.

	A	B	C	D
	D4			
1	Savings Plan			
2				
3	Rate	Time	Future Value	Monthly Deposit
4	0.075	4	7500	
5	0.075	3	7500	
6	0.075	2	7500	
7	0.075	1	7500	

Figure 5-10 **The Savings Plan worksheet**

3. In cell D4, write a formula using the appropriate function to compute the amount of monthly savings required to reach your goal of $7,500 in four years.

4. Complete the worksheet by writing similar formulas in cells D5 through D7, adjusting the time value in each new formula.

5. Save the file as svplan.xls.

2. Saving for a car

Now that you have your car paid off, you have decided to save the amount of the car payment in anticipation of buying a new car in three years. You want to know how much money you will have amassed at the end of the three years.

1. Start Excel, and open a new worksheet, if necessary.

2. In cell A3, type the value 412.50, the amount you plan to save each month.

3. In cell B3, type the value .055, the interest rate you are currently getting at your bank.

4. In cell C3, type the value 3, the number of years you plan to save.

5. Write a formula, using the appropriate financial function, that will compute the value in three years of the money you save each month.

6. Save the file as car.xls.

3. Tracking your grades

For this problem, you will create a small worksheet to track your performance on assignments for a class of your choosing.

1. Start Excel, and open a new workbook, if necessary.

2. In cell A1, type the course number and course title of the course you are going to track.

3. In cell A2, type the semester or term and the year of the course.

4. In row 4, type assignment headings (Lab 1, Lab 2, for example), ending with the column headings Average, Minimum, and Maximum.

5. In row 5, type your score for each assignment. Make sure that you use the same criterion for each score—in other words, if you enter one score as a percentage, you enter all scores as a percentage).

6. In the cell under the Average heading, write a formula using the AVERAGE function that will compute the average score of your assignments.

7. In the cell under the Minimum heading, write a formula that will compute the minimum score you have received thus far.

8. In the cell under the Maximum heading, write a formula that will compute the maximum score you have received thus far.

Examine the summary scores carefully. Why do you think you did better on one assignment than the rest? Why do you think you performed poorly on one assignment? Use this information to help you identify your strong and weak study skills.

9. Save the file as grades.xls.

4. Counting the days

You have a big trip planned and decide to write a fun formula that will compute the number of days between now and the day you leave.

1. Start Excel, and open a new workbook, if necessary.

2. In cell A3, type the date on which you are to leave for vacation (make one up if you don't have any real plans).

3. In cell B3, use the TODAY function to print today's date.

4. In cell C3, write a formula using the appropriate function to determine the number of days between the current day and your departure date.

   The TODAY function will update the date automatically each time you open this worksheet. So, if you open the worksheet a week from now, a new date will appear in cell B3 and a new countdown number will appear in cell C3.

5. Enter appropriate column headings for each of the three columns in rows 1 and 2.

6. Save the file as holiday.xls.

In-Depth Projects

1. Tracking sports scores

For this problem, you will track your favorite sports team's score over a period of four games and write formulas to generate summary statistics.

1. Start Excel, and open a new worksheet.

2. Using the worksheet shown in Figure 5-11 as a model, enter data about the team you are tracking and their scores for the last four games.

	A	B	C	D	E	F
	F4					
	A	**B**	**C**	**D**	**E**	**F**
1	Indiana Hoosier Basketball					
2						
3		Opponent	Home/Away	Opponent Score	Hoosier Score	Win/Loss
4	Game 1	Cincinnati	Away	63	98	
5	Game 2	Purdue	Home	72	75	
6	Game 3	Michigan	Home	79	80	
7	Game 4	Northwestern	Away	68	74	
8						
9	Average					
10	Minimum					
11	Maximum					

Figure 5-11 The Teamrec worksheet

3. Name the score range in column D Opponent_Score and the score range in column E Team_Score.

4. Write a formula using the IF function in column F that will print the word *Win* or *Loss,* depending on your team's performance.

5. In cell D9, write a formula using the named cell ranges that will compute the average score of the opponent teams and the average score of your team in cell E9.

6. In cell D10, write a formula using the named cell ranges that will compute the minimum score of the opponent teams and the minimum score of your team in cell E10.

7. In cell D11, write a formula using the named cell ranges that will compute the maximum score of the opponent teams and the maximum score of your team in cell E11.

8. Save the file as teamrec.xls.

2. Creating an animal shelter worksheet

You decided to volunteer time at the local animal shelter. When the shelter discovered that you knew how to use Excel, they asked you to design a system for managing animals that are brought in to the shelter and that are adopted from the shelter.

1. Design a worksheet that will store information on the following categories: Breed; Gender; Spayed/Neutered; Color; Day In; Day Out; Total Days; Advertise.

2. Enter at least five rows of data into the worksheet for the first six columns. For animals that have not been adopted, use the date 1/1/01.

3. In the Total Days column, write a formula using the appropriate function that will compute the total number of days an animal has been in the shelter. Copy this formula so that every animal in the worksheet has a Total Days number assigned.

4. In the Advertise column, write a formula using the appropriate function that will print the word *Yes* in the cell if the animal has been in the shelter more than five days and the word *No* in the cell if the animal has been in the shelter less than five days. Copy this formula so that every animal in the worksheet has a Yes or No in its row.

5. Save the file as shelter.xls.

CASE STUDIES

Coffee-On-The-Go:

Creating a Loan Worksheet

In this chapter, you learned to use built-in functions, which provide a powerful way to build formulas. You will apply those skills to the Coffee-On-The-Go case study.

Open a new workbook, and use built-in functions to create a loan worksheet. You need to borrow $30,000. If you borrow the money for 15 years, the interest rate is 7%. If you borrow it for 30 years, the interest rate is 9.75%. Show what the monthly payments would be for the different rates and time periods.

Save the file as payment, and print it out.

CASE STUDIES

Videos West:

Using FUNCTIONS

In this chapter, you learned to use built-in functions. You will apply those skills to build a worksheet which analyzes data for Videos West.

1. Open a new worksheet.
2. Create the following worksheet:

Title	Quantity	Price
Golf like a Pro	12	19.99
Tips on Hunting	5	14.99
Tai Chi for Health	10	19.99
Quit Smoking on Your Own	7	9.99
Buy Your Own Home	12	14.99
Baseball Tips	10	19.99
Beaded Jewelry	7	14.99
Jogging Tips	11	14.99
Take Control of Your Debt	12	9.99
Addiction Awareness	10	21.99
Eating for your Health	3	14.99
Christmas Decorations	5	7.99
Skiing Your Best	9	9.99

Tennis Pros Talk	10	9.99
Hobbies for Profit	5	9.99
Yoga for your Health	7	14.99
Start Your Own Business	9	14.99

3. Move to column D, and add the label reorder in cell D1.

4. Write a formula using the IF function, which looks at the quantity column and places the word *Reorder* in the column D if the quantity is below 10 and places the word *OK* in column D if the quantity is equal to or greater than 10.

5. Copy the IF formula to all cells with data in column D.

6. Save the file as reorder.

7. Print the worksheet.

Chapter 6

Using Multiple Spreadsheets

Objectives
- Creating Multiple Worksheets
- Navigating Sheets
- Deleting, Copying, Moving, and Hiding Sheets
- Copying and Moving Data among Sheets
- Creating Formulas Using Multiple Sheets
- Using Multiple Workbooks
- Creating Formulas Using Multiple Workbooks

Key Terms

TERM	DEFINITION
Sheet Tabs	the markers at the bottom of the worksheet window that enable you to switch between open worksheets
Source Sheet	the sheet from which data is being copied or linked
Target Sheet	the sheet to which data is being copied
Remote Sheet	the sheet to which data is being linked
Static Operation	any procedure that does not automatically update data

One of the nicest things about working in the Windows environment is that you can use multiple applications and files at one time. Before Windows and before computers had enough system resources (RAM) for large and complex operations, people were forced to create gigantic spreadsheets to hold all the data about a particular subject because it was impossible to work with multiple worksheets at one time. All that has changed, however, and now it is not only possible but very easy to work with multiple worksheets and workbooks in Excel.

Objective 1: Creating Multiple Worksheets

Each time you start a new workbook (file), it has sixteen worksheets. You can enter and store data in each of these sixteen worksheets and easily share data among sheets. It has become common practice to use several smaller sheets to hold related data rather than storing the data in one large worksheet. There are several reasons for this. Smaller sheets are easier to work with. You can see most, if not all, of the data at a glance. Compartmentalizing your data into smaller worksheets also makes it possible to work with only the data you need at the moment.

Entering data in multiple sheets

sheet tabs   When you are ready to create a multisheet workbook, open a new workbook file. At the bottom of the Excel window, you will see *sheet tabs*, which you can use to move from sheet to sheet. To make a sheet active, click its tab and it will come to the front of the window to become the active worksheet.

Exercise 1: Creating a multisheet workbook

In this exercise, you will create three small worksheets in one workbook.

1. Boot your computer and start Excel, if necessary.

   A new, untitled worksheet appears on the screen. Notice that Sheet1 is the active sheet by default.

2. Enter the data shown in Figure 6-1. Be sure to use a formula to compute the totals in row 9.

	A	B	C	D
1	Keys			
2	Date	Cate	Markel	Schwinn
3	8/19/94	$ 2.75	$ 8.32	$ 12.15
4	9/1/94	$ 1.75	$ 1.75	$ 1.75
5	9/3/94	$ 0.75	$ 2.75	$ 1.75
6				
7				
8				
9	Totals	$ 5.25	$ 12.82	$ 15.65

Figure 6-1   **The Keys worksheet**

3. Click the Sheet2 tab at the bottom of the Excel window.

   A new, blank worksheet appears.

4. Enter the data shown in Figure 6-2, again using a formula to compute the totals in row 8.

E12	↓		
A	**B**	**C**	**D**
1 Photocopies			
2			
3 Date	Cate	Markel	Schwinn
4 8/15/94	234.95	362.89	12.72
5 8/25/94	200.03	581.83	14.95
6 9/1/95	186.72	32.54	193.92
7			
8 Totals	621.7	977.26	221.59

Figure 6-2 The Copies worksheet

[handwritten margin notes:] Keys | Photocopic Bals. | printer keys: highlight Edict Copy Balance Book Hight edit past Special

5. Click the Sheet3 tab at the bottom of the Excel window to make the third worksheet in the workbook active.

6. Enter the data shown in Figure 6-3.

F12	↓			
A	**B**	**C**	**D**	**E**
1 O'Malley Accounts				
2	Opening Balance	Keys	Photocopies	Current Bal
3 Cate	$ 5,000.00			
4 Markel	$ 5,000.00			
5 Schwinn	$ 2,000.00			

Figure 6-3 The Balance worksheet

7. Save the file as accounts.xls.

Note that all three worksheets are saved under the one workbook name.

Assigning names to worksheets

After you have data entered into multiple worksheets, it is generally a good idea to name each worksheet so that you can easily differentiate one worksheet from another. When you rename a worksheet, the new name replaces the generic sheet number at the bottom of the screen. You can rename a sheet by double-clicking the sheet tab and typing the new name in the dialog box, or you can use the Sheet Rename command located under the Format menu.

Exercise 2: Renaming worksheets

In this exercise, you will name the three worksheets created in Exercise 1.

1. Click the Sheet1 tab to make it the active worksheet.

2. Double-click the sheet tab.

   A dialog box like the one shown in Figure 6-4 appears.

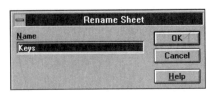

```
┌─────────────────────────────────────┐
│ ─        Rename Sheet                │
│ Name                    ┌────────┐   │
│ ┌─────────────────────┐ │   OK   │   │
│ │Keys                 │ └────────┘   │
│ └─────────────────────┘ ┌────────┐   │
│                         │ Cancel │   │
│                         └────────┘   │
│                         ┌────────┐   │
│                         │  Help  │   │
│                         └────────┘   │
└─────────────────────────────────────┘
```

Figure 6-4   The Rename Sheet dialog box

3. In the Name field, type Keys and click OK.

   The sheet tab at the bottom of the window now has the word *Keys* in it.

4. Double-click the Sheet2 tab, and rename this worksheet Copies.

5. Double-click the Sheet3 tab, and rename the worksheet Balance.

6. Save the file and leave it on the screen for further work.

TIP Another way to rename a sheet tab is to click the sheet tab name with the right mouse button to access the shortcut menu. Choose Rename from the shortcut menu, and rename the sheet tab.

Objective 2: Navigating Sheets

As you have probably already discovered, navigating between worksheets is a fairly straightforward task. If you have your sheets named, it is easy to click the tab of the desired sheet at the bottom of the window. If you don't have your sheets named, however, you will need to browse through all sheets that contain data. To do this, use the First, Previous, Next, and Last buttons to the left of the sheet tabs, as shown in Figure 6-5. When you click the First or Last button, you are taken automatically to Sheet1 or Sheet16, respectively. When you click the Next button, you are taken to the next sheet in sequence; the Previous button takes you to the previous sheet in the sequence.

TIP Drag the bar to the left of the horizontal scroll bar to view more or fewer sheet tabs. Double-click this bar to return to the default setting.

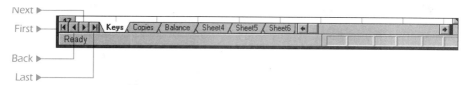

Figure 6-5 The sheet navigation buttons

Exercise 3: Moving among worksheets

In this exercise, you will practice using the sheet buttons to move among worksheets in the workbook.

1. Click the First button ⏮ to make the Keys worksheet active.

2. Click the Last button ⏭.

   There is no data in worksheet 16.

3. Click the First button again ⏮ and then click the Next button ▶ once.

   The Copies sheet should be the active worksheet.

4. Click the Next button ▶ again.

The Balance sheet is now the active worksheet.

5. Click the Previous button ◀ once.

You are now back at the Copies worksheet.

Objective 3: Deleting, Copying, Moving and Hiding Sheets

Once you begin to work with multiple worksheets in a workbook, you may find that you need to manipulate not only the data in the sheets, but the sheets themselves. Excel enables you to delete unnecessary sheets, to make a copy of a sheet, and to change the order of the worksheets by moving one or more sheets.

Deleting worksheets

Although Excel is rather generous in its automatic assignment of sixteen worksheets to each workbook, it is a good idea to delete any unused sheets so that the size of your file is not unnecessarily large. You can delete sheets one at a time, or you can select a group of sheets to be deleted all at once. In either case, you can use the Delete Sheet command located under the Edit menu.

TIP   If you rarely need all sixteen worksheets, change the default sheet number to a lower number by opening the Tools menu, choosing Options, accessing the General sheet, and changing the number of sheets in the workbook.

Exercise 4: Deleting unnecessary sheets

In this exercise, you will delete Sheet4 through Sheet16 of the Accounts workbook so that the file size is not too large.

1. Using the sheet buttons, make Sheet4 the active sheet.
2. From the Edit menu, choose Delete Sheet.

    Excel displays a warning message asking if you really want to delete the selected sheet or sheets.

3. Click OK.

    Sheet4 is deleted, and Sheet5 now follows the Balance worksheet.

4. Make Sheet5 the active sheet.
5. Hold down (SHIFT), and click the tabs for Sheet6 through Sheet16, using the sheet buttons if necessary.
6. Issue the command to delete the selected sheets.
7. You should now have only three worksheets in the workbook.
8. Save the file as account1.xls.

TIP   You can also delete a sheet by using the shortcut menu. Move the mouse pointer to the sheet tab, click the right mouse button to access the shortcut menu, and select Delete. The same warning message appears as does when you delete a sheet the long way.

Copying worksheets

If you have several worksheets with similar structures or data, you may want to copy the first sheet to several others, saving time and effort in typing data. In addition to copying sheets to the same workbook, you can also copy one or more sheets to a different workbook file.

To copy a worksheet, make the sheet you want to copy the active sheet. From the Edit menu or sheet tab shortcut menu, choose Move or Copy Sheet. A dialog box like the one shown in Figure 6-6 will appear. Excel will ask where you want the sheet to be located and whether a copy of the sheet should be made. Provide the appropriate information, and Excel will create a new sheet in the workbook if it does not already have sixteen sheets.

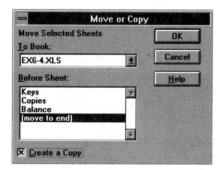

Figure 6-6   **The Move or Copy dialog box**

Exercise 5: Creating a new sheet by copying

In this exercise, you will create a new sheet in the workbook by copying the Balance worksheet to a new location.

1. Make the Balance worksheet the active sheet.

2. Move the mouse pointer to the sheet tab label, click the right mouse button to access the shortcut menu, and choose Move or Copy.

   The dialog box shown in Figure 6-6 appears.

3. Select (Move to End), and click in the Create a Copy check box.

4. Click OK to close the dialog box.

   The copied sheet, named Balance(2), becomes the active sheet. (If you needed a blank sheet, you could clear the contents of the entire worksheet and rename the sheet or open the Insert menu and choose Worksheet.)

5. Rename the new sheet Extra.

6. Save the file as account2.xls.

Making backups

The more you learn to do in Excel, the more time and effort you have invested in the files you have created and, just as importantly, the more you trust the program to manage your important documents. Because of these factors, you need to remember to make back up copies of your files for safekeeping. If you are saving your files on a hard drive, you should keep backup copies on data disks. If you are saving your files on a data disk, make a diskcopy of the floppy onto another floppy. Hard drive and floppy drive failures do happen, and they always happen when you least expect them and can least afford them. The more you use the computer, the more you may be tempted to trust it and not make backups, but Murphy's Law of Computing states that this is exactly the time your disk will fail!

Moving sheets

In addition to deleting and copying sheets, you can also change the order in which the sheets appear by moving a sheet. The process of moving a sheet is identical to that of copying except that you don't click the Create a Copy check box in the Move or Copy dialog box. A shortcut method for moving a sheet is to drag the sheet tab from its original location to its new location in the tab order.

Exercise 6: Moving a sheet to a new workbook

In this exercise, you will move the Extra worksheet to a new workbook.

1. Make the Extra sheet the active worksheet.
2. From the Edit menu, choose Move or Copy Sheet.
3. In the dialog box, pull down the To Book list box and select (New Book).
4. Click OK.

   Excel opens a new book and places the contents of the Extra worksheet in the new workbook in the Sheet1 position.

5. Save the new workbook as extra.xls and close it.
6. Save the account2.xls file as account3.xls.

Hiding and unhiding sheets

Although it is nice to have the name of the sheet displayed in the sheet tabs at the bottom of the window, it is sometimes desirable to keep one or more sheets hidden from view. This is especially true if you are showing a sheet to people and don't want them to see the names of the other sheets saved in the workbook. If you are showing employees their current tax withholding levels in one worksheet and they see a sheet tab named Salaries, for example, the employees may be tempted to look at the salaries of their fellow employees.

When you want to hide a worksheet from view, use the Sheet Hide command under the Format menu. This will remove the sheet's name from the sheet tabs at the bottom of the window. To restore the sheet's name and continue working with the sheet, use the Sheet Unhide command and then select the sheet you want to unhide.

Exercise 7: Hiding and unhiding the Balance worksheet

In this exercise, you will practice hiding and unhiding the Balance worksheet in the Account workbook.

1. Make the Balance sheet the active sheet in the workbook.
2. From the Format menu, choose Sheet Hide.

   The sheet's name is removed from the sheet tabs at the bottom of the window, and there is no way to get to the sheet.

3. From the Format menu, choose Sheet Unhide.

4. From the dialog box, select the Balance sheet and click OK.

    The Balance sheet once again appears in the sheet tabs, and you can now move to that sheet and work with it.

Objective 4: Copying and Moving Data among Sheets

target sheet

As was noted earlier, you will occasionally need to copy or move data among worksheets in a single workbook. As you know from earlier chapters, copying and moving data saves time and reduces the risk of error.

Copying data among worksheets

When you copy text among worksheets, there are no special considerations to be made. You select the cell or cells you want to copy, issue the Copy command, move to the *target sheet*, and paste the cells. When you copy values that are generated by formulas, however, you must use the Paste Special command so that only the values get pasted, not the underlying formulas. Figure 6-7 shows the Paste Special dialog box.

Figure 6-7   **The Paste Special dialog box**

Table 6-1 describes the options in the Paste Special dialog box.

Table 6-1   **Paste Special dialog box options**

OPTION NAME	DESCRIPTION
All	pastes the entire contents of the cell
Formulas	pastes only the formulas in the cell
Values	pastes only the values generated by the original formula in the target cell, not the formulas themselves
Formats	pastes only the cell formats, not contents, into the target cell
Notes	pastes only the attached notes to the cell, not contents
None	completely replaces the contents of the target cell with the copied cells
Add	adds the values and formulas of the copied cells to the target cells
Subtract	subtracts the values and formulas of the copied cells from the target cells
Multiply	multiplies the values and formulas of the copied cells by the target cells

continued

Table 6-1   Continued

OPTION NAME	DESCRIPTION
Divide	divides the contents of the target cell by the values and formulas of the copied cells
Skip Blanks	causes Excel not to copy blank cells
Transpose	shifts a row of data into a column or a column of data into a single row

Exercise 8: Copying account data from one worksheet to another

In this exercise, you will copy the Keys and Copies totals from their respective worksheets to the Balance worksheet.

1. Make the Keys worksheet the active sheet.
2. Select the range B9:D9.
3. Press ⌈CTRL⌉+⌈C⌉, or from the Edit menu, choose Copy.
4. Click the Balance sheet tab, and make cell C3 the active cell.
5. From the Edit menu, choose Paste Special.

    The Paste Special dialog box, shown in Figure 6-7, appears.

6. In the Paste column, click beside the Values option.
7. At the bottom of the box, click beside the Transpose option.
8. Click OK.

    The values from the Keys worksheet are transposed into a column and copied into column C of the Balance worksheet.

9. Make the Copies worksheet the active sheet.
10. Select cells B8:D8 and copy them.
11. Make cell D3 of the Balance worksheet the active cell.
12. Use the Paste Special command to transpose the copied cells and paste only the values into column D.
13. Write a formula in column E to compute the account balance of each person listed, subtracting key and photocopy charges from their beginning balances.
14. Save the file as account4.xls.

Moving data from one sheet to another

Occasionally, you will want to reorganize your worksheets so that they better meet your needs. When this happens, you may want to move some or all the data from one sheet to another. This is especially true when you are dividing a large worksheet into several smaller worksheets.

When you move data from one worksheet to another, you must be careful that any values generated by formulas remain constant during the move.

Any time data is moved, always take a minute to examine the moved data to make sure that it is correct.

source sheet To move data from one sheet to another, select the range of cells to be moved, cut the text from the original or *source sheet*, and then use the Paste or Paste Special command to paste the data into the target sheet. The data will be deleted from the original worksheet and pasted into the target sheet.

Exercise 9: Moving account data

In this exercise, you will create a copy of the Balance worksheet and move some data from the original Balance worksheet to the Balance(2) worksheet.

1. Make the Balance worksheet the active sheet.
2. Move the mouse pointer to the sheet tab, open the shortcut menu, and choose Move or Copy.
3. Make the appropriate selections to create a copy of the sheet, and place the copy at the end.
4. Select the entire contents of the Balance(2) sheet (the one you just created).
5. From the Edit menu, choose Clear All.

   The entire contents of the Balance(2) sheet are deleted.
6. In the Balance sheet, select the range A5:E5.
7. Click the Cut button ✂ in the toolbar, or from the Edit menu, choose Cut.
8. Make the Balance(2) sheet the active sheet, and make cell A5 the active cell.
9. Click the Paste button 📋, or from the Edit menu, choose Paste.

   The row of data is pasted into the Balance(2) worksheet.
10. Now move the data in Balance(2) to its original location in the Balance sheet, using the steps described in this exercise,.
11. Save the file as account5.xls.

Objective 5: Creating Formulas Using Multiple Sheets

So far you have worked with formulas and functions that complete operations on the data within one worksheet. You can, however, write formulas and functions that will use data from multiple sheets (and even multiple workbooks).

Think about the Account worksheet that you have been building in the exercises of this chapter. Currently, the data from the Keys and Copies worksheets has been copied into the Balance worksheet. While this does enable you to compute the balance on each of the three accounts, it is a

static operation *static operation*, meaning that when the data is copied into the worksheet, it will not be automatically updated if the data from the original worksheet is updated; you will have to copy the Keys and Copies totals each time you want to get an account balance.

A much more efficient method for getting the Keys and Copies charges is to use a function to locate the totals in the two worksheets and place those totals in the Balance worksheet. When you want to use cell references from a different sheet in a formula, type the name of the sheet, followed by an exclamation point and then the cell references, for example, =SUM(KEYS!B3:B5).

Exercise 10: Using HLOOKUP to update the Balance sheet

In this exercise, you will use the HLOOKUP function to get totals from the Keys and Copies worksheets and place those totals in the Balance worksheet. Before you begin writing the formula, you should make a printout of the Keys and Copies worksheets to make writing the formula easier.

1. Make the Keys worksheet the active sheet, and print a copy of the sheet by clicking the Print button on the Standard toolbar or by opening the File menu and choosing Print

2. Make the Copies worksheet the active sheet, and print a copy of the sheet.

3. In the Balance sheet, clear the contents of the range C3:D5.

4. Make cell C3 the active cell, and click the Function Wizard button f_{x}.

5. In the Function Wizard, select Lookup & Reference from the category column and HLOOKUP from the function name column, and then click Next to move to Step 2.

6. Try to determine what information goes into each component of the function. If you need help, look at Figure 6-8.

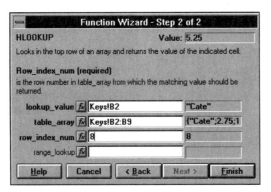

Figure 6-8 *The entry Keys! tells Excel to look in the Keys worksheet for the data in the function*

7. When you have finished filling in Step 2 of the Function Wizard, click Finish. Excel should print the value 5.25 in cell C3 of the Balance worksheet. Check the value in cell B9 of the Keys worksheet. It should be the same value.

8. Using the formula in cell C3 as an example, write formulas for cells C4, C5, D3, D4, and D5, using the HLOOKUP function and the appropriate worksheet.

   Notice that the formulas in row E automatically update each time a new value is placed in columns C and D.

9. Save the file as account6.xls.

Objective 6: Using Multiple Workbooks

While it is most common to use multiple sheets within the same workbook to manage related data, it is possible and useful to use data in multiple workbooks. You may want to keep all payroll-related worksheets in one workbook, all employee benefits worksheets in another workbook, and a general accounting ledger with information from both the payroll and benefits workbooks in a separate workbook. Keeping this data in separate workbooks not only helps make the data more manageable by keeping it in smaller chunks, but it also provides an added means of security. Because the information is in separate workbooks, the workbooks can be protected separately, with only authorized personnel having access to the data in each workbook.

Creating a new file

You create a new workbook file, as you know, by opening the File menu and choosing New. A new workbook is created, with the default of sixteen empty worksheets. Enter the data into this workbook as you would any other workbook.

Exercise 11: Creating a general ledger workbook

In this exercise, you will create a workbook that will store summary information from multiple accounts, including the O'Malley account with which you worked in the Balance worksheet of the Account workbook.

1. Click the New button 🗋 on the Standard toolbar, or from the File menu, choose New to start a new workbook.

   A new workbook appears on the screen, with 16 blank worksheets.

2. Enter the worksheet shown in Figure 6-9, complete with formatting.

3. Save the file as ledger.xls.

A12 ↓			
	A	**B**	**C**	**D**
1	General Faculty Expenditure Accounts			
2				
3		Cate	Markel	Schwinn
4	Computer Equipment	$4,350.17	$6,091.83	$14,987.63
5	O'Malley			
6	Supplies and Equipment	$ 176.32	$ 97.63	$ 13.85
7	WorkStudy	$3,412.98	$7,837.64	$ 6,121.89

Figure 6-9 **The Ledger workbook**

Navigating among workbooks

When you work with multiple workbooks, it is very important to pay attention to the title bar at the top of the Excel window so that you are working with the right workbook at all times. Because worksheets have so many similar characteristics, it is quite easy to make several changes in the wrong worksheet or workbook before realizing what you have done. Taking a few seconds to check the title bar can save you hours of reconstructing a worksheet.

When you work with multiple workbooks, you navigate among the open workbooks by using the Window menu. The bottom portion of this menu lists all open workbooks, as shown in Figure 6-10. To move to a different workbook, select the workbook you want to use from the list of open workbooks.

Figure 6-10 **The Window menu lists all open workbooks**

Exercise 12: Switching workbooks

In this exercise, you will use the Window menu to switch between open workbooks.

1. Open the Window menu, and select account6.xls.

   The Account6 workbook appears on the screen.

2. Open the Window menu again, and select ledger.xls.

   The Ledger workbook becomes the active workbook.

3. Leave both files open for further work.

FEATURE

Saving workspaces

When you work with multiple workbooks in Excel, you can save the screen positions, window sizes, and workbook file names in a special file called a workspace file. The workspace file does not store the actual workbooks but stores the settings information about each workbook. If you have several workbooks that you always use together, it is a good idea to save them in a workspace. When you open a workspace file, each workbook saved in the workspace is automatically opened, sized, and positioned on the screen, ready for work in the same configuration you last selected.

To save a group of workbooks in a workspace, first make certain that all necessary workbooks are open. Then from the File menu, choose Save Workspace. Excel will prompt you for a workspace file name. Note that the file extension for a workspace is .XLW. Enter the file name for the new workspace, and click OK to finish saving it. To open a workspace, open the File menu and choose Open. From the list of files shown, select the .XLW file that contains the workspace you want to open and click OK. All the workbooks in the workspace will be opened.

Objective 7: Creating Formulas Using Multiple Workbooks

Just as it is possible to use data from multiple sheets in a formula, it is also possible to use data from multiple workbooks in a formula. When you do this, you need to specify the workbook name, the sheet name, and the cell reference as part of the formula, for example, =SUM([Account6.xls]Keys!B3:B5). Note that the workbook name is placed between brackets ([ ]).

Exercise 13: Getting data from the Account6 worksheet

In this exercise, you will write a formula in the Ledger worksheet that uses data obtained from the Account6 worksheet.

1. Make the Balance worksheet of the Account6 workbook the active sheet.
2. Note the cell references for the O'Malley balances for each of the three faculty members (the range E3:E5).
3. Make the Ledger workbook the active book.
4. In cell B5, write a formula using the HLOOKUP function that will locate Cate's O'Malley balance in the Balance sheet of the Account6 workbook.
5. Write a similar formula for Markel in cell C5 of the Ledger worksheet and for Schwinn in cell D5 of the Ledger worksheet.

   The Ledger worksheet should now be complete.
6. Make the Balance sheet of the Account6 workbook the active sheet.

7. Lower the Opening Balance for Cate from 5000 to 3000, and note the change in the balance.

8. Switch back to the Ledger workbook, and examine Cate's O'Malley balance.

remote sheet

Because the workbooks are linked through the HLOOKUP formula, the data in the *remote sheet*, the Ledger workbook, is automatically updated whenever the cells involved in the formula are updated in the source sheet, the Balance sheet of the Account6 worksheet.

9. Save the Ledger workbook as ledger1.xls, and close it.

10. Save the Account6 workbook and close it.

11. Exit Excel or continue with the problems at the end of the chapter.

Chapter Summary

This chapter focused on data management using multiple worksheets and workbooks. You have seen how related data can be stored in separate worksheets and workbooks within Excel and how data from separate sheets and books can be used in formulas and functions.

Review Questions

True/False Questions

_____ 1. A worksheet and a workbook are the same thing.

_____ 2. To insert a new sheet into a workbook, use the Insert, Sheet command.

_____ 3. When a sheet is hidden, you cannot see the sheet name or the sheet's contents.

_____ 4. To reference a different sheet in a formula, type the sheet name, followed by an exclamation point and then the cell reference.

_____ 5. You cannot use data from different worksheets in a formula.

Multiple Choice Questions

_____ 6. When copying cells with formulas from one sheet to another, you should paste

A. the entire contents of the cell into the new location.

B. only the format of the cell into the new location.

C. only the values of the cell into the new location.

D. only the notes of the cell into the new location.

_____ 7. To delete multiple sheets at one time, hold down which key while selecting the sheet tabs?

A. Ctrl

B. Shift

C. Alt

D. F9

_____ 8. Which of the following formulas accurately references cells in a different worksheet?

A. =AVERAGE([Cars]!Prices)

B. =AVERAGE(Cars!Prices)

C. =AVERAGE(Cars:Prices)

D. =AVERAGE!Cars(Prices)

_____ 9. Which of the following formulas accurately references cells in a different workbook?

A. =MIN!Trucks(Fords!E3:E7)

B. =MIN([Trucks]Fords!E3:E7)

C. =MIN(Trucks[Fords]!E3:E7)

D. =MIN((Trucks)Fords!E3:E7)

_____ 10. To switch from one open workbook to another, select a file name from which listing?

A. Files, Open

B. View, Worksheets

C. Edit, Worksheets

D. the Window menu

Fill-in-the-Blank Questions

11. The default number of worksheets opened with a new workbook is _____.

12. To quickly return to Sheet1, click the _____ button.

13. To copy a column of cells into a row of cells, use the _____ option in the Paste Special command.

14. To insert a worksheet into a workbook, you must _____.

15. Two advantages of keeping data in multiple workbooks are _____ and _____.

Acumen-Building Activities

Quick Projects

1. Adding to the savings plan

Now that you know what it will take to reach your savings goal of $7,500, you want to see if it is possible to save even more—$10,000, if you stretch out the time span to the full four years.

1. Open the svplan.xls workbook you created in the last chapter.
2. Copy all the data, including formulas, from Sheet1 to Sheet2. Be sure to put the data in the same cell range in Sheet2 as it is in Sheet1.
3. Edit the Sheet2 worksheet so that your goal is $10,000 instead of $7,500.
4. Check your formulas and edit them, if necessary.
5. Name Sheet2 $10,000 and Sheet1 $7,500.
6. Save the file as svplan2.xls.

2. Planning for your new car

In the last chapter, you created a worksheet that determined the amount of money you would have saved at the end of three years. Now that you know how much money you'll have to work with, you've decided to compare the purchasing of three cars you like.

1. Open the car.xls file you created in the last chapter.
2. Name Sheet1 Financial.
3. In Sheet2, type the names of three cars you like and their current prices. Be sure to provide appropriate column headings for each column you create.
4. In a new column, write a formula that will compute the future cost of the car based on 6 percent inflation over the three-year period. Copy the formula for each of the three cars.
5. In the next column, write a formula that will determine the amount of money you'll still need in order to buy each car after you have used your car savings. Be sure to reference the correct cell in the Financial worksheet to get this value.
6. Name Sheet2 Autos and save the file as car2.xls.

3. Tracking grades in multiple classes

Because tracking your grades for one class helped you determine which study strategies worked and which ones didn't, you've decided to track the grades in another class, with hopefully the same result.

1. Open the grades.xls worksheet you created in the last chapter.
2. Assign Sheet1 the name or number of the course you are tracking.
3. In Sheet2, create another worksheet to track your grades in a second course. Be sure to include appropriate column headings, formatting, and the summary statistics (average, min, and max).
4. Assign Sheet2 the name or number of the course you are tracking.
5. Save the file as grades2.xls.

4. Budgeting your trip

You have decided that if you really scrape, you can save $8 a day for spending money on your next trip. For this problem, you will create a worksheet and formula that will keep a running total of your savings.

1. Open the holiday.xls file you created in the last chapter.
2. Name Sheet1 Days.
3. In Sheet2, type the value -8 in cell A3. The negative value indicates that this is outgoing money (a debit from your personal spending money).
4. In cell B3, enter a formula that will find the number of days remaining until your trip from the Days worksheet and multiply that by the value in cell A3, to determine the amount of money you can save between now and the trip date. Be sure to reference the information in the Days worksheet correctly in the formula.
5. Name Sheet2 Potential Savings, and save the file as holiday2.xls.

In-Depth Projects

1. Tracking players

For this problem, you will build on the Teamrec worksheet you created in the last chapter so that you can track individual players on your team.

1. Open the teamrec.xls workbook, and name Sheet1 Games.
2. In Sheet2, create a worksheet to track the individual performance of at least three players during the four games you recorded in the Games worksheet. If you want to, track each player's performance on more than one variable (for example, scores, rebounds, and assists).
3. Write a formula that will total each variable you are tracking for each game (for example, total number of assists by all three players for game 1).
4. Name Sheet2 Players.

5. In the Games worksheet, create a new column called Player Totals. Write a formula in this column that uses the HLOOKUP or VLOOKUP function to calculate the total scores for each game from the Players worksheet.

6. Copy this formula with appropriate changes to the remaining three games.

7. Save the file as teamrec2.xls.

2. Updating the shelter system

Assume that the animal shelter employees have been working with your worksheet for a week or so and have some suggestions for changes. They think each animal should be assigned a case number so that the animal is easier to track in the system. They also think that a related file should be created containing the names of owners or adopters and a reason why their pet ended up at the shelter.

1. Open the shelter.xls worksheet you created in the last chapter.

2. Insert a new column in front of column A, and type the column heading Case #.

3. Use a unique case number (for example, 1, 2, 3, 4, 5) for each animal in the shelter.

4. Name Sheet1 Check-in-out.

5. In Sheet2, create a worksheet that will store Case #, Date In, Date Out, Owner, and Reason, and name Sheet2 Owner Info.

6. In the Check-in/out sheet, copy the Case #, Date In, and Date Out information to the Owner Info sheet for each animal that has been checked out.

7. Save the file as shelter2.xls.

CASE STUDIES

 **Coffee-On-The-Go:** **Using Multiple Worksheets to Create Income Projections**

In this chapter, you learned to create multiple worksheets. You can use this capability to analyze data for Coffee-On-The-Go.

1. Open the Income spreadsheet.

2. Copy the Income spreadsheet to sheets 2 and 3.

3. Edit the title in Sheet2 so that the year is 1996 and the title in Sheet3, 1997.

4. Rename Sheet1 1995; Sheet2, 1996; and Sheet3, 1997.

5. Save the file as income3.

6. Print all the sheets.

CASE STUDIES

Videos West:

Using Multiple Worksheets

In this chapter, you learned to create multiple worksheets. You can use this capability to analyze data for Videos West.

1. Open the Revenue4 spreadsheet.

2. Copy Sheet1 to sheets 2, 3, and 4.

3. Edit each sheet so that the second one represents Quarter Two: April, May, and June; the third one represents Quarter Three: July, August, September; and the fourth one represents Quarter Four: October, November, and December. Name Sheet1 1st Quarter; Sheet1 (2), 2nd Quarter; Sheet1 (3), 3rd Quarter; and Sheet1 (4), 4th Quarter.

4. Increase the Total Expenses for each month—in the 2nd Quarter sheet by 3%, in the 3rd Quarter sheet by 4%, and in the 4th Quarter sheet by 5%.

5. Insert a new sheet in front of the four existing sheets, and name the new sheet Summary.

6. In the Summary sheet, create formulas which total the Net Sales, Gross Profit, Operating Expenses, and Net Income/Loss for the four quarters.

7. Format as necessary.

8. Save the file as revenue5.

9. Print the four quarters and the totals sheets.

Chapter 7

Printing Reports

Key Terms

TERM	DEFINITION
Preview	the process of viewing a document before it is printed. The preview shows the document exactly as it will appear when printed.
Zoom In	the process of magnifying a portion of miniaturized text
Zoom Out	the process of leaving a magnified view of text and returning to the miniaturized view
Page Break	the point in a document at which a new page begins
Portrait Orientation	the default print direction which prints across the short (8.5 inches) edge of a page
Landscape Orientation	the alternative print direction which prints across the long (11 inches) edge of a page
Scaling	the process of reducing or enlarging a document to make it fit within a certain area on a page
Dots Per Inch (DPI)	the measurement used to judge print quality. The higher number of dots per inch, the higher the print quality.
Margins	the white space surrounding a document
Header	text that is printed at the top of each page
Footer	text that is printed at the bottom of each page

TERM	DEFINITION
Dialog Buttons	buttons in a dialog box which return specific results, such as a page number or current date
Print Area	the range of cells in a worksheet to be printed
Print Titles	column and row headings that are printed at the top of each page

When spreadsheet programs first came on the market in the late 1970s, they had what would be considered very limited functionality by today's standards. One of the features they did provide, however, was the capability of printing. Over the years, printing options have become more and more refined in spreadsheet programs, and now you can create professional reports with the spreadsheet program itself.

preview   In Excel, you can print reports that are simple or quite complex. Excel has a series of tab sheets for setting print options such as the print direction, placement of the worksheet on the page, text at the top and bottom of the page, and the components of the worksheet that should be printed. You can obtain a *preview* of the worksheet at any time to see how the actual printed output will really look.

Objective 1: Printing Simple Reports

page breaks   Although you have already printed several worksheets, two options can be used to make the printing process go more smoothly: obtaining a Print Preview and inserting *page breaks*.

Viewing a Print Preview

When you have a file to print, it is a good idea to use the Print Preview command found on the Standard toolbar or under the File menu to examine your worksheet before you actually send it to the printer. When you issue this command, Excel displays your worksheet in miniaturized format, as shown in Figure 7-1. The format is designed to enable you to see structural flaws such as data that runs across cells or cells that run across page breaks. You can use the Zoom button to get a closer, more readable view of your data. Clicking the Zoom button a second time returns the view to the miniaturized format.

Figure 7-1   **A Print Preview of the Balance worksheet**

Exercise 1: Obtaining a Print Preview

In this exercise, you will preview the Balance worksheet in the Account6 workbook.

1. Boot your computer, and start Excel, if necessary.
2. Open the workbook file account6.xls, and make the Balance worksheet the active sheet.
3. Select the range A1:E5.
4. Click the Preview button on the Standard toolbar, or from the File menu, choose Print Preview.

   Excel displays the preview version of the Balance worksheet so that you can see the entire page. Notice that Excel automatically places the worksheet name at the top of the page and a page number at the bottom of the page.

zoom in 5. Click the Zoom button at the top of the window to *zoom in* on the data.

   Excel increases the size of the view so that you can read the data.

zoom out 6. Click the Zoom button again to *zoom out* of the data, returning to the original preview format.

7. Click Close to close Print Preview.

> **TIP** If you are working with a multiple-page worksheet, you can preview multiple pages using the Next and Previous buttons in Print Preview mode.

Printing multipage reports with page breaks

Even simple reports sometimes require more than one page when printed. When this is the case, you may need to exert some control over where the page breaks occur so that the flow of your worksheet is clear. To insert a page break, make the row which should begin on the new page the active row. From the Insert menu, choose Page Break. A dotted line will be inserted on the screen to represent the page break (the dotted line doesn't get printed). To remove the page break, open the Insert menu and choose Remove Page Break.

Exercise 2: Inserting page breaks

In this exercise, you will copy data from the Keys and Copies worksheets into the Balance(2) worksheet to make it longer than one page. You will then insert a page break in a logical location.

1. Make the Keys worksheet the active sheet.
2. Select the range A1:D9, and issue the Copy command.
3. Make the Balance(2) worksheet the active sheet and cell A1 the active cell.
4. Use the Paste command to paste the copied data into the Balance(2) worksheet.

5. In the Balance(2) worksheet, select the range A1:D9.

6. Using the fill handle in the lower right corner of the range border, fill the worksheet through cell D100.

   The data from the Keys worksheet is repeated approximately 11 times within the one-hundred row range.

7. Click the Preview button 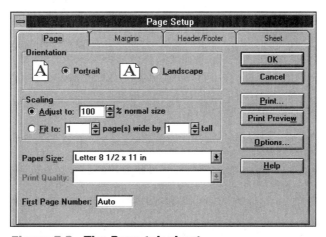 to view the worksheet.

8. Close Print Preview and return to the Balance(2) worksheet.

9. Scroll down to row 51 of the worksheet.

   The dotted line indicates where the page break occurs.

10. With cell A46 the active cell, open the Insert menu and choose Page Break.

    The dotted page break line is moved up a few lines so that the sixth iteration of the Keys worksheet is not split between two pages.

11. Choose Print Preview again to make sure the page break is in the right location this time.

12. Close the Print Preview window, and keep the worksheet on the screen for further use.

Objective 2: Defining Page Setup Options

Excel's default Page Setup options work well in most situations, but there may be times when you will want to use different settings so that your printed report fits nicely on the page. The Page tab sheet, shown in Figure 7-2, enables you to define the direction the worksheet should be printed on the page, the size of the worksheet, the size of the paper, and the page number settings.

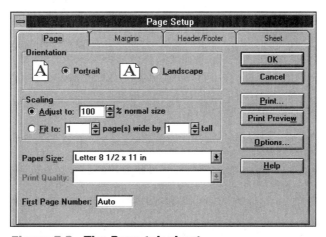

Figure 7-2 **The Page tab sheet**

Setting the orientation

portrait orientation; landscape orientation

The printing term orientation refers to the direction in which a document is printed on paper. *Portrait orientation* is the default setting in which the document prints parallel to the short edge (8.5 inches) of the paper. In *landscape orientation,* the document prints parallel to the long edge (11 inches) of the paper. Landscape orientation is often used when printing worksheets because sheets tend to be wider rather than longer.

Exercise 3: Changing the page orientation

In this exercise, you will practice changing the page orientation and previewing the changed worksheet.

1. With the Account6 workbook on the screen, make the Balance worksheet the active sheet.
2. Select the range A1:E5, open the File menu, and then choose Page Setup.

   The Page Setup dialog box appears, as shown in Figure 7-2.
3. Click the Page tab to access the page settings.
4. Click the Landscape option, and then click Print Preview to see the changed print orientation.

   The Print Preview of the Balance worksheet appears. Notice that the width available is about twice the width required by the worksheet; your worksheet will probably look better and be more effective if you print it in portrait orientation rather than landscape.
5. Click the Setup button to return to the Page Setup dialog box.
6. Click the Portrait option to return the orientation of the page to portrait.

Scaling the worksheet to the page

scaling

Another way to fit your worksheet on the page is to reduce or enlarge its size when it is printed. This is generally referred to as *scaling* the worksheet to the page. When you scale a worksheet down, all components of the worksheet get smaller: the text, the worksheet grid—everything. Conversely,

FEATURE

Saving print styles as views

An additional print feature not presented in this chapter is the View feature. You can save print settings, areas, and titles to a specific view, with multiple views per workbook. Saving the settings to a view ensures that you get the same printout of your document each time. It also saves you the time of redoing all the print and page setup settings. To learn more about views, use Excel's on-line Help feature to search for the word *view.*

when you scale a worksheet up, all components become larger. You can manually adjust the scale of the printed worksheet by clicking the arrows beside the scale percentage in the Page tab sheet. You can also have Excel scale the worksheet automatically by setting the number of pages you want your worksheet to fill. This saves you the trial-and-error estimating and manually reducing the worksheet. As always, you should use the Print Preview option to make sure your changes achieve the desired result.

Exercise 4: Changing the worksheet scale

In this exercise, you will change the scale of the Balance worksheet. This exercise assumes that the Page tab sheet is still showing on the screen.

1. In the Page tab sheet, click the down arrow in the Scaling portion of the sheet until the scale is 75%.
2. Click Print Preview to view the results of the changed scale.
3. Click the Close button to return to the worksheet.
4. Make the Balance(2) worksheet the active sheet.
5. From the File menu, choose Page Setup, and access the Page tab sheet.
6. In the scaling portion of the sheet, click beside the Fit to option.

   Excel automatically fits the data into the specified number of page widths and lengths.
7. Click Print Preview.

   Excel displays a Reducing rate in the lower left corner of the window. How much does Excel have to reduce the two-page worksheet to make it fit on one page?
8. Click Setup to return to the Page tab sheet.

Setting the paper size

dots per inch (DPI)

Most laser printers and even some dot-matrix printers enable you to print on paper size other than the standard 8 ½-by-11 inches. Excel enables you to select different paper sizes in the Page tab sheet if your printer supports sizes other than the standard. Depending on which printer you have installed, you may also be able to change the print quality. Print quality is measured in *dots per inch* or *dpi*. The higher the number, the higher the quality of print. For example, most low-cost laser printers print at 300 dpi. More expensive laser printers print at 600 dpi. Most typesetting printers print at 12000 dpi.

The final element of the Page tab sheet is the First Page Number setting. The default setting is Auto, which automatically numbers the first page printed 1; the second page, 2; and so on. If your worksheet is just one page of a larger report, you can manually set the page number by selecting the field and replacing the Auto setting with a number.

Exercise 5: Changing paper size, print quality, and page numbering

In this exercise, you will change the paper size, the print quality setting, and the page number to be printed as the first page.

1. Pull down the Paper Size list box, and examine the options you have.

   The number of paper size options is dependent on the type of printer you have. You may have several options, or you may have none.

2. If the list box is available, select the Legal (8½" x 14") paper size.

3. Select Auto in the First Page Number field, and type the number 2.

4. Click OK or Print Preview to view the effect of these changes.

   How much reduction does Excel have to make this time to fit all the data in the Balance(2) worksheet onto a single page of legal-size paper?

5. Zoom in on the preview, scroll to the bottom of the document, and make sure that the page number is 2.

6. Click the Zoom button again to zoom out.

7. Click Setup to return to the Page tab sheet.

8. Restore the Page settings so that Excel scales the document to 100%, prints on 8½-by-11-inch paper, and automatically prints the first page number.

9. Click OK to close the Page Setup dialog box.

Objective 3: Setting Page Margins

margins;
headers;
footers

The Margins tab sheet of the Page Setup dialog box, shown in Figure 7-3, enables you to set *margins*, the location of *headers* and *footers*, and the position of the worksheet on the printed page.

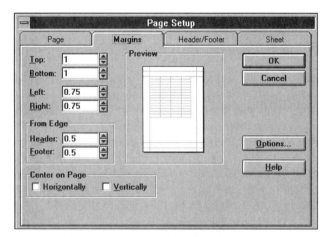

Figure 7-3   **The Margins tab sheet**

Setting margins

Margins are an important component of any printed document. Studies have shown that people need white space, or margins, in the documents they read in order to differentiate among the various components of the document. You have probably experienced having someone hand you a printed document and the entire page looks black because the text is dense and the margins are minuscule. Documents like this are difficult to read and cause eyestrain. Because worksheets have lots of little parts (cells), margins can give readers' eyes a break and can help them understand the contents of the worksheet more readily.

Although you can set the top, bottom, left, and right margins from as small a setting as zero, most printers, especially laser and ink jet printers, require at least a half-inch margin on all sides. The default margin settings in Excel are one inch on the top and bottom and three-quarters of an inch on the sides. To change any of these settings, click the dialog box up or down arrow beside the margin you want to change. You can also select the current margin setting and type in the desired setting. The Preview portion of the Margins tab sheet shows the effect of any margin changes.

Exercise 6: Changing the margins

In this exercise, you will change the margins in the Balance worksheet.

1. Make the Balance worksheet the active sheet.
2. From the File menu, choose Page Setup.
3. From the Page Setup dialog box, click the Margins tab.

   The Margins tab sheet, shown in Figure 7-3, appears.
4. Increase the left margin to 1 ½ inches by clicking the up arrow three times.
5. Increase the right margin to 1 ½ inches by clicking the up arrow three times.

   The effect of the margin changes can be seen in the Preview portion of the tab sheet.

Changing the location of headers and footers

Margin settings affect only the data in the worksheet proper—they do not affect information in headers and footers such as page numbers and worksheet titles. If you have header and footer information, you may want to set the headers away from the edge of the page but leave enough room so that they don't overlap the data in the worksheet. Thus, the header and footer setting should always be smaller than the margin setting. For example, a footer might be set at .5 inch while the bottom margin is set at 1 inch. This setting ensures that the footer will be printed within the margin space and not run into text from the document.

More paper, not less

When computers first became popular in the early-to-mid 1980s, one of the advantages claimed by those who used them and those who sold them is that computers would help us become a paperless society. In the years since those claims were made, several studies have been conducted which indicate that offices and homes with computers consume almost twice as much paper as they did before they had computers. Why? The hypothesis is that since it is possible to create "the perfect document," most of us try, try, and try again until our document is just the way we want it. So instead of printing just one version, we print two or three until we are happy with the document. You can do your part to spare the environment all this waste of paper by always doing a Print Preview of your document before you print. Closely examining your document before you put it on paper can save thousands of sheets of paper each year.

Exercise 7: Spacing headers and footers

In this exercise, you will increase the amount of space for headers and footers.

1. On the Margins tab sheet, increase the header's distance from the edge to 1 inch by clicking the up arrow twice.

2. Increase the footer's distance from the edge to 1 inch by clicking the up arrow twice.

3. Examine the changes in the Preview portion of the tab sheet.

Positioning the document on the page

Although you can change the margins to realign your document on the page, an easier way is to let Excel do it automatically. Excel can center the document horizontally on the page (so that the worksheet is centered between the left and right margins) or vertically on the page (so that the worksheet is centered between the top and bottom margins on the page) or both horizontally and vertically.

Exercise 8: Centering the worksheet on the page

In this exercise, you will center the worksheet on the page vertically and horizontally.

1. On the Margins tab sheet, click the Horizontally and Vertically check boxes.

2. Examine the result in the Preview portion of the tab sheet.

Objective 4: Creating and Editing Headers and Footers

Excel automatically prints the worksheet title in the header of a document and the page number in the footer of a document. While this may be enough information for some small worksheets, you should generally provide more information in the header or footer so that readers know exactly what information the worksheet is providing and when it was printed. There are few things more frustrating than trying to balance an account only to discover that you are working with an old copy of a worksheet.

The Header/Footer tab sheet is shown in Figure 7-4. Notice that the default title and page number are automatically entered. You can change this information by selecting one of the other built-in headers or footers from the pull-down list box or by creating a custom header or footer.

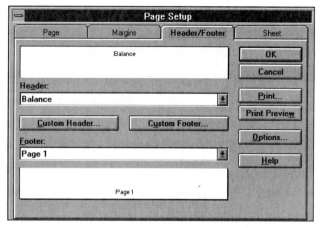

Figure 7-4 **The Header/Footer tab sheet**

Using a built-in header and footer

Excel uses the information in the software registration screen and the summary information attached to the workbook, as well as the workbook name and worksheet name, to offer several different built-in headers and footers. Figure 7-5 shows the available built-in headers on the author's computer. To replace the default header with one of the built-in headers, select the desired header from the list.

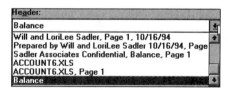

Figure 7-5 **Built-in headers available to the owner of the software**

Exercise 9: Changing the built-in header and footer

In this exercise, you will change the default header and footer to one of the other built-in headers and footers.

1. Click the Header/Footer tab to display the Header/Footer tab sheet shown in Figure 7-4.

2. Pull down the Header list box, and select an alternative header.

3. Pull down the Footer list box, and select an alternative footer.

4. Click Print Preview to see what the new headers look like.

5. Click Setup to return to the Header/Footer tab sheet.

Creating custom headers and footers

If none of the built-in headers or footers is appropriate, you can create your own custom header or footer. When you click one of the custom buttons, the Custom Header dialog box like the one shown in Figure 7-6 appears.

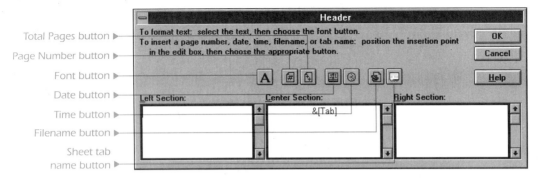

Total Pages button ▶
Page Number button ▶
Font button ▶
Date button ▶
Time button ▶
Filename button ▶
Sheet tab
name button ▶

Figure 7-6 **The Header dialog box**

Notice that the dialog box splits the width of the printed page into three sections: the left section, the center section, and the right section. Click in the section in which you want to add information to the header, and use the *dialog buttons* to change the font of the text or automatically enter the page number, number of total pages, date, time, name of the file, or name of the sheet. Click OK to apply the changes and close the dialog box.

dialog buttons

Exercise 10: Making a custom header and footer

In this exercise, you will create a custom header and footer for the Balance worksheet.

1. Click the Custom Header button in the Header/Footer tab sheet.
    A dialog box like the one shown in Figure 7-6 appears.
2. Click in the Left Section box to anchor the I-beam, and then click the Filename button 🖳
    A code for the file name, account6.xls, appears in the box.
3. Click in the Center Section box, and then click the Sheet name button 🖳
    A code for the sheet name appears in the center box.
4. Click in the Right Section box, and then click the Date button 🖳
    A code for the date appears in the right box.
5. Click OK to apply the changes and close the dialog box.
6. Click the Custom Footer button in the Header/Footer tab sheet.
    The Footer dialog box opens.
7. Click in the Left Section box, and type your full name.
8. Click in the Center Section box, and click the Time button 🕗.
9. Click in the Right Section box, and click the Page Number button 🖳.
10. Click OK to apply the changes and close the dialog box.

11. Click Print Preview to view your custom header and footer.

12. If the header and footer are satisfactory, click Print to print the worksheet. (If you need to change an element in the header or footer, return to the Page Setup dialog box and edit the header or footer by clicking the appropriate button, making the necessary changes, and then clicking OK.)

13. Click Close to return to the worksheet.

Objective 5: Defining Sheet Components to Print

The final set of page setup settings to be discussed are the sheet components. Sheet components, which are set from the Sheet tab sheet shown in Figure 7-7, include the range of cells to print, titles to appear at the top and left side of each worksheet page, additional printer settings, and the page order in which sheets are to be printed.

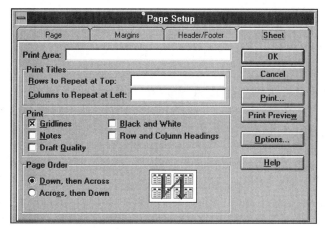

Figure 7-7   **The Sheet tab sheet**

Defining the print area and print titles

print area The *print area* is the portion of the worksheet that is to be printed. You can define the print area by entering cell coordinates for the range (for example, A1:D5) or by clicking in the Print Area field and then dragging the mouse pointer through the range of cells to print in the worksheet. (Note: This works only if you move the dialog box so that you can actually see the range of cells you want to select.)

print titles *Print titles* are column and row headings that print at the top and left side of each page subsequent to the page on which they are found. By using print titles, you can have multipage worksheets with the column and row headings automatically reprinted on each page. Enter the coordinates for a cell range or drag through the desired cell range in the worksheet to set row titles and column titles.

Exercise 11: Defining the print area and adding print titles

In this exercise, you will define the print area for the Balance worksheet and add print titles.

1. In the Balance worksheet, select cells A3:E5.
2. Using the fill handle, drag the cell range to E95.
3. From the File menu, choose Page Setup and click the Sheet tab to display it.

   The Sheet tab sheet, as shown in Figure 7-7, appears.
4. Click in the Print Area field, and type A1:E95.
5. Click in the Rows to Repeat at Top field, and type B2:E2.
6. Click in the Columns to Repeat at Left field, and type A3:A5.
7. Click Print Preview to see the effect of the changes you've just made.

   Excel displays the preview pages. Unfortunately, the header and footer runs into the data on the first page.
8. Click the Setup button to return to the Page Setup dialog box.
9. Click the Margins tab, and change the From Edge header and footer settings to .5.
10. Click OK to return to the Print Preview.

    The Print Preview recalculates the space on the page and then displays the corrected page layout. If you click on Next, you will see that the column and row titles are repeated on the second page.
11. Click Close and return to the worksheet.

Defining print components

In addition to telling Excel which parts of the worksheet it needs to print, you also have the option of telling Excel how to print the worksheet. Referring back to Figure 7-7, you can print the gridlines of the worksheet and any attached notes. You can print in draft quality (fewer graphics and no gridlines), black and white (as opposed to shades of gray or color if you have a color printer), and you can choose whether to print row and column headings. Each option is enabled only if the check box beside it contains an *X*.

Exercise 12: Viewing the worksheet without gridlines

In this exercise, you will deselect the Gridlines option and preview the worksheet without the separating lines.

1. Select the range A1:E5, open the File menu, and choose Page Setup.
2. Click the Sheet tab, and click the check box beside Gridlines to deselect the option.

3. Click Print Preview to see the worksheet without gridlines.

   Do you think the gridlines make the worksheet easier or more difficult to read?

4. Click Close to return to the worksheet.

Determining page order

This final Sheet option is the Page Order setting. This setting is applicable only if you have a worksheet that is more than one page wide *and* more than one page long. When you have a worksheet that is two pages wide and two pages long and you choose to print down and then across, Excel prints and numbers the two left halves of the worksheet first (page 1 and page 2) and then the two right halves (page 3 and page 4). When you choose to print across and then down, using the same worksheet example, Excel prints the upper left half as page one, the upper right half as page two, the lower left half as page three, and the lower right half as page four.

Exercise 13: Changing the page order

In this exercise, you will copy additional worksheet information to add width to the Balance worksheet. You will then use the Page Setup settings to change the page order of the worksheet for printing.

1. In the Balance worksheet, select the range A3:E95.

2. Click the Copy button in the Standard toolbar.

3. Make cell F3 the active cell, open the Edit menu, and choose Paste.

   The range is copied, doubling the width of the worksheet.

4. From the File menu, choose Page Setup and click the Sheet tab.

5. In the Print Area, change the setting to A1:J95.

6. In the Page Order section, click Across and then Down.

7. Click Print Preview to see the results of this change. Pay special attention to the page numbers.

8. Click Close to close the Print Preview.

9. From the File menu, choose Close.

   Excel asks if you want to save the changes made to the worksheet.

10. Click No so that none of the changes to the Account6 worksheet are saved.

11. Exit Excel at this time or continue with the problems at the end of the chapter.

Chapter Summary

In this chapter, you explored the various options available for page setup and printer setup. You learned to print specific portions of a worksheet, to add headers and footers to your document, to add print titles, and to print with or without gridlines. By using these settings, you can create informative and persuasive reports in Excel.

Review Questions

True/False Questions

_____ 1. You can edit data in cells when you are in Print Preview mode.

_____ 2. Excel automatically inserts page breaks, and you have no control over where they occur.

_____ 3. Orientation refers to the direction a document is printed on the page.

_____ 4. It is good practice to use the smallest possible margins when printing a worksheet.

_____ 5. Print titles are row and column headings that are printed at the top of each new page.

Multiple Choice Questions

_____ 6. Which one of the following orientations forces Excel to print the worksheet along the long side of the page?

A. portrait

B. pastoral

C. landscape

D. urban

_____ 7. To change the size of the worksheet so that it will fit on one page you should

A. shrink the worksheet.

B. change the font of all data in the worksheet to a small size.

C. insert page breaks.

D. scale the worksheet.

_____ 8. The number of paper size alternatives available to you depends on

   A. the type of printer you have.

   B. the type of paper you have.

   C. the version of Excel you have.

   D. the type of computer you have.

_____ 9. A header's distance from the edge of the paper must be

   A. greater than the top margin.

   B. less than the top margin.

   C. greater than the bottom margin.

   D. less than the bottom margin.

_____ 10. When printing a worksheet that is at least two pages wide and two pages long,

   A. it is best to print across and then down.

   B. it is best to print down and then across.

   C. either A or B

   D. none of the above

Fill-in-the-Blank Questions

11. To get a magnified view of a Print Preview, _____.

12. Page breaks are represented by _____ in the worksheet.

13. _____ orientation works best for wide worksheets.

14. Print quality is measured in _____ .

15. Text that is printed at the bottom of every page is called a(n) _____ .

Acumen-Building Activities

Quick Projects

1. Printing your savings plan

In this problem, you will print the Svplan worksheet.

Open the svplan2.xls worksheet. Make the appropriate settings to center the worksheet on the page horizontally and vertically. Print the $7,500 worksheet. Save the file as svplan3.xls.

2. Printing the car plan

For this problem, you will add a custom footer to your Autos worksheet and print it.

Open the car2.xls worksheet. Make the Autos sheet the active sheet. Issue the appropriate commands and dialog box settings to create a custom footer with your full name in the center of the page. Place the workbook name in the left section and the sheet name in the right section. Print the sheet, and save the file as car3.xls.

3. Printing the Grades workbook without gridlines

In this problem, you will print one of the sheets from the Grades workbook without gridlines.

Open the grades2.xls file. Select the sheet you want to print. Make the appropriate menu and command selections to print the worksheet without gridlines. Print the worksheet, and save the file as grades3.xls.

4. Printing the Days worksheet

For this problem, you will change the margins in the Days sheet and print it.

Open the holiday2.xls workbook. With the Days sheet as the active sheet, make the appropriate selections to change the top and bottom margins to three inches and the left and right margins to one and one-half inches. Print the worksheet. Save the file as holiday3.xls.

In-Depth Projects

1. Creating a custom header for the Teamrec workbook

For this project, you will create a custom header for the Teamrec workbook and then print the Games worksheet.

Open the teamrec2.xls workbook. In the Games worksheet, make the appropriate selections to create a custom header. The header should have the following components: file name in left section, date in center section, and sheet name in right section. Create a custom footer with the following components: time in left section; your full name in center section, and page number in right section. Print the file. Save the file as teamrec3.xls.

2. Changing the orientation of the Shelter workbook

For this problem, you will change the orientation of the Check-in-out worksheet and add a built-in header. You will then print the worksheet.

Open the shelter2.xls workbook. With the Check-in-out sheet as the active sheet, make the appropriate selections to change the orientation to landscape. Select one of the alternative built-in headers. Print the worksheet. Save the file as shelter3.xls.

CASE STUDIES

**Coffee-On-
The-Go:**

Creating a Budget Deviation Analysis

In this chapter, you learned to enhance your printouts. You will use those skills to enhance the printout of the following budget worksheet for Coffee-On-The-Go.

1. Create the budget deviation analysis as shown. Use formulas and functions to compute the totals, deviation (Budget minus Actual), percent of deviation (Deviation divided by Budget), and net profit.

	Actual for Month	Budget for Month	Deviation	% Deviation
Sales	3,850	4,000		
Cost of Goods	1,000	900		
Gross Profit				
Operating Expenses:				
Utilities	450	500		
Advertising	500	500		
Miscellaneous	75	100		
Total				
Fixed Expenses:				
Salaries	1,200	1,200		
Benefits	150	100		
Taxes	100	100		
Insurance	425	400		
Licenses	75	100		
Total				
Total Expenses				
Net Profit (Gross Profit on Sales minus Total Operating Expenses)				

2. Format the worksheet.

3. Widen columns as necessary.

4. Save the file as deviate.

5. Format the spreadsheet with a header that prints the file name and sheet name in the left section, date in the center section, and your name in the right section.

6. Scale the worksheet to fit on one page, if necessary, and print the worksheet.

CASE STUDIES

Videos West: Printing

In this chapter, you learned to enhance your printouts. You will use those skills to enhance the printout of the Revenue worksheet for Videos West.

1. Open the revenue5 file.

2. Select settings to print in landscape orientation.

3. Add the header Videos West Quarterly Forecast in the top left section and a page number in the footer.

4. Print the worksheets.

5. Save the file as revenue6.

Chapter 8

Creating Charts

Key Terms

TERM	DEFINITION
Chart	a graphical representation of data in a worksheet
Chart Gallery	a collection of chart types (pie, bar, column, and so on) from which to choose
X-Axis	the horizontal boundary line of a chart
Y-Axis	the vertical boundary line of a chart
Category Axis	an alternate term for the X-axis, used because the X-axis generally plots categories of information
Value Axis	an alternate term for the Y-axis, used because the Y-axis generally plots values by which data is measured
Legend	a key that identifies the colors or symbols representing elements of data in a chart
Embedded Chart	a chart that is embedded into the worksheet for which it is representing data
Chart Sheet	a chart that is stored as a separate sheet in the workbook
Data Series	a group of cells being plotted in a chart
Plot Area	the background on which the chart rests

TERM	DEFINITION
Tick Mark	the large and small marks that intersect the Y-axis line
Scale	the distance between each tick mark
Logarithmic Scale	forces the distance between each tick mark to be exponential (for example, 1, 10, 100, 1000, 10000, and so on)

charts
In grade school, you probably learned how to plot data on graph paper using a ruler and colored pencils. While that process might have seemed fun at the time, creating *charts* or graphical displays as an adult is tedious work and, when done by hand, often inaccurate.

chart sheet
Most full-featured spreadsheet programs have the capability of transforming data into many different kinds of charts, and Excel is no exception. Excel enables you to embed a chart directly into a worksheet so that the chart is saved as part of the worksheet or as a separate sheet, called a *chart sheet*. In either case, Excel has many chart options that will help you make effective charts for presentations and easier data interpretation.

Objective 1: Creating Charts with the ChartWizard

In preceding chapters, you have seen how the Function Wizard can be used to complete a function in a guided step-by-step process. In addition to the Function Wizard, Excel has also included a ChartWizard to help take some of the guesswork out of creating charts. The ChartWizard helps you select the data to chart and the type of chart in which to display your data and then the wizard guides you through the process of adding chart components.

Starting the ChartWizard

embedded chart
The ChartWizard icon is located in the Standard toolbar. When you have entered data into a worksheet, you can click the ChartWizard to create an *embedded chart* within the worksheet. You must then define the area of the worksheet where you want the chart to be placed (think of this as Step 0 in the chart-making process). You define this area by dragging the mouse pointer across a range of cells that should be reserved for a chart.

Exercise 1: Starting ChartWizard and defining the range to be charted

In this exercise, you will open the Account6 worksheet you have built in previous chapters, and you will begin the process of embedding a chart within the worksheet.

1. Boot your computer, and start Excel, if necessary.
2. Open the file account6.xls.
3. Make the Balance worksheet the active sheet.

4. Click the ChartWizard tool ![icon] in the Standard toolbar.

   A flashing border appears around the active cell, and the status bar at the bottom of the screen tells you to drag in the document to create a chart.

5. Move the mouse pointer to cell A8 and drag to cell E16, and then release the mouse button.

   Step 1 of the ChartWizard, shown in Figure 8-1, appears on the screen.

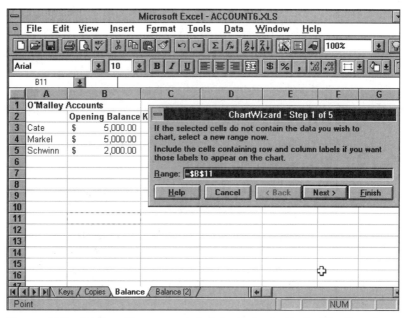

Figure 8-1   Define the range of data to be included in the chart

Defining the data range

After you have defined the chart location in the worksheet, the first ChartWizard step—defining the data to be charted—appears on the screen, as shown in Figure 8-1. The ChartWizard will attempt to guess the correct chart range, but you must check this range and make any changes to it if necessary.

The data range of a chart is generally the range of cells that includes any data you want to display in the chart, along with the associated column and row headings. You generally do not include cells devoted to the worksheet title or explanatory text.

You can define the range by manually typing the range into the Range field in the Step 1 dialog box of the ChartWizard, or you can drag the Step 1 dialog box to a blank portion of the screen so that you can see your data and then drag through the range of cells to be included in the chart. After the appropriate range has been selected, click Next to continue with the next step.

Exercise 2: Completing Step 1 of the ChartWizard

In this exercise, you will select the range to be included in the chart for the Account6 worksheet.

TIP You can also preselect the range to be charted before you access the ChartWizard.

1. With the Step 1 dialog box on the screen, drag the dialog box down so that you can see the entire contents of the worksheet.
2. Select the range A2:E5.

   This range appears in the Range field of the dialog box, in absolute cell address format.
3. Click Next to continue with Step 2.

   The Step 2 dialog box, shown in Figure 8-2, appears.

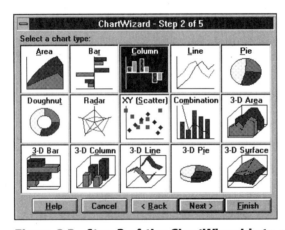

Figure 8-2 **Step 2 of the ChartWizard is to select a chart type**

Selecting a chart type and format

chart gallery As Figure 8-2 shows, Excel provides you with a *chart gallery* of fifteen chart types. By default, the ChartWizard formats your data for a column chart. However, you can override this setting by clicking on a different chart type. A general rule of thumb to keep in mind is that pie charts, no matter what style, are used to show proportions or parts of a whole while all other charts help you compare different data in different ways.

When you have chosen a chart type, click the Next button to move to the next step in the ChartWizard. The third step of the ChartWizard, as shown in Figure 8-3, is to select a format for the desired chart type. Notice that Excel again attempts to guess at the most appropriate chart format. As usual, you can override Excel's choice by clicking on a different chart format.

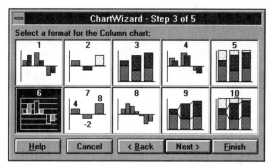

Figure 8-3   *Step 3 of the ChartWizard asks you to select a chart format*

At this point, you may want to experiment a little to see what other chart types and formats Excel has to offer. To do this, click the Back button in the Step 3 dialog box to return to Step 2. Select a different chart type, and click Next to see the available chart formats. You can repeat this experimentation as many times as you like to see the full extent of chart type and format offerings.

Exercise 3: Exploring chart types and formats

In this exercise, you will experiment with the various chart types and formats available in Excel.

1. With the Step 3 dialog box on the screen, click the Back button to return to the chart type dialog box.

   The Step 2 dialog box (refer to Figure 8-2) appears on the screen.

2. Select a different chart type, and then click Next to see the format options for the new chart type.

3. Repeat Steps 1 and 2 until you have explored as many chart types and formats you as want.

4. Finish this exercise by selecting the Column chart type from the Step 2 dialog box and the sixth column format from the Step 3 dialog box.

5. Click Next.

   Step 4 of the ChartWizard appears, as shown in Figure 8-4.

6. Leave Step 4 of the ChartWizard on the screen for the next exercise.

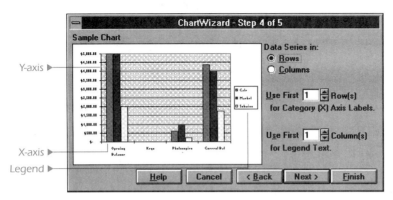

Y-axis ▶

X-axis ▶

Legend ▶

Figure 8-4   The sample chart appears as Step 4 of the ChartWizard

Viewing the sample chart

Y-axis; value axis; X-axis; category axis

Step 4 of the ChartWizard displays a sample chart and offers you several options for changing the sample. First, notice some components of the chart. The *Y-axis*, often called the *value axis* because it is the axis upon which values or measurements are generally displayed, is the vertical border of the chart. The horizontal border of the chart is called the *X-axis* or *category axis*; the categories that are being valued or measured are generally displayed along this line. The small box to the right of the chart is called the *legend*. Although it is not very readable in the chart sample, the legend explains what each column represents.

legend

data series

In addition to the sample chart display, Excel also provides you with several options. First, you can change the way the worksheet data is interpreted in the chart by changing the location of the *data series*—the columns or rows upon which Excel categorizes the chart. Notice that Excel has automatically used the data series across rows A through E, displaying data by account (keys, copies, balance) rather than by person. If you wanted to display the data by person (Cate, Markel, Schwinn), you would change the data series to columns.

This step also enables you to select which row (or column, if the data series is in columns) to use for the category axis labels and which column (or row, if the data series is in columns) to use for the legend text.

At this step, you should carefully examine the effectiveness of the selected chart type and format. If you think there is a better way to display your data, now is the time to click the Back button twice and select a different chart type and chart style. Of course, you can always edit the chart later, but it is much easier to edit within the context of the ChartWizard.

Exercise 4: Making changes to the sample chart

In this exercise, you will experiment with the sample chart.

1. With the Step 4 dialog box on the screen, click the Columns option to change the data series from Rows to Columns.

   Excel immediately changes the sample worksheet so that the data is organized by person and then by beginning balance, copies, keys, and current balance. Excel also changed the category axis labels and the legend.

2. Click Back twice to return to Step 2 of the ChartWizard.

3. Select the pie chart type, and click Next.

4. Accept the default pie chart format, and click Next.

   Excel shows what proportion each person's current balance is of the entire balance.

5. Change the data series to Rows.

   Excel attempts to show the proportions the previous balance, keys, copies, and current balance make of the total. This is a completely invalid chart because Excel is displaying the wholes (the balances) as well as the parts (the keys and copies data).

6. Experiment with as many other chart types and formats as you want. The more you explore, the easier it will be for you to choose the best chart type quickly later on.

7. Return the ChartWizard settings to a Column chart type in format number 6, with the data series in columns.

8. Click Next to continue with the last ChartWizard step.

   The Step 5 dialog box, shown in Figure 8-5, appears.

9. Leave the ChartWizard on the screen for the next exercise.

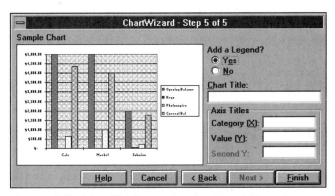

Figure 8-5   The final step in the ChartWizard process

Entering chart legends and titles

The final step in creating a chart is to add or remove a chart legend and enter text for a chart title and for axis titles. By default, Excel automatically places a legend in any non-pie chart. If you do not want a legend to appear, you can remove the legend and increase the size of the plot area in the chart by clicking the No option beneath the Add a Legend question.

In most cases, you will want a title for your chart so that the reader has some understanding of why the chart was created. You can manually enter a title for the chart in the Chart Title field, or you can enter the cell address of worksheet data that should be used as a chart title.

Finally, you can provide titles for both axes by manually entering title text or defining a cell address of worksheet data to be used as axis titles. When you are finished with this step and are satisfied with the overall look of the chart, click Finish to complete creating the chart.

Exercise 5: Finishing the chart

In this exercise, you will put the finishing touches on the Account6 chart.

1. In the Chart Title field, type the text O'Malley Account as of 9/15/94.
2. In the Category title field, type Faculty Member.
3. Click Finish to complete the chart.

    Excel displays a rather squished-looking chart, shown in Figure 8-6, of the range A8:E16 in the worksheet.

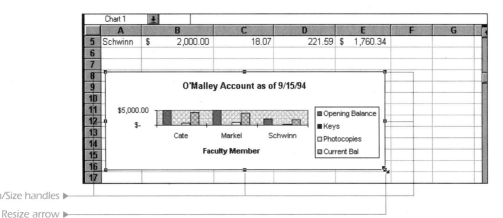

Selection/Size handles ▶

Resize arrow ▶

Figure 8-6 **The completed chart**

4. Move the mouse pointer to the lower right corner of the chart outline so that the mouse pointer changes to a resize arrow, as shown in Figure 8-6.

5. Drag the chart corner down to cell E20.

   The chart expands to display values at $1,000 intervals on the value axis.

6. Save the file as account7.xls.

   Because the chart is embedded in the worksheet, both the chart and the sheet will be saved in the same file.

Objective 2: Creating Chart Sheets

While embedding a chart within a worksheet is convenient, it is often more efficient in the long run to create a stand-alone chart— a chart that is used in the worksheet but that is in a separate sheet. By creating stand-alone charts in separate sheets, you can easily create electronic presentations, using charts without showing any of the underlying data.

You create a stand-alone chart sheet by selecting the data range to be included in the chart and then opening the Insert menu and choosing Chart, As New Sheet. Issuing this command starts the ChartWizard and places the finished chart in the sheet to the left of the current sheet.

Exercise 6: Creating a new chart sheet

In this exercise, you will create a new chart sheet that shows the proportion of the total O'Malley funds spent on copies and keys.

1. With the Balance sheet as the active sheet, select the range C2:D5.

2. From the Insert menu, choose Chart, As New Sheet.

   The ChartWizard opens with Step 1.

3. Make sure that the data range in Step 1 of the ChartWizard is accurate, and click Next.

4. In Step 2 of the ChartWizard, select the pie chart type and click Next.

5. In Step 3 of the ChartWizard, select the 7th pie chart format and click Next.

6. In Step 4 of the ChartWizard, make sure that the data series is taken from Rows and click Next.

Tasteful Charts

If you are lucky enough to have a color printer, you can make use of the available colors in the Patterns tab sheet of the Format Series dialog box. Remember, however, that colors, like fonts, can distract the reader from the data. Use pleasing, conservative colors, alternate lights and darks, and avoid clashing colors. For those using black and white charts, consider how the charts are to be viewed. Are they going to be seen as overhead projections? Will the patterns be recognizable from the back of the room? If your chart is going to be duplicated, will the darker patterns bleed into a black blob, and be indistinguishable from the adjoining data series. If so, try alternating dark and light patterns. Finally, if your presentation is really important and you don't have a color printer, you might consider going to one of the copy stores in your area. Most are now equipped with PCs and popular software, as well as color printers. For a small fee, you can print your charts and overheads on color printers.

7. In Step 5 of the ChartWizard, type the chart title as Proportion of O'Malley Account Expenditures.

8. Click Finish.

   The completed chart appears in a new chart sheet that precedes the Balance worksheet, as shown in Figure 8-7.

9. Save the file as account8.xls.

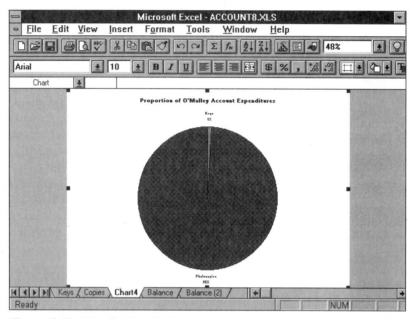

Figure 8-7   The finished pie chart

Objective 3: Formatting Charts

When you have created a chart using the basic formatting provided in the ChartWizard, you can use many other formatting options to make your chart easier to read and to emphasize certain components of the chart. These options are available from the menu or by double-clicking the portion of the chart you want to change. The following sections discuss formatting the

plot area   *plot area* and data series, axes, legend, gridlines, chart title, and axis titles.

Formatting the data series and plot area

If you double-click on a column or piece of a pie chart or if you choose Selected Data Series from the Format menu, a dialog box appears containing six tab sheets, as shown in Figure 8-8.

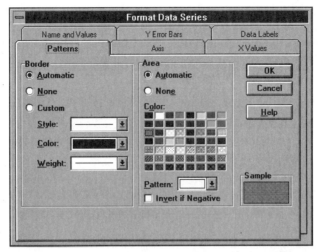

Figure 8-8   The Patterns tab sheet of the Format Data Series dialog box

Table 8.1 describes the options available on each tab sheet.

Table 8-1   Tab sheet name options and their descriptions

TAB SHEET NAME	OPTION	DESCRIPTION
Patterns	Border	draws a border around the selected column or pie piece
	Area	fills the column or pie piece with the specified color or pattern
Axis	Plot Series On Primary Axis	draws the data along the main axis
	Plot Series On Secondary Axis	adds a second axis from the data and draws the data according to the secondary axis
X-Values	X-Values	identifies the cell or cells used as the identifying marks for the X-axis
Name and Values	Name	the location of the cell containing the name or label of the data being plotted
	Y-Values	the cell or cells that are to be measured along the Y-axis
Y Error Bars	Display	the symbol used to denote potential error in the data series
	Error Amount	the type of value used to express potential error (percentage, standard deviation, for example)
Data Labels	None	prohibits the display of a label on or next to a data series
	Show Value	displays the actual value of the column or pie piece.
	Show Label	displays the label for the data series. This works well if your chart is quite long and X-axis labels are far away from the data being shown.

If you double-click the background portion of a chart, the Format Plot Area dialog box appears. This dialog box enables you to select a plot area border and background color and pattern. The border and area selection options are identical to those shown in the Format Data Series dialog box shown in Figure 8-8.

Exercise 7: Changing the plot area and data series colors

In this exercise, you will change the background color of the plot area, the colors for each of the four values being displayed, and the data labels for each plotted data series.

1. Make the Balance worksheet the active worksheet, and click in the chart to make it active.

   The selection/size handles should appear around the edge of the chart.

2. Double-click the Opening Balance column in Cate's section of the chart.

   The Format Data Series dialog box appears, as shown in Figure 8-8.

3. In the Area section of the Patterns tab sheet, select the bright blue color with no pattern and click OK.

   Each Opening Balance column is now represented by bright blue.

4. Double-click one of the Photocopies columns in the chart, select a bright yellow to represent this category from the Patterns tab sheet, and then click OK.

5. Double-click one of the Current Balance columns in the chart, and select the bright purple (orchid) color.

6. Click the Data Labels tab to access that sheet, select the Show Value option, and click OK to close the dialog box.

   The current balance for all three faculty members is displayed in purple, and the actual current balance amount is printed above the column.

7. Double-click the background of the chart to access the Format Plot Area dialog box.

   The Format Plot Area dialog box appears on the screen.

8. In the Area section, select the lightest shade of gray with no pattern, and then click OK to close the dialog box.

   The chart now displays three bright colors on a light gray background field. This chart is much easier to read than it was using the default colors assigned by Excel.

9. Save the file as account9.xls.

Formatting axes

You can make many changes to both the Y-axis and X-axis of a chart to make the chart more readable. In the chart with which you have been working, one of the big problems is that you can't read the keys value because it is so small compared to the other values being displayed. You can correct

tick mark   this problem by changing the *tick mark* value in the Y-axis. Tick marks are the marks that intersect the Y-axis and that generally have values assigned to them. Figures 8-9 and 8-10 show the options available for changing tick

scale   marks and the *scale* on which they are displayed.

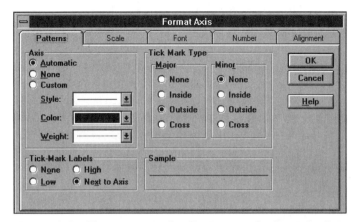

Figure 8-9   You can use the Patterns tab sheet to determine the pattern of the tick marks

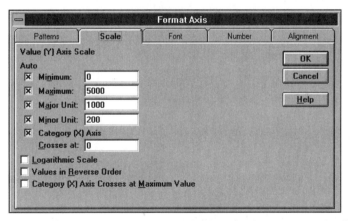

Figure 8-10   You can use the Scale tab sheet to set the incremental values for tick marks as well as to determine the intersection of the X- and Y- axes

In addition to editing patterns and scales, you can also edit the font, font size (which is generally too small), style of axis labels, the formatting of numbers along the axes, and the alignment of text along the axes.

Exercise 8: Changing the tick mark scale

In this exercise, you will change the scale of the tick marks on the Y-axis so that the keys data will be displayed.

1. Double-click one of the values on the Y-axis to access the Format Axis dialog box.

   The Patterns tab sheet, shown in Figure 8-9, appears on the screen.

2. Click the Scale tab to make it the active sheet.

logarithmic scale

3. Click the check box beside Logarithmic Scale and click OK.

   The scale of the chart changes so that the tick marks are not displayed in even increments (1000, 2000, for example) but rather so that all data is meaningfully displayed on the chart.

4. Change the color of the keys columns by double-clicking one of the keys columns to access the Format Data Series dialog box.

5. On the Patterns sheet, select cyan blue (a light but bright blue) from the color palette and click OK to close the tab sheets.

   Each data series is now displayed in a bright color and is easy to see on the chart, as shown in Figure 8-11.

6. Save the file as acct10.xls.

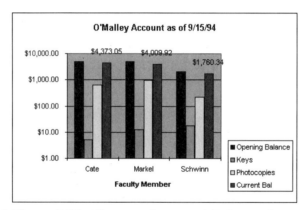

Figure 8-11   The new, improved Balance chart

Formatting legends

If you double-click on the legend in the chart, the Format Legend dialog box appears on the screen. The Patterns sheet is the standard tab sheet for determining borders and colors. The Font tab sheet is for selecting font, font size, and style. The Placement sheet enables you to tell Excel where to place the legend within the chart. Your choices are bottom, corner, top, right, and left.

Exercise 9: Moving the legend

In this exercise, you will move the legend to a different location in the chart.

1. Double-click the legend in the Balance chart to open the Format Legend dialog box.

2. Click the Placement tab sheet to access it.

3. Click the option beside Top, and click OK to close the tab sheet.

    The legend expands across the top of the chart, just below the chart title.

4. Save the file as acct11.xls.

Formatting gridlines

When you double-click on a gridline, Excel opens the Format Gridlines dialog box with Patterns and Scale tab sheets. The Patterns tab sheet enables you to select whether you want gridlines and, if you do, how wide the gridlines should be and what color the gridlines should be. The Scale tab sheet is the same one available in the Format Axis dialog box (refer to Figure 8-10) and enables you to alter the scale of the Y-axis.

Exercise 10: Changing the weight and color of the gridlines

In this exercise, you will change the weight and color of the gridlines in the Balance chart.

1. Double-click one of the gridlines in the Balance chart to open the Format Gridlines dialog box.

    The Patterns sheet of the Format Gridlines dialog box appears.

2. From the Color list box, select the burgundy color (the first color in the second row).

3. From the Weight list box, select the second weight line—a thin solid line.

    Notice that the sample displays the new colored gridline.

4. Click OK to close the tab sheet, and examine your ever-evolving chart.

5. Save the file as acct12.xls.

Formatting chart and axis titles

The final two elements which can be formatted are the chart and axis titles. The options for these two elements are identical. You can format the patterns, the font, and the alignment. To access the tab sheets, double-click on the element you want to format.

Exercise 11: Formatting the chart title

In this exercise, you will increase the font size of the chart title to make it more readable.

1. Double-click the chart title text.

    The Format Chart Title dialog box appears on the screen.

2. Click the Font tab to access that sheet.

3. Change the Size to 12 (or something approximately two values larger than the current setting), and click OK.

    The title appears in much larger text than anything else in the chart.

4. Save the file as acct13.xls.

FEATURE

Visually Interesting Charts

One of the charting features not covered in this chapter is the Picture Marker feature. Excel enables you to draw a picture from scratch or copy a picture from another resource and paste it into a chart so that the picture is the data series marker rather than a standard column or bar. The picture can be stacked to show quantities, as shown in Figure 8-12, or stretched along the Y-axis, as shown in Figure 8-13.

To use a picture rather than a chart, locate or create a picture that you want to use and copy the picture to the Clipboard. In Excel, select the data series portion of a previously-created chart (the columns or bars), and then paste the picture into the chart. Double-click on the data series to open the Format Data Series dialog box. Access the Patterns tab sheet if it is not already in front, and select Stretch to force the picture to stretch along the Y-axis, select Stack to force the picture to stack along the Y-axis, or select Stack and Scale to set the number of pictures to appear along the Y-axis, based on the number of items being represented (for example, one picture for every item being represented, two to one, and so on).

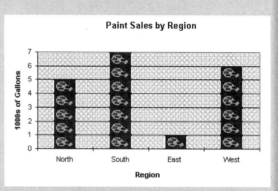

Figure 8-12 The standard column data series marker is replaced with stacked paint icons

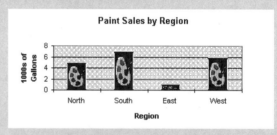

Figure 8-13 The Paint icon can be stretched along the Y-axis

Objective 4: Naming and Moving Charts

By this point, you are probably beginning to think of the many things you can do with Excel's charting feature. As you create multiple charts in chart sheets, some management issues arise that are quite easy to deal with once you know the strategies. By assigning names to chart sheets, you can keep track of which chart is which. By moving chart sheets around in the sheet order, you can create a presentation of charts that is logical and easy to follow.

Naming chart sheets

You name chart sheets by using the Format menu to access the Sheet, Rename command. When you do this, the new chart sheet name appears on the sheet tab at the bottom of the screen.

 TIP Remember, you can also rename sheets by double-clicking the sheet tab.

Exercise 12: Naming the pie chart

In this exercise, you will assign a meaningful name to the pie chart created earlier in this chapter.

1. Double-click the Chart1 sheet tab at the bottom of the screen to make the pie chart the active sheet.

   The Rename Sheet dialog box appears.

2. In the dialog box, type the name O'Malley Pie and click OK.

   The pie chart sheet is now named O'Malley Pie in the sheet tab.

3. Save the file as acct14.xls.

Moving chart sheets

You can move a chart sheet from one location to another within the sheet order, just as you would a regular worksheet. If you have several chart sheets, it is a good idea to organize them in the order that you use them or in the order in which you plan to present them. To move a chart sheet, make the chart sheet the active sheet. From the Edit menu, choose Move or Copy Sheet. When the dialog box appears, click the name of the sheet you want the chart sheet to follow, or click (move to end) to make the chart sheet the last sheet in the series. A faster method for moving sheets is to drag the tab of the sheet to the new location among the other tabs.

Exercise 13: Moving the O'Malley pie chart sheet

In this exercise, you will move the O'Malley pie chart sheet to the end of the worksheets.

1. Make the O'Malley pie chart sheet the active sheet.

2. Drag the sheet tab so that it follows the Balance(2) worksheet.

   The chart sheet changes location and now follows the Balance(2) worksheet.

3. Save the file as acct15.xls.

Objective 5: Previewing and Printing Charts

After you have your charts created and formatted, you will probably want to print the chart. Although most printers still print only in shades of gray (from black to white), color printers are becoming more common and less costly to purchase and maintain. If you are preparing a chart for an important presentation or you are going to make overhead slides (acetates) of your charts, you should consider going to a photocopy store that has computers and paying the extra money to get color output. Your presentation will be more effective and more visually interesting in color than in black and white.

Regardless of whether you choose to have color or black-and-white output, the printing process is the same. As was stated in an earlier chapter, you should always do a Print Preview before sending any document to the printer, and charts are no exception.

Previewing embedded charts

You can print embedded charts with their associated worksheet or by themselves. To preview the chart and worksheet data, open the File menu and choose Print Preview. The chart and worksheet will be displayed. You may need to resize the chart so that it fits on the page with the worksheet, or you may need to change the orientation of the page. If you want to preview an embedded chart without the worksheet data, you must double-click the chart to make it active, then open the File menu, and choose Print Preview. Only the chart will be displayed on the preview screen.

Exercise 14: Previewing the embedded chart

In this exercise, you will preview the embedded chart with the associated worksheet data and without it

1. Make the Balance worksheet the active sheet, and deselect any elements of the chart that are currently selected by clicking outside the chart area.

2. Click the Preview button 🔍 on the Standard toolbar.

   A preview showing the data and the chart appears on the screen.

3. Use the magnifying glass to zoom in on the chart and then zoom back out.

4. Close the Preview window.

5. In the Balance worksheet, double-click the chart to make it active.

6. Click the Preview button 🔍.

7. This time the preview shows only the chart.

8. Close the preview window.

Previewing chart sheets

In addition to previewing embedded charts, you can also get a Print Preview of a chart sheet. To do this, make the chart sheet the active sheet and then issue the Print Preview command.

Exercise 15: Previewing the O'Malley pie chart

In this exercise, you will preview the O'Malley pie chart.

1. Make the O'Malley pie chart sheet the active sheet.

2. Click the Preview button 🔍.

   The chart is displayed in Preview mode. Zoom in and out as necessary to see the details of the chart.

3. Close the Preview window.

Printing charts

After you have obtained a preview of a chart and are relatively certain that the chart is formatted as you want it, you are ready to print the chart. The procedure for printing charts is identical to the procedure used to preview charts except that you choose the Print command rather than the Print Preview command.

Exercise 16: Printing the charts

In this exercise, you will add your name as footer information to the O'Malley pie chart and the embedded chart in the Balance worksheet and then print the charts.

1. Make the O'Malley pie chart sheet the active sheet if it is not already.
2. From the File menu, choose Print.
3. From the dialog box, click Page Setup to access the Page Setup dialog box.
4. Click the Header/Footer tab to access that sheet.
5. Type your full name as the left section footer, and close the dialog box by clicking OK.
6. Click OK again to close the Page Setup dialog box.
7. Click OK a third time to send the chart to the printer.

   Collect your printout from the printer. Make sure that the page you get has your name at the bottom.
8. Make the Balance worksheet the active sheet, and double-click the chart to make it active.
9. Complete Steps 2 through 7 again to print your name as a left section footer.

   Collect the printout from the printer, making sure that you get your work.
10. Save the file as acct16.xls.
11. Save any other open workbooks at this time and exit Excel or continue with the problems at the end of this chapter.

Chapter Summary

In this chapter, you learned how to present worksheet data graphically in the form of a chart. You learned how to use the ChartWizard to create charts and how to edit and format each element of the chart by double-clicking the element to be changed. You learned how to set the scale, tick marks, and patterns for the chart itself, as well as how to format explanatory and title text surrounding the chart. Finally, you learned how to print the chart, either by itself or in conjunction with its associated data.

Review Questions

True/False Questions

_____ 1. Excel can create only charts which are embedded in the worksheet.

_____ 2. The X-axis of a chart is also referred to as the category axis.

_____ 3. Pie charts are especially good for showing data as it evolves over a period of time.

_____ 4. The Y-axis of a chart is also referred to as the category axis.

_____ 5. Chart sheets are named Chart1, Chart2, and so on, by default.

Multiple Choice Questions

Use the worksheet below to answer the multiple choice questions.

	A	B	C	D	E
1	**Sales by Region by Quarter**				
2					
3	**Region**	**1st Quarter**	**2nd Quarter**	**3rd Quarter**	**4th Quarter**
4	North	$ 2,789,126	$ 3,000,125	$ 3,590,829	$ 3,193,893
5	South	$ 3,981,838	$ 4,583,298	$ 4,883,928	$ 4,900,002
6	East	$ 1,992,581	$ 2,803,928	$ 2,918,238	$ 2,809,381
7	West	$ 3,500,318	$ 3,987,918	$ 4,019,283	$ 3,898,192

_____ 6. With the range A3:E7 as the data series to be charted, which one of the following chart types would <u>not</u> be appropriate for showing sales over the entire four quarters?

A. column

B. pie

C. bar

D. line

_____ 7. To plot the data by region, which one of the following settings must be made?

A. Data series in columns

B. All data in series

C. Data series in rows

D. X-axis range is A3:E3

_____ 8. To plot the data by quarter, which one of the following settings must be made?

   A. Date series in columns

   B. All data in series

   C. Data series in rows

   D. Y-axis range is A1:A7

_____ 9. Which of the following ranges would be meaningful as a pie chart?

   A. B4:E7

   B. B4:E4

   C. B4:B7

   D. both B and C

_____ 10. Which one of the following scales would best display the data in a column chart?

   A. Logarithmic scale

   B. Minimum=$0; Maximum=$5,000,000 with $1,000 increments

   C. Minimum=$1,000,000; Maximum=$5,000,000 with $500,000 increments

   D. Minimum=$2,000,000; Maximum=$5,000,000 with $1,000 increments

Fill-in-the-Blank Questions

11. When the values being plotted cover a wide numeric range, the _____ scale can be used to plot all values.

12. When you want to print the actual value of a data series being plotted, use the _____ option in the Format Data Series tab sheet.

13. The short lines that intersect the Y-axis are called _____.

14. To print an embedded worksheet without the associated worksheet data, you must _____ before choosing the File, Print command.

15. When working with several chart sheets, you may want to _____the sheets to change the order in which they appear.

Acumen-Building Activities

Quick Projects

1. Plotting your savings plan

In this project, you will add some additional data to the svplan.xls worksheet and then chart the data.

Open the svplan3.xls worksheet, and click the $10,000 sheet tab. In cell E3, type the column heading Monthly Income. In cell E4, type the value 1600, and copy this value to cells E5:E7. In cell F3, type the column heading After Savings. In cell F4, write a formula that will compute how much you have left over after you have set aside your savings amount each month, in positive notation. Copy this formula to cells F5:F7. Adjust the column widths in columns E and F so that they are wide enough to accommodate the data, and format the values in columns E and F as currency with no decimal places.

Select the range D3:F7, and click the ChartWizard button ▨. Follow the steps in the ChartWizard, using the suggested chart type and format to create an embedded column chart with an appropriate title. Print the worksheet and chart with your name in the left footer section. Be sure to make the chart and data fit on one page. Save the file as svplan4.xls, and close the file.

2. Plotting the car plan

In this project, you will graphically display your car-buying plans based on data in the car3.xls worksheet.

Open the car3.xls worksheet. Select all cells that contain data, and click the ChartWizard button ▨. Make the appropriate selections to create a line graph, plotting the data series in rows and using the first row for X-axis labels and the first column for legend information. Enter text appropriate for a chart title. Size the chart on the screen so that none of the X-axis labels are wrapped at odd points and so that the data is easy to read. Edit the data series for the Chrysler LaBaron so that its line and symbol are cyan blue (light bright blue). Edit the plot area so that the background of the chart is light gray. Print the chart and associated worksheet on one page. Save the file as car4.xls, and close the file.

3. Charting your grades

In this project, you will chart your grades for one of the courses you tracked in the grades3.xls worksheet. Notice how much easier it is to read the chart data than the worksheet data in this particular case.

Open the grades3.xls worksheet. Select one of the sheets to chart. Select the column headings and raw data (no average, minimum, or maximum) to chart.

Click the ChartWizard button ▨, and create an embedded line chart with appropriate chart, X-axis, and Y-axis titles. Be sure to include your name in the chart title. Print the chart by itself (no worksheet data should be included in the printout). Save the file as grades4.xls, and close the file.

4. Creating chart sheets in the Svplan worksheet

For this project, you will create four chart sheets to go along with the Svplan worksheet.

Open the svplan4.xls worksheet, and make the $10,000 sheet the active sheet. Select the range D3:E4 and insert a chart as a new sheet. From the ChartWizard, select the pie chart type, approve the default pie chart format, and enter an appropriate chart title. Name the chart sheet 4-yr pie. Return to the $10,000 sheet, select the range D3:E3. Hold down ⌐CTRL⌐, and select the range D5:E5.

(Note: ⌐CTRL⌐ enables you to put cells in a range that are not connected to other cells in the range. This is a great shortcut to use when creating charts.)

Create a new chart sheet, make a pie graph, add an appropriate title, and name the sheet 3-yr pie. Create 2-year and 1-year pie charts, using the methods described in previous steps. Be sure to give appropriate chart titles and chart tab names. Save the file as svplan5.xls, print any of the charts you want, and close the worksheet.

In-Depth Projects

1. Charting team performance

In this project, you will create two charts to help analyze team performance over the first four games.

Open the teamrec3.xls worksheet, and make the Games sheet active. Select the range B3:B7, and then hold down ⌐CTRL⌐ and select D3:E7 so that two ranges that are not contiguous are selected. Create a new chart sheet using a column chart type, the default column format, data series in columns, with appropriate chart and axis titles. Edit the data series for your home team, and make the series your predominate school color and name the chart sheet By Game. Using the same data range as before, create a second chart sheet using the column chart type and default column format, this time placing the data series in rows. Add appropriate chart and axis titles. Edit the plot area so that it is a solid light gray and name the chart sheet By Score. Print both chart sheets, adding your full name in the left footer section of each chart. Save the file as teamrec4.xls.

2. Charting individual player's performance

In this project, you will work again with the Teamrec4 worksheet to chart individual player performance.

Open the teamrec4.xls worksheet if necessary. Create a chart sheet, using the chart type that will best display comparisons between the team members you have tracked over the period of four games. Edit the chart sheet so that colors, gridlines, plot area, and scale are used effectively. Create chart and axis titles that indicate what the chart is attempting to show. Assign the chart sheet an appropriate name. Create a custom header that will print the worksheet name in the left section, your name in the center section, and the workbook name in the right section. Create a custom footer that will print the date in the left section, the page number in the center section, and the time in the right section of the chart sheet. Save the file as teamrec5.xls.

CASE STUDIES

Coffee-On-The-Go: **Creating Charts**

In this chapter, you learned to create and enhance charts. You will use those skills to create and enhance charts for the following spreadsheet for Coffee-On-The-Go.

1. Create the following spreadsheet, which represents the number of units sold per type of drink per quarter.

	Qtr 1	Qtr 2	Qtr 3	Qtr 4
Espresso	2,000	2,100	2,400	1,900
Cappuccino	1,700	1,500	2,100	1,800
Latte	1,500	1,600	1,500	1,600
Mocha	2,200	2,300	2,000	2,100
House	4,000	4,100	3,900	4,000
Tea	500	300	1,000	900

2. Create an embedded bar chart of the data.
3. Enhance the chart with titles, legend, and gridlines.
4. Print the chart and the spreadsheet together.
5. Change the chart type three times, and print all the charts.
6. Save the file as types.

CASE STUDIES

 **Videos West:**   **Creating Charts**

In this chapter, you learned to create and enhance charts. You will use those skills to create and enhance charts for the Revenue spreadsheet for Videos West.

1. Open the revenue3 file.
2. Increase the Utilities by $100 for February and by another $100 for March. Increase the Office Supplies by $50 for February and by another $50 for March.
3. Copy the month headings from row 4 to row 14.
4. Create a chart of the individual Operating Expenses (not the totals) for the three months.
5. Enhance the chart with titles, legends, gridlines, and patterns.
6. Print the chart.
7. Print the spreadsheet and the chart together.
8. Change the chart type three times, and print all the charts.
9. Save the file as revchart.

Acumen Critical Thinking Milestone

Individual Project:

Buying a Puppy

You have been thinking about buying a new puppy but are having trouble deciding which kind to get. You want a small- to medium-sized dog that is good tempered, not prone to barking, and whose breed has generally good health. Go to the library and find the following information for Lhasa Apsos, Shelties, Cocker Spaniel, and ShihTzus: cost for a pet-quality dog, average life span; average veterinary costs (assume $75/year minimum). Record this information in an Excel worksheet. Create a chart sheet that contains pie charts for each of the four breeds, showing the cost breakdown of the total cost for each dog. Name the chart sheet bydog. In the sheet with the data, create an embedded chart that compares the costs in each category for each dog. Give the chart appropriate titles and formatting. Save the file as dog.xls, and print both sheets with headers that include your name and the sheet name and footers that include the page number.

Team Project:

Gathering Crime Statistics

Assume that your team has been assigned to write a report on crime in your area. Collect monthly crime statistics for rape, assault, murder, drunk driving, and disorderly conduct from your local or campus police department for the last two years. Create a worksheet that will store and display this information. Be sure to format column widths so that the data fits in the columns. Create a column chart that shows the annual totals for each crime category. Include a legend and explanatory titles. Save the file as crime.xls. Write a short report or commentary based on the statistics you collected. Include references to the data in the worksheet and chart. Print the worksheet, chart, and report, making sure that the names for each of your team's members is on the printout.

Part 3

Advanced Features

Chapter 9

Working with Lists

Key Terms

TERM	DEFINITION
Database	a file, containing information about people or objects, that is broken down into standard categories
List	Excel's term for a database
Fields	the categories used to group information. Columns in a worksheet are considered to be database fields.
Records	the contents of several fields that describe an object or individual. In Excel, rows in a worksheet are records.
Sorting	the process of rearranging the data in a database list according to a set of specified rules
Criteria	rules used to locate, sort, or calculate data in a worksheet
Primary Key	the first field used in a sort procedure
Comparison Criteria	rules, placed in a separate location of the worksheet, that are used to carry out database functions

database; list

Spreadsheet programs have many unique capabilities but also incorporate features like charting generally found in other stand-alone programs. An important Excel feature is the program's capability of organizing and locating data using methods similar to those of *database* programs. With Excel, you can define a series of rows and columns as a *list* and then manipulate the

sorting   data in the list by *sorting* the information in a certain order, by searching for information within the list, and by using database functions on the data in the list.

list;   A *list* is Excel's term for a database. A database is a contiguous range of
records;   cells organized into *records* (rows) and *fields* (columns). Think back to the
fields   checkbook example used early in this text. You made column headings for date, check number, description, amount, and so on. These headings are database fields. Each row contained information about a unique entry (the check number) but used the same standard fields to organize the information. In database terminology, a row is a record. A worksheet containing multiple records and fields is sometimes called a database.

Objective 1: Sorting a List

In Excel, you don't have to do anything special to make a worksheet a database or list. Excel automatically assumes that at some point you will
criteria   want to sort or reorganize your data based on a set of rules or *criteria*. When you sort a list, Excel physically and permanently rearranges the rows in your worksheet. For this reason, you must use extreme caution when sorting a list and remember to use the Undo command (available from the Standard toolbar or the Edit menu) immediately if the list is not sorted correctly.

Sorting on a single field

The Sort command is located under the Data menu. Figure 9-1 shows the Sort dialog box. Notice that you can sort on three fields.

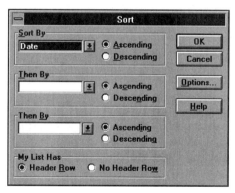

Figure 9-1 **You can use the Sort dialog box to determine which fields to sort on and the order in which the data should be sorted**

primary key   The field listed first is called the *primary key*; Excel will sort on the data in that field first, then the data in the next field listed, and then the data in the third field listed. Excel also enables you to determine whether you want your list sorted in ascending (A...Z, 1....100) or descending (Z...A, 100...1) order.

You also can tell Excel to ignore the first row in the sort range if the first row contains only headers (column headings/field names) so that the headers won't be included in the sort.

By clicking the Options button, you can also tell Excel to pay attention to the case of the characters being sorted (uppercase is sorted before lowercase) and in which direction to sort (top to bottom or left to right). Figure 9-2 shows the Sort Options dialog box.

Excel also includes two sort buttons on the Standard toolbar. The Sort Ascending button ![A-Z down] automatically sorts the selected range in ascending order, using the data in the first selected column as the primary key. The Sort Descending button ![Z-A down] automatically sorts the selected range in descending order, again using the data in the first column as the primary key. These buttons do not access the Sort dialog box, nor do they allow you to determine which field is to be used as the primary key. For these reasons, these buttons should be viewed as shortcuts for doing simple, one-field sorts only.

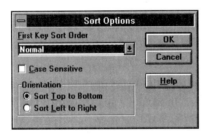

Figure 9-2 **The Sort Options dialog box**

Exercise 1: Sorting the Copies worksheet on a single field

In this exercise, you will duplicate the data portion of the Copies worksheet into a new location on the worksheet and then sort the duplicate list.

1. Start Excel, if necessary.
2. Open the file acct16.xls, and make the Copies worksheet the active sheet.
3. Copy the range A3:D8 to A13:D18.
4. Select the range A14:D16.
5. From the Data menu, choose Sort.

   The Sort dialog box, shown in Figure 9-1, appears.
6. In the Sort By field, open the list box and select Date.
7. Click the Descending radio button.

8. Click the No Header Row radio button, and then click OK.

   The data is rearranged by date so that the most recent charges appear at the top of the range and the oldest charges appear at the bottom of the range. Compare the newly sorted data with the original data set in cells A3:D8. Notice that none of the data was altered and that the totals remain the same.

9. Save the file as sort1.xls.

Sorting on multiple fields

As stated earlier, you can sort on more than one field from the database. Using multiple fields for sorting comes in handy when you have identical data in multiple rows of the database. If you have a worksheet that contains columns for last name, first name, and middle initial, for example, you will probably want to sort using the last name as the primary key and the first name as the secondary key. This way, if there are two people with the same last name, Excel will sort them in proper alphabetical order using their first names (Smith, Roger will appear before Smith, William in the sorted list, for example). To sort using multiple fields, enter field names or column locations in the second and, optionally, third sort criteria fields.

Exercise 2: Sorting Keys using multiple fields

In this exercise, you will sort the Keys worksheet on amount and date.

1. In the sortl.xls workbook, make the Keys worksheet the active sheet.
2. Copy the range A2:D9 to A12:D19.
3. Select the range A13:D15.
4. From the Data menu, choose Sort.

   The Sort dialog box shown in Figure 9-1 appears.

5. In the Sort By field, type the criteria Column B, and define the order as Ascending.
6. In the second criteria field, type Column A, and define the order as Ascending.
7. Click the radio button beside No Header Row at the bottom of the dialog box, and then click OK.

   The data is sorted in ascending order first by amount in column B and then by date.

8. Save the file as sort2.xls.

Objective 2: Using Data Forms

You can view your list record by record using the Form command located under the Data menu. The Form dialog box is shown in Figure 9-3. In addition to this more traditional database view, the Form dialog box also enables you to create new records, edit and delete existing records, and search for specific records within the list.

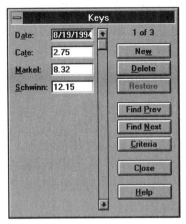

Figure 9-3 **The Form dialog box displays the worksheet title in the dialog box title bar**

Navigating records using the Form

When you open the Form dialog box, you can view each record in the list by using the scroll bar. Clicking the up arrow in the scroll bar moves up one record; clicking the down arrow in the scroll bar moves down one record. You can also use the Find Prev button to move up and the Find Next button to move down.

Exercise 3: Navigating the list

In this exercise, you will practice using the scroll bar and buttons to move from record to record in the Form.

1. With the Keys worksheet on the screen, make cell A12 the active cell.
2. From the Data menu, choose Form.

   A dialog box similar to the one shown in Figure 9-3 appears.
3. Click the down arrow in the scroll bar once to move to record 2.

   Notice that the record counter in the top right corner of the dialog box displays *2 of 3*, showing you the exact position within the database list.
4. Click the down arrow again to display record 3.
5. Click the Find Prev button to move up in the database and display record 2.
6. Click the Find Next button to move back down to record 3.
7. Click Close to close the dialog box.

Adding new records in the Form

You can append a new record to the end of the database list by opening the Form dialog box, clicking the New button, entering the data for the new record, and clicking New again. The new data is added to the bottom of the list in the worksheet and appears as a new record number in the form. Note that when you add new records to a list that has been sorted, you must resort the list to place the added records in the proper order.

Exercise 4: Adding a new record to the Keys list

In this exercise, you will add a new record to the duplicate Keys list in the Keys worksheet, using the Form dialog box.

1. Make cell A12 of the Keys worksheet the active cell, if it isn't already.
2. From the Data menu, choose Form.

   The Form dialog box appears.
3. Click New.

   The fields in the left side of the dialog box are cleared, and the I-beam is anchored in the Date field.
4. In the Date field, type 8/27/94.
5. Press TAB to move to the Cate field, and type 2.10.
6. Press TAB again to move to the Markel field, and type 3.25.
7. Move to the Schwinn field, and type 4.80.
8. Click New again to complete the addition.

   The new data appears in the worksheet, and the fields in the Form dialog box clear so that you can enter another new record if you want.
9. Close the Form dialog box, and save the file as sort3.xls.

Editing and deleting records using the Form

Using worksheet database lists for personal information

Many people use spreadsheet programs like Excel to keep track of not only business and financial records, but also personal records such as names, addresses, phone numbers, and birthdays of friends and relatives. The Sort feature discussed in this chapter makes it easy to reorganize your list with just a few keystrokes so that you can easily view the list in alphabetical order, ZIP code order, or perhaps by birthday or anniversary. If you use Excel as a birthday or anniversary reminder and employ the Sort feature, you may never miss another important date again!

In addition to adding new records, the Form dialog box also enables you to edit and delete existing records in the database list. To edit data in a record, use the navigation buttons or scroll bar arrows to move to the record you want to edit and then make the desired change in the record. The worksheet data will be updated when you move to a new record. If you make a change to a record and then decide you want to undo the change, click the Restore button before moving to a new record.

To delete a record in the list, use the navigation buttons or scroll bar arrows to move to the record you want to delete, and then click Delete. A dialog box asking you to confirm this command appears. Click OK to complete the Delete operation, Cancel to abort the Delete operation, or Help to get help with this command. If you choose to confirm the deletion, the record will be removed from the list.

Exercise 5: Editing and deleting records

In this exercise, you will edit a record in the Keys list and delete the record you added in the last exercise.

1. With the Keys worksheet as the active sheet, make cell A12 active.

2. From the Data menu, choose Form.

3. Move to record 3, and change the entry for Cate from 2.75 to 12.75.

4. Move to record 4, the new record you added in the last exercise.

5. Click Delete to delete the record.

   A warning dialog box appears, asking you to confirm the operation.

6. Click OK to confirm the delete operation, and close the Form dialog box.

7. Save the file as sort4.xls.

Searching for specific records

comparison criteria

One of the most useful features available in the Form dialog box is the Criteria option, which enables you to enter *comparison criteria* to use to locate a specific record within the list. This option is especially helpful if you are working with a large worksheet that contains rows and columns beyond the width of your computer screen or if you want to quickly go to a record to edit or delete it.

To use this feature, open the Form dialog box and click Criteria. All the fields are cleared, and you can enter a comparison operator (=, <, >, <=, >=, <>) followed by specific information for which to look. If you wanted to locate the records for the date August 19, 1994, for example, you would type =8/19/94 in the Date field. When the search criteria has been entered into the fields, click Find Next to locate the next record that matches the criteria. If multiple records match the search criteria, clicking Find Next will cycle you through each of the matching records until you find the exact record for which you are looking.

Exercise 6: Searching for data

In this exercise, you will search the Keys worksheet for a specific value.

1. With the Keys worksheet as the active sheet, make cell A12 the active cell.

2. From the Data menu, choose Form to access the Form dialog box.

3. Move to the top of the list—to record 1.

4. Click Criteria.

   All the fields in the list are cleared.

5. Anchor the I-beam in the Schwinn field, and type =1.75.

6. Click Find Next.

   Record 2 from the list displays, showing an exact match of the search criteria.

7. Click Find Prev.

   Record 1 from the list displays, again showing an exact match.

8. Close the Form dialog box.

Objective 3:   Using Database Functions

Database functions are a special subset of Excel's regular functions that work specifically within a database list. Database functions all begin with the letter *D*. Table 9-1 lists some commonly used database functions.

Table 9-1   **Database functions**

FUNCTION NAME	DESCRIPTION
DAVERAGE	averages values in a database
DCOUNT	counts the number of occurrences of an item in a database
DGET	extracts the value from a single cell in the database
DMAX	returns the maximum value found in a database
DMIN	returns the minimum value found in a database
DSUM	returns the sum of a set of values in a database

Each function shown in Table 9.1 requires three arguments: database, field, criteria. The database argument is the range of cells that comprises the database itself. The field argument is the column that contains the data to be used in the function. The criteria is the range of cells that contains the criteria (comparison operators). Using a criterion range enhances your capability to ask questions about your data.

Figure 9-4 shows an expanded checkbook worksheet. The range A1:F12 is the database. A criteria range has been created below the database, in cells A15:F16, the range in which comparison operators are entered to locate specific data in the database list. Cell B19 contains a formula using the DCOUNT function to count the number of entries in the Debit field that are greater than one hundred dollars. The function returns the value 4, which is the number of checks that have been written that are greater than $100.00.

FEATURE

Exporting data

After working a bit with the database features of Excel, you may decide that the kind of data analysis you want to do requires a full-featured database program. You can easily export the data from an Excel worksheet into a database program like Microsoft Access in a number of ways. You can copy the data you want to use in Access from an Excel worksheet to an Access table. You can also save the Excel worksheet as a DIF (data interchange format) file, which Access can open and interpret. To save a file using a different file format, open the File menu and choose Save As. When the dialog box appears, click the list box underneath Save File as Type and select the file type you want to save. Be sure to give the exported data a new file name so that you don't overwrite the existing Excel file.

	B19			=DCOUNT(A1:F12, D1, A15:F16)		
	A	**B**	**C**	**D**	**E**	**F**
1	Check #	Date	Description	Debit	Credit	Balance
2	5274	9/2/94	Hardware store	$ 57.63		$2,701.73
3	5275	9/2/94	Grocery store	$ 102.83		$2,598.90
4	5276	9/3/94	Veterinarian	$ 78.20		$2,520.70
5		9/5/94	Pay check		$2,751.43	$5,272.13
6	5277	9/5/94	Cash	$ 100.00		$5,172.13
7	5278	9/6/94	City Gas Co.	$ 38.00		$5,134.13
8	5279	9/6/94	Telephone Co.	$ 52.87		$5,081.26
9	5280	9/6/94	Water Co.	$ 9.87		$5,071.39
10	5281	9/6/94	Car Insurance	$ 372.68		$4,698.71
11	5282	9/7/94	Mortgage	$ 807.86		$3,890.85
12	5283	9/7/94	Car Payment	$ 412.50		$3,478.35
13						
14	Criteria Range					
15	Check #	Date	Description	Debit	Credit	Balance
16				>100.00		
17						
18	Summary:					
19	Count	4				

Figure 9-4   Using a database function to locate information in the database list

Writing a simple database function

As stated in Table 9-1, the DCOUNT function counts the number of occurrences of a certain kind of information in the database list. You use a criteria range to set the rules for data to be counted. The rules in the criteria range can be simple, like the one shown in Figure 9-4, or more complex.

Exercise 7: Using DCOUNT

In this exercise, you will set up a criteria range in the Keys worksheet and use the DCOUNT function to count the number of key charges over $1.00.

1. With the Keys worksheet as the active sheet, make cell A19 the active cell.

2. In cell A19, type the text Criteria Range and boldface the cell entry.

3. Copy the data from the range A12:D12 to the range A20:D20.

4. In cell B21, type the comparison information >1.00.

   This information tells Excel to include only data that is greater than 1.00 in the operation of the formula.

5. In cell A24, type the label Summary and boldface the entry.

6. In cell A25, type the label Cate Count, and adjust the column width if necessary.

7. In cell B25, write a formula that includes a DCOUNT function that will use the database range A12:D15, the field B12, and the criteria range A20:D21.

   The function should return the value 2 since there are two values in the field that meet the criterion.

8. Save the file as dcount1.xls.

Using multiple comparisons

You have seen how it is possible to use one comparison for a field. It is also possible, however, to enter multiple comparisons for multiple fields and multiple comparisons for the same field. To use multiple comparison operators in multiple fields, add additional criteria range. Refer back to Figure 9-4. If you wanted to narrow your search to a single date, you would type the desired date (for example, =9/6/94) in cell B16. Then the count formula would count only the number of checks written on 9/6/94 that were greater than $100. The value returned would be 1.

In addition to using multiple criteria in different fields, you can also use multiple criteria for the same field. Referring again to Figure 9-4, suppose that you wanted to know how many checks you wrote on 9/6/94 that were less than $100 but greater than $25. To do this, you would add a second debit column in the criteria range and then enter the modified criteria, as shown in Figure 9-5.

	B19	↓		=DCOUNT(A1:F12, D1, A15:G16)			
	A	B	C	D	E	F	G
1	Check #	Date	Description	Debit	Credit	Balance	
2	5274	9/2/94	Hardware store	$ 57.63		$2,701.73	
3	5275	9/2/94	Grocery store	$ 102.83		$2,598.90	
4	5276	9/3/94	Veterinarian	$ 78.20		$2,520.70	
5		9/5/94	Pay check		$2,751.43	$5,272.13	
6	5277	9/5/94	Cash	$ 100.00		$5,172.13	
7	5278	9/6/94	City Gas Co.	$ 38.00		$5,134.13	
8	5279	9/6/94	Telephone Co.	$ 52.87		$5,081.26	
9	5280	9/6/94	Water Co.	$ 9.87		$5,071.39	
10	5281	9/6/94	Car Insurance	$ 372.68		$4,698.71	
11	5282	9/7/94	Mortgage	$ 807.86		$3,890.85	
12	5283	9/7/94	Car Payment	$ 412.50		$3,478.35	
13							
14	Criteria Range						
15	Check #	Date	Description	Debit	Debit	Credit	Balance
16		=9/6/94		<100	>25		
17							
18	Summary:						
19	Count	2					

Figure 9-5 By duplicating the field name in the criteria range, you can enter multiple criteria

Exercise 8: Modifying the COUNT

In this exercise, you will edit the Keys worksheet criteria range so that you can count and total the key expenditures for Cate that are greater than 1.00 between the dates 8/1/94 and 9/1/94.

1. With the Keys worksheet as the active sheet, move the range B20:D21 to C20:E21.

2. Copy the cell A20 to cell B20.

   You now have two Date columns in the criteria range.

3. In cell A20, type the comparison criteria >=8/1/94.

4. In cell B20, type the comparison criteria <=9/1/94.

   The value generated by the DCOUNT formula remains the same since both values greater than 1.00 were within the date range criteria.

5. In cell A26, type the label Cate Sum-Aug-Sept., adjusting the column width if necessary.

6. In cell B26, enter a formula using the DSUM function that will total all key charges for Cate between August 1 and September 1, 1994 that are greater than $1.00.

   The formula returns the value 14.5.

7. Save the file as dcount2.xls.

Specifying OR Relationships

In the preceding exercises, you have specified criteria in what is known as an AND relationship. That is, the first date, the second date, and the dollar value criteria all had to be met in the Keys worksheet in order for the record to be counted and summed. As a general rule, multiple criteria placed in the same row of the criteria range are said to be in an AND relationship.

You can specify an OR relationship, in which at least one of the criteria given must be met, by placing the criteria on separate rows. OR relationships are especially useful when you want to group categories of data together. Notice in Figure 9-5 that check number 5277 was written for cash. This is equivalent to getting cash from an ATM. If, at the end of the month, you wanted to see how much money you had withdrawn from your account to have as cash (as opposed to purchasing an item or paying bills), you could enter the criteria =Cash in cell C16 and =ATM in cell C17.

Exercise 9: Using OR relationships

In this exercise, you will use the Keys worksheet to specify an OR relationship between two dates to get the maximum values from two dates.

1. With the Keys worksheet as the active sheet, clear all contents from row 21 of the worksheet.

2. In cell A21, type '=8/19/94.

3. In cell A22, type '=9/1/94.

4. In cell A27, type the label Cate Max.

5. In cell B27, type a formula using the DMAX function that will locate the maximum value using the database range A12:D15, the field range B12, and the criteria range A20:E22.

   Excel returns the value 12.75.

6. Save the file as dcount3.xls.

Chapter Summary

In this chapter, you have learned both the similarities and differences between spreadsheet applications and database applications. You have learned that Excel treats a contiguous block of cells as a database list and that you can sort, search, and edit the list using commands found in the Data menu. You have also learned how to use database functions to ask questions about your data and to locate data that meets specific criteria.

Review Questions

True/False Questions

_____ 1. In Excel, you must define a database area using the Define command before you can perform database operations.

_____ 2. In Excel, a column is a record and a row is a field.

_____ 3. Database programs are used to organize large amounts of data and generate professional reports.

_____ 4. The Form dialog box enables you to add, edit, and delete records to a database list.

_____ 5. Valid comparison operators are AND, OR, and NOT.

Multiple Choice Questions

	A	B	C	D	E	F	G	H
1	LastName	FirstName	Street Address	City	State	Zip	Phone	Birthday
2	Adams	Claire	3271 Northwest Drive	Bloomington,	IN	47402	812-555-3928	4/25/65
3	Alan	Maurice	871 Faculty Drive	Bloomington,	IN	47401	812-555-3929	8/12/47
4	Alan	Ann	236 Woodlawn	Bloomington,	IN	47402	812-555-9281	6/13/46
5	Allen	James	1000 S. Jordan	Bloomington,	IN	47403	812-555-9183	3/19/52
6	Caswell	Austen	1083 College Ave.	Bloomington,	IN	47404	812-555-3810	5/12/41
7	Percival	Pete	391 Southdowns	Bloomington,	IN	47401	812-555-9173	7/18/55
8	Rodriguez	Sarali	1298 Faculty Drive	Bloomington,	IN	47402	812-555-2918	9/12/62
9	Sheehan	Marc	1738 Longview	Bloomington,	IN	47402	812-555-0938	2/11/57
10	Stager	Sue	1937 Sparrow Lane	Bloomington,	IN	47403	812-555-3918	10/22/59
11	Thatcher	Paula	9382 Windfree Lane	Bloomington,	IN	47404	812-555-9904	11/3/60
12	Yoon	Elesia	916 Olcott Drive	Bloomington,	IN	47403	812-855-3811	5/19/62

Figure 9-6 Use this worksheet for questions 6-10

_____ 6. In the worksheet shown in Figure 9-6, what is the database range?

A. A1:H1

B. A1:H12

C. A2:H12

D. none of the above

_____ 7. The worksheet shown in Figure 9-6 is sorted on which field?

A. LastName

B. FirstName

C. Both LastName and FirstName

D. City

_____ 8. To sort the worksheet shown in Figure 9-6 so that birthdays are in chronological order starting with January, you would have to

A. sort on Birthday in descending order.

B. sort on Birthday in ascending order.

C. use the DATESTRING function to change the dates to character strings and then sort alphabetically in ascending order.

D. manually rearrange the data because you can't accomplish this task with an Excel command.

_____ 9. To count the number of people in the list shown in Figure 9-6 who were between the age of fifty and fifty-two on October 1, 1994, you would have to enter which one of the following criteria?

A. In the Birthday field of the criteria range, type >=50 in the first row and <=52 in the second row.

B. In the Birthday field of the criteria range, type >=50,<=52.

C. Make two Birthday fields in the criteria range. Type >=50 in the first field and <=52 in the second field.

D. none of the above

_____ 10. To locate the oldest person in the list shown in Figure 9-6, which one of the following functions would be most appropriate?

A. DCOUNT

B. DMIN

C. DAVERAGE

D. DMAX

Fill-in-the-Blank Questions

11. Rules that tell Excel which data to use in a calculation are called
_____.

12. When two comparison criteria are placed on separate rows in a criteria range of a database list, a(n) _____ relationship is created between the two criteria.

13. When two comparison criteria are placed on the same row in a criteria range of a database list, a(n) _____ relationship is created between the two criteria.

14. To obtain a more traditional database view of the records in a database list, use the _____ dialog box.

15. If you sort a database incorrectly, you should issue the _____ command immediately to return the database to its original state.

Acumen-Building Activities

Quick Projects

1. Sorting the savings plan

In this project, you will open the savings plan worksheet created in earlier chapters and sort it.

Open the file svplan5.xls. Select the range A3:F7 and sort it in ascending order, using Time as the primary key. Check the database list to make sure the sort yielded the appropriate results, and then save the file as svplan6.xls.

2. Sorting the Car worksheet

In this project, you will open the car worksheet that you created in earlier chapters and sort it alphabetically based on the name of the car.

Open the file car4.xls. Select the range A2:D5 and sort the database in ascending order alphabetically by car. Notice how the associated chart changes based on the changes in the worksheet. Save the file as car5.xls.

3. Using database functions to make a decision

In this project, you will use the truck9.xls worksheet created in an earlier chapter. You will create a criteria range and use several database functions to help make a decision about which truck to buy.

Open the file truck9.xls. In cell A15, type the label Criteria Range. Copy cells A4:F4 to cells A16:F16 and cell F16 to cell G16. Enter the criteria to locate all trucks that are within the price range of $25,000 to $32,000, inclusively. In cell A22, write a formula using the appropriate function to determine the number of trucks in the list that fall within the criteria range you specified. Save the file as truck10.xls.

4. Examining stock values

In this project, you will use the stock3.xls worksheet created in an earlier chapter. You will create a criteria range and write a formula to determine the average stock price on Mondays.

Open the file stock3.xls. Type the label Criteria Range in cell A16. Copy the column headings from the worksheet into the criteria range. Enter the appropriate information to calculate only records for the day Monday. In cell A22, type the label Avg. Monday Price and adjust the column width, if necessary. In cell B22, write a formula, using the appropriate function, that will compute the average price of your stock on Mondays. Save the file as stock4.xls.

In-Depth Projects

1. Organizing team information

For this project, you will work with the Teamrec worksheet to organize the data so that it is easier to read. You will also write a formula that will locate the lowest and highest score from the list of home games.

Open the file teamrec5.xls. Make the Games sheet the active sheet. Sort the worksheet using the Home/Away field as the primary key and the Opponent field as the secondary key. Create a criteria range below the data area within the worksheet. Set the comparison criteria so that only Home games are used in calculations. Below the criteria range, write a formula that will locate the highest score for your team of all home games recorded. Beneath the formula, write a formula that will locate the lowest score for your team of all home games recorded. Save the file as teamrec6.xls.

2. Organizing shelter sheets

In this project, you will sort the Shelter3 worksheet prepared in an earlier exercise and then write a formula to compute the average number of days animals that are picked up spend in the shelter.

Open the file shelter3.xls. Make the Check-In-Out sheet the active sheet. Sort the list using Gender as the primary key. Create a criteria range below the data area of the worksheet. Set the criteria so that the database function will look only at records in which the dog was checked out prior to 1/1/01. Below the criteria range, write a formula, using the appropriate function, that will compute the average number of days animals that are picked up from the shelter spend in the shelter. Save the file as shelter4.xls.

CASE STUDIES

Coffee-On-The-Go:

Creating a database

In this chapter, you learned to create a database list. Coffee-On-The-Go wants to do direct mailing to their customers, so you are going to use your skills to create a customer database.

1. Create the following database.

```
Joe Smith
Attorney-at-Law
123 Ninth St.
Eugene, Or 97401

Mary Jones
Eugene Medical Plaza
567 Second St.
Eugene, Or 97401

Albert Barry
U.S. Bank
987 Pearl St.
Eugene, Or 97401

Sue Brown
Center College
123 First St.
Eugene, Or 97403

Barb Swan
Attorney-At-Law
456 Oak St.
Eugene, Or 97401

Mary Barns
The Federal Building
876 Main St.
Eugene, Or 97403
```

```
Norman White
Investments Plus
651 Main St.
Eugene, Or 97401

George Williams
Golds Travel Agency
345 Oak St.
Eugene, Or 97401

Will Peters
Eugene Medical Plaza
567 Second St.
Eugene, Or 97401

Henry Jones
The Federal Building
876 Main St.
Eugene, Or 97401
```

2. Sort the database on last name.
3. Find the name in the database of anyone who works at the Eugene Medical Plaza.
4. Find the name in the database of anyone whose last name begins with the letter *B*.
5. Find the name in the database of anyone who works on Main St.
6. Print the database.
7. Save the file as customer.

CASE STUDIES

 **Videos West:**

Creating Databases

In this chapter, you learned to create databases. You will apply those skills by creating an inventory database and an invoice for Videos West.

1. Open a new worksheet.
2. Move to column L and create the following database.

Number	Type	Title	Rating	Price
A110	01	Golf like a Pro	PG	19.99
A111	01	Tips on Hunting	R	14.99
A200	02	Tai Chi for Health	PG	19.99
A211	03	Quit Smoking on Your Own	PG	9.99
A222	04	Buy Your Own Home	PG	14.99
A333	01	Baseball Tips	PG	19.99
A444	05	Beaded Jewelry	PG	14.99
A445	02	Jogging Tips	PG	14.99
A455	04	Take Control of Your Debt	PG	9.99
A456	03	Addiction Awareness	R	21.99
A555	03	Eating for your Health	PG	14.99
A556	05	Christmas Decorations	PG	7.99
A567	01	Skiing Your Best	PG	9.99
A666	01	Tennis Pros Talk	PG	.99
A667	05	Hobbies for Profit	PG	9.99
A777	02	Yoga for your Health	PG	14.99
A888	04	Start Your Own Business	PG	14.99

3. Sort the database by Title, and print the results.
4. Sort the database first by Type and then by Title, and print the results.
5. Sort the database by Price, and print the results.
6. Find all videos which are Type 01, and print the results.
7. Find all videos which are Type 02 and cost less than $15.00, and print the results.
8. Find all videos which are Type 04 or 05, and print the results.
9. Find all videos which are not Type 01, and print the results.
10. Sort the database so that it is in its original order, that is, sorted by Number.
11. Create an invoice. In cell A6, type Video Number. In cell A7, type Video Title. In cell A8, type Video Price.
12. In cell B6, type A110. In cells B7 and B8, write a formula using the VLOOKUP function that will locate the video title and price respectively, based on the video number in cell B6.
13. Save the file as videos.

Chapter 10

Using Macros

Key Terms

TERM	DEFINITION
Macro	a group of keystrokes and commands stored as a procedure that can be executed from a single menu selection or keystroke
Macro Sheet	a worksheet that contains the commands used in macros. In Excel, macro sheets are named Module1, Module2, and so on.
Shortcut Key	a keystroke combination used to execute a macro
Global Macros	macros that can be used with any Excel workbook
Interactive Macros	macros that ask for and accept input from users
Variable	a storage place for text or values used in macro code

As you know by now, Excel provides many features that make working with worksheets relatively quick and easy. One of those features is creating macros.

macros   *Macros*, as defined in Chapter 1, are special programs that contain a series of commands to carry out a task in Excel. Macros make repetitive tasks easy because they can be called through a menu selection or keystroke combination. Macros also make repetitive or complex tasks safer to execute by ensuring consistent use of procedures.

In order to use a macro, you must first plan the keystrokes and commands to be contained in the macro and then record those commands. You then must run the macro to see if it works and edit the macro to add functionality and correct any problems. This process is sometimes carried out several times before you get the macro to work exactly the way you want it to work.

Objective 1: Recording Macros

In Excel, macros can be created using two different methods. The first method is to record the keystrokes to be contained in the macro. You do this by turning the keyboard recorder on, making the menu selections and keystrokes necessary, and then turning the keyboard recorder off. Everything you do while the recorder is on is stored as a command in a
macro sheet   *macro sheet*, a separate worksheet used to store macro commands.

The second method for creating macros is to create a new macro sheet and write the commands directly into the macro sheet. This method requires that you know the macro language (a subset of Microsoft's Visual Basic programming language) and some fundamental programming concepts. Since both of these are beyond the scope of this book, you will be using the record method to create macros.

Planning the macro

Before you record a macro, you must first carefully plan the keystrokes to place within the macro. Although nothing is ever written in stone on the computer, you probably know from experience that it is much easier to do a little planning ahead of time than to spend time correcting mistakes after the fact. This basic principle holds true in writing macros.

If you know Excel well, you may want to just mentally think through the steps you will store in a macro. If you still have to look through several menus before finding the command you want to locate, it is probably a good idea for you to write down each command and keystroke to be used in the proper order before you record the macro.

Exercise 1: Writing the macro keystrokes

In this exercise, you will write down the exact keystrokes necessary to create a macro that will boldface, underline, and italicize the selected text and automatically reset the width of its column. You will need a pencil and paper for this exercise.

1. On a piece of paper, write the command to boldface selected cells.
2. On the next line, write the command to italicize selected cells.
3. On the third line, write the command to underline selected cells.

4. On the fourth line, write the command to Autofit the column width.

5. Save this piece of paper for subsequent exercises.

Starting the Macro Record process

Before you actually start recording the macro, there are several things that Excel requires you to do. To start the process, open the Tools menu and choose Record Macro. From the submenu that appears, choose Record New Macro. A dialog box like the one shown in Figure 10-1 will appear. The Macro Name is, by default, named Macro1. If you had already created one macro in this work session, the default macro name would be Macro2, and so on. In general, you should give a meaningful name to your macros so that you can easily tell what they do when you look at a list of macro names in a list box. The Description field offers one default option, similar to those available in the default print header and footer dialog boxes.

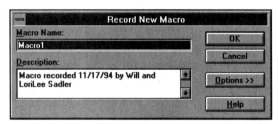

Figure 10-1 **The Record New Macro dialog box asks for a macro name and description**

An expanded Record New Macro dialog box appears when you click the Options button. In this dialog box, as shown in Figure 10-2, you can set the macro name and description, force the macro name to appear in a menu, assign a macro to a keystroke combination or *shortcut key*, define the storage place for the macro, and define the language the macro is to be written in. The last two options in this dialog box bear further discussion.

shortcut key

By default, macros are stored on a new sheet in the open workbook. This enables you to use the macro with any sheet in the workbook, but not in other workbooks. You can also choose to store macros in a new workbook. When you do this, you can use the macro with any sheet in the new workbook but, again, not with sheets outside that workbook. Finally, you can store macros in a personal macro workbook. This is a special workbook file created by Excel the first time you record a macro. The macros stored in this workbook can be used with any Excel workbook and are therefore sometimes referred to as *global macros;* they can be used globally. The personal macro workbook is a file named personal.xls and is opened each time you start Excel.

global macros

The macro language you choose to use is also an important decision. Prior to version 5.0, Excel used its own macro language. This macro language was relatively easy to use but was limited in power and capability. Power users of Excel needed more functionality, and the programmers at Microsoft decided that rather than write an entirely new programming language, they would incorporate a subset of their very popular Visual Basic programming language into Excel. This language gives you the capability of creating powerful macros that you can, if you desire, export to a stand-alone Visual Basic program. If you don't need all this functionality and if you already have macros created in the Excel 4.0 macro language, you can use that language rather than Visual Basic.

Exercise 2: Setting the macro options

In this exercise, you will set the options for the macro that you will create in Exercise 3.

1. Start Excel, if necessary.
2. With a new, blank worksheet on the screen, make cell A1 the active cell.
3. From the Tools menu, choose Record Macro.
4. From the submenu, choose Record New Macro.
5. When the dialog box shown in Figure 10-1 appears, click Options.

   The Record New Macro option dialog box appears (see Figure 10-2).

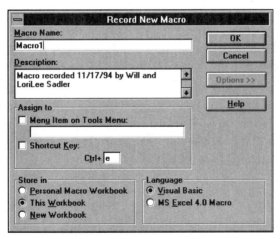

Figure 10-2 **You can use the Record New Macro options dialog box to define the name, description, menu and shortcut associations, and storage location for the new macro**

6. In the Macro Name field, delete the Macro1 default name and type Full_Format as the macro name.
7. Make sure that the macro is being stored in the current workbook (This Workbook) and that the language is Visual Basic.
8. Leave this dialog box on the screen for further use.

Recording the macro

Now that you have completed all the preparatory steps for creating the macro, you are ready to do the actual recording. Try to be as careful as possible when recording. Make sure that you choose the correct menu items and commands. If you make a mistake, keep going; you will edit the mistakes later.

Exercise 3: Recording the Format macro

In this exercise, you will enter the keystrokes to be contained in the Format macro.

1. With the Record New Macro dialog box still on the screen, click OK.
2. Type the first keystroke command you wrote out for Exercise 1.
3. Type the remaining keystroke commands you wrote for Exercise 1.
4. Click the Stop button ■.

Objective 2: Executing Macros

Now that you have written and recorded your first macro, it is time to execute it to make sure that it does what you wanted it to do. You'll be surprised at the number of times the macro doesn't work quite the way you thought it would!.

To run the macro, select the cell or range of cells on which you want the macro to act, open the Tools menu, and then choose Macro. A dialog box like the one shown in Figure 10-3 will appear. Click the macro name to select it, and then click the Run button. The macro will run, and the selected cells will be changed.

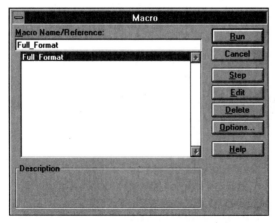

Figure 10-3 **The Macro dialog box lists all macros created**

Exercise 4: Executing the macro

In this exercise, you will run the Full_Format macro.

1. Make cell B1 the active cell.
2. Type your full name in the cell (first, middle, and last name).
3. From the Tools menu, choose Macro.
4. Select the Full_Format macro from the window, and then click Run.
5. Save the file as mac1.xls.

Objective 3: Examining and Editing Macro Code

When you store a macro in the current workbook, Excel stores the macro in a separate sheet at the end of the sheet range. You can view this sheet and make changes to it, just as you would any worksheet.

Examining the Full_Format code

You can view the underlying program code of a macro by switching to the macro sheet, named Module1, which is located after the last sheet in the workbook. Figure 10-4 shows the Full_Format macro from the Module1 sheet. Notice that the lines with apostrophes preceding the text are comment lines and are not acted upon by the macro itself. The macro commands are stored in a subroutine, abbreviated Sub so that you can have multiple macros stored in one sheet.

Comment lines ▶——

```
' Full_Format Macro
' Macro recorded 11/17/94 by Will and LoriLee Sadler
'
'
Sub Full_Format()
    Selection.Font.Bold = True
    Selection.Font.Italic = True
    Selection.Font.Underline = xlSingle
    Selection.EntireColumn.AutoFit
    Selection.Font.Bold = True
    Selection.Font.Italic = True
    Selection.Font.Underline = xlSingle
    Selection.EntireColumn.AutoFit
    With Toolbars(8)
        .Left = 484
        .Top = 26
    End With
End Sub
```

Figure 10-4 **The Visual Basic macro commands for the Full_Format macro**

Exercise 5: Examining the macro

In this exercise, you will move to the Module1 sheet and examine the macro that you created in Exercise 4.

1. Click the Last button ▶️ in the sheet tab section to move to the last sheet in the workbook.

2. Click the Module1 sheet tab to make it the active sheet.

3. Examine the sheet carefully. How does it differ from the one shown in Figure 10-4?

Editing the macro code

You can make changes to the macro by editing the macro sheet. You can add features to the macro by adding new commands, you can take features away by deleting commands, or you can alter the commands currently in the sheet so that they act in a different way.

Exercise 6: Editing the Full_Format macro

In this exercise, you will remove one of the formatting options from the Full_Format macro.

1. Make Module1 the active sheet if it isn't already.

2. Use the mouse to select the third line of the macro code (not counting the comment lines)—the line with the italic instruction.

3. Press (DELETE) to erase the line.

4. Make Sheet1 the active sheet again, with cell B3 the active cell.

5. Type your full name, as you did in cell B1.

6. Run the macro, and examine the difference between cells B1 and B3 to make sure that the changes you made to the macro took effect.

7. Save the file as mac2.xls.

Objective 4: Binding Macros to Menus, Keys, and Buttons

Excel enables you to assign or attach macro code to a menu, an alphanumeric key, or a graphical object, such as a button. When you attach a macro to a menu, Excel displays the name of the macro in the last portion of the Tools menu. If you want to execute a macro from the keyboard, you can assign a shortcut key combination such as Ctrl+b. Shortcut keys should be mnemonic so that you can easily remember them. Finally, you can add a button to your worksheet and attach a macro to the button. Assigning a macro to a graphical button is especially useful when other people, who may or may not have much computer experience, will be using your macros. You should experiment with all three methods of binding to find the one that works best for you.

Adding macros to menus

To add a macro to a menu, you must edit the macro options. You can do this by opening the Macro dialog box and clicking the Options button (refer to Figure 10-3). Figure 10-5 shows the subsequent dialog box, in which you can type a macro description, assign the macro to a menu item in the Tools menu and define the text to be displayed in the menu, and assign status bar text for the menu selection. When you have completed the dialog box, click OK to apply the changes.

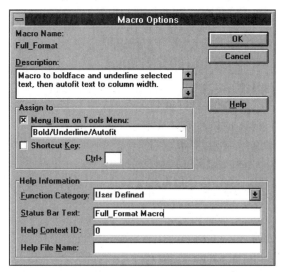

Figure 10-5   The Macro Options dialog box

Exercise 7: Adding the Full_Format macro to the Tools menu

In this exercise, you will complete the dialog box shown in Figure 10-5 to add the Full_Format macro to the Tools menu.

1. With Sheet1 as the active sheet, open the Tools menu and choose Macro.
2. Click the Full_Format macro name, and click the Options button.
3. Click in the Description field, and type the description shown in Figure 10-5.
4. Click the Assign to Menu Item on Tools Menu check box, and type the text shown in the figure.
5. Finally, type the Status Bar Text as shown in Figure 10-5, and click OK.
6. Click Close to close the Macro dialog box.
7. In Sheet1, open the Tools menu.
8. Drag the mouse pointer down to the Bold/Underline/Autofit macro name, and examine the status bar.
9. Drag the mouse pointer outside of the menu bar and release the mouse button so that no selection is made.
10. Save the file as mac3.xls.

Binding a macro to a shortcut key

In addition to adding a macro to a menu, you can also bind the macro to a key combination or shortcut key. This is especially useful to people who type fast. When you bind a macro to a shortcut key, you need to assign

Macros live on

When spreadsheet programs first became popular in the early '80s, writing macros was a tedious and difficult process, requiring many hours and lots of patience. In those days, unfortunately, writing macros was also a necessary evil; features like toolbars and power buttons did not exist. Spreadsheet users spent hours writing macros to complete operations like underlining and boldfacing text in selected cells or formatting selected cells as currency. Today those tasks are trivial since they are available, quite literally, at the click of a button. Macros are still important, however, and they have expanded the capabilities of spreadsheet programs such as Excel beyond the wildest dreams of those early spreadsheet developers and users.

only a single letter. Excel, by default, assigns the Control key (Ctrl) to be the combination key. It is a good idea to assign a letter name that is a mnemonic for the macro. If you assign an uppercase letter as the alpha key, Excel will make the shortcut key combination Ctrl+Shift+X, where X is the capital letter you assign. If you assign a lowercase letter as the alpha key, Excel uses only the Ctrl key in the shortcut key combination.

Exercise 8: Assigning a shortcut key to the Full_Format macro

In this exercise, you will assign a shortcut key to the Full_Format macro so that the macro can be run from the keyboard.

1. With Sheet1 as the active sheet, open the Tools menu and choose Macro.
2. From the Macro dialog box, click the Full_Format macro name and click Options.
3. In the Macro Options dialog box, click the check box beside Shortcut Key.
4. In the Ctrl+ box, type the letter f.
5. Click OK to apply the changes, and click Close to close the Macro dialog box.
6. In cell B5, type the name of the person sitting beside you (or someone else's name, if no one is sitting with you).
7. Click off cell B5, and then back on to reselect it.
8. Press ⌷CTRL⌷ + ⌷F⌷ to run the Full_Format macro.
9. Save the file as mac4.xls.

Attaching a macro to a button on a sheet

There may be times when you want to assign a macro to a graphical button rather than a menu or a shortcut key. This is especially true if you are developing a worksheet system with macros that others will be using.

To assign a macro to a button on a sheet, you must first display the Drawing toolbar. Access this toolbar by clicking the Draw button on the Standard toolbar. The Drawing toolbar, as shown in Figure 10-6, appears on the worksheet as a movable toolbar. Click the Create Button button on the Drawing toolbar, click in the worksheet where you want the button to be placed, and then drag the button rectangle until it is the size you desire. When you release the mouse button, the Macro dialog box will appear. Select the name of the macro you want to attach to the button, and click OK. Finally, use the selection arrow from the Drawing toolbar to select the button and change the text of the button to something meaningful.

Figure 10-6 **The Drawing toolbar contains the Create Button button**

Exercise 9: Attaching the Full_Format macro to a sheet button

In this exercise, you will create a sheet button and attach the Full_Format macro to the button.

1. With Sheet1 as the active sheet, click the Draw button 🔲 in the Standard toolbar.

    The Drawing toolbar appears.

2. Click the Create Button 🔲 to create a new button.

3. Drag the mouse pointer in row 2 across columns E, F, and G, and release the mouse button.

4. Select the Full_Format macro and click OK.

5. If it is not already selected, click the selection arrow (the arrow to the right of the Create Button button on the Drawing toolbar), and then click the new button in the worksheet to select it.

6. Anchor the I-beam inside the new button, and delete the text Button1.

7. Type the text Bold/Underline/Autofit into the new button.

8. Click outside the button to deselect it.

9. Click the select arrow again to deselect it.

10. In cell B7, type another name in the worksheet and press ⏎ ENTER.

11. Make cell B7 active again, and click the Bold/Underline/Autofit button to try it out.

12. Save the file as mac5.xls.

Objective 5: Writing Interactive Macros

interactive macros

You have seen how easy it is to create a macro that does relatively easy tasks, like formatting a cell or a group of cells. Writing more complex and usually more useful macros that have some form of interactivity in them is relatively easy, too. *Interactive macros* are macros that ask for and accept user input.

variable You can add an element of interactivity to a recorded macro (or one that you have created using Visual Basic) by editing the macro so that the user is asked for input and that input is stored in a *variable*— a holding place or container for text and numbers. The program code for accomplishing this task is shown here, with line numbers added for easier referencing.

```
(1)' PayScale Macro
(2)' Macro recorded 11/17/94 by Will and LoriLee Sadler
(3)'
(4)' Keyboard Shortcut: Ctrl+P
(5)'
(6)Sub PayScale()
(7)  Pay = InputBox( _
(8)  prompt:="Please enter the pay scale.", _
(9)  default:="5.65")
(10)  ActiveCell.FormulaR1C1 = Pay
(11)End Sub
```

Table 10-1 describes the purpose and function of each line.

Table 10-1 Explanation of macro lines

Line 1	Comment line telling what the name of the macro is
Line 2	Comment line telling when the macro was recorded and by whom
Line 3	Blank comment line
Line 4	Comment line describing the keyboard shortcut
Line 5	Blank comment line
Line 6	Beginning of the subprocedure called PayScale
Line 7	Assign the variable Pay to hold the contents of the function InputBox
Line 8	Prompt the user for input
Line 9	Enter a default input of 5.65
Line 10	Enter the contents of Pay into the current cell
Line 11	End the subprocedure

Exercise 10: Writing an interactive macro

In this exercise, you will write the macro shown above, first by recording a noninteractive version and then editing the code to add interactivity.

1. Make Sheet1 the active sheet if it isn't already, and make cell C1 the active cell.
2. From the Tools menu, choose Record Macro.
3. From the submenu, choose Record New Macro.
4. When the dialog box shown in Figure 10-1 appears, click Options.
5. In the Macro Name field, delete the Macro1 default name and type PayScale as the macro name.
6. Click the check box beside Shortcut Key and type the letter p in the field.

7. Make sure that the macro is being stored in the current workbook (This Workbook) and that the language is Visual Basic.

8. Click OK to begin recording the macro.

9. In cell C1, type 5.65.

10. Click the Stop button ■ to stop the macro recorder.

11. Make Module2 the active sheet.

12. Edit the macro so that it looks exactly like the one shown in Figure 10-7, with the exception of the record date and person.

```
' PayScale Macro
' Macro recorded 11/17/94 by Will and LoriLee Sadler
'
' Keyboard Shortcut: Ctrl+P
'
Sub PayScale()
    Pay = InputBox( _
        prompt:="Please enter the pay scale.", _
        default:="5.65")
    ActiveCell.FormulaR1C1 = Pay
End Sub
```

Figure 10-7 The Visual Basic code for the PayScale macro

13. Make Sheet2 the active sheet, and make cell B1 the active cell.

14. Run the macro from the Tools menu.

15. Type a new value of 3.75 and press (↵ ENTER).

16. Make cell B3 the active cell, and run the PayScale macro again. Accept the default value of 5.65 by pressing (↵ ENTER) when the input dialog box appears.

17. Save the file as mac6.xls.

Objective 6: Displaying Message Boxes in Macros

Another way to add interactivity to a macro is to display a message box that asks users to click on a button and then takes action on that button click. To display a message box, you must use the MsgBox function in Visual Basic. This function accepts as many as five arguments but requires only two. The three arguments that you will be concerned with are Prompt, Buttons, and Title. The Prompt argument holds the text of the message box. The Buttons argument determines the type of buttons to be displayed (Yes, No, OK, Cancel, and so on). The Title argument gives the message box a title in the top border.

The MsgBox function is generally used in conjunction with an IF statement. If one button is pressed, the macro is to do one thing. If another button is pressed, the macro is to do something different. Following is an example of the MsgBox function used in conjunction with an IF statement.

```
(1)' PayScale Macro asks user to format cell then enters
pay scale.
(2)' Macro recorded 11/17/94 by Will and LoriLee Sadler
(3)'
(4)' Keyboard Shortcut: Ctrl+p
(5)'
(6)Sub PayScale()
(7)'Declare Variables section
(8)Prompt = "Format the value as Currency?"
(9)Style = vbYesNo
(10)Title = "Format Currency"
(11)'
(12) Response = MsgBox(Prompt, Style, Title)
(13) If Response = vbYes Then
(14) Selection.NumberFormat = "$#,##0.00_);($#,##0.00)"
(15) Else
(16) Selection.NumberFormat = "General"
(17) End If
(18) Pay = InputBox( _
(19) Prompt:="Please enter the pay scale.", _
(20) default:="5.65")
(21) ActiveCell.FormulaR1C1 = Pay
(22)End Sub
```

FEATURE

Portable global macros

This chapter briefly discussed the notion of global macros—macros that are available to all workbooks. Global macros are stored in a file named personal.xls in Excel. This file starts out as a hidden file, and you must unhide the file using the Window Unhide command before you can edit anything in the file. The personal.xls file is special not only because it stores global macros but also because of the way it operates. Each time Excel is started, the personal.xls workbook is opened automatically. This means that all macros stored in this workbook immediately become available to all other open workbooks.

If you are working on a shared computer (in a computer laboratory or classroom), you can save your personal.xls workbook to a floppy disk. To use your macros, start Excel and open the personal.xls file from your disk, and then open other workbooks with which you want to work. This will make your personal.xls file portable and enable you to take your custom macros wherever you go.

Table 10-2 describes the purpose and function of each line of code shown.

Table 10-2   Explanation of macro lines

Line 1	Name of macro and description comment
Line 2	Date and creator of macro comment
Line 3	Blank comment line
Line 4	Shortcut key definition
Line 5	Blank comment line
Line 6	Beginning of PayScale subprocedure
Line 7	Comment line defining the beginning of a variable declaration list
Line 8	Define the variable Prompt to store the message
Line 9	Define the variable Style to store the button style
Line 10	Define the variable Title to store the message box title
Line 11	Blank comment line
Line 12	Define the variable Response to store the MsgBox function and arguments
Line 13	If the button pressed was the Yes button, do line 14
Line 14	Format the cell for currency with 2 decimal places
Line 15	If the button pressed was not Yes, do line 16
Line 16	Format the current cell as general
Line 17	End the IF structure
Line 18-22	The PayScale macro created in the last exercise (see table 10-1)

Exercise 11: Editing the PayScale macro to add a message box

In this exercise, you will edit the PayScale macro so that it looks exactly like the macro shown in Figure 10-8.

```
'
Sub PayScale()
'Declare Variables section
Prompt = "Format the value as Currency?"
Style = vbYesNo
Title = "Format Currency"
'
    Response = MsgBox(Prompt, Style, Title)
        If Response = vbYes Then
            Selection.NumberFormat = "$#,##0.00_);($#,##0.00)"
            Else
            Selection.NumberFormat = "General"
        End If
    Pay = InputBox( _
        Prompt:="Please enter the pay scale.", _
        default:="5.65")
    ActiveCell.FormulaR1C1 = Pay

End Sub
```

Figure 10-8   The PayScale macro with a format message box

1. Make Module2 the active sheet if it isn't already.
2. Edit the PayScale macro so that it is identical to the one shown in Figure 10-8, with the exception of the comment lines at the top.
3. Make Sheet3 the active sheet.
4. From the Tools menu, choose Macro.
5. From the Macro dialog box, select PayScale and click Run.
6. Click Yes.
7. Accept the default by pressing `⏎ ENTER`.
8. Save the file as mac7.xls, and exit Excel at this time or continue with the exercises at the end of this chapter.

Chapter Summary

In this chapter, you began to explore the power of macros and of the Visual Basic programming language. You learned that repetitive tasks can be made simpler and less prone to error by creating macros that accomplish the task. You learned how to edit macros to make them accept user input and how to create a test in a macro so that specific activities are carried out only when a criterion is true.

Review Questions

True/False Questions

_____ 1. The only way to create macros is to record them.

_____ 2. When recording a macro, every keystroke and menu selection is recorded.

_____ 3. Macros can be bound to an Alt+key combination.

_____ 4. Macros can be run only from the Tools menu.

_____ 5. Global macros are stored in the global.xls sheet.

Multiple Choice Questions

_____ 6. The Visual Basic function call to display a dialog box on the screen that accepts keystrokes from the user is

    A. UserBox().

    B. InputBox().

    C. MsgBox().

    D. AskBox().

_____ 7. The code fragment Selection.NumberFormat = "General" is a(n)

    A. statement.

    B. object.

    C. method.

    D. property.

_____ 8. The code fragment Style = vbOKCancel is a(n)

    A. variable declaration.

    B. property.

    C. object.

    D. method.

_____ 9. The Visual Basic function used to display a message box with buttons is

    A. UserBox().

    B. InputBox().

    C. MsgBox().

    D. AskBox().

_____ 10. Workbook macros are stored in

    A. macro sheets.

    B. modules.

    C. .XLM files.

    D. .XLB files.

Fill-in-the-Blank Questions

11. Macros that will work with any open workbook are called _____.

12. Macros that will work with any open workbook must be stored in _____.

13. An alternative macro language in Excel is _____.

14. Macros can be attached to a _____, which appears on worksheets.

15. Macros that ask for and accept user input are called _____ macros.

Acumen-Building Activities

Quick Projects

1. Writing a percent format macro

For this project, you will record a macro that will format the selected cells as percent, with two decimal places, and alter the width of the column to accommodate the data.

Open a new workbook in Excel. Write the necessary steps to record your macro so that you will be well organized when the recorder is turned on. Name the macro Percent, and record your macro. Stop the macro recorder when you have finished the tasks described in the introduction to this project. In cell B3, type .0689831 and press (⏎ ENTER). Reselect cell B3 and run your macro. If the macro doesn't work, make the necessary corrections and try again. Save the file as sp1.xls.

2. Setting macro options

For this project, you will set the macro options for the macro you wrote in Project 1 above.

With the file sp1.xls on the screen, access the macro options screen for the Percent macro. Select the appropriate options for the following macro settings: macro name visible in the menu; macro executed by the shortcut key (CTRL) + (SHIFT) + (P); status line reads Format cell as percentage with 2 decimal places. Save the file as sp2.xls.

3. Recording a template worksheet

For this project, you will record a macro that will fill in the column and row headings of a blank worksheet.

With the file sp2.xls on the screen, make Sheet 2 the active sheet. Record a macro called Days that will enter the days of the week (Monday, Tuesday, Wednesday, and so on) in row three starting at column B and then change the column width of all columns in the range so that the data fits in the columns. Record a macro called Times that will enter twelve hours of the day, starting with 8:00 a.m. and ending with 8:00 p.m. in one-hour intervals in column A, starting in row four. Edit the options for both macros so that they have appropriate status line text, appear in the Tools menu, and are executed by (CTRL) + (SHIFT) + (D) (for the Days macro) and (CTRL) + (SHIFT) + (T) (for the Times macro). Rename Sheet2 schedule, and save the file as sp3.xls.

4. Combining two macros

For this project, you will combine the Days and Times macro into one macro called Schedule.

With the sp3.xls workbook on the screen, move to the Module1 sheet. Edit the Days macro so that it includes the Times macro. You will have to make changes to two lines of code so that the proper range is selected for Monday and 8:00. Edit the name of the sub procedure so that the new combined macro is called Schedule. Move to Sheet3, and run the Schedule macro. If there are problems, go back to the Module1 sheet and edit the macro, debugging until the macro works properly. Save the file as sp4.xls.

In-Depth Projects

1. Adding interactivity to the sp4.xls macro

For this project, you will add a message box to the sp4 macro to ask the user if they want to enter the days of the week in English or German. If the user chooses German, Excel must print the days of the week in that language rather than English. The German translation for the days, starting with Monday, is Montag, Dienstag, Mittwoch, Donnerstag, Freitag, Samstag, and Sonntag.

Open the file sp4.xls, and make Module1 the active sheet. Add a MsgBox function and appropriate variables to form a message box with the text, Print the days in German?, the style vbYesNo, and the title Language. Add an IF statement that will act upon the user's button choice and print the days of the week in German if the button choice is yes, or English if the button choice is no. Test the macro in sheet4. Save the file as german.xls.

2. Writing an interactive sort macro

For this project, you will create a quick expense category worksheet, shown in Figure 10-9, to categorize your daily expenses. You will then record a macro that sorts the worksheet data first by category, then by date, and then by amount. You will then add a button to the worksheet that will execute the macro when clicked. Finally, you will add two additional rows of data to the worksheet and resort the data using the button you just created.

	A	B	C
1	Date	Category	Amount
2	10/11/94	Entertainment	27.5
3	10/11/94	Food	32.5
4	10/12/94	Cash	50
5	10/15/94	Hardware	48.59
6	10/15/94	Cleaning	12.8
7	10/15/94	Entertainment	6.5
8	10/15/94	Food	98.31
9	10/16/94	Church	250
10	10/17/94	Car	12.8
11	10/18/94	Cleaning	8.5
12			
13			

Figure 10-9   ***The Expense Category worksheet***

Open a new workbook, and create the expense category worksheet shown in Figure 10-9. Record a macro called ExpenseCategory that will sort the data in the worksheet according to the criteria given above. Create a button on the worksheet called Category Sort. Add two new rows of data in rows 12 and 13 of the worksheet, showing any expenses you have. Select the range of the worksheet that contains data, and click the Category Sort button to test it. The worksheet should be resorted to include the new data. Save the file as expense.xls.

CASE STUDIES

Coffee-On-The-Go: Creating Macros

In this chapter, you learned to create macros. You will use those skills to automate inputting text into a spreadsheet for Coffee-On-The-Go.

1. Create a macro called COTG that will enter Coffee-On-the-Go and the address (700 Oak Street, Eugene, OR 97401), and then format the address by changing the font and increasing the font size.
2. Save the file as COTG.

CASE STUDIES

Videos West: Creating Macros

In this chapter, you learned to create macros. You will use those skills to automate inputting text into a spreadsheet for Videos West.

1. Open the Video spreadsheet.
2. Create a macro which places the company name and address on the invoice, starting in cell A1. The address is Videos West, 1211 Second St., Fairbanks, Alaska 99791.
3. Have the macro increase the font size and place a border around the name.
4. Save the macro as vidwest.
5. Save the file as vidmac.

Chapter 11

Customizing Excel

Objectives

■ Exploring Visual Basic
■ Customizing Existing Toolbars
■ Creating Toolbars

Key Terms

TERM	DEFINITION
Applet	a slang term for a small computer application that runs inside a larger application
Pixel	the smallest unit of measurement on the computer screen. Each dot that creates an image is one pixel and is represented by one bit, which has no color if the bit is turned off and has color if the bit is turned on.
Bit-mapped Image	an image that is made up of pixels which have been turned on or off
Configuration File	a file that stores settings, including toolbar information, for a program

In Chapter 10, you learned how to create macros and you worked briefly with Visual Basic to create interactive macros. This chapter concentrates on creating applications within Excel. To do this, you must work more extensively with Visual Basic to better understand the elements of the programming language and how it can increase your capability to create powerful applications within Excel. In addition to creating macros, Excel enables you to create libraries of macros that can be used in conjunction with one another. Finally, you can create customized toolbars to work with your macro libraries so that the user of your application has an entire operating environment in which to work.

Objective 1: Exploring Visual Basic

applet

Visual Basic (VB) is a powerful and relatively easy-to-use programming language that enables you to create Windows applications. The subset of Visual Basic Excel is designed to help you create applications or *applets* within Excel. Although you were able to do some work with VB in the last chapter without knowing much about programming and the syntax of the Visual Basic programming language, you can't go much further without some fundamental programming concepts.

The syntax of the VB language is broken into five elements: functions, methods, objects, properties, and statements. By understanding the purpose and some of the commands in each of these elements, you will better grasp how to formulate and develop Visual Basic code. Table 11-1 describes these five elements in more detail.

When less is more

Many people use spreadsheet programs such as Excel to create custom applications for their own work or for others to use within their office or company. One of the features of Excel that these developers often make use of is the capability of customizing the toolbars so that the required tools are visible. Because toolbars present a lot of information and functionality in a very small space, they can be daunting to many users. Many times, only a few of the tools on the toolbars are actually used. One of the reasons people create custom applications is to simplify a complex task and to reduce the amount of spreadsheet experience the user needs in order to complete the task efficiently and effectively. Reducing the visual elements of the application, like limiting the toolbar, can be very effective in creating a streamlined, specialized application.

Table 11-1   The five Visual Basic elements

ELEMENT	USE
Functions	return a character string or value based on arguments given to the function name
Methods	perform a procedure on a specific object, such as clearing formulas from a range of cells
Objects	directly manipulate objects such as buttons, borders, charts, dialog boxes, and so on
Properties	get the attributes or properties of objects and enable them to be changed
Statements	commands that are used within a program to act on values returned by functions and that provide control structure, such as in an If...Then...Else statement

Getting Visual Basic help

Excel comes with a small Visual Basic reference manual, but you will find more complete help on-line in the Visual Basic reference. To get help with the Visual Basic programming language, you can open the Help menu, choose Contents, and choose *Programming with Visual Basic*. The Visual Basic Reference contents then appear, as shown in Figure 11-1. Use this help system just as you would the regular Excel Help system.

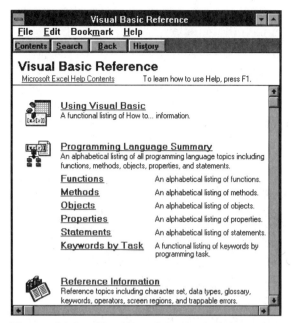

Figure 11-1   **The Visual Basic Reference manual available from the Help menu**

Exercise 1: Getting Visual Basic help

In this exercise, you will use the on-line Visual Basic Reference manual to look up several of the statements and function names used in the macros in Chapter 10.

1. Boot your computer and start Excel if necessary.
2. From the Help menu, choose Contents.
3. From the Contents list, select *Programming in Visual Basic*.

   The Visual Basic Reference shown in Figure 11-1 appears.
4. Click the word *Functions* to get an alphabetical listing of functions.

   A function list similar to the one shown in Figure 11-2 appears.

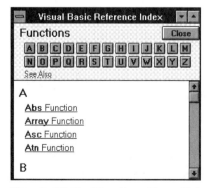

Figure 11-2   **The Functions list**

5. Click the I button to go to the section of the list with function names beginning with the letter *I*.

6. From the list of functions beginning with the letter *I*, click InputBox.

   The Help file for the InputBox function appears. Notice that the function name is given, followed by a brief definition of what the function does, and then the syntax for using the function.

7. Read through the InputBox Help. When you have finished reading, click the Example link at the top of the screen to see an actual example of the function in a piece of code.

   Because most people learn how to program primarily from seeing examples, Excel includes a program example of every element in the Visual Basic Reference.

8. When you have finished reading the example screen, click Close to close the example window.

9. Click Back to go back to the Visual Basic Reference contents list.

10. Look for the Help file on the function MsgBox. Be sure to look at the Example code as well as the Help file.

11. Close the Help file when you have finished.

Examining the PayScale macro code

Now that you know a little bit more about the elements of the Visual Basic programming language, you should reexamine the macro code written in the last chapter to be sure that you can identify each element and how the elements work together. This section describes the first half of the PayScale macro in detail.

```
Sub PayScale()
```

The Sub statement is a control statement that denotes the beginning of a procedure. The End Sub statement closes the PayScale sub procedure, marking its end. Every Sub statement must have a corresponding End Sub statement.

```
Prompt = "Format the value as currency?"
Style = vbYesNo
Title = "Format Currency"
```

The variable declaration section assigns a variable name (Prompt, Style, Title), to longer strings of text or, in the case of Style, to an actual valid button style in Visual Basic.

```
Response = MsgBox(Prompt, Style, Title)
```

The Response variable is assigned to the MsgBox function, which uses the arguments stored in the variables Prompt, Style, and Title.

```
If Response = vbYes Then
Selection.NumberFormat = "$#,##0.00_);($#,##0.00)"
```

The If statement begins a control structure which checks to see which button was pressed in the message box and then acts on the button accordingly. If the button pressed was the Yes button, then the property of the selected cell or cells is changed to the numeric format defined in the Then statement.

```
Else
Selection.NumberFormat = General
End If
```

The Else statement is part of the If control structure. If the Yes button was not the one pressed, then the property of the selected cell or cells should be set to the general numeric format. Finally, the If control structure is ended with an End If. Every If statement must have a matching End If statement.

Exercise 2: Finishing the technical description of the PayScale macro

In this exercise, you will complete the technical description of the PayScale macro begun in this section. You may do this exercise with your favorite word processing program or with pencil and paper.

1. Using the macro code shown in Figure 11-3, complete the technical description of the PayScale macro, starting with the word *Pay*. You should define each element as a function, method, object, property, or statement, and describe what it does in relationship to the rest of the program. Be sure to use the Visual Basic Reference materials that are available on line if you need help.

```
'
Sub PayScale()
'Declare Variables section
Prompt = "Format the value as Currency?"
Style = vbYesNo
Title = "Format Currency"
'
    Response = MsgBox(Prompt, Style, Title)
        If Response = vbYes Then
            Selection.NumberFormat = "$#,##0.00_);($#,##0.00)"
            Else
            Selection.NumberFormat = "General"
        End If
    Pay = InputBox( _
        Prompt:="Please enter the pay scale.", _
        default:="5.65")
    ActiveCell.FormulaR1C1 = Pay

End Sub
```

Figure 11-3   The PayScale macro

2. Give your technical description to your instructor.

Using sample macro code to write programs

As stated earlier, most people learn to program by looking at program code that has already been written. There are a couple of ways to obtain and use sample code to help you write macros in Visual Basic.

If you want to do something simple in a macro but don't know where to look to find some starter code, an easy way to get help is to record as much of the functionality as you can in a macro, using the macro recorder. This can save a lot of time when writing code, especially when you begin to set properties of items. This starter code will give you the basic outline of the macro program, leaving only the more complex functionality for you to fill in. You already used this method in Chapter 10 when you recorded a macro and then edited it to add functionality.

An alternative to recording bits and pieces of macros is to use Excel's built-in macro samples, stored in a subdirectory of the Excel directory called Examples. There are two full applets that are built from macros: one for managing a bookstore and another for working with airline sales data. A third file contains code fragment samples for a variety of tasks. The code from each of these modules can be copied and pasted into your own macro modules and then edited to meet your needs.

Exercise 3: Exploring sample code

In this exercise, you will open the sample applications, examine the under-lying code, and run the code to see how it works.

1. From the File menu, choose Open.
2. From the File Open dialog box, double-click the Examples directory.
3. Double-click the bookst.xls file name to open this application.

    The Bookstore Application opens, as shown in Figure 11-4.

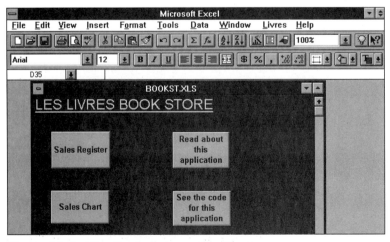

Figure 11-4   **The Bookstore application**

4. Click the Maximize button in the worksheet window so that the sheet tabs appear at the bottom of the screen.

5. Click the Sales Register button.

The MSSeller dialog box appears on the screen, as shown in Figure 11-5.

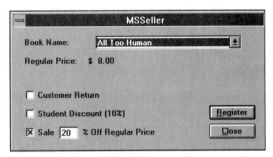

Figure 11-5   The MSSeller dialog box

6. Open the list box for Book Name, and view the list of books available for selling.

7. Click the Student Discount check box.

8. Deselect the Sale check box.

9. Click the Register button.

The MSReceipt dialog box displays, as shown in Figure 11-6. Notice that the macro does all the correct calculation based on the options checked in the preceding dialog box.

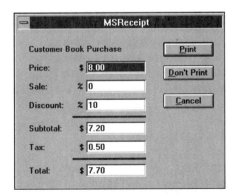

Figure 11-6   The MSReceipt dialog box

10. Click Cancel to exit the MSReceipt dialog box, and click Close to close the MSSeller dialog box and return to the Interface sheet.

11. Click the About this Application sheet and read the information stored there.

12. Click the Start and Finish Code sheet tab.

   The Visual Basic toolbar appears in the window, along with the macro code that begins and ends the application. Examine the application code carefully. Can you tell what it is doing?

13. Close the bookst.xls file without saving the changes to the file.

Objective 2: Customizing Existing Toolbars

In Excel, you can modify existing toolbars by creating and deleting toolbar buttons—buttons that are located on the toolbar rather than on the worksheet. Modifying toolbar buttons is especially useful in the following three situations:

- When you have created an application, such as the Bookstore application, and require a special functionality on the toolbar
- When you have created an application or a group of worksheets that requires only a subset of the Excel functionality
- When you have one or more global macros stored in your personal.xls macro sheet that is used with many workbooks

Adding a custom button to the toolbar

To add a custom button to the toolbar, open the View menu and choose Toolbars. The dialog box shown in Figure 11-7 will appear. Remember that this dialog box enables you to select which toolbars appear in the Excel window at any given time. You can, however, click the Customize button to create a new toolbar.

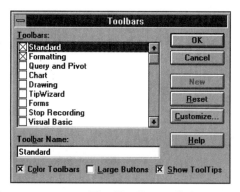

Figure 11-7 **The Toolbars dialog box**

When you click the Customize button, a new dialog box, shown in Figure 11-8, appears that has button icons organized by function. Buttons to which you can assign macros are at the bottom of the list under the Custom category.

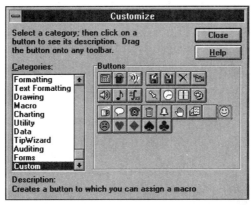

Figure 11-8 You can use the Customize dialog box to select the buttons to be placed on the custom toolbar

Select a button from the list, and drag it to the desired location on the toolbar of your choice (you can add a custom button to any toolbar, not just the Standard toolbar). Excel will ask you to identify the macro to be associated with the button. Select a macro from the list, and click OK. Click Close to close the Customize dialog box. The new button appears on the toolbar and may cause some buttons to be displayed beyond the border of the window. Scroll right to see any remaining buttons.

Exercise 4: Adding a button to the Formatting toolbar

In this exercise, you will add a button to the Formatting toolbar to represent the Full_Format macro written in the last chapter.

1. Open the file mac7.xls.
2. From the View menu, choose Toolbars.

   The Toolbars dialog box, shown in Figure 11-7, appears.
3. From the Toolbars dialog box, choose Customize.

   The Customize dialog box, shown in Figure 11-8, appears.
4. In the Categories column, select the Custom category.
5. Select the fish icon ![fish icon], the third one from the left on the top row, and then drag the icon so that it rests on the right side of the Underline button in the Formatting toolbar.

   The alignment buttons move to the right to make room for the new icon, and the Assign Macro dialog box appears.
6. From the Assign Macro dialog box, select the Full_Format macro and click OK.
7. Click Close to close the Customize dialog box.
8. Move the mouse pointer over the Fish icon.

   The status line should read *Full_Format Macro*, but the ToolTip should be labeled *Custom*.

9. In cell D5, type a few characters of text. Click off the cell to deselect it, and then back on to reselect it.

10. Click the fish button 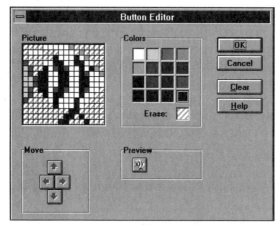 to format the cell.

The contents of the cell are formatted as boldfaced, underlined, and the column width is adjusted, if necessary.

Changing the button image

If you thought your choice of button images was pretty limited in the Customize dialog box, you're not alone. Excel comes with only a few pre-defined custom buttons because you can make your own button image. In Excel, you can personalize your work environment and create button images that truly represent the process they will execute (that is, if you are a good artist!).

pixel; bit-mapped image
You can create custom button images using Excel's Button Editor. This editor enables you to turn specific *pixels* or bits on the screen on and off, to form an image. Figure 11-9 shows the *bit-mapped image* (the image bit-by-bit or pixel-by-pixel) of the fish button you added to the Formatting toolbar in the preceding exercise. To change the image, pick a new color from the Colors palette and click in the pixel you want to change. The Preview area shows each change as it will appear in the button. Use the Move arrows to move the entire image up, down, left, or right in the button area. To clear the entire image and start over, click Clear.

Figure 11-9   You can use the Button Editor utility to change the image of predefined buttons or to create a new image for a custom button

Exercise 5: Creating a new image for the Full_Format button

In this exercise, you will create a new image for the Full_Format button using the Button Editor.

1. With the mac7.xls workbook on the screen, position the mouse pointer on the fish button [fish icon].

2. Press the right mouse button to access the shortcut menu.

   The Toolbar shortcut menu is displayed, as shown in Figure 11-10.

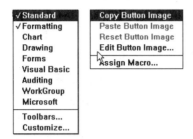

Figure 11-10 You can access the Toolbar shortcut menu and the Button shortcut menu by pressing the right mouse button while pointing to the toolbar

3. From the Toolbar shortcut menu, choose Customize.

   The Customize dialog box appears.

4. Move the mouse pointer back up to the fish icon [fish icon], and press the right mouse button again to access the Button shortcut menu.

   The Button shortcut menu, as shown in Figure 11-10, appears.

5. From the Button shortcut menu, choose Edit Button Image.

   The Button Editor, as shown in Figure 11-9, appears.

6. Click Clear to clear the contents of the button.

   The fish disappears, and the edit box is filled with erase marks.

7. Create a custom button image of your choosing for the Full_Format macro. You may want to draw a sketch of your image on paper first.

8. When you have finished creating the image and are satisfied with the preview of the button image, click OK.

   The Button Editor closes.

9. Click Close to close the Customize dialog box.

   Your new button image appears in place of the fish button.

10. Try it out to make sure that it still works.

Deleting buttons from existing toolbars

There may be times when you want to delete buttons from existing toolbars to make the Excel work environment exactly fit the needs of the application you have written or the work that an employee is to be doing. Deleting unnecessary buttons from the toolbars reduces the possibility of selecting a wrong button.

To delete a button, access the Customize dialog box, and then drag the button you want to delete off the toolbar. The button will be deleted, and the remaining buttons will moved left on the toolbar.

Exercise 6: Deleting buttons from the toolbars

In this exercise, you will delete several buttons from the Standard and Formatting toolbars.

1. Place the mouse pointer on a toolbar.
2. Press the right mouse button to access the Toolbar shortcut menu.

   The Toolbar shortcut menu, as shown in Figure 11-10, appears.
3. Choose Customize from the menu.

   The Customize dialog box appears.
4. Place the mouse pointer on the Format Painter button ⊘ in the Standard toolbar (the 10th button from the left), and drag the button off the toolbar.

   The button disappears, and the remaining buttons in the Standard toolbar move left.
5. Move the mouse pointer to the Borders button ▦ on the Formatting toolbar, and drag it down off the toolbar to remove it.

   The button disappears, and the remaining buttons move left.
6. Close the Customize dialog box.

FEATURE

Creating an interface screen
In this chapter, you examined the bookst.xls application. One of the things you may have noticed about this application is that the opening screen on the Interface sheet didn't look like a worksheet at all. If you clicked around the large buttons, however, you probably noticed that there were cells beneath the large colored background. You can make this kind of interface screen easily by coloring in a block of cells using the Format Cells command. This command brings up the Format Cells dialog box. When you format the pattern of the selected cells with a different color, the gridlines are blocked out and you can simulate a solid screen. When you paste buttons onto the screen, make them larger than the Excel default to give your custom screen a definitely non-worksheet look.

Managing customized toolbars

Now that you know how to add and remove buttons, you need to know how to keep track of these customized versions of the toolbars. The developers at Microsoft realize that you may not always want to use a customized set of toolbars—that you may want to use the standard toolbars that are shipped with Excel. For this reason, they have separated the toolbar information into a separate Excel file called excel5.xlb. Each time you exit the program, this file is updated with any changes you have made to the toolbars. You can rename this file to something meaningful, such as format.xlb, so that you **configuration** know that this is the *configuration file* to use when you want the Full_Format **file** button on the Formatting toolbar. After you have renamed the excel5.xlb file, you should start the Excel program again and reset the toolbars so that the excel5.xlb file will hold the settings for the standard Excel toolbars.

Exercise 7: Saving and resetting the excel5.xlb file

In this exercise, you will exit the Excel program and rename the excel5.xls file to a more meaningful file name. Then you will restart Excel and return the toolbar settings to their default configuration.

1. Make sure that you have saved any worksheets you have developed while working through these exercises.

2. Exit the Excel program.

3. From the Program Manager window, double-click the Main program-

   group icon Main .

4. From the Main program group window, double-click the File Manager

   program-item icon File Manager .

5. Scroll through the directories listed in the left column until you find the Windows directory (ask your instructor for exact details on this directory's name).

6. In the right half of the window, locate the excel5.xlb file and click the file name.

7. From the File menu, choose Copy.

   A Copy dialog box, similar to the one shown in Figure 11-11, appears.

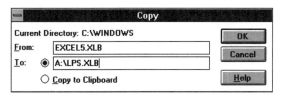

Figure 11-11   The Copy dialog box

8. In the To field of the Copy dialog box, type A:\, followed by your three initials and the file extension .xlb.

9. Click OK to complete the Copy operation.

10. Start Excel again, and access the Toolbar shortcut menu by pointing to one of the toolbars and clicking the right mouse button.

11. Choose Toolbars from the menu.

12. In the Toolbars dialog box, click the Reset button.

The Standard toolbar changes back to its default settings, with the Format Painter button back in place. The Formatting toolbar again displays the Borders button but no longer displays your Full_Format macro button.

13. Exit Excel again so that the default settings are saved in the excel5.xlb file.

TIP To use your customized.XLB file, start Excel and then open the.XLB file that contains your settings. Remember that these settings will automatically be saved to the excel5.xlb file when you exit Excel, so be sure to reset the toolbars before you exit the program.

Objective 3: Creating Toolbars

In addition to modifying existing toolbars by adding and deleting buttons, you can also create new toolbars for your customized applications and set those toolbars to open automatically when an associated workbook file is opened.

Creating a new toolbar

To create a new toolbar, you must access the Toolbars dialog box, type a new toolbar name, and then click the New button. Excel will then ask you to fill in the toolbar with buttons from the button categories in the Customize dialog box. You can select any of the standard buttons and use buttons that you have created.

Exercise 8: Creating the PayScale toolbar

In this exercise, you will create a custom toolbar for hourly employees to use when they work with payroll information.

1. Start Excel, if necessary, and open the mac7.xls file.

2. Please the mouse pointer on a toolbar, and click the right mouse button to access the Toolbar shortcut menu.

The Toolbar shortcut menu appears, as shown in Figure 11-10.

3. From the menu, choose Toolbars.

The Toolbars dialog box appears.

4. In the Toolbar Name field, delete the toolbar name shown and type PayScale.

5. Click New.

   The Customize dialog box appears. To the left of the dialog box, a small window also appears (probably with the letter *P* showing in the window title area). This is the basic outline of your toolbar.

6. From the File category of the Customize dialog box, drag the File Open icon ![File Open icon] into the new PayScale toolbar.

   The toolbar expands, and the File Open button appears.

7. Drag the File Save ![File Save icon], File Print ![File Print icon], and File Print Preview ![File Print Preview icon] icons onto the PayScale toolbar.

8. From the Edit category of the Customize dialog box, drag the Undo ![Undo icon] and Repeat (Redo) ![Redo icon] buttons onto the PayScale toolbar.

9. From the Custom category of the Customize dialog box, drag the smiley face button ![smiley face icon] onto the PayScale toolbar.

   The Assign Macro dialog box appears, asking which macro to attach to the button.

10. Select the PayScale macro, and click OK.

11. From the Utility category of the Customize dialog box, drag the Help button ![Help icon] onto the PayScale toolbar.

12. Click Close to close the Customize dialog box.

    Your PayScale toolbar should now look like the one shown in Figure 11-12.

Figure 11-12 **The completed PayScale toolbar**

Attaching a custom toolbar to a workbook

Now that you have created a specialized toolbar for working with payroll data, it is a good idea to attach the toolbar to the payroll data workbook. By attaching the toolbar to the workbook, the toolbar will be displayed automatically each time the workbook is opened.

To attach a toolbar to a workbook, you must first go to a module sheet within the workbook. If you don't have a module sheet (because you have not created any macros), use the Insert Macro Module command to create one. From the module sheet, open the Tools menu and choose Attach Toolbars. Excel will display a dialog box like the one shown in Figure 11-13. Use this dialog box to copy all desired custom toolbars into the workbook workspace. Then save the workbook file and exit Excel. The next time you start Excel and open the workbook, the custom toolbar will open automatically.

Exercise 9: Attaching the PayScale toolbar to the mac7 workbook

In this exercise, you will attach the PayScale toolbar to the mac7 workbook and save the file as mac8.xls.

1. With the mac7.xls workbook on the screen, make Module2 the active sheet.
2. From the Tools menu, choose Attach Toolbars.

   The dialog box like the one shown in Figure 11-13 appears.
3. Select the PayScale toolbar from the Custom Toolbars window, and click Copy to copy it into the Toolbars in Workbook window.
4. Click OK to close the dialog box.
5. Save the workbook file as mac8.xls, and exit Excel.
6. Restart Excel and open the mac8.xls workbook file.

   The PayScale toolbar appears in the work area.
7. Close the worksheet, and exit Excel or continue with the projects at the end of this chapter.

Chapter Summary

In this chapter, you explored the Visual Basic programming language in greater detail than in the preceding chapter. You learned the five basic components of the Visual Basic language, how to get help on each of those components, and two strategies for writing macros in Visual Basic. The remainder of the chapter was devoted to customizing the Excel environment by creating custom buttons to be placed on toolbars and custom toolbars. You learned how to manage these custom settings by copying the excel5.xlb file and how to attach a custom toolbar to a workbook.

Review Questions

True/False Questions

_____ 1. The If...Then...Else... control structure in Visual Basic is a function.

_____ 2. Most of the reference materials for Visual Basic can be found under the Help menu in Excel.

_____ 3. A good way to develop Visual Basic code is to look at code examples from other applications.

_____ 4. Excel does not allow you to add a custom button to an existing toolbar.

_____ 5. In Excel, you can attach a custom toolbar to a worksheet.

Multiple Choice Questions

_____ 6. A function in Excel works similarly to what in Visual Basic?
   A. function
   B. property
   C. object
   D. statement

_____ 7. To clear formulas from a range of cells in Visual Basic, you use a
   A. function.
   B. method.
   C. statement.
   D. none of the above

_____ 8. To alter or create a new image for a button, you must use the
   A. Image Editor.
   B. drawing tools.
   C. Pattern dialog box.
   D. Button Editor.

_____ 9. When altering the image on a button, you actually turn what off and on?
   A. pixels
   B. picas
   C. dots
   D. bytes

_____ 10. A specialized application that is written to work inside a more general application is referred to as a(n)
   A. custom application.
   B. single-use application.
   C. applet.
   D. single-purpose application.

Fill-in-the-Blank Questions

11. An image that has been created by turning pixels on and off is called a
_____.

12. By pointing to a toolbar and clicking the right mouse button, you can
access the _____.

13. Toolbar information is saved in a file called _____.

14. To restore toolbars to their default settings, click the _____
button on the Toolbars dialog box.

15. When you create a new toolbar, the toolbar appears in the
_____ area of the screen.

Acumen-Building Activities

Quick Projects

1. Creating an essentials toolbar

In this project, you will create a customized toolbar that has only the
essential toolbar elements for creating a worksheet, doing a Print Preview,
saving the worksheet, and printing the worksheet.

Open a new workbook in Excel. Delete all buttons from the Standard toolbar except those mentioned above. Exit Excel and rename the excel5.xlb
file to ch11-1.xlb. Start Excel and reset the toolbars.

2. Replacing Standard toolbar buttons

In this project, you will replace the Sort Ascending and Sort Descending
buttons on the Standard toolbar with buttons to delete a column and
delete a row.

Open a new workbook in Excel. Delete the Sort Ascending and Sort
Descending buttons from the Standard toolbar. Access the Customize dialog box for toolbars and select the Edit category. Copy the buttons for
Delete Row and Delete Column into the space made available when you
deleted the two sort buttons. Exit Excel and copy the excel5.xlb file to the
file ch11-2.xlb. Start Excel and reset the toolbars.

 TIP   Click on a button in the Customize dialog box to see a description of the button.

3. Creating a custom formula bar

In this project, you will create a custom formula bar that displays common formula operators.

Open a new workbook and create a new, custom toolbar called Formula Writer. Place the following formula icons in the toolbar: equals sign; addition; subtraction; multiplication; division; left parenthesis; right parenthesis. Save the file as ch11-3.xls, and close the workbook.

4. Attaching the Formula Writer toolbar to a worksheet

In this project, you will attach the Formula Writer toolbar created in Quick Project 3 to a worksheet.

Open a new workbook. Set the toolbar settings so that the Formula Writer toolbar is displayed. Insert a macro module, and attach the Formula Writer toolbar to the workbook. Save the file as ch11-4.xls.

In-Depth Projects

1. Creating navigation macros

In this project, you will copy sample macro code that comes with Excel and edit that code so that it provides fast worksheet navigation.

In Excel, open the file samples.xls from the Excel\Examples subdirectory. From the contents listing, select Moving and Selecting from the Visual Basic Procedures column. In the Moving and Selecting module sheet, locate the macro code that begins with Sub VB_Variable_Move(). Select all the code for this macro and click the Copy button ▣.

Open a new workbook, insert a macro module, and click Paste ▣. Make Sheet1 the active sheet, and type column headings in row 3 as follows: Column A, Name; column B, Title; column C, Office Address; column D, Phone; column E, Fax. You have data to complete only the name and phone entries at this time. You will edit the macro that you copied from the samples.xls file so that a single keystroke will move the cell pointer over several columns after you have typed a name and back to column A after you have typed the phone number.

Make the Module1 sheet the active sheet. Select the macro code, and make a duplicate copy in the Module1 sheet so that there are two copies of the same macro. Edit the first copy so that the macro name is Right2. Edit the name of the second macro so that it is Left3. The first macro will move the cell pointer right two columns (from the Name column to the Phone column). The second macro will move the cell pointer left three columns (from the Phone column to the Name column on a new row).

Edit the Right2 macro so that it moves zero rows and two columns. Be sure to edit the description so that it reflects these changes. Edit the Left3 macro so that it moves left three columns (you will use a negative 3 (−3) to move left), and edit the description so that it is accurate.

Change the options on the Right2 macro so that it can be executed with the shortcut key CTRL + R . Change the options on the Left3 macro so that it can be executed with the shortcut key CTRL + L .

In Sheet1, type a name in column A, press TAB and press CTRL + R . The cell pointer should move to column D. Type a phone number, press ↵ ENTER , and then press CTRL + L . The cell pointer should move to column A. Save the file as navigate.xls.

2. Making buttons easier to create

In this project, you will place the Create Button button on the Formatting toolbar in place of the Borders button.

Open a new workbook and access the Customize dialog box. Delete the Borders button from the Formatting toolbar. In the dialog box, select the Utility category and locate the Create Button icon. Copy this icon into the Formatting toolbar in the position where the Borders icon used to be. Exit Excel. Copy the excel5.xlb file to a new file called button.xlb. Start Excel and reset the toolbars. Exit Excel.

CASE STUDIES

 **Coffee-On-The-Go:**

Creating a Macro Library

In this chapter, you learned to customize your worksheet. One of the most effective ways to customize and automate a worksheet is to create macros that are saved together in a single workbook or library. You will create another useful macro for Coffee-On-The-Go.

1. Open the file cotg.xls.
2. Because many budgets and other worksheets need the months of the year across a range of cells, create a macro named Months which creates columns for the months in a worksheet.
3. Save the file as cotg2.xls.

CASE STUDIES

Videos West: **Creating a Macro Library**

In this chapter, you learned to customize your worksheet. An effective way to customize and automate a worksheet is to create macros that you can save together in a single workbook or library. You will create several useful macros for Videos West.

1. Open a new worksheet.
2. Create the five macros named and described below:

MACRO NAME	DESCRIPTION
Dollar	formats for currency with 0 decimal places
Comma	formats for comma with 0 decimal places
Center	aligns text in center of cell
Save	saves a previously saved workbook with the same name
Print	prints the worksheet

3. Save the file as macros.

Chapter 12

Using Advanced Features

Key Terms

TERM	DEFINITION
What-if Problems	problems that are generally formed by questions such as "What happens if I do *x* instead of *y*?"
Data Tables	tables that demonstrate the outcome of a problem when different variables are used in computing the solution
One-input Tables	data tables for which one item has a set of variables to be computed
Two-input Tables	data tables in which two items have a unique set of variables which must be computed
Scenario	a set of input values saved with a name for easy viewing and management
Changing Cells	the cells affected or changed by input values in a scenario
PivotTables	an analysis mechanism whereby complex data in worksheets is summarized in dynamic tables, called crosstabs in Excel 4.0

The goal of this text is to help you become a competent user of Excel for beginning and intermediate tasks and to help you understand the possibilities in using the advanced features of the program. This final chapter briefly covers two specialized tasks that you may find critical to your work some **what-if problems** day: solving *what-if problems* and summarizing complex worksheet data.

Objective 1: Solving What-If Problems

As human beings, we solve what-if problems every day of our lives. Will I have enough time to go to the grocery store before the movie starts? Do I have enough money left over this month to splurge on a new suit? Should I pay the full balance on my credit card or spread it out over another few months? All these questions are categorized as what-if problems because they rely on the person asking the question to evaluate several pieces of information before making the decision.

Excel provides several tools for solving what-if problems that make looking at all the options quick and easy to do. The easiest tool to use is Goal Seek.

Using Goal Seek

Goal seeking (sometimes called backsolving or backward chaining) is the process of starting with a desired outcome and working backwards until you find all the inputs that make the outcome possible. If you have a goal of saving $250.00 each month, for example, you can start with that answer and work your way backward through a problem with the Goal Seek to determine how much money you should pay on variable-pay bills such as credit cards.

Exercise 1: Using Goal Seek to determine credit card payments

In this exercise, you will create a quick worksheet that displays your monthly income, fixed and variable expense summaries, and the amount of money left over. You will then use the Goal Seek feature to determine how to reach your goal by manipulating the variable expenses amount.

1. Start Excel and open a new workbook, if necessary.
2. Type the worksheet shown in Figure 12-1. Use the SUM function to total the minimum and maximum payments in the variable expenses section and a simple subtraction formula to compute the After Expenses total (monthly income minus expenses).

	A	B	C	D	E	F
	D15					
1						
2						
3	Monthly Income	$2,850.00		Variable Expenses	Min	Max
4	Fixed Expenses	$1,837.00		Master Card	$ 32.00	$1,287.37
5	Variable Expenses	$ 131.00		Diner's Club	$ 28.00	$ 238.31
6	After Expenses	$ 882.00		Optima	$ 71.00	$3,298.12
7				Subtotal	$131.00	$4,823.80
8						

Figure 12-1   The Payoff worksheet

3. Make cell B6 the active cell.

4. From the Tools menu, choose Goal Seek.

   The dialog box shown in Figure 12-2 appears.

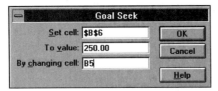

Figure 12-2 **The Goal Seek dialog box**

5. In the To Value field, type 250.00, since the goal is to have $250.00 left for savings.

6. In the By Changing Cell field, type B5, since this is the field you want to change.

7. Click OK.

   Excel presents you with the suggested solution, as shown in Figure 12-3, and asks you to confirm the answer by clicking OK. If you do this, Excel will replace the original data in cell B5 with the solution from the Goal Seek process.

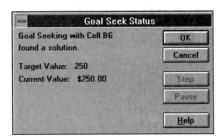

Figure 12-3 **The solution to the Goal Seek problem**

8. Click OK to accept the solution.

   Excel replaces the original value in cell B5 with the new value. You now know that you have $763.00 to divide between your credit card payments.

9. Save the file as payoff.xls.

Using data tables

As you have seen, the Goal Seek feature provides a quick way of determining the inputs required to reach a desired output. One of the limitations of Goal Seek is that it can adjust only one variable at a time. If you had multiple variable expenses in different categories, Goal Seek would not be much help in **data tables** solving your problem. When this is the case, you may use *data tables*.

Data tables are Excel worksheets containing input values in a row or column that can be used to solve what-if problems. Excel has two kinds of data tables: *one-input tables* and *two-input tables*. You can use a one-input table to see how changes in one variable affect one or more formulas in your worksheet. You can use a two-input table to see how changes in two variables affect one or more formulas in your worksheet.

one-input tables
two-input tables

C11		=PMT(C6/12, C7, -C8)	
	A	**B**	**C**	**D**
1				
2				
3		Car Loan Analysis		
4				
5		Downpayment	$ -	
6		Interest Rate	0.075	
7		Time (months)	60	
8		Loan Amount	$ 42,000.00	
9				
10			Payments	
11			$ 841.59	
12		0.04		
13		0.05		
14		0.062		
15		0.075		

Figure 12-4   The skeleton of a one-input data table

Figure 12-4 shows the initial setup of a one-input table. Cell C11 contains a formula which computes the payment (using the PMT function) of the information in the loan analysis. Cells B12 through B15 contain the input values for the interest rate. When you issue the Table command from the Data menu, Excel fills in the range C12 to C15 with the monthly car payment amount based on the interest rates stored in the input cells, as shown in Figure 12-5.

C15		{=TABLE(,C6)}	
	A	**B**	**C**	**D**
1				
2				
3		Car Loan Analysis		
4				
5		Downpayment	$ -	
6		Interest Rate	0.075	
7		Time (months)	60	
8		Loan Amount	$ 42,000.00	
9				
10			Payments	
11			$ 841.59	
12		0.04	$ 773.49	
13		0.05	$ 792.59	
14		0.062	$ 815.89	
15		0.075	$ 841.59	

Figure 12-5   The completed one-input loan analysis worksheet

Trust your judgment

Although Excel provides excellent problem-solving tools, you should never completely trust the solution of any problem-solving tool (no matter how advanced). Good decision-makers use a variety of tools to resolve complex problems. There are no tools to help you factor in common sense and everyday knowledge about your world, and sometimes these elements of a problem are far more important than the "factual" elements that a problem-solving tool can handle. So, if Excel tells you one thing and your gut tells you something else, weigh the two solutions against one another before making a decision. Contrary to popular belief, the computer is *not* always right!

Exercise 2: Creating a one-input table

In this exercise, you will create a one-input table using the data shown in Figure 12-4.

1. Save and close any open workbooks you have on the screen, and open a new workbook.

2. Enter the data shown in Figure 12-4. Be sure to use the PMT function in a formula to compute monthly payments in cell C11.

3. Format cells C5 and C8 and cells C11 through C15 as currency with two decimal places, and adjust the column width to accommodate this data.

4. Select the range B11:C15.

5. From the Data menu, choose Table.

   A dialog box like the one shown in Figure 12-6 appears.

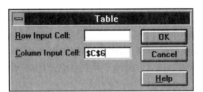

Figure 12-6   The Table dialog box asks for row and column input cell addresses

6. Type the absolute cell reference $C$6 in the Column Input Cell field, and click OK.

   The dialog box closes, and Excel computes the payment amount based on each interest rate in the input range, as shown in Figure 12-5.

7. Save the file as loan.xls.

Using two-input tables

Often it is necessary to analyze data using two variables rather than just one. To do this, you can use a two-input table. In a two-input table, the second set of variables are displayed horizontally in a row above the vertical values for the one-input table. When the Table command is issued, both variables are computed and a matrix is formed by filling in the area between the column inputs and the row inputs, as shown in Figure 12-7.

C11		=PMT(C6/12, C7, -C8)				
A	B	C	D	E	F	G

1						
2						
3	Car Loan Analysis					
4						
5	Downpayment	$ -				
6	Interest Rate	0.075				
7	Time (months)	60				
8	Loan Amount	$ 42,000.00				
9						
10		Payments				
11		$841.59	24	36	48	60
12		0.04	$1,823.85	$1,240.01	$ 948.32	$773.49
13		0.05	$1,842.60	$1,258.78	$ 967.23	$792.59
14		0.062	$1,865.25	$1,281.53	$ 990.23	$815.89
15		0.075	$1,889.98	$1,306.46	$1,015.51	$841.59

Raw inputs ▶ (row 9)

Column inputs ▶ (row 13)

Figure 12-7   The results of a two-input table

Exercise 3: Creating a two-input table

In this exercise, you will edit the loan.xls workbook to create a two-input table.

1. With the loan.xls workbook on the screen in the active window, select the range C12:C15.
2. From the Edit menu, choose Clear All to clear the contents of this range.
3. Move the interest rate percentages from B12:B15 to C12:C15.
4. Enter the loan months shown in the range D11:G11 in Figure 12-7.
5. Select the range C11:G15.
6. From the Data menu, choose Table.

   A dialog box like the one shown in Figure 12-6 appears.

7. In the Row Input Cell field, type $C$7.
8. In the Column Input Cell field, type $C$6.
9. Click OK.

   The table routine runs, and Excel fills in the matrix for payments based on the two variables—interest rate and time.

10. Save the file as loan2.xls.

Using scenarios to manage problem-solving

scenario   In Excel, you can create multiple input ranges, called *scenarios*, to examine and solve problems. Think about the car loan analysis for a minute. It would have been nice to be able to define a best-case scenario (lowest interest rate and a monthly payment that was affordable), a realistic-case scenario (higher interest rate, longer loan term, and lower monthly payments), and a worst-case scenario (high interest rate, five-year loan term, and relatively low monthly payments). In the best-case scenario, you pay the least interest, thereby reducing your loss. In the worst-case scenario, you pay the most interest and increase your loss.

By developing scenarios and using Excel's Scenario Manager to manage the various scenarios for a problem, you can easily project multiple outcomes of a problem based on a set of input data.

changing cells

To develop a scenario, you must first set up the worksheet structure so that the *changing cells*, cells that will change based on the different scenarios, are present in the worksheet. The changing cells represent the location of the result based on whatever scenario is in force at a given time. After the basic worksheet structure is created, you must enter values to be plugged into the changing cells for the various scenarios. It is a good idea to name the ranges containing the values for each scenario. If you have a range of values that represent a set of assumptions based on low sales data, for example, you might want to name the range *Low Sales* for easy recognition.

After you have created the input values for the scenarios, you must create the scenario using the Scenario Manager. To do this, open the Tools menu and choose Scenarios. The Scenario Manager dialog box will appear, and you will be asked to enter the range of cells that are the changing cells, a name for the scenario, and comments or a description of the scenario. You will then be asked to define the data that will be placed into the changing cells. This is the input data.

When you have created all your scenarios, you can display each scenario by using the Scenario Manager dialog box to select a scenario. The data in your worksheet will change based on the results of the scenario.

Exercise 4: Creating funding scenarios

In this exercise, you will create three funding scenarios for a public radio station fund drive, based on previous years' funding data, as shown in Figure 12-8.

FEATURE

Got a problem? Let the Solver help!
One of the what-if problem-solving tools not discussed in this chapter is Excel's Solver. The Solver solves complex problems with multiple variables as inputs and multiple formulas in the worksheet or changing cells range. The Solver can work with existing database lists and scenarios to evaluate and solve problems with three or more variable components. If you have complex problems that require this kind of power, consult Excel's on-line Help for information and step-by-step instructions for using the Solver.

	A	B	C	D
1			Fund Drive '95	
2				
3	Last Year's Goal:	$ 160,000.00	Last Year's Actual:	$ 161,281.00
4	This Year's Goal:	$ 175,000.00	This Year's Actual:	$ -
5				
6	94 Information:		95 Information	
7	Number of Pledges	2617	Number of Pledges	
8	Avg. Amt of Pledge	$ 61.63	Avg. Amt of Pledge	
9	Avg. Difference 93-94	6.00%	Avg. Difference 94-95	
10				
11				
12		Input Values for Worst Case	Input Values for Realistic Case	Input Values for Best Case
13	Number of Pledges	2538	2696	2748
14	Avg. Amt of Pledge	$ 59.78	$63.48	$64.71
15	Avg. Difference 93-94	-3.00%	3.00%	5.00%
16				

Figure 12-8   The Fund Drive worksheet with scenario inputs

1. Save and close any open workbooks.
2. Enter the data shown in Figure 12-8. Be sure to adjust column widths so that all data fits in the columns and to format the data in the columns appropriately.
3. Enter a formula in cell D4 that multiplies the number of pledges for 1995 by the average pledge amount for 1995.
4. Name the range B13:B15 WorstCase.
5. Name the range C13:C15 RealCase.
6. Name the range D13:D15 BestCase.
7. From the Tools menu, choose Scenarios.

    The Scenario Manager dialog box appears.
8. Click Add to add a new scenario.

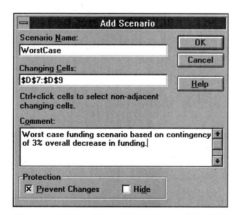

Figure 12-9   The Add Scenario dialog box

9. Fill in the Add Scenario dialog box as shown in Figure 12-9, and click OK.

    A Scenario Values dialog box appears.

10. In the Scenario Values dialog box, type =B13 in the top field, B14 in the middle field, and B15 in the bottom field. These cells contain the values that will be used to fill in the changing cells in the worst-case scenario.

11. Click OK.

    The WorstCase scenario appears in the Scenario Manager dialog box.

12. In the Scenario Manager dialog box, click Add again.

13. In the Add Scenario dialog box, type the Scenario Name RealCase, the Changing Cells $D$7:$D$9, and the Comment Realistic case scenario of 3% increase over previous year based on last six years of fund drive., and then click OK.

14. In the Scenario Values dialog box, enter the correct input values for the RealCase scenario and click OK.

    The RealCase scenario name now appears in the Scenario Manager dialog box.

15. Add a third scenario, named BestCase, using the same changing cells range and the comment Best-case scenario based on NPR projections for 95 fiscal year. Enter the appropriate values in the Scenario Values dialog box, and click OK.

16. From the Scenario Manager dialog box, click the WorstCase scenario and click Show. Move the Scenario Manger dialog box so that you can see the data in the worksheet.

    The data has changed to reflect the worst-case scenario.

17. Show the best-case scenario and the real-case scenario.

18. Close the Scenario Manager dialog box.

19. Save the file as fund.xls.

Objective 2: Summarizing Data with PivotTables

crosstabs PivotTables (referred to as *crosstabs* in Excel 4.0) are a way to create and examine customized summaries of complex data. PivotTables take data from Excel lists (databases) and form dynamic interfaces that enable you to see only the data you need to see at any one time. Figure 12-10 shows data and an example of a PivotTable created from the acct15.xls worksheet used in preceding chapters.

	A	B	C	D	E
1	O'Malley Accounts				
2	Name	Opening Balance	Keys	Photocopies	Current Bal
3	Cate	$ 5,000.00	$ 5.25	$ 621.70	$ 4,373.05
4	Markel	$ 5,000.00	$ 12.82	$ 977.26	$ 4,009.92
5	Schwinn	$ 2,000.00	$ 18.07	$ 221.59	$ 1,760.34
6					
7					
8	Name	(All)			
9					
10	Data	Total			
11	Sum of Opening Balance	$ 12,000.00			
12	Sum of Keys	$ 36.14			
13	Sum of Photocopies	$ 1,820.55			
14	Sum of Current Bal	$ 10,143.31			

Figure 12-10   The acct15.xls worksheet is easily converted to a PivotTable for quick summaries

The list box in Figure 12-10 enables you to view a summary of the worksheet data by individual name (Cate, Markel, or Schwinn), or, as you can see in the figure, a summary for everyone in the worksheet (All). Imagine the Acct worksheet with 1500 cells of data rather than just a mere five rows. A PivotTable would be critical to summarizing the data in such a large worksheet.

Using the PivotTable Wizard

As with most multistep processes, Excel provides you with a PivotTable Wizard to guide you through the creation of simple PivotTables. More complex PivotTables may require you to use menu commands to alter or adjust the PivotTable format.

Exercise 5: Creating the Acct PivotTable

In this exercise, you will use the acct15.xls workbook to create a PivotTable, as shown in Figure 12-10.

1. Save and close any open workbooks.
2. Open the acct15.xls workbook, and drag the chart down to cell A40 so that there is room for the PivotTable to be inserted between the worksheet and chart.
3. In cell A2, type the column heading Name.

NOTE   PivotTables required that all columns have column headings.

4. Select the range A2:E5.
5. From the Data menu, choose PivotTable.

   Step 1 of the PivotTable Wizard appears, asking you to tell Excel the source of the data for the PivotTable.

6. Click the radio button beside Microsoft Excel List or Database, and click the Next button.

   Step 2 of the PivotTable Wizard appears. The range $A$2:$E$5 should already be filled into the Range field since you preselected the range before starting the Wizard.

7. Click Next.

   Step 3 of the PivotTable Wizard appears. Figure 12-11 shows the completed Step 3.

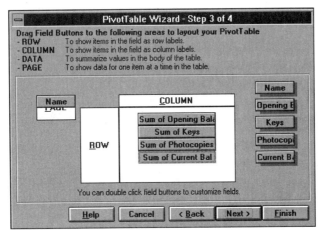

Figure 12-11 The completed Step 3 of the PivotTable Wizard defines the layout of the PivotTable

8. Drag the Name field from the column on the right side of the dialog box onto the Page placeholder on the left side of the dialog box, as shown in Figure 12-11.

   This causes the PivotTable to show the data for one person at a time in the table.

9. Drag the remaining four fields from the right side of the dialog box into the Data area of the dialog box, as shown in Figure 12-11 and click Next.

   The fourth and final step of the PivotTable Wizard appears.

10. In the PivotTable Starting Cell field of Step 4, type A7, which is a blank cell in the worksheet, and click Finish.

    The PivotTable appears, starting in cell A7.

11. Adjust any column widths, as necessary.

12. Open the list box in the PivotTable and select Cate.

    The values for Cate's record appear in the table.

13. Select Schwinn from the list box.

14. Select All from the list box.

15. Save the file as pivot.xls.

Editing fields in a PivotTable

After you have created the basic PivotTable layout using the PivotTable Wizard, you can edit the individual fields in the table so that the table is exactly as you want it. You can edit fields so that the summary data is computed differently than the default (sum). Figure 12-12 shows the PivotTable Field dialog box, in which you make changes to the selected field. Notice that in addition to changing the summary computation, you can also format the number style of the values in the cells, as well as delete the field from the PivotTable.

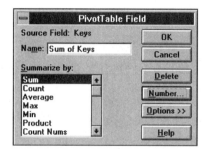

Figure 12-12   The PivotTable Field dialog box

Exercise 6: Editing the PivotTable

In this exercise, you will edit the PivotTable you created in Exercise 5 so that the values displayed in the table are in the appropriate number format.

1. Make cell A10 the active cell, and click the right mouse button to access the PivotTable shortcut menu.

2. From the menu, choose PivotTable Field.

   The PivotTable Field dialog box, shown in Figure 12-12, appears.

3. Click Number.

   The Format Cells dialog box appears.

4. From the dialog box, select Currency format with 2 decimal places (the third currency format style shown), and click OK to close the Format Cells dialog box.

5. Click OK to close the PivotTable Field dialog box.

6. Select the remaining summary fields, and format them as Currency with 2 decimal places.

7. Save the file as pivot2.xls.

8. Exit Excel or continue with the exercises at the end of this chapter.

Chapter Summary

In this chapter, you have worked with two important advanced features: problem-solving tools and PivotTables. Problem-solving tools such as Goal Seek and scenarios help you analyze the facts and factor in variables that exist in every real-world problem. PivotTables enable you to analyze complex worksheet data in a dynamic table environment so that you can see exactly what you need to see at any given time.

Review Questions

True/False Questions

_____ 1. When using the Goal Seek feature in Excel, you must know the answer to the problem.

_____ 2. The Goal Seek feature can use as many as three variables.

_____ 3. When using tables, you must know the answer to the problem.

_____ 4. Data tables can factor as many as four variables.

_____ 5. PivotTables were referred to as crosstabs.

Multiple Choice Questions

_____ 6. When using a two-input table, the first input range is in a column and the second is in a

    A. cell.

    B. formula.

    C. row.

    D. separate sheet.

_____ 7. Input ranges in a data table provide input to

    A. cells.

    B. formulas.

    C. functions.

    D. all of the above

_____ 8. Scenarios are

    A. named input ranges.

    B. stories written in Excel.

    C. named problems.

    D. none of the above

_____ 9. In order to create a PivotTable from a list in Excel, all columns must have

    A. data.

    B. values.

    C. headings.

    D. formulas.

_____ 10. When a field is placed in the Page portion of a PivotTable, it

    A. causes a page break between each occurrence of the field when printed.

    B. causes the field name to be printed as a header.

    C. causes data in the field to be displayed one item at a time.

    D. none of the above

Fill-in-the-Blank Questions

11. Problems that require the evaluation of one or more variables in order to find a solution are called _____ problems.

12. The Goal Seek feature can evaluate _____ variable(s) at a time.

13. Data tables that evaluate two variables at a time are called _____ .

14. PivotTables are generally used to _____ complex data.

15. Each worksheet element in a PivotTable is called a _____ .

Acumen-Building Activities

Quick Projects

1. Varying the down payment on the car

For this project, you will edit the loan.xls worksheet (not Loan2) to calculate a variable down payment rather than an interest rate.

Open the file loan.xls. Type 5000 in cell C5. Type .068 in cell C6 for the interest rate. Enter the formula that will subtract the down payment amount from the total loan amount in cell C8. In the range B12:B16, type the series 1000, 2000, 3000, 4000, 5000 as the variable down payment amounts. Issue the Table command to compute the monthly payments based on the variable down payment. Save the file as down.xls.

2. Finding an affordable new car

Assume that you need a new car and can spend up to $420 per month for a car payment over the next three years. New car interest rates are 6.8%. In this problem, you will use the Goal Seek feature to determine the amount of money you can spend on a new car.

Open a new workbook, and create row headings for Price of Car, Interest Rate, Term (in months), and Goal Price. Enter the information given in the problem introduction above into the appropriate cells. In the Goal Price cell, enter a formula which will compute the monthly payment based on the information given. Use a Goal Seek to find the original price of a car. Save the file as auto.xls.

3. Computing a tax table

For this project, you are asked to use the Table command to quickly create a sales tax table.

Open a new workbook. In cell B3, type Item Price. In cell B4. type Sales Tax. In cell C3, type 1. In cell C4, type .55. In cell C6, enter a formula that will compute the sales tax on the value cell C3. In cell B7, type the value .5. In cell B8, type the value 1.0. In cell B9, type the value 1.5. Use the fill handle to fill column B with values in increments of 50 up through 30.00. Use the Table command to compute the tax on each of the variable item prices in column B. Format all values in the worksheet as currency with 2 decimal places. Save the file as salestax.xls.

4. Determining the break-even point

For this project, you are asked to use Excel to determine the number of people required to attend a conference in order to break even financially.

Open a new workbook. In cell A1, type Number of Registrants; in cell A2, type Conference Rate; in cell A3, type Conference Expenses. In cell B2, type 475. In cell B3, enter a formula that will multiply the number of registrants by the conference rate. Format cells B2 and B3 for currency with two decimal places, and adjust the column widths in column A and B if necessary. Use Excel's what-if tools to determine the number of registrants needed to pay for the expenses of the conference, which are $79,821.62. Save the file as conf.xls.

In-Depth Projects

1. Using scenarios to analyze your house sale

In this project, you will develop three scenarios that examine the best-case scenario, realistic-case scenario, and worst-case scenario for selling your house.

Open a new workbook and set up a worksheet with row headings for Sale Price, Realtor Fees, Mortgage Balance, and New Downpayment. You want to list your house for $115,000, the realtor fees are 7% of the sale price of the house, and your mortgage balance is $90,000. New Downpayment is the difference between the selling price minus the realtor fees and mortgage balance—the amount of cash you will have to use as a down payment on a new home.

Develop a best-case scenario in which you sell your house for the asking price without using a realtor. Develop a realistic-case scenario in which you sell your house for $112,000 with the assistance of a realtor. Develop a worst-case scenario in which you sell your house for the amount you paid for it two years ago ($109,000) through a realtor. Name the scenarios appropriately. Run each scenario to make sure it works. Save the file as house.xls.

2. Estimating your income

In this project, assume that you have just taken a job, on a commission basis, as a sales assistant in an appliance store. You make 12% of everything you sell but receive no additional salary. You have determined that you must earn at least $1600 a month. You have already sold $13,000 worth of appliances this month, and there are still two weeks to go.

Create a new workbook and set up a worksheet with row headings for Sales Total and Commission Earned. Enter your current sales in the Sales Total row and a formula that computes your commission based on the value in the Sales Total row.

Develop three scenarios for the month. The first scenario, called WorstCase, should assume that you sell no more appliances between now and the end of the month. The second scenario, called RealCase, assumes that you sell the same amount in the last two weeks of the month as you did in the first two weeks. The third scenario, called BestCase, assumes that you sell one and one-half times as much in the last two weeks of the month as you did in the first two weeks.

Run all three scenarios to make sure that they work. Format all cells appropriately. Which scenario enables you to meet your monthly income goal? Save the file as earnings.xls.

CASE STUDIES

Coffee-On-The-Go:

Creating a Frequency Distribution

In this chapter, you learned to summarize data by creating PivotTables. You will use those skills to create a PivotTable for Coffee-On-The-Go's beverage types.

To better demonstrate how well different beverages sell, you decide to create a PivotTable of the Types worksheet.

1. Open the types.xls worksheet.
2. In cell A3, type the heading Type.
3. Create a PivotTable from the data list in the worksheet, using Type as the Page component and Qtr 1, Qtr 2, Qtr 3, and Qtr 4 as the summed data. Start the PivotTable two rows below the data.
4. Save the file as typepiv.xls.
5. Print the worksheet with the PivotTable displaying all beverage types.

CASE STUDIES

 **Videos West: Creating a What-If Table**

In this chapter, you learned to analyze data by using what-if. You will apply those skills for Videos West by creating a what-if analysis table.

To analyze the effects of borrowing $120,000 to increase the video inventory, you can create a two-input table to compare the various terms of the loan the bank is offering.

1. Open a new worksheet.
2. In cell A3, type Loan Amount:.
3. In cell A4, type Months:.
4. In cell A5, type Interest:.
5. In cell A6, type Monthly Payment:.
6. Input the Loan Amount of 120,000 in cell B3, 24 in cell B4, .09 in cell B5, and a formula that computes the monthly payment in B6.

   The four interest rates are 9%, 11%, 12% and 12.5%.

   The terms of the loan are for 24, 36, and 48 months.
7. Create a table that calculates the monthly payments for the four rates at each of the three terms.
8. Save the file as whatif.
9. Print the worksheet.

Acumen Advanced Features Milestone

Individual Project:

Gathering Census Information

You are wanting to relocate and are beginning to think about jobs and where you might like to live. You have targeted three major cities as possible living locations: Chicago, Illinois; St. Louis, Missouri; and Minneapolis, Minnesota. Go to the library (or use the World Wide Web on the Internet), and examine 1990 census data for these three cities. Record the data for average income, ethnic composition of the population, average family size, and average education level. Create a database list in Excel that displays this data in a meaningful way. Sort the list by average income. Create a chart that will graphically display the similarities and differences among the three cities. Save the file as census and print the worksheet and chart.

Team Project:

Nutrition Study

You have been asked to do a group paper on the nutritional habits of college students. A quick poll of your group shows that you all eat fast food more than any other kind of food. Your group decides that each member should collect nutritional information on menu items from their favorite fast food restaurant. When the data has been collected from several restaurants, enter it into a worksheet. Be sure to include the item name, the number of calories, and the number of fat grams for each item. Create a PivotTable of the data that will summarize the data by restaurant and by item (for example, Hamburger, Cheeseburger, Pizza, and so on). Save the file as food.xls. Using a word processing program, write a short summary of your data and conclusions that you can draw about the eating habits of college students, and refer to specific cell locations or the PivotTable in the Food worksheet for examples. Print both the Food worksheet and the report. Make sure that each group member's name appears on both documents, and turn the documents in to your instructor.

Index for Microsoft Excel 5.0 for Windows

Quick Preview

Microsoft Access 2.0

Microsoft Access 2.0 is a database management system that can be used by people at all skill levels for storing data and displaying information. MS-Access is easy for beginners and has powerful features that help you build tables to store data, construct queries to manipulate data, and generate forms and reports to display data. This Quick Preview shows you some of these features.

Activity 1: Creating a Database File

The first step in using MS-Access is to create a database file. The database file acts as a container that holds your data, tables, forms, and reports.

1. Start Microsoft Windows.

   The Program Manager window opens.

2. Double-click the MS-Access Group icon.

   The MS-Access Group window opens.

3. Double-click the MS-Access icon.

   The MS-Access main screen opens.

4. Click File/New Database from the top menu.

   The New Database dialog box opens.

5. Accept the name db1.mdb and click OK.

   You have just created a database file.

Activity 2: Creating a Table

tables
wizard

The next step is to create a table. Your data is stored in organized groups called *tables*. You will use the MS-Access Wizards to create a table in which to store your data. A *Wizard* is a program within MS-Access that leads you through the steps necessary to perform a task—in this case, creating a table.

1. The Database window is open at the Table listing. There are no tables in the list.
2. Click New.

   The New Table dialog box appears.
3. Click Table Wizards.

   The Table Wizard dialog box appears.
4. From the Sample Tables list on the left, select Mailing List.
5. From the Sample Fields list in the middle, select MailingListID.
6. Click the box with the > symbol to move a copy of MailingListID from the Sample Fields list to the Fields in My New Table list.
7. Move the following entries in the Sample Fields list to the Fields in My New Table list by repeating Steps 5 and 6:

   FirstName
   LastName
   Address
   City
   State
   PostalCode.
8. Click Next at the bottom of the dialog box.
9. When the next dialog box appears, leave the suggested Mailing List as the name of your table and let MS-Access set the primary key for you.
10. Click Next at the bottom of the dialog box.
11. Select the Enter Data Directly Into the Table response to the question, What do you want to do?
12. Click Finish at the bottom of the dialog box.

    The MS-Access Table Wizard creates the Mailing Labels table for you and opens it. You are ready to begin adding data.

Activity 3: Entering Data into the Database

Now that you have created a database and a table in the database, you are ready to enter data into the table.

1. Press (TAB) to move to the First Name column and type *your first name*.
2. Press (TAB) to move to the Last Name column and type *your last name*.
3. Press (TAB) to move to the Address column and type *your street address*.
4. Press (TAB) to move to the City column and type *the name of the city you live in*.
5. Press (TAB) to move to the State column and type *the name of the state you live in*.
6. Press (TAB) to move to the Postal Code column and type *your zip code*.
7. Press (↵ ENTER) to complete the first record.

8. Repeat Steps 1 through 7 to create three additional records containing the names and addresses of friends or classmates.

   You now have four records in your Mailing List table.

9. Click File/Save Record to save the data you entered.

10. Click File/Save Table to save the table you created.

11. Click File/Close to close the datasheet and return to the Database window.

Activity 4: Generating a Mailing Labels Report

Now that you have data in your table, you can print this information as mailing labels. You will use the MS-Access Wizards to create a mailing labels report. You can then preview this report and send it to the printer.

1. The Database window for database.db1 is open at the table listing. Click the Report tab on the left.

   The Report window opens. There are no reports in the list.

2. Click New.

   The New Report dialog box appears.

3. Click the down arrow located to the right of the Select a Table/Query box.

   A drop-down menu appears with the entry Mailing List highlighted.

4. Click Mailing List.

   Mailing List pops into the Select a Table/Query box.

5. Click the Report Wizards button.

   The Report Wizards dialog box appears.

6. Highlight the Mailing Labels Wizard. Click OK.

   The Mailing Labels Wizard dialog box appears.

7. In the Available Fields list, highlight the FirstName entry.

8. Click the > button located to the right of the FirstName entry in the Available Fields list.

   A copy of First Name moves to the Label Appearance list.

9. Click the Space button located below the Available Fields list.

10. Highlight LastName in the Available Fields list. Click the > button.

    First Name and Last Name are now on the first line of the Label Appearance list; they are separated by a space.

11. Click the Newline button.

    A new line appears on the Label Appearance list.

12. Highlight Address in the Available Fields list. Click the > button.

    Address appears on the second line of the Label Appearance list.

13. Click Newline to start a new line.

14. Scroll down the Available Fields list to show City, State, and PostalCode.

15. Highlight City in the Available Fields list. Click the > button to move it to the Label Appearance list.

16. Click Comma, then Space to add a comma and a space after City in the Label Appearance list.

17. Highlight State in the Available Fields list. Click the > button to move it to the Label Appearance list.

18. Click Space twice to add two spaces after State in the Label Appearance list.

19. Highlight PostalCode in the Available Fields list. Click the > button to move it to the Label Appearance list.

20. Click Next at the bottom of the Mailing Label Wizard dialog box.

21. Highlight LastName as the field by which you want to order the list. Click the > button to move it to the Sort Order list.

22. Click Next at the bottom of the Mailing Label Wizard dialog box.

23. Highlight Avery #5161, 1" × 4", 2 across, when asked for the size of the label. Accept English as the unit of measure and Sheet Feed as the label type.

24. Click Next at the bottom of the Mailing Label Wizard dialog box.

25. Accept the default values for text appearance. Click Next.

26. Accept See Mailing Labels as They Will Look Printed. Click Finish.

    The Mailing Label Wizard creates the Mailing Label report for you and displays the Print Preview screen.

Activity 5: Printing a Mailing Labels Report

The Print Preview screen allows you to preview your report before sending it to the printer. By clicking on the report itself, you can zoom in to see specific sections of the report or zoom out to see the general layout of the report. Once you are satisfied with the appearance of the report, you can print it.

1. At the Print Preview screen, test the zoom feature: Click the report several times to zoom in and out.

2. From the top menu choose File/Print.

   The Print dialog box appears.

3. Accept the print range of All. Click OK.

   Your mailing labels are now printing.

4. Exit Print Preview by clicking the Close Window icon at the far left of the top toolbar.

   You are returned to the Report Design Mode screen.

5. Select File/Save to save the report.

   The Save As dialog box appears, prompting you for a report name.

6. Type MailingLabelsReport as the report name. Click OK.

7. Select File/Close to close the report and return to the Database window.

Activity 6: Ending Your MS-Access Session

It is important to end your MS-Access session properly. Improper exit procedures—such as turning off your computer in the middle of an MS-Access session—could cause you to lose data. Here's the correct way to end an MS-Access session.

1. From the Database window, choose File/Close Database.

   The active database is shut down.

2. Choose File/Exit.

   The MS-Access session is terminated. You are returned to the MS-Access group, in the Program Manager screen.

Part 1

Fundamentals

Chapter 1

Database Fundamentals

Key Terms

TERM	DEFINITION
Data	raw facts—for example, a data item might be a name, street address, or phone number
Information	organized data that can be used to assist in the decision-making process
Database	an organized, related collection of data
Database Management System	a computerized record-keeping system that stores data, manages a database, and presents data to a user on request
Flat-file Data Manager	a type of database that stores data in a single file
Relational Database	a type of database that stores data in separate, but related, groups called tables
Database File	a computer file that contains an MS-Access database
Table	a collection of data related to a single topic, such as customer information
User Interface	the screens used to interact with a computer or computer program

TERM	DEFINITION
Network	a system that connects computers so that people can communicate with each other and share data files, printers, and hardware
Report	a printed listing of data from the database, organized to provide information used in evaluating and making decisions
Form	a screen display of a single record from a table in the database that is used for inputting, outputting, and displaying data
Report Writer	a database tool used to design, build, and produce printed reports without the user having to write code in a computer programming language
Icon	a small picture on the computer screen that represents a program, such as MS-Access, or a task, such as opening a file
Dialog Box	a pop-up window that assists you in some task, such as choosing a file
Minimize a Window	reduce an MS-Access window to an icon
Maximize a Window	enlarge an MS-Access window to fill the entire screen.
On-line Help System	the computerized version of the *MS-Access User's Guide*, which contains information about MS-Access
Cue Card	an on-line tutorial that guides you through a complicated task, such as editing a table; a part of the MS-Access on-line help system
Context-sensitive Help	a feature of the MS-Access on-line help system that allows you to access information relevant to what you are doing by pressing F1
Wizard	a predefined set of instructions built into MS-Access that automates the steps required to perform a task; a part of the MS-Access on-line help system

Computing technology has revolutionized the way we live and do business. With the desktop computer standard in most offices and many homes, there is a demand to organize the vast amount of information at our fingertips: Enter the database and the database management system.

database programmers

Database management systems were once found only in large corporations. They were an intricate set of programs that were exceedingly complicated to use and maintain. Only specially trained people (called *database programmers*) knew how to extract information from the database. Today's database management systems are very different: just as complex on the inside, but user-friendly on the outside.

Objective 1: Introduction to Databases

SIGNS, Ltd. is a small business that makes and sells signs. The owner is considering developing a database to track sales and customer calls and has called in a database systems consultant to discuss this project. Listen in on the conversation between the owner of SIGNS, Ltd. and the consultant.

Owner: People keep telling me I need a database, but they all have different ideas about what a database really is. Can you tell me the *real* definition of a database?

database   *Consultant*: A *database* is an organized collection of related data from which you extract information. This Rolodex on your desk can be considered a database. It's organized—you have each card in alphabetical order—and from it you can extract phone numbers, names, and where a customer's office is located.

Owner: How does a database differ from a database management system?

database   *Consultant*: A database is a collection of related facts. A *database manage-*
management   *ment system* is a set of computer programs that stores and manages those
system   facts. If the database is stored on a *network*, the database management system
network   makes the database accessible to anyone connected to the network. The data stored in the database becomes a shared resource throughout the company.

The database management system allows you to build a nice, user-friendly
user interface   *user interface* to work with. The user interface makes it easy for you to add data, change data already stored in the database, or get rid of old data that has outlived its usefulness. It helps you manipulate the data and extract useful information so that you can make better-informed decisions. This
report writer   information can be formatted by the *report writer*, which is also part of the database management system. The report writer produces paper reports for distribution—for example, invoices for your customers or end-of-year purchase reports that help your customers track what they've bought from you over the past twelve months. And the database management system acts as a security guard—only people who are supposed to get into the database can do so.

Owner: Just a minute. I thought information and data were the same thing—you're telling me they're not?

data   *Consultant*: Actually they're not the same. *Data* is raw facts. You rearrange
information   or recombine data to produce useful *information* that can help you make decisions. For instance, your company sells several types of signs to customers, and you have a list of customers. That is your data. When you're having a sale on a specific type of sign, you sort through your customer list, extracting the names of only those customers who have purchased that type of sign in the past. That is information.

Owner: So how can a database help my company?

Consultant: What you now do manually you can do with a computerized database management system in a fraction of the time. For example, it probably takes an hour or so to sort through all your customers to find those who have purchased a specific type of sign. It then takes several hours to prepare the mailing for the sale notices. With a database system you could complete these tasks in a few minutes.

With your sales data stored in a database, you could generate reports of sales activity—which products are selling and which are not—and adjust your inventory and sales efforts to meet the demand. Also, you could track overdue accounts.

If you had all your product inventory information stored in the database, you could enter customer orders into the database and see immediately which items are in stock and which need to be ordered. You could track and manage your inventory by assigning a reorder point value to each inventory item and generate a daily report listing which items need to be reordered. The possibilities are endless.

Owner: Right now I keep customer lists in my word processor and product lists and sales in my spreadsheet. Isn't that a sort of database?

Consultant: Yes it is. Each list is a file—a collection of data related to a single topic. It is very much like the earliest and simplest of the database management systems for the personal computer. These database manage **flat-file data** ment systems, which are still used today, are called *flat-file data managers.* **managers** They allow only for a single type of data in a database file, such as your customer listing or sales figures.

Word processors, spreadsheets, and flat-file data managers are a fine way to keep track of short lists and simple sets of data. But as your company grows and you need to get more and more information out of these lists, they will fall short. You will need to combine and extract data from the **relational** different sets of data, and unless you have your data stored in an inte **database** grated, *relational database*, this will be very difficult to do.

Owner: What do you mean by relational?

Consultant: A relational database stores data in separate groups, called **tables** *tables.* Each table stores information about a single topic, such as customer data or outstanding orders. The relational database connects these database tables so that you might, for example, print a list of all customers who have outstanding orders. To make these connections, the database must know how the two tables are related. When you define these relationships between tables, you are building a relational database.

Owner: Well, I think we need a relational database, and MS-Access sounds like an interesting product. How do I find out more about it?

Consultant: Please follow me to the next section.

Objective 2: Starting the Software

icons Your computer should be turned on and running MS-Windows. The Program Manager window will be visible. It contains the Program Group *icons*, which are small pictures. Each of these icons represents a group of programs. Find the Program Group icon labeled Microsoft Access, MS-Access, or simply Access. When you select a Program Group icon you open a window for that group; the window contains icons for the programs. The MS-Access Group window may include the MS-Access icon, a Readme Help icon, and a Setup icon.

Cue Cards When you start MS-Access, the Cue Cards window may appear. *Cue Cards*, which are part of the MS-Access on-line help system, are tutorials that walk you through various complicated tasks, such as editing a table. If the Cue Cards window is open, simply close it. You will see it again the next time you start MS-Access. When time permits, you should investigate the contents of the Cue Cards window.

Exercise 1: Starting MS-Access

This exercise teaches you to start MS-Access from the MS-Windows Program Manager.

1. Double-click the Microsoft Access Program Group icon in the Windows Program Manager screen to open the MS-Access Program Group (Fig. 1-1).

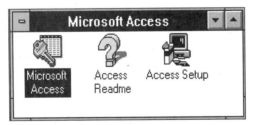

Figure 1-1 MS-Access Program Group icons

2. Double-click the Microsoft Access icon to start MS-Access.
3. If the Cue Cards window appears, close the window by double-clicking the small box in the upper, left corner of the Cue Cards window.

   You are now in the MS-Access main window.

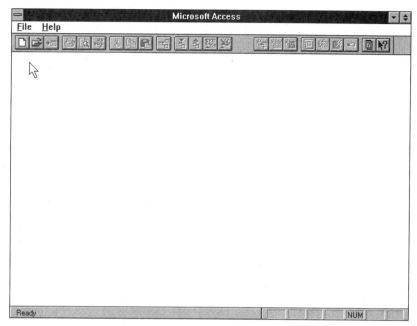

Figure 1-2 **MS-Access Main window**

The Father of Modern Computing . . .

. . . was a nineteenth-century Englishman named Charles Babbage (1791–1871). He never built an operational computer himself, but his ideas laid the foundation for modern computing devices and methods.

Charles Babbage began work on the Difference Engine in 1822. This machine was designed to automate the calculation of the roots of polynomials. The British Navy used these calculations to produce astronomical tables for navigation. While developing the Difference Engine, Babbage began work on a much more powerful Analytical Engine. The Analytical Engine was designed as a general-purpose computing machine that employed the basic concepts of a modern-day digital computer. For nearly 40 years, Babbage labored at his plans, producing thousands of detailed drawings of this steam-driven computing machine that would accept punched-card input of both program instructions and data, perform any arithmetic operation under the direction of the mechanically stored set of instructions, and produce either punched-card or printed output. Babbage died before he could make his dream a reality.

Babbage's Analytical Engine was finally finished in 1991–92 from his original designs. It was sponsored and displayed by the Science Museum in London, England. The Analytical Engine works exactly as Babbage predicted it would.

Objective 3: Mouse and Keyboard Commands

You can use either the mouse or the keyboard to navigate MS-Access screens and menus. When you start MS-Access, you see a nearly empty window. The title bar reads, "MS-Access." Directly below the title bar is the menu bar, which has only two options, File and Help. Notice that the letters F and H are underlined on the screen. The convention for all MS-Windows programs is that you can choose these menu items with the key combination ⟨ALT⟩ + (underlined letter). To use the File menu, you click File or press ⟨ALT⟩+⟨F⟩. The underlined letter is not necessarily the first letter of the word.

When you choose a menu item, a list of actions drops down below the item you choose. Once the drop-down menu is opened, there are three ways to choose an action: (1) select an item by pressing the appropriate letter (this time without ⟨ALT⟩), (2) use the arrow keys to highlight the item and press ⟨← ENTER⟩, or (3) use the mouse to select the item. You can also use a combination of keystrokes and mouse clicks.

Exercise 2: Using the keyboard and mouse to open a database file

MS-Access comes with sample database files. You can open and close these files to familiarize yourself with the mouse and keyboard actions. MS-Access normally places the sample files in a directory called \access\sampapps.

1. From the File menu, click the Open Database icon.

dialog box

The Open Database dialog box opens to help you select a database file (Fig. 1-3). A *dialog box* is a pop-up window that assists you in some task, such as choosing a file.

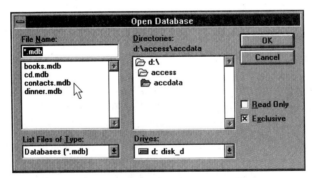

Figure 1-3 Open Database dialog box

2. Change to the directory where the sample database files are stored.
3. Double-click nwind.mdb to open the NorthWind Traders database.

The database window entitled Database: NWIND opens (Fig. 1-4). Leave it on the screen while you continue with the next objective.

Figure 1-4   NorthWind Traders database window

Objective 4: Elements of the Screen

minimize
maximize

At the top of the screen is the title bar, which displays the title "Microsoft Access." To the left of the title bar is the box used to close MS-Access. To the right are two arrows that *minimize* (reduce the MS-Access window to an icon on the screen) and *maximize* (enlarge the MS-Access window to fill the entire screen) the MS-Access window. These arrows are standard MS-Windows controls.

Below the title bar is the main menu bar. Below the main menu bar is the toolbar, which contains a row of icons. Some icons are dimmed, which means they are not available at this time. When you position the cursor over an icon, a small balloon-box appears with a description of the icon. At certain times a longer description of the icon is shown in the lower left corner of the screen. These descriptions appear for the dimmed icons as well.

database file

The icon on the far left is used to create a new database file. It looks, appropriately, like a blank sheet of paper. The *database file* is the MS-Access file that contains all the tables you create, all the data you enter, and all the other database objects. The database filename always ends with the extension .mdb.

on-line help
system

The icon just to the right of the new database file icon looks like an open file folder. This is the icon for opening an existing database file. The two icons at the far right with question marks are for Cue Cards and on-line help. The *on-line help system* contains descriptions and definitions of everything used in MS-Access.

Exercise 3: The MS-Access Main window: icons

In this exercise, you learn to use the first of the MS-Access help functions by positioning the cursor over various icons.

1. Position the cursor over one of the icons in the top toolbar and wait.

   A balloon box with information (Fig. 1-5) and a description in the lower left corner appear for that icon.

2. Repeat Step 1 for several other icons.

Figure 1-5   Toolbar with balloon-box help windows for icons

FEATURE

How can I get a copy of that database?

You will probably develop databases for groups to which you belong, such as Little League, church groups, and social organizations. At work, you may produce contact directories, sales leads organizers, or branch office personnel rosters. At home, your video tapes, CDs, photographs, and even the contents of your freezer can be databased. As you develop useful databases in MS-Access, your friends, coworkers, and neighbors may ask for copies so they can use them. How do you provide copies? Most likely your friends will not want to buy MS-Access, and you know that you cannot legally install your copy on their computers, for copyright reasons.

There is an easy solution. You can buy a product called the MS-Access Developer's Toolkit. It costs several hundred dollars but is a one-time investment. With this product you can legally compile and distribute your databases with no further royalties or payments to Microsoft. As long as your friends have computers that will run MS-Windows, they can install your program and databases like any other Windows software package. They can run the programs, use the forms, add their own data, and generate reports and mailing labels; a nice, legal solution that makes everyone happy!

Objective 5: Elements of the Menu System

The opening screen for MS-Access shows only two menu options, File and Help. Clicking either of these options causes a menu box to drop down. The File menu opens and closes database files and lists the maintenance operations that you can perform on your databases. The Help menu is the gateway to the on-line help system and the Cue Cards.

Exercise 4: The MS-Access Main window: menu choices

This exercise teaches you to use the MS-Access menu system.

1. Click File on the main menu bar to drop down a list of options (Fig. 1-6).

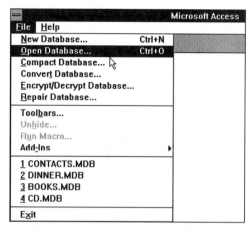

Figure 1-6 File menu drop-down menu

The options you will work with in later exercises are New Database, Open Database, Close Database, and Exit. Do not select any of these options yet.

2. Press ⌈ESC⌋ or click anywhere on the screen outside of the drop-down menu box to exit from this menu.

Objective 6: *Event-Driven versus Menu-Driven Applications*

You have probably heard the term event-driven application. What does it mean? Consider the Database: NWIND window on the screen. At the top of the window is a row of buttons: New, Open, and Design. Down the left side are tabs: Table, Query, Form, Report, Macro, and Module. Because MS-Access is event-driven, *you* decide what to do next. You can open a table to look at data, edit the design of a table, or use any one of the other MS-Access features. When you click a button or tab, the program interprets the click as an event—that is, a command to do something. It then runs the program code associated with that event.

In a menu-driven application, you have a list of choices, but the list is limited. You are forced to step through the program just as the programmer designed it.

Exercise 5: Looking at an example of event-driven programming

In this exercise, you will investigate the NorthWind Traders database to see a good example of an event-driven application. You will learn important navigation skills inside an MS-Access application.

1. In the Database window, click the Form tab to show a list of forms.
2. Use the arrow keys to move down the list until the Main Switchboard entry is visible.
3. Double-click Main Switchboard on the list to open NorthWind Traders (Fig. 1-7).

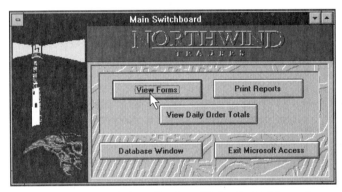

Figure 1-7   NorthWind Traders Main Switchboard

4. Click the View Forms button.

   A second switchboard, the Forms Switchboard, opens (Fig. 1-8). It shows six buttons, which allow you to do different things, such as look at customer information or modify product information.

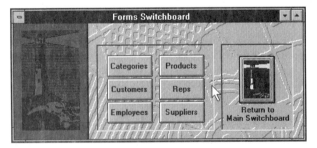

Figure 1-8   NorthWind Traders Forms Switchboard

5. Double-click the dash in the small box at the upper left corner of the Forms Switchboard.

   You are returned to the Main Switchboard.

6. Double-click the dash in the small box at the upper left corner of the Main Switchboard.

The Main Switchboard closes, and you are returned to the Database window, without having to exit MS-Access.

Objective 7: The On-Line Help System

There are several ways to ask MS-Access for help. The first is to click the Help option on the top menu bar. The drop-down menu that appears contains a table of contents for the help system, a search option for tracking down help topics by keywords, and the Cue Cards discussed earlier.

On the top toolbar, at the far right, is an icon with an arrow and a question mark. When you click this icon, it stays active and changes color. The cursor changes to a copy of the arrow and question mark. You then position the cursor over any menu item or icon and click; the MS-Access help information for that specific menu item or icon appears.

A quick way to invoke Cue Cards is to use the Cue Cards icon. Just to the left of the Help icon is the Cue Cards icon, which looks like a stack of cards with a question mark on top.

context-sensitive help MS-Access also has *context-sensitive help* available. When you press ⌐F1⌐, MS-Access knows where you are in the software and provides information relevant to whatever you are doing.

form When working with MS-Access, you create forms to help with data entry. A *form* displays one record at a time from a table of a database. You also build reports in MS-Access. A report is used to output data to either the **report** screen or a printer. A *report* is a listing of data from the database, organized to provide information that can be used in making decisions.

Wizards As you design tables, reports, and forms, you will encounter the *Wizards*, predefined sets of instructions built into MS-Access that guide you through particular tasks. The Wizards ask questions and then take over. For example, they can produce a table, form, or report for you. They differ from Cue Cards: Using Cue Cards is like having someone stand behind you and tell you what to do next; using a Wizard is like having someone take over the keyboard and do the work for you.

Exercise 6: Examining the on-line help system

During this exercise, you will investigate some of the features of the MS-Access help system.

1. Choose Help/Contents from the top menu.

The MS-Access Help Contents menu appears on the right of the screen (Fig. 1-9).

Figure 1-9 **The On-Line Help menu**

2. Click Cue Cards from the list.

   The MS-Access Cue Cards window appears. Examine the available choices.

3. Click the dash in the upper left corner of the Cue Cards window. Choose Close.

4. Click the dash in the upper left corner of the Help window. Choose Close.

5. Click the Help icon on the top toolbar.

   The cursor changes to an arrow and a question mark (Fig. 1-10).

Figure 1-10 **The Help cursor**

6. Position the changed cursor over the Print icon and click.

   MS-Access Help opens at the Print Command (File menu) page.

7. Double-click the dash in the upper left corner of the Help window.

   MS-Access Help closes.

Objective 8: Exiting the Software

Now you must close the database and exit from the software. You should never turn off your computer while any program is running because you risk losing data. Since you make business decisions based on information from your database, this risk is not acceptable. Always (1) close the database, (2) close MS-Access, (3) exit from MS-Windows, and (4) turn off your computer.

Exercise 7: Exiting from the database

This exercise teaches you how to exit properly from the database. If you are finished with MS-Access, then you can close it.

1. Click File/Close Database.

   The NorthWind Traders database closes.

2. Click File/Exit.

   MS-Access is terminated.

Chapter Summary

This chapter introduced the concept of a database and a database management system (DBMS). You learned how companies use DBMSs and what they can do for companies. You took a guided tour through MS-Access and the NorthWind Traders database. You looked at the screens and moved around using both the mouse and the keyboard. We discussed the differences between menu-driven and event-driven applications. You looked at the on-line help system, which is always available with MS-Access, and learned about the Cue Cards and the Wizards. You also learned how to leave MS-Access properly so that the data stored in your database will not be corrupted.

Review Questions

True/False Questions

_____ 1. Data and information are the same thing.

_____ 2. A database is a collection of unrelated facts.

_____ 3. An event-driven program forces you to move through the application step-by-step.

_____ 4. A relational database allows you to organize your data into related groups called tables.

_____ 5. With on-line help you can search using specific keywords.

Multiple-Choice Questions

_____ 6. A computerized record-keeping system that stores, manages, and retrieves data on demand is called a
  A. Wizard.
  B. database.
  C. database management system.
  D. user interface.

_____ 7. Organized data that is used in the decision-making process is called
  A. information.
  B. a database.
  C. a report.
  D. a flat-file data manager.

_____ 8. A database user interface
  A. helps you manage data.
  B. allows you to view data.
  C. helps you enter data and change data already stored in the database.
  D. all of the above.

_____ 9. When you need step-by-step instructions to accomplish a task you look for the
  A. Wizards.
  B. Cue Cards.
  C. on-line help table of contents.
  D. instructor.

_____ 10. When you are finished with MS-Access and ready to shut it down, you should
  A. turn off your computer.
  B. exit MS-Windows without closing MS-Access.
  C. close the database you are working with, then close MS-Access.
  D. close MS-Access, then close the database you are working with.

Fill-in-the-Blank Questions

11. A person interacts with his/her computer through a _____.

12. MS-Access is a database management system that needs to run in the environment known as _____.

13. Programs that allow you to choose what you want to do next are called _____.

14. You can select menu commands by using the key combination _____ + the appropriate underlined letter.

15. Helpful information that is relevant to where you currently are in MS-Access is called _____.

Acumen-Building Activities

Quick Projects

1. Opening the NorthWind Traders Database Main Switchboard.

1. Start MS-Access. From the File menu click the Open Database icon.

2. Change to the directory where the sample database files are stored and double-click nwind.mdb to open the NorthWind Traders database.

3. Click the Form tab in the Database window.

4. Click the Main Switchboard entry in the list to highlight it (you may have to scroll down the list to find it). Click Open.

2. Using Print Preview.

1. In the NorthWind Traders database, at the Main Switchboard screen, click the Print Reports button.

2. In the Print Reports dialog box, click the Sales by Category option of Report to Print.

3. Highlight Dairy Products. Click Print Preview.

4. When the report appears on the screen, use the zoom-in and zoom-out features to examine the report.

3. Using context-sensitive help.

1. From the Print Preview screen, press (F1) to invoke context-sensitive help.

2. Read the on-screen information about Print Preview.

3. Position the cursor over the green lettering that reads `Print Preview button` and click once. Read about the Print Preview icon. Click to close the pop-up help box.

4. Position the cursor over the green lettering that reads `Close button` and click once. Read about the Close icon.

5. Exit help and return to the Print Preview screen. Click File/Exit from the top menu.

6. Return to the Main Switchboard. Click File/Close from the top menu.

7. Close the Main Switchboard.

4. Using on-line help and Cue Cards.

1. From the Database window, click the Help menu and choose Cue Cards.

2. Click See a Quick Overview. Click the Databases button.

3. Read the page on What Is a Database? Click Next in the lower right corner.

4. Read A Microsoft Access Database. Click Next.

5. Close the Cue Cards. Close the NorthWind Traders database. Close MS-Access.

In-Depth Projects

1. Designing the CD database.

You have a large collection of music CDs. Managing them is becoming difficult, and you are looking at computerizing.

In coming chapters, you will design and build a database in which you can record information about your collection of CDs. You'll create a table, designating the title, artist, recording label, music classification, length, release date, and cost of each CD. You'll then create a second table to store the track information for each CD. Then you will establish a relationship between the two tables, so you can extract information from the CD database.

From specifications we provide, you will design and develop a user interface for the CD database. You will create forms to assist you in data entry and reports to list what is in the database.

For now, write out a list of the data you would store in a database for your CD collection and the reports you would want to see from such a database.

2. Designing the Dinner Party database.

You belong to a social organization that meets periodically for dinner parties and would like to track the events better. In coming chapters, you will design and build a database in which you can record information about these dinner parties. The first table includes information about the people in your group—their names, addresses, phone numbers, dietary restrictions, likes, and dislikes. The second table includes information about each dinner party—when, where, and what was served. A third table keeps track of which people attended each dinner party. Then you will establish a relationship between these three tables, so you can extract information from the Dinner Party database.

You will design and develop a user interface for the Dinner Party database. You will create forms to assist you in data entry and reports to list what is in the database. For now, write out a list of the type of data you want to store in a dinner party database and what kind of information you want to extract.

CASE STUDIES

Coffee-On-The-Go:

Introduction

In this case study, you will create and use a database of employees for a business called Coffee-On-The-Go. This chain of espresso stands is located in many cities in the Pacific Northwest. The business sells various types of coffee drinks and teas, along with muffins and cookies. The coffee booths are all located in busy areas and are accessible by automobile and by foot.

You will be provided with more information in the chapters that follow.

CASE STUDIES

Videos West:

Introduction

In this case study, you will create and use a database for a video business located in Fairbanks, Alaska. This business has operated a video rental store in downtown Fairbanks for two years. The owners of Videos West are planning to expand the business by including a retail line of special interest videos available to the entire state by mail order.

You will be provided with the information to complete the database for the new venture in the chapters that follow.

Chapter 2

Designing A Database

Objectives
- Creating a Database File
- Designing the Tables in a Database
- Understanding Data and Field Types
- Determining Relationships
- Setting a Primary Key
- Creating a Database Table
- Editing a Database Table
- Saving the Database Table
- Printing a Definition of the Database Table

Key Terms

TERM	DEFINITION
Field	a data item that is part of a database table and that is defined when you create the table; related fields are grouped together to form a record
Field Name	the name assigned to a field at the time it is defined
Data Type	the different types of data that MS-Access recognizes and supports; a data type is assigned to a field when it is defined
Record	a collection of related fields, such as customer information or inventory information; records of the same type make up a database table
Relationship	an association between two tables in a database that allows you to combine data items from each table and display them in the same form or report

TERM	DEFINITION
One-to-One Relationship	a situation where each record in one table is related, or linked, to one and only one record in another table
One-to-Many Relationship	a situation where each record in one table is related, or linked, to more than one record in another table
Many-to-Many Relationship	a situation where many records in one table are related or linked to many records in the second table
Primary Key	a field of a table whose contents can be used to identify each row in the table; no two primary keys can have the same value within the same table
Database Report	a report that contains information on a table of the database, listing the fields, data types, field lengths, primary key assignments, and so on
Table Wizard	a predefined set of instructions built into MS-Access that builds a table for you

Before you begin any database development, you must ask yourself: What am I going to use the database for? What kind of data am I going to collect? How am I going to collect it? What kind of reports am I going to produce? To make your database work well for you, you must understand its purpose and what it is intended for.

Database design is the first step of database development and is usually done with pencil and paper. You wouldn't think of building a plane without a set of engineering blueprints. Neither should you plunge ahead with database development until you have a clear design to work from.

Time spent on design is not time wasted. Rather, it cuts down on database development time. Perhaps more important, a good design will allow you to be productive and expand your database in response to future needs.

First you must decide what data is to be stored and how to divide the data items into appropriate groupings. Next you create the database and its tables according to the way you group the data items. Then you assign specific characteristics for each data item, such as a field name and data type. You will change some of these characteristics once the table has been created. Next you print out the Table Structure report, and finally you save the table structure.

Objective 1: Creating a Database File

MS-Access stores all the information about a database in one file on your disk. All MS-Access database files have the extension .mdb. You must create the database file before you can proceed.

Exercise 1: Creating a new database file

This exercise teaches you how to create a new, empty database file.

1. Start MS-Access. Click File.
2. Click New Database to bring up the New Database dialog box (Fig. 2-1).

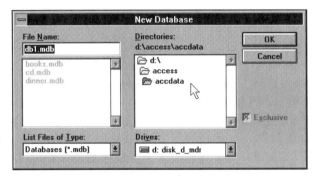

Figure 2-1 **New Database dialog box**

3. In the File Name window type contacts.mdb.
4. Move to the Drives window in this dialog box.

Verify that the drive shown is where you want to save the database file.

5. Move to the Directories window in this dialog box.

Verify that the directory shown is where you want to save the database file.

6. Click OK.

MS-Access creates your database. It moves you to the Database window, so that you may begin adding new tables (Fig. 2-2).

Figure 2-2 **MS-Access Database window**

Objective 2: Designing the Tables in a Database

Now that you have built your database file, you can think seriously about what to put in it. Write down what you want this database to do. Is it meant to keep track of your collection of compact discs? Is it meant to track statistics gathered during a research project? Is it a database that underlies an order-entry system? Each of these three databases would be designed differently.

Once you know the purpose of the database, list the type of output you want. Paper reports, electronic reports, computer files, and merge files are types of database output. Also decide what information will be in the reports. A report can be as simple as a listing of your CD titles or as complex as a customer invoice. If you understand what you want to get out of a database, then you know what you need to put into it. Working backwards like this is often the most efficient method of determining what data items you need to store in a database.

Let's design a sample database: a sales contact database. In such a database, you would store a person's name, address, phone number, the company he or she works for, and so on. To begin, list these data items on a piece of paper—do not start keying them into the database until you have

field   thought the design through. Each data item will become a field. A *field* is a data item that is part of a database table. Related fields—for example,

record   name, address, and phone number—are grouped together to form a *record*. Each contact person will become a record in the contacts table.

field name   Assign each data item a proper *field name*. MS-Access allows you to use long table names and field names for ease of recognition. It even permits you to use spaces in these names, such as First Name. However, the technique most favored among MS-Access database designers is to leave out all spaces and join words, indicating the beginning of each word with an uppercase letter, as in FirstName.

Make a list of how you will want to sort your sales contacts. This helps you organize the data. If you list first name, last name, company name, street address, city, state, and zip code as separate data items, then you can sort your database by first name, to find Mary's phone number, or by city and zip code, to organize your sales calls when you're in Denver.

Consider if you are storing too much information in any one field. Are you storing a person's full name in one field? It may be easier to store it in two fields, such as FirstName and LastName. Having the last name stored separately from the first name allows sorting by either first or last name.

Consider if you are storing too little information in any one field. Did you split the street address into separate fields for number, street, and apartment or suite? Do you need this much detail? If you are a door-to-door salesperson, you may need to know which of your customers live on Baker Street. But if you are keeping a database of batting statistics for the local Little League team, this design would be too detailed.

Exercise 2: Designing the tables of a database

This exercise shows you how to lay out the design of the sales contact database on paper.

1. Make a list of the data items you will store in your sales contact database.
2. Give each data item a proper field name.
3. Mark the fields on which you will sort the data.
4. Consider if you are storing too much information in any one field.
5. Consider if you are storing too little information in any one field.

Objective 3: Understanding Data and Field Types

data type   You should choose an appropriate *data type* for each field. MS-Access has a number of data types from which you can choose, as described in Table 2-1.

Table 2-1   MS-Access data types

DATA TYPE	DESCRIPTION	EXAMPLE
Text	The data type used to store letters, numbers, and special characters (*&^%$#@!). Can be up to 255 characters long.	123 West High St.
Memo	A text data type with a maximum length of 64,000 characters. Use this data type for notes, comments, or long fields (greater than 255 characters). There are some restrictions imposed on this data type, so use it carefully.	Any kind of text message or number can be stored.
Number	A data type used to store numbers. There are many numeric data types.	1
Byte	A number data type, stores values from 0 to 255 (no fractions).	1
Integer	A number data type, stores values from –32,768 to 32,767 (no fractions).	32,000
Long Integer	A number data type, stores values from –2,147,648 to 2,147,647 (no fractions).	1,100,000
Single	A number data type, stores values with six digits of precision (scientific notation). This data type can store fractions.	4.25
Double	A number data type, stores values with ten digits of precision (scientific notation). This data type can store fractions.	.0000000001
Date/ Time	The data type used to store date and/or time values.	1/01/94, 5:34 P.M.
Currency	The data type used to store money values, up to 15 digits on the left side of the decimal point and 4 digits on the right side. Displayed in forms and reports in the currency format, as shown.	$1.00

continued

Table 2-1   Continued

DATA TYPE	DESCRIPTION	EXAMPLE
Counter	A number automatically incremented by MS-Access whenever a new record is added to a table. Counter fields are most often used as primary keys. They are maintained within MS-Access and cannot be updated by the user.	0000001
Yes/No	A data type used when one of two possible answers is needed, such as yes/no, true/false, 0/1. There are some restrictions imposed on this data type, so use it carefully.	0
OLE Object	A data type used to store graphics, video, sound, or other computer programs, such as spreadsheets, in the database. There are some restrictions imposed on this data type, so use it carefully.	

When choosing a data type for a field, consider the following:

1. Will this field store a date and/or time, a money value, or some graphic?

If a date or time, select the Date/Time data type.

If a money value, use the Currency data type.

If a graphic or sound/video clip, use the OLE Object data type.

Otherwise, proceed.

2. What is the maximum size of the data to be stored in the field?

If one of two letters or numbers, use the Yes/No data type.

If over 255 characters, use the Memo data type.

Otherwise, proceed.

3. Will you need to do arithmetic on the data that you have stored in this field?

Use one of the number data types, determined by (1) the largest and smallest value you will ever need to store and (2) whether you will need to store fractions or only whole numbers.

Otherwise, proceed.

4. Will you be storing letters, numbers, and special characters in a field?

Use the Text data type.

Objective 4: Determining Relationships

relationship

Look at the tables and determine if there are any relationships between your tables. A *relationship* is a special association between two tables in a database. This association allows you to combine data items from two tables and display them in the same form or report.

A relational database is composed of data grouped into tables. These tables are related to one another in one of three ways: one-to-one, one-to-many, and many-to-many.

one-to-one relationship

A *one-to-one relationship* is when a record in one table is related or linked to one and only one record in a second table. A student's on-campus address information might be stored in one table, while the student's parent/guardian information might be stored in a second table. The student has one campus address record in one table related to one parent information record in a second table.

The link that joins these two tables in the one-to-one relationship is a data field that is present in both tables. In the example, the StudentID field is a field in the Student table as well as the StuParentInfo table. When the value of StudentID in a record in the Student table matches the value of StudentID in a record in the StuParentInfo table, you have a link established between these two tables.

primary key

The StudentID field is an excellent candidate for the primary key. A *primary key* has a value that is unique. Since no two students will have the same student ID number, the ID number is unique and suitable as the primary key. Most often the primary key field is used to link two related tables.

one-to-many relationship

A *one-to-many relationship* is when a record in one table is related or linked to many records in a second table. In our example, each department at Central University offers many courses, but each course, with its own unique course number, is offered by only one department. In this case, one table contains data describing each department (the Department table), and a second table describes each class (the Class table). The relationship between the Department table and the Class table is a one-to-many relationship; each record in the Department table is related to many records in the Class table.

many-to-many relationship

A *many-to-many relationship* is where many records in one table are related or linked to many records in a second table. On campus, many students take many classes, and each class has many students. Student information is stored in the Student table. Class information is stored in the Class table. A student registers for many classes each term, and a class includes many students. This constitutes a many-to-many relationship.

Keeping in mind the different types of relationships you can have in a relational database, you must determine the kinds of relationships between tables.

Objective 5: Setting a Primary Key

Once you have determined the relationships between tables in your database, select a field in each table to serve as a primary key. Remember, the data values in a primary key field must uniquely identify each row in the table.

If you don't have a field in a table that is a good primary key, you might have to create one. StudentID, CustomerID, and InvoiceNumber are all typical primary key fields. While it is not absolutely necessary to set a primary key for each table, MS-Access functions faster and more efficiently if you do. It is always a good idea to assign a primary key to each table in your database.

Objective 6: Creating a Database Table

Table Wizard

MS-Access has many Wizards to help you create database objects, one of which is the Table Wizard. The *Table Wizard* is a set of instructions that prompts you for certain information and then builds a table for you. You can build a table without the help of the Table Wizard, but the best practice in most cases is to let the Table Wizard build a basic table for you and then modify the table to fit your needs.

Exercise 3: Creating the database tables

This exercise shows you how to use the Table Wizard to construct the first table in your contact database.

1. At the Database window, make sure the Table tab is selected and click New.

The New Table dialog box pops up.

2. Choose the Table Wizards button to activate the Table Wizard (Fig. 2-3).

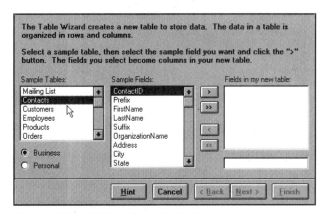

Figure 2-3   Table Wizard window

3. Highlight Contacts in the Sample Tables box.

The list of fields in the Sample Fields box changes to show the suggested fields for a Contacts table.

4. Highlight the ContactID field in the Sample Fields list. Click the single right arrow button to the right of the Sample Fields.

A copy of the ContactID field is moved to the list entitled Fields in my new table, and the Sample Fields highlight bar moves down to the next entry in the list.

5. Select the following fields from the Sample Fields list: FirstName, LastName, OrganizationName, Address, City, State, PostalCode, Country, WorkPhone, HomePhone, Note, and Photograph.

TIP   A quick way to select an item from the Sample Fields list is to double-click on it. The first click highlights the item; the second click selects it.

6. Click the Next> button.

The Next dialog box of the Table Wizard appears, asking you about table names and primary keys (Fig. 2-4).

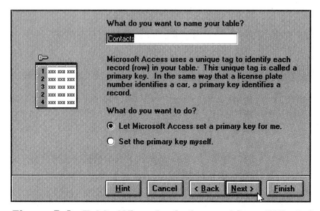

Figure 2-4   Table Wizard window asking, "What do you want to name your table?"

7. This Wizard dialog box asks you for a name for your table. MS-Access suggests Contacts. This seems reasonable, so leave it as is.

8. Check that Let MS-Access set a primary key for me is selected, then click Next.

The final Table Wizard window appears (Fig. 2-5).

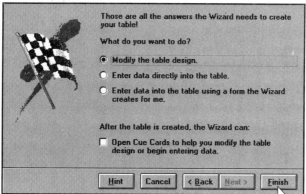

Figure 2-5 **Table Wizard Window with a checkered flag**

9. Click the Modify the table design button, and then the Finish button.

The Table Wizard builds your table and then exits, presenting you with the table in design view, so you can modify it.

Objective 7: Editing a Database Table

The Table Wizard is a helpful starting point for creating a table, but you will probably want to make some changes to the table it builds for you. In Exercise 4, you will modify some of the fields in the Contacts table.

Adding field descriptions

You should add some descriptive text to identify better the fields in the table. It is good practice to annotate each field when you create a table.

Exercise 4: Editing an existing field: adding field descriptions

The Table Wizard does not supply descriptions of each field when it builds a table, so you should add descriptions to document the fields you created. At the moment, your screen displays the Table Design window (Fig. 2-6).

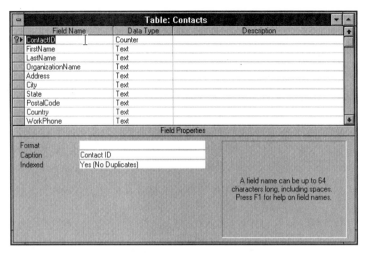

Figure 2-6   **Table Design window**

1. Use TAB, →, or the mouse to move the cursor to the top row of the Description field. Type Automatic counter, primary key.

2. Move the cursor to the Description column for the FirstName field and type Given name.

3. Add descriptions for the remaining fields.

Objective 8: Saving the Database Table

It is always a good idea to save your tables as you work on them and again when you end an editing session.

Exercise 5: Saving a database table

1. Click File/Save to save your work.

2. Close the Design window by clicking File/Close.

The First Computer Programmer . . .

. . . was a woman, Lady Augusta Ada Byron (1815 – 1853), the Countess of Lovelace and daughter of the poet Lord Byron. She worked closely with Charles Babbage, the father of the modern computer, developing program instructions for his Analytical Engine. In 1978, the Department of Defense (DOD) staged a competition to select a programming language as the standard for all software development within the DOD. They selected the language Ada, which was named after Augusta Ada. Today the DOD still uses Ada as the programming language for its embedded computer systems on airplanes, ships, and rockets.

Objective 9: Printing a Definition of the Database Table

database report

When you build tables in your database you should print out information about each table. This *database report* gives you documentation for each table—for example, when the table was created, when it was last updated, and how many records are in the table. The report also contains information on each field or column in the table, the relationships this table has with other tables, and how those relationships are defined.

Exercise 6: Printing out a table definition

1. In the Database window, click the Table tab. Make sure the Contacts table is highlighted.
2. Select File/Print Definition.

The Print Table Definition dialog box appears (Fig. 2-7).

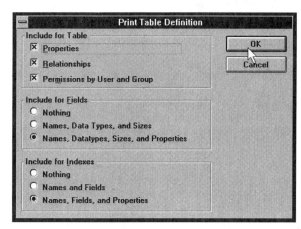

Figure 2-7   Print Table Definition dialog box

3. Select the following options for the Table Definition report:

   - Include for Table: Properties; Relationships; Permissions by User and Group
   - Include for Fields: Names, Data Types, Sizes, and Properties
   - Include for Indexes: Names, Fields, and Properties

4. Choose OK.

The Table Definition report Object Definition appears in Print Preview. (A table is an MS-Access object.) Scroll through the report, clicking the cursor to zoom in and out on any portion of the report.

⚠ WARNING If you want to print out this report, be sure that your computer is connected to a printer and that the printer is turned on.

FEATURE

What's in a name?

Here are some thoughts on how to handle a seemingly easy subject that is full of pitfalls — how to divide up the name field.

The simplest method is to split your names into two fields: one for last names, the other for first name plus middle initials. You will find that this accommodates both Wolfgang A. Mozart and J. Sebastian Bach.

However, name fields can be handled many different ways. Consider the following list:

- John Doe
- John M. Doe
- J. Martin Doe
- Dr. John M. Doe, III
- J. Martin Doe, III Ph. D.

And what about hyphenated, combined, and prefixed names like Forbes-Hamilton, Van Der Waal, and MacTavish? Or double last names such as Jacqueline Kennedy Onassis? You may consider using FamilyName and GivenName instead of FirstName and LastName.

Many societies reverse the order of their names: The well-known Japanese actor Toshiro Mifune is called Mifune Toshiro. It is important to be culturally, politically, and technically correct.

5. Click the Print icon.

The Print dialog box pops up (Fig. 2-8). You can print the entire report (six pages) or just a few pages. Check with your instructor to determine your best set of options for printing all or part of this report.

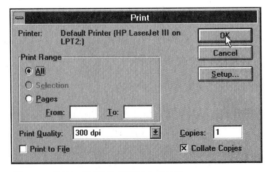

Figure 2-8 **Print dialog box**

6. To exit Print Preview, click the Open Door icon in the left corner.
7. Click File/Close Database to close the database.
8. Click File/Exit to shut down MS-Access.

Chapter Summary

The first part of this chapter discussed database design and some of the techniques used to develop a good design. You started with paper and pencil and determined (1) what the purpose of the database is and (2) what kind of information you want to get out of the database. That helped you to decide what kind of data to store and how to organize the data in the tables of the database. We discussed the types of relationships between the tables of the database and the criteria used to determine primary key assignments.

In the second part of this chapter, you built a table for your contacts database, then made some changes to the fields in the table. You learned how to print out a database report and save the table.

Review Questions

True/False Questions

_____   1. Before writing code, you need not take time to design your database program.

_____   2. If you understand what you want from a database, then you will understand how to design your database.

_____   3. It is a good idea to keep your database files in a directory separate from the MS-Access software.

_____   4. Every record in a table should have a unique identifier, called a primary key.

_____   5. A one-to-one relationship involves only one table.

Multiple-Choice Questions

_____ 6. All MS-Access database files have the extension

A. .mbd

B. .mdt

C. .mdb

D. .dta

_____ 7. A Table Wizard will

A. select data types for you.

B. show you the different colors and design options available for your table.

C. enter data into the table for you.

D. guide you through the table-building process and construct a table for you.

_____ 8. The primary key of a table

A. uniquely identifies each record in the table.

B. can be maintained only by MS-Access.

C. can be maintained only by the user.

D. speeds up operations on the database.

_____ 9. You would make a field a number field if

A. you will be doing calculations on the contents of the field.

B. the contents of the field will be number values.

C. the contents of the field will not be number values.

D. the field will hold decimal values.

_____ 10. If you need to store long messages or notes that will exceed 255 characters, you must use the data type called

A. text.

B. memo.

C. double.

D. long.

Fill-in-the-Blank Questions

11. MS-Access stores all the information about a database in _____ file on your hard drive.

12. When designing your database and choosing table and field names, it (is, is not) a good idea to use spaces in the names.

13. In a _____ relationship, each record in one table is related to many records in a second table.

14. The field in a table that contains a group of unique values that can uniquely identify each row of the table is called a _____.

15. To store money values in a field, you would use the _____ data type.

Acumen-Building Activities

Quick Projects

1. Creating a new Books database.

1. Start MS-Access. Click File/New Database.
2. In the File Name window type books.mdb.
3. Move to the Drives window in this dialog box. Make sure that the drive shown is where you want to save the database file.
4. Move to the Directories window in this dialog box. Make sure that the directory shown is where you want to save the database file. Click OK.

2. Creating a new table.

This exercise is a continuation of Quick Project #1.

1. At the Database window, with the Table tab selected, click New.
2. Choose the Table Wizards button.
3. Under Sample Tables, choose Personal. Scroll through the list and choose Book Collection.
4. From the Sample Fields list, choose the following fields and move them to the Fields in My Table list: BookCollectionID, Title, ISBNNumber, PublisherName, DatePurchased, Pages, and Note.
5. Click the Next button. Name your table MyBooks.
6. Choose Set the Primary Key Myself. Click Next.
7. Accept that BookCollectionID will be unique for each record and choose Numbers and/or letters I enter when I add new records. Click Next.
8. Click Modify the table design. Click Finish.

3. Adding field descriptions to the MyBooks table.

This exercise is a continuation of Quick Project #2.

1. Type these descriptions for the corresponding field names:
2. Save your changes by clicking File/Save.
3. Close the Design window. Click File/Close.

FIELD NAME	DESCRIPTION
BookCollectionID	Primary key of this table; unique identifier for each book.
Title	Title of the book
ISBNNumber	Assigned ISBN number.
PublisherName	Name of the publishing house.
DatePurchased	When this book was purchased.
Pages	Number of pages in the book.
Note	Subject, notes, and comments.

4. Printing out a report for the MyBooks table.

This exercise is a continuation of Quick Project #3.

1. Highlight MyBooks in the Database window. Select File/Print Definition.
2. Use the default options for this table. Choose OK.
3. Look at the Print Preview presentation of this report and use the zoom feature.
4. If you are connected to a printer, click the Print icon.
5. Choose File/Close. Choose File/Close Database.

In-Depth Projects

1. Creating the CD database.

1. Create a new database file and call it cd.mdb.
2. Create a new table using the Table Wizard. From the Personal Sample Tables list, use MusicCollection. Select MusicCollectionID, Title, GroupName, RecordingLabel, YearReleased, and PurchasePrice, in that order, and add them as fields in your new table.
3. Name your new table CDCollection, and let MS-Access set the primary key for you.
4. Indicate that you want to modify the table design, then tell the Table Wizard that you are finished.
5. In the Description column of the CDCollection table, add some text describing each field. Notice that MusicCollectionID is the primary key for this table.
6. Save the changes and close the Design Mode screen.
7. Print the Table Definition using the default options or, if you are not connected to a printer, carefully examine the Print Preview output.
8. Exit from Print Preview and close the database.

2. Creating the Dinner Party database.

1. Create a new database file and call it dinner.mdb.
2. Create a new table using the Table Wizard. From the Personal Sample Tables list use Guests. Select GuestID, FirstName, LastName, Address, City, State, PostalCode, HomePhone, and HealthProblems, in that order, and add them as fields in your new table.
3. Name your new table DinnerGuests and let MS-Access set the primary key for you.
4. Indicate that you want to modify the table design, then tell the Table Wizard that you are finished.
5. In the Description column of the DinnerGuests table, add a line of description for each field. GuestID is the primary key for this table. For the description of HealthProblems, type Dietary restrictions.
6. Save the changes and close the Design Mode screen.
7. Print the Table Definition using the default options or, if you are not connected to a printer, carefully examine the Print Preview output.
8. Exit from Print Preview and close the database.

CASE STUDIES

 **Coffee-On-The-Go:** **Creating a Database**

In this chapter, you learned how to create a database and a database table. You will use those skills to create an employee table for Coffee-On-The-Go.

1. Create a database file Coffee.mdb.
2. Create the following employee table:

Field	Type	Size
EmployeeID	Text	10
Last	Text	20
First	Text	9
Location	Text	2
Sex	Text	1
Salary	Currency	
Start	Date/Time	
Current	Yes/No	

3. Make EmployeeID the primary key for this table.
4. Save the table as Employee.
5. Print the table definition.

CASE STUDIES

 **Videos West:** **Creating a Database**

In this chapter, you learned how to create a database and a database table. You will use those skills to create an inventory table for Videos West.

1. Create a database file Video.mdb.
2. Create the following inventory table:

Field	Type	Size
VideoID	Counter	–
Type	Text	2
Title	Text	30
Cost	Currency	
Retail	Currency	
Quantity	Numeric/Integer	3
Rating	Text	2
Release	Date	

3. Make VideoID the primary key for this table.
4. Save the table as Inventory.
5. Print the table definition.

Chapter 3

Adding Records to the Database

Objectives

- Opening a Database File
- Using the Datasheet View to Add Records
- Using the Form Wizard to Create a Basic Data Entry Form
- Using the Form View to Add Records
- Generating a Quick Report with the Report Wizard

Key Terms

TERM	DEFINITION
Datasheet	a display of many records from a table of the database with the data arranged in rows and columns
Form Wizard	a predefined set of instructions built into MS-Access that assists in building a form by asking questions and then constructing a form
Browse Mode	a mode of operation that allows you only to view the records in your database
Edit Mode	a mode of operation that allows you to browse, make changes, and add records to your database
Data-Entry Mode	a mode of operation that allows you only to add records to your database
Report Wizard	a predefined set of instructions built into MS-Access that assists in building a report by asking questions and then constructing a report

You need to add data to your database so that you can extract information. Data can be added directly to the database tables using the datasheet view of the database or a data-entry form. In this chapter, you will add data to the database using both techniques. You will use the MS-Access Form Wizard to build a quick data-entry form to help you enter the data. Then you will use the MS-Access Report Wizard to generate a quick report so you can have a list of the data that you entered into the database.

MS-Access forms are usually screen displays that show a single record at a time from a database table. They are used to enter data into the database and display data from the database, record by record. Reports are printed on paper or distributed electronically and display organized information from the database.

datasheet The *datasheet* of an MS-Access database presents many records from a single table in a spreadsheet format. You can enter data directly into the datasheet. The Form Wizard helps you quickly build a form that is more suitable for data entry. Once you have some data in the database, you can use the Report Wizard to generate a quick report.

Objective 1: Opening a Database File

In order to continue working with the Sales Contact database you created in Chapter 2, you must first open that database file. There are three different ways to open an MS-Access database file. The first way is to use the icons on the upper toolbar. When you first start MS-Access, you will see a screen that is blank except for the menu and toolbar at the top and the status bar at the bottom, which reads "Ready." On the toolbar, the second icon from the left looks like an open folder. Clicking on this icon will open the Open Database dialog box.

The second way to open a database file is to use the top drop-down menu. By selecting the File option on the menu, then selecting the Open Database option from the drop-down menu that appears, you open the Open Database dialog box.

If you have recently used the database file you are seeking, then the third method may be the quickest: Select the File menu; near the bottom of the drop-down menu, just above Exit, is a list of recently used database files. You can select any file from this list.

Exercise 1: Opening a database file

1. Start MS-Access. Click the Open Folder icon of the top toolbar (Fig. 3-1).

Figure 3-1 Opening a database with the Open Folder icon

The Open Database dialog box pops up (Fig. 3-2), allowing you to select your drive, directory, and database file.

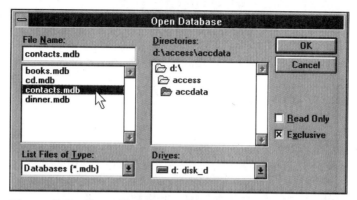

Figure 3-2   **Open Database dialog box**

2. Click Cancel.

   Now you will open the database file using the third method we discussed.

3. Click File on the menu bar (Fig. 3-3).

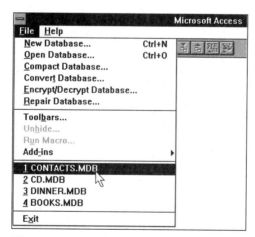

Figure 3-3   **MS-Access File menu**

4. Click the entry for contacts.mdb at the bottom of the drop-down menu.

   The Database window opens (Fig. 3-4).

Figure 3-4 **The Database window**

Objective 2: Using the Datasheet View to Add Records

You can add records directly to the datasheet. The datasheet looks much like a spreadsheet, with data arranged in rows and columns. Each row represents a single record; each column represents a single field of data.

When you add data to a field in the datasheet and the text you type is longer than the space shown on screen, the text scrolls to the left as you type it in. Notice that the table columns are identified by field captions, which (unlike field names) contain spaces for clarity.

Exercise 2: Adding records to the database using the Datasheet view

In this exercise, you will type several records directly into the datasheet.

1. Make sure the Contacts table is highlighted in the Database window. Click the Open button to open the datasheet (Fig. 3-5).

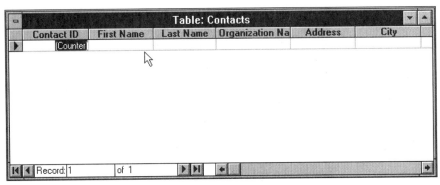

Figure 3-5 **Contacts database in Datasheet view**

2. Position the cursor in the first row of the First Name column and type John S.

   The counter field, ContactID, is immediately assigned a value by MS-Access.

3. Using TAB, move to the first row of the Last Name column and type Adams.

4. Enter the following data for each field:

The First U.S. Government Database . . .

. . . was developed by the Census Bureau to help with the 1890 census. The 1880 census took seven years to tabulate by hand. A government engineer and statistician named Herman Hollerith came up with an idea to facilitate counting. The 1890 census data was stored on cards with holes punched in them. Hollerith then built devices to punch the holes and other devices to sort the cards. Cards were "read" by electromechanical devices equipped with wire brushes that touched the cards. When the brush encountered a hole, it completed a circuit in an electromechanical counter. Using Hollerith's equipment and ideas, the Census Bureau completed the 1890 census count one month after the data was entered onto punch cards. The complete set of tabulations, including information that had never before been gathered because of the enormity of the task, was finished in under two years.

FIELD CAPTION	DATA
Organization Name:	Antiques Unlimited
Address:	47 Main Street
City:	Boston
State:	MA
Postal Code:	01738
Country:	USA
Work Phone:	1241234567 (Don't worry about parentheses around the area code or the hyphen in a seven-digit phone number; the format mask inserts those for you. Type only the digits, without any spaces.)
Home Phone:	1249742525
Note:	A real nice guy, likes to golf on Wednesdays.
Photo:	(no entry)

5. Press TAB to finish the record entry.

6. Save your work by selecting File/Save Record.

Exercise 3: Resizing a column of the datasheet

You can change the size of the columns in a datasheet so that you can see more and work better as you add and edit data. (If you have used Microsoft Excel, then you already know how to resize an MS-Access datasheet column.)

1. Position the cursor on the right boundary of the Address column.

   The cursor will change to a short vertical line intersected by a horizontal double arrow.

2. Drag the column boundary to the right to widen the column until it is large enough to display the full address (Fig. 3-6).

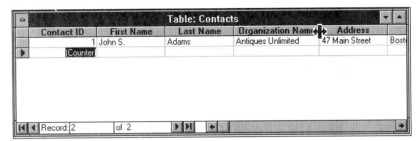

Figure 3-6   Resizing columns on the datasheet

3. Move to the State column. Position the cursor over the right boundary line of the State column label until the cursor changes shape.

4. Drag the right boundary line of the State column to the left, making the State column narrower.

5. Move to the Note column. Resize the Note column, making it wider so you can read a reasonable portion of the text contained within.

6. Save your changes by selecting File/Save Table. Close the datasheet using File/Close. Choose Yes when asked if you want to save the layout changes.

Objective 3: Using the Form Wizard to Create a Basic Data Entry Form

Form Wizards

There is a second way to enter data into the database: Use a data-entry form. You can easily and quickly build a data entry form using the MS-Access Form Wizards. The *Form Wizards* are programs built into MS-Access that assist in building a form by asking questions and constructing a form.

One of the MS-Access Form Wizards builds a very simple default form (MS-Access calls it an AutoForm) from a single table, with all the fields arranged in a single column. In later chapters, you will rearrange the position of the fields on the form and add some advanced features that will make your form more useable.

Exercise 4: Creating a basic data-entry form

The Form Wizard asks you several questions and then generates a default data-entry form for the Contacts table.

1. Make sure you're at the Database window and click the Form tab.

   The Forms window opens. At this point, you will have no forms in the list.

2. Click the New button to begin designing a new form (Fig. 3-7).

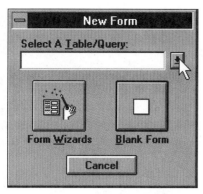

Figure 3-7   New Form menu

3. Click the down arrow to the right of the Select a Table/Query box.
   The drop-down menu appears with Contacts highlighted.
4. Click the highlighted Contacts entry in the list.
   Contacts pops into the Select a Table/Query box.
5. Click the Form Wizards button to initiate the Form Wizards (Fig. 3-8).

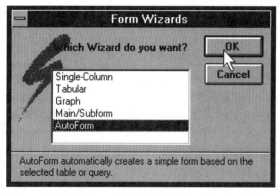

Figure 3-8   Form Wizards dialog box

6. Select AutoForm from the list of Wizards. Click OK.
   MS-Access builds the default data-entry form.
7. Save your work by clicking File/Save Form As from the top menu.
   The Save As dialog box appears.
8. Type QuickForm. Click OK (Fig. 3-9).

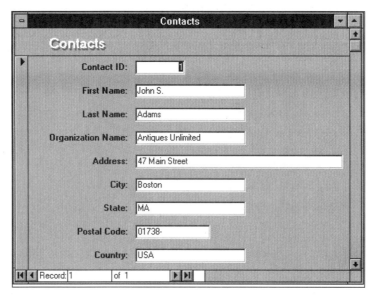

Figure 3-9 **A new form**

Objective 4: Using the Form View to Add Records

Browse mode

While working on a form, you have available three modes of operation: Browse mode, Data-Entry mode, and Edit mode. When you first open a form in MS-Access you are in *Browse mode:* You can search through the database and look at all your records. You can browse through the records using $\boxed{\text{CTRL}}$+$\boxed{\text{PAGE DOWN}}$ and $\boxed{\text{CTRL}}$+$\boxed{\text{PAGE UP}}$. You can also use the controls at the bottom of the form to scroll through the records. If your database is shared on a network, anyone on the network may browse the same data at the same time. You cannot make changes to the data in the database while in Browse mode.

Data-Entry mode

If you want to add new records to the database and do not need to view any of the data already stored in the table, then you want to use *Data-Entry mode*. While you enter a new record into the database, only you have access to that record. Other people on the network have to wait until you have saved the new record before they can view it.

Edit mode

When you want to be able to do a combination of tasks—browse the data, change or delete a record, and add a record—you want to be in *Edit mode*. While you are in Edit mode, you and others on your network will be able to browse all records in the database. Only when you begin to change the data in a record will others on the network be denied access to that record. As soon as you save the record, the record becomes available to others on the network.

Exercise 5: Adding records in Form view, Edit mode

In this exercise, you will add several records to the table using the data-entry form you created.

1. Click the right arrow with the vertical bar at the bottom of the form so that the last record in this table is displayed.
2. Click the single right arrow at the bottom of the form to switch to Data-Entry mode.
3. Press ⎯TAB⎯ to move to the First Name field and add the following data to the database:

FIELD CAPTION	DATA
First Name:	George
Last Name:	Langford
Organization Name:	Langford Trucking
Address:	1 Farm Road
City:	Mount Vernon
State:	VA
Postal Code:	00111
Country:	USA
Work Phone:	7032341234
Home Phone:	7032344321
Note:	Very cautious, very quality conscious.
Photo:	(no entry)

4. Press ⎯↵ ENTER⎯ to move to the next record.
5. Press ⎯TAB⎯ to move to the First Name field and add the following data:

FIELD CAPTION	DATA
First Name:	G. David
Last Name:	Swenson
Organization Name:	Swenson Adventure Tours
Address:	24 Bear Creek Road
City:	Smyrna
State:	TN
Postal Code:	27238
Country:	USA
Work Phone:	6156667777
Home Phone:	6156677773
Note:	Loves adventure and travel.
Photo:	(no entry)

6. Save your records by selecting File/Save Record from the top menu.

Exercise 6: Adding records in Form view, Data-Entry mode

In this exercise, you will add some records to the table using the same form. This time you will be in Data-Entry mode.

1. Select Records/Data Entry from the top menu.

   Notice that the record count at the bottom of the form has changed from `Record: 3 of 3` to `Record: 1 of 1`.

2. Press (TAB) to move to the First Name field and enter the following data:

FIELD CAPTION	DATA
First Name:	Margaret
Last Name:	Moore
Organization Name:	Liberty Insurance, Inc.
Address:	145 Independence Ave.
City:	Philadelphia
State:	PA
Postal Code:	01873
Country:	USA
Work Phone:	2152221111
Home Phone:	2152201234
Note:	In line for promotion to VP.
Photo:	(no entry)

3. Press (↵ ENTER) to move to the next record.

4. Press (TAB) to move to the First Name field and add the following data:

FIELD CAPTION	DATA
First Name:	John P.
Last Name:	Jones
Organization Name:	Jones Shipbuilding
Address:	19 Harbor Lane
City:	Mystic
State:	CT
Postal Code:	03728
Country:	USA
Work Phone:	2038003333
Home Phone:	2034544242
Note:	A dynamic personality.
Photo:	(no entry)

5. Save your records by selecting File/Save Record.

6. Add the following data while in Data-Entry mode:

Roger S. O'Leary
Western Surveying Company
2525 Forest Lane
Walla Walla, WA 94372 USA
Work: 509 989 1000
Home: 509 988 8877
"Likes to go camping."
(No photo)

Robin H. Clark
Western Surveying Company
270 Butte Meadows
Boise, ID 82919 USA
Work: 208 544 1111
Home: 208 543 1234
"Is into river rafting."
(No photo)

Ignacio Chavez
Western Surveying Company
348 Embarcadero
San Francisco, CA 91118 USA
Work: 415 222 8880
Home: 415 221 7777
"Has been a surveyor for many years."
(No photo)

Hiroshi Kanzaki
Western Surveying Company
897 Green Mtn. Boulevard
Portland, OR 93456 USA
Work: 503 565 7878
Home: 503 522 2334
"Doing well with his map-making business."
(No photo)

Wendy Monteleone
Monteleone Legal Services
1478 27th Avenue SW
Washington, DC 01728 USA
Work: 202 344 1212
Home: 202 341 1122
"Legal services at reasonable fees."
(No photo)

7. Select File/Save Record. Select File/Close.

Objective 5: Creating a Quick Report with the Report Wizard

Now that you have some data in your database, you can generate a report. Remember: The real justification for a database is information retrieval, not data storage. A report, printed to paper or circulated electronically by a network mail system, is an excellent way to disseminate information throughout your company. In the following exercise, you will use the MS-Access Report Wizard to build a default report from data in the Contacts table.

Report Wizard
The *Report Wizard* allows you to generate a quick report that can be used to check data that you have recently input. Generating a quick report is similar to generating a quick form. You tell MS-Access that you want to create a new report. It asks which table you want to use. Then the Report Wizard takes over. The generated report lays out the fields in a single column, one below the other. As you gain experience, you will let the Wizards build forms and reports and then modify their appearance to suit your requirements.

After you generate the quick report, you will have a chance to preview it before printing it out. You may direct the output from the report to Microsoft Word or Excel using the buttons just to the right of the center screen. In most cases, however, you will print the report from MS-Access.

FEATURE

Entering large amounts of data into your database
If you have a large quantity of data in another format—for example, a mailing list in a word-processing format or a list of data items in a spreadsheet program— you do not have to retype the data into your MS-Access database. MS-Access has an Import option to bring the external data into your MS-Access database tables. The Import function is part of the File menu and is quite simple to use.

Exercise 7: Generating a quick report

In this exercise, you will generate a quick report using the MS-Access Report Wizard. Your starting point is the Database window.

1. Click the Report tab in the Database window.

    The Reports window appears; there are no reports listed yet.

2. Click the New button to begin designing a new report.

3. Click the down arrow to the right of the Select a Table/Query box.

4. Click the highlighted Contacts entry in the list.

    Contacts pops into the Select a Table/Query box.

5. Click the Report Wizards button to initiate the Report Wizards (Fig. 3-10).

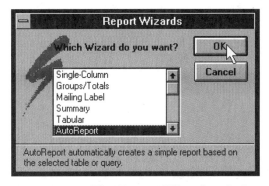

Figure 3-10 **The Report Wizards window**

6. Select AutoReport from the list of Wizards and click OK.

   MS-Access builds the default report. When the report is finished, you will be at the Print Preview screen (Fig. 3-11). Take a minute to explore some of the options on this screen. Position the cursor over each option in turn (but do not click the mouse), and balloon-box help information will appear to tell you what each button does. If you have a printer connected, you may now print your report.

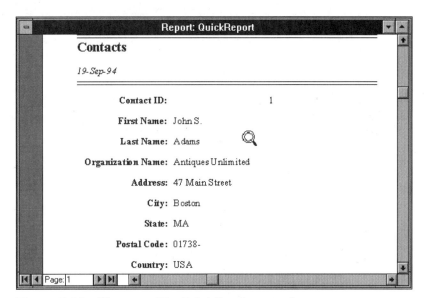

Figure 3-11 **The report in Print Preview mode**

7. To print the report, click the Printer icon to bring up the Print dialog box.

8. Accept All for the print range and press OK. Your report is printing.

9. Exit Print Preview by clicking the Close Window icon on the far left of the toolbar. You are returned to the Report Design Mode screen.

10. Click File/Save As. Name the report QuickReport. Click OK to save your work.
11. Click File/Close to exit the report.
12. Close the database.
13. Close MS-Access.

Chapter Summary

There are two ways to enter data into an MS-Access database. You can use the Datasheet view (rows and columns) or you can use a data-entry form, which you can easily create using the Form Wizard. When you wish to present information, you may do so using a printed report generated by the Report Wizard. Whether you are designing a form or a report, you can use a Wizard to generate a first draft, which you may then modify to your own specifications.

Review Questions

True/False Questions

_____ 1. A datasheet is a view of a single database table.

_____ 2. Reports display organized information from the database.

_____ 3. You cannot enter data directly into the Datasheet view of an MS-Access table.

_____ 4. The real reason for a database is data storage.

_____ 5. The default report created by the MS-Access Report Wizard lays out data in two, side-by-side columns.

Multiple-Choice Questions

_____ 6. Forms are most often used for

A. generating reports for circulation to the rest of the office.

B. entering and displaying data on the screen.

C. making backups of the database.

D. assistance in creating tables.

_____ 7. A dialog box

    A. keeps up a running conversation with your MS-Access database.

    B. is a pop-up screen.

    C. assists the user in performing some special function.

    D. B and C

_____ 8. MS-Access lists recently used databases under which menu entry?

    A. File

    B. Edit

    C. Window

    D. Help

_____ 9. Which MS-Access Wizard would you use to build a data-entry form?

    A. the Table Wizard

    B. the Query Wizard

    C. the Report Wizard

    D. the Forms Wizard

_____ 10. An excellent way to disseminate information throughout your company is to

    A. chat with your fellow employees at the water cooler.

    B. send your boss a memo.

    C. generate a database report and circulate it electronically using the network mail facility.

    D. not say anything; it's not part of your job description.

Fill-in-the-Blank Questions

11. The Datasheet view of an MS-Access table resembles a
_____.

12. To resize a column in Datasheet view, you _____ the right column boundary until the column is the size you want.

13. For data entry, the Form view is _____ user-friendly than the Datasheet view.

14. Reports are used to _____ information.

15. The facility used to preview a report before printing it is called the _____ screen.

Acumen-Building Activities

Quick Projects

1. Resize a column of the datasheet using the Books database.

1. Click File/Open Database to open the Books database. Open the table MyBooks.
2. Position the cursor on the right boundary of the BookCollectionID column label.
3. Drag the column boundary to the left to make the column narrower so that only the Book of BookCollectionID is showing.
4. Position the cursor over the right boundary line of the Pages column. Drag the right boundary line of the Pages column to the left making it narrower.
5. Select File/Save Table. Close the datasheet.

2. Build a quick form for MyBooks.

This exercise is a continuation of Quick Project #1.

1. From the Database window, click the Form tab. Click the New button to begin designing a new form.
2. Click the down arrow. Choose MyBooks for the Select a Table/Query.
3. Click the Form Wizards button. Select AutoForm. Click OK.
4. Click File/Save Form As. Name the form frmBook. Click OK.

3. Add records to MyBooks.

This exercise is a continuation of Quick Project #2.

1. In the BookCollectionID field, type 1.
2. Press ⬚TAB to move to the Title field and add the following data to the database:

FIELD	DATA
Title	Summer of the Danes
ISBNNumber	0-7472-3564-3
PublisherName	Headline
DatePurchased	3/12/94
Pages	311
Note	A medieval whodunnit. The Eighteenth Chronicle of Brother Cadfael.

3. Press ⬚↵ ENTER to move to the next record.
4. In the BookCollectionID field, type 2.

FIELD	DATA
Title	Relativity
ISBNNumber	0-517-029618
PublisherName	Crown
DatePurchased	6/01/90
Pages	164
Note	The special and general theories of relativity.

5. Add a third record using the following data:

FIELD	DATA
Title	Friday
ISBNNumber	1-03-061516-X
PublisherName	Holt Rinehart Winston
DatePurchased	7/23/91
Pages	368
Note	Recreational reading.

6. Add a fourth record using the following data:

FIELD	DATA
Title	One Up On Wall Street
ISBNNumber	0-1401-27925
PublisherName	Penguin
DatePurchased	11/30/93
Pages	318
Note	How to make money in the stock market.

7. Save your records. Close the form.

4. Build a quick report for MyBook.

This exercise is a continuation of Quick Project #3.

1. Click the Report tab in the Database window. Click New for a new report.

2. Select MyBooks for the Select a Table/Query. Click the Report Wizards button.

3. Select AutoReport from the list of Wizards and click OK.

4. Look at the Print Preview presentation of this report using the zoom feature.

5. If you are connected to a printer, click the Print icon and print out the report.

6. Exit Print Preview and click the Close Window icon. Select File/Save As.
7. Name the report rptBooks. Click OK. Choose File/Close to close the report.
8. Close the Book database by clicking File/Close Database.

In-Depth Projects

1. Quick forms and reports for the CD database.

1. Open the CD database. Create a new form for the CDCollection table using the Form Wizard. It will be an AutoForm.
2. When the form opens, enter some data. You may use the data suggested below or your own. Remember: The MusicCollectionID field is a counter, which will be incremented automatically, so Tab to the Title field to begin data entry.

TITLE	GROUP NAME	RECORDING LABEL	YEAR RELEASED	PURCHASE PRICE
Star Wars	London Symphony Orchestra	RSO	1977	20.00
Evangeline	Evangeline	MCA	1992	12.00
Canyon Trilogy	R. Carlos Nakai	Canyon Records	1989	14.00
Cusco 2002	Cusco	Higher Octave Music	1993	12.00
Question of Balance	Moody Blues	Threshold	1970	11.00

3. After you have finished entering the data, save your records.
4. Save the form and name it frmCD. Close the form.
5. Create a new report for the CDCollection table using the Report Wizard. It will be an AutoReport.
6. Print the report or, if you are not connected to a printer, examine carefully the Print Preview output.
7. Save the report, calling it rptCD, and close it. Close the CD database.

2. Quick forms and reports for the Dinner Party database.

1. Open the Dinner database. Create a new form for the DinnerGuests table using the Form Wizard. It will be an AutoForm.
2. When the form opens, enter some data. You may use the data suggested below or your own. Remember: The GuestID field is a counter, which will be incremented automatically, so Tab to the FirstName field to begin data entry.

FIRST NAME	LAST NAME	ADDRESS	CITY	STATE	POSTAL CODE	HOME PHONE	HEALTH PROBLEMS
Linda	Smith	231 Poplar Street	Golden	CO	80401	303-677-3241	
John	Baccus	89 Maple Grove	Littleton	CO	80123	303-757-9976	allergic to peanuts
Mary	Cummings	717 Shady Lane	Applewood	CO	80413	303-636-3357	
Fred	Wood	14 Fox Hunt Road	Lakewood	CO	80119	303-925-4546	
Sue	Woolrich	67 Genessee Point	Englewood	CO	80017	303-423-5531	

3. After you have finished entering the data, save your records.
4. Save the form and name it frmGuests. Close the form.
5. Create a new report for the DinnerGuests table using the Report Wizard. It will be an AutoReport. Print the report or, if you are not connected to a printer, examine carefully the Print Preview output.
6. Save the report, calling it rptGuests. Close the Dinner database.

CASE STUDIES

Coffee-On-The-Go: **Adding Records**

In this chapter, you learned to add records to a database. You will use those skills to add records to the Coffee database for Coffee-On-The-Go.

1. Open the Coffee database.
2. Open the Employee table.
3. Add the following records:

1	Smith	Sue	01	F	15,000	1/3/89	y
2	Lowe	George	02	M	12,000	3/30/91	y
3	White	Albert	01	M	15,000	4/1/90	n
4	Jones	Jerry	01	M	14,000	3/15/93	y
5	Smyth	Sally	03	F	18,000	1/4/90	y
6	Meyers	Judy	01	F	14,000	4/1/94	y
7	Miller	Mark	03	M	12,000	3/8/88	n
8	Smithsonian	Gerry	02	M	16,000	2/3/94	y
9	Ryan	Randy	01	M	14,000	3/3/90	n
10	Hart	Henry	01	M	18,000	4/2/90	y
11	Gold	Jane	04	F	15,000	12/20/89	y
12	Williams	Larry	04	M	17,000	9/15/90	y
13	Black	Ann	03	F	13,000	6/4/93	y
14	Pope	Nancy	01	F	17,000	8/1/92	y
15	Frances	Mary	04	F	14,000	4/2/90	n

4. Save the Employee table.
5. Print a quick report of the data.

CASE STUDIES

 **Videos West:**   **Adding Records**

In this chapter, you learned to add records to a database. You will use those skills to add records to the Video database for Videos West.

1. Open the Video database.
2. Open the Inventory table.
3. Add the following records:

01	Golf Like a Pro	7.99	19.99	10	PG	5/1/93
01	Tips on Hunting	3.99	14.99	5	R	6/1/90
02	Tai Chi for Health	9.99	19.99	3	PG	6/1/94
03	Quit Smoking on Your Own	5.99	9.99	5	PG	7/15/93
04	Buy Your Own Home	6.99	14.99	4	PG	5/1/92
01	Baseball Tips	9.99	19.99	2	PG	6/1/92
05	Beaded Jewelry	5.99	14.99	1	PG	5/15/93
02	Jogging Tips	6.99	14.99	2	PG	8/1/93
04	Take Control of Your Debt	5.99	9.99	3	PG	5/1/92
03	Addiction Awareness	14.99	21.99	6	R	7/1/94
03	Eating for Your Health	5.99	14.99	7	PG	8/1/94
05	Christmas Decorations	3.99	7.99	1	PG	12/2/92
01	Skiing Your Best	9.99	19.99	3	PG	3/1/91
01	Tennis Pros Talk	5.99	9.99	1	PG	1/1/94
05	Hobbies for Profit	5.99	9.99	2	PG	2/1/94
02	Yoga for Your Health	9.99	14.99	3	PG	6/1/91
04	Start Your Own Business	5.99	14.99	7	PG	5/1/93

4. Save the Inventory table.
5. Print a quick report of the data.

Chapter 4

Editing a Database

Key Terms

TERM	DEFINITION
Delete a Record	remove a record from a database
Update a Record	change a data value within a record that is currently in a database
Input Mask	a user-defined template attached to a field of a table or form that aids in data entry; MS-Access contains several pre-defined input masks for commonly-used fields such as PhoneNumber and SocialSecurityNumber

Some database tables, such as a list of state abbreviations, are relatively static. Other database tables, such as a list of contacts or employees, change often. As your business changes, so will the data you store in your database. You must keep your databases current by adding, editing, and deleting records and modifying table structures as necessary.

Objective 1: Adding a Field Using the Table Design View

The easiest way to add a new field is to copy an existing field using the cut and paste method; this method copies all the characteristics of the old field and transfers them to the new field. Alternatively, you can create a new field from scratch.

input mask   An *input mask* is a special property that you can assign to a field in a table. It is a template that formats the data entered into the field by specifying where data is to be entered, what kind of data is allowed, and how many characters are allowed. Although you define the input mask for a field in a table, when you build a form from the table the input mask remains.

Adding a New Field to the Table Using Cut and Paste

Databases evolve as you use them. You design the database carefully, use the database for a while, and then realize that you need a field not included in the original design. MS-Access makes it easy to add fields to your database tables.

Exercise 1: Adding a new field to the table using cut and paste

When you created the Contacts table you included the fields WorkPhone and HomePhone. For a business contact database, you should include a fax number as well.

1. Start MS-Access, and open the Contacts database. Open the Contacts table in Design mode.
2. Scroll down to the HomePhone row of the Field Name column.
3. Position the cursor in the left margin of the row to the left of the H in HomePhone; the cursor arrow changes shape and points into the row.
4. Click the mouse to highlight the row (Fig. 4-1).

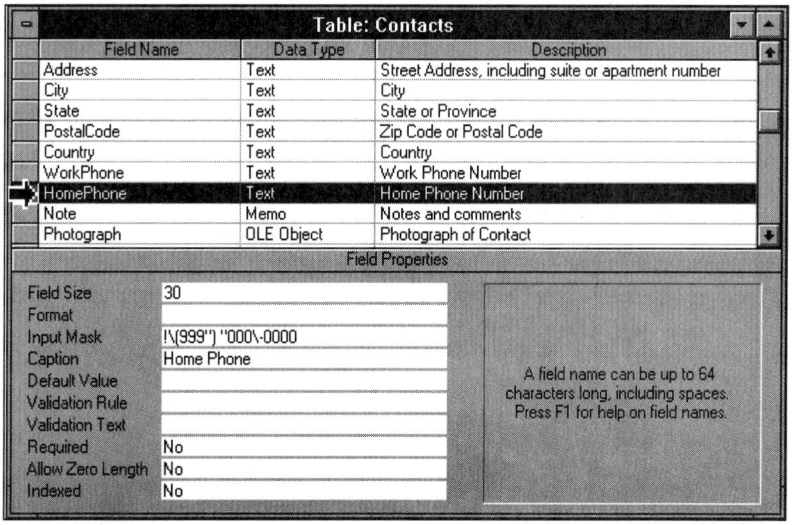

Figure 4-1   Table Design window with HomePhone highlighted

5. Click Edit/Copy to place a copy of HomePhone on the Windows clipboard.

6. Click Edit/Insert Row to insert an empty row above HomePhone.

7. Click Edit/Paste to place a copy of HomePhone in the blank row.

8. Type Fax in the Field Name column and Fax Number in the Description column.

    Note: MS-Access will not accept two identical field names in the same table, so you must change the name of the new field when you add a field by copying.

9. Press F6 to move into the Field Properties box. Type Fax Number in the Caption row.

10. Press F6 to return to the field definitions (Fig. 4-2). Click File/Save to save your work.

Field Name	Data Type	Description
Address	Text	Street Address, including suite or apartment number
City	Text	City
State	Text	State or Province
PostalCode	Text	Zip Code or Postal Code
Country	Text	Country
WorkPhone	Text	Work Phone Number
Fax	Text	Fax Number
HomePhone	Text	Home Phone Number
Note	Memo	Notes and comments
Photograph	OLE Object	Photograph of Contact

Table: Contacts

Field Properties

Field Size	30
Format	
Input Mask	!\(999") "000\-0000
Caption	Fax Number
Default Value	
Validation Rule	
Validation Text	
Required	No
Allow Zero Length	No
Indexed	No

The field description is optional. It helps you describe the field and is also displayed in the status bar when you select this field on a form. Press F1 for help on descriptions.

Figure 4-2 Table Design window with the Fax field added

Creating a New Field from Scratch

You need a field to record the number of employees in a company. You will use this field to find candidates for the on-site computer classes you offer. Because you will perform calculations on this data, it must be a numeric field.

Exercise 2: Adding a new field to the table from scratch

There is no similar field to copy, so you will create a new field from scratch.

1. Open the table Contacts in Design mode. Scroll to the empty row below the field named Photograph. Type NumEmployees in the Field Name column.

2. Press TAB or ← ENTER to move to the Data Type column.

3. Click the down arrow at the right side of the box and choose Number from the list. Press F6 to move to the Field Properties box (Fig. 4-3).

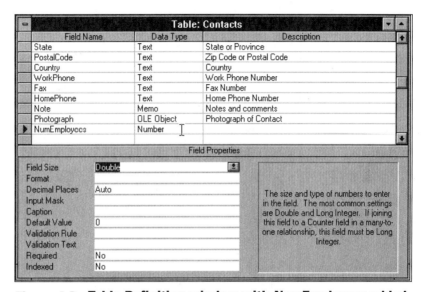

Figure 4-3 **Table Definition window with NumEmployees added**

4. Use the down arrow at the right of the box to see a list of the available numeric data types (Fig. 4-4) and choose Integer.

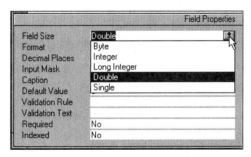

Figure 4-4 **Field Properties window with numeric data types listed**

5. In the Field Properties box, move to the Caption line and type Number of Employees. Press F6 to return to the Definition window.

6. Move to the Description column, type Number of employees who work for this company. Click File/Save to save your work.

7. Switch to Datasheet view. Input the following values for Fax and NumEmployees:

FIRST NAME	LAST NAME	FAX	NUMBER OF EMPLOYEES
John	Adams	(124)123-9874	8
George	Langford	(703)234-1111	85
G. David	Swenson		50
Margaret	Moore	(215)222-1010	1259
John P.	Jones		2
Roger S.	O'Leary	(509)989-3333	14
Robin H.	Clark	(208)544-1100	10
Ignacio	Chavez	(415)222-8000	49
Hiroshi	Kanzaki	(503)565-7888	26
Wendy	Monteleone	(202)727-4444	2

Objective 2: Deleting a Field Using the Table Design View

Occasionally you will design a table and include fields that are not useful. Deleting fields from a table is very simple and quick, but be sure that you will not need the data stored in the deleted fields—the data is deleted from the database along with the field.

Exercise 3: Deleting a field from the database table

In this exercise, you will delete the Photograph field.

1. Switch back to Design view, and move the cursor to the Photograph field. Click the margin to the left of the P in Photograph to highlight the entire field.
2. Press (DELETE) on your keyboard to remove the field.

NOTE If you accidentally delete the wrong row, you can recover, but only if you act immediately. Select Edit/Undo to restore the deleted row. A dialog box appears, telling you "If you delete this field, you will lose the data it contains. Continue anyway?"

3. Click OK.
4. Click File/Save to save your work. Click File/Close to leave Table Design mode.

Objective 3: Changing a Record Using the Datasheet or Table View

update a record You can use the Datasheet view to *update a record*—that is, change one or more data values within a record that is currently in a database. This method is most efficient when you have only a few changes to make. The Datasheet view displays multiple records in a row-and-column format, letting you view many records at one time. How you move to a field in the datasheet affects how MS-Access handles the data you input. If you use Tab and the arrow keys to move to a field, all the data in the field is highlighted, and anything you type will replace what is currently in that field. If you use the mouse to position the cursor in the field, whatever you type will be inserted at the cursor position, and the rest of the text will be moved to the right.

Exercise 4: Changing records in Datasheet view

John S. Adams is on an extended vacation, so your contact at his antique shop will be his cousin Sam Adams. Also, Margaret Moore informed you that the Liberty Insurance Co. has changed its name to Liberty Shield Insurance, Inc.

1. Open the Contacts table in Datasheet view. (TAB) to the FirstName field for John S. Adams. Type Sam and press (TAB) or (↵ ENTER).

2. Position the cursor between Liberty and Insurance in the Organization Name field of the Margaret Moore record. Click once. Type Shield and add a space before or after this word, as necessary (Fig. 4-5).

Contact ID	First Name	Last Name	Organization Name	Address	City
1	Sam	Adams	Antiques Unlimited	47 Main Street	Boston
2	George	Langford	Langford Trucking	1 Farm Road	Mount vernon
3	G. David	Swenson	Swenson Adventure Tc	24 Bear Creek Road	Smyrna
4	Margaret	Moore	Liberty Shield Insuranc	145 Independence A	Philadelphia
5	John P.	Jones	Jones Shipbuilding	19 Harbor Lane	Mystic
6	Roger S.	O'Leary	Western Surveying Cor	2525 Forest lane	Walla Walla
7	Robin H.	Clark	Western Surveying Cor	270 Butte meadows	Boise
8	Ignacio	Chavez	Western Surveying Cor	348 Embarcadero	San Francisco
9	Hiroshi	Kanzaki	Western Surveying Cor	897 Green Mountain I	Portland
10	Wendy	Monteleone	Monteleone Legal Serv	1478 27th Avenue S\	Washington

Record: 1   of 10

Figure 4-5 Contacts table in Datasheet view with changes

3. Position the mouse at the end of the OrganizationName field after the Co. Use (← BACKSPACE) to remove the Co. and the space preceding it. Type, Inc.

4. Save your changes by selecting File/Save Record. Close the datasheet.

Objective 4: Changing a Record Using the Form View

G. David Swenson has moved his Adventure Tours from Smyrna to Nashville; this means you need to update his record. In the following exercise, you will use the Form view to make the modifications.

Exercise 5: Changing a record in Form view

In this exercise, you will make changes to the record for G. David Swenson.

1. In the Database window, click the Form tab. Open the QuickForm.

2. Click on the right, single arrow at the bottom of the form repeatedly until you find the record for G. David Swenson. (TAB) to the Address field.

3. Type 101 Chase Lane. Press (↵ ENTER) to move to the City field.

4. Type Nashville. Press (↵ ENTER) twice to move to the PostalCode field.

5. Press (DELETE) to remove the PostalCode value. You don't know the new postal code, but you need to remove the old value because it is no longer valid.

6. Repeat Step 5 to remove the data values for the WorkPhone, Fax, and HomePhone fields.

7. (TAB) to the Note field, press (F2), and type Just moved from Smyrna to Nashville. This comment will be added to the notes already in the field.

8. Select File/Save Record. Close the QuickForm.

Objective 5: Deleting Records Using the Datasheet or Table View

delete records

You decide to remove certain people—retirees and those with whom you have lost contact—from your database so that it will run more quickly and take up less disk space. This means you will *delete records.*

You can delete records using either the Datasheet or Form view—these two views are essentially the same. When you delete records using the Datasheet view, you can delete one or more records at the same time. In Form view, you can only delete one record at a time: You must first open the form, select the record you want to delete, and then delete it.

When you delete a record from the database, you can change your mind and cancel the delete command. MS-Access asks if you want to save your changes. If you choose OK, the record is deleted.

Exercise 6: Deleting a single record using the Datasheet or Table view

Open the Contacts table in Datasheet view. Move to the record for John P. Jones, who has recently retired and is living on his yacht, and delete it.

1. Open the Contacts table in Datasheet view and select the record for John P. Jones.

2. Click the arrow in the left margin of the datasheet to highlight the entire record (Fig. 4-6).

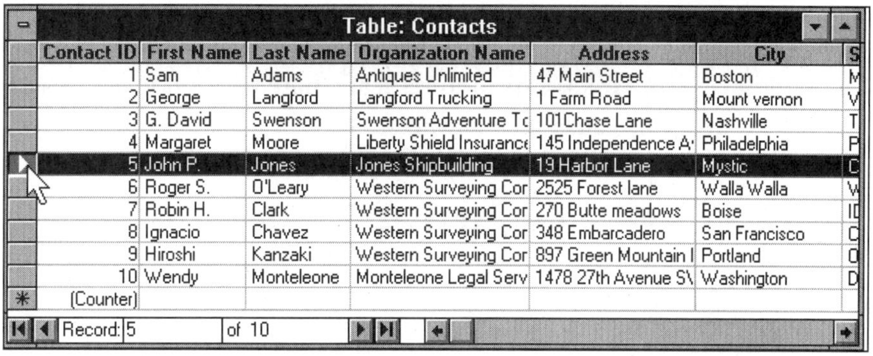

Table: Contacts

Contact ID	First Name	Last Name	Organization Name	Address	City	S
1	Sam	Adams	Antiques Unlimited	47 Main Street	Boston	M
2	George	Langford	Langford Trucking	1 Farm Road	Mount vernon	V
3	G. David	Swenson	Swenson Adventure Tc	101Chase Lane	Nashville	T
4	Margaret	Moore	Liberty Shield Insuranc	145 Independence A	Philadelphia	P
5	John P.	Jones	Jones Shipbuilding	19 Harbor Lane	Mystic	C
6	Roger S.	O'Leary	Western Surveying Cor	2525 Forest lane	Walla Walla	W
7	Robin H.	Clark	Western Surveying Cor	270 Butte meadows	Boise	ID
8	Ignacio	Chavez	Western Surveying Cor	348 Embarcadero	San Francisco	C
9	Hiroshi	Kanzaki	Western Surveying Cor	897 Green Mountain I	Portland	O
10	Wendy	Monteleone	Monteleone Legal Serv	1478 27th Avenue S\	Washington	D
(Counter)						

Record: 5 of 10

Figure 4-6 Contacts table in Datasheet view with John P. Jones record highlighted

3. Press DELETE to remove the record.
4. Click OK in the dialog box to confirm that you want to delete this record.

   Mr. Jones is gone from your database and MS-Access has updated all the necessary tables.

Exercise 7: Deleting multiple records using the Datasheet or Table view

Your contacts O'Leary, Clark, Chavez, and Kanzaki have moved. You want to delete their records. Their records are listed consecutively in the database, so you can remove them in one operation.

1. Highlight the entire O'Leary record by clicking the left margin of the datasheet.
2. Hold the left mouse button down and drag the cursor down the table until Clark, Chavez, and Kanzaki are also highlighted (Fig. 4-7).

   (To highlight several consecutive records, you can click the first record in the block, hold down Shift, and click the last record in the block.)

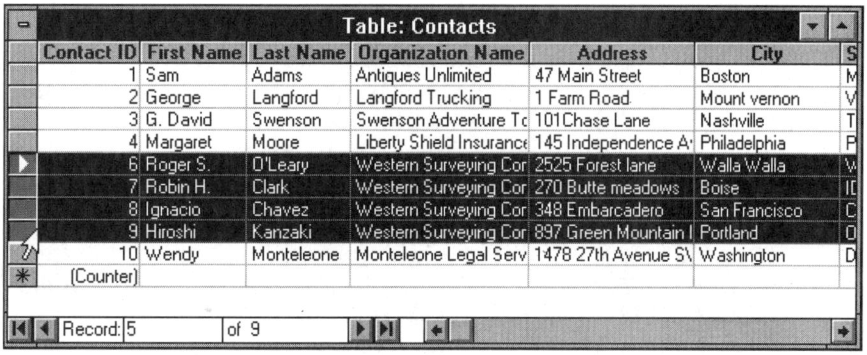

Table: Contacts

Contact ID	First Name	Last Name	Organization Name	Address	City	S
1	Sam	Adams	Antiques Unlimited	47 Main Street	Boston	M
2	George	Langford	Langford Trucking	1 Farm Road	Mount vernon	V
3	G. David	Swenson	Swenson Adventure Tc	101Chase Lane	Nashville	T
4	Margaret	Moore	Liberty Shield Insuranc	145 Independence A	Philadelphia	P
6	Roger S.	O'Leary	Western Surveying Cor	2525 Forest lane	Walla Walla	W
7	Robin H.	Clark	Western Surveying Cor	270 Butte meadows	Boise	ID
8	Ignacio	Chavez	Western Surveying Cor	348 Embarcadero	San Francisco	C
9	Hiroshi	Kanzaki	Western Surveying Cor	897 Green Mountain I	Portland	O
10	Wendy	Monteleone	Monteleone Legal Serv	1478 27th Avenue S\	Washington	D
(Counter)						

Record: 5 of 9

Figure 4-7 Contacts table in Datasheet view with four records selected

3. Select Edit/Delete or press (DELETE).

4. When the dialog box appears asking you to confirm your deletion, click Cancel to indicate that you do *not* want to delete these records.

5. Close the datasheet.

The Gender Gap and Computers . . .

. . . is real, according to *Newsweek* magazine (May 16, 1994). Multiple studies done on households across the country show that nearly one-third of American families have at least one computer in the home, but most of those are purchased and operated by males. Could this be male-bonding in the digital age? After all, to the truly converted, computers are a virtual religion, complete with icons (on-screen graphics), relics (obsolete hardware and software), and prophets (Microsoft's Bill Gates). Females tend to think of computers as something to be *used*, like a dishwasher or microwave, but certainly not something worthy of obsession or worship.

From the report Computers in American Schools (University of Minnesota), we find that until about the fifth grade boys and girls are equally interested in computers. Then, when children begin to identify more strongly with their sex, we see a definite drift— boys toward computers, girls away from computers. These paths seem to continue throughout life. Even though women have made great strides in occupations formerly dominated by men, such as law and medicine, they have yet to enter the computer industry in significant numbers. The National Science Foundation released a report that states that men earning computer-science and related degrees outnumber women by 3 to 1, and the gap appears to be growing.

Objective 6: Deleting Records Using the Form View

The Form view is most often used for data entry, but it can also be used for changing or deleting records. You will be able to change or delete only the record that is on the screen.

Exercise 8: Deleting a record using the Form view

You want to remove Wendy Monteleone from your list of contacts. You must first select the record before you can delete it.

1. Open the QuickForm. Use the buttons at the bottom of the form to find the record for Wendy Monteleone.

2. Select the record by clicking Edit/Select Record.

3. Press (DELETE) to remove the record. Click Cancel when MS-Access asks if you want to save your changes. Close the form.

Objective 7: Locating Records

Once you have many records in a database, you will find it a chore to page through them looking for a particular record. Fortunately, you you can use the Find dialog box, in either Datasheet or Form view, to locate specific records quickly.

The Find dialog box is opened by clicking the binoculars icon on the top toolbar, pressing Ctrl+F, or selecting Edit/Find from the top menu. Using one of these three mthods, call up the Find dialog box.

Notice the options in the Find dialog box. Let's assume you want to find the record George Langford. You could change the Where condition to Start Of Field, type Lang, and thus find all records that begin with Lang. Of course, MS-Access would find Langdon and Langston as well, if they were records in your database.

Exercise 9: Finding a record in Datasheet view

In this exercise, you will find a record in the database by opening the datasheet, selecting the field to be searched, and specifying the search criteria.

1. Open the Contacts table in Datasheet view. Position the cursor at the top of the Last Name column until it changes to a black down-turned arrow.
2. Click the Last Name label.

   The entire column is selected for the search operation.
3. Click the binoculars icon to open the Find dialog box.

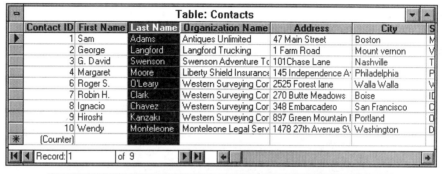

Figure 4-8   Contacts table in Datasheet view with the Find dialog box open

4. Type Langford in the Find What field (Fig. 4-8) and press ⏎ ENTER.

   MS-Access finds the record for George Langford.
5. Click the Close button to close the Find dialog box.

   The record for George Langford is highlighted in the datasheet.
6. Close the datasheet.

Objective 8: Locating and Replacing Data

You sometimes need to find one or more records in your database and update the information they contain. The Replace procedure is very similar to the Find procedure. However, when replacing information, you specify not only the data you want to find, but the data you want to input in its place.

You can replace data values one record at a time, or you can replace a value in all the records at the same time. You should use this method only when you are sure that you want to substitute a new value for every occurrence of the old value in *all* records.

When you perform a Find-and-Replace operation on more than one record at a time, you make multiple changes to the data in your database. You must confirm these changes in a separate step. Also, the Edit/Undo option does not work after multiple changes are made.

Exercise 10: Locating and Replacing Data

Western Surveying Company has changed its name to Precision Surveys, Inc. You have several contacts at Western Surveying. Find and replace the outdated data with the current data.

1. Open the QuickForm and move to the Organization Name field.
2. Click Edit/Replace on the top menu. The Replace dialog box opens.

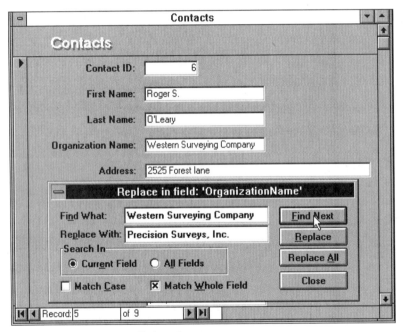

Figure 4-9   Replace dialog box

3. Type Western Surveying Company in the Find What box. Press ⌷TAB⌷.
4. Type Precision Surveys, Inc. in the Replace With box. Press ⌷↵ENTER⌷.

    The first record with Organization Name Western Surveying Company has been found (Fig. 4-9). Now replace the old organization name with the new one.

5. Click Replace to modify the O'Leary record.
6. To change the rest of the outdated values, click Replace All.

    All the outdated records are changed. The pop-up dialog box indicates that MS-Access has reached the end of its search.

7. Select Yes when asked if MS-Access should continue searching from the beginning of the records. Click OK when the next pop-up dialog box appears.

   MS-Access has reached the end of the records and has made all the replacements you requested.

8. Click OK when you are warned that this operation cannot be undone.

9. Click Close to exit the Replace dialog box. Close the Contacts QuickForm.

FEATURE

Tips on table design

When you create fields in a table, do not give the same name to two fields. MS-Access will not accept two identical field names in the same table.

When you add a field to a table, you can insert it anywhere in the table; you do not have to add it to the end of the table. Simply highlight the row *below* where you want the new field to appear and press Insert.

The Field Name, Caption, and Description fields often contain the same information, but they do not have to. The Field Name is the name given to a data item when it is created as part of the table. It can be as long as 64 characters, but you should try to keep it between 12 and 20 characters. Don't use embedded spaces in the field name; rather, use the mixed-case naming convention we introduced earlier. The Caption is a label that appears on forms and reports. If you do not specify a Caption, MS-Access automatically creates one from the Field Name. If you create your own Captions, make them descriptive but short. The Description is the place to spell out the purpose or use of a field. Indicate in the Description column when a field is a primary key or when it relates to other tables. Identification fields and Code fields might need an explanation to make them understandable to others. You should always document your work, and the Description column is the place to do just that.

Chapter Summary

In this chapter, you learned how to udpate your database by editing records and removing out-of-date records, find specific records in the database using the Find operation, and search for and replace data values with the Find-and-Replace function. You learned how to perform these database maintenance operations using both the Datasheet and Form views.

Review Questions

True/False Questions

_____ 1. A database is only as accurate and current as the data it contains.

_____ 2. Once you press Del to delete a record in Datasheet view, you have no way to reverse that action.

_____ 3. In Datasheet view, you cannot delete more than one record at a time.

_____ 4. In Form view, you cannot delete more than one record at a time.

_____ 5. When using the Find dialog box to locate a record, MS-Access shows only records that match exactly the text you type.

Multiple-Choice Questions

_____ 6. You make changes to the data in your database because

    A. you want accurate information.

    B. you want current, timely information.

    C. you want the data in your database to be correct.

    D. All of the above.

_____ 7. When in Data-Entry or Update mode on the datasheet, scrolling allows you to

    A. move the cursor from field to field.

    B. continue entering text even after you have apparently filled the field.

    C. switch from Form to Datasheet view.

    D. enter the same data in several consecutive records.

_____ 8. You can open a form from the Database window by

    A. highlighting the form name and clicking Open.

    B. typing OPEN form_name> at the command line.

    C. double-clicking the form name.

    D. either A or C

_____ 9. When deleting records from the database, you must

    A. use the mouse to position the cursor in the field you want to delete, then press Del.

    B. press Ctrl+Alt+Del.

    C. first select the record, then delete it.

    D. Choose File/Remove from the top menu.

_____ 10. When performing a Find-and-Replace operation, you must
   A. position the cursor in the field you want to change and select File/Replace from the top menu.
   B. first select the field and then type in the old and new data values.
   C. select Edit/Replace from the top menu without first indicating the field.
   D. press Ctrl+Alt+Repl.

Fill-in-the-Blank Questions

11. To move from field to field in a form, you can use the _____ key.
12. To move from field to field in a form and highlight the contents of the field selected, you would use the _____ key.
13. One way to open the Search dialog box is to click the _____ icon on the top toolbar.
14. The _____ operation locates all records that meet the criteria you have specified.
15. The _____ operation locates all records that meet the criteria you have specified and replaces the data with the new value you specify.

Acumen-Building Activities

Quick Projects

1. Creating a new field in the table MyBooks.

1. Open the Books database. Open the table MyBooks in Table Design mode.
2. Highlight the row ISBNNumber by clicking the margin to the left of Field Name. Press INSERT.
3. Type Author in the Field Name column. Choose Text as the data type.
4. Press F6 to move to the Field Properties box. In the Indexed row select Yes (Duplicates OK). Press F6 to return to the Definition window.
5. In the Description column, type Author of the book.
6. Click File/Save. Exit Table Design mode.

2. Regenerating the AutoForm for MyBooks to include the new field.

This exercise is a continuation of Quick Project #1.

1. Click the Form tab in the Database window.
2. Make sure .frmBook is highlighted. Press DELETE. Click OK.

3. Create a New form using the table MyBooks and the Form Wizards.

4. Select AutoForm. Save your work (File/Save Form As). Name the new form frmBooks. Click OK.

3. Changing records in MyBooks.

This exercise is a continuation of Quick Project #2.

1. For Book ID #1, (TAB) to the Author field and type Ellis Peters.
2. For Book ID #2, (TAB) to the Author field and type Albert Einstein.
3. For Book ID #3, (TAB) to the Author field and type Robert Heinlein.
4. For Book ID #4, (TAB) to the Author field and type Peter Lynch.
5. Save your work by clicking File/Save Record.

4. Finding a record in the Form view from MyBooks.

This exercise is a continuation of Quick Project #3.

1. Press (SHIFT)+(TAB) to return to the Title field. Click the binoculars icon on the toolbar.
2. Type Danes in the Find What field. Make sure the Where field is set to Any Part of Field. Click Find First. Drag the Find dialog box down to the bottom of the screen so you can see the record underneath.
3. Click the Find Next button in the dialog box to find any additional entries for Danes. Check through the records from the beginning.
4. Close the Find dialog box. Close the form. Save your changes.
5. Close the Books database.

In-Depth Projects

1. The CD database.

1. Open the CD database. Open the table CDCollection in Table Design mode.
2. Add two new fields. Insert the field Length between YearReleased and PurchasePrice. Make it a number/integer data type. Modify the caption by typing Length in Minutes. In the Description field, type How long is this CD? Add the field Classification to the end of the Field Name list. Make it a text data type. In the Description field, type What type of music is this?
3. Save the changes you made and close the Table Design Mode window.
4. Go to the Forms listing in the Database window and delete the form frmCD.
5. Create a new form using the Auto Form option of the Form Wizards. Save the form, calling it frmCDs. Leave the new form open.
6. Modify the data currently in CDCollection. You may use the data suggested below, which is a continuation of the data from the previous chapter, or your own.

TITLE	LENGTH	CLASSIFICATION
Star Wars	75	Movie theme
Evangeline	39	Cajun/Country
Canyon Trilogy	59	Native American flute
Cusco 2002	41	New Age symphonic
Question of Balance	38	Symphonic Rock

7. After you have entered the data, save your records.

8. Close the form. Close the CD database.

2. The Dinner Party database.

1. Open the database dinner.mdb. Open the table DinnerGuests in Table Design mode.

2. Add two new fields to the end of the Field Name list. The first field is Likes: Make it a text data type and type Specific food preferences as the Description. The second field is Dislikes: Make it a text data type and type Specific culinary dislikes for the Description.

3. Save the changes you have just made and close the Table Design Mode window.

4. Go to the Forms listing in the Database window and delete the form frmGuests.

5. Create a new form using the Auto Form option of the Form Wizards. Save the form, calling it frmGuests. Leave the new form open.

6. Modify the data currently in DinnerGuests. You may use the data suggested below, which is a continuation of the data from the previous chapter, or your own. Maximize the form to facilitate data entry.

FIRST NAME	LAST NAME	LIKES	DISLIKES
Linda	Smith	chocolate	
John	Baccus	fajitas	cauliflower
Mary	Cummings	lemon squares	
Fred	Wood	strawberry trifle	whole tomatoes
Sue	Woolrich	salads	fish

7. After you have entered the data, save your records. Close the form.

8. Go to the Report listing in the Database window and delete the report rptGuests.

9. Create a new report using the Report Wizard.

10. Examine your report on the Print Preview screen. Then, if you are connected to a printer, print out the report.

11. Save the report, calling it rptGuests.

12. Close the report. Close the Dinner Party database.

CASE STUDIES

Coffee-On-The-Go: **Editing a Database**

In this chapter, you learned to edit a database. You will use those skills to edit the Employee table for Coffee-On-The-Go.

1. Open the Coffee database.
2. Open the Employee table.
3. Change Henry Hart's name to Harry Hart.
4. Change Nancy Pope's location from 01 to 02.
5. Change the spelling of Jerry Jones's first name to Gerry.
6. Delete Mary Frances from the database.
7. Save the changes to the Employee table.
8. Print a quick report of the data.
9. Close the database.

CASE STUDIES

Videos West: **Editing a Database**

In this chapter, you learned to edit a database. You will use those skills to edit the Inventory table for Videos West.

1. Open the Video database.
2. Open the Inventory table.
3. Delete the video Christmas Decorations.
4. Change the retail price of Yoga for Your Health to $19.99.
5. Change the video Baseball Tips to Baseball Pitching Tips.
6. Change the quantity of Start Your Own Business from 7 to 3.
7. Save the changes to the Video database.
8. Print a quick report of the data.
9. Close the database.

Acumen Fundamentals Milestone

Individual Project:

the Scouts Cookie Sale Database

Scout Troop #99 is getting ready to launch its annual cookie sale. Troop Master Wilson wants to track sales this year to find out who is selling in which neighborhoods and where they need more penetration.

Mrs. Wilson will need a table to store information about the scouts (ScoutNbr, ScoutName), customers (CustomerNbr, CustomerName, Address, HomePhone), and sales (ScoutNbr, CustomerNbr, CookieType, NbrBoxes).

There are eight scouts in Troop #99: Andrea, Ariel, Cathy, Debby, Laura, Mandy, Michelle, and Rachel. There are six cookie types: Chocolate Chip, Coconut Macaroon, Lemon Crisp, Mint Wafer, Peanut Butter, and Vanilla Sandwich. Instead of building a separate table for the cookies, Mrs. Wilson has chosen to use a reference list in the form when entering cookie sales.

1. Design the database on paper. Identify the tables of the database and the fields within each. Give each field a proper field name. Designate the primary key for each table. Mark the fields on which you will sort the data as candidates for indexing. Make sure that you will be able to create relationships between tables as needed.
2. Create the tables in MS-Access. Choose appropriate data types for each field. Add meaningful comments to each field. Assign a primary key to each table as designated by your design.
3. Create Quick Forms. Populate the Scout table. Record this week's cookie sales.
4. Generate Quick Reports to print out the data in your database.

Team Project:

the Community Recreation Center Database

Your project group has been assigned to develop a database to track activities at the local Community Recreation Center. The Rec Center services both the community and the nearby University. Students from the

University can use the Rec Center if they have paid their annual student activity fee. The student activity fee can be considered a purchased membership. Faculty members from the University and residents of the community must purchase a membership before they can use the facilities. Faculty membership fees are slightly less than those for people from the community.

The Rec Center has four racquetball courts and six tennis courts. These courts may be reserved up to one week in advance. A member can make many reservations, but each court can only be reserved for one hour at a time.

Members of the Rec Center are allowed to check out sports equipment to use at the facility. When members check out the equipment, an equipment-issue form is completed listing the member's number, the member's name, the equipment being used, and the date and time that the equipment was checked out. The member gets one copy; a second copy is kept by the Rec Center staff. When the equipment is returned, the equipment-issue form is updated with the date and time of the return. Staff employed by the Rec Center monitor the checkout and use of the sporting equipment and make reservations for use of the racquetball and tennis courts.

All the members of your project group will have to work together to design this database on paper. In addition to determining the tables and their relationships, list the kinds of reports that will be required by the management of the Rec Center. Include equipment-issue receipts, listings of court activity, membership listings, mailing listings, mailing labels, and letters to the membership about upcoming events.

Designate one member of your project group as the Database Administrator. This person is responsible for creating tables and relationships, designating primary keys and indexes, and implementing validation rules as requested by the members of the team.

Designate a second member of your project group as the Forms Designer. This person is responsible for the design and implementation of the data-entry forms and any underlying queries for the Rec Center database.

A third member of your project group will serve as the Report Designer. This person is responsible for the design and implementation of the reports and any underlying queries for the Rec Center database.

All members of the project team will share data-entry responsibilities equally. When changes to any object of the database are required, each member first confers with the others before making a modification. The project team members report to each other on a regular basis about their activities and coordinate development of the Rec Center database with each other.

The Full Project Team

Design the database on paper. Identify the tables of the database and the fields within each. Give each field a proper field name. Designate the primary key for each table. Mark the fields on which you will sort the data as candidates for indexing. Make sure that you will be able to create relationships between the tables as needed. Record this week's new members, reservations, and equipment issues.

The Database Administrator

Create the tables in MS-Access. Choose appropriate data types for each field. Add meaningful comments to each field. Assign a primary key to each table as designated by your design. Generate database reports.

The Forms Designer

Create Quick Forms. Populate the Courts and Equipment Inventory table.

The Report Designer

Generate some Quick Reports to print out the data.

Part 2

Critical Thinking

Chapter 5

Changing and Customizing Tables

Objectives
- Creating a Relationship Between Two Tables
- Sorting Records
- Changing Field Size and Format
- Adding Validation Rules to Tables
- Creating Indexes
- Making a Backup of the Database

Key Terms

TERM	DEFINITION
Database Application	a combination of data, input and output modules, and business rules that turn raw data into useable information
Database Integrity	a measure of the accuracy and correctness of the data stored in a database
Null	a condition that indicates missing or unknown data
Referential Integrity	a rule that states that you cannot have records on the many side of a one-to-many relationship that are not linked to a record on the one side of that same relationship
Orphan Records	records that were once part of a one-to-many relationship on the many side that have been abandoned because the related record on the one side was changed or deleted
Cascade Update	a change made in the value of a primary key field on the one side is passed along to the related record(s) on the many side in a one-to-many relationship
Cascade Delete	an automatic deletion of records on the many side that occurs when the related record on the one side is deleted

TERM	DEFINITION
Join	a database operation that connects related records in two or more tables so that data can be accurately extracted and displayed from the related tables in a single form or report
Index	a list of unique values built from a column of a table that helps you find a record quickly
Validation Rule	a business rule that limits data being entered into the database
Database Backup	a copy of the database file, which is made as a safety measure

database application   A *database application* is a combination of the data, the input and output modules, and the business rules that turn raw data into useable information. Before you start building applications, you must create relationships between tables. You can then combine data from different tables and output them to forms and reports.

Often you will need to sort records in a specific order, such as Last Name, State, or Zip Code. With MS-Access you can sort in ascending or descending order.

After using the database for a while, you may need to change a field size or format. Or you may want to prevent incorrect data from being entered. Adding validation rules to your database application will help prevent these problems.

MS-Access uses a technique called Rushmore to find data quickly, even in large databases. To take advantage of this technique, you must use queries or reports that are based on fields that are indexed. Therefore, carefully choosing which fields to index helps when retrieving your data.

Two routine maintenance steps that are often neglected are compacting, or compressing, the database and making a regular backup copy of the database.

Objective 1: Creating a Relationship Between Two Tables

To create a relationship between two tables, you must build a table that can be related, or linked, to an existing table.

Building a Related Table

Your Contacts table includes fields for home, work, and fax phone numbers. Three phone number fields may not be enough, since people have pagers, cellular phones, car phones, and 800 numbers. You can add more fields to the Contacts table for each extra phone number, but you would have to add a separate field for each type. Using a second, related table, you can employ a more efficient method of handling multiple phone numbers.

Exercise 1: Building a phone number table

Instead of using the Table Wizard, you will build the Phone Number table from scratch.

1. Start at your Contacts database with the Tables tab selected.
2. Click New.
3. Click the New Table button (Fig. 5-1).

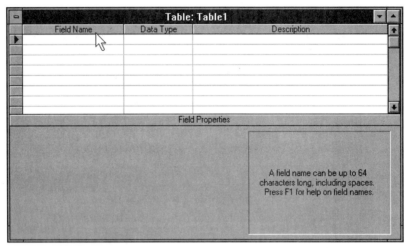

Figure 5-1   New Table Definition window

4. Type ContactID in the first row of the Field Name column.
5. TAB to the Data Type column. Click the arrow in the box at the right of the column to open a list of data types. Click Number.
6. Press F6 to move down to the Field Properties box.
7. Click the arrow in the box at the right of Field Size to open a list of numeric data types. Click Long Integer.

   You must use the Long Integer data type for this field because you will be relating it to the ContactID in the Contacts table, which is a counter data type. MS-Access uses the Long Integer type internally for all its counter fields.

8. Type Contact ID in the Caption field. Press F6 to return to the Field Definitions.

   Spaces are acceptable in the Caption field, as this is just a label for the field.

9. Move the cursor to the first row of the Description column and type Contact ID. Press ⏎ ENTER.
10. Move the cursor to the second row of the Field Name column and type PhoneNumber. Press ⏎ ENTER. Leave the data type as Text.
11. Press F6 to move down to the Field Properties box. Move to the Input Mask field and click the button to the right of the field.

12. The Save Table dialog box appears asking to save the table now. Click Yes.

13. When prompted for a table name, type PhoneNumbers. Choose OK.

14. When prompted for a primary key, click No.

    The Input Mask Wizard dialog box appears (Fig. 5-2). The first option listed is phone number.

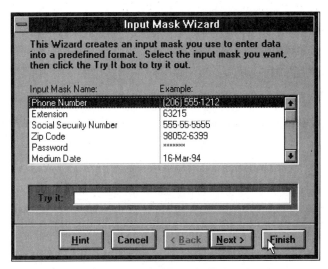

Figure 5-2 **Input Mask Wizard dialog box**

15. Phone Number is already highlighted, so click Finish.

    MS-Access builds the input mask for you.

16. Type Phone Number in the Caption field.

17. Press (F6) to return to the Field Definition box. Move to the Description field.

18. Type Phone Number and press (← ENTER).

19. Move the cursor to the third row of the Field Name column and type PhoneType. Press (← ENTER).

20. Leave the field type as Text. Press (F6) to move to the Field Properties box. Type Type of Phone Number for the caption.

21. Press (F6) to return to the Field Definition box. Type the description Type of Phone Number.

22. Click in the left margin of the Table Definition window, so that the entire first row is highlighted.

23. Hold down (SHIFT) and click the margin of the PhoneNumber field so that *both* lines are highlighted. Release (SHIFT).

24. Click the Set Primary Key icon on the Toolbar to create a two-line primary key.

    Both ContactID and PhoneNumber show key symbols in their left margins (Fig. 5-3).

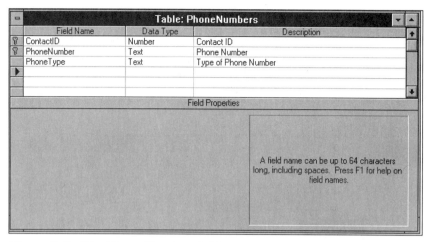

Figure 5-3   The PhoneNumber table

25. Choose File/Save to save your new table. Choose File/Close to exit.

Defining Relationships Between Tables

referential integrity

orphan records

Now that you have two tables designed to be linked, you can specify how they are related. MS-Access provides help when you are defining relationships between tables. It takes care of important details, including *referential integrity*, which means that MS-Access will not let you delete a record from one table that has related records in another table. Such a deletion would result in *orphan records*—records that were once part of a one-to-many relationship on the many side that have been abandoned because the related record on the one side was deleted.

database integrity

Referential integrity is part of database integrity. *Database integrity* is a measure of the accuracy and correctness of the data stored in a database. If there are orphan records in your database, you have inaccurate data.

cascade update

MS-Access protects against orphan records by giving you two options after you choose to Enforce Referential Integrity. *Cascade Update* Related Fields modifies related records for you when you change the value of a primary key. For example, if you change an employee number from AB133 to AB103, all records in other tables associated with that employee will have their employee number data values changed from AB133 to AB103.

cascade delete

Cascade Delete Related Fields deletes related records in other tables when you remove a record from the first table. For example, if you remove an employee's record from the Personnel table, all records in other tables associated with that employee are also removed.

join

A connection or link between tables that have related data is known as a *join*. There are several different types of joins, and MS-Access explains each type of join in easy-to-understand language. You select the tables, connect the fields that are common to the two tables, and choose the type of join needed.

Exercise 2: Creating a relationship between two tables

In this exercise, you will create a relationship between the Contacts and PhoneNumbers tables.

1. At the Database window choose Edit/Relationships from the top menu.

   The Add Table dialog box opens, with the Contacts table highlighted (Fig. 5-4).

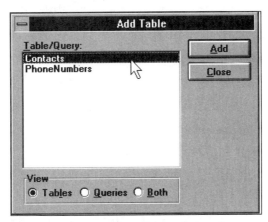

Figure 5-4 The Add Table dialog box

2. Click the Add button to include the Contacts table in the relationship.
3. Highlight the PhoneNumbers table, add it to the relationship by clicking Add.
4. Close the Add Table dialog box (Fig. 5-5).

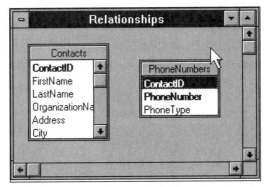

Figure 5-5 The Relationships dialog box with the PhoneNumbers table added

5. Place the cursor over the ContactID field in the Contacts table and hold down the left mouse button. Drag the cursor to the right until it is over the ContactID field in the PhoneNumbers field. Release the mouse button (Fig. 5-6).

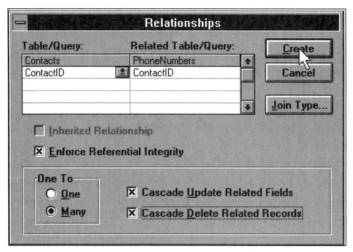

Figure 5-6   **The Relationships dialog box**

6. In the Relationships dialog box, click Enforce Referential Integrity. Note that the One-To-Many option is chosen for you.

7. Click the option boxes to turn on Cascade Update Related Fields and Cascade Delete Related Fields.

   An X appears in each box to show that the option is selected.

8. Click Join Type to open the Join Properties dialog box (Fig. 5-7).

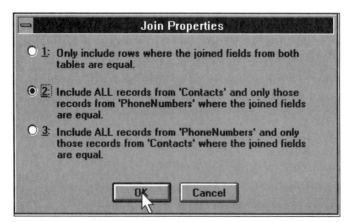

Figure 5-7   **The Join Properties dialog box**

9. Select the second option from the list of Join Types. Click OK.

The Join Properties dialog box closes and returns you to the Relationships dialog box.

10. Click Create to create the relationship.
11. Click File/Save Layout to save the relationship. Close the Relationship window.

FEATURE

Using indexes

MS-Access can retrieve data most rapidly when it is performing the search on an indexed field. As we said before, you want to index the fields you use most often for sorting, such as LastName and PostalCode, and those that link or join two tables together, such as ContactID. However, you do not want to index every field in a table. Each time you enter a new record into the database, the index must be updated to include the new data, thus slowing MS-Access performance.

Objective 2: Sorting Records

When you look at or print out data from your database, you want the data to be organized. For example, you might want to list your contacts by last name or by city. Sorting in MS-Access is quick and easy because only the screen display or report is sorted. MS-Access does not actually rearrange the data on the disk. If you close and open the form, it reverts to its original data storage order.

Exercise 3: Sorting records in the DataSheet view

In this exercise, you will sort records in ascending and descending order.

1. Open the Contacts table in Datasheet view and position the cursor in the Last Name column.
2. Click the Sort Ascending icon on the toolbar.

   The records are sorted in ascending order by the Last Name (Fig. 5-8).

Contact ID	First Name	Last Name	Organization Name	Address	City	S
1	Sam	Adams	Antiques Unlimited	47 Main Street	Boston	M
8	Ignacio	Chavez	Precision Surveys, Inc.	348 Embarcadero	San Francisco	C
7	Robin H.	Clark	Precision Surveys, Inc.	270 Butte Meadows	Boise	ID
9	Hiroshi	Kanzaki	Precision Surveys, Inc.	897 Green Mountain l	Portland	O
2	George	Langford	Langford Trucking	1 Farm Road	Mount vernon	V
10	Wendy	Monteleone	Monteleone Legal Serv	1478 27th Avenue S\	Washington	D
4	Margaret	Moore	Liberty Shield Insurance	145 Independence A'	Philadelphia	P
6	Roger S.	O'Leary	Precision Surveys, Inc.	2525 Forest lane	Walla Walla	W
3	G. David	Swenson	Swenson Adventure Tc	101 Chase Lane	Nashville	T
(Counter)						

Record: 1 of 9

Figure 5-8   The Contacts table in Datasheet view sorted by last name

3. Position the cursor in the Organization Name column and click the Sort Ascending icon.

    The records are sorted in ascending order by organization name.

4. Position the cursor in the Contact ID column list and click the Sort Descending icon.

    In descending sort, the most recently entered data is positioned at the top.

5. Close the Datasheet view.

Objective 3: Changing Field Size and Format

After using the database for a while, you might discover that some fields are too short. You can easily change the length of a field, but think carefully before you reduce the size of a field because long data items may be truncated. For example, if you reduce a field from 30 to 20 characters, data items stored in this field between 21 and 30 characters long will be cut off.

Exercise 4: Changing field size

The PostalCode field is currently 20 characters long. For longer zip codes, including nine-digit zip codes and Canadian postal codes, a 10-character field will suffice, but we will shorten the field to 12 characters to be safe.

1. At the Database window with the Table list showing, highlight the Contacts table.

2. Open the Contacts table in Table Design mode.

3. Move to the PostalCode field. Press (F6) to switch to the Field Properties box.

4. Change the Field Size from 20 to 12.

5. Click File/Save.

    A dialog box appears warning that you may lose data.

6. Click OK. Click File/Close.

Objective 4: Adding Validation Rules to Tables

validation rule   A *validation rule* is a business rule that becomes part of the database. Validation rules put restrictions on the data you may enter.

The rule you will implement is that all entries in your contact database must have a Last Name. In the language of databases, the LastName field "is not null." A null data value is one that indicates that a field has been left blank intentionally. The validation rule Is Not Null means that the field cannot contain a blank space or null value.

Exercise 5: Validation rule: every record must have a LastName value

In this exercise, you will create a validation rule.

1. Open the Contacts table in Design mode.
2. Move to the LastName field and press F6 to shift to the Field Properties box.
3. Go to the Validation Rule field and type Is Not Null.

   You should explain validation rules to the user in the Validation Text field.

4. TAB to the Validation Text field and type Please enter a last name (Fig. 5-9).

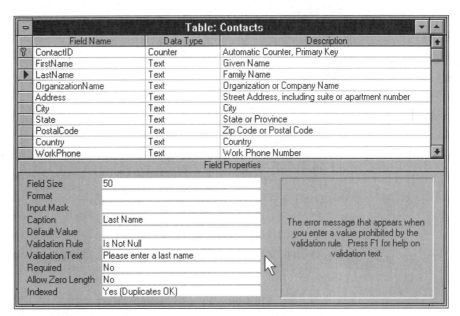

Figure 5-9 *The Contacts table in Design view with the LastName validation rule*

5. Click File/Save.

   A message appears on the screen. It offers to check your table for entries that conflict with the new rule. You know that all your records have an entry for LastName, so click No.

6. Click File/Close.

Objective 5: Creating Indexes

index

To retrieve data from a database efficiently, you should search on an indexed field. An *index* is a database structure built by MS-Access that acts like the index of a book—it tells MS-Access where to look for a piece of information. You want to index the fields that you use most often to sort, such as LastName and PostalCode, as well as those you use to link or join two tables, such as ContactID.

Exercise 6: Creating an index on the State field

Since you often sort your Contacts database by State, you should build an index for the State field.

1. Open the Contacts table in Table Design mode and click View/Indexes.

   The Index Definition window opens with Indexes: Contacts in the window header (Fig. 5-10).

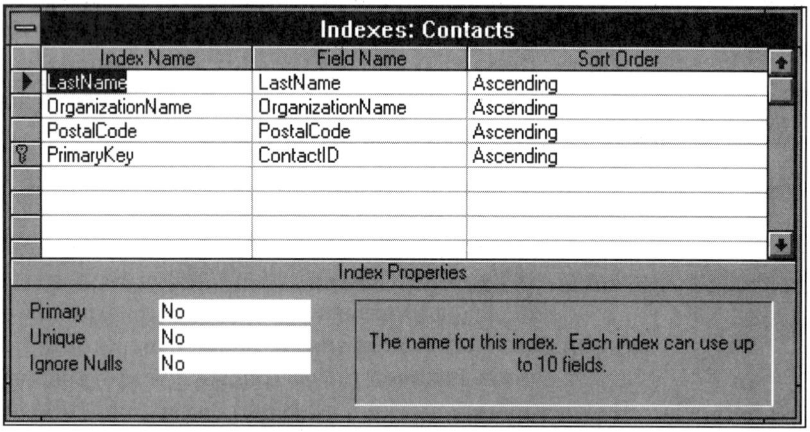

Figure 5-10   Index Definition window

2. Move to the first empty row in the Index Name column and type State.

3. Move to the Field Name column and click the down arrow to show a list of fields (Fig. 5-11).

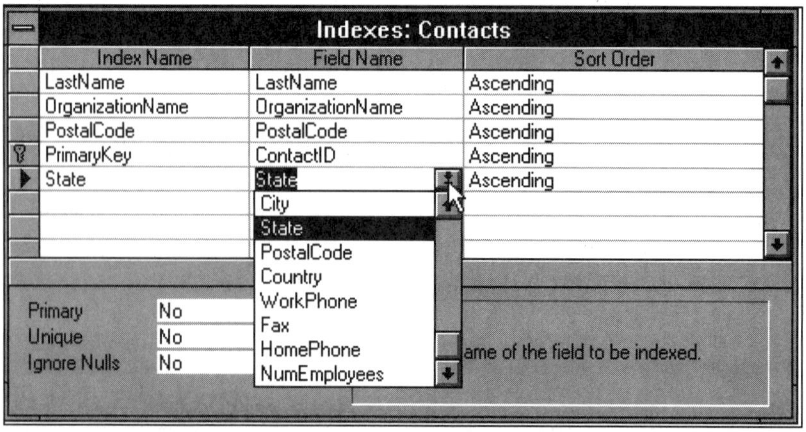

Figure 5-11   *Index Definition window showing a list of fields*

The Term "Computer Bug" Was First Used . . .

. . . in 1947 when the late Mary Grace Hopper was investigating a problem with an early computer. She could not figure out why the program she had written was not running as it should, so she looked inside the computer's memory, or "core" as it was called then. She found a dead moth lying on the memory assembly. When she removed it, her program worked fine. From then on, computing errors became known as "bugs," and chasing down and fixing errors became known as "debugging."

Mary Grace Hopper taped the moth to her logbook next to that day's entry. The logbook and the moth are on display at the U.S. Naval Museum in Dahlgren, Virginia.

4. Click the State field. Leave the Sort Order column as Ascending.
5. Close the Index Definition window. You have just indexed the State field.
6. Save your changes. Close the Table Design window.

Objective 6: Making a Backup of the Database

One cannot overemphasize the importance of backup copies for your database. You will come to rely on your databases; if you lose them, it is hard to recover from the loss. The primary copy of your database is on the hard disk. You should always keep a backup copy of your database on a floppy disk. Make backups regularly and store one copy in a different location, away from your hard drive.

There are two ways to make backups of your database. The first is by using MS-Windows File Manager to copy the .mdb file onto a floppy disk or tape. The second way is to use the MS-Access Compact facility.

As you change your database—building forms and reports and making design changes to the tables—MS-Access adds the changes to the database file. When you delete data records, MS-Access reclaims the space that the records occupied but does not reuse it. Gradually, the database grows and becomes disorganized. Compacting it reorganizes and reduces the size of the database file.

When you compact the database, you can compact it into a new database with a new name, or you can compact it into itself. If you compact and save your database into a new database on a floppy disk, the new database can act as your backup copy. Then you can compact the database into itself on your hard disk, recovering some disk space in the process.

Exercise 7: Making a backup of your database

The following exercise shows you how to use the MS-Windows File Manager to make a backup of your database.

1. Close the Contacts database (File/Close Database). Minimize MS-Access.
2. Use the MS-Windows File Manager to make a copy of the contacts.mdb file, preferably to a different hard disk, floppy disk (if your database is small enough), tape, or different computer on the network.

3. If you have backup software, you can use it to backup to a floppy disk or tape. MS-DOS V6 has a backup program that runs from DOS or Windows and will backup to a floppy disk.

Exercise 8: Compacting the database

This exercise shows you how to use the MS-Access Compact facility to backup your database. You will compact contacts.mdb into a new database called cont_bak.mdb, which becomes your backup file.

1. Make sure all your databases are closed.

2. Select File/Compact Database. The Compact Database dialog box appears (Fig. 5-12).

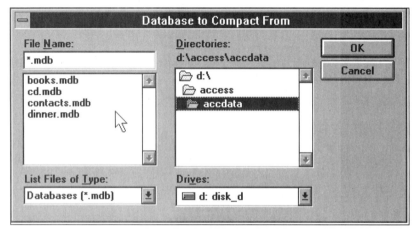

Figure 5-12 **The Compact Database dialog box**

3. Select contacts.mdb file as the Database to Compact From. Select OK.

   The Database to Compact Into dialog box appears.

4. Type cont_bak.mdb as the new filename. Click OK.

   You may specify a different directory or disk. MS-Access produces a compacted backup of your database. When it finishes, you can open the database and begin using it or exit from MS-Access.

Chapter Summary

In this chapter you learned how to establish a relationship between two tables, sort data, and adjust field sizes to better fit your needs. You implemented validation rules that define acceptable data for the database. You indexed the State field to improve MS-Access performance when searching that field. After making all these changes, you compacted and made a backup copy of the database.

Review Questions

True/False Questions

_____ 1. Two tables in a relational database can be associated only in a one-to-one or one-to-many relationship.

_____ 2. Violating referential integrity might result in orphan records.

_____ 3. The connection between two related tables is known as a *joint*.

_____ 4. To make MS-Access run faster, you should index every column in the table.

_____ 5. You should make periodic backups of your database to avoid a disastrous loss of data.

Multiple-Choice Questions

_____ 6. During a cascade delete,

A. a record in the table of the many is deleted, which results in all related records in that table being deleted.

B. a record in the table of the many is deleted, which results in the related record in the table of the one being deleted.

C. a record in the table of the one is deleted, which results in all related records in the table of the many being deleted.

D. a record in the table of the one is deleted, which results in all related records in that table being deleted.

_____ 7. A database object built from one or more fields of a base table that is used to assist in doing searches for specific data values is called a(n)

A. relational table.

B. index.

C. cascade update.

D. validation rule.

_____ 8. If you want to rearrange the order of the records in a datasheet, you perform a

A. join.

B. compact.

C. reformat.

D. sort.

_____ 9. The technique used by MS-Access to retrieve data from a database very rapidly is called

    A. Rushmore.

    B. Denali.

    C. Everest.

    D. McKinley.

_____ 10. The procedure used to reclaim space within the database that has been vacated by deleted records is called a database

    A. backup.

    B. compression.

    C. compaction.

    D. format.

Fill-in-the-Blank Questions

11. The kind of relationship in which each record in one table is related or linked to many records in a second table is called a _____ relationship.

12. Database integrity is the measure of the _____ of the data stored in a database.

13. When a data item does not have a value, it is called _____.

14. A format rule, usage rule, or business rule coded into a database table or form is called a _____.

15. You must be careful if you shorten a field of a table because you could _____ the data already stored in the field.

Acumen-Building Activities

Quick Projects

1. Sorting records in the MyBooks form.

1. Open the Books database. Open the form frmBooks. `TAB` to the Title field.

2. Click the Sort Ascending icon on the top toolbar.

3. Use the controls at the bottom of the form to scroll through the records to verify that they are sorted by book title.

4. `TAB` to the Author field and click on the Sort Ascending icon.

5. Browse the records to verify that they are sorted by author.

6. Click File/Close to close the form.

2. Build and test a validation rule for MyBooks.

This exercise is a continuation of Quick Project #1.

1. Open the table MyBooks in Design mode.
2. Move to the Title FieldName and press ⒡⒍ to shift to the Field Properties box.
3. Go to the ValidationRule field and type is not null.
4. ⒯⒜⒝ to the ValidationText field and type Please enter a book title.
5. Save your changes (File/Save). Answer Yes when MS-Access asks to test the data in the table with the new validation rule.
6. Choose File/Close to leave Table Design mode. Click the Form tab and Open frmBooks. Click Records/Data Entry from the top menu.
7. Type in the following data, leaving the Title field blank.

BOOKCOLLECTIONID	5
Title	
Author	Tony Hillerman
ISBNNumber	0-06-100017-5
PublisherName	Harper
DatePurchased	5/31/94
Pages	299
Note	A southwest Native American mystery.

8. Click File/Save Record. Click OK to close the message box warning you not to leave the book Title blank.
9. Return to the Title field and type Skinwalkers.
10. Choose File/Save Record. Close the form.

3. Creating an index on the ISBNNumber field.

This exercise is a continuation of Quick Project #2.

1. Open the table MyBooks in Table Design mode. Move the cursor to the FieldName ISBNNumber.
2. Press ⒡⒍ to move into the Field Properties box and move the cursor to the Indexed field.
3. Click the drop-down list box and select Yes (duplicates OK).
4. Save your changes by selecting File/Save. Close the Table Design window.

4. Compacting a database into itself.

This exercise is a continuation of Quick Project #3.

1. Close the Books database. Select File/Compact Database.
2. Select books.mdb as the Database to Compact From and click OK.
3. Type books.mdb as the File Name for the Database to Compact Into and click OK.
4. Click Yes when asked to confirm this action.

In-Depth Projects

1. The CD database.

1. Open the CD database. Create a New table without using the Table Wizard. Use the following field names, data types, descriptions, and field properties.

FIELD NAME	DATA TYPE	DESCRIPTION	FIELD PROPERTIES
MusicCollectionID	number	Part of primary key; connects this table to CDCollection.	Field size: long integer
TrackNbr	number	Second part of the primary key; track number.	Field size: byte
TrackTitle	text	Title of the song or track.	Field size: 50 Validation rule: is not null
TrackTime	date/time	How long is this track or song?	Format: short time

2. Highlight the first two lines of the table by holding down (SHIFT) and clicking each line in the left margin.

3. Click the Primary Key icon to create a two-line primary key. Both MusicCollectionID and TrackNbr will show key symbols in their left margins.

4. Save the table and name it Tracks. Close the Design window for the Tracks table.

5. Open table CDCollection in Table Design mode.

6. Modify Field Name title by changing field size from 20 to 50. Save these changes.

7. Close the Design window for the CDCollection table.

8. Create a relationship (Edit/Relationships) between CDCollection and Tracks. Link the two tables with the MusicCollectionID field. Enforce referential integrity. Indicate that this is a One-To-Many relationship. Turn on Cascade Update Related Fields and Cascade Delete Related Records. Choose Join. Type number 2.

9. Save the layout (File/Save Layout). Close the Relationships window.

10. Create an AutoForm for the table Tracks using the Form Wizard.

11. Save the new form, calling it frmTracks and add data. You may use the data suggested below, which is a continuation from previous chapters, or your own.

MUSICCOLLECTIONID	TRACKNBR	TRACKTITLE	TRACKTIME
1	1	Main Title	
1	2	Imperial Attack	
1	3	Princess Leia's Theme	
1	4	The Desert and the Robot Auction	
2	1	Bayou Bay	4:01
2	2	If I Had a Heart	4:06
2	3	Am I a Fool	3:51
2	4	Hey Rene	3:25
3	1	Song for the Morning Start	4:07
3	2	Daybreak Vision	1:44
3	3	Ancestral Home	4:44
4	1	Seaplanet	3:47
4	2	Australia	6:07
4	3	Island Turtles	3:59
5	1	Question	
5	2	How Is It (We Are Here)	
5	3	And the Tide Rushes In	
5	4	Don't You Feel Small	

12. Save your records after you have finished entering the data.

13. Close the Tracks form. Close the CD database.

2. The Dinner Party database.

1. Open the Dinner database. Create a New table without using the Table Wizard. Use the following field names, data types, descriptions, and field properties.

FIELD NAME	DATA TYPE	DESCRIPTION	FIELD PROPERTIES
DinnerID	counter	Primary key.	
Place	text	Where is the dinner party held?	Field size: 50
Date	date/time	What day is the dinner party?	Format: short date Input mask: short date Indexed: yes (duplicates OK)
Time	date/time	What time is the dinner party?	Format: medium time Input mask: medium time
Occasion	text	What, if any, is the occasion?	Field size: 50
Comments	memo	Notes about the dinner party.	

2. If prompted to save the table during this process, do so. Name it Dinners. Let MS-Access create the primary key. (It will make DinnerID the primary key of the table.)

3. When building the date and time input masks, do not attempt to customize the mask. Accept the default design. Save and close the Dinners table.

4. Create a second New table without using the Table Wizard. Use the following field names, data types, descriptions, and field properties.

FIELD NAME	DATA TYPE	DESCRIPTION	FIELD PROPERTIES
GuestID	number	Part of the primary key; links to the table DinnerGuests.	Field size: long integer
DinnerID	number	Second part of the primary key; links to the table Dinners.	Field size: long integer

5. Save the table, naming it GuestList. Do not create the primary key when prompted.

6. Highlight both lines of the table by holding down ⟨SHIFT⟩ and clicking each line in the left margin.

7. Click the Primary Key icon to create a two-line primary key. Both GuestID and DinnerID will show key symbols in the left margin.

8. Save the table GuestList and close the Design window for the table Guestlist.

9. To create a set of relationships (Edit/Relationships) for the tables DinnerGuests, GuestList, and Dinners, add these tables to the Relationships window in the order listed.

10. Link DinnerGuests to GuestList using the GuestID field. Enforce referential integrity. Indicate that this is a One-To-Many relationship. Turn on Cascade Update Related Fields and Cascade Delete Related Records. Choose Join. Type number 1.

11. Link Dinners to GuestList using the DinnerID field. Enforce referential integrity. Indicate that this is a One-To-Many relationship. Turn on Cascade Update Related Fields and Cascade Delete Related Records. Choose Join. Type number 1.

12. Save the layout (File/Save Layout) and close the Relationships window.

13. Create an AutoForm for the table Dinners using the Form Wizard.

14. Save the new form and call it frmDinners.

15. Add some data using the Dinners form. You may use the data suggested below, which is a continuation from previous chapters, or your own.

PLACE	DATE	TIME	OCCASION	COMMENTS
Fred's house	02/13/94	02:00 PM	Valentine's Day dinner	Had a lovely time despite the snow-storm. A super seven-layer Valentine's cake.
Mary's house	04/03/94	11:00 AM	Easter brunch	A wonderful sampling of Eastern European dishes.
Observatory Park	05/29/94	12:00 PM	Memorial Day picnic	Deep southern cooking, Cajun and Creole, fried chicken and all the fixins.
Linda's house	07/19/94	04:00 PM	Midsummer BBQ	A feast of smoked ribs and smoked turkey, salads and side dishes.
Sue's house	08/30/94	06:00 PM	Linda's birthday	Southeast Asian menu and a big birthday cake.

16. Save your records after you have finished entering the data. Close the Dinners form.

17. Create an AutoForm for the table GuestList using the Form Wizard. Save the new form, calling it frmGuestList.

18. Add some data using the Dinners form. You may use the data suggested below, which is a continuation from previous chapters, or your own.

GUESTID	DINNERID
1	1
2	1
3	1
4	1
5	1
1	2
2	2
3	2
4	2
3	3
4	3
5	3
1	4
2	4
3	4
4	4
5	4

continued

GUESTID	DINNERID
1	5
2	5
3	5
4	5
5	5

19. Save your records. Close the GuestList form.

20. Create a new report from the Dinners table using the Report Wizard. It will be an AutoReport.

21. Examine your report on the Print Preview screen and, if you are connected to a printer, print out the report.

22. Save the report, calling it rptDinners. Close the report. Close the Dinner database.

CASE STUDIES

Coffee-On-
The-Go:

Working with Tables

In this chapter, you learned to create relationships between two tables. You will use the skills you have learned so far to create another table and link it to the Employee table for Coffee-On-The-Go.

1. Create the following table:

Field	Type	Size
Location	Text	2
Name	Text	15
Union	Yes/No	1
Benefits	Text	20

2. Name the table Benefits. Make Location the primary key.

3. Add the following data:

Location	Name	Union	Benefits
01	Portland	Y	Blue Cross
02	Eugene	N	none
03	Seattle	Y	Washington HMO
04	San Diego	N	California HMO

4. Establish a relationship between the Employee table and the Benefits table. The Location field is used to connect the two.

5. Open the Employee table, and make the following changes:

   Create an index on the LastName field.

   Create an index on the Location field.

Delete the index on the LastName field.

Change the width of the LastName field to 15.

Add a new field and name it Union.

Delete the Union field.

6. Print both tables.

7. Save your changes and close the database.

CASE STUDIES

 **Videos West:** **Working with Tables**

In this chapter, you learned to create relationships between two tables. You will use the skills you have learned so far to create another table and link it to the Inventory table for Videos West.

1. Create the following table:

Field	Type	Size
Type	Text	2
Name	Text	20
Vendor	Text	20

2. Name the table Vendor. Make Type the primary key.

3. Add the following data:

Type	Name	Vendor
01	Sports and Outdoors	Outdoor Video Productions
02	Fitness	Better Bodies Videos
03	Health and Medicine	Medical Video Corp.
04	Finances	Financial Video, Inc.
05	Hobbies	Craft Video Productions
06	Languages	Language Videos, Inc.

4. Establish a relationship between the Inventory table and the Vendor table. Use Type as the common field to connect the two.

5. Open the Inventory table, and make the following changes:

Create an index on the Title field.

Create an index on the Type field.

Delete the index on the Title field.

Change the width of the Title field to 35.

Add a new field and name it Number Sold.

Input data into the Number Sold field.

6. Print both tables.

7. Save your changes and close the database.

Chapter 6

Creating Forms

Objectives

- Creating a Form
- Using the Form Wizard
- Editing a Form
- Deleting Fields on a Form
- Moving Fields on a Form
- Adding and Changing Text on a Form
- Adding Boxes, Lines, and Color
- Controlling Numeric Input
- Controlling Character Input
- Using a Form

Key Terms

TERM	DEFINITION
Form	an interactive screen that connects the user and the database management system; it can be used for both entering and displaying data
Calculated Field	a field on a form that displays the result of a calculation based on data stored in the database
Reference Table	a table of static data—that is, data whose values don't change often—such as state abbreviations or zip codes
Properties Sheet	an MS-Access window in which you can view or modify the properties of a selected object on a form
Handle	a marked position at a corner or side of a form object in Form Design view that allows you to modify the size of that object
Toolbox	a set of tools available in Form Design mode that you use to place objects and controls on a form

TERM	DEFINITION
Palette	an MS-Access window available in Form Design mode that contains color choices, box special effects, and border-line styles and widths
Font	a typeface that can be applied uniformly to all letters, numbers, and symbols within a document; the font style is typeface, while the font size is the size of the typeface are measured in points
Text Box	an MS-Access object on a form; a control that provides a place to view or update data from the database
Label	an MS-Access object on a form; a control that displays descriptive characters on a form

Forms   *Forms* are used for data entry or displaying data on the computer screen. Using Forms offers more flexibility than entering data in Datasheet view. With a form, you can select fields from a table to view. You can also combine data from more than one table in a form. You can use the form to check the values of data you enter to ensure that they are within acceptable ranges. You can build a calculated field—that is, a field on a form that displays the result of a calculation based on data stored in the database—such as Totals or Subtotals. We will discuss calculated fields in Chapter 9.

The best way to start designing your form is with the MS-Access Form Wizards. Once you have the form on the screen, you can modify it by adding or deleting fields, moving fields, and adding or changing text. You can add boxes, lines, and color to delineate the various parts of the form. Visual cues guide the user and make the form easier to use. You customize the form **toolbox** using the set of tools in the toolbox and the color palette. The *toolbox* is a **palette** set of tools that places objects and controls on a form. The *palette* is a window that contains color choices, box special effects, and border-line styles and widths.

Objective 1: Creating a Form Using the Form Wizards

You have already used the Form Wizards to create a QuickForm for the Contacts table. When you use the Form Wizards this time, you will exert more control over the final product.

Exercise 1: Creating a form using the Form Wizards

In this exercise, you will build a new form based on the Contacts table.

1. Start at the Contacts database with the Form tab highlighted. Click New (Fig. 6-1).

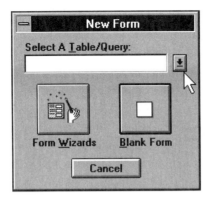

Figure 6-1 **New Form dialog box**

2. In the New Form dialog box select the Contacts table. Click Form Wizards.

3. Select the Single-Column Form Wizard. Click OK (Fig. 6-2).

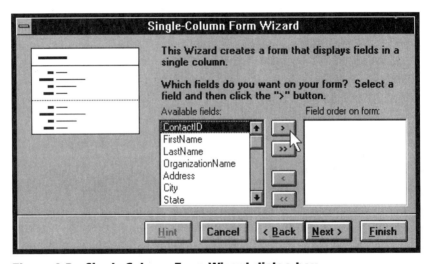

Figure 6-2 *Single-Column Form Wizard dialog box*

4. Move ContactID and FirstName from the list of available fields to the Field Order on Form column by highlighting the field name and then clicking the single right arrow.

5. Move the other fields to the Field Order on Form box by clicking the double right arrow. Click Next.

6. Choose the Embossed style. Click Next (Fig. 6-3).

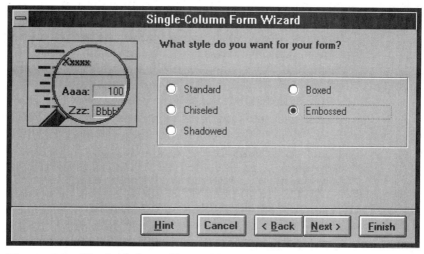

Figure 6-3 **Single-Column Form Wizard: styles**

7. Leave the form title as Contacts and select the option to open the form with data in it. Click Finish to complete building the form and view the results.

8. Save the form (File/Save Form). Type Contacts for the form name. Click OK (Fig. 6-4).

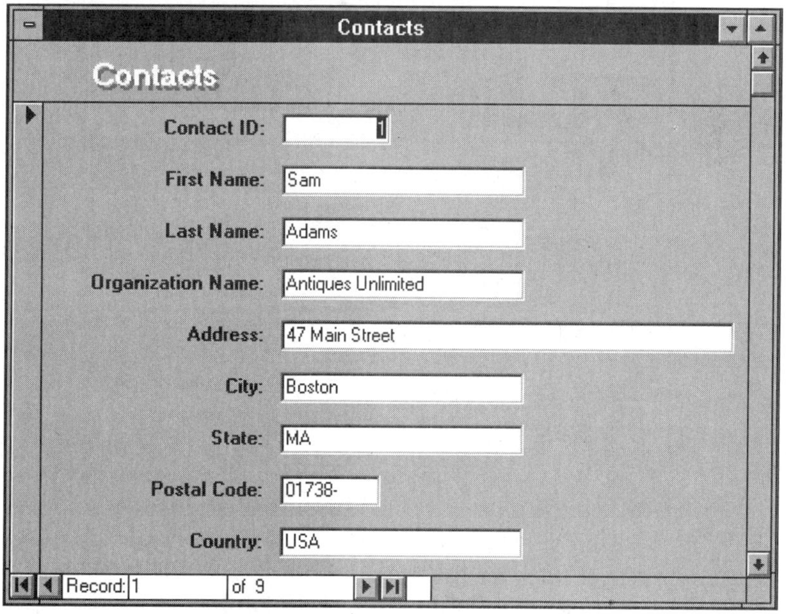

Figure 6-4 **Newly-created Contacts form**

Objective 2: Editing a Form

To make a form easier to use, you want to adjust the vertical spacing between fields and rearrange objects on the form so everything fits comfortably on a single page. This avoids time-consuming scrolling.

Editing a Form: Deleting Fields on a Form

To delete a field, you must identify the field and then remove it.

⚠️ **WARNING** MS-Access has a one-level Undo feature. When you delete a field, you can undo the deletion if you act at once. However, if you perform another operation after deleting a field, you can no longer recover the deleted field.

Exercise 2: Editing a form: deleting fields

In this exercise, you will first delete the NumEmployees field and then undo the deletion.

1. Click View/Form Design.
2. Maximize your form by clicking the up arrow in the upper right corner of the Form window (Fig. 6-5).

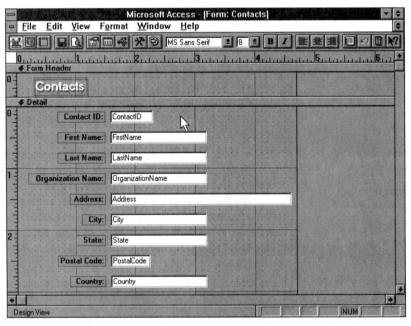

Figure 6-5 The Contacts form in Design view, maximized

3. Click anywhere on the NumEmployees field (Fig. 6-6).

handles The corners of the field show handles. The *handles* on an object allow you to resize it.

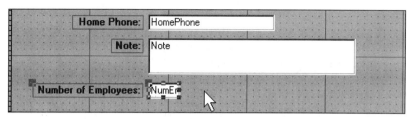

Figure 6-6 **The Contacts form with the NumEmployees field selected**

4. Press `DELETE` to remove the NumEmployees field.
5. Click Edit/Undo Delete to recover the NumEmployees field. Click File/Save.

Editing a form: moving fields on a form

Mail-Order Processing . . .

. . . is a good example of a how forms are used. The data entry system used by a mail-order company to take orders is a set of forms that are part of a database. Customer information (name, address, phone number) is entered and used to update the Customer table. During data entry, the form may automatically fill in the state field as soon as the zip code is typed. To do this, the form uses a reference, or lookup, table that contains a list of zip codes for each state. A *reference table* is a table of static data—that is, data whose values do not change. Next, the customer supplies an item number. As the operator types in the item number, the description of the item is filled in automatically from a reference table of inventory information. The form displays information as it accepts new data. If the customer supplies an item number that is out of stock, a small dialog box appears on the screen warning that the item is back ordered. When the order is complete, the shipping charge, sales tax, and total cost are displayed on the screen. All three values are calculated in the form.

You can move and resize fields. You can move more than one field at a time by drawing a box around a group of fields with the mouse. MS-Access provides formatting tools that help you space fields evenly on a form.

Exercise 3: Moving fields manually

You will move several of the fields around the Contact form. Then you will use the MS-Access alignment tools to make the fields align properly.

1. Draw a box around the ContactID and FirstName fields so that both fields and their labels are selected at once. (You accomplish this by drawing a box around these objects. First, position the mouse where you want the upper left corner of the box. Hold down the left mouse button and drag the cursor where you want the the lower right corner of the box. Then release the mouse button.)

2. Position the cursor over one of the selected fields until the cursor changes from an arrow to a hand (Fig. 6-7).

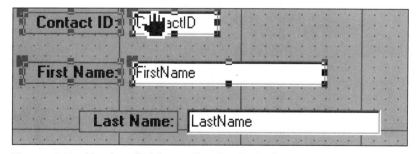

Figure 6-7 **Moving fields on the Contacts form**

3. Hold down the left mouse button and move the cursor to the left. The fields move with the cursor. When the labels are 0.75" from the left margin, release the mouse button.

4. Position the cursor over the right margin of the form. The cursor changes from an arrow to a double-headed horizontal arrow with a vertical crossbar. Drag the margin to the 6" line on the top ruler and release the mouse button.

   If the ruler is not visible, click View/Ruler to make it visible.

5. Move the LastName field so that it lines up horizontally to the right of the FirstName field.

6. Click the vertical ruler to the left of the FirstName field.

   The cursor changes to a horizontal arrow, and all objects on a horizontal line to the right are selected.

7. From the top menu, click Format/Align/Top.

   The FirstName and LastName fields and labels are aligned.

8. Draw a box around the remaining fields and labels from OrganizationName to NumEmployees.

9. Press (PAGE UP) so that you can see what you are doing in the next step.

10. Hold down (CTRL) and press the (↑) repeatedly until the fields are positioned closer to the top of the form.

11. Click anywhere on the form background to deselect the fields (Fig. 6-8).

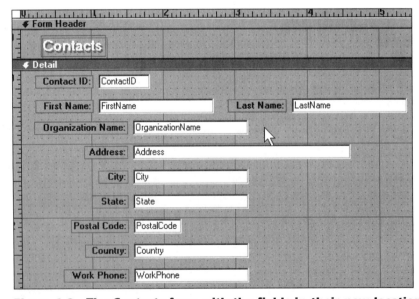

Figure 6-8 **The Contacts form with the fields in their new locations**

12. Click File/Save to save your work.

Exercise 4: Moving fields with the format tools

In this exercise, you will re-adjust the spacing between fields on a form.

1. Select all the fields in the Detail section by drawing a box around them.
2. Click Format/Vertical Spacing/Make Equal.
3. Click Format/Vertical Spacing/Decrease. Repeat as necessary until all the fields fit on the screen.
4. Deselect the fields by clicking the form background. Click File/Save.
5. Reduce the size of the form by dragging the bottom margin up to just below the NumEmployees field.
6. Click the Form view icon.

   The whole form now fits on the screen (Fig. 6-9).

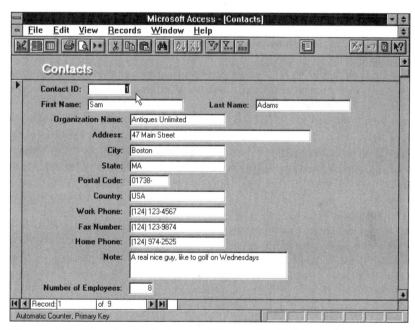

Figure 6-9 **The Contacts form with smaller field spacing**

Editing a Form: Adding and Changing Text

If a field name is not descriptive enough, you can change it. You can add, delete, or modify the text already in place. These labels are derived from the Caption, which you entered when you defined the table and fields. If you did not supply a caption then, the field name is used as a label.

Exercise 5: Changing the text

In this exercise, you will change the label of a field and reduce the label's size.

1. Switch to Design view. Click the *label* Organization Name to select it. (Don't click the OrganizationName field.)

2. Position the cursor inside the label; it will change from an arrow to an I-beam.

3. Place the I-beam between "Organization" and "Name" and click.

4. Remove the word "Name" from the label.

5. Click the box surrounding the label to select it.

6. Resize the box with the mouse by dragging the handle on the left side of the box.

7. Draw a box around the fields from Organization to NumEmployees and move them to the left, aligning them with the ContactID and FirstName fields (Fig. 6-10).

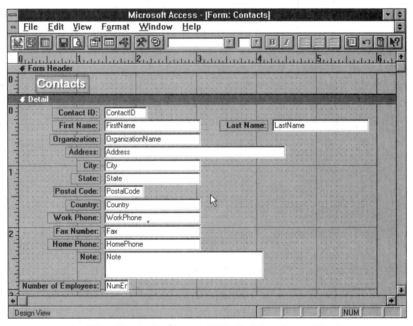

Figure 6-10 **The Contacts form with fields aligned left**

8. Draw a box around the fields, from ContactID to NumEmployees. Do not include the labels.

9. Click Format/Align/Left to align the fields. Click File/Save to save your work.

Objective 3: Adding Boxes, Lines, and Color

text box All text added to the form must be in a text box. A *text box* provides a place to view and update data. You use the Toolbox to add a text box to the form. The Toolbox icon looks like a crossed wrench and hammer. When you click it, the toolbox appears on the screen. You can position it anywhere, dragging it to the top, bottom, or either side of the screen. Once you position it, the Toolbox turns into a horizontal or vertical toolbar.

> **⚠ WARNING** Be careful of MS-Access's terminology: A text box is used to input data values and is associated with a field in the database. In the following exercise, you will add text to a label, which is simply placing text on a form.

Exercise 6: Adding a label

font In this exercise, you will add a label to the screen to identify the application and its author, then change the *font*, or typeface, and font size to make the text easier to read.

1. Click the Toolbox icon and position the Toolbox along the top of the window.

2. Click the Label button, then move to the open area at the right of the form.

   The cursor changes to an "A" with a plus sign (+) above and to the left of it.

3. Position the plus sign where you want the upper left corner of your label box. Hold down the left mouse button and drag the cursor diagonally down and to the right to create a box about 1.5" deep by 2" wide. Release the left mouse button.

4. Click the cursor in the box and type

   Contact Database (⎡CTRL⎤+⎡↵ ENTER⎤))

   by (*your name here*) (⎡CTRL⎤+⎡↵ ENTER⎤))

   Copyright (*year*)

   Do not press ⎡↵ ENTER⎤ at the end of each line, or MS-Access will assume that you are finished typing and exit from the label box. Instead, press ⎡CTRL⎤+⎡↵ ENTER⎤ to indicate the end of each line.

5. Click outside the box, then on the outer edge of the box to select it.

   The font name and size information are displayed on the top toolbar.

6. Click the down arrow to the right of the Font Name box and select a font from the list.

7. Click the down arrow to the right of the Font Size box and select a font size.

8. Click the Center-Align Text icon, which is to the right of the Font Size box, to center the text in the box. Adjust the size of the box if necessary (Fig. 6-11).

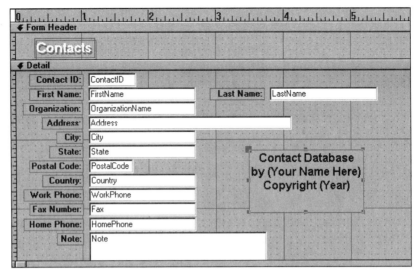

Figure 6-11   The Contacts form with a copyright label.

9. Click File/Save.

Exercise 7: Adding lines

To emphasize the ownership notice, you will place a line under the label box.

1. Click the Line icon on the toolbox.
2. With the mouse, draw a line under the label box. Position the cursor 0.25" below the left edge of your label box. Hold down the left mouse button, drag the cursor horizontally to the right side of the label box, and release the button.
3. Draw another line just below the first.

Exercise 8: Adding boxes and color

The color of any object on a form can be changed by selecting it and click-ing the color palette. In this exercise, you will use the Edit/Undo option to return the object to its previous color.

1. Click the Rectangle icon in the toolbox.
2. Draw a rectangle to cover the copyright notice and the lines below.

   This new box should be slightly larger than the copyright notice box and lines, and it should hide them.
3. Click the Palette icon on the toolbar.
4. Click the Clear option for the Back Color bar on the palette so that you can see your notice again.
5. Click the text of the copyright notice to select it. Click a colored square in the Fore Color bar of the palette.

   The text changes color. Find a color you like.

6. Change the background color. Find a Fore Color/Back Color combination that you like (Fig. 6-12).

7. Close the palette by clicking its icon on the toolbar. Close the Toolbox the same way. Click File/Save.

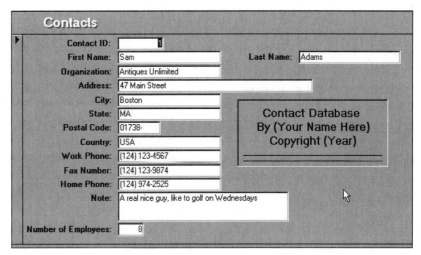

Figure 6-12   The Contacts form with a colored copyright box

Objective 4: Controlling Numeric Input

As we discussed in Chapter 5, you need to control input data to prevent errors in the data entered into your database. Input masks and validation rules are two forms of control that can be used in forms. But it is better design to place input masks and validation rules in the table field definitions so that these rules apply to every object that uses those fields. Sometimes you will need to control input masks on the data-entry form.

If you modify an input mask in a form, then the change affects only data that is entered through this form. It does not change how the data is stored.

properties sheet In the following exercise, you will use a *properties sheet*, which allows you to view and modify the properties of a selected object. Every object on a form has a properties sheet that shows the set of properties specific to that type of object. Even the form itself has a properties sheet.

Exercise 9: Controlling numeric input

In this exercise, you will modify an input mask to control how the zip code is input.

1. Click the PostalCode field to select it.

2. Click the Properties icon on the toolbar.

3. Move to the Input Mask entry in the properties sheet and change the entry to 00000.

4. Tab out of the Input Mask entry and click File/Save to save your work (Fig. 6-13).

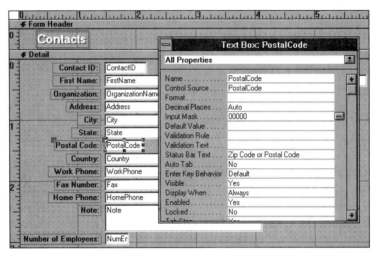

Figure 6-13   Contacts form with its properties sheet modified

Objective 5: Controlling Character Input

Controlling character input is very similar to controlling numeric input. Validation rules and input masks are used to control text characters input into the database. The Format option is another tool used to control text when it is input. For instance, you can automatically convert lowercase letters to uppercase letters during data entry. However, when you use this feature, the text is stored in the database exactly as typed, even if it is typed in lowercase letters.

Exercise 10: Controlling the State field

In this exercise, you will control the State field data that is input so that it appears in uppercase letters on the form.

1. Click the State field to select it.

2. Click the Format row in the properties sheet. Type the greater-than symbol (>).

3. TAB out of the Format row. Click File/Save to save your work.

In this exercise, you changed the State field on the form only. It is a good idea to make this same change at the table level so that the data in the State field will display in uppercase letters wherever it appears. The next time you open the Contacts table in Design mode, make this same change to the State field. This ensures the values are stored throughout the database as uppercase letters.

4. Close the Properties box by clicking the Properties icon on the toolbar.

FEATURE

Storing different types of data in MS-Access
When you created the Contacts database in Chapter 2, you included a field called Photograph. (We later deleted this field in Chapter 4.) This field is an example of MS-Access's ability to store objects in databases. You can store pictures, voice or music recordings, and full-motion video. These stored objects are produced by other software applications and are known as OLE objects. An OLE object is a piece of information created in a Windows application that supports Object Linking and Embedding technology. This technology allows you to store an image generated by a graphics design package, a scanned photograph, or a video clip from a video capture program. You can edit movies that you record with your camcorder and use segments in other applications. The applications for OLE objects are limitless: Imagine selecting a destination in a travel database and being able to view a short movie about that place in a window on your computer screen, or storing employee photographs along with personnel records.

Over the next few years, OLE technology will become more prevalent as the traditional report gives way to multimedia presentations.

Objective 6: Using the Form

From the Database window, with the Forms tab selected, you should see a list that includes the Contacts form that you built and the quick form you created in Chapter 3. Now you can open the form, browse the records, and add records.

Exercise 11: Browsing Records

1. Open the Contacts form. Maximize the form.
2. Browse the records using [PAGE UP] and [PAGE DOWN].
3. Browse the records using the controls at the bottom of the form.

Exercise 12: Adding Records

In this exercise, you will place the form in Data-Entry mode and add a record.

1. Click the New button on the toolbar.
2. Enter the following data:
   Tom Lincoln
   Lincoln Log Homes, Inc.
   1278 Acadia Avenue
   Peoria, IL 37482 USA

WorkPhone: 282-383-1193 Fax 282-383-1195 HomePhone 282-384-1914

Note: This company has lots of potential for growth with the recent surge in homebuilding and the back-to-nature movement that seems so strong in many parts of the country.

NumEmployees 37

NOTE   When typing text into a memo field, pressing ⏎ ENTER is interpreted as the end of your data entry in this field. At the end of a line, continue typing, and the text will wrap around. If you want to start a new line while entering text, press CTRL + ⏎ ENTER .

3. Click File/Save Record.

4. Close the database and exit from MS-Access.

Chapter Summary

In this chapter, you learned how to make forms work for you. You started with a form generated by the Form Wizard and then customized it. You learned how to remove unnecessary fields, the difference between a text box and a label, and how to modify static text and labels on a form. You rearranged the fields on the form to make the form easier to use, then added text, lines, and boxes to give the user visual clues. You investigated the use of color on a form and how it can add to the form's functionality. Using a properties sheet, you added numeric and character controls to the form to assist with data entry.

Review Questions

True/False Questions

_____   1. You should wait until all editing changes are completed before saving a new form.

_____   2. Forms are used only for data entry.

_____   3. A field on a form will use the input mask defined for that field in the underlying table if you have not changed the input mask in the form's properties sheet.

_____   4. Changing the color of one field on a form changes the color of the other fields on that form.

_____   5. A form can show data from more than one table.

Multiple-Choice Questions

_____ 6. The spacing between fields on a form can be adjusted by using:

A. Ctrl+arrow keys.

B. the mouse.

C. the Format/Horizontal (or Vertical) Spacing command.

D. Any of the above.

_____ 7. The default label that is used for a field on a form is

A. the field name as defined in the table.

B. the caption as defined in the table.

C. the caption as defined in the table unless it is blank in which case the field name is used.

D. blank. The Form Designer must add the label.

_____ 8. Which of the following zip codes would be rejected by an input mask of 00000\-9999 ?

A. 12345-2829

B. 12345-28

C. 1234

D. 12345

_____ 9. To add color, special effects, and border-line styles to your form, you would use the

A. pallete in Design view.

B. toolbox in Design view.

C. properties sheet in Design view.

D. properties sheet in Form view.

_____ 10. To control numeric input when using your form, you would use a feature called

A. a control mask.

B. a data-entry mask.

C. an edit mask.

D. an input mask.

Fill-in-the-Blank Questions

11. _____ are a major component of the interface between user and database.

12. A _____ is a table of static data that is used to assist data-entry operations by offering a list of values from which the operator can choose.

13. The entries in a field on a form can be automatically modified so that they will be displayed in all uppercase letters by entering a _____ character in the Format row of the properties sheet.

14. In Form Design view, the colors of a field can be changed using the
_____ .

15. In order to delete a field in Form Design view, you would select the field and press _____ .

Acumen-Building Activities

Quick Projects

1. Creating a form using the Form Wizards

1. Open the Books database and move to the Forms listing. Begin building a New form.
2. Select the table MyBooks and use the Form Wizards.
3. Select the Single-Column Form Wizard. Click OK.
4. Click the double right-arrow button to move all fields from Available Fields to Field Order on Form. Click Next.
5. Select the Embossed style. Click Next.
6. Name the form Books. Select Open the form with data in it. Select Finish.
7. Click File/Save Form. Name the form Books and click OK.

2. Moving fields around the Books form.

This exercise is a continuation of Quick Project #1.

1. Switch to Form Design mode and maximize the form.
2. Draw a box around the Pages text box and label to select both and reposition the Pages field 0.5" to the right of the DatePurchased field.
3. Select both fields and click Format/Align/Bottom.
4. Select both the text field and the label for Note. Press ⎯CTRL⎯+⎯↑⎯ to move the note up, closing the gap in the form.
5. Position the cursor over the right edge of the form until it changes shape. Drag the right margin line to the 6" position on the top ruler to widen the form.
6. Click File/Save to save your work.

3. Resizing fields on the Books form.

This exercise is a continuation of Quick Project #2.

1. Click and select the BookCollectionID text box.
2. Shorten the box. Position the cursor on the right vertical edge of the box until it changes to a horizontal arrow. Drag the edge to the left to the 2.5" position on the top ruler.

3. Resize the Title text box. Drag the right side of the box to the right to the 4" position on the top ruler.

4. Click File/Save to save your work.

4. Drawing boxes and using color on the Books form.

This exercise is a continuation of Quick Project #3.

1. Open the toolbox by clicking its icon on the top toolbar.

2. Click the Rectangle icon in the toolbox and draw a rectangular box to cover the bottom three fields of the form (DatePurchased, Pages, and Note).

3. Click the Palette icon on the upper toolbar.

4. With the rectangular box still selected, click the BackColor/Clear button.

5. Adjust the size of the rectangular box to fit comfortably around the three fields.

6. Select the labels of the three fields in the box and change the color of the text from black to dark blue by selecting Fore Color on the palette.

7. Change the background color of the labels by selecting Back Color on the palette from pale grey to a color of your choice.

8. Click the form background and change the color to aqua.

9. Close the palette by clicking its icon on the toolbar.

10. Close the toolbar by clicking its icon on the toolbar. Click File/Save.

11. Return your form to normal size by clicking the lower double-headed arrow in the upper right corner. Widen the window by dragging the right side to the right.

12. View your finished design by clicking View/Form.

13. Close the form (File/Close). Close the Book database.

In-Depth Projects

1. The CD database.

1. Open the CD database and create a New form from the table CDCollection using the Single-Column Form Wizard. Add the fields to the new form in the following order:

MusicCollectionID

Title

GroupName

RecordingLabel

PurchasePrice

Length

YearReleased

Classification

2. Select a Shadowed style, name the form CDCollection, and select Open the form with data in it.

3. Save your new design and name it frmCDCollection.

4. Switch to Form Design mode and maximize the form to make it easier to work with.

5. Widen the form by moving the right edge to the 5" position on the top ruler.

6. Draw a box around YearReleased, selecting the label, text box, and underlying shadow.

7. Reposition YearReleased 0.5" to the right of LengthInMinutes and align the two fields along the bottom.

8. Reposition Classification by moving it up, closing the gap between it and the above line.

9. Save your work.

10. Lengthen the Title text box by moving the right edge to the 4" position on the top ruler.

    Hint: Use ⌈SHIFT⌋ to carefully select both layers of the text box (the active display and the underlying shadow) and enlarge both at the same time.

11. Enlarge the text boxes for GroupName, RecordingLabel, and Classification by dragging all three to the 4" position on the top ruler.

12. Save your work.

13. Click the Palette icon to open it.

14. Click the form background. Choose a back color and modify the color of the background. Modify the color of the other objects (labels and text boxes) if you want to. Your goal is to make the form easy to use and pleasant to look at.

15. Close the palette. Close the Toolbox.

16. Return your form to normal size, resizing the window if necessary.

17. Save your work. View your finished design.

18. Close the form. Close the CD database.

2. The Dinner Party database.

1. Open the Dinner database and create a New form from the table DinnerGuests using the Single-Column Form Wizard. Add the fields to the new form in the following order:

   GuestID

   FirstName

   LastName

   HomePhone

   Likes

   Dislikes

   HealthProblems

Address

City

State

PostalCode

2. Choose a style, name the form DinnerGuestList, and select Open the form with data in it.

3. Save your new design and name it frmDinnerGuest2.

4. Switch to Form Design mode and maximize the form to make it easier to work with.

5. Widen the form by moving the right edge to the 6" position on the top ruler.

6. Reposition LastName so that it is on the same line as FirstName and align the two.

7. Reposition Dislikes so that it is on the same line as Likes and align the two.

8. Move HomePhone, Likes, and Dislikes up to close the gap in the form.

9. Move HealthProblems, Address, City, State, and PostalCode up to close the gap in the form.

10. Delete the State label. Shorten the State text field. Reposition it so that it is on the same line as City.

11. Reposition the PostalCode field so that it is on the same line as City and State. Align the three fields (City, State, and PostalCode).

12. Shorten the form by dragging the bottom of the form up to just below the City, State, and PostalCode fields.

13. Save your work.

14. Draw a box around Likes, Dislikes, and Health Problems. Click the Palette icon.

15. Make the back color of the newly drawn box clear.

16. Select all the fields and labels inside the box. Click Format/Bring to Front.

17. Select the box and choose a back color for the box that contrasts with the form. Experiment with color combinations.

18. Close the palette.

19. Return your form to normal size and resize the window if necessary so that you can see your modifications.

20. Save your work. View your finished design.

21. Close the form. Close the Dinner database.

CASE STUDIES

Coffee-On-The-Go: **Creating Forms**

In this chapter, you learned to create forms. You will use those skills to create an on-line data entry form for the Coffee-On-The-Go Coffee database.

1. Open the Coffee database.
2. Create a data entry form for the Employee table.
3. Move fields and change the text to make the screen easy for data entry.
4. Enhance the screen form with lines or boxes.
5. Allow only F or M in the Sex field.
6. Allow only numbers greater than 8,000 in the Salary field.
7. Add two records using the form.
8. Save the form and close the database.

CASE STUDIES

Videos West: **Creating Forms**

In this chapter, you learned to create forms. You will use those skills to create an on-line data entry form for the Videos West Video database.

1. Open the Video database.
2. Create a data entry form for the Inventory table.
3. Move fields and change the text to make the screen easy for data entry.
4. Enhance the screen form with lines or boxes.
5. Allow only PG or R in the Rating field.
6. Allow only numbers greater than 1.00 in the Retail field.
7. Add two more videos to the database using the form.
8. Save the form and close the database.

Chapter 7

Querying a Database

Key Terms

TERM	DEFINITION
Query	a question about data stored in database tables or a request to perform an action on data
Criteria	conditions and restrictions imposed on data in order to limit the information presented in the results of a query
Query Wizard	a predefined set of instructions built into MS-Access that assists in building a query by asking questions and then constructing a query
Recordset	the list of records that result from running a query
Operator	the means used to set conditions and compare values

query   A *query* is a question about data stored in a database. You use a query whenever you want to extract specific information from database tables. For example. a query might ask for a list of all the people from the Contacts database who live in the state of Colorado.

In a previous chapter, you learned how to find a particular record in a table, searching, for example, on a specific zip code. When you perform this type of search, MS-Access takes you to the record you want, but still shows all other data in the table. Suppose that you want to make a list of all your contacts in a specific zip code. You could do so by repeating your MS-Access search until you find all entries in the table with that zip code. Even then, you would have to keep a handwritten list of each record. What you really want is for MS-Access to list *only* the records that meet your cri-

criteria   teria. *Criteria* are conditions and restrictions imposed on data to limit the information presented by a query. That is exactly what a query can do: It provides a list of specified records, sorts them in whatever order you wish, and then allows you to print out the list in a report.

A simple query might be, "List all contacts with LastName of Smith." This query has to match only one condition: Last name is Smith. A query can match many conditions or selection criteria, such as "Show me all customers in the state of Oregon who have placed orders this month and have an outstanding balance of more than $1000."

A query can combine data from more than one table. As an example, suppose you are in charge of information systems for a mail-order company. Your Inventory table contains information about back-ordered items. The Orders table contains information about customer orders. The Customers table contains address information for each customer. The sales manager decides to send a discount coupon to all customers who are waiting for back-ordered products. To do this, she needs a set of mailing labels. So you build a query that says, "Get the name and address (from the Customers table) for each customer who has an outstanding order (from the Orders table) for a back-ordered item (from the Inventory table)." In a later chapter, you will build a multitable query. For now, just use the Contacts table.

In a previous chapter, you built forms using a table as the foundation. In many cases, you will build forms and reports that use a query rather than a table for the underlying data. This is especially true if you want to combine data from more than one table on the form or report. The order-entry form, or an invoice, combines the customer data and shipping information with a list of items ordered.

A query is not always built to extract information directly from the database tables. It can be constructed to use the output from another query as the starting point.

Query Wizard   Queries can be constructed using the Query Wizard. The *Query Wizard* is a predefined set of instructions built into MS-Access that assists in building a query. It differs from the Form and Table Wizards in that it contains four specific Wizards; each is used for generating a special-purpose query. In most cases, you will design the query yourself rather than use the Query Wizard.

Queries can also be used to perform actions on the database, such as deleting selected records or adding data from one table to another.

recordset   The list of records that results from running a query is called a *recordset*. A recordset can be thought of as a virtual table. It is not written to your hard disk and disappears as soon as you close the results window. If you want to see the list again, you need to run the query again. When you open a form or a report built on a query, the query retrieves the information. This is beneficial because the form or report always shows current information. If the query results were stored, you would run the risk of looking at old data.

Objective 1: Setting Up Queries

Begin with MS-Access running and the Database window open. You will set up a new query and define which table the query will use. Next, you will select some fields from the table for the query. You can do this by double-clicking the field name or dragging and dropping the field name from the list to the query. Finally, you will run the query to see the resulting recordset. In the recordset, the fields appear in the same order in which they appear in the query—that is, the order in which you choose them. This might be different from the order in which they appear in the original table.

Exercise 1: Setting up a simple query

You will build a simple query to select FirstName, LastName, OrganizationName, and State from the Contacts table.

1. Click the Query tab in the Database window. Click New to build a new query.

2. Click New Query.

    The Select Query Design window opens with the Add Table dialog box (Fig. 7-1).

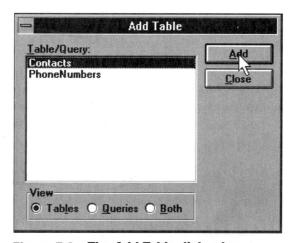

Figure 7-1   **The Add Table dialog box**

**Database Marketing:
Did You Know That . . .**

. . . marketers can target
smaller and more special-
ized segments of the population as a result of newer,
faster, more powerful computers and database man-
agement systems? This new
business enterprise, called
database marketing, is
becoming critical to the success of many companies in
the United States and
thoughout the world.
According to a survey by
Donnelly Marketing, Inc.,
56% of manufacturers and
retailers are currently building marketing databases,
and 85% believe they will
need marketing databases if
they are to stay competitive
into the next decade. It is
one of the most important
marketing developments of
the 1990s (*Business Week,*
September 5, 1994).

Massive parallel processing,
which can be done easily
by supercomputers, is being
used to divine which cus-
tomers are likely to buy what
products and when. Big
credit-card companies, air-
lines, and insurance companies are jumping on the
data-mining bandwagon in
an effort to get an edge on
the competition. A Gartner
Group vice president pre-
dicts that sales of parallel-
processing computers could
expand tenfold, to $5 billion
by the end of 1998, as a result
of this explosion in database
marketing. While marketing
types are plunging ahead,
academics are warning of
possible problems. One business professor warned that
"the fallout could be nasty if
companies start abusing their
new found information. The
companies doing this have a
big responsibility. Otherwise
there will be an information
Chernobyl" (*The Wall Street
Journal,* August 16, 1994).

3. Double-click Contacts to select the Contacts table and click Close.

   The table, with a list of fields, appears in the Query Design window. Note that at the top of the list is an asterisk. This means that all fields in the table are included.

4. Double-click FirstName to add this to the list of fields in the query.

5. Double-click LastName, OrganizationName, and State to add them to the list of fields in the query.

   (Alternatively, you can drag and drop the field name from the table to the query list.)

6. Click the Run icon (which shows an exclamation point) to see the results of your query (Fig. 7-2).

First Name	Last Name	Organization Name	State
Sam	Adams	Antiques Unlimited	MA
George	Langford	Langford Trucking	VA
G. David	Swenson	Swenson Adventure Tours	TN
Margaret	Moore	Liberty Shield Insurance Inc.	PA
Roger S.	O'Leary	Precision Surveys, Inc.	WA
Robin H.	Clark	Precision Surveys, Inc.	ID
Ignacio	Chavez	Precision Surveys, Inc.	CA
Hiroshi	Kanzaki	Precision Surveys, Inc.	OR
Wendy	Monteleone	Monteleone Legal Services	DC
Tom	Lincoln	Lincoln Log Homes, Inc.	IL

Select Query: Query1 — Record: 1 of 10

Figure 7-2   Query results

Objective 2: Specifying Criteria

The resulting recordset shows four fields: FirstName, LastName, OrganizationName, and State. The records are shown in the order in which they are stored in the database. It would make more sense to specify criteria to sort the records in alphabetical order by last name. In addition to sorting the results, you can specify criteria that restrict the output to a limited set of records. For example, you might want to see only the contacts at Precision Surveys, Inc.

Exercise 2: Specifying sort criteria

In this exercise, you will sort the results of the previous query by last name.

1. Return to Design mode by clicking the Design View icon on the toolbar.

2. In the Query Design window, click the Sort row under the Last Name column.

3. Click the down arrow and choose Ascending from the list.

4. Click the Run icon to see the results of your query (Fig. 7-3).

First Name	Last Name	Organization Name	State
Sam	Adams	Antiques Unlimited	MA
Ignacio	Chavez	Precision Surveys, Inc.	CA
Robin H.	Clark	Precision Surveys, Inc.	ID
Hiroshi	Kanzaki	Precision Surveys, Inc.	OR
George	Langford	Langford Trucking	VA
Tom	Lincoln	Lincoln Log Homes, Inc.	IL
Wendy	Monteleone	Monteleone Legal Services	DC
Margaret	Moore	Liberty Shield Insurance Inc.	PA
Roger S.	O'Leary	Precision Surveys, Inc.	WA
G. David	Swenson	Swenson Adventure Tours	TN

Record: 1 of 10

Figure 7-3   Query results, sorted by LastName

Exercise 3: Specifying selection criteria

You will now limit the results of the previous query by OrganizationName.

1. Return to Design mode by clicking the Design View icon on the toolbar.

2. In the Query Design window, click the Criteria row, under the Organization Name Column.

3. Type ="Precision Surveys, Inc." Be sure to include the quotation marks.

WARNING   You must enclose the name of the company in quotation marks because there are spaces in the name. If you do not, you will see a dialog box on the screen telling you that there is a syntax error in the query.

4. Click the Run icon to see the results of your query (Fig. 7-4).

   The results include only those contacts who work for Precision Surveys. The records are still sorted by last name because you did not modify the sort instruction from the previous exercise.

First Name	Last Name	Organization Name	State
Ignacio	Chavez	Precision Surveys, Inc.	CA
Robin H.	Clark	Precision Surveys, Inc.	ID
Hiroshi	Kanzaki	Precision Surveys, Inc.	OR
Roger S.	O'Leary	Precision Surveys, Inc.	WA

Record: 1 of 4

Figure 7-4   Query results, sorted by LastName with only Precision Surveys, Inc. contacts

Objective 3: Using Operators

operators To specify more complex criteria, you use operators. *Operators* set conditions and compare values. For example, operators such as less than (<) or greater than (>) are normally used with numeric fields—for example, credit limits or number of employees. Operators such as Like are used with text fields—for example, names and addresses. It is possible to set criteria on fields which do *not* show in the results. You will see an example of this in Exercise 4.

Exercise 4: Using operators

You have a training class that you offer to companies who want to improve their employees' computer skills. Normally you teach this class at a computer lab, and people come to you. But for companies with 50 or more employees, it is more cost-effective for you to go to their office. You want a listing of all the companies in your contact database with 50 or more employees. Modify the existing query to produce the list. Run the query. Then modify the query so that the NumEmployees field does not show in the recordset, as you might if you were producing mailing labels from this list.

1. Return to Design mode by clicking the Design View icon on the toolbar.
2. Double-click on NumEmployees in the list of fields to add it to the query.
3. Delete the condition from the OrganizationName field.
4. Move to the Criteria row under the NumEmployees column. Type >49. The > symbol means greater than. You could type >=50 , meaning greater than or equal to 50, but it is more efficient to specify greater than 49.
5. Run the query (Fig. 7-5).

First Name	Last Name	Organization Name	State	NumEmployees
George	Langford	Langford Trucking	VA	85
Margaret	Moore	Liberty Shield Insurance Inc.	PA	1259
G. David	Swenson	Swenson Adventure Tours	TN	50
*				0

Select Query: FirstQuery — Record: 1 of 3

Figure 7.5   Query results with NumEmployees greater than 49

6. Return to Design mode by clicking the Design View icon on the toolbar.
7. Click the box in the Show row under NumEmployees to remove the X.
8. Run the query again.

The list looks the same as last time except that the NumEmployees field is *not* shown in the results.

Objective 4: Matching Approximate Values

Sometimes, you do not want to search for an exact match, as you did in Exercise 4. For example, let's say you cannot remember the exact name of Precision Surveys, Inc. You remember only "Precision *something*." In this case, you use the Like operator and give the query a pattern to search for.

The Like operator searches for records that are similar to the values you type in the query. You specify what you want to match and then add an asterisk. The asterisk indicates that any characters are acceptable. Suppose you specify that you want to search for records where State Like Mi*. (Assume that you are using complete state names rather than two-letter state codes.) This query results in records from Minnesota, Mississippi, and Missouri because the first two letters match. Now you change the requirement to State Like Mis*. Now only records from Mississippi and Missouri will be listed. What would the results be for the query State Like M*?

Exercise 5: Approximate searches

In this exercise, you will use the pattern-matching capabilities of the Like operator to find a match.

1. Return to Design mode by clicking the Design View icon on the toolbar.
2. Delete the >49 condition in the NumEmployees column.
3. In the Query Design window, click the Criteria row under the Organization Name Column.
4. Type Like Prec*.

   MS-Access adds quotation marks when you move the cursor out of the cell.

First Name	Last Name	Organization Name	State
Ignacio	Chavez	Precision Surveys, Inc.	CA
Robin H.	Clark	Precision Surveys, Inc.	ID
Hiroshi	Kanzaki	Precision Surveys, Inc.	OR
Roger S.	O'Leary	Precision Surveys, Inc.	WA

Select Query: FirstQuery

Record: 1   of 4

Figure 7-6   Query results, sorted by LastName with only Precision Surveys, Inc. contacts

5. Click the Run icon to see the results of your query (Fig. 7-6).
6. Close the query by clicking File/Close.
7. When asked if you want to save changes to the query, save it as FirstQuery.

FEATURE

MS-Access naming conventions

MS-Access allows you to use embedded spaces when naming objects—such as tables, forms, and queries—but this is not a good practice for two reasons: (1) A space in a table or form name is considered a character. If, from a form or report, you reference a table that has an embedded space in its name and accidentally type two spaces instead of one, the form or report will not recognize the table name. This kind of error is easy to make but hard to track down, making it very frustrating to deal with. (2) Compatibility with other database management systems is another issue. At the time of this writing, no other database management system allows embedded spaces in the names of tables, fields, forms, or reports. The power and purpose of MS-Access is to allow quick and easy connectivity to other database management systems. But to do so, MS-Access object names must conform to industry-standard naming conventions. You may think now that you will never need to integrate an MS-Access application with that of another database management system. But think of the hundreds of thousands of Paradox and dBase databases already in place in front offices across the country. Think of the millions of Oracle, Ingres, Sybase, Informix, and DB/2 databases in back offices. It makes sense to follow prevalent naming conventions for database objects today, so that you can take advantage of existing database resources tomorrow.

Objective 5: Using the Query Wizard

There are certain situations in which the Query Wizard can help you. One such situation is finding duplicate records in your database. This is not an overwhelming task when your database is small. But as your database grows, you will find that the number of duplicate records grows. (How many times have you received multiple copies of the same catalog from a company?) Once you know how to build a query to find duplicate records, you can prevent this mistake from annoying *your* contacts.

Exercise 6: Using the Query Wizard to find duplicate records

In this exercise, you will look for duplicate company names. These are not true duplicate records, because they refer to different people. But this exercise will illustrate the technique of finding duplicate information. Start at the Database window with the Queries tab selected.

1. Click New. Click Query Wizards (Fig. 7-7).

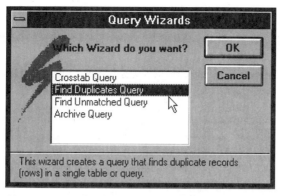

Figure 7-7   Query Wizards dialog box

2. Double-click the Find Duplicates Query field (Fig. 7-8).

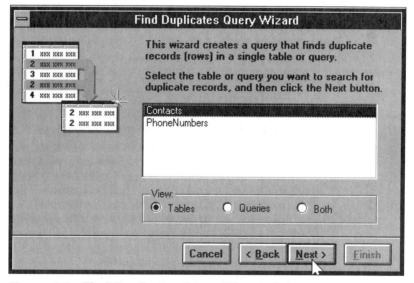

Figure 7-8   Find Duplicates Query Wizard dialog box

3. Highlight the Contacts table and click Next.
4. Double-click the OrganizationName field to select it as the field in which to look for duplicate values. Click Next.
5. Select the following additional fields for the output results by double-clicking each: FirstName, LastName, City, and State.
6. Click Next.
7. At the checkered flag screen, accept the default values and click Finish (Fig. 7-9).

Organization Name	First Name	Last Name	City	State
Precision Surveys, Inc.	Hiroshi	Kanzaki	Portland	OR
Precision Surveys, Inc.	Ignacio	Chavez	San Francisco	CA
Precision Surveys, Inc.	Robin H.	Clark	Boise	ID
Precision Surveys, Inc.	Roger S.	O'Leary	Walla Walla	WA

Figure 7-9 List of duplicate records

8. Save your query. If prompted for a name, accept the MS-Access suggestion.
9. Close the query (File/Close).

Objective 6: Selecting Unique Values

Normally, a query returns all records that meet the specified criteria. But there are times when you do not want all the records; instead, you need a list of unique values from a field or fields. For example, suppose you wonder if you have at least one person from every state in your contact database, which contains thousands of records. A simple query on the state field produces a list of the state values for all the records but does not answer your question. If you tell the query that you want only unique values, then the output list will show only the first occurrence of each state value. If you look at the status bar at the bottom of the screen, the total number of records is shown. If this number is less than 50, then you know that you do not have a contact in every state.

Exercise 7: Selecting Unique Values

Every object in MS-Access—whether a form, field, report, or query—has associated properties. By changing a setting in the Query properties, you can request only unique values in the results.

1. At the Database window click New to begin building a new query.
2. In the New Query dialog box, click New Query.
3. Double-click Contacts to select the Contacts table.
4. Click Close to close the Add Table dialog box.
5. Double-click State in the list of fields to add it to the query.
6. Click anywhere on the background of the query window, then click the Properties icon on the toolbar to open the Query Properties window (Fig. 7-10).

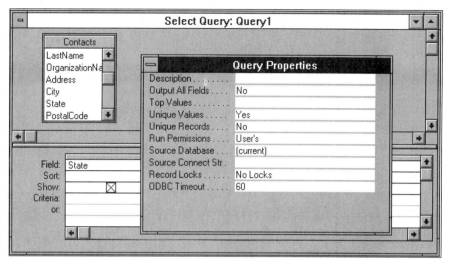

Figure 7-10   **The Query Design window with the Query Properties dialog box open**

7. Change the setting for Unique Values to Yes and run the query.

   A list of states in which you have contacts appears (Fig. 7-11).

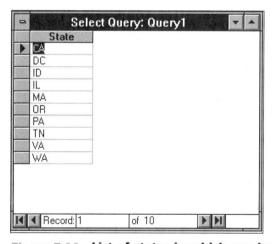

Figure 7-11   **List of states in which you have contacts**

Objective 7: Saving the Query

Save the query you have built so that you can use it as the basis for forms and reports. You can modify it and extend it. If you make copies of this query under different names, you can modify the copies to perform other queries.

Many MS-Access developers start query names with the lowercase letters "qry," as in qryMailingList. This helps identify the file as a query, which has two benefits: (1) When you build forms and reports, you can easily distinguish a table from a query and (2) when you modify a form or report, it will be obvious how you built it—with a table or query. You can extend this naming convention to tables, forms, and reports by beginning the filenames with tbl, frm, or rpt, respectively.

Exercise 8: Save the query

Save the query with an appropriate name.

1. Click File/Save Query As.
2. Type qryUniqueState for the query name and click OK.
3. Click File/Close to close the query design window.
4. Click File/Close Database to close the database. Exit from MS-Access.

Chapter Summary

Queries are used to extract information from the database. A query can show information that meets certain conditions. The results can be sorted and the fields displayed in a desired order. Approximate searches simplify matching data. Special-purpose queries, generated by the Query Wizard, simplify tasks such as finding duplicate records in a table.

Remember: The main purpose of a database is information retrieval. To do this well, a database must be able to store and manage data efficiently. The query is the real key to turning raw data into useful information. It harnesses the power of the relational database to give you precisely the information that you want to see.

Review Questions

True/False Questions

_____ 1. A query can contain only fields from one table.

_____ 2. A form or report can be based on the results of a query instead of a table.

_____ 3. You can set selection conditions on one field and sort the results of the query on a different field.

_____ 4. You always build queries using the Query Wizard.

_____ 5. The results of a query are stored on disk in a recordset.

Multiple-Choice Questions

_____ 6. To find all records in the Contacts table with a state value of AZ, you would use the following criterion for the state code:

A. =AZ.

B. ="AZ".

C. Like "AZ".

D. Any of the above.

_____ 7. To find duplicate records in a table,

A. print out the table and look for similar records on the printout.

B. build a query to list the records in the table and run the query twice.

C. use the Query Wizard to build a query to find duplicate records.

D. None of the above. There is no way to find duplicate records in a table.

_____ 8. To list only companies with more than 100 employees, you would set the NumEmployees criterion to

A. <100.

B. >100.

C. >99.

D. >=99.

_____ 9. Which of the following statements about sorting in a query is incorrect:

A. The records may be sorted in ascending or descending order.

B. The sort can be done only on an indexed field.

C. The records must be sorted on a field that appears in the output recordset.

D. The sort can be done in addition to other selection criteria.

_____ 10. To set criteria on a field, but exclude the field from the results of the query, you would

A. set the criterion for that field to =NULL.

B. click the box in the Show row to remove the X.

C. not include the field in the query.

D. set the criterion for this field to "invisible."

Fill-in-the-Blank Questions

11. To set conditions such as greater than, less than, or like, you use comparison _____.

12. The output from a query is called a _____.

13. Conditions that you set to limit output data are known as _____.

14. A form or report can be built on either a _____ or _____.

15. You want to find your contacts at a company whose name you recall is "*something* Surveys" but you forget what that *something* is. So you build a query where the criterion for OrganizationName is Like "_____".

Acumen-Building Activities

Quick Projects

1. **Setting up a simple query for MyBooks.**

   1. Open the Books database. Click the Query tab in the Database window.
   2. Create a New Query without using the Query Wizard.
   3. Add MyBooks to the Query Design window. Click Close.
   4. Double-click Title, Author, and Pages to add them to the query.
   5. Click the Run icon to run the query.
   6. Return to Query Design mode.
   7. In the Query Design window, in the Title column, click the Sort row and choose Ascending from the list.
   8. Run the query.

2. **Specifying selection criteria in the MyBooks query.**

   This exercise is a continuation of Quick Project #1.

   1. Return to Query Design mode.
   2. In the Query Design window, in the Title column, click the Criteria row and type Friday.
   3. Run the query and check the results.

3. **Using operators in the MyBooks query.**

   This exercise is a continuation of Quick Project #2.

   1. Return to Query Design mode.
   2. Delete the criteria from the Title column.
   3. In the Pages column of the Criteria row, type >= 300.

4. Run the query and check the results. Return to Query Design mode.

5. Click the box in the Show row of the Pages column to remove the X so that this field will not appear in the query output.

6. Run the query again and compare the results to the previous query.

4. Doing approximate searches in the MyBooks query.
This exercise is a continuation of Quick Project #3.

1. Return to Query Design mode.

2. Delete the criteria in the Pages column and turn Show back on.

3. In the Author column of the Criteria row, type like *peter*.

4. Click the Run icon and check the results.

5. Save the query by clicking File/Save Query and name it qryFirst.

6. Close the query by clicking File/Close.

7. Close the Books database.

In-Depth Projects

1. Querying the CD database

1. Open the CD database.

2. Create a New query without using the Query Wizard.

3. Add the table CDCollection to the Query Design screen.

4. Choose Title, GroupName, RecordingLabel, and Length for the query.

5. Sort the query in ascending order by Title and run the query.

6. Return to Query Design mode.

7. Modify the query to find those CDs with length greater than or equal to 45 minutes, run the query.

8. Return to query design mode.

9. Delete the condition in the Length column.

10. Modify the query to find those CDs recorded by M*B* and run the query.

11. Return to Query Design mode.

12. Delete the condition in the GroupName column.

13. Save the query and name it qryFirst.

14. Close the query.

15. Close the CD database.

2. Querying the Dinner Party database.

1. Open the Dinner database.

2. Create a New query without using the Query Wizard.

3. Add the table DinnerGuests to the Query Design screen.

4. Choose FirstName, LastName, City, Likes, and Dislikes for the query and run the query.

5. Return to Query Design mode.

6. Modify the query to sort the output in ascending order by City and run the query.

7. Return to Query Design mode.

8. Save this query and name it qryGuestByCity.

9. Close this query.

10. Create a New query without using the Query Wizard.

11. Add the table Dinners to the Query Design screen.

12. Choose Date, Time, Place, and Occasion for the query.

13. Sort the query by Date in descending order and run the query.

14. Return to Query Design mode.

15. Modify the query to find the Valentine's Day dinner and run the query.

16. Return to Query Design mode.

17. Delete the previous search condition.

18. Modify the query to find those dinners held after 5:00 P.M. and run the query.

WARNING This is a tricky one. When searching a date or time data type, use the pound symbol (#) as you would the quotation mark (") for a search of a text field. For example, to find those dinners that started at noon, your search criteria would look like =#12:00PM#.

19. Save the query and name it qryDinnerDates.

20. Close the query.

21. Close the Dinner database.

CASE STUDIES

Coffee-On-The-Go: **Querying a Database**

In this chapter, you learned to set up queries to a database. You will use those skills to select records from the Coffee-On-The-Go Employee table based on a query.

1. Open the Coffee database.
2. Open the Employee table.
3. Set up a query to see all employees who work in location 01. Print the results.
4. Set up a query to see all employees who make more than $15,000. Print the results.
5. Set up a query to see all current employees. Print the results.
6. Set up a query to see all employees who started working for the company before 1990. Print the results.
7. Set up a query to see all female employees. Print the results.
8. Save the query and close the Coffee database.

CASE STUDIES

Videos West: **Querying the Database**

In this chapter, you learned to set up queries to a database. You will use those skills to select videos from the Videos West Inventory table based on a query.

1. Open the Video database.
2. Open the Inventory table.
3. Find all the videos which cost $5.99. Print the results.
4. Find all the videos with a retail price of $14.99. Print the results.
5. Find all the videos in the 01 category. Print the results.
6. Find any videos which have Tennis in the title. Print the results.
7. Find all the videos produced before 1992. Print the results.
8. Save the query and close the Video database.

Chapter 8

Creating Reports

Objectives
- Understanding the Report Wizard
- Using the Report Wizard
- Modifying the Report—Removing and Moving Fields
- Adding and Changing Fields
- Modifying the Page Footer
- Modifying the Page Header and Report Header
- Adding Lines and Boxes
- Formatting Data in a Report
- Saving a Report
- Previewing a Report
- Printing a Report

Key Terms

TERM	DEFINITION
Report	information output from a database on paper or in electronic form
Formatting	establishing a pattern for the display, storage, or printing of data
Report Header	a section of a report that appears before the page header on the first page of the report, often containing a title, logo or picture
Report Footer	a section of a report containing report summary information that appears after the page footer at the end of the report
Page Header	a section of a report that appears at the top of every printed page of the report, often containing the title and date of the report
Page Footer	a section of a report that appears at the bottom of every printed page of the report, often containing the page number

report   A *report*, whether printed or on the screen, is used to distribute information from the database. Printed documents, e-mail messages, and mailing
labels are all reports. A report extracts current data from the database each
time you run it and acts as a snapshot of the information in the database as
it exists at the time the report is run.

When you build a report in MS-Access, you are actually building a template
or pattern. You define how you want the data to appear in the report—the
fonts, spacing, organization of the data on the page, and page numbering.

formatting   These specifications are called the *formatting* of the report. Once you have
the report saved on your hard disk, you may run it as often as needed.

Objective 1: Understanding the Report Wizard

You have the choice of building a new report from scratch or using a Report
Wizard. The Report Wizard, like the Form Wizard, ensures that the information you want appears on the report. Like the Form Wizard, the layout of
that information is very simple. The Report Wizard is a good starting point
from which you can customize the appearance of the report.

Objective 2: Using the Report Wizard

The Report Wizard offers a selection of reports, some of them fairly complex. In the Quick Preview, you were introduced to the Mailing Label
report. This time you will use the Single-Column report.

Exercise 1: Using the Report Wizard to generate a default report

In this exercise, you will use the Report Wizard to generate a report of
your contacts. Begin with the Contacts database window open and the
Reports tab selected.

1. Click New.

2. Select the Contacts table, then click Report Wizards (Fig. 8-1).

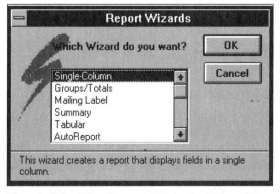

Figure 8-1   **The Report Wizards dialog box**

3. Double-click Single-Column in the Report Wizard dialog box.

   The Single-Column Report Wizard dialog box opens (Fig. 8-2).

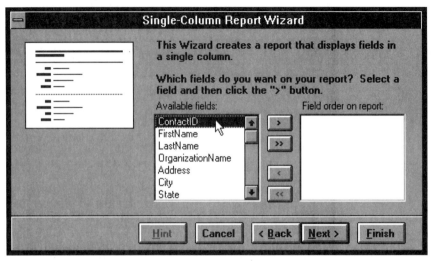

Figure 8-2 **The Single-Column Report Wizard dialog box**

4. Move the following fields from the List of Available fields to the Field order on report list: FirstName, LastName, OrganizationName, Address, City, State, PostalCode, and WorkPhone.

5. Click Next.

6. Move the LastName field then the FirstName field to the sort order list. Click Next.

7. Choose a style. Click Next.

8. When the checkered flag screen appears, click Finish.

   The report appears in Preview mode (Fig. 8-3).

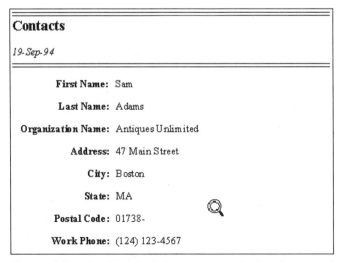

Figure 8-3 **The Single-Column report in Preview mode**

Electronic Mail Coming of Age

Electronic mail use, within companies and over the Internet, has exploded in the last few years. E-mail was meant to facilitate communication and reduce the amount of paper in the office. What we have now is network lines cluttered with broadcast FYI memos and invitations to holiday parties, most of which are printed out on paper before they are ever read! Many industry insiders who were once champions of e-mail have removed their e-mail address from their business cards and turned over the keys to their e-mail boxes for others to handle. For example, Bill Gates, head of Microsoft Corporation, had a "bozo filter" installed on his e-mail account after a national magazine published his Internet address. The filter passes along messages from identified associates and flings the rest into limbo. What this world needs is intelligent e-mail helper software that can sort and categorize e-mail. How about a book entitled, *Miss Manners on Electronic Mail*?

On the more positive side, there are now e-mail services for the blind. International Discount Communications, a small New Jersey company, offers e-mail services for the visually handicapped. Their software interfaces with standard e-mail software, converts digital messages to voice messages, and then places a telephone call to the recipient. The message can either be read aloud to the individual or saved to a voice-mail box (*Internet World*, October 1994).

Objective 3: Modifying the Report— Removing and Moving Fields

The report produced by the Single-Column Report Wizard shows the data you requested, but not necessarily as you might like it arranged. You can move fields, change labels, and reduce the amount of space allotted to each record. To modify a report, you must switch to Design mode. In Design mode, the report is divided into sections: the report header, page header, detail, page footer, and report footer.

In the next exercise, you will remove some field labels. The label on a report is like the label on a form—it is static text taken from either the field name in the table or the caption in the Field Properties box. Removing a data field is similar to removing a report label.

Exercise 2: Modifying the report: removing fields

In this exercise, modify the report layout by deleting some field labels.

1. From Print Preview, click the Close Window icon to switch to Design mode (Fig. 8-4).

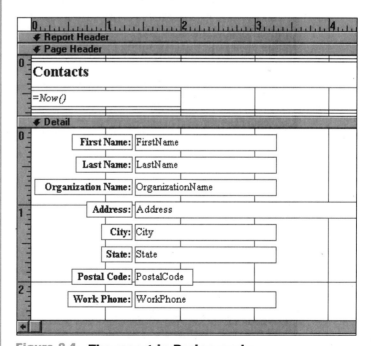

Figure 8-4 **The report in Design mode**

2. Drag the right edge of the report to widen it to 6".

    It may help to maximize the report window so that you can see more of the report.

⚠WARNING A common problem encountered when printing reports is that every other printed page is blank. This occurs when the report is too wide for the page. If this happens, check your margin settings and decrease the width of the page.

3. Click the label Last Name, then press ⌐DELETE⌐.

   Do not delete the data field. The label is the text in bold characters to the left of the field.

4. Repeat Step 3 for the State and Postal Code labels.

Exercise 3: Modifying the report: moving fields

1. Drag the LastName field and position it to the right of the FirstName field.

2. Drag the State field to position it to the right of the City field.

3. Reduce the size of the State field to allow for two character state codes.

4. Drag the PostalCode field to position it to the right of the State field.

5. With the mouse, draw a box around the OrganizationName, Address, City, State, and PostalCode fields. Drag this box up to move the fields closer to the name fields.

6. Move up the WorkPhone field to just below the City field.

7. Drag the bottom border of the Detail section to just below the WorkPhone field.

8. Click the Print Preview icon to see what the report looks like (Fig. 8-5).

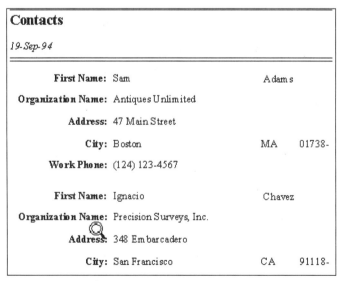

Figure 8-5 The modified report

9. Click the Close Window icon to return to Design mode.

Objective 4: Adding and Changing Fields

After reviewing the report, you decide that the fax number ought to appear as well. This is also a good time to modify the label for the name field.

The toolbar at the top of the screen contains a Field List icon. When you click this icon, you see a list of the fields in the table or query upon which you built the report. To add a field to the report, drag it from the field list and drop it on the report.

Exercise 4: Adding a field

1. Click the Field List icon.
2. Drag the Fax field from the list and drop it on the report to the right of the WorkPhone field.
3. Click the Field List icon to close the Field List window.
4. Adjust the position and size of the Fax field so that it aligns with the surrounding fields.
5. Click the Print Preview icon to see what the report looks like with the fax numbers added.
6. Click the Close Window icon to return to Design mode.

FEATURE

Concatenating names in MS-Access

How many times have you received mail that is meant to appear as if it is addressed to you personally but is obviously a mass mailing? The giveaway is the space between the first and last names. In order to allow for long first names, the FirstName field on the report has to be larger than needed for the average name. Here is how to make such mailings look better by eliminating that space.

1. Delete the LastName field completely.
2. In the FirstName field, change the entry to read
   = [FirstName] & " " & [LastName]

Make sure you include the equals sign and use the square brackets. The space between the quotation marks is the amount of space you will see between the first and last names on your report.

To do the same for the city, state, and zip code, eliminate the State and PostalCode fields and change the entry in the City field to read

=[City] & " " & [State] & " " & [PostalCode]

You may need to enlarge the Name and City fields since they now show more information than before.

Exercise 5: Changing a field

The label on the line that contains the names currently reads First Name:. You want it to read Name:.

1. Position the cursor over the First Name label (*not* the data field) and click. The field is selected, and the cursor turns into an I-beam.
2. Position the cursor between the words First and Name and click again. The cursor changes to a vertical line.
3. Use the (← BACKSPACE) to delete First.
4. Click anywhere outside this label to complete the edit (Fig. 8-6).

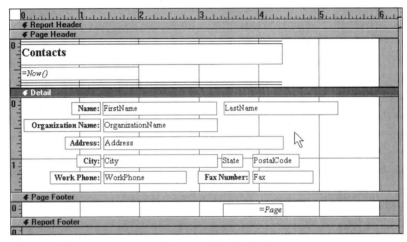

Figure 8-6 **The report with modified labels**

5. Click PrintPreview to see what the report looks like.
6. Click the Close Window icon.

Objective 5: Modifying the Page Footer

page footer   The *page footer* is a section of the report that appears at the bottom of every page and often contains the page number. Anything in the page footer will show on every page of a report. The Report Wizard builds a page footer that is very plain. You can change the page footer to include more information— for example, "Page 1 of 12" or however many pages are in your report.

Exercise 6: Modifying the page footer

1. Scroll down the report until you see the Page Footer section (Fig. 8-7).

Figure 8-7 **The Page Footer section**

2. Double-click the PageNumber field to open the Properties box.

3. Click the Control Source line in the Properties box.

4. Use (← BACKSPACE) or (DELETE) to remove the entry for Control Source.

5. Click the button with the three dots to the right of the Control Source line to open the Expression Builder (Fig. 8-8).

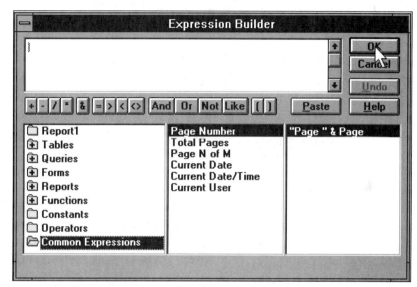

Figure 8-8 The Expression Builder window

6. Click Common Expressions at the bottom of the list of objects.

7. Double-click Page N of M in the list of Common Expressions. Click OK.

8. Click the Properties Box icon to close the Properties box.

9. Click PrintPreview to review the changes to the report.

10. Click CloseWindow to return to Design mode.

Objective 6: Modifying the Page Header and Report Header

page header The *page header* is a section of the report that can contain information such as the report title or date. It appears at the top of every page of the report. You will modify the page header to use the space more efficiently. The Report Wizard includes lines in the page header. Now that the report is wider, you need to lengthen those lines for a more balanced look.

report header The *report header* is a section of the report that may contain a title, picture, or logo that appears on the first page of the report. The Wizard did not build a report header, so you will add one, including your name so you can easily identify your report as it comes off the printer. The report header can be used to create a cover or title page for the report.

report footer
The *report footer* is a section of the report that may contain summary information. It appears at the end of the report. Report footer information follows page footer information.

Exercise 7: Modifying the page header

First you need to shorten the space for the title. Then you will move the date up to the same line as the title. The current date is automatically put on the report using the =Now() command.

1. Click the Contacts title box in the page header (Fig. 8-9).

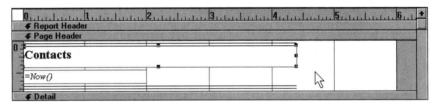

Figure 8-9 The Page Header section

2. Use the right handle to decrease the size of the box to 3".
3. Reduce the size of the Date field to about 1.25".
4. Move the Date field box to the right of the Contacts title box.
5. Click the top horizontal line.
6. Hold down (SHIFT) and carefully click the other three lines.
   All four lines are now selected.
7. Press (SHIFT)+(→) repeatedly to extend the line to about 5.8".
8. Select the two lower lines and move them up to just under the title box.
9. Drag the bottom margin of the Page Header section to just below the lower of the two lines (Fig. 8-10).

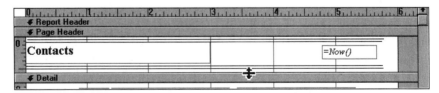

Figure 8-10 The Page Header section with changes

10. Use PrintPreview to see the effects of your changes. Return to Design mode.

Exercise 8: Adding a report header and title

In this exercise, you will add a report header with a report title.

1. Place the cursor on the line that divides the report header from the page header and drag it down about 1".
2. Click the Label button in the Toolbox.

   (If the Toolbox is not already open, you will need to open it.)
3. Move the cursor to the Report Header section.

   The cursor changes to a cross-hair with the letter A below it.
4. Use the mouse to draw a box about 4" wide by 0.5" deep in the Report Header section.

   When you release the mouse button, you will see a blinking vertical line at the right side of the box. The line indicates that you can type text into the box.
5. Type *your name* in the box.

   The text is small because it uses the default font, which is small. You will enlarge the font in a later exercise.

Objective 7: Adding Lines and Boxes

You can add visual impact to your report with lines and boxes.

Exercise 9: Adding lines

To separate your new report header from the page header, draw lines above and below the text box you just created. Then modify the properties of the lines to make them thicker.

1. Click the Line icon in the toolbox. Draw a horizontal line above the report title.
2. Repeat Step 1 to draw a horizontal line below the report title.
3. Select both lines.
4. Click the Properties icon on the toolbar to open the Properties box.

   The title of the Properties box reads Multiple selection. This indicates that you have selected more than one object.
5. Click the Border Width entry in the Properties box.
6. Click the arrow that appears on the right of the Border Width entry.
7. Click the 2 pt value and close the Properties box.
8. If necessary, reduce the size of your Report Header area.
9. Use PrintPreview to see the effects of your changes (Fig. 8-11), then return to Report Design mode.

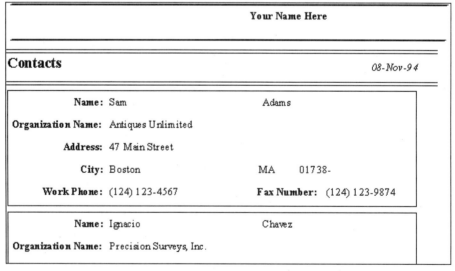

Your Name Here

Contacts　　　　　　　　　　　　　　　　　　　　　　　　　　08-Nov-94

Name: Sam	Adams	
Organization Name: Antiques Unlimited		
Address: 47 Main Street		
City: Boston	MA　　01738-	
Work Phone: (124) 123-4567	**Fax Number:** (124) 123-9874	

Figure 8-11　**The report with lines added**

Exercise 10: Adding boxes

To visually separate each record from the surrounding records on the page, add a box around the whole record in the Detail section. It will seem as though all your data disappears because you have placed the box on *top* of the fields. All you have to do is position the box *behind* your fields, and your data will reappear.

1. Click the Rectangle button in the Toolbox.
2. Using the mouse, draw a box around all the fields in the Detail section.
3. Click Format/Send to Back on the menu bar to make the fields visible.

Your Name Here

Contacts　　　　　　　　　　　　　　　　　　　　　　　　　　08-Nov-94

Name: Sam	Adams
Organization Name: Antiques Unlimited	
Address: 47 Main Street	
City: Boston	MA　　01738-
Work Phone: (124) 123-4567	**Fax Number:** (124) 123-9874

Name: Ignacio	Chavez
Organization Name: Precision Surveys, Inc.	

Figure 8-12　**The report with a box added**

4. Use PrintPreview to see the effects of your changes (Fig. 8-12), then return to Design mode.

Objective 8: Formatting Data in a Report

Formatting a report includes changing font types and sizes, rearranging items on the screen, changing the spacing between lines, and modifying the appearance of the printed report. All the fonts on your computer that are available to MS-Windows applications are available in MS-Access. The fonts on your computer may vary from those available on another computer depending on the fonts installed on each and the printer connected to each. If you are in doubt as to which font to use, Arial comes with MS-Windows and is a plain font suitable for titles and headlines.

Exercise 11: Changing fonts

The name you typed into the report title is still displayed in the default font. In this exercise, you will make the name larger and change the font style of the title in the page header to italic.

1. Click the box that surrounds your name on the report title.

   On the top toolbar, a font name and size are listed in the viewing areas of two drop-down list boxes (Fig. 8-13).

Figure 8-13 **Fonts on the toolbar**

2. Click the arrow on the font-name drop-down box to show a list of available fonts.
3. Select a font.
4. Click the arrow on the font-size drop-down box.
5. Select a font size from the list or type a value.

   (Try 24-point type and adjust this value up or down, as necessary.)
6. Click the Center-Align Text icon on the toolbar.

   This centers the text within the text box, not the report. To center the text on the report, move the box or enlarge the box so that it is as wide as the report.
7. Click the Contacts title in the page header to select it.
8. Click the Italic icon on the toolbar (Fig. 8-14).

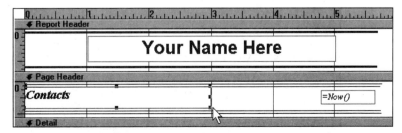

Figure 8-14 **Modified report header**

9. Use PrintPreview to see the effects of your changes. Return to Design mode.

Objective 9: Saving the report

If you have not already done so, save the report.

Exercise 12: Saving the report

1. Click File/Save As on the menu bar.
2. When prompted for a report name, type rptContactList. Click OK.

Objective 10: Previewing the Report

When you use Print Preview, the screen changes. The button bar is considerably different. It shows a restricted set of options—those that you need while in Print Preview. Even the cursor changes; it looks like a magnifying glass. This is a visual reminder that by clicking once you can zoom in to magnify a section of a report or zoom out to see the full page.

Exercise 13: Print Preview mode

1. Click the Print Preview icon on the toolbar.
2. Use the balloon help to examine the function performed by each icon on the button bar.
3. Use the zoom feature, clicking the mouse button to zoom in and out. Move around the page and examine the report.
4. Click the Print Setup icon.

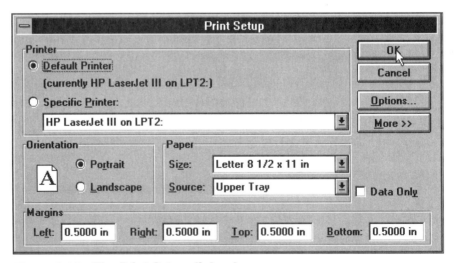

Figure 8-15 **The Print Setup dialog box**

The Print Setup dialog box opens (Fig. 8-15). This is where you can set the margins of the report or change to a different printer. Leave the default values unless you are told to change them.

5. Click Cancel to exit from the Print Setup dialog box.

Objective 11: Printing a Report

Print out the first page of your report. Take a minute to look over this first page; if it looks the way you want it to, print the entire report. The report header contains your name, so you can identify your report even if it is printed along with someone else's.

Exercise 14: Printing the report

1. Click the Print icon to open the Print dialog box.
2. In the Print Range From: and To: boxes, type 1. Click OK.
3. Check the report. Make sure it looks the way you want it to. If it does not, go back to Design mode and correct any problems.
4. If all is well, click the Print icon. Select All for the Print Range. Click OK.
5. Exit from Print Preview mode.
6. Exit from Report Design mode.
7. Close the database and exit from MS-Access.

Chapter Summary

In this chapter, you used the Report Wizard to generate a report, which you then modified by moving, deleting, and adding fields. You changed the page header and footer and added a report header. You added visual accents such as lines and boxes. You changed the formatting of the report. Once you were satisfied with the report, you previewed it and then printed it.

Review Questions

True/False Questions

_____ 1. The Today() function is used to put the current date on a report.

_____ 2. The width of the report generated by the Report Wizard can be changed later.

_____ 3. MS-Access can use any fonts on your computer that are recognized by MS-Windows.

_____ 4. The report header appears on every page of the report.

_____ 5. The Print Preview option prints out only the first page of the report.

Multiple-Choice Questions

_____ 6. To provide visual clues about important items on a report, you can use

    A. fonts.

    B. boxes.

    C. lines.

    D. Any of the above.

_____ 7. To add lines and boxes to a report, you use the

    A. toolkit.

    B. toolbox.

    C. toolbar.

    D. tollbooth.

_____ 8. The title that appears at the top of each page in a report is called the

    A. title bar.

    B. report header.

    C. page header.

    D. page footer.

_____ 9. If every other page of your report prints out blank, you should

    A. check the width of your report page.

    B. print only every other page.

    C. check the margin settings.

    D. A and C

_____ 10. The report header can be used to

    A. identify the author of the report.

    B. specify the title of the report.

    C. show when the report was generated.

    D. All of the above.

Fill-in-the-Blank Questions

11. The _____ section of the report contains the line-by-line listing of the database records.

12. To add a text data field to a report, you would begin by clicking the _____ icon on the toolbar.

13. The margins of a report can be changed using the File/_____ option.

14. Changing the appearance of a report by modifying fonts, layout, and spacing is known as _____ the report.

15. To make the page number appear near the bottom edge of each page, you would place the page () in the _____ section of the report.

Acumen-Building Activities

Quick Projects

1. Using the Report Wizard for MyBooks.

1. Open the Books database. Click the Reports tab. Click New for a new report.
2. Select the table MyBooks. Click Report Wizards. Double-click Single-Column.
3. Move the following fields from the List of available fields to the Field order on report list: Title, Author, PublisherName, ISBNNumber, and Note. Click Next.
4. Sort by Title. Click Next.
5. Choose the Executive style and Portrait orientation. Click Next.
6. Accept the default title and options. Click Finish.

2. Modifying the detail area of the MyBooks report.

This exercise is a continuation of Quick Project #1.

1. Click the Close Window icon to return to Report Design mode. Maximize the screen.
2. Drag the right edge of the report to the 6" mark on the ruler.
3. Lengthen the Title field by drawing it out to the 3" mark on the ruler.
4. Reposition the Author field and label so that they are on the same line as Title.
5. Modify the label of ISBNNumber to read ISBN. Resize the label.
6. Reposition the ISBN label so that it is on the same line as Publisher. Align both and move them up closer to the line that contains Author and Title.
7. Lengthen the Note field so that it stretches across the page. Move it up closer to the line that contains Publisher and ISBN.
8. Preview the results.

3. Modifying the title area of the MyBooks report.

This exercise is a continuation of Quick Project #2.

1. Return to Design mode. Click the MyBooks title box in the page header.
2. Use the right handle to decrease the size of the box to 3".
3. Change the font style to italic and the font size to 18 point.
4. Reduce the size of the date field to about 1.5". Right-align the text.
5. Position the Date field box on the right side of the report.
6. Hold down ⇧SHIFT and carefully select the two lower horizontal lines. Move them up to just below the Title field.
7. Press ⇧SHIFT + → to extend these lines to the right margin of the report.
8. Hold down ⇧SHIFT and carefully select the top two lines. Press ⇧SHIFT + → to extend these lines to the right margin of the report.

9. Adjust the size of the page header to make it smaller.
10. Preview your work.

4. Adding visual impact to the MyBooks report.

This exercise is a continuation of Quick Project #3.

1. Return to Design mode.
2. Click the Rectangle button in the toolbox.
3. Using the mouse, draw a box around all the fields in the Detail section.
4. Click the Format/Send to Back option on the menu bar.
5. Adjust the size of the Detail area leaving 0.25" of space below the lowest box.
6. Preview your work. Return to Report Design mode.
7. Save your report (File/Save As) and name it rptBookList.
8. Close the Report Design screen.
9. Close the Books database.

In-Depth Projects

1. Building a report for the CD database.

1. Open the CD database and go to the Reports window.
2. Build a New single-column report from the table CDCollection using the Report Wizards.
3. Include the following fields in the report: Title, GroupName, RecordingLabel, Length, YearReleased, and Classification.
4. Sort first by Classification, then by Title. Select your own style and use Portrait orientation. Accept the default title and options and click Finish. Preview the results.
5. Return to Report Design mode. Make the report 6" wide.
6. Position GroupName and RecordingLabel so they are on the same line and aligned along the top.
7. Position LengthInMinutes and YearReleased so they are on the same line and aligned along the top. Move them closer to the line above.
8. Reduce the size of both LengthInMinutes and YearReleased to a little over 0.5" each.
9. Position Classification directly beneath LengthInMinutes.
10. Adjust and refine the position of the fields as appropriate.
11. Drag the border of the Detail section to within 0.25" of the bottom of Classification.
12. Preview your work. Return to Report Design mode.
13. Decrease the size of the CDCollection title box in the page header to 3" and change the font style to italic.
14. Reduce the size of the date field to 1.5" and right-align the text.
15. Move the Date field box to the right side of the report, aligning it and the title field along the top.

16. Move the two lower horizontal lines up to just below the title field and extend all four lines to the right margin of the report.
17. Adjust the size of the page header to make it smaller.
18. Preview your changes. Return to Report Design mode.
19. Using the Toolbox, draw a rectangle around all the fields in the Detail section of the report and send it to the back so that the fields are superimposed on the rectangle.
20. Preview the effects of your changes. Return to Report Design mode.
21. In the page footer, move the page number to the right margin of the report.
22. Create a label box on the left side of the page footer, type *your name*, and left-align it within the label box.
23. Save your report and call it rptCDList. Print the report after previewing it.
24. Close the Report Design screen. Close the CD database.

2.   Building a report for the Dinner Party database.

1. Open the Dinner database and go to the Report window.
2. Build a New single-column report from the table Dinners using the Report Wizards.
3. Include the following fields in the report: Place, Date, Time, and Occasion.
4. Sort by Date. Select your own style and use Portrait orientation.
5. Name this report Dinner List. Accept the other defaults and click Finish.
6. Widen the report to 6".
7. Position Date, Time, and Occasion on the same line.
8. Adjust the size of the Detail section.
9. In the page header, position the Date field near the right margin and right-align it.
10. Italicize the Dinners title field.
11. Adjust the position and length of the horizontal lines in the page header.
12. Adjust the size of the page header.
13. Draw a box around all the fields in the Detail section of the report and send it to the back so that the fields are superimposed on the rectangle.
14. Move the page number in the page footer close to the right margin of the report.
15. Create a label box on the left side of the page footer, type *your name*, and left-align it within the label box.
16. Preview your report, then print it out.
17. Save your report and call it rptDinnerList. Close the Report Design screen.
18. Build a second New report from the table DinnerGuests. Make it the same type of report as rptDinnerList. Include the following fields: FirstName, LastName, Address, City, State, and PostalCode.
19. Sort by LastName, then FirstName.
20. Modify this report as you did rptDinnerList.

21. Preview your work and print it out. Save the report and call it rptDinnerGuestList.

22. Close the Report Design screen. Close the Dinner database.

CASE STUDIES

Coffee-On-The-Go:

Creating Reports

In this chapter, you learned to create reports. You will use those skills to create reports for Coffee-On-The-Go.

1. Open the Coffee database.
2. Create a report that includes only the following fields from the Employee table:

   Last
   First
   Salary
   Current

3. Enhance the report to include a title, formatting, and lines.
4. Preview the report.
5. When you are pleased with the report, print it.
6. Save the report and close the Coffee database.

CASE STUDIES

Videos West:

Creating Reports

In this chapter, you learned to create reports. You will use those skills to create reports for Videos West.

1. Open the Video database.
2. Create a report that includes only the following fields from the Inventory table:

   Title
   Retail
   Quantity
   Rating

3. Enhance the report to include a title, formatting, and lines.
4. Preview the report.
5. When you are pleased with the report, print it.
6. Save the report and close the Video database.

Acumen Critical Thinking Milestone

Individual Project:

the Scouts Cookie Sale Database

It occurs to Mrs. Wilson that, in addition to the home phone number, she needs to record the work number for each customer, so she decides to add that number to the Customer table. She also decides to add some validation rules—like not being able to leave the customer's name or address blank.

After working on the data-entry form to make it more visually appealing and entering this week's cookie sales, she decides to build some queries and generate reports to see who is selling the most cookies and what is the best-selling variety. Then Mrs. Wilson makes a backup of the database.

1. Add WorkPhone to the Customer table. Insert some validation rules to avoid nulls in CustomerName and Address. Enter this week's cookie sales.
2. Modify the data-entry form. Adjust the fields so that all can be viewed on the screen without scrolling. Add features (lines, boxes, color) to make the form visually appealing and easy to use.
3. Build a query to determine how cookie sales are going and who is selling how much. Build another query to determine the best-selling cookie type.
4. Create reports on the previous two queries. Make a database backup.

Team Project:

the Community Rec Center Database

The Forms Designer in your project group has decided to make the forms more useful by adding visual clues to facilitate data entry and repositioning the fields on the forms to avoid scrolling. Also, the type of membership field on the Members form should not be left empty. The Forms Designer and the Database Administrator must confer to decide where to insert this validation rule: in the form or Members table.

The Report Designer has decided to generate more informative listings, such as which members are using the facilities, which members are checking out equipment, and how much equipment is currently on loan.

The entire project team will work together to enroll this week's new members into the Rec Center database and record reservations and equipment issue. Then the Database Administrator will make a backup of the Rec Center database.

The Full Project Team

Confer on the best place to position the validation rule regarding the Type of Membership field. Insert the rule. Record this week's new members, reservations, and equipment issues.

The Database Administrator

If appropriate, add the validation rule for Type of Membership to the Members table. Confer with project team members to ensure that all data items they need to capture have corresponding fields in a table of the Rec Center database. Make a backup of the database.

The Forms Designer

Enhance the quick forms. Reposition the fields to eliminate scrolling and add visual appeal to enhance data entry. Add any validation rules or input masks that you deem appropriate. Confer with your colleagues before making these changes to make sure they agree with you.

The Report Designer

Create the following reports: (1) which members are using the facilities, (2) which members are checking out equipment, and (3) how much equipment is currently on loan.

Part 3

Advanced Features

Chapter 9

Advanced Query Operations

Objectives
- Using Compound Conditions
- Specifying Ranges
- Using the Not Operator
- Prompting for Criteria
- Calculated Values in Queries
- Creating Multitable Queries

Key Terms

TERM	DEFINITION
Compound Condition	a set of criteria that are combined within a query

Building a simple query with one condition is not the only type of query you can construct. You can combine several conditions within one query. If your database contains thousands or hundreds of thousands of records, you can use queries to extract a subset of the data by specifying ranges of values.

Objective 1: Using Compound Conditions

compound query

When we first studied queries in this book, we said that if a query were written in English, it would read, "Show me only data where . . . " If you were to write a compound condition in English, it might read, "Show me only data where . . . *and* . . ." A *compound query* is a set of criteria that are combined within a single query. For example, you could query, "Show me all records where the City is Burlington *and* the State is Colorado," because you want data from Burlington, Colorado, but not from Burlington, Vermont. Another type of compound query might read, "Show me only data where . . . *or* . . . ," as in "Show me all the orders we have received from Washington *or* Oregon."

When designing a compound condition, take time to consider how the criteria will be interpreted by MS-Access. If your queries are producing unexpected results, then the combination of criteria you used is incorrect. An example will clarify this point.

Big Brother Is Still Watching

The on-line services you use are compiling data about you every time you log on. Your social security number, credit card numbers, where you live, what you do, what interests you have—all this information is now available for sale. One service can offer the last-known address for any person in the U.S. Another service can tell you how long someone has had a certain phone number or has lived in a particular place and who else lives there. A third service can give you information on how to obtain state driving records.

  A new type of job—that of Information Detective—is forming around this oversupply of data. These high-tech detectives negotiate massive databases and sell their skills to answer questions about people. What does your nanny's driving record look like? The homebuilder you are considering contracting—has he ever filed for bankruptcy? This new employee you just hired—did she really earn the degree listed on her job application? One such agency, which works out of Annandale, Virginia, charges clients $4.00 an hour to provide them with information they are looking for.

  The U.S. House of Representatives is working on the draft of a bill that will require all telecommunications companies, including on-line services, to tell consumers what information is being collected and how it will be used.

Suppose you want to send a letter to all your contacts in Florida who work at companies with more than 50 people. In English, the query would read, "Show me a list of contacts where the state is Florida and the number of employees is greater than or equal to 50." This is interpreted by MS-Access to read, "Show me a list of contacts where (state *equals* Florida) *and* (the number of employees *is greater than or equal to* 50)." The conditions are compounded, so the second condition further restricts the limits imposed by the first condition.

You should have an idea of the type of results you expect from a query. If you are running a report based on a query, run the query first or use Print Preview to make sure you have the records you are getting the results you expect.

How would you write the query to include all your contacts in Florida and Georgia? If you write, "Show me a list of contacts where the state equals Florida and Georgia," you will not see any names in the results. Why? Think about what the query is really saying. Nobody lives in *both* Florida and Georgia—they live in one state or the other. Your query asked for names where both conditions were met—no contacts matched, so no names appeared in the output list. What you really meant was, "Show me a list of contacts where the state equals Florida *or* the state equals Georgia."

The distinction between And compound conditions and Or compound conditions is very important to understand. MS-Access provides considerable help in building queries, but you still have to be very careful to say exactly what you mean.

Exercise 1: Compound conditions: And

Write a query that uses two conditions connected by And. The two conditions combine to restrict the output recordset and act on two different fields. Your starting point is at the Contacts Database window with the Query tab selected.

1. Open the query FirstQuery in Design mode.

   The query should include only the fields FirstName, LastName, OrganizationName, State, and NumEmployees.

2. Delete the condition for OrganizationName and set the condition for NumEmployees to >49. Make sure that the Show box for NumEmployees is checked (Fig. 9-1).

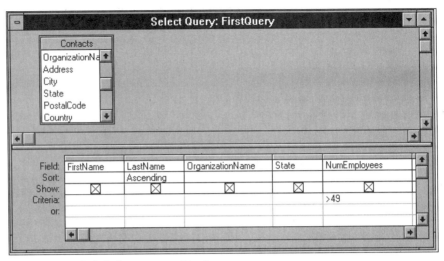

Figure 9-1 **Initial query criteria**

3. Run the query by clicking the exclamation point on the toolbar.

   The results show all your contacts in companies with 50 or more employees.

   The list includes Moore, Langford, and Swenson.

4. Return to Design mode.

5. In the State column on the Criteria line, type = VA.

   It is important that this goes on the same line as the >49 in the NumEmployees column. Criteria on the same line are combined using the And operator.

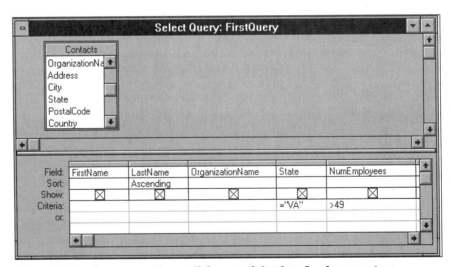

Figure 9-2 **Compound conditions with the And operator**

6. Run the query again.

    Now you will see only the contacts where both conditions are met. The list shows only Langford.

7. Return to Design mode.

Exercise 2: Compound conditions: Or

Write a query that uses two conditions connected by the Or operator. Records that meet either condition are returned.

1. Delete the =VA from the Criteria line.

2. Type =ID on the next line.

    This row is labeled or:. The two criteria are combined using the Or operator (Fig. 9-3).

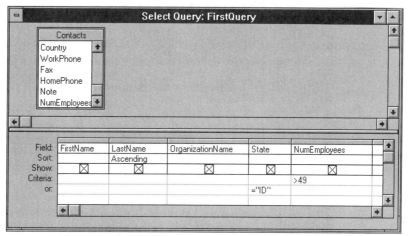

Figure 9-3 Compound conditions with the Or operator

3. Run the query.

    You will see a list of contacts in companies with 50 or more employees, and also any contacts in Idaho, without regard to the number of employees.

4. Return to Design mode.

Exercise 3: Compound conditions on the same field

How would you construct a query that retrieves data from two or more states? One way is to list the states.

1. Delete the =ID condition from the Or line and type = VA or PA on the Criteria line.

2. Run the query.

    The results show your contacts in Virginia and Pennsylvania for companies with 50 or more employees.

3. Return to Design mode.

Objective 2: Specifying Ranges

Often you will need to extract records from a database where some field has a value that falls within a specified range of values. What if you want contacts from a group of states? You can use the In operator to list the State names. Then you search for records where the State name is in the list.

The Between operator can be used to find, for example, a list of companies with 20 to 200 employees or orders dated between January 1 and July 4. The Between operator is inclusive: Your order list will include orders placed on New Year's Day and the Fourth of July.

If you ask for a list from the Contacts database with last names between A and M, you will see names from Adams to Kanzaki on the list. But you will not see Monteleone or Moore. Why not? Because Mo comes after M when you sort alphabetically. There are two solutions to this possible problem. You can look for names between A and MZZ. Or you could search between A and N. You must know your data in order to specify the correct search criteria.

Exercise 4: Compound conditions: In

Look for people in Virginia, Pennsylvania, or Washington, DC.

1. Delete = VA or PA from the Criteria row.
2. Type IN (VA, PA, DC) in the Criteria row.
3. Delete >49 from the NumEmployees column (Fig. 9-4).

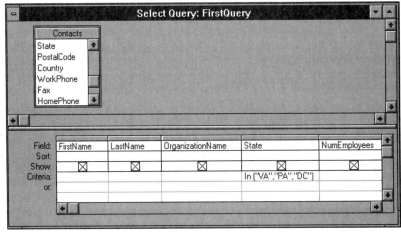

Figure 9-4　Compound conditions with the In operator

4. Run the query.

   You will see the records for Langford, Moore, and Monteleone. These are people in the two states that you specified and the District of Columbia.

5. Return to Design mode.

Exercise 5: Compound conditions: Between

Look for last names that start with letters between A and M.

1. Clear the In condition from the State column.
2. In the LastName column of the Criteria row, type between A and M (Fig. 9-5).

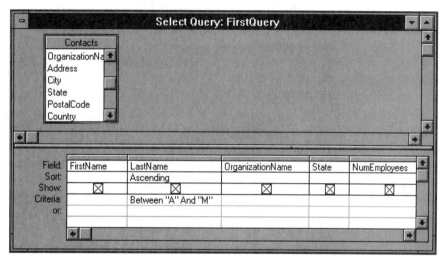

Figure 9-5   Compound Conditions with the Between operator.

3. Run the query.

   Monteleone and Moore are not on the list because Mo sorts alphabetically after M.
4. Return to Design mode.
5. Change the Criteria condition to between A and MZZ. Run the query.

   Monteleone and Moore are now on the list.

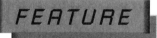

Queries and security

Even when you are building a form based on only one table, you may want to think about using a query instead of a table. One reason for doing so is security. Take the example of employee records. They usually contain sensitive information, such as pay level and performance reviews. You want to design a form so that the clerical staff in the personnel department can enter routine information without having access to confidential data. First, you build a query, selecting only the open information fields. You set permissions so that the query cannot be changed. Then you build the form on that query. Even if a staff member has the Form Design mode available, he or she can modify only the display of the fields selected in the query. The staff member cannot get to the confidential data in the table.

Objective 3: Using the Not Operator

Not is a special compound condition. It reverses or inverts the effects of other conditions. Records that would have been selected in a regular query are excluded. Records that would have been omitted now make up the output recordset. Sometimes it is easier to specify what you do *not* want than to describe what you *do* want.

To search for all the contacts in Arkansas you use the query Like AK. How do you find all the contacts *not* in Arkansas? Simply change the condition to Not Like AK. It is easier to exclude one state than to create a query that includes 49 states.

There is one potential pitfall when using the Not operator. If a State field is not filled in, it has a value of Null. This record shows up in the out-of-state list because the null value is indeed Not Like AK. To circumvent this situation, add a validation rule to the table that makes State a required field, as you did with the LastName field. You might consider imposing the same rule on any field that you plan to use as the basis for a query.

Exercise 6: Using the Not operator to reverse the selection criteria

When you ran the query in Exercise 1 with no restrictions on The State field, you saw three records. When you restricted the state to VA, you saw only one record. If you reverse the state condition, the other two records will be listed.

1. Delete the Between condition from the Criteria row in the LastName column.
2. Type <>VA on the Criteria row in the State column.
   <> means "not equal to."
3. Type >49 under NumEmployees on the Criteria row (Fig. 9-6).

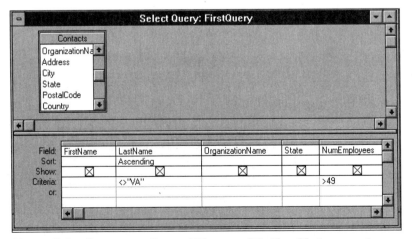

Figure 9-6 Compound conditions with the Not operator

4. Run the query.

> Moore and Swenson are listed, and Langford, from Virginia, is not shown.

5. Return to Design mode.

6. Type Not in front of the >49 in the NumEmployees column. Run the query.

> Now the list shows all the contacts who are not in Virginia and who work at companies with less than 50 employees. There's another way to do this.

7. Return to Design mode.

8. Change the Not >49 entry to <50. Run the query. The results are the same as the previous query. Return to Design mode.

Objective 4: Prompting for Criteria

The previous queries used criteria coded into the query. If you want to look at a list of contacts for each state, you could build fifty queries with each specifying one state in the Criteria row. This is not a good technique. A better way is to build one query with a prompt that asks you which state you want. You can build prompt queries that use approximate matches to the data, or you can build prompt queries that require exact matches. You can combine prompts and normal criteria or even prompt for input values on more than one field.

Exercise 7: Prompting for criteria

Modify the query so that it prompts you for the state code in which you want to see contacts. Then change the prompt so that you can search for a specific last name.

1. Clear all the criteria from the query.

2. In the criteria row of the State column, type [Enter a two-letter State code]. Make sure you include the square brackets.

3. Run the query. When prompted for a State code, type PA and click OK (Fig. 9-7).

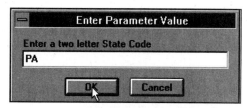

Figure 9-7 **The Prompt dialog box**

> You will see a list of your contacts in Pennsylvania.

4. Switch back to Design mode.

5. Run the query again. When prompted for a State code, type ID and click OK.

    You will see a list of your contacts in Idaho.

6. Switch back to Design mode.

7. Delete the prompt from the Criteria row of the State column.

8. In the Criteria row under LastName, type Like [Enter a Last Name].

9. Run the query. When prompted for a last name, type Lan*.

    The record for Langford is shown. Here you combined the Like operator with the prompt, so you can search for names when you know only part of the spelling.

⚠WARNING You can combine a prompt and the Between operator—you will be prompted for a range of values. This does not work with the In operator. If you execute a prompt using the In operator, MS-Access will crash without warning, and you may lose data.

10. Return to Design mode.

11. Click File/Save As and save the query as qryPromptLastName.

12. Close the query.

Objective 5: Calculated Values in Queries

We mentioned before that you should not store computed data in a table. The better approach is to compute the data as necessary so that it is always current and correct. Some typical examples of computed data are totals, subtotals, and averages. Often it is useful to know the count of the number of records in a table or the number of records that match the criteria in a query.

Exercise 8: Calculated totals in queries

First, find the total number of records in your database. Then determine how many records you have in each state. Finally, calculate the average number of people employed by your contact companies in each state.

1. Start at the Database window with the Query tab selected.

2. Click New, then New Query.

3. At the Add Table dialog box, select Contacts. Click Add. Close the dialog box.

4. Double-click ContactID to add it to the query.

5. On the menu bar, click View/Totals.

    A new line appears in the query specification. This line is labeled Total:. The default value is Group By.

6. Click the Group By value to show a list of options (Fig. 9-8).

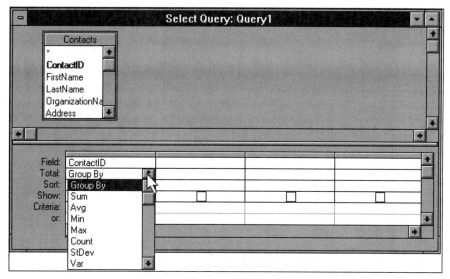

Figure 9-8 **Total Option menu**

7. Select Count from the list and run the query.

   You will see that you have ten records in the database.

8. Return to Design mode.

9. Double-click State in the list of fields for the Contacts table to add it to the query. Leave the Group By value in the Total row. Run the query.

   You have a list of the number of contacts in each state (Fig. 9-9). Because your Contact database is small, this table is not very revealing. It would be more informational if you had a large number of records in the database.

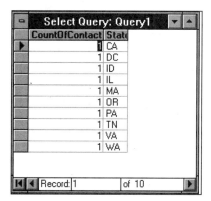

Figure 9-9 **Contacts by state**

10. Return to Design mode.

11. Click the ContactID entry in the Field row and select NumEmployees from the list that appears.

12. Click the Count value in the Total row and change it to Avg. Run the query (Fig. 9-10).

    This query shows you the average number of people employed by your contact companies, grouped by state.

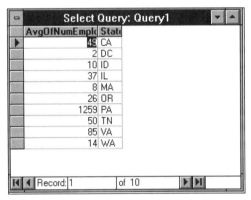

Figure 9-10   Average number of employees, grouped by state

13. Save the query as qryAvgNumEmp. Close the query.

Objective 6: Creating Multitable Queries

The most common reason for using queries is to extract related data from two or more tables at the same time. This capability is unique to relational databases, and you do it with a query.

It is recommended that the relationships between the tables be established before you create the query. While this is not absolutely necessary (MS-Access generally can deduce the relationships as it runs the query), there is a chance that you may see unexpected results if MS-Access deduces the relationships incorrectly. Also the query will run faster if the relationships are predefined. The relationships between the tables used in the following exercises were established in Chapter 5. But you will have to add some data to the second table before you can use it in a query.

Exercise 9: Adding data to a second, related table

Begin this exercise at the Database window.

1. Open the PhoneNumbers table in Datasheet view.

2. Add the following values to the table:

CONTACT ID	PHONE NUMBER	PHONETYPE
1	(124) 123-4567	Work
2	(703) 234-1234	Work
3	(615) 232-4505	Pager
3	(615) 459-5245	Home
3	(615) 666-7070	Fax
4	(215) 222-1111	Work
6	(509) 989-1000	Work
7	(208) 544-1111	Work
8	(415) 222-8880	Work
9	(503) 565-7878	Work
10	(202) 344-1212	Work
11	(282) 383-1193	Work

Exercise 10: Multitable Queries

You have two tables in your Contacts database: the main Contacts table and the secondary PhoneNumbers table. You want to print a telephone directory that shows each contact's name, company, and phone numbers. Construct a query to list the required information. Start at the Database window with the Queries tab selected.

1. Click New, then New Query.

   The Query Design window opens with the Add Table dialog box on top.

2. Double-click the Contacts table to add it to the query.

3. Double-click the PhoneNumbers table to add it to the query.

4. Click Close to close the dialog box (Fig. 9-11).

   The line between the two tables represents the relationship defined in Chapter 5. There is a 1 next to the Contacts table and the infinity symbol next to the PhoneNumbers table. This indicates that between the Contacts and PhoneNumbers tables there is a one-to-many relationship.

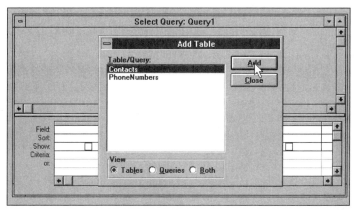

Figure 9-11   Query Design window with multiple tables

5. Double-click the LastName, FirstName, and OrganizationName fields from the Contacts table to add them to the query.

6. Double-click the PhoneNumber and PhoneType fields from the PhoneNumbers table to add them to the query.

7. Click View/Table Names to show the table names in the Query Design window (Fig. 9-12).

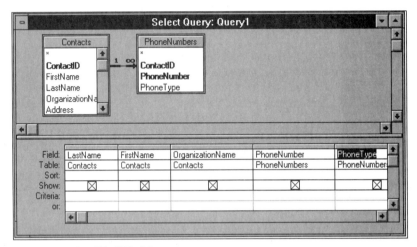

Figure 9-12   Multitable query

8. Under LastName, click in the Sort row and select Ascending. Run the query.

Last Name	First Name	Organization Name	Phone Number	Type of Phone Number
Adams	Sam	Antiques Unlimited	(124) 123-4567	Work
Chavez	Ignacio	Precision Surveys, Inc.	(415) 222-8880	Work
Clark	Robin	Precision Surveys, Inc.	(208) 544-1111	Work
Kanzaki	Hiroshi	Precision Surveys, Inc.	(503) 565-7878	Work
Langford	George	Langford Trucking	(703) 234-1234	Work
Lincoln	Tom	Lincoln Log Homes, Inc	(282) 383-1193	Work
Monteleone	Wendy	Monteleone Legal Serv	(202) 344-1212	Work
Moore	Margaret	Liberty Shield Insuranc	(215) 222-1111	Work
O'Leary	Roger S.	Precision Surveys, Inc.	(509) 989-1000	Work
Swenson	G. David	Swenson Adventure Tc	(615) 666-7070	Fax
Swenson	G. David	Swenson Adventure Tc	(615) 459-5245	Home
Swenson	G. David	Swenson Adventure Tc	(615) 232-4505	Pager

Select Query: qryPhoneList

Record: 1   of 12

Figure 9-13   Results of a multitable query

9. Save the query as qryPhoneList.

10. Close the database and exit from MS-Access.

Chapter Summary

In this chapter, you built complex queries using compound conditions to specify multiple criteria. You learned how to use operators to combine criteria and the difference between the And operator and Or operator. You used the In and Between operators to specify ranges of data values. You made your queries more flexible by prompting for criteria instead of building them into the query. You saw how to compute values in a query. The concept of multitable queries was introduced, and you built a query using two tables from your Contacts database.

Review Questions

True/False Questions

_____ 1. It is a good idea to define relationships between tables before using them in a multitable query.

_____ 2. Requesting records from one state Or another will result in only those records from the first state being returned.

_____ 3. The Between operator returns records that are between the values you specify, but not those that are equal to the values you specify.

_____ 4. A query can show data that is not in the database tables but is computed from stored data.

_____ 5. The In operator returns the same data as the Or operator.

Multiple-Choice Questions

_____ 6. To match a list of specific values for a selection condition, you would use the

   A. Between operator.

   B. Like operator.

   C. In operator.

   D. Inclusive operator.

_____ 7. To find records for all states except New Hampshire, you would set the criterion on the state field to

   A. Unlike "NH".

   B. Not Like "NH".

   C. Like "NH" Not!

   D. Except "NH".

_____ 8. If you have not defined a relationship between two tables before building a query, MS-Access will

    A. deduce the relationship automatically.

    B. show an error message on the screen.

    C. run the query, but give the wrong results.

    D. ask for the relationship to be specified.

_____ 9. Which of the following statements about MS-Access queries is untrue?

    A. You can set multiple conditions on one field.

    B. A query can be used as the basis for a form or report.

    C. The values for the selection criteria can be specified when the query is run.

    D. A query run every week will show the same data.

_____ 10. If you want to find the contacts who live in New Mexico and work for companies with fewer than twelve people, you would

    A. set the criterion in the State column to "NM".

    B. set the criterion in the NumEmployees column to "<12".

    C. set the criterion in the State column to "NM" and set the criterion in the NumEmployees column to "<= 12".

    D. set the criterion in the State column State to "NM" and set the criterion in the NumEmployees column to "< 12".

Fill-in-the-Blank Questions

11. When you store a field that is computed from other fields, you endanger the _____ of the database.

12. The Not condition is used to _____ the effects of the specified criteria.

13. To select records with a last name of White, Whittle, or Whitton, but not Whyte or Whistler, you would specify LastName Like

_____.

14. To perform computations, such as totals and averages, in a query, click on the _____ / _____ (*two words*) menu option.

15. It is possible for MS-Access to _____ the user for a value for a criterion whenever the query is run.

Acumen-Building Activities

Quick Projects

1. Compound queries of MyBooks using And.

1. Open the Books database and create a New Query without using the Query Wizard.
2. Add the table MyBooks to the Query Design screen.
3. Include in the query the following fields in the following order: Title, Author, ISBNNumber, PublisherName, Pages, and Note.
4. Sort by Title in ascending order.
5. Run the query. Check the contents and return to the Query Design window.
6. In the Title column of the Criteria row, type like *walk*.
7. In the Note column of the Criteria row, type like *mystery*. Run the query.

   The output from the query is restricted to one row, if you are using the data set provided by the authors. The single record returned contains the value Skinwalkers in the Title field and mystery in the Note field.

2. Compound queries of MyBooks using Or.

· This exercise is a continuation of Quick Project #1.

1. Return to Query Design mode and delete the criterion from the Title column.
2. Modify the criterion in the Note column so that it reads like *market*.
3. In the next line down, which is labeled or:, type like *relativity*. Run the query.

   The output from the query is restricted to two rows, if you are using the data set provided by the authors. One of the records returned contains the value market in the Note column; the other contains the value relativity.

3. Querying for a range of values with MyBooks.

This exercise is a continuation of Quick Project #2.

1. Return to Query Design mode. Delete the criterion from the Note column.
2. In the Pages column of the Criteria row, type between 300 and 350. Run the query.

   The output from the query shows two rows, if you are using the data set provided by the authors. Each of these books has between 300 and 350 pages.

4. Using Between to exclude a set of records in MyBooks.

This exercise is a continuation of Quick Project #3.

1. Return to Design mode.
2. Modify the criterion in the Pages column by typing not between 300 and 350. Run the query.

   Three rows are output, if you are using the data set provided by the authors. The first book has 164 pages, the second has 299, and the third has 368. None of the three has between 300 and 350 pages.
3. Save the query by clicking File/Save Query and call it qryCompound. Click OK.
4. Close the Query Display screen. Close the Books database.

In-Depth Projects

1. Advanced queries in the CD database.

1. Open the CD database and go to the Query window.
2. Create a New query without using the Query Wizard. Use only the table CDCollection. Include in the query the following fields in the following order: Title, YearReleased, and Classification.
3. Sort by Title in ascending order.
4. Run the query. Check the contents and return to the Design Mode window.
5. Find those CDs that are classified as rock or country. Run the query.
6. If you are using the data set provided by the authors you will have two rows returned: Evangeline (Cajun/Country) and Question of Balance (Symphonic Rock).
7. Return to Query Design mode. Remove the criterion from the Classification column.
8. Find those CDs that were released between 1970 and 1990. Run the query.
9. If you are using the data set provided by the authors you will have three rows returned: Canyon Trilogy (1989), Question of Balance (1970), and Star Wars (1977).
10. Return to Query Design mode. Remove the criterion from the YearReleased column.
11. Find those CDs that have the values Wars or 2002 in their Title field. Run the query.
12. If you are using the data set provided by the authors, you will have two rows returned: Star Wars and Cusco 2002.
13. Save the query and name it qryCompound. Close the query.
14. Create a New query without using the Query Wizard. Use the tables CDCollection and Tracks for the query.
15. Include in the query the following fields in the following order: from table CDCollection: Title and GroupName; from table Tracks: TrackTitle and TrackTime.
16. Sort by Title in ascending order. Run the query.

17. If you are using the data set provided by the authors, you will have 18 rows returned.
18. Save this query and name it qryJoin.
19. Close the query. Close the CD database.

2. Advanced queries in the Dinner database.

1. Open the Dinner database and go to the Query window.
2. Create a New query without using the Query Wizard. Use the table Dinners.
3. Include in the query the following fields in the following order: Date, Time, Occasion, and Place.
4. Sort by Date in ascending order.
5. Run the query. Check the contents and return to the Design Mode window.
6. Find those Dinners that were held between 02/01/94 and 06/01/94. Run the query.
7. If you are using the data set provided by the authors, you will have three rows returned: 02/13/94, 04/03/94, and 05/29/94.
8. Return to Query Design mode. Remove the criterion from the Date column.
9. Find those dinners that were either birthdays or BBQs. Run the query.
10. If you are using the data set provided by the authors, you will have two rows returned: 07/19/94 (midsummer BBQ) and 08/30/94 (Linda's birthday).
11. Save this query and name it qryComplexDinner. Close the query.
12. Create a New query without using the Query Wizard. Use the table DinnerGuests for the query.
13. Include in the query the following fields in the following order: FirstName, LastName, and HomePhone.
14. Sort by LastName in ascending order. Check the contents and return to the Design Mode window.
15. Find those DinnerGuests who live in the 757 phone exchange. Run the query.
16. If you are using the data set provided by the authors, you will have one row returned: John Baccus ((303) 757-9976).
17. Save this query and name it qryComplexGuest. Close the query.
18. Create a New query without using the Query Wizard. Use the tables DinnerGuests, GuestList, and Dinners—in that order—for the query.
19. Include in the query the following fields in the following order: from table Dinners: Date and Place; from table DinnerGuests: FirstName and LastName.
20. Sort by Date in ascending order. Run the query.
21. If you are using the data set provided by the authors, you will have 22 rows returned.
22. Save the query and name it qryTripleJoin.
23. Close the query. Close the Dinner database.

CASE STUDIES

Coffee-On-The-Go: Using Advanced Queries

In this chapter, you learned to create advanced queries. You will use those skills to create queries for the Coffee database for Coffee-On-The-Go. You may, if you wish, save each query.

1. Open the Coffee database.
2. Set up a query to find only the employees Smith and Smyth. Print the results.
3. Set up a query to find the employees Smith, Smyth, and Smithsonian. Print the results.
4. Find all female employees who make $15,000 or more. Print the results.
5. Find all male employees who no longer work for the company. Print the results.
6. Find all male employees who work for location 01 and make more than $14,000. Print the results.
7. Find all female employees who started working for the company after 1991. Print the results.
8. Close the database.

CASE STUDIES

Videos West: Using Advanced Queries

In this chapter, you learned to create advanced queries. You will use those skills to create queries for the Video database for Videos West. You may, if you wish, save each query.

1. Open the Video database.
2. Find all videos which cost $9.99 and have a retail price of $14.99. Print the results.
3. Find all videos released after 1993 which sell for $9.99. Print the results.
4. Find all the videos in the 01 category with a retail price of $9.99. Print the results.
5. Find all the 02 videos with a PG rating. Print the results.
6. Find all the videos in the 03 or the 04 category. Print the results.
7. Find all the videos which are not in the 01 category. Print the results.
8. Close the database.

Chapter 10

Advanced Forms

Objectives
- Providing a List of Choices
- Displaying Yes/No Values
- Creating a Command Button
- Including Data from More Than One Table in a Form

Key Terms

TERM	DEFINITION
Command Button	a button, icon, or control placed on a form that performs a predefined action when the user clicks it
List Box	a box on a form that shows a list of acceptable values
Combo Box	a box on a form that accepts text input or shows a list of acceptable values
Auto Expand	a feature of the combo box that completes the data entry for you after you type the first few letters of an item in the list of allowed values
Check Box	a box on a form used to display a Yes/No value; the box contains an X if the value is Yes or True and is empty if the value is No or False
Option Button	a control on a form used to make one choice among several items
Toggle Button	a control on a form that shows normal for a No value and depressed for a Yes value
Subform	a form that shows data inside a main form; the subform is built from a table that is related to another table used to build the main form

Forms can be used for browsing through the database, but they can do more than serve as a backdrop for your data. They can actively assist with data entry. They can show lists of items from which you can choose a value rather than having to type it. Forms can also include *command buttons,* which are buttons, icons, and controls on a form that perform predefined actions when you select them. They speed movement around and between forms. You can build forms that display data from more than one table.

command buttons

Objective 1: Providing a List of Choices

In earlier chapters, you learned to put restrictions on some data fields. You made sure that State codes were shown as uppercase characters and that telephone numbers were entered according to an input mask. These techniques help avoid confusion and inconsistency in data entry. With these goals in mind, how would you handle a field like the PhoneType field? How would you prevent one person entering "Office" and someone else entering "Work" as the value in your database's PhoneType field? The answer is to provide a standard list of values, which everyone in the organization must use. You do this with a combo box or a list box. The *combo box* displays a list from which you can either choose or type a value. The *list box* is more restrictive; it shows a list of acceptable values from which you can choose one. The combo box has a really nice feature called *Auto Expand:* You type in the first few letters of the value you want and the combo box finishes entering the data for you. Depending on your needs, you would use either the combo or list box.

combo box

list box

Auto Expand

When creating a combo box, you can incorporate the list of values into the combo box and form. This is a good scheme for a short list that does not change often. For longer lists of values or lists with values that change constantly, you can design the combo box to refer to a table in the database. Another feature of the combo box is that it can be restricted like a list box; you can limit the data entered to just those values in the combo box list.

Exercise 1: Building a combo box

In this exercise, you will build a form for the PhoneNumbers field. Then you will replace the PhoneType field with a combo box. Start by opening the Contacts database and selecting the Form tab.

1. Click New to build a form for the PhoneNumber table.
2. Select the PhoneNumbers table and click Form Wizards.
3. Use the Autoform Wizard.

   Now that you have the PhoneNumbers form (Fig. 10-1), you can begin to modify it.

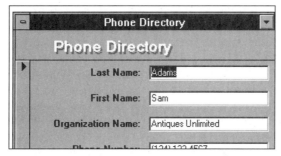

Figure 10-1 **PhoneNumbers form**

4. Switch to Form Design mode and maximize the Form window. Be sure the Toolbox is open and the Control Wizards button in the Toolbox is depressed.

5. Delete the PhoneType Field and its label.

6. Click the Combo Box button in the Toolbox.

   The button will stay depressed and the cursor will change as you move it to the Detail section of the form.

7. Draw a box approximately where the PhoneType box used to be.

   The Combo Box Wizard dialog box opens (Fig. 10-2).

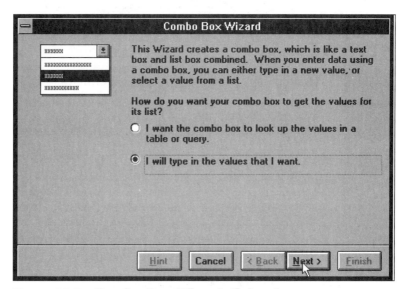

Figure 10-2 **Combo Box Wizard dialog box**

8. Select the option: I will type in the values that I want. Click Next.

9. Tell the Wizard that you only want one column in the box. Use ⟨TAB⟩ to move to the column to begin data entry.

10. Type the following values, one per line, and press $\boxed{\leftarrow \text{ENTER}}$ after each value: Work, Home, Fax, Pager, Cellular, Direct, 800 line, Data line, and 2nd line.

The items appear in the list in the order in which you type them (Fig. 10-3).

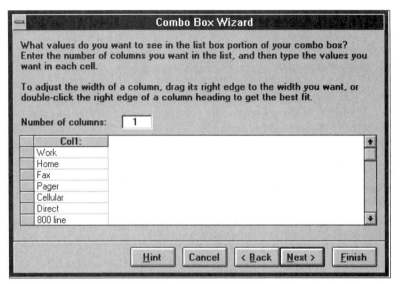

Figure 10-3 Combo Box Wizard, entering the list of values

11. Click Next.

12. Click the option: Store that value in this field. Select the PhoneType field, then click Next.

13. Type Type of Phone Number for the name of the combo box. Click Finish.

14. Adjust the size and placement of the combo box and label.

15. Switch to Form view to test your changes (Fig. 10-4).

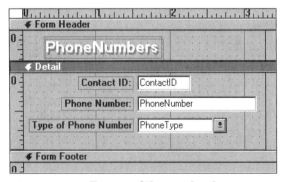

Figure 10-4 Form with combo box

16. Click the arrow to the right of the combo box to see the list of allowed values. Select Cellular.

17. Now type direct in the box. Notice that you do not need to type the entire word; MS-Access fills in the value using its Auto Expand feature.

18. Enter values for Home and Work. Watch Auto Expand in action.

Exercise 2: Limiting input values

You want to limit the values entered to those listed in the combo box. You must go back to Design mode to change the properties of the combo box.

1. Return to Design mode and click the combo box to select it.

2. Click the Properties icon to open the Properties box (Fig. 10-5).

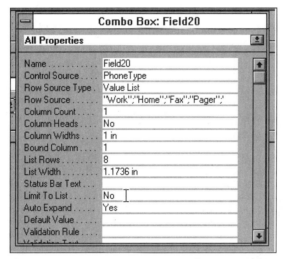

Combo Box: Field20

All Properties

Name	Field20
Control Source	PhoneType
Row Source Type	Value List
Row Source	"Work";"Home";"Fax";"Pager";
Column Count	1
Column Heads	No
Column Widths	1 in
Bound Column	1
List Rows	8
List Width	1.1736 in
Status Bar Text	
Limit To List	No
Auto Expand	Yes
Default Value	
Validation Rule	

Figure 10-5 Properties box for the combo box

Notice the fourth item from the top of the box: the Row Source, which lists values. This is where you edit the list.

TIP You can give yourself more space to work by pressing (SHIFT)+(F2) to zoom the box to a larger size. Make your edits and click OK to close the zoom box.

3. Scroll down the properties list until you see the entry Limit to List. Change this value to Yes.

4. Close the Properties box and return to Form view.

5. Type Office in the combo box. Press (← ENTER).

You see a message telling you that what you typed is not a valid entry and you must match a value in the list (Fig. 10-6). Once you close the message box, MS-Access helpfully pops up the list of choices for you.

Figure 10-6 **Message box following an invalid data entry**

6. Select Work, which is a valid entry from the list.
7. Click File/Save Form As. When prompted for a name, type frmPhoneNumbers.
8. Click File/Close.

Telecommuting, Boom or Bust?

The number of virtual offices is swelling and more and more people are opting to telecommute to their jobs. Integrated Services Digital Network (ISDN) connections, which are used for high-speed data communications and are necessary to connect to corporate networks, are increasing dramatically. There are estimates that the number of basic-rate ISDN lines will double from 1993 to 1994.

At the same time, the companies that are moving their workers into telecommuting positions are facing some very real problems. An office in the home means there is no clear definition between work hours and off hours, which can lead to employee burnout. One vice-president has been trying to figure out how to stop her home-office staff from sending faxes in the middle of the night. "People are now thinking and working on the job 12 to 18 hours a day." Other companies tend to misuse the situation, expecting their employees to produce more than what could normally be done in an eight-hour day.

Some companies have had great success with telecommuting. Following the Los Angeles earthquake in January of 1994, Pacific Bell made a special effort to offer telecommuting opportunities to its workers. Nine months later, 90% of the people who took advantage of the "telecommuting relief package" are still working from home, 50% of whom are working five days per week. Almost half of those who started telecommuting in January had never considered it before, and more than half have managerial responsibilities (*Investor's Business Daily*, September 29, 1994).

But despite Pacific Bell's success, the Conference Board reports that fewer than 1% of employees at 155 businesses nationwide are telecommuters. "Some 75% of those surveyed say their greatest hurdle is convincing managers that employees can be productive and properly supervised when they work from home," says the report (*The Tampa Tribune*, October 2, 1994).

Objective 2: Displaying Yes/No Values

As you use your database, you will refine it to make it more useful. You might add a Christmas card field to the Contacts table. For such a field, a simple Yes/No value would suffice. Either the contact is on your Christmas card list or is not. On the form, all you need is a check box. A *check box* is a small square box that contains an X for a Yes value and is blank for a No value. You click the box to turn the checkmark on or off for yes or no.

check box

Alternatively, you could use an option button or toggle button for this field. An *option button* is round and shows a black center for a Yes value and a white center for a No value. Normally, option buttons are grouped

option button

toggle button

together and are used to select one of several options. They are also known as radio buttons. A *toggle button* appears pressed down for a Yes value and raised up for a No value. It is used to trigger some action inside the form and is not often used for a simple Yes/No selection.

FEATURE

Dialing out from MS-Access

If your computer has a modem, you can have MS-Access dial telephone numbers for you. It's easy to add an autodialer command button to your form. Follow the steps below:

1. Open the form in Design mode.

2. Place a command button on the form.

3. When the Wizard opens, select the Miscellaneous category and choose the autodialer option. Leave the Telephone icon in place.

4. For the button's name, type cmdAutodial.

5. Size and position the button. Switch to Form view and test.

The autodial feature is simple to use. In Form view, click a telephone number field and click the autodial command button. The autodialer shows you which number it will dial. It even has an option to include a prefix, like a 9, for an outside line. It will dial the number and tell you when to pick up the phone.

Exercise 3: Displaying Yes/No values with a check box

In this exercise, you will add a Yes/No field and values to the Contacts table. Then open the Contacts form and add a check box.

1. Start at the Database window, with the Table tab selected.

2. Select the Contacts table and click Design.

3. Add a new field at the end of the table. Name the field ChristmasCard.

4. Make the field type Yes/No and set the default value in the properties box to No.

5. Switch to Datasheet view, saving the table when prompted.

6. Change the ChristmasCard value to Yes for the following names: Clark, Kanzaki, Monteleone, Moore, and Swenson.

7. Close the table, return to the Database window, and click the Form tab.

8. Select Contacts, click Design, and maximize the window.

9. Click the Check Box icon in the toolbox.

10. Position the cursor in the Detail section, and draw a box for the control. (Place this box to the right of the Address field.)

11. Open the Properties box (Fig. 10-7).

At the top of the Properties box, you will see Check Box.

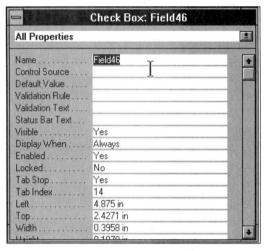

Figure 10-7   Properties box for Check Box

12. Click the Control Source line of the box, then click the down arrow.

A list of fields in the Contacts table appears.

13. Select the ChristmasCard Field.

14. Click the label for the check box.

15. Type Christmas Card: in the Caption field and close the Properties box.

16. Position and size the label and check box appropriately.

17. Switch to Form view and browse through the records (Fig. 10-8).

Note that there is an X in the check box for only those contacts for whom you changed the option to Yes—that is, Clark, Kanzaki, Monteleone, Moore, and Swenson.

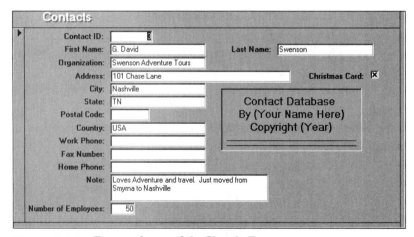

Figure 10-8   Form view with Check Box

18. Add O'Leary to the Christmas Card list by clicking the check box when his record is on the screen.

19. Drop Kanzaki from the list by clicking the check box when his record is on the screen.

20. Close the form, saving the changes when prompted.

Objective 3: Creating a Command Button

There are some operations that you perform regularly on a form, such as go to another form or close a form. You can build a command button that will do these things for you automatically, instead of having to select a menu item or navigate your way around the Database window.

Exercise 4: Creating a command button

In this exercise, you will put a command button on the Contacts form to close the form.

1. Open the Contacts form in Design mode.

2. Click the Command Button icon in the toolbox.

3. Draw a box for the button to the right of the Note field.

    The Command Button Wizard dialog box appears (Fig. 10-9).

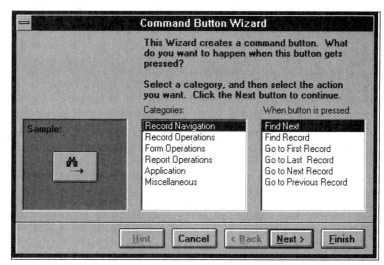

Figure 10-9 **Command Button Wizard dialog box**

4. Select Form Operations from the Categories list, then Close Form from the list of actions. Click Next.

5. Choose any of the available options for the "look" of the button—a stop sign, an exit door, or just a text message. You can abbreviate the text to Close. Click Next.

6. Name your button cmdClose when prompted, then click Finish.

7. Position and size the button appropriately.

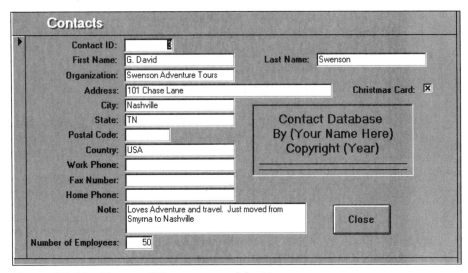

Figure 10-10   Form with command button

8. Save the form with your changes. Switch to Form view (Fig. 10-10).

9. Click the Close button, and your form will close.

Objective 4: Including Data from More Than One Table in a Form

The easiest way to display data from more than one table in a form is to base the form on a query. In the query, you select fields from related tables, then build a form using the query just as you would a table. The data from the two tables appears on one form. When two tables have a one-to-one relationship, this is the best approach.

subform   If two tables have a one-to-many relationship a better method is to use a Form Wizard to build a form and *subform*. The main record (from the one) is displayed on the form and the associated data (from the many) is displayed on the subform. The subform is presented as a datasheet so that many records can be displayed at once.

Exercise 5: A Multitable form

You will use the Form Wizard to build a form based on a query you created in Chapter 9. Then you will modify the PhoneType field to a combo box, as you did in Exercise 1.

1. Start at the Database window with the Form tab selected. Click New.

2. Select qryPhoneList and click the Form Wizard button.

Make sure that you select the query, not the PhoneNumbers table.

3. Select the Single-Column Form Wizard and click OK.

4. Click the double arrow to select all the fields for the form, then click Next.

5. Select a style, then click Next.

6. For the form title, type Phone Directory. Accept the defaults and click Finish to see the form in Form view.

Figure 10-11   Multitable form

7. Switch back to Design mode.

8. Delete the PhoneType field and its label.

9. Create a combo box, as you did in Exercise 1, to replace the PhoneType field you just deleted. Use the same values for the list. The label will read Type of Phone Number. Adjust the size and placement of the combo box on the form. Switch to Form view (Fig. 10-12). Test the combo box.

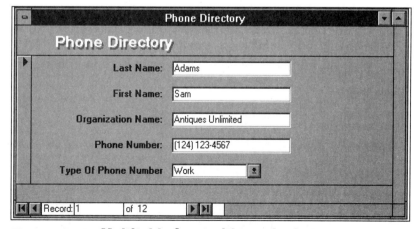

Figure 10-12   Multitable form with combo box

10. Save the form as frmPhoneList. Close the form.

Exercise 6: Building a form and subform

In this exercise, you will use the Contacts and PhoneNumber tables to build a form and an associated subform.

1. Start at the Database window with the Form tab selected.
2. Click New, select the Contacts table, then click the Form Wizards button.
3. Select the Main/Subform Wizard and click OK to open the Wizard dialog box (Fig. 10-13).

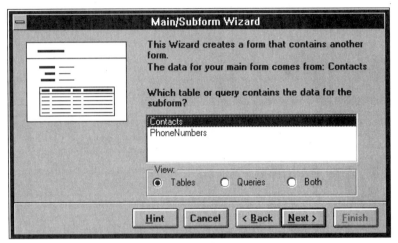

Figure 10-13 **Main/Subform Wizard dialog box**

4. Select the PhoneNumbers table for the subform and click Next.
5. Select the following fields for the main form: LastName, FirstName, and OrganizationName. Click Next.
6. Select the following fields for the subform: PhoneNumber and PhoneType. Click Next.
7. Select a style for your form. Click Next.
8. For the form title, type Contacts + PhoneNumbers. Click Finish.

   A dialog box appears, telling you that you have to save the subform.
9. Click OK to close the dialog box.
10. Save the subform as frmSubPhones.

   The Wizard will finish building the form (Fig. 10-14).

Figure 10-14   **Form with subform**

11. Browse through the records using the controls at the bottom of the main form.

    The numbers in the subform change as the Contact in the main form changes.

12. Find the record for David Swenson.

    Note the multiple entries in the subform.

13. Click File/Save Form As and save the form as frmContactsPhoneList.

14. Close the form, close the database, and exit from MS-Access.

Chapter Summary

In this chapter, you learned how to create more complex forms that can assist you with your work. You learned how to limit the data input to a range of permitted values and how to pop up that list on the form when needed. You became familiar with using check boxes to display and change Yes/No values. Your form now includes command buttons to perform various functions. You learned another way to display data from more than one table—by using a form and subform.

Review Questions

True/False Questions

_____ 1. A list box on a form can show a list of values from a table.

_____ 2. When using a form with a subform, the field that joins the two tables must appear on the form.

_____ 3. The Auto Expand feature makes the box on a form bigger when you type in more text than the field can display.

_____ 4. The only way to show data from two related tables is to join them with a query.

_____ 5. A check box for a field contains an X if the field's value is Yes.

Multiple-Choice Questions

_____ 6. You can create a command button on a form to
   A. close a form.
   B. add a new record.
   C. save a record.
   D. Any of the above.

_____ 7. For a multiple-choice question on a form with only one correct answer, you would use
   A. a check box.
   B. a toggle button.
   C. an option button.
   D. Either A or B.

_____ 8. To restrict a combo box to accept only permitted values, you would
   A. base the combo box on a table containing only the permitted values.
   B. type a list of permitted values in the Row Source in the Properties box.
   C. set the Auto Expand option to Yes in the Properties box.
   D. set the Limit to List option to Yes in the Properties box.

_____ 9. You can use a check box to display values from
   A. a memo field.
   B. a date field.
   C. a Yes/No field.
   D. an option field.

_____ 10. The values found in a combo box come from

    A. a list typed in the Row Source row of the Properties box.

    B. a table.

    C. a query.

    D. Any of the above.

Fill-in-the-Blank Questions

11. A _____ box on a form can show a list of values or accept values that you type in the box.

12. You can turn the Auto Expand feature on or off by switching to _____ mode and changing the Auto Expand setting in the _____ box.

13. Pressing _____ zooms a box in which you are typing.

14. Associated records from tables in a one-to-many relationship can be shown on a form and _____.

15. A _____ button can be placed on a form and designed to perform an action on that form.

Acumen-Building Activities

Quick Projects

1. Building a combo box for MyBooks.

1. Open the Books database. Open the table MyBooks in Design mode.

2. Add two new fields—BookCover and ReadYet—to the end of the list of field names and assign each field the following data types, descriptions, and properties.

FIELD NAME	DATA TYPE	DESCRIPTION	FIELD PROPERTIES
BookCover	text	Type of book	FieldSize: 20
ReadYet	yes/no	Have you read the book yet?	Caption: Read Yet? Default Value: No

3. Save the changes and close the Table Design window.

4. Open the form frmBooks in Design mode. Maximize the Design window. Make sure that the toolbox is visible and the Control Wizards button is depressed.

5. Widen the form to 5.5". Reduce the length of the BookCollectionID field. Lengthen the Title field. Place a combo box on the form alongside the Author field.

6. From the Combo Box Wizard, select the option to type in the values that you want for the list. Click Next. You want only one column in the box. Make the following entries, one per line, in column one: Hard Bound, Soft Bound, Paperback, and Magazine. Click Next.

7. Click the Store that value in this field option and store the value in the field BookCover. Click Next.

8. Type Book Cover: for the combo box label. Click Finish.

9. Adjust the size and placement of the combo box and label. Resize the window to normal and adjust the size of the window so you can see the combo box.

10. Save the form. Switch to Form view. Fill in the categories as follows:

Summer of the Danes	Soft Bound
Relativity	Hard Bound
Friday	Hard Bound
One Up On Wall Street	Soft Bound
Skinwalkers	Paperback

2. Limiting input values with MyBooks.

This exercise is a continuation of Quick Project #1.

1. Return to Form Design mode and click the combo box to select it.
2. Open the Properties box and change the Limit to List option to Yes.
3. Close the Properties box and return to Form view.
4. Go to the third record (Friday), move to the combo box, and type Paper Back. Press ENTER.
5. A dialog box appears because you entered an invalid entry. Click OK to remove the dialog box.
6. Select Paperback from the list in the combo box.
7. Save your work. Close the form.

3. Inserting a Yes/No field into MyBooks.

This exercise is a continuation of Quick Project #2.

1. Return to Form Design mode. In the Toolbox, click the CheckBox icon.
2. Position the cursor below the BookCover combo box and click once to place the check box.
3. Open the Properties box, click Control Source, and select ReadYet.
4. Click the label for the check box and type Read Yet? in the Caption row of the Properties box. Close the Properties box.
5. Size the label and position both the label and the check box appropriately.
6. Save your changes.

7. Switch to Form view and mark those books you have read.

8. Save your changes.

4. Building a Close Form command button for MyBooks.

This exercise is a continuation of Quick Project #3.

1. Return to Design mode and click the Command Button icon in the toolbox.

2. Place the button in the form header to the right of the title MyBooks.

3. From the Command Button Wizard, select FormOperations from the Categories list. Select CloseForm from the list of actions. Click Next.

4. Choose text and Close Form. Click Next.

5. Name this button cmdCloseForm. Click Finish.

6. Save your changes. Switch to Form view to test the button.

7. Click the Close button. Close the Books database.

In-Depth Projects

1. Advanced forms for the CD database.

1. Open the CD database and go to the Query window.

2. Open the form frmCDCollection in Design mode and delete the Classification field and its label.

3. Create a new combo box to replace Classification. Position the cross-hairs at the upper left corner of the remaining shadow box and click.

4. In the Combo Box Wizard, select the option to type in the values that you want for the combo box list. There is only one column in the box, with the following entries: Cajun/Country, Classical, Country & Western, Easy Listening, Jazz, Movie Theme, Native American Flute, New Age Symphonic, Rock & Roll, and Symphonic Rock.

   Adjust the column width accordingly.

5. Store the combo box values in the Classification field.

6. For the label, type Classification. Click Finish. Adjust the size and placement of the combo box and label. Resize the shadow box.

7. Resize the window to normal and adjust the size so that you can see the Classification field. Save the form.

8. Switch to Form view. Test the new combo box. Close the CDCollection form.

9. Create a New form using the table CDCollection. Use the Form Wizards to build a main form and subform. Use the table Tracks for the subform.

10. For the main form, choose the following fields from the table CDCollection: Title, GroupName, and RecordingLabel.

11. For the subform, choose the following fields from the table Tracks: TrackNbr, TrackTitle, and TrackTime.

12. Choose your style. Name the form CDCollection and Tracks.

13. Save the subform and name it frmSubTracks.

14. Browse the main form. Find Cusco 2002 and add these track entries:

4	Erosian	5:39
5	Ancient People	4:25
6	Unknown Paradise	3:50
7	Didjeridoo	3:35
8	From a Higher Point	5:13
9	Earth Waltz	3:16

15. Save the data. Scroll through the new entries of the subform.

16. Save the form and name it frmCDPlusTracks.

17. Close the form. Close the CD database.

2. Advanced forms for the Dinner database.

1. Open the Dinner database. Open the query qryTripleJoin in Design mode.

2. Add DinnerID and GuestID to the query. Remove Sort in ascending order from the Date column. Choose Sort in ascending order on the FirstName column.

3. Run the query. Save the query. Close the query.

4. Create a New form using the table Dinners. Use the Form Wizards to build a Main/Subform. The query qryTripleJoin will be used for the subform.

5. For the main form, choose the following fields from the table Dinners: Place, Date, Time, Occasion, and Comments.

6. For the subform, choose the following fields from the query qryTripleJoin: GuestID, FirstName, and LastName.

7. Choose your style. Name the form Dinners and Guests. Open the form.

8. Save the subform and name it frmSubGuests. Browse the main form.

9. Switch to Form Design mode. Adjust the size of the main form and subform as necessary to show data for both. Switch back and forth between Form Design mode and Form View mode to look at the form as it will be used.

10. Save the main form and name it frmDinnerAndGuests.

11. Create a command button from the toolbox. Position it on the open space to the right of Date and Time.

12. From the Command Button Wizard select FormOperations, then select CloseForm.

13. Select the Exit picture and name the command button cmdExit. Click Finish. Position and size the button.

14. Save the form. Switch to Form view. Click the Close button. Close the Dinner database.

CASE STUDIES

Coffee-On-The-Go: **Advanced Forms**

In this chapter, you learned advanced techniques for creating forms. You will apply those skills to create a form for Coffee-On-The-Go.

1. Create a form which includes fields from both the Employee and the Benefits tables.
2. Create a combo box for the Location field that offers the user a list of choices.
3. Using the Form, add three new records.
4. Save your changes and close the database.

CASE STUDIES

Videos West: **Advanced Forms**

In this chapter, you learned advanced techniques for creating forms. You will apply those skills to create a form for Videos West.

1. Create a form which includes fields from both the Inventory and the Vendor tables.
2. Create a list box for the Vendor Name field that offers the user a list of choices.
3. Using the Form, add three new records.
4. Save your changes and close the database.

Chapter 11

Advanced Reports

Key Terms

TERM	DEFINITION
Grouping	logically organizing data in a report by dividing it into groups based on the value of a field in the report

grouping

When you generate a report from a database, you want to organize the data, which can be sorted in various ways. Exactly how it is sorted depends on the data and the purpose for which it is being used. If you want a telephone directory listing, you sort by last name. A set of mailing labels is sorted by postal code. You can also group the data in your reports. *Grouping* means logically organizing data in a report by dividing it into groups based on the value of a field in the report. An example of grouping is a list of engine-part numbers, grouped by a prefix that indicates which factory makes each part.

A report often contains data which is calculated from other data. As you build more complex reports, you will find that you need to incorporate data from more than one table. You may need to change reports to sort and group the data in a different manner.

Objective 1: Sorting Data

In a database, data is stored in a certain order. However, as you have already learned, your report need not show the data in that same order. By changing settings in the report, you can control how the data is presented.

MS-Access makes this easy—there is a Sorting and Grouping icon on the top toolbar. When you open the Sorting and Grouping dialog box, notice the default values in the box. If you build a report from a query that has sorted or grouped data, the Report Wizard uses this information to define the sorting or grouping scheme in the report.

Exercise 1: Sorting data

In this exerise, you will use the report that you built in Chapter 8 and modify it to sort the output in different ways.

1. Open the Contacts database and select the Report tab.
2. Open the report rptContactList in Design mode.
3. Click the Sorting and Grouping icon on the menu bar. The Sorting and Grouping dialog box opens (Fig. 11-1).

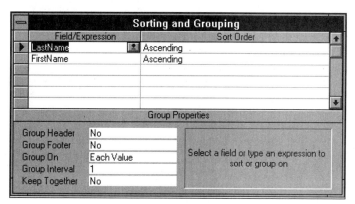

Figure 11-1   *Sorting and Grouping dialog box*

4. Use Print Preview to verify that the report is being sorted by LastName and then FirstName. Return to Design mode.
5. Click LastName in the Field/Expression list, then click the down arrow at the right of the box. Select PostalCode.
6. Click the margin of the box to the left of the F in FirstName.

   To delete an entry, you must select the entire line and then delete it.
7. Press (DELETE) to remove the FirstName sort. When prompted, confirm that you do want to delete this line.
8. Preview the report to verify that it is sorted by PostalCode. Return to Design mode.
9. Change the sort field to OrganizationName.
10. Preview the output (Fig. 11-2). Return to Design mode.

Name: Sam	Adams
Organization Name: Antiques Unlimited	
Address: 47 Main Street	
City: Boston	MA 01738-
Work Phone: (124) 123-4567	**Fax Number:** (124) 123-9874

Name: George	Langford
Organization Name: Langford Trucking	
Address: 1 Farm Road	
City: Mount Vernon	VA 00111-
Work Phone: (703) 234-1234	**Fax Number:** (703) 234-1111

Name: Margaret	Moore
Organization Name: Liberty Shield Insurance Inc.	
Address: 145 Independence Ave.,	
City: Philadelphia	PA 01873-

Figure 11-2   **The new report sorted by OrganizationName**

Objective 2: Grouping Data

You can sort records in a report without grouping them. You can define groupings only for sorted fields. Why? In order to separate the data into groups based on the value of some field, you must first sort the data on that field.

When you group data, you have the option of adding a header, a footer, or both to the group. For example, if you group by company name, you can add a header that shows the name of each company. You can keep a group of records all together on one page in a report. In other words, if all the records for a group do not fit on the current page, MS-Access begins a new page. This happens, except when there are too many records to fit on a single page. In that case, MS-Access simply ignores the request to keep all the records of the group together.

Exercise 2: Grouping data

In this exercise, you will use the same report as in Exercise 1 to group the data. You will group on OrganizationName and add a group header to identify the group. You must specify what will be in the group header.

1. In the Sorting and Grouping dialog box, change the GroupHeader value to Yes.

   The symbol on the OrganizationName line changes from an arrowhead to the Sorting and Grouping symbol with an arrowhead. This indicates that the OrganizationName field is being used to group the data.

2. Move the dialog box out of the way and scroll until you see the OrganizationName header section.

3. Increase the height of this section to 0.6".

4. Click the Field List icon on the toolbar to open the list of fields.

5. Drag the OrganizationName field from this list and drop it in the OrganizationName header section. Click the Field List icon on the toolbar to close the list of fields.

6. Delete the label from the newly added field. Change the field font to Arial, 14 point. Enlarge the field, if necessary.

7. Preview the report. Find Precision Surveys, Inc. (Fig. 11-3).

    The header is shown once and then the four contacts are listed—but they are not in alphabetical order.

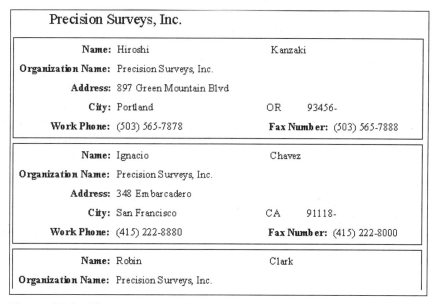

Figure 11-3   The grouped report

8. Return to Design mode. In the Sorting and Grouping dialog box, add a second sort line, using LastName in Ascending order.

9. Preview the report. Return to Design mode.

Exercise 3: Keeping data together within groups

Sometimes on a report the records in a group are split between two pages. In this exercise, you instruct MS-Access to keep all the records in a group on a single page.

1. In the Sorting and Grouping dialog box, make sure that the OrganizationName line is selected.

2. Change the Keep Together value to Whole Group.

3. Preview the report. The contacts from Precision Surveys appear together. Return to Design mode.

Objective 3: Creating Calculated Fields

In a previous chapter, you learned how to calculate totals and subtotals in queries. We said that any value that can be calculated from other data values should not be stored in the database. It is possible to calculate values in a report, so even if the table or query does not contain the value which you need, you can compute it on the report.

MS-Access has available a wide range of functions that may be used in the calculation of fields. These include SUM, AVG, and COUNT.

Calculated fields can be placed anywhere in the report. One common place for calculated fields is the group footer, where they summarize the records that appear in the Detail section.

FEATURE

Mail merge

You can use records from your database to print out "personalized" letters. This is called a mail merge. It is possible to send data from an MS-Access table or query directly into a word processor. However, you can do mail merge tasks completely within MS-Access. You can build a form letter in MS-Access and have it fill in the names and addresses of those people in your database to whom you want to send the letter. You build a query to extract just the names and addresses you need. Then you create the form letter, which is actually a report with a lot of text on it. On the report, you add the database fields that make up the inside address and salutation. You can add formatting for a professional appearance; you can even build your own letterhead. As a final touch, you can use the same query to generate a set of mailing labels to go with the letters.

Exercise 4: Calculated fields in the group footer

In this exercise, you will add a group footer and specify what will appear in it. Start with a count of the number of records in each group.

1. In the Sorting and Grouping dialog box, change the Group Footer setting to Yes.
2. Scroll down the form to the OrganizationName footer.
3. Create a text box in the footer. You may need to open the Toolbox if it is not already visible.
4. Change the label for the text box to Number of Contacts in the Organization:. Enlarge the label if necessary.
5. Click the text box that is currently labeled Unbound.

   Unbound means that the box is not yet tied to a field or expression.

6. Replace Unbound, typing =Count (ContactID) in its place.

7. Click the text box again to select it. Click the Left-Align icon on the toolbar to align the value along the left edge of the box, close to the label (Fig. 11-4).

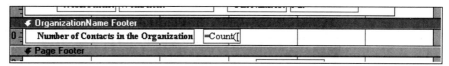

Figure 11-4 Calculated fields in the group footer

8. Preview the report (Fig. 11-5). Return to Design mode. Close the Sorting and Grouping dialog box.

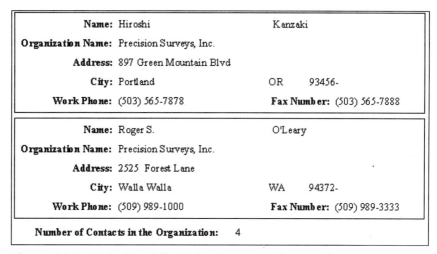

Figure 11-5 Calculated fields in the group footer of the report

9. Save the report. Print the report. Close the report

Objective 4: Including Data from More Than One Table in a Report

A report can be built from more than one table or query. The easiest way to build a report that includes data from multiple tables is to first build a query that selects the data from the tables. Then you can use the Report Wizard to build the report.

Often, for ease of data entry and efficiency in storage, you will use codes in your database. A typical example is the two-letter state code. Instead of storing California, you just store CA. Anyone who enters a large amount of data appreciates such abbreviations, but you may want to show the full word rather than the code on a printed report. Perhaps you are producing a report for clients who are unfamiliar with the shorthand codes used for product names or part numbers. How do you change a code into a full word? The best method is to use a reference or look-up table.

In Exercise 5, you will build a small reference table of states so that you can use it in a report. Once you have built the table, you can use it for other forms, reports, and queries. It can be tied to a list or combo box on a form, so you can pop up a list of states during data entry. MS-Access allows you to use tables from other databases, so you can refer to this reference table while working on other databases. This is known as attaching a table. Some database designers like to keep all their code reference tables—such as state codes, country telephone codes, postal codes—in one database. They attach to these tables from whatever other database they might be using. This has a real benefit: when you change a code or the meaning of a code, you change it in only one place. For every table in which that code is used, the value is automatically updated. Of course, if you plan to distribute your database applications to others, you have to remember to include the .mdb file with the code reference tables.

Exercise 5: Building a report that uses more than one table

Previously you built a multitable query that combined the Contacts and Phone Number tables. In this exercise, you will use this query as the basis for the next report. The layout of the report reflects the relationship between the two tables.

1. Start a New report. Select qryPhoneList. Use the Report Wizards.
2. Select the Groups/Totals Report Wizard. Click OK.
3. Click the double arrow to move all the fields into the report. Click Next.
4. Select LastName as the field to group by. Click Next.
5. Leave the group order as Normal. Click Next.
6. Select PhoneType as the field to sort by. Click Next.
7. Pick a style for your report. Click Next.
8. Give the report the title Contacts and Phone Numbers.
9. Turn off the Calculate Percentages option. Click Finish (Fig. 11-6).

   The phone numbers for Swenson are listed as a subgroup under his name.

Swenson Adventure Tours		
	(615) 666-7070	Fax
	(615) 459-5245	Home
	(615) 232-4505	Pager

Figure 11-6   Multitable report grouped by last name

10. Print the report. Exit from Print Preview to return to Design mode.

Telemedicine: the Promise and the Obstacles

The promise of telemedicine was great: to bring specialized medical diagnostics and care to rural America. The concept was simple: digital communications links from country hospitals to urban diagnostics centers would enable specialists at urban centers to visually "examine" patients at rural hospitals.

But promise and reality clash as the use of and support for telemedicine is lacking. Physicians trained in conventional diagnostic techniques are reluctant to embrace the new technology. Still unresolved are the issues of licensing—which governing body will regulate medicine practiced across state or international lines? Reimbursement is an issue. And equipping rural hospitals with the means to practice telemedicine has certainly not been cost-effective.

Fewer than 1000 teleconsultations happened on the North American continent in 1993. With so little success thus far, the speculation is that telemedicine, despite its great potential, will be a long time establishing itself.

Exercise 6: Changing the grouping in the report

The last report was grouped by LastName. Now you will change the report to group by OrganizationName.

1. Click the Sorting and Grouping icon to open the dialog box.
2. Click LastName and change it to OrganizationName.
3. Change PhoneType to LastName and set the Group Header option to Yes.
4. Add a third row using the field PhoneType (Fig. 11-7).
5. Close the Sorting and Grouping dialog box.

Figure 11-7 **Multitable report grouped by OrganizationName**

An extra header row appears. If you leave it blank, you will not see all the contacts in a company that has more than one contact. The report will print the LastName only when the OrganizationName changes, so you will see only the first contact at each company. There is a way to resolve this.

6. Use Print Preview to confirm the problem, checking the Precision Surveys listing. Return to Design mode.
7. Click LastName in the OrganizationName header. Hold down SHIFT and click the FirstName field to select it at the same time. Do not select the OrganizationName field.
8. Press CTRL+X to delete these fields and put them on the Windows clipboard.
9. Move to the LastName header section and press CTRL+V to paste these fields into that section (Fig. 11-8).

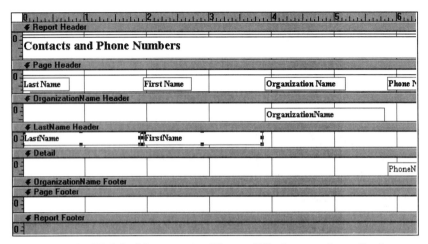

Figure 11-8   **Multitable report with modified group-by criteria**

10. Preview the report to verify that it now lists all the contacts at Precision Surveys in a group.

11. Save the report as rptBusinessPhone. Print the report. Close the report.

Exercise 7: Building a reference table for a report

1. Start at the Database window with the Tables tab selected.

2. Click New. Click New Table to begin a new table layout.

3. Make the first field StateCode. Set it to a text field with field size 2.

4. Make the second field StateName. Set it to a text field with field size 24.

5. Switch to Datasheet view, saving the table as tblrefState when prompted. Do *not* create a primary key for this table. Enter the following pairs of values:

CA	California
CT	Connecticut
DC	District of Columbia
ID	Idaho
MA	Massachusetts
OR	Oregon
PA	Pennsylvania
TN	Tennessee
VA	Virginia
WA	Washington

6. Close the table and return to the Database window.

7. Click the Query tab. Click New. Click New Query.

8. Add the Contacts and tblrefState tables to the query.

9. Drag and drop the State field from the Contacts table onto the StateCode field in the tblrefState table to establish the relationship.

10. Include all fields from both tables in the query output by double-clicking the asterisk at the top of each table's field listing (Fig. 11-9).

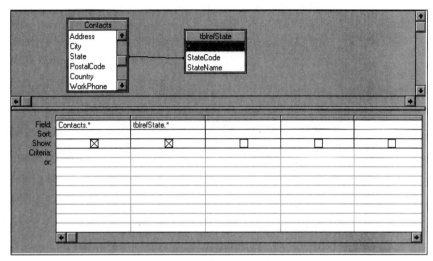

Figure 11-9 Building the query with a reference table

11. Close the query. When prompted for a name, save as qryContactsAndStates.

Exercise 8: Including data from a reference table in a report

In this exercise, you will use the Mailing Labels Wizard. In addition to mailing labels, this wizard can produce a directory-type listing with multiple columns per page. In this exercise, you will build the report and then substitute the full state names for the corresponding state codes.

1. Start at the Database window with the Report tab selected.
2. Click New, select qryContactsAndStates, and use the Report Wizards.
3. Select the Mailing Label Wizard.
4. From the list of Available fields, select FirstName. Select Space.
5. From the list of Available fields, select LastName. Select Newline.
6. From the list of Available fields, select Address. Select Newline.
7. From the list of Available fields, select City. Select Space twice.
8. From the list of Available fields, select StateName. (Make sure that you select the StateName field, not the State field). Select Space twice.
9. From the list of Available fields, select PostalCode (Fig. 11-10).

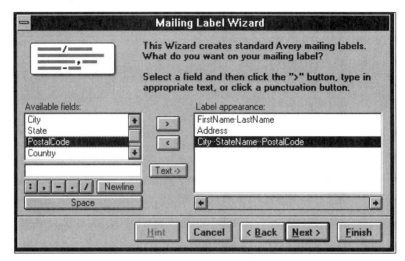

Figure 11-10 **Building the report with a reference table**

10. Click Next, choose sort by LastName, and click Next.

11. Choose the 5162 labels. Click Finish.

    Check the line that contains City, StateName, and PostalCode. The state names are shown in full (Fig. 11-11). Return to Design mode.

Margaret Moore	Roger S. O'Leary
145 Independence Ave.,	2525 Forest Lane
Philadelphia Pennsylvania 01873	Walla Walla Washington 94372-

Figure 11-11 **The report with full state names**

12. Use Format/Report Header-Footer to add a report header. Insert a label from the toolbar. Type your name in the label.

13. Print the report.

14. Save the report as rptContactsMailing. Close the report.

15. Close the database, then exit MS-Access.

Chapter Summary

In this chapter, you modified your reports to group and sort data. You learned how to add calculated fields. Using a multitable query, you built a report that shows data from more than one table. You modified the report to change the sorting and grouping. The idea of reference tables was introduced. You built a reference table, used it in a multitable query to modify how the data was presented, and created a report with the modified data.

Review Questions

True/False Questions

_____ 1. You can sort data in a report without grouping it.

_____ 2. You can group data in a report without sorting it.

_____ 3. When a report is based on a query, the data on the report must be sorted in the same order as the data in the query.

_____ 4. To use a reference table from another database, you must copy it into your current database.

_____ 5. Calculated fields can be placed anywhere in a report.

Multiple-Choice Questions

_____ 6. A report can be constructed from
  A. a query.
  B. a table.
  C. any number of queries and/or tables.
  D. Any of the above.

_____ 7. Arranging a list of data items in groups based on a common data value is called
  A. grouping.
  B. sorting.
  C. an array.
  D. ordering.

_____ 8. Arranging a list of data items in ascending or descending order is called
  A. grouping.
  B. sorting.
  C. an array.
  D. ordering.

_____ 9. By placing a calculated field in the footer section of a report, you summarize the records that appear in the report
  A. header section.
  B. footer section.
  C. grouping section.
  D. detail section.

_____ 10. If a field is unbound, it
  A. can be moved anywhere on the report.
  B. is not tied to a field or expression.
  C. has no limits on the values which it can accept.
  D. has no validation rules.

Fill-in-the-Blank Questions

11. A field on a report does not have to be stored in the database, it can be _____ from other fields.

12. If you want to group records in a report based on the value of a field, you indicate this in the _____ in the Report Design screen.

13. If you want to add up the number of records displayed in a group, you use the _____ function in the report footer.

14. A table that is used to decode values from other tables is called a _____ table.

15. If you want to use a table from another database, you can _____ it to the database you are currently using.

Acumen-Building Activities

Quick Projects

1. Sorting data in a report for MyBooks.

1. Open the Books database. Go to the Reports window.
2. Confirm that rptBookList is sorted by Title.
3. In Report Design mode, click the Sorting and Grouping icon.
4. Change the sort field from Title to Author and leave it in ascending order.
5. Run the report and check the sort order. Return to Design mode.

2. Building a group header for MyBooks.

This exercise is a continuation of Quick Project #1.

1. In the Sorting and Grouping dialog box, change the Group Header value to Yes to open an AuthorHeader section in the report.
2. Delete the label from the Author field. Drag the Author field from the Detail section into the AuthorHeader section and position it on the left side of the Header section. Make it bold and italic.
3. Preview the report. Return to Design mode.

3. Inserting page breaks into the report for MyBooks.

This exercise is a continuation of Quick Project #2.

1. Close the Sorting and Grouping dialog box. Open the Properties dialog box.
2. Click in the AuthorHeader section. Make sure the Properties box reads Section:GroupHeader0.
3. Set the ForceNewPage property to BeforeSection.
4. Preview the report. Return to Design mode.

4. **Calculating totals in the report for MyBooks.**

This exercise is a continuation of Quick Project #3.

1. Close the Properties dialog box. Open the Sorting and Grouping dialog box.
2. Change the Group Footer setting to Yes.
3. Place a text box on the right edge of the footer. Resize the label and modify it to read Number of Books by this Author:.
4. Modify the text in the Unbound box, changing it to read =Count (BookCollectionID).
5. Left align Count(BookCollectionID). Preview the report.
6. Return to Design mode. Close the Sorting and Grouping dialog box.
7. Save the report. Close the report. Close the Books database.

In-Depth Projects

1. Advanced reports for the CD database.

1. Open the CD database. Go to the Query window.
2. Modify query qryCompound. Remove the selection criteria from any of the columns. Add GroupName after Title; add Length to the end of the query.
3. Run the query to check it. Save the changes. Close the query.
4. Create a New report using qryCompound and the Report Wizards.
5. Make it a Tabular report and use all fields available. Sort by Title. Pick your style. Type CD Collection Detail Report as the name of the report.
6. Exit Print Preview. In Design mode, in the report footer, change the =Sum(YearReleased) to =Avg(YearReleased). Preview the report.
7. Print the report. Exit Print Preview. Close the report. Save it, naming it rptDetail.
8. Create a second New report using qryJoin and the Report Wizards.
9. Make it a Groups/Totals report and use all fields available. Group by Title, then GroupName. Use Normal grouping for each. Sort by TrackTitle. Pick your style. Type CD Report as the name of the report.
10. Print the report. Exit Print Preview. Close the report. Save it, naming it rptGroup.
11. Close the CD database.

2. Advanced reports for the Dinner database.

1. Open the Dinner database.
2. Create a New report using qryGuestByCity and the Report Wizards.
3. Make it a Tabular report and use all fields available. Sort by FirstName. Pick your style. Type Listing of Guests By City as the name of the report.
4. Print the report. Exit Print Preview. Close the report. Save it, naming it rptGuestsByCity.

5. Create a second New report using qryTripleJoin and the Report Wizards.

6. Make it a Groups/Totals report and use only the Date, Place, FirstName, and LastName fields. Group by Date. Use Normal grouping. Sort by FirstName. Pick your style. Type Dinner Report as the name of the report.

7. Exit Print Preview. In Detail view, left align the Date field in the Date Header section. Preview the results.

8. Print the report. Exit Print Preview. Close the report. Save it, naming it rptGroup.

9. Close the Dinner database.

CASE STUDIES

Coffee-On-The-Go: **Advanced Reports**

In this chapter, you learned advanced techniques for creating reports. You will apply those skills to create reports for Coffee-On-The-Go.

1. Create a report which includes data from both the Employee and Benefits tables.

2. Group the data in the report by the Location field.

3. Sort the records by Last Name within each location.

4. Calculate the average of all the salaries.

5. Print the report.

6. Save the report and close the database.

CASE STUDIES

Videos West: **Advanced Reports**

In this chapter, you learned advanced techniques for creating reports. You will apply those skills to create reports for Videos West.

1. Create a report which includes data from both the Inventory and Vendor tables.

2. Group the data in the report by the Type field.

3. Sort the records by Title within each type.

4. Calculate the total number of videos in the quantity field.

5. Print the report.

6. Save the report and close the database.

Chapter 12

Macro Basics

Key Terms

TERM	DEFINITION
Macro	a set of instructions that performs a sequence of tasks
Macro Group	a group of associated macros that run independently but are usually related or similar in function
Autoexec Macro	a macro that runs every time the database opens

macro A *macro* is a set of instructions that performs a sequence of tasks. If you have experience with a word processor, you may have used macros. But macros in MS-Access differ from macros in a word-processing program. When you create a macro in a word-processing program, you record it by performing a task once while the program keeps track of the steps. Then you can replay the recorded macro. There is no macro recording option in MS-Access. The macros must be built by the database designer. Fortunately, MS-Access provides a lot of help during this process. In word-processing programs, macros are run by pressing a key combination—for example, Alt+P to print the current page. MS-Access uses command buttons and other controls to run macros.

Objective 1: What Is a Macro?

In MS-Access, a macro consists of a set of instructions stored in the database that can be used whenever required. In the Database window, one of the tabs is marked Macro. This is where the macros are stored. You can run macros directly from this tab list, but, more commonly, macros are associated with controls on forms. In this chapter, you will build a macro, put a command button on a form, and associate the command button with the macro so that when you click the button, the macro will run.

Another way to run a macro is to connect it to a field on a form. When you enter data in the field, the macro automatically performs some action, such as checking to see if an item is in stock.

autoexec macro The *autoexec macro* is a unique macro. When you open a database, MS-Access looks for the autoexec macro and runs it. You can use this special macro to open a form when you start an MS-Access database.

macro group MS-Access allows you to put associated macros in a *macro group*. The macros within a group run independently but are related. For example, you may choose to put all the macros for one form in a group. This grouping makes it easier to maintain the database.

Objective 2: Creating a Macro

When you build a macro you must decide what you want the macro to do and how it will be activated. The first step is to create the macro in the Macro Design window of the database. Then you build controls or command buttons and connect the macro to these controls or command buttons.

In Exercise 1, you will build a macro that will be activated by a command button on the Contacts form. When you push the button on the Contacts form, the macro opens the frmPhoneNumbers form and shows you the phone numbers for the person who is currently displayed on the Contacts form. Then you will build a second control button on the frmPhoneNumbers form, which will be attached to another macro. This second macro will close the frmPhoneNumbers form and return you to the Contacts form.

Exercise 1: The Macro Design window

In this exercise, you will familiarize yourself with the Macro Design window.

1. Start at the Database window with the Macro button selected. Click New.

   The Macro Design window opens (Fig. 12-1). The toolbar for this window is very different from others you have seen.

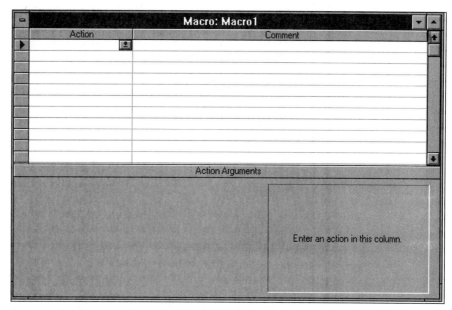

Figure 12-1   The Macro Design window

2. Use the balloon help to check the five buttons on the left of the toolbar (Fig. 12-2).

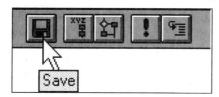

Figure 12-2   The Macro Design Window toolbar

The first button is the Save button, which is used to save the macro to the hard disk. The second and third buttons add the names and conditions columns to the Macro Design window. The fourth button runs the macro. The fifth button runs the macro one step at a time; this is used for debugging.

Exercise 2: Creating a macro

In this exercise you will build your first macro.

1. Make sure that the Macro Name column is in the Design window; if not, click the Macro Names button on the toolbar to add it.

2. In the first row of the Macro Name column, type OpenfrmPhoneNumbers.

3. Move to the Action column, click the down arrow, and select the action Open Form.

   The Action Arguments box opens at the bottom of the window (Fig. 12-3). The arguments in this box describe the action you have chosen.

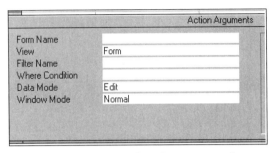

Figure 12-3 The Action Arguments box

4. In the Action Arguments box, click the Form Name row and then select frmPhoneNumbers.

5. Click the Where Condition row, then click the little button with the three dots, which appears at the right side of the row.

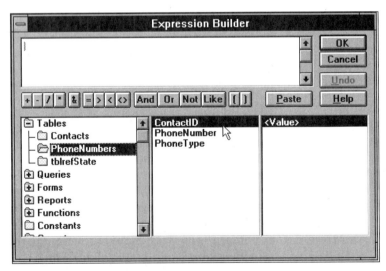

Figure 12-4 The Expression Builder

   The Expression Builder opens (Fig. 12-4), where you set up the link that opens the frmPhoneNumbers form with only the records related to the record on the Contacts main form.

6. Double-click Tables in the lower left window. When the sublist opens, double-click PhoneNumbers.

7. Double-click ContactID in the middle window.

   The first part of the expression appears in the upper window.

8. Click the button with the equals sign.

9. In the lower left window, double-click Forms.

10. In the sublist, double-click AllForms. Double-click Contacts.

11. Double-click ContactID in the center window.

   The expression is complete (Fig. 12-5). It states that the ContactID value should be the same on both the Contact form and the frmPhoneNumbers form.

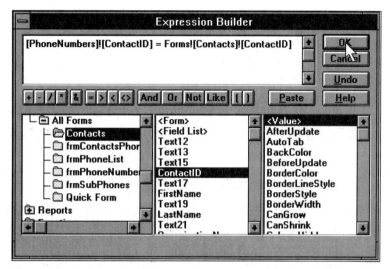

Figure 12-5   **The Expression Builder with the completed expression**

12. Click OK to close the Expression Builder and return to the Macro Design window. Type Open the frmPhoneNumbers form. in the Comments column.

13. Click on the second row of the Action column below the OpenForm command. Select the action Maximize.

   This will maximize the frmPhoneNumbers form when it is opened by the macro.

14. Type Maximize the frmPhoneNumbers form in the Comments column.

Objective 3: Saving a Macro

You must save a macro before you can use it. The name you give the macro when you save it is not the same as the macro name that you supplied while building the macro. What you are saving and naming is actually the macro group. A macro group can contain more than one macro. Think of the name you supplied earlier as the name of a macro and the group name you will supply in Exercise 3 as a macro family name.

Exercise 3: Saving the macro

1. Click the Save icon to save the macro. Name it mcrConPhone (Fig. 12-6).

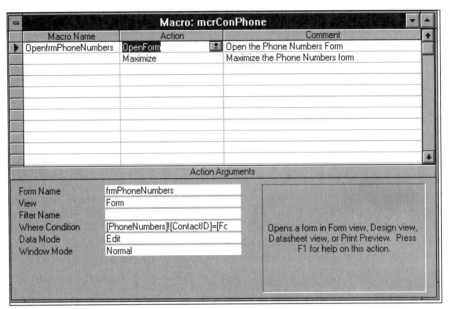

Figure 12-6 The Macro Design window with the completed macro

2. Close the Macro Design window.

Objective 4: Running a Macro

Usually, macros are not run from the Macro window. Most often they are run by pressing an associated command button. This makes sense since most macros are designed to perform a specific task within a form.

Exercise 4: Running the macro

In this exercise, you will run the macro from the Macro window. The macro prompts you for a value for ContactID because, running alone, it cannot get the value of ContactID from the Contacts form. In order for this macro to work, the Contacts form must be open, which it currently is not.

1. At the Database window with the Macro tab selected and mcrConPhone highlighted, click Run.

2. When the dialog box appears requesting a value for ContactID, click Cancel.

Where Are We Going?
Some schools of thought maintain that in the very near future all objects in a computer will have underlying databases and that the computer's operating system will effectively be a database management system. All documents will be stored and managed by a document retrieval system, which is a type of database management system. Your address book will be maintained electronically in a name and address database, which will be accessible by every application that needs an address or a phone number. Your daily schedule will be maintained as a database. Phone calls will be routed through your computer, with the caller identified and announced on your screen before you pick up the phone. The call, of course, will be added to a received-calls database.

All systems will be fully integrated. If a customer calls to check on an order, you can look up the order status and tell immediately if the order has been shipped. You can fax a copy of the air-bill number if the order was shipped or issue an investigation form if the order has not gone out yet—all from the databases accessed by your personal computer.

Data storage technology is advancing rapidly. But without good information retrieval interfaces, the data will remain just data. Whenever you design a database application, remember—databases are for information retrieval, not just for data storage.

Exercise 5: Connecting the macro to a form

In this exercise, you will add a command button to the Contacts form that will run the macro and open the PhoneNumbers form with the data from the contact name shown on the Contacts form.

1. Open the Contacts form in Design mode. Make sure that the Toolbox is visible.

2. Place a command button on the form, just above the Close button.

3. When the Command Button Wizard dialog box opens, select Miscellaneous. Select Run Macro (Fig. 12-7). Click Next.

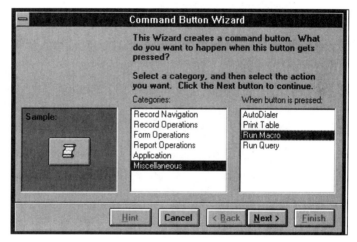

Figure 12-7   The Command Button Wizard dialog box

4. From the list of macros, select mcrConPhone.OpenfrmPhoneNumbers (Fig. 12-8). Click Next.

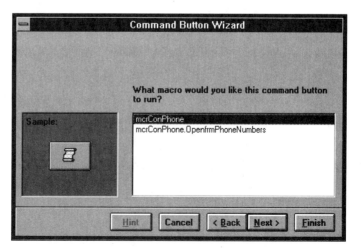

Figure 12-8   The Command Button Wizard dialog box with a list of macros

Note the naming convention. The macro you selected is named *macro family name.macro name.*

5. Click the Show All Pictures option and select Phone 1 from the list. Click Next.

6. Name the button ConPhone. Click Finish.

7. Switch to Form view (Fig. 12-9).

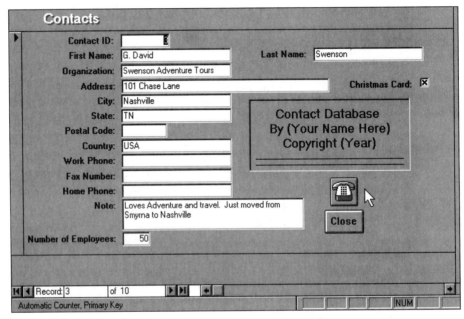

Figure 12-9 The Contacts form with the macro button

8. Find Swenson's contact record and click the button with the telephone on it.

   The frmPhoneNumbers form opens.

9. Browse through the records. Notice that they all belong to Swenson. You cannot see the phone numbers for any of your other contacts.

10. Close the frmPhoneNumbers form.

    You have to use File/Close or click the box in the upper left corner of the form.

12. Close the Contacts form, saving your changes.

Objective 5: Modifying a Macro

It is not very convenient to use File/Close or click the box in the upper left corner of the form each time you want to close the secondary form. To remedy this, you will put a close button on frmPhoneNumbers. You will add this macro as a second macro in the macro group you created earlier.

While you are making changes to mcrConPhone, there is another subtle change you should make. Remember what happeneed when you tried to run this macro on its own? The results were not what you expected. You can ensure that the macro will not accidently execute by inserting a blank line above the first line of instruction in the macro group.

Exercise 6: Making multiple macro modifications

In this exercise, you will put a button on frmPhoneNumbers that will call a macro and close the form.

1. Open the macro group mcrConPhone in Design mode.
2. Click anywhere in the top row of the macro. Then click Edit/Insert Row. A blank row is inserted at the beginning of the macro group.
3. Position the cursor in the Macro Name column two lines below the end of the OpenfrmPhoneNumbers macro and type ClosefrmPhoneNumbers.
4. Click the Action column and select Close.

FEATURE

Macros and event procedures

You may be wondering about the difference between the Close Form button you built in Chapter 10 and the one in this chapter, which runs a macro. The first one, which you built with the Command Button Wizard, actually has some program code behind it. If you examine the properties of this button, you will find something called an Event Procedure in the On Click property. This means that it runs a code snippet—a DoCmd Close—each time the button is clicked. The code, which is shorthand for "do the Close command from the menu bar," works as if you had selected File/Close. This is part of the programming language called Access Basic, which underlies everything that happens in MS-Access.

The last tab in the Database window is Modules. What is a module? Like a macro group, it can be a collection of small programs or code snippets. Each can be called from within a form or a report. While the macro is built by specifying a series of steps, the module is written in Access Basic.

5. In the Object Type row in the Action Arguments window, select Form. Then in the Object Name row, select frmPhoneNumbers.

6. Type Close frmPhoneNumbers in the Comments column (Fig. 12-10).

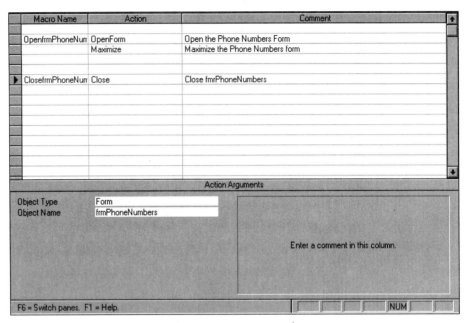

Macro Name	Action	Comment
OpenfrmPhoneNum	OpenForm	Open the Phone Numbers Form
	Maximize	Maximize the Phone Numbers form
ClosefrmPhoneNum	Close	Close frmPhoneNumbers

Action Arguments

Object Type	Form
Object Name	frmPhoneNumbers

Enter a comment in this column.

F6 = Switch panes. F1 = Help.   NUM

Figure 12-10 The macro with changes

7. Close the macro, saving your changes.

8. Open the form frmPhoneNumbers in Design mode. Place a command button on this form below the PhoneType field.

9. When prompted, select Miscellaneous, then select Run Macro.

10. When asked for the name of the macro, select mcrConPhone.ClosefrmPhoneNumbers. Click Next.

11. When prompted for the button face, check the Show All Pictures box and select the Exit Door button. Click Next.

12. Call the button cmdClosePhoneNumbers and click Finish.

13. Close the form, saving your changes.

14. Open the Contacts form in Form view.

15. Scroll to Swenson's record, then click the Phone button to open the Phone Numbers form.

16. Click the Exit Door button to close this form and return to the Contacts form.

17. Close the Contacts form by clicking the Close button on the form.

Objective 6: The Autoexec Macro

The autoexec macro performs a special function. When you first open your database, MS-Access looks for this macro. Whatever instructions are in this macro are run automatically. The most common use of the autoexec macro is to open a form so that the user can begin to browse or enter data. But you could use autoexec to generate a report every morning as you open the database with the previous day's sales figures and automatically e-mail it to your head office. In Exercise 7, you will build a simple autoexec macro to open the Contacts form.

Exercise 7: Building the autoexec macro

1. Start at the Database window with the Macro tab selected. Click New.

    In this example, the autoexec macro has only one entry in its macro group.

2. On the first line of the Action column, select or type OpenForm.

3. In the Name row of the Action Arguments form, select the Contacts form.

    This is the form that will open automatically when you open the Contacts database.

4. On the second line of the Action column, select Maximize.

    This will enlarge your Contacts form to fill the screen.

5. Click File/Save As to save the macro as autoexec.

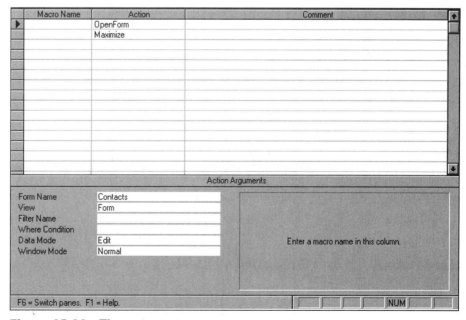

Figure 12-11   The autoexec macro

6. Close the macro and return to the Database window.
7. Highlight the autoexec macro. Click Run.

   The Contacts form opens and fills the screen.
8. Click the Close button to close the form.
9. Click File/Close Database to close the database. Click File/contacts.mdb to open it again. Do not exit from MS-Access.

   The database opens to a maximized Contacts form.
10. Close the form.

TIP Once the autoexec macro is in the Macro list, the database will open automatically at the form designated in the macro. To bypass autoexec, hold (SHIFT) as you click the database name to open it. You can disable autoexec by renaming or deleting it.

Objective 7: Debugging a Macro

There may be times when your macro does not work as you expected. How do you find the cause of the problem? The best method is to use the built-in macro debugger to step through the macro—that is, to execute each instruction and then pause to see what happens.

Exercise 8: Stepping through a functioning macro

In this exercise, you will step through a macro that works correctly. This will give you an idea of what to expect in the debugging process.

1. Start at the Database window with the Macro tab selected. Open mcrConPhone in Design mode.
2. Depress the Single Step button on the toolbar.
3. Close the Macro Design window, saving the changes when prompted.
4. Open the Contacts form in Form view.
5. Click the button to open the Phone Numbers form.
6. Click Step repeatedly to execute the macro one step at a time (Fig. 12-12).

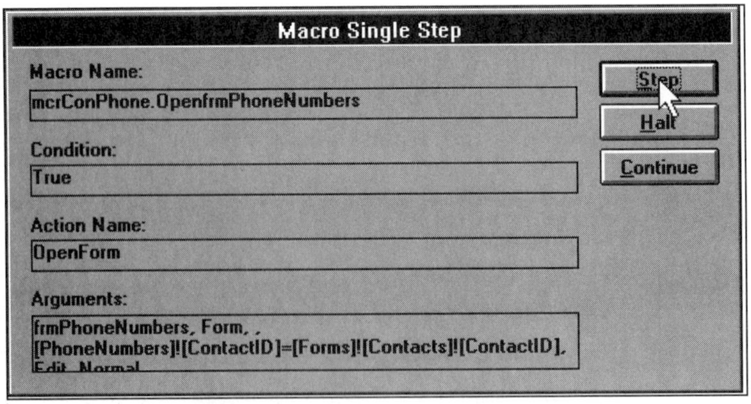

Figure 12-12 The Macro Single Step window

7. Click the button to close the Phone Numbers form.

8. Click Step to run the second macro.

9. Close the Contacts form.

Exercise 9: Stepping through a macro with an error

Now, you will introduce an error into the macro and step through it. In this case, you know where the problem is, so watch what happens.

1. Open the macro mcrConPhone in Design mode.

2. Change the Action Arguments of the Open Form action so that the form name reads xxfrmPhoneNumbers. (There is no such form.) The Single Step button should still be depressed.

3. Close the macro, saving the changes when prompted.

4. Open the Contacts form in Form view.

5. Click the button to open the Phone Numbers form. Step through the macro.

   After the first step, a dialog box appears that reads, "There is no form named 'xxfrmPhoneNumbers'" (Fig. 12-13).

Figure 12-13 **An error dialog box**

6. Close the dialog box.

   The macro halts, showing you the instruction it was executing when it encountered the first error (Fig. 12-14). If you were truly debugging a macro you would fix this problem, then step through the macro again until it ran correctly.

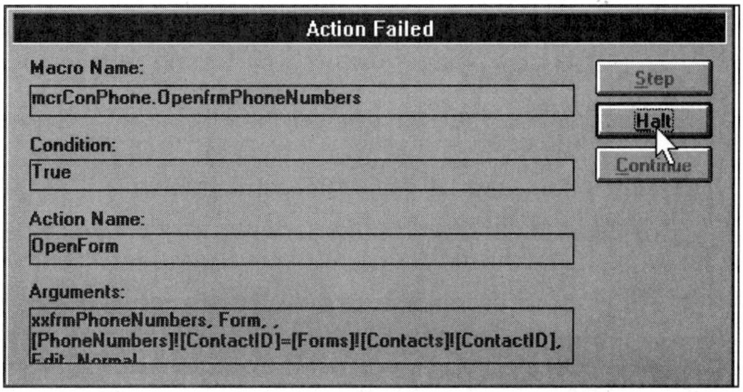

Figure 12-14 **The Macro Action Failed dialog box**

7. Click the Halt button to stop the macro.

8. Close the Contacts form.

9. Open the macro mcrConPhone in Design mode, remove the xx from the form name, and click the SingleStep button so that it is no longer depressed.

   Now the macro will run correctly.

10. Close the Macro Design window, saving your changes.

11. Close the database, and exit from MS-Access.

Chapter Summary

In this chapter, you learned how to automate your application with macros. Macros can make moving between forms easier and can execute sets of instructions for you whenever you require. You learned that macros have to be built and then tied to a command button or a field on a form. The special autoexec macro runs automatically when the database is opened. To debug a macro, you can step through it one instruction at a time until you find the cause of the problem.

Review Questions

True/False Questions

_____ 1. You can record an MS-Access macro and play it back later as needed.

_____ 2. When you step through a macro, you will see every error as it happens.

_____ 3. Each macro within a group performs only one action.

_____ 4. You can bypass the autoexec macro by holding down Shift as you open the database.

_____ 5. MS-Access macros can be run with an Alt+key combination.

Multiple-Choice Questions

_____ 6. An MS-Access macro is

A. a sequence of strokes on the keyboard.

B. a set of instructions that performs a sequence of tasks.

C. program code.

D. a form or report with embedded graphics.

_____ 7. The macro that MS-Access runs when the database opens is called

    A. autoexec.bat.

    B. autoexec.

    C. autoexec.mdb.

    D. mcrAutoexec.

_____ 8. Macros can be used to

    A. open a form.

    B. print a report.

    C. dial a telephone number.

    D. Any of the above.

_____ 9. When building a command button with the Command Button Wizard, you can place on the button

    A. a picture.

    B. text.

    C. text and a picture.

    D. text or a picture.

_____ 10. The instructions used to further define a macro action are called

    A. Macro Actions.

    B. Macro Arguments.

    C. Action Arguments.

    D. Argument Actions.

Fill-in-the-Blank Questions

11. A set of related macros is called a _____.

12. The _____ is used when building a macro and constructing the code needed to link two forms.

13. The _____ command in an Open Form macro makes the form fill the screen when it opens.

14. The parameters that you specify to describe an action in a macro are called _____.

15. To debug a macro, you _____ through it instruction by instruction.

Acumen-Building Activities

Quick Projects

1. Create a Sort-by-Title macro and command button for MyBooks.

1. Open the Books database. Go to the Query window.
2. Create a New query without using the Query Wizard. Use the table MyBooks.
3. Drag each field from the table onto the Query window. Sort by Title in ascending order. Test the query.
4. Save the query, naming it qrySortByTitle. Close the Query Design window.
5. Go to the Macro window. Create a New macro.
6. Skip the first row in the Macro Design window. In the second row of the Macro Name column, type SortByTitle. In the Action column choose ApplyFilter. In the Comments column, type Sort the Books by Title. In the Filter Name row of the Action Arguments box, type qrySortByTitle.
7. Save the macro, calling it mcrSort. Close the macro.
8. Go to the Forms window. Open frmBooks in Design mode and maximize the form.
9. Place a command button on the form near the top at the 5" line.
10. From the Command Button Wizard, select Miscellaneous, then select Run Macro. Select mcrSort.SortByTitle. Put text on the command button and type Sort By Title. Name the command button cmdSortByTitle. Click Finish.
11. Resize the button if necessary. Save the changes.
12. Switch to Form view. Test the button. Close the form.

2. Create a Sort-by-Subject macro and command button for MyBooks.

This exercise is a continuation of Quick Project #1.

1. Go to the Query window. Create a New query without using the Query Wizard. Use the table MyBooks.
2. Drag each field from the table onto the Query window. Sort by Author in ascending order. Test the query. Save the query, naming it qrySortByAuthor. Close the Query Design window.
3. Go to the Macro window. Open mcrSort in Design mode.
4. In the fourth row of the Macro Name column, type SortByAuthor. In the Action column, choose ApplyFilter. In the Comments column, type Sort the Books by Author. In the Filter Name row of the Action Arguments box, type qrySortByAuthor. Save the changes. Close the macro.

5. Go to the Forms window. Open frmBooks in Design mode and maximize the form.

6. Place a command button on the form near the SortByTitle button.

7. From the Command Button Wizard, select Miscellaneous, then select Run Macro. Select mcrSort.SortByAuthor. Put text on the command button and type Sort By Author. Name the command button cmdSortByAuthor. Click Finish.

8. Resize the button so it is the same size as the first button. Save the changes.

9. Switch to Form view. Test the button. Close the form.

3. Create a Print Preview macro and command button for MyBooks.

This exercise is a continuation of Quick Project #2.

1. Go to the Macro window. Create a New macro.

2. In the second row of the Macro Name column, type PrintPreview. In the Action column choose, DoMenuItem. In the Comments column, type Preview the form before printing. In the Menu Bar row of the Action Arguments box, select Form. In the Menu Name row, select File. In the Command row, select Print Preview. Save the changes, call the macro mcrPrint. Close the macro.

3. Go to the Forms window. Open frmBooks in Design mode and maximize the form.

4. Place a command button on the form.

5. From the Command Button Wizard, select Miscellaneous, then select Run Macro. Select mcrPrint.PrintPreview. Place the Preview Document picture on the command button. Name the command button cmdPrintPreview. Click Finish.

6. Resize and reposition the button if appropriate. Save the changes.

7. Switch to Form view. Test the new button. Exit from Print Preview. Close the form.

4. Create an autoexec macro for MyBooks.

This exercise is a continuation of Quick Project #3.

1. Go to the Macro window and create a New macro.

2. On the first line of the Action column, select Open Form. In the Comments column, type The autoexec macro. In the Form Name row of the Action Arguments box, select frmBooks.

3. On the second line of the Action column, select Maximize.

4. Save the macro, naming it autoexec. Close the macro.

5. In the Database window, highlight autoexec and click Run.

6. Close the form. Close the Books database.

In-Depth Projects

1. Link CDs and Tracks for the CD database.

1. Open the CD database. Create a New macro.
2. Skip the first row in the Macro Design window. In the second row of the Macro Name column, type OpenTracks. In the Action column, choose Open Form. In the Comments column, type Open the Tracks form. In the Form Name row of the Action Arguments box, type frmTracks. Use the Expression Builder for the Where condition.
3. Double-click Tables and double-click Tracks. Double-click MusicCollectionID.
4. Click the equals sign.
5. Double-click Forms. Double-click AllForms. Double-click frmCDCollection. Double-click MusicCollectionID. Click OK.
6. Save the macro, naming it mcrOpenSub. Close the Macro Design window.
7. Open frmTracks in Design mode. Position the Form window in the lower right portion of the screen. Open the Properties box. Find the entry for PopUp and change it to Yes. Close frmTracks and save the changes.
8. Open frmCDCollection in Design mode and maximize the form. Place a new command button in the header area.
9. From the Command Button Wizard, select Miscellaneous, then select Run Macro. Choose the macro mcrOpenSub.OpenTracks. Select the picture Subform and name the command button cmdOpenTracks. Click Finish. Save your changes.
10. Switch to Form view. Test the Subform command button. Scroll through the tracks for the CD you have selected on the main form. Close the Track subform.
11. Go to the next CD on the main form. Click the Subform command button and scroll through the tracks for that CD. Close the Tracks subform. Close the CDCollection main form. Save any changes if prompted to do so. Close the CD database.

2. Creating an autoexec and a Print Report macro for the Dinner database.

1. Open the Dinner database and go to the Macro window.
2. Create a New autoexec macro. On the first line of the Action column, type OpenForm. In the Form Name row of the Action Arguments box, select frmDinnerGuest2. Add a comment to the Comments column.
3. On the second line of the Action column, select Maximize.
4. Save the macro as autoexec.
5. Create a second New macro.
6. Skip the first row. In the second row of the Macro Name column, type CurrentRec. In the Action column, choose Open Report. In the Comments column, type Print preview the current record before

printing. In the Report Name row of the Action Arguments box, type rptGuests; Leave the view as Print Preview. Use the Expression Builder for the Where condition and choose Tables/ DinnerGuests/ GuestID/ = /Forms/All Forms/frmDinnerGuest2/GuestID. Your expressions should look like [DinnerGuests]![GuestID] = Forms![frmDinnerGuest2]![GuestID]. Save the changes and call the macro mcrPrint. Close the macro.

7. Go to the Forms window. Open frmDinnerGuest2 in Design mode and maximize the form.

8. Lengthen the Detail section of the form. Place a command button at the bottom of the Detail section on the right side.

9. From the Command Button Wizard, select Miscellaneous, then select Run Macro. Select mcrPrint.CurrentRec. Place text on the command button and type Print Current Profile. Name the command button cmdCurrentRec. Click Finish.

10. Save the changes. Switch to Form view. Test the button. Exit from Print Preview. Close the form. Close the Dinner database.

CASE STUDIES

Coffee-On-The-Go: Using Macros

In this chapter, you learned to create macros. You will apply those skills to create a macro for Coffee-On-The-Go.

1. Create a macro of your own choosing which automates a task.
2. Test the macro.
3. Debug and edit the macro as necessary.
4. Save the macro and close the database.

CASE STUDIES

Videos West: Using Macros

In this chapter, you learned to create macros. You will apply those skills to create a macro for Videos West.

1. Create a macro of your own choosing which automates a task.
2. Test the macro.
3. Debug and edit the macro as necessary.
4. Save the macro and close the database.

Acumen Advanced Features Milestone

the Scouts Cookie Sale Database

Mrs. Wilson finds her Cookie Sales database to be very useful. She decides to build a multitable form so she can enter this week's cookie sales without having to switch back and forth between two different forms. She will add a command button so she can go directly to the Sales form and enter the type of cookie and number of boxes purchased. She is thinking about adding some combo boxes to assist with data entry, specifically on the scout's name and cookie type. Then she will build some new reports. One report will list all customers, what cookies they have ordered, and how much of each cookie type they have each ordered. A second report will list cookies by type and the total number of each cookie type sold. A third report will list the scouts and the cookies each has sold, grouped by type with a total number of sales for each scout.

Mrs. Wilson also wants to build an autoexec macro that will open this new multitable data entry form when she starts up the Cookie Sales database. She is thinking that she might like to have command buttons on the form that run macros to sort by different fields, too. Finally, Mrs. Wilson plans to make a backup of her database.

1. Build a multitable data-entry form. Make the Scout table the main form and the Customer table the subform. Put a command button on this form to go directly to the Sales form. Put the command button on the Sales form to return to the main form.

2. Build combo boxes on these forms to assist with data entry. Put a combo box on the Sales form to list the cookie types. Put a combo box on the Main form to facilitate choosing the scout's name. Add this week's cookie sales.

3. Create three new reports.

- A list of all customers, what cookies they have ordered, and how much of each type.
- A list of cookies by type and total number of each sold.
- A report that groups cookie sales by scouts, then by what type of cookies each has sold. Add subtotals for the cookie groups and totals for each scout.

4. Create an autoexec macro to open the mutitable form when the Cookie Sales database is opened. Create a command button on the main form to sort by scout name, and a second command button on the Sales form to sort by cookie type. Make a backup of the Cookie Sales database.

Group Project:

the Community Rec Center Database

The Forms Designer decides to make some multitable forms to handle reservations and equipment issue. There will have to be command buttons placed on the forms to switch from one to the other. The Forms Designer must confer with the rest of the project team to design the forms so that they are easy to use and functional.

The Report Designer decides that the center needs to print equipment-issue receipts when a member checks out a piece of equipment. It would be best to do this directly from the Equipment Issue multitable form. Also, it would be very nice to be able to give each member a reservation slip when he or she makes a reservation to use a tennis court. The Report Designer wants to do this directly from the Reservations multitable form. In addition, the Report Designer would like to generate form letters with mailing labels to send to the members, notifying them of the annual Rec Center Holiday Party.

The Database Administrator decides to create an autoexec macro to bring up the Reservations multitable form when the Rec Center database is started. The entire project team will work together to enroll this week's new members into the Rec Center database and to record reservations and equipment issue. Then the Database Administrator will make a backup of the Rec Center database.

The Full Project Team

Confer to design the best way for navigating through the new multitable forms for reservations and equipment issue. Compose the wording of the letter to the membership about the holiday party. Record this week's new members, reservations, and equipment issues.

The Database Administrator

Create the autoexec macro so that the Reservations multitable form opens when the Rec Center database is brought up (if the rest of the project team agrees with this decision). Assist with the creation of any macros needed by the Forms Designer. Make a backup of the database.

The Forms Designer

Create two new multitable forms, one for making reservations to use the courts, a second for recording equipment issue. Add command buttons to switch back and forth between the two forms as well as to navigate elsewhere in the database. Confer with the project team members as to the best design.

The Report Designer

Create the equipment-issue receipts and confer with the Forms Designer about where and how to place a command button on the form to generate them. Create the reservations slips and confer with Forms Designer about where and how to place a command button on the forms to generate them. Create a general mailing to the membership, notifying them of the upcoming holiday party. Generate a set of mailing labels to accompany the letters.

Index for Microsoft Access 2.0